Religion
and Contemporary
Western Culture

Religion
and Contemporary
Western Culture

SELECTED READINGS

Edited by Edward Cell

Nashville   ABINGDON PRESS   New York

RELIGION AND CONTEMPORARY WESTERN CULTURE

Copyright © 1967 by Abingdon Press

Library of Congress Catalog Card Number: 67-14980

SET UP, PRINTED, AND BOUND BY THE
PARTHENON PRESS AT NASHVILLE,
TENNESSEE, UNITED STATES OF AMERICA

To
my mother and father

Preface

The aim of this book is to present, at an introductory level, leading theories of the relation of religion and culture and to show their application to specific areas of contemporary Western culture. In this way these theories may be better understood and evaluated. Each will tend to reflect a greater concern for and understanding of some aspects of culture than others; yet, each must be evaluated in terms of its adequacy to the entire range of cultural creativity. Then, too, by this procedure these theories can be related more directly to the situation of cultural crisis in which we are living, and their relevance to our situation—their power to illuminate it—is surely a question of primary importance.

There are difficulties, however, concerning how the words "religion and culture" are to be understood. "Culture" may be defined as the way of life of a people and includes their language, art, literature, religion, philosophy, science, technology, education, ethics, law, and political system. But the term "religion" is used in many different ways, and its meaning will vary from one theory of religion and culture to another. For example, it may refer to one area or function of culture, or it may mean something that runs through all areas of culture; it may be defined in terms of belief in a divine being, or it may be defined more broadly to mean one's basic commitments. This is not simply a matter of words. One's use of the term "religion" will reflect his basic philosophical position. What one is to mean by "religion," then, is itself part of the problem of how one is to understand the relation of religion and culture. Moreover, as the opening chapter on "The Question of Religion" attempts to indicate, this whole issue is intimately bound up with our cultural crisis. For these reasons the readings have not been selected in light of any preconceived idea about the nature of religion. Rather, the aim has been to present leading approaches to this issue in contemporary Western thought as they find expression in the discussion of religion and culture.

From the perspective of this particular concern, the discussion presented by the readings may be seen as moving in two directions. In one direction, the discussion takes place between leading theistic positions within Christianity—the Roman Catholic, neo-orthodox, postliberal, and Tillichian. In the other direction, a dialogue is maintained between theism and leading forms of the protest that nature is all that there is—specifically, the Freudian, the Marxist, the existentialist (Read, Esslin, Sartre, and Fromm), and the analytic philosophy of Wisdom and Ayer.

There are two closely related reasons for giving major attention to Christian thought. First, there is simply the fact that Christianity is the leading institutional religion in the West. But, more fundamentally, Western culture has had its foundation in Christianity to such a degree that the relation of Western culture to religion is inseparable from its relation to the Christian tradition. Indeed, to a large extent, the crisis in Western religion is the crisis in Christianity. Even nontheistic forms of humanism are not understandable apart from the Christian heritage of our culture, for they have important roots in that tradition, and much of their vitality frequently has been expended on, and even derived from, their protests against certain aspects of that same tradition. Extensive attention to Christian thought, therefore, has seemed not only justifiable but necessary. Regrettably, since decisions to include are also decisions to exclude, this has resulted in the omission of the important work of such Jewish thinkers as Buber, Heschel, and Herberg.

The fact that Western culture is so intimately bound up with the heritage of Christianity has led to a second criterion for our selections. This is the concern to present leading interpretations of the relation of Christian faith to culture as they have been classified in H. Richard Niebuhr's *Christ and Culture*. Specifically, focus has been given to the "Christ Above Culture," "Christ and Culture in Paradox," and "Christ the Transformer of Culture," positions described in the selection from Niebuhr in section two.

The basic criteria for selection, then, have been the presentation of leading positions concerning (1) the nature of religion as this is seen in terms of the relation of religion and culture, and (2) the relation of Christian faith and culture. Within this framework, selections have been preferred which will be most readable for college students at an introductory level, although several readings of importance have been included which are fairly difficult.

The selection of the particular areas of culture to be studied also was made with several considerations in mind. First of all, the aim has been to include a wide range of cultural functions—specifically, the expressive functions of art and literature; the cognitive functions of philosophy, psychotherapy, and science; and the practical functions of man's socioeconomic and political orders. Second, attention has been given to those areas of culture which seem to be particularly interesting to the undergraduate. Third, those areas have been preferred which seem to reflect most vividly our situation of cultural crisis.

The introductions to each section have been kept extremely brief in order to allow maximum space for the readings. They consist of the kind of comment that has seemed helpful to give in class in preparation for an assignment. In addition to suggesting perspectives from which to approach the readings, the aims have been (1) to raise some of the questions or to invite some of the comparisons which seemed less likely to occur to the reader on his own, (2) to supply information which may be helpful, and (3) occasionally to summarize key points from the more difficult readings. Above all, however, the concern has been to let the reader do his own thinking.

I wish to thank the many persons who helped in the preparation of this book. I am particularly indebted to Professors George Thomas, Jack Padgett, William Halverson, Fred Holder, and Paul Bosley for their criticisms and suggestions; to Mrs. Barbara Long and Miss Mary Lou Simpson for their assistance in preparing the manuscript; and to my wife, Mary, who has been helpful in so many ways. And, finally, it has been possible to use a good proportion of the selections which were my first choice, and I am grateful to those who so kindly have given permission to use their work.

EDWARD CELL

Contents

I
Religion

EDWARD CELL

The Question of Religion

Have you not heard of that madman who lit a lantern in the bright morning hours, ran to the market place, and cried incessantly, "I seek God! I seek God!" As many of those who do not believe in God were standing around just then, he provoked much laughter. . . .

"Whither is God" he cried. "I shall tell you. *We have killed him*—you and I. All of us are his murderers. But how have we done this? How were we able to drink up the sea? Who gave us the sponge to wipe away the entire horizon? What did we do when we unchained this earth from its sun? Whither is it moving now? Whither are we moving now? Away from all suns? Are we not plunging continually? . . . Do we not hear anything yet of the noise of the gravediggers who are burying God? Do we not smell anything yet of God's decomposition? Gods too decompose. God is dead. . . . Is not the greatness of this deed too great for us? Must not we ourselves become gods simply to seem worthy of it? There has never been a greater deed; and whoever will be born after us—for the sake of this deed he will be part of a higher history than all history hitherto."

. . . It has been related further that on that same day the madman entered divers churches and there sang his *requiem aeternam deo*. Led out and called to account, he is said to have replied each time, "What are these churches now if they are not the tombs and sepulchers of God?" [1]

The subject of "Religion and Contemporary Western Culture" has an urgency about it which is expressed by Nietzsche's prophetic words. With these strokes, his pen becomes the seismographic needle for a culture shaken at its very foundations, an instrument making early record of the now commonplace judgment that we are in a situation of crisis. He indicates the depth of this crisis by proclaiming that it is particularly beneath Western religion that the ground has cracked, and so one is not surprised to find that our religious thought seems to have become, more than anything else, the interpretation of Nietzsche's proclamation.

The main outlines of this situation seem fairly clear. First of all, we have come to see our time as a period of cultural transition. Now a culture is simply the way of life of a particular people. It is expressed in their technology and social system as well as in their arts, their philosophy and religion, and their science. Cultural transition, then, means that an old way of life is dying because it is no longer adequate to changing conditions, and consequently, a new way of life is coming to birth. To return to our earlier metaphor,

[1] From *The Portable Nietzsche*, ed. and trans. by Walter Kaufmann. Copyright 1954 by The Viking Press, Inc. Reprinted by permission of The Viking Press, Inc.

the foundations of our culture are shifting, and the shock is being suffered by every dimension of our way of life, be it the religious, the aesthetic, the scientific, the economic, or any other.

In the second place, there seems to be little doubt that the heart of this transformation is to be found in the tremendous achievements of science, together with the vast technological advances which science has made possible. In the judgment of many, it is in science that we find the most authentic and creative expression of the contemporary human spirit. Through his deep participation in this mode of expression, man, it seems, has profoundly changed his relationship to himself and to the reality around him. Particularly have our *images* of self and world been reshaped, which means that they are no longer the images provided by the world view of traditional Christianity.

Here, then, is a third feature of our crisis, namely, that our sensibilities seem no longer to be shaped by Christianity—not, at least, in the form in which it has found expression in earlier periods of culture. The Christian artifacts, together with the religious holidays and cultic practices, which have been bequeathed to us from earlier periods, are to many little more than vestigial remnants. Even such once powerful words as "God," "sin," "grace," "salvation," and the like now increasingly present themselves as strange intruders from a different world. In effect, they seem lifeless.

Insofar as it is true that the images by which most men live are no longer those of traditional Christianity, we are faced with the problem of what this means for our understanding of religion and its place in culture. To deal with this problem we need to consider two very different, though not necessarily incompatible, judgments concerning the nature of this impact that science and technology have had on our way of life. On the one hand, the resulting images

may be seen as liberating. In this case the death of God will symbolize the dismissal of those aspects of traditional Christianity which now seem to have been obstacles to human growth and achievement. On the other hand, other images seem to have been produced which are expressions of man's progressive dehumanization of himself. Seen from this perspective, the death of God really says something about man's loss of his own humanity.

If we turn first to the liberating consequences that our scientific activity allegedly has had on our way of understanding, appreciating, and shaping ourselves and our world, we can quickly get to the heart of our subject by considering a commonly held interpretation of supernaturalism. Supernaturalism, according to this view, is the belief that a world exists beyond the natural world which is inhabited by one or more divine beings and that these beings exercise power over the natural world. This belief is seen by many to belong to those stages in man's cultural development in which he had an overwhelming sense of being at the mercy of the forces of nature. By imagining these forces to be controlled by supernatural powers which are personal, he achieved the comforting hope that he might be able to influence these powers in behalf of his interests. However, as man has gained increasing mastery over nature through science and concomitant advances in technology, he gradually has lost his sense of helplessness and with it his need to believe in the supernatural. He has become more and more this-worldly and can say, quite readily, "This world is all that there is and it is enough."

This naturalism has been fostered by science in numerous ways. To mention just two, there is first the emphasis on man's continuity with the other animals which has a number of sources in our scientific activities. The work of Darwin is an example. Second, there is the way in which anthropology, sociology, and psychology have undermined belief in supernaturally based absolutes by displaying religious and ethical ideas as having many elements which are relative to the cultures in which they appear and even to the personal histories of those holding them.

But we are not concerned here to trace in detail the way in which science has changed our ways of seeing things, for the basic tension with traditional religious belief seems to grow out of the new sense of strength which man has discovered through his scientific pursuits. It is on this fundamental source of tension that we wish to focus our attention.[2] Nor is man's new sense of himself limited to naturalistic forms of expression. It may, in fact, be helpful to discuss our problems by developing an analogy from the work of a theist.

Dietrich Bonhöffer has suggested that in his spiritual situation modern man is analogous to the young man who has "come of age." His childhood was a situation of dependency. Not only did he depend upon his parents for his physical needs, but he also existed in a state of spiritual dependency, leaning on their authority intellectually, morally, and religiously. But, having reached adulthood, he now assumes the responsibility for himself, including his commitments and beliefs. To be sure, along with achievement and joy come failure and suffering, but he "cannot go home again." One could call this the death of daddy. Analogously, in his childhood man looked to God for a bountiful harvest, for a revealed truth concerning the final meaning of life, and for a set of absolute moral laws. The mark of man's adulthood, however, is his assumption of responsibility for the meaning he creates, the ethics he seeks to live by, and the relation in which he stands

to nature. It is, perhaps, strikingly indicative of this maturity that men frequently experience a sense of immense relief when they surrender their belief in the supernatural.

What, then, does all this mean for our understanding of religion and its place in culture?

Some believe that religion should be identified with belief in the existence of one or more divine beings and that this belief is relative to certain stages in man's cultural development. It is rooted in man's sense of helplessness. From this they conclude that religion should be given up because this sort of belief is now only an obstacle to man's further development.

Others believe that we should distinguish between that in religion which is relative to a particular culture and that which is an essential part of the human situation. But there is considerable difference of interpretation concerning just what it is about religion that abides throughout cultural change.

On the one hand, many naturalists bid us distinguish between belief in divine beings and man's aspirations toward those values which he regards as most worthy of his active concern. Freed of the supernaturalism relative to an earlier culture, we may focus more fruitfully on the genuine religious question of which ideals, among those having the possibility of a progressive human achievement in this world, are most worthy of our allegiance.

On the other hand, there are those who wish to retain a belief which, first of all, does not identify God with some aspect of the natural finite world and yet, secondly, need not be tied strictly to the supernaturalistic conceptions from which many have come to be so alienated. Man's need for God, they believe, can be interpreted in ways which do not

[2] For a brief introduction to many facets of the impact of science on traditional Christian belief, see L. Harold DeWolf, *Trends and Frontiers in Religious Thought* (Nashville: The Board of Education of The Methodist Church, 1955), pp. 7-18.

suggest the dependencies of childhood. The sort of dependence on the human plane that blocks maturation is that in which someone relies on another to do for him that which he can and should do for himself. In effect, he evades certain exercises of his powers which are a part of responsible, mature selfhood. But we also need each other in countless ways, such as for love and understanding, which have nothing to do with a failure to develop and use our personal powers. "Coming of age," then, does not necessarily mean that one must cease to feel any need for relationship with his father. May not one say, similarly, that man has an essential need for God but that, as he comes of age, it no longer involves the kind of need that finds its appropriate analogue in the need of the child for its father?

From this point of view, what seems required is a shift away from interventionist conceptions of God. Instead of thinking of God as intervening in certain situations, in the sense of acting as one force along side of the other forces involved but powerful enough simply to override them, one develops another side of traditional thought—the belief that God acts in everything according to its nature or mode of being.[3] The question at issue here, in other words, is this: When God acts in the life of a human being, does this action have an essential relation to the powers of that person so that it does not take place apart from the active play of those powers, or is this action something which is merely done *to* him, something which is entirely strange to him, something to which he is simply passive? Is it not in this latter conception that parallels are to be found to childish dependencies? Consider, for example, the child's need to believe that his father will intervene to protect him from anything terrible—an intervention that has no essential relation to the child's very minimal powers. As he matures, he comes to rely more and more upon his own power and courage. He does not ask his father to make decisions for him, fight his battles, assume his responsibilities, or the like. Yet his relationship with his father may have an important bearing upon his independent actions. From this relationship, if it is one of mutual acceptance and respect, he may derive much personal strength and courage on which he draws in facing his own anxieties or greater insight by which he makes his own decisions.

Analogously, we may conceive of divine providence to mean that God will intervene to prevent anything too terrible from happening. Or providence may mean that, whatever happens, "nothing in all creation can separate us from the love of God" and that by this relationship with God we gain the strength and courage to face even the worst and to continue to affirm life in spite of it.

To extend one side of the analogy a bit further, the young man "come of age" may choose his father as one of the persons to whom he feels particularly responsible concerning the way in which he conducts his life. At times his father may even take the initiative to challenge something about his life or to confront him with an unhappy image of himself. Similarly, without being interventionists, many maintain that if we are not separated from the love of God then our deepest sense of ourselves is inseparable from feeling every use of our powers to be a response to God. And sometimes through the loving challenge of another human being, God's love may break into our lives to confront that in us which is unloving.

Lest this father-son analogy be pushed unduly, however, let us consider our question in terms of those events to which the biblical writers responded as

---

[3] See, for example, Thomas Aquinas, *Summa Theologica*, Pt. I, Q. 8, a. 1. Aquinas, it should be noted, did not limit his conception of God's acts to this particular doctrine.

acts of God. In the Exodus, for example, is God acting in the sense of doing things which are quite unrelated to Moses' own human powers, such as creating a path through a body of water? Or is it rather that in Moses' exercise of his own powers in delivering his people from bondage some persons experienced not just a human presence and concern but also a numinous or divine presence and concern? The same could be asked with respect to Jesus' acts of reconciling love, or the actions of the prophets, and so on.

The same issue is faced concerning revelation. On the interventionist side we have the propositional view of revelation which pictures God as handing down through the passive instrumentality of the Bible writers both ethical and religious statements which we are to believe and obey. On the other hand revelation may be understood in terms of the events in which God is encountered. Just as one man reveals himself to another through his actions, so God is revealed through his actions. Faith has to do with man's response to God as he meets Him in these actions rather than an acceptance of propositionally revealed truths.

The question, let us remember, is whether the forms of belief in God which allegedly function so as to thwart the development of our human potentialities are rightly to be seen as tied to interventionist conceptions. The issue is, of course, far more complex than a brief treatment can suggest. But one must at least stress the difficulty in clearly defining what is to be meant by the concept of intervention and also the significantly different ways in which one might understand what human maturity means and so what in religious belief is to be regarded as an expression of immature dependency. Suppose, for example, that one believes that God has revealed certain truths which the human mind is incapable of achieving by its own powers but which do not contradict any truths

which the human mind does achieve and to which one can respond in a meaningful way. One does not find here any clear analogue to the evasion of the use of one's own power by leaning on the powers of another. Of course, one may regard the very willingness to entertain such a belief as itself the expression of a yearning to prolong immaturity. But the point is that the issue is not clear cut.

What one finds, then, is that people may agree in giving up certain beliefs as interventionist yet disagree concerning other beliefs. Such disagreement is perhaps most deep-seated with respect to the belief in a life after death. Are we to believe that God intervenes, resurrecting us to a new life after we die? To those who reject this belief it is as though man in his childhood was unable to face his finitude and needed to believe that his father would forever protect him from it by giving him unending life, but in coming of age man can accept and affirm his life for what it is, including the fact that it moves toward a final end. To reject the hope for a divine intervention here, however, is not at all to deny that the courage to make this affirmation is grounded finally in one's relationship with God. Others see it quite differently, believing that if there is nothing beyond the grave, then man lives his life in a context that is fundamentally hostile to him. Consequently, although he may courageously resign himself to the situation, it is not in his power fully to affirm such a life. He has no choice but to live defensively and with a mistrust that undercuts the self-giving that might otherwise be a genuine potentiality. God, they maintain, intervenes that man may be more rather than less.

Up to this point we have been pursuing the thesis that man has glimpsed a newfound strength in his scientific and technological activities. We have presented the question of whether this alleged spiritual transformation is to be

17

symbolized by a dismissal of the holy or by subtle transformations in the meaning of the word "God"—transformations, that is, in the way in which we experience and respond to that which is ultimate. But suppose that we now go on to ask this question: If our sense of ourselves and our situation may be symbolized at least in part by, say, Cape Kennedy and the conquest of space, is it not also symbolized for us by Hiroshima and the destruction that rains out of space? For many, it is this side of things which stands out as they reflect upon our spiritual situation. In view of its brutality and chaos, our age has been called an age of anxiety, of meaninglessness, of lostness. From this perspective the death of God is seen rather differently.

"How indeed," asks Maritain, "could God still live in a world from which his image, i.e. the free and spiritual personality of man, is fading away?" The trend of Western culture, says Tillich, has been a trend "towards ever-increasing *loss* of religious consciousness." As Buber views it, "The fact that it is so difficult for present-day man to pray . . . and the fact that it is so difficult for him to carry on genuine talk with his fellow-men are elements of a . . . lack of trust, . . . an innermost sickness." In effect, then, the question many would pose is this: "Is not the death of God simply one side of man's dehumanization of himself—one side of man's progressive alienation from others, from nature and even from himself?" If we can say, "God is dead," can we not also say in the same sense that "Nature is dead," "My neighbor is dead," "I myself am dead"? One thinks, for example, of Kafka's "The Metamorphosis" or Sartre's *The Condemned of Altona* in which Franz proclaims that man is dead. Our scientific preoccupations have tempted us to see the world solely in its objectifiable dimensions, a conglomeration of mere things of which man is simply another —a thing.[4] And the by-product of our technology has been that we think of ourselves as consumers, as cogs in the industrial machine, as role players whose significance lies solely in our membership in the group. Living, thus, in a mass culture, preoccupied with the quantifiable and the consumable, we have steadily lost our capacity to respond to the personal and, with it, our capacity to respond to God.

Here, then, is a very different view of the effect of our scientific and technological advances. One may, of course, see truth in both interpretations. But if one gives considerable weight to the depersonalizing aspect of our situation, a rather different view of man is indicated than is true for those who would emphasize the liberating side. While the latter often tend to see man's problems particularly in terms of his struggle to master nature, those who are especially sensitive to the existing patterns of the antihuman tend rather to see man as being a problem to himself in a way that is somehow inescapable. What do we see, they ask, in man's use of his marvelous mastery of nature if it is not simply another version of the same old story of man's tendency to misuse even the finest of his powers? And if this is true, then surely modern man's relationship with God is characterized much less by maturation than it is by rebellion. This, for example, is the substance of

---

[4] There are many other ways as well in which it is claimed that we have allowed science to have a dehumanizing effect on us. The sense of our continuity with the other animals, which we touched on earlier, may well liberate us from damaging tendencies to reject something of our basic nature. But may it not be emphasized to such an extreme that it undermines our sense of the significance of the differences between man and the rest of the animals? Or, to take yet another example from our earlier discussion, the undermining of belief in supernaturally based absolutes may well encourage a fuller and more responsible use of our powers of judgment. But if relativism is carried to an extreme, does it not undercut the significance of such discernment and discrimination by seeing the results as mere reflections of our particular situation?

Karl Barth's reaction to the conclusion of his former student, Bonhoeffer, that man has come of age. Has not Bonhoeffer simply misinterpreted his discovery that men have edged God out of the world? Hasn't he misjudged the depth of man's alienation from God?

Man's rebellion against God, which is the other side of his refusal to accept his status simply as man and his consequent misuse of his powers, has been given quite varied interpretation. Let us briefly consider one which will allow us to return to the analogy of the relation of father and son. Beginning with the birth of his conscience, the child experiences the inner division which we call guilt and feels a subconscious hostility toward that which he sees as making him guilty. Insofar as his father has been the one who has introduced some sort of moral law into his life, the child feels a hatred toward his father as the source of his divided condition, his war with himself. Just this, it is claimed, is the condition of man before God. Every man feels hostility toward his own existence and toward that which he somehow feels is the source of its being what it is—a guilty existence. Nothing can separate us from the love of God, but man finds in his split condition a motivation to reject that love.[5]

From this point of view, man's rebellion (and his consequent misuse of his powers) is seen to find expression in every area of life including his religion itself. Religion often functions as a substitute for relationship with God, so that the term "God" is then really being used to refer to some idol such as the interests of one's own nation, or one's concern to maintain a state of righteousness which elevates him over others, and so forth. Religion, in effect, may itself be a leading expression of the death of God.

We have seen, then, that the widespread alienation from traditional Christianity which allegedly characterizes our contemporary situation may be interpreted from two very different, though not incompatible, points of view. On the one hand, our culture is seen in terms of liberation and maturity; on the other, in terms of dehumanization and rebellion. One may find himself hard pressed to judge between these two just as in the young man's struggle for independence it may be difficult to discern the extent to which he is striving for healthy maturity and how far he is rebelliously refusing relationship. This problem has played a prominent part in the selection of these readings. In view of this, the reader may wish to consider some of the following readings on religion which could be valuable additions to the readings in this book.

John Dewey, *A Common Faith* (New Haven: Yale University Press [1934]; paper, 1960), pp. 1-11, 27-33, 49-57. Dewey argues against *religion,* in the sense of belief in the supernatural, as a carry-over from earlier cultures in which men felt relatively helpless in the face of the forces of nature and as an obstacle to "the realization of distinctively religious values inherent in natural experience" (p. 28). He advocates a *religious* faith by which he means "the unification of the self through allegiance to inclusive ideal ends . . . worthy of controlling our desires and choices" (p. 33). Ideals must be tested by experience to determine their worth and their possibility of progressive realization.

Sigmund Freud, *The Future of an Illusion* (Anchor ed.; Garden City: Doubleday & Company, 1961). For Freud supernaturalism is the product of man's sense of helplessness and its association with the sense of helplessness he had as a child. Thus, belief in God is the projection onto the universe of the

---

[5] See, for example, Paul Tillich, *The Shaking of the Foundations* (New York: Charles Scribner's Sons [1948]; paper, 1955), pp. 133-34, 107.

buried memories of one's father in those days when one felt so helpless and yet protected. Freud's own psychiatric experience indicated to him "that religion is comparable to a childhood neurosis," and yet he was "optimistic enough to suppose that mankind will surmount this neurotic phase, just as so many children grow out of their similar neurosis." (p. 87) As men come to rely on their own resources, they will, through science, achieve whichever of those wishes are possible for which they now look to God.

Maurice Cornforth, *Introduction to Dialectical Materialism* (3rd ed.; New York: International Publishers, 1963), volume III, chapter 7. All ideas, including those of religion, are seen by the Marxist as reflections of the existing relations of production. But men are seldom conscious of this character of their religious ideas and so may accept these ideas without realizing that they are really accepting nothing more than a disguised expression of the existing relations of production. Thus "the world of the supernatural always serves as the guardian of the basic fabric of society" (p. 81). The economic class in power, moreover, will strongly promote these ideas because it benefits from the preservation of the existing economic relations, although very seldom will it be aware of this motivation. Religious ideas, then, "constitute a class-motivated system of deception, a mode of disguising the real social relations in the interests of a definite class" (p. 89).

Gustave Weigel and Arthur G. Madden, *Religion and the Knowledge of God* (Spectrum ed.; Englewood Cliffs, N. J.: Prentice-Hall, 1961), chapter 2. Supernaturalism is strongly defended. Religion is defined in terms of activity directed toward a supernatural being; faith is the assent of the whole man to divinely revealed truths, and the goal of life is an other-worldly salvation. Revelation consists of three moments: the preparation, the encounter, and the reflec-

tion. The first is our dissatisfaction with this world. "Guilt, suffering, disappointment, trials, the incompleteness of the finite, all can draw the attention of the human being toward a horizon beyond the finite . . ." (p. 21). The second, the moment of encounter, is not a direct awareness of God. Rather, God elevates or fortifies both the intellect and will, so that the intellect, under this unnatural push of the will, "directs its light on the revelation. The revelation now becomes luminous and is humanly acceptable as the manifestation of God. Simultaneously there is a recognition in terms of logical processes that the revelation can be safely accepted . . ." (p. 22). The culmination of the encounter is "the acceptance of the revelation as true because God is the testifying revealer." In the third moment—the reflection—one can draw out some of the implications of the revelatory encounter for thought and action.

Peter L. Berger, *The Precarious Vision* (Garden City: Doubleday & Company, 1961), chapter 9. This neo-orthodox writer makes a sharp distinction between religion and faith, and consequently welcomes the antireligious critiques of religion—such as those of Freud and Marx. Religion is man's attempt to reach God. It is an attempt to give "ultimate meaning to his life" (p. 169), "to give an illusion of security in a very insecure world" (p. 170), and to provide "a basis of morality, of law and order, of respectability . . ." (p. 173). Religion seeks to undermine the strength and freedom of "man come of age" because he feels no need of religion. Unlike religion, Christian faith is based on a revelation which comes to us *entirely from outside* of ourselves and our world and places all of life, including religion, under judgment. It is at "one point," namely "Jesus Christ, that God has allowed himself to be found" (p. 166), and this revelation calls us to responsible freedom in the world and to the hope of a life beyond the grave. The separation of

God and world is more radical than that to be found in the previous reading from Weigel.

Paul Tillich, "Religion as a Dimension in Man's Spiritual Life," reprinted in *Theology of Culture,* ed. Robert C. Kimball (New York: Oxford University Press, 1959). Concerning his position, Tillich notes that "some Christian theologians [Peter Berger, for example] will ask whether religion is here considered as a creative element of the human spirit rather than as a gift of divine revelation. . . . Then some secular scientists will ask whether religion is to be considered a lasting quality of the human spirit instead of an effect of changing psychological and sociological conditions" (p. 3). Both groups reject Tillich's affirmative answers to these questions, because both "define religion as man's relation to divine beings" (p. 4). Religion is rather the experience of a depth in all of man's spiritual life, the experience of something that concerns us ultimately, something about which we are unconditionally serious, something which "gives substance, ultimate meaning, judgment, and creative courage to all functions of the human spirit" (p. 9). Religion in the narrower sense of a special activity should function to open up the experience of the ultimate or holy in all areas of life, and one reason

that it provokes such passionate resistance from the secular world is that again and again it pretends to be the ultimate which it can only really point to.

For those with special interest in Tillich's point of view, the readings included in this book may be seen as representing (1) various forms of naturalism,[6] (2) various forms of supernaturalism—if this term be used very broadly, and (3) the attempt of Tillich and others to work out a position somewhere between these two. For those of differing interests, other groupings will doubtless suggest themselves as more fruitful. Every system of grouping or classification, however, has the value and the danger of drawing attention to some similarities and differences at the cost of neglecting many other similarities and differences.

In conclusion, the aim of this chapter has been to raise some questions about the religious condition of man in contemporary Western culture. Is he liberated? Is he orphaned? Is he like the prodigal who has not yet come to himself by rediscovering who he is and whose he is? Or is he, rather, like the prodigal who has remembered his father but does not know how to relate to him —knowing only that it cannot be in the old way?

---

[6] The nontheistic selections share the naturalistic contention that "nature is all that there is," but not all of them embrace the belief of naturalism that one should rely solely on scientific method to attain knowledge.

II
Religion and Culture

Introduction

The term "culture" is used here in its broad sense to mean the entire way of life of a people. Fortunately, most of the selections in this book follow this usage. Emil Brunner, however, frequently uses the phrase "civilization and culture" to mean the same thing that we mean here by "culture." This, as he explains, reflects a distinction which German writers have been concerned to make but which Brunner himself is not concerned with, and thus it need not preoccupy the reader. Brunner, in fact, tends to use the terms "civilization" and "culture" interchangeably.

As the introductory chapter has indicated, the reader will find the term "religion" used with a number of very different meanings. Great care must be taken, then, to avoid confusing these meanings in comparing one selection with another.

The first two selections represent two of the foremost nonreligious interpretations of culture in the West today, the Marxist and the Freudian. Although White is not a Marxist and would not be happy about this association, his central thesis concerning culture is identical with that of Marx, namely, that technology is the basic determinant of culture. At the same time, since White is an anthropologist, this selection has the value of presenting a good deal of material from contemporary anthropology on the subject.[1] Norman Brown, on the other hand, is an avowed Freudian, although, as this selection will make clear, he departs from Freud in (1) entertaining a hope for a transformation of culture which Freud did not share and in (2) rejecting certain of Freud's ideas which are incompatible with this hope.

It is recommended that particularly careful study be given to the third selection, by Niebuhr, because it is of basic importance to the rest of the book. Niebuhr discusses five types of interpretation of the relation of the Christian's faith to his cultural concerns, and the last three of these were held foremost in mind in selecting the readings. One may find it helpful, consequently, to refer back to Niebuhr's discussion frequently in the course of the readings. Particularly important in this respect is the relation of the concepts of creation, fall, and redemption to the Christian's interpretation of culture. Is culture seen more in terms of the essential goodness of creation or in terms of the conditions of distortion or corruption symbolized by the fall? Is redemption understood in such a way that it takes place within the cultural process or apart from it?

The next three readings interpret man's relationship to culture on the basis of a belief that his ultimate destiny lies in a life to come after this life.

---

[1] This is not meant to imply, of course, that White's interpretation represents any consensus among anthropologists.

However, they express varying degrees of tension between religion and culture, and although Brunner and Kean are both neo-orthodox Protestants, the reader might ask whether, in this respect, Brunner seems any closer to Kean than he does to the Roman Catholic position of Dawson.[2]

In the next reading, by Tillich, any idea of a world beyond this world or a life beyond this life is rejected. But man is seen to exist in two different orders or dimensions of reality, the finite and the ultimate, which interpenetrate each other. In this way considerable tension is retained between religion and culture even though the two are seen as essentially inseparable. Tillich seeks to show this interpenetration—the fact that "the Unconditioned of which we have an immediate awareness . . . can be recognized in the cultural and natural universe"—in two ways, one positive and one negative.[3] Positively he seeks to show that "in every cultural creation . . . an ultimate concern is expressed, and that it is possible to recognize the unconscious theological character of it."[4] The "negative way of recognizing the unconditional element in man and his world" is by "the analysis of the finitude of the finite in the light of the awareness of the Unconditioned," an analysis which focuses on "concepts like contingency, insecurity, transitoriness, and their psychological correlates anxiety, care, meaninglessness."[5]

The reading from Meland represents a postliberal movement in Protestantism in which reality is seen as a process and God is understood to be known through his creative activity at the most fundamental level of that process. Meland rejects, then, the neo-orthodox view that God breaks into our cultural processes from outside them. God works within the flow of events to create a feeling orientation or structure of experience that makes possible the most creative human activity.

The final selection, from Harvey Cox, does not present an explicit theory about the relation of religion and culture. Rather, it interprets our present cultural situation in terms of his belief that the secularization of man—his "coming of age"—is the work of God, and thus it stands in interesting contrast with some of the previous selections. It is important here to keep in mind the distinction Cox draws between "secularization" and "secularism."

Secularization implies a historical process, almost certainly irreversible, in which society and culture are delivered from tutelage to religious control and closed metaphysical world-views. . . . Secularism, on the other hand, is the name for an ideology, a new closed world-view which functions very much like a new religion.[6]

---

[2] Neo-orthodoxy is an attempt, usually on the part of former liberals, to restore what they regard as the essential doctrines of Luther and Calvin, but without closing their eyes to significant developments since that time, such as the radical work of modern biblical criticism. For further information concerning this sort of disagreement within neo-orthodoxy, the reader may wish to refer to a discussion between Brunner and Karl Barth in *Nature and Grace* (London: The Centenary Press, 1946), or to a discussion between Barth and Reinhold Niebuhr in *The Christian Century*, LXV (October 27, 1948), 1138-40, and LXVI (February 16, 1949), 201-4, and LXVI (February 23, 1949), 234-36.

[3] "The Two Types of Philosophy of Religion" reprinted from *Union Seminary Quarterly Review*, I, 4 in *Theology of Culture*, p. 26.

[4] *Ibid.*, p. 27.

[5] *Ibid.*, p. 26.

[6] *The Secular City* (New York: The Macmillan Company, 1965), pp. 20-21.

LESLIE A. WHITE

Technology as the Basis of Culture*

Man is unique: he is the only living species that has a culture. By *culture* we mean an extrasomatic, temporal continuum of things and events dependent upon symboling. Specifically and concretely, culture consists of tools, implements, utensils, clothing, ornaments, customs, institutions, beliefs, rituals, games, works of art, language, etc. All peoples in all times and places have possessed culture; no other species has or has had culture. In the course of the evolution of primates *man* appeared when the ability to symbol had been developed and become capable of expression. We thus define man in terms of the ability to symbol and the consequent ability to produce culture.

Man, as an animal, possesses a number of characteristics which qualify him for culture. Among these may be mentioned erect posture, which frees the forelimbs for nonlocomotory activities; an opposable thumb, which makes the hand an effective grasping organ; stereoscopic, chromatic vision; gregariousness; and possibly a few other traits. But the most important qualification of all is the ability to symbol.

We call the ability freely and arbitrarily to originate and bestow meaning upon a thing or event, and, correspondingly, the ability to grasp and appreciate such meaning, *the ability to symbol.* . . .

Dogs "can understand words and sentences," as Darwin observed long ago. And today laboratory rats can distinguish the food meaning of green circles from the electric-shock meaning of red triangles. But this is not symboling. In neither case does the animal originate and bestow the meaning; it is man who does this. And in each case dog and rat grasp the meanings with their senses because these meanings have become so identified with their physical bases through the operation of the conditioned reflex that sensory comprehension becomes possible.

Darwin declared that "there is no fundamental difference between man and the higher mammals in their mental faculties," that the difference between them consists "*solely* in his (man's) almost infinitely larger power of associating together the most diversified sounds and ideas . . . the mental powers of higher animals do not differ *in kind,* though greatly *in degree,* from the corresponding powers of man" (italics supplied).[1] This view has been held by many psychologists down to the present day. It can be readily demonstrated, however, that this is not the case; that the difference between the mind of man and that of subman is indeed one of kind, not merely one of degree; that man's mind is unique among all species of living beings.

There are many things that man can do that no other creature is capable of. Only man can appreciate the difference between holy water and ordinary water; no ape, rat, dog, or any other subhuman animal can have the slightest conception of the meaning of holy water. Many primitive peoples distinguish parallel cousins from cross-cousins; all peoples classify their relatives, distinguish cousin from sibling, uncle from grandfather, etc. No subhuman animal can do this; no monkey can tell an uncle from a

[1] Charles Darwin, *The Descent of Man,* 1904, Chaps. 3, 18.

cousin. No nonhuman animal can remember the Sabbath to keep it holy; in fact, he cannot distinguish the Sabbath from any other day, and he can have no conception whatsoever of holiness. . . .

Man and culture originated simultaneously; this by definition. . . . The time of man's and culture's origin cannot be fixed with precision, of course, but one million years ago represents a fair consensus among authorities of the date of their beginning.

We may assume that culture came into being in the following way: Neurological evolution in a certain line, or lines, of anthropoids culminated eventually in the ability to symbol. The exercise of this ability brought culture into existence and then perpetuated it. We may elucidate and justify this conception by showing that culture in all parts and aspects is dependent upon symboling, or, more specifically, upon articulate speech. For this purpose we may divide the components of culture into four categories: ideological, sociological, sentimental or attitudinal, and technological.

The ideological sector of culture is composed of beliefs, and all beliefs—at least all beliefs of man as a human being—are dependent upon symboling, or articulate speech, for their origin and for their perpetuation. . . .

The sociological component—i.e., the customs, institutions, rules and patterns of interpersonal behavior, etc.—of cultural systems likewise is dependent upon articulate speech. . . . How could one distinguish between mine and thine, or right and wrong, or know what is a polite and acceptable way to behave toward one's mother-in-law, or how to dispose of the dead, etc., without verbal expression and communication? It is plain, therefore, that the behavior of man as a human being[2] in his social life is dependent upon symboling.

With regard to sentiments, or attitudes, as components of culture, we find the same situation. The feelings or attitudes that constitute the subjunctive aspect of the mother-in-law taboo, for example, require symboling for their existence. . . .

But how is it with the technological sector of culture, the manufacture and use of tools and implements? The definition of man as the tool-using animal, often attributed to Benjamin Franklin —but with a justification open to question—is obsolete. Apes not only use tools with ease, skill, and versatility; they make or "invent" them as well. They seem to be almost as much at home with tools that require a fine and delicate touch as with those requiring great muscular strength. One ape may learn the use of a tool from another by observation and imitation. But for all this, there is a profound difference between man's use of tools and the technology of anthropoid apes. The use of tools in the human species is, on the whole, a cumulative and progressive process; it is this that distinguishes neolithic from paleolithic cultures, and the Age of Coal and Steel from the Middle Ages. In the human tool process, one generation may begin where the preceding generation left off. It is otherwise with the anthropoids. Tool using with them is not a cumulative or progressive process; each generation begins where its predecessor began. There is no reason to believe that apes are any farther along technologically today than they were ten, or a hundred, thousand years ago. Why this great difference? . . .

. . . In the author's essay "On the Use of Tools by Primates,"[3] he has gone to

---

[2] A portion of the behavior of man is not symboled and is therefore not human. Coughing, scratching, yawning, etc., are examples of this.

[3] *Journal of Comparative Psychology*, vol. 34, pp. 369-74, 1942.

considerable length to show, specifically and concretely, how symbolizing and language have transformed the nonprogressive, noncumulative tool process of anthropoids into a cumulative and progressive process in the human species. . . .

The function of culture. The purpose and function of culture are to make life secure and enduring for the human species. All species of living beings behave in such a way as to perpetuate their kind. Subhuman species execute this behavior by somatic means, i.e., with their bodies, muscles, organs, etc. Man, as a mere animal, also employs his bodily organs in life-sustaining behavior. But as a human being man employs the extrasomatic tradition that we call culture in order to sustain and perpetuate his existence and give it full expression. We may think of culture, then, as an extrasomatic mechanism employed by a particular animal species in order to make its life secure and continuous. . . .

We might express the functions of culture in another way: the purpose of culture is to serve the needs of man. These needs may be divided into two categories: (1) those that can be served only by exploiting the resources of the external world; and (2) those that can be served by drawing upon the resources of the human organism only. Man needs food and materials of many kinds for clothing, utensils, ornaments, etc.; these must be obtained, of course, from the external world. But man has inner, psychic, social, and "spiritual" needs that can be fed and nourished without drawing upon the external world at all. Man needs courage, comfort, consolation, confidence, companionship, a feeling of consequence in the scheme of things that life is worthwhile, and some assurance of success. It is the business of culture to serve these needs of the "spirit" as well as the needs of the body.

Life is continued only by effort. Pain, suffering, lonesomeness, fear, frustration, and boredom dog man's steps at almost every turn. He requires companionship, courage, inspiration, hope, comfort, reassurance, and consolation to enable him to continue the struggle of life. Cultural devices serve man here. Mythologies flatter, encourage, and reassure him. By means of magic and ritual he can capture the illusion of power and control over things and events; he can "control" the weather, cure disease, foresee the future, increase his food supply, overcome his enemies. Various devices relate him to the spirit world so that he may enjoy the blessings and avoid the wrath of the gods. Cosmologies give him answers to all fundamental questions, of life and death and the nature of things. Thus culture gives man a sense of power and of confidence. It assures him that life is worth living and gives him the courage to endure it. It comforts and sustains him when he meets defeat or frustration. It provides him with companions, divine as well as human. It attacks boredom and manages at times to make life pleasurably exciting and of fine flavor. In short, culture gives man the illusion of importance, omnipotence, and omniscience. These inner spiritual—or intraorganismal—needs of man are of course as real as those for food, shelter, and defense; in fact, they might be felt even more keenly. And these needs must be served if man is to succeed in the struggle of life.

There are institutions or customary practices in virtually every culture that have as their prime, if not sole, purpose association among members of the community or some members of it. There are tribal or community feasts and festivals. There are clubs and societies, both secret and nonsecret. Groupings of this sort are, perhaps, especially conspicuous in a culture like our own where the individual would be lost in the vast structures of government, economics, and industry without some small group within which he may have intimate and personal association with his fellows.

29

The almost innumerable fraternal orders, lodges, and clubs of all kinds in our culture testify to the ubiquity and magnitude of the need for the annihilation of solitude and loneliness, the need for the moral and psychological support that comes from membership in a relatively small, intimate, personal group. The sociological sector of cultural systems thus serves the "inner," psychic, "spiritual"—or "moral" as Durkheim would put it—needs of man just as the ideological—the mythological, theological, philosophical and even the scientific—sector does.

And even the technological sector is not immune; it, too, provides satisfactions that are not utilitarian or technological in character. Craftsmanship, the process of doing or making something, can and often does provide the craftsman with pleasures and satisfactions quite apart from the product made or the fruits of its use. Carving a perfect canoe paddle, grinding a symmetrical stone ax, weaving a basket, making a spear, a cradle board, etc., as technological processes can yield psychic satisfactions in and by themselves. . . .

Relationship between man and culture.
. . . Culture was brought into being by the actions of man; it is supported and maintained in the same way. It could not be otherwise, then, that culture should be determined *in a general way,* in its structure and behavior as a system, by the nature—the bodily structure and capabilities—of man. Had culture been produced by a race of supercats, supercows or superants, instead of a race of supersimians, it would have been quite different from what it is with us, because cats, cows and ants are fundamentally different in their natures from simians —as well as from each other. The nature of man, i.e., his bodily structure and functions, makes possible certain developments within, and also imposes certain limitations upon, the culture-building process. Our culture would be

quite different if man could subsist only upon plants, or upon a single genus of plant, instead of being omnivorous. Our culture is a function of our vision to a certain extent; it would be otherwise if our vision were achromatic and non-stereoscopic. The continuous activity of our sexual life, instead of a rutting season, has a profound effect upon our social organization, as we shall see later. . . .

But if there is a significant and fundamental generic relationship between man and culture, there is no instance of a specific relationship between a grouping—a physical type, race, tribe, or nation—of mankind and a type of culture. Few people would wish to argue that the physical type of the Chinese disposes them to eat with chopsticks or to write with a brush rather than with a pen. But there are many who believe that a people's "temperament" shapes their political, social, or economic system—they are by nature aggressive, submissive, individualistic, communistic, etc. These beliefs receive no support, however, from scientific evidence. Peoples differ in physical type, of course, and they may differ temperamentally also. But we do not know what these differences may be, nor how to identify and measure them, and much less to determine their effect upon cultural differences. We do know that the influence of culture upon the behavior of peoples is so powerful, so overriding, that we may be sure that such temperamental differences as may exist among peoples is slight and insignificant in comparison. And there is good reason to believe that the phenomena, or qualities, called temperament are not innate, or biologically determined, at all, but are produced by cultural influence.

In the man-culture situation, therefore, we may consider man, the biological factor, to be a constant; culture the variable. . . . This means that the biological factor of man is irrelevant to various problems of cultural interpretation such

30

as diversities among cultures, and processes of culture change in general and the evolution of culture in particular. . . .

The culture of mankind in actuality is a one, a single system; all the so-called cultures are merely distinguishable portions of a single fabric. The culture of mankind as a whole may be considered temporally as a flowing stream, or nontemporally as a system, or as both, i.e., as a system in a temporal continuum. . . .

It is only when and in so far as cultures can be considered significantly apart from their relations and contacts with other cultures that they can be treated as systems. Failure to realize this has led to serious error in the past in ethnological theory. Thus it was pointed out by opponents of the theory of cultural evolution that "a given culture" did not have to pass through certain stages of development in order to reach a certain point because this point could be reached as a consequence of cultural diffusion. . . . Actually, of course, the evolutionists did not say that every culture, or every people, had to pass through a certain sequence of stages, but that processes of cultural development had to go through a certain series of stages. . . .

TECHNOLOGY: THE BASIS AND DETERMINANT OF CULTURAL SYSTEMS

Through logical analysis we have distinguished four kinds of components of cultural systems: technological, sociological, ideological, and sentimental, or attitudinal. . . . The fact that these four cultural categories are interrelated, that each is related to the other three, does not mean that their respective roles in the culture process are equal, for they are not. The technological factor is the basic one; all others are dependent upon it. Furthermore, the technological factor determines, in a general way at least, the form and content of the social, philosophic, and sentimental sectors.

The technological basis of cultural systems is rather easily demonstrated. All living organisms can maintain themselves as individuals and perpetuate themselves as species only if a certain minimum adjustment to the external world is achieved and maintained. There must be food, protection from the elements, and defense from enemies. These life-sustaining, life-perpetuating processes are technological in a broad, but valid, sense, i.e., they are carried on by material, mechanical, biophysical, and biochemical means.

If it be argued that technologies could not exist without ideas—and it is of course a matter of empirical observation that technologies do not exist apart from ideas—and that therefore tools are dependent upon ideas, it may be countered, first, that ideas can be significant and effective in the maintenance of life only by receiving expression through technological means, and hence are dependent upon them whereas the technological culture is significant directly. Secondly, in associations of technologies and ideas, one can account for idea systems in terms of technologies, and technologies can be explained in terms of the physiochemical, mechanical means of adjustment of one material body to another. But if one explains technologies in terms of ideas, the ideas are either unexplained or are accounted for by appeal to other ideas, which amounts to the same thing.

It is fairly obvious that the social organization of a people is not only dependent upon their technology but is determined to a great extent, if not wholly, by it, both in form and content. As a matter of fact, a social system might well be defined as the way in which a society makes use of its particular technology in the various life-sustaining processes: subsistence, protection from the elements, defense from enemies, combating disease, etc. The activities of hunting, fishing, gathering, farming, tending herds and flocks, mining, and

31

all the processes by means of which raw materials are transformed and made ready for human consumption are not merely technological processes; they are social processes as well.[4] And *as* social processes they are functions of their respective technological processes; as the latter change, so will the former. The processes of combating disease, "controlling" the weather, providing protection against the elements and defense against enemies, are likewise social processes. Social systems have, therefore, like technological systems, subsistence, health, protection, and defense coordinates. Of these, the subsistence function is the most important because all others are dependent upon it. Thus, hunting, herding, gathering, fishing, farming, mining, manufacturing, and transportation will influence, each in its own way, and in proportion to its magnitude, the form and content of a social system. Any society will have many. In addition to the exploitation and processing of materials taken from nature, any social system will be determined by medical, protectional, and military technological factors as well. . . .

The influence of technology upon social organization is expressed in two ways. First, there is the *direct* effect of technological instruments upon the behavior of human organisms. A bow and arrow, digging stick, clock, or steam engine produces certain orbits, or patterns, of behavior. Secondly, these patterns must be related to each other on the social level, in order to make a coherent, integrated social system possible. The manner in which this interrelationship of social patterns takes place is conditioned by their own structure and function, which are in turn technologically determined. Thus, a brotherhood of railroad trainmen is a grouping formed upon the basis of patterns of behavior that are formed directly by the use of locomotives, cars, etc. And society must have means to relate this brotherhood to other social groupings and so incorporate it into society as a whole. The effect of technology upon social organization is thus exercised directly through the use of tools, utensils, etc., and indirectly in the process of interrelating the social patterns formed directly by the technology.

To be sure, it may not be practically possible to account for minute differences of social system in terms of technology as a determinant. . . . But inability to do this would not necessarily mean that our thesis is invalid. It is not always possible to observe microscopic events effectively with a macroscopic spyglass.

If social institutions are shaped by the operation of technologies, then social change will tend to follow technological change. But the institutional response to technological change may not be immediate. Institutions come to have an inertia of their own. The articulation of one institution within a social structure may tend to preserve the institution intact, also. . . . Secondly, as we have seen, a social phenomenon is the resultant not merely of *one* technological factor but of many. The denotation of the avuncular relationship by a single reciprocal term is, we may say, a minute and particular expression of the cooperation, integration, and solidarity required by the group in order to make life secure. But to break this down into all its technological determinants, such as all the tools, weapons, utensils used by a tribe, might prove to be an impossible task, even with more adequate means of

---

[4] . . . This is in sharp contrast to the view of Boas which he and his disciples used to combat the theory of cultural evolution. "The early attempts of Morgan to associate social organization and economic condition have proved to be fallacious. . . . We have simple industries and complex organization, or diverse industries and simple organization." Franz Boas, "Some Problems of Methodology in the Social Sciences," *Race, Language and Culture*, The Macmillan Company, New York, 1940, pp. 266-67. . . .

analysis than we now possess. Thirdly, as we have already pointed out, a social element may serve to interrelate and integrate other social elements that have been formed directly by the technological factor, and is consequently the indirect rather than direct result of technological influence. This would, of course, make correlation between the social and the technological even more difficult. Finally, we would reply to the demand that we interpret details of kinship systems and other social forms in terms of technological influence by asking, "If they are not determined technologically, either directly or indirectly, how then are they determined?" Alternative explanations would seem to be instinct, ideas, and free will.

Instinct can probably be dismissed at the outset; no one, we dare say, would want to argue that any cultural form is determined by genes and chromosomes. If ideas determine social forms, what determines the ideas? We have touched upon this point before. To argue that a people determines its social organization by its own free will and choice[5] really explains nothing and shuts the door to further inquiry as well. . . .

A close correlation between types of philosophy and types of technology can be established. . . .

The philosophy, or ideological component, of every culture thus far is made up of naturalistic and supernaturalistic elements. The role of each in any given situation is determined by the underlying technology. Supernaturalism flourishes best where man's control over his relations with the external world, with the realm outside his own ego, is least. . . . In occupations in preliterate cultures like hunting, fishing, combating illness, warfare, and in dealing with the weather, where control over things and

events is relatively slight, supernaturalism luxuriates. In the course of cultural development, as control has increased, supernaturalism waned. Knowledge and understanding increase as the material, mechanical, physiochemical means of adjustment and control are improved and extended. Witness, for example, the great effect wrought upon knowledge, belief, and outlook—i.e., upon philosophy—by the telescope and microscope; by such advances in agriculture as irrigation, draining, use of artificial fertilizers, and plant breeding; by technological explorations in the physical, chemical, biological, geological, meteorological, and astronomical realms. Astronomy and mathematics—geometry especially—may be regarded to a great extent as byproducts of agriculture.

An explanation of a philosophy requires more than an appeal to technological determinants alone. A philosophy is an expression in verbal forms, of experience. . . .

The expression of experience arising from technological sources is conditioned by passing through the medium of a social system, and this medium may refract the expression in one way or another. A primitive tribe, a feudal order, an industrialized capitalist society will each have its philosophy conditioned by its respective social, political, and economic institutions. Furthermore, much of human experience is of institutions themselves directly. . . .

We may say, then, that philosophies are determined by technologies (1) directly and (2) indirectly, through social systems.

Our theory of technological determination does not enable us to deal with microscopic details in philosophy any more than in the realm of social organization. We cannot explain in terms

---

[5] Ruth Benedict appears clearly to take this view. "The great arc along which all the possible human behaviors are distributed is far too immense and too full of contradictions for any one culture to utilize even any considerable portion of it. Selection is the first requirement . . . any society selects some segment of the arc of possible human behavior" which they then "capitalize in their traditional institutions. . . ." *Patterns of Culture,* Houghton Mifflin Company, Boston, 1934, pp. 237, 254.

of technology why, for example, in one culture there is a belief in three souls per person whereas in another there is a belief in only one. But it must be remembered that our theory specifies generic kinds of belief rather than specific beliefs. Philosophically, there is no difference in kind between a belief in one soul and a belief in three. The difference between a belief in soul or souls and a belief in protoplasm can, however, be accounted for technologically. We can distinguish various types of philosophy and correlate them with types of technology. Thus, any cultural anthropologist could tell in advance what type of philosophy would be correlated with an upper Paleolithic type of technology, for example. Hunting, fishing, farming, etc., each has its philosophic reflexes and emphases. As a theoretical principle, the proposition that in the system that is culture, philosophy is determined by technology in its type, emphasis, orientation, and generic content is illuminating and fruitful.

The application of the theory of technological determination to the category *sentiments* in culture is less significant than its use in the social and philosophic spheres. . . .

Ideals of beauty in women may in some instances be correlated rather closely with the mode of subsistence as technologically determined. In cultures where technological control over food supply is slight and food is frequently scarce as a consequence, a fat woman is often regarded as beautiful. In cultures where food is abundant and women work little, obesity is likely to be regarded as unsightly. In some societies, a sun-browned skin in women was a mark of the lower class of peasants, for example. Ladies, on the other hand, took great pains to preserve a fair skin. In other cultures, e.g., our own today, the pallid skin is a mark of the urban working girl who sees little of the sun, whereas the well-tanned girl is one who can afford to spend much time on golf courses or bathing beaches. The attitude toward sun-browned skins is here reversed. The social systems involved are of course shaped by their respective technologies.

Sentiments pertaining to the distinction between "we" and "they" groups on the tribal, national, and international levels are of course tremendously powerful and significant in social intercourse. Size of social unit is especially relevant here. In some situations we find small groups, each with its independence, integrity, and solidarity. Individuals within these groups owe allegiance to them, respectively, and regard all groups save their own as inferior or hostile. In the course of social evolution, however, a number of these separate and sovereign groups may become united in a single political entity. A synthesis of a number of rival loyalties into a common allegiance follows. What produces this change of sentiment? The answer is, of course, the forces that made small political units obsolete and their amalgamation inevitable. And these forces were those of technology, specifically those exercised in production, commerce, communication, transportation, and warfare. Evolution toward larger political units is at bottom a technological affair. Those who think a world state can be brought about by playing upon the sentiments of citizens directly have the cart before the horse. It is not a changing sentiment that turns the wheels of social evolution. Rather, it is the alteration of social and political groupings by the operation of technological forces that determines the direction and scope of the sentiment. . . .

A word of caution is in order here, however. In emphasizing the dominant and determining role of technology, one should not lose sight of the influence exerted upon technology by social, philosophic, and sentimental factors. To assert the preeminence or dominance of technology is not to deny all power and influence to other factors. We insisted at the very outset upon the interaction and interrelationship of all aspects of culture, even though the roles played by each were not equal in magnitude of influence. Having demonstrated the dominance of the technological factor in the culture process, it would be well to cite a few examples of influence exerted upon technology by other kinds of factors.

Technologies exist and function within social systems and are consequently conditioned by them. A social system may stimulate the technology it embraces, encourage full and free exercise of its functions, and promote its growth and development. Or it may restrict free technological exercise and expression and impose curbs upon its growth....

Much the same observations can be made with regard to philosophies or sentiments. They, too, may aid or oppose free expression of growth of the technologies which, respectively, they embrace. A set of beliefs may oppose medical technology, for example. Certain attitudes or sentiments might do likewise.

We are confronted by no theoretical problem when social systems, philosophies, and sentiments promote the free and full expression of the technological process. But what becomes of our theory of technological determinism if social or philosophic factors may successfully oppose the technology?...

The motive power of a culture, so to speak, lies in its technology, for here it is that energy is harnessed and put to work. But the magnitude of this motive power is always finite, however great it may be. Now when a technology of a given magnitude of strength or power is opposed by nontechnological cultural elements, be they social, ideational, or emotional, what happens? The answer is obvious. The technology overcomes this opposition if it is strong enough to do so; if it is not strong enough, then it

must submit. If a technology is powerful enough to break up a social system that thwarts it, it does so and brings a new system into existence. If it is not sufficiently powerful, then it must submit to the restrictions. The same remarks will apply to philosophies and sentiments also as curbs upon technology.

It is important to recognize the fact that these observations are not concessions made to an opponent of our theory of technological determinism. This theory states merely that of the various classes of forces within a cultural system, technology is the basis and the motive power of the system. It does not assert that it is omnipotent, independent of conditions and subject to no limitations....

[RELIGION AND CULTURE]

Benedict has asserted that religion is independent of technology, that man "can *at any stage of technological development* create his gods *in the most diverse form.*"[6] But this is manifestly not true. In cultures where the superiorities of animals over man are manifest on every hand—in size, strength, and special abilities like those of the cobra, skunk, seal, eagle, or mole—the attitude of man is not the same as it is in cultures where man's supremacy—thanks to his technology—is undisputed. In primitive cultures man did not consider himself both superior and unique, nor even *primus inter pares;* he was merely one of the animals and often so inferior that they became his gods. The prevalence of animal gods—the bear, snake, eagle, coyote—on preliterate, tribal cultural levels, the wide occurrence of half-man, half-beast gods in the cultures of the Bronze age—such as gods with the heads of cats or birds, or the bodies of bulls or hippos, in Egypt and Mesopotamia—

---

[6] Ruth Benedict, "Anthropology and the Humanities," *American Anthropologist,* vol. 50, p. 589, 1948.

and the emphasis upon anthropomorphic deities in modern cultures cannot be without significance, although these correlations are not yet well understood.

The social experience of primitive man in societies based upon kinship is reflected in his mythologies. Not only are subhuman species his neighbors, they are often his friends and even his kinsmen. "I *am* a kangaroo," says an Arunta in identifying himself with his totem. And in myths and tales, lower animals and birds can assume the human form; all animals can speak and intermarry freely with man. In Christian cultures, by contrast, man alone has a soul and his nonhuman kin are degraded to the level of beasts. Apropos of Benedict's pronouncement about the independence of religion from technology and stages of social evolution, we may observe that no primitive culture is capable of having a deity who is " (Christ) the *royal* master" or "Great God our *King*," just as alphabets, keystone arches, and tempered steel are incompatible with Emu totems, Sun Youth, and Spider Grandmother.

Cultural systems are self-consistent, as they are coherent, and integrated. A primitive society goes with a primitive technology, and both are reflected and expressed by a primitive philosophy. . . .

Gods are the supernaturalization of factors that significantly affect the lives of men. These factors vary with habitat and degree of cultural development. In primitive, preliterate cultures the most significant factors tend to become sociocultural. In primitive cultures, the forces that pressed hardest upon man and determined his weal and woe were those of nature: the sun, wind, and rain; disease germs; powerful predators, or an abundance of game. In civil societies, the significant forces are social: economic and political. The privation, hunger, toil bondage, or technological unemployment of the masses of civil society are not due to nature's niggardliness or

hostility; they are features of a social system. The power, wealth, and ease of the upper classes may be ascribed to the favor of the gods, but if so this favor is made manifest and expressed in a kind of social system. The existence of slavery, serfdom, levies, usury, and taxation is to be attributed to a kind of social system, a type of society produced by intensive cultivation of cereals with plow and oxen, rather than to forces of nature. There may be gods of war in civil society, but battles are always fought by men who are commanded by kings and blessed by priests; and it is human beings, organized in political and military systems, who kill, conquer, and subjugate one another.

In the great urban cultures of antiquity, therefore, the most significant factors affecting the lives of the people, great and small alike, were those of *society,* of sociocultural systems in their technological and institutional aspects. Society and god became one. The almighty, immortal, and ethical power that is civil society was expressed in the conception of a deity in the heavens and in the person of a ruler on earth. Sometimes the king was only the earthly representative—the "tenant farmer," as he was sometimes called—of the deity; sometimes he was a god himself or the descendant of a god. Society, god, and ruler are a triad of concepts that constitute a unity; they are but three expressions of the same phenomenon. Eventually the concept of one supreme deity emerges. . . .

Theologies reflect political organization and exercises of power and authority as well as agriculture and the succession of the seasons. We can cite only a few instances of this for ancient Egypt as suggestive of what an adequate study of Bronze Age cultures might do in this respect. . . .

In ancient Egypt, as Breasted has shrewdly observed, theological thinking was "brought into close relationship with political conditions."[7]

The struggle between Akhenaten (Ikhnaton), "the Heretic King," and the priesthoods of Egypt during the fourteenth century B.C. found its expression in theology. The emergence of the doctrine of monotheism was a means employed by the pharaoh to oppose the priests: Aton, the disk, or sun, god, was declared to be the only god, and the pharaoh was his chief priest; the other deities were declared to be nonexistent, and therefore Akhenaten attempted to close their temples and abolish their priesthoods. It was an attempt, says Moret, to "break the power of the priests of Amon lest they should dethrone the kings."[8] He also makes the shrewd observation that "this appropriation of the property of the temples shows us what lay beneath the religious revolution, *the economic and political objects of the rupture.*"[9] In this bitter struggle between the two components of the special mechanism of integration of the nation, state and church, the pharaoh and his one god, Aton, were defeated. The victors razed the temple of Aton, and inscriptions pertaining to the "heresy" were expunged from monuments and public buildings. The god Amon, through his priests, triumphed.

The change from nationalism to imperialism, too, is reflected in Egyptian theology. In the Pyramid Age the sun god ruled only Egypt, and in the hymns of the day we find him standing guard at her frontiers "where he builds the gates which restrain all outsiders from entering his inviolable domain." But after Egyptian forces had conquered foreign lands and established an empire, the supreme god of Egypt became the Lord of the Universe. As Breasted has observed, "monotheism is but imperialism in religion."[10]

NORMAN O. BROWN

Culture as Sublimation*

There is a qualitative distinction between men and animals; but the distinction is based on what is perhaps only a quantitative phenomenon, namely, the peculiar prolongation of infancy in the human species. In the case of man, the prolongation of infancy and the postponement of puberty give infantile sexuality a longer period in which to mature, and at the same time parental

[7] James H. Breasted, *A History of Egypt,* rev. ed., Charles Scribner's Sons, New York, 1909, p. 359.
[8] Alexandre Moret, *Kings and Gods of Egypt,* G. P. Putnam's Sons, New York, 1912, p. 45.
[9] Alexandre Moret, *The Nile and Egyptian Civilization,* Alfred A. Knopf, Inc., New York, 1927, p. 324.
[10] James H. Breasted, *The Development of Religion and Thought in Ancient Egypt,* Charles Scribner's Sons, New York, 1912, pp. 312, 315.

care shelters it from the reality-principle. Under these conditions infantile sexuality achieves a full bloom to which there can be no parallel in other species of animals. Hence there is a conflict in the sexual life of man, as there is not in other animals. In man infantile sexuality is repressed and never outgrown; repression (and consequently neurosis) distinguishes man from the other animals. The result is that genital organization is a tyranny in man because his peculiar infancy has left him with a lifelong allegiance (i.e., fixation) to the pattern of infantile sexuality.

Thus Freud's theory of infantile sexuality is an essential part of his theory of neurosis, so that he puts this concept on the same level of importance as his concept of repression and the unconscious, and says that psychoanalysis stands or falls by the expansion of the idea of the "sexual function" as opposed to the narrower one of a "genital function." The therapeutic value of the concept of infantile sexuality as an aid in the psychiatric treatment of those individuals whose neurosis has reached the point of incapacitating them for practical living is not the issue here. What matters is the flood of light which the concept of infantile sexuality throws on the universal neurosis of mankind and on his ultimate nature and destiny.

In Freud's theory of infantile sexuality there is first of all a critique of the genital function and an implied rejection of genital intercourse—"free love" and the orgasm—as a solution to the sexual problem. Not only is there an implied critique of D. H. Lawrence; there is an implied critique of superficial followers of Freud himself, and even some great ones (Abraham, Reich, Fenichel), who have idealized the "genital character" as a way out of the human neurosis. Thus Fenichel: "The ability to obtain full satisfaction through genital orgasm makes the physiological regulation of sexuality possible and thus puts an end to the damming up of instinctual energies, with its unfortunate effects on the person's behavior."[1] This appearance of finding the solution to the world's problems in the genital has done much to discredit psychoanalysis: mankind, from history and from personal experience, knows better. How perilous the pitfalls are that lie on both sides of the psychoanalytical path can be seen in the sad career of Wilhelm Reich. A man with keen insight into the sociological implications of psychoanalysis, he foundered on the theory of infantile sexuality (as do the neo-Freudians) and ended up in a glorification of the orgasm as the solution to all social and bodily ailments.

Freud sees conflict—in his earlier theory, between the pleasure-principle and the reality-principle; in his later theory, between Eros and Death—in the genital act itself. He distinguishes fore-pleasure and end-pleasure in sexual intercourse. The fore-pleasure is the preliminary play with all parts of the body, and represents a perpetuation of the pure polymorphous perverse play of infantile sexuality. The end-pleasure in the orgasm is purely genital and postpubertal.

From the Freudian point of view the subordination of fore-pleasure to end-pleasure in sexual intercourse is a compromise concealing a conflict between the desire of the immortal child in us for pure polymorphous play and the reality-principle which imposes genital organization on us. This conflict explains the fact that while it is not true, as the Church father said, that *post coitum omne animal triste,* it is true of the human animal: the immortal child in us is frustrated, even in the sexual act, by the tyranny of genital organization. Hence the attempt to overthrow

---

[1] Fenichel, *The Psychoanalytic Theory of Neurosis,* p. 496. Cf. Abraham, *Selected Papers,* pp. 407-15; Reich, *The Function of the Orgasm.*

genital organization in certain practices of mysticism—mysticism being able, as Freud said, "to grasp certain relations in the deeper layers of the ego and the id which would otherwise be inaccessible." [2] The heretical Christian sect known as Adamites, who sought to recapture in this life the innocent eroticism of Adam before the Fall, practiced *coitus reservatus,* intercourse without orgasm, that is to say, pure fore-pleasure.[3] If he knew psychoanalysis, Needham would not be so puzzled that in Taoist mysticism *"coitus reservatus* should have been considered so valuable for mental health." [4]

For Freud, the clue not only to normal adult sexuality but to our whole repressed and hidden ultimate essence lies in infantile sexuality. This is not a proposition to which we take kindly. Ignorance and fear, both of them the results of repression, together with the noble illusion, fostered by our higher aspirations, that we are all soul and no body, set in motion one or another of a number of mechanisms of intellectual flight whenever the topic of sexuality is taken seriously. If deference to the scientific attitude has induced a certain broad- or open-mindedness toward the general topic, the specific details are more than we can take, and we slip into the evasion of abhorrence or amusement. We are likely to withdraw our willingness to listen when we are told that infantile sexuality is polymorphously perverse. And Freud must mean that polymorphous perversity is the pattern of our deepest desires. How can this proposition be taken seriously?

If we divest ourselves of the prejudice surrounding the "perverse," if we try to be objective and analyze what infantile sexuality is in itself, we must return again to the definition. Infantile sexuality is the pursuit of pleasure obtained through the activity of any and all organs of the human body. So defined, the ultimate essence of our desires and our being is nothing more or less than delight in the active life of all the human body. That this is Freud's notion becomes abundantly clear if we examine the specific nature of the "perverse" components in infantile sexuality. They include the pleasure of touching, of seeing, of muscular activity, and even the passion for pain.[5] It is therefore perfectly consistent, and implies no change of view, when in his later writings Freud added the term "life instinct" as synonymous with what he in other contexts called "the sexual instinct," "Eros," or "libido." And there is no difference between Freud's notion of the ultimate essence of the human being and William Blake's when he said, "Energy is the only life, and is from the Body. . . . Energy is Eternal Delight." As with the concept of repression and the unconscious, so in his concept of the libido Freud appears less as an inventor of unheard-of novelties than as one who grasped in rational and scientific form intuitions which have haunted the imagination of poets and philosophers throughout the modern or Romantic period of our intellectual history.

Freud and Blake are asserting that the ultimate essence of our being remains in our unconscious secretly faithful to the principle of pleasure, or, as Blake calls it, delight. To say this is to call in question the psychological assumptions upon which our Western morality has been built. For two thousand years or more man has been subjected to a systematic effort to transform him into an ascetic animal. He remains a pleasure-seeking animal. Parental discipline, religious denunciation of bodily pleasure, and philosophic exaltation of the life of reason have all left man overtly docile,

---

[2] *New Introductory Lectures on Psychoanalysis,* p. 106.
[3] Cf. Huxley, *Tomorrow and Tomorrow,* pp. 289-301; Eliade, *Le Yoga,* pp. 250, 267, 270, 396.
[4] Needham, *Science and Civilization in China,* II, 149.
[5] *The Basic Writings of Sigmund Freud (Three Contributions to the Theory of Sex),* pp. 599-602.

but secretly in his unconscious unconvinced, and therefore neurotic. Man remains unconvinced because in infancy he tasted the fruit of the tree of life, and knows that it is good, and never forgets. . . .

The realm of the unconscious is established in the individual when he refuses to admit into his conscious life a purpose or desire which he has, and in doing so establishes in himself a psychic force opposed to his own idea. This rejection by the individual of a purpose or idea, which nevertheless remains his, is repression. "The essence of repression lies simply in the function of rejecting or keeping something out of consciousness." [6] Stated in more general terms, the essence of repression lies in the refusal of the human being to recognize the realities of his human nature. The fact that the repressed purposes nevertheless remain his is shown by dreams and neurotic symptoms, which represent an irruption of the unconscious into consciousness, producing not indeed a pure image of the unconscious, but a compromise between the two conflicting systems, and thus exhibiting the reality of the conflict. . . .

For the evidence on which the hypothesis of the repressed unconscious is based entails the conclusion that it is a phenomenon present in all human beings. The psychopathological phenomena of everyday life, although trivial from a practical point of view, are theoretically important because they show the intrusion of unconscious intentions into our everyday and supposedly normal behavior.

Even more theoretically important are dreams. For dreams, also "normal" phenomena, exhibit in detail not only the existence of the unconscious but also the dynamics of its repression (the dream-censorship). But since the same dynamics of repression explained neurotic symptoms, and since the dreams of neurotics, which are a clue to the meaning of their symptoms, differ neither in structure nor in content from the dreams of normal people, the conclusion is that a dream is itself a neurotic symptom.[7] We are all therefore neurotic. At least dreams show that the difference between neurosis and health prevails only by day; and since the psychopathology of everyday life exhibits the same dynamics, even the waking life of the "healthy" man is pervaded by innumerable symptom-formations. Between "normality" and "abnormality" there is no qualitative but only a quantitative difference, based largely on the practical question of whether our neurosis is serious enough to incapacitate us for work.[8]

Or perhaps we are closer to the Freudian point of view if we give a more paradoxical formulation; the difference between "neurotic" and "healthy" is only that the "healthy" have a socially usual form of neurosis. At any rate, to quote a more technical and cautious formulation of the same theorem, Freud says that from the study of dreams we learn that the neuroses make use of a mechanism already in existence as a normal part of our psychic structure, not of one that is newly created by some morbid disturbance or other.[9] . . .

And furthermore, it is a Freudian theorem that each individual neurosis is not static but dynamic. It is a historical process with its own internal logic. Because of the basically unsatisfactory nature of the neurotic compromise, tension between the repressed and repress-

[6] Collected Papers, IV, 86. Cf. A General Introduction to Psycho-Analysis, pp. 304, 358-59; The Ego and the Id, II; New Introductory Lectures on Psychoanalysis, pp. 25-26.

[7] A General Introduction to Psycho-Analysis, pp. 87, 236, 307, 368, 464; New Introductory Lectures on Psychoanalysis, pp. 15, 26.

[8] A General Introduction to Psycho-Analysis, pp. 367-68, 464, 65; New Introductory Lectures on Psychoanalysis, p. 80; Collected Papers, II, 120; Collected Papers, IV, 337; Delusion and Dream and Other Essays, p. 5.

[9] The Basic Writings of Sigmund Freud (The Interpretation of Dreams), p. 539.

ing factors persists and produces a constant series of new symptom-formations. And the series of symptom-formations is not a shapeless series of mere changes; it exhibits a regressive pattern, which Freud calls the slow return of the repressed. It is a law of neurotic diseases, he says, that these obsessive acts increasingly come closer to the original impulse and to the original forbidden act itself.[10] The doctrine of the universal neurosis of mankind, if we take it seriously, therefore compels us to entertain the hypothesis that the pattern of history exhibits a dialectic not hitherto recognized by historians, the dialectic of neurosis.

A reinterpretation of human history is not an appendage to psychoanalysis but an integral part of it. The empirical fact which compelled Freud to comprehend the whole of human history in the area of psychoanalysis is the appearance in dreams and in neurotic symptoms of themes substantially identical with major themes—both ritualistic and mythical—in the religious history of mankind. The link between the theory of neurosis and the theory of history is the theory of religion, as is made perfectly clear in *Totem and Taboo* and *Moses and Monotheism*. . . .

Psychoanalysis must view religion both as neurosis and as that attempt to become conscious and to cure, inside the neurosis itself, on which Freud came at the end of his life to pin his hopes for therapy. Psychoanalysis is vulgarly interpreted as dismissing religion as an erroneous system of wishful thinking. In *The Future of an Illusion,* Freud does speak of religion as a "substitute-gratification"—the Freudian analogue to the Marxian formula, "opiate of the people." But according to the whole doctrine of repression, "substitute-gratifications"—a term which applies not only to

poetry and religion but also to dreams and neurotic symptoms—contain truth: they are expressions, distorted by repression, of the immortal desires of the human heart.

The proper psychoanalytical perspective on religion is that taken in *Moses and Monotheism,* where Freud set out to find the fragment of historic and psychological truth in Judaism and Christianity. Even Marx—in the same passage in which the notorious formula "opiate of the people" occurs—speaks of religion as "the sigh of the oppressed creature, the heart of a heartless world." [11] But Marx, lacking the concept of repression and the unconscious—that is to say, not being prepared to recognize the mystery of the human heart—could not pursue the line of thought implied in his own epigram. Psychoanalysis is equipped to study the mystery of the human heart, and must recognize religion to be the heart of the mystery. But [it] can go beyond religion only if it sees itself as completing what religion tries to do, namely, make the unconscious conscious; then psychoanalysis would be the science of original sin. Psychoanalysis is in a position to define the error in religion only after it has recognized the truth. . . .

Then the historical process is sustained by man's desire to become other than what he is. And man's desire to become something different is essentially an unconscious desire. The actual changes in history neither result from nor correspond to the conscious desires of the human agents who bring them about. Every historian knows this, and the philosopher of history, Hegel, in his doctrine of the "cunning of Reason," made it a fundamental point in his structural analysis of history. Mankind today is still making history without having any conscious idea of what it really wants or under what conditions it

---

[10] *The Basic Writings of Sigmund Freud (Totem and Taboo)*, p. 831; cf. p. 875; *Collected Papers,* III, 454; *Collected Papers,* IV, 93; *Inhibitions, Symptoms and Anxiety,* pp. 61, 71; *Moses and Monotheism,* pp. 122-29, 201.

[11] Marx, *Der historische Materialismus,* p. 264.

would stop being unhappy; in fact what it is doing seems to be making itself more unhappy and calling that unhappiness progress.

Christian theology, or at least Augustinian theology, recognizes human restlessness and discontent, the *cor irrequietum*, as the psychological source of the historical process. But Christian theology, to account for the origin of human discontent and to indicate a solution, has to take man out of this real world, out of the animal kingdom, and inculcate into him delusions of grandeur. And thus Christian theology commits its own worst sin, the sin of pride. . . .

SUBLIMATION

The link between psychoanalysis and the science of human culture is the concept of sublimation. If psychoanalysis is right, virtually the totality of what anthropologists call culture consists of sublimations. Freud not only regards "higher mental operations, scientific, artistic, ideological activities" as sublimations of sexual energy, but also the less high but more fundamental cultural activity of work. The emotional ties which bind the individual members of a particular culture into a unity, as well as individual and social character structures, are also said to be effects of sublimation. . . .

Sublimation changes both the aim and the object of the instinct, so that "what was originally a sexual instinct finds some achievement which is no longer sexual but has a higher social or ethical valuation"; with his scientific integrity, he immediately adds, "These different features do not as yet combine to form an integral picture." [12] He here and elsewhere stresses that sublimation involves on the one hand the desexualization of the aims of the sexual instinct and on the other hand their socializa-

tion. But it is not clear how desexualization and socialization take place, or even what these terms mean. The connection between infantile sexuality and culture is postulated, not explained. Attacking the problem from the side of culture, Freud asserts that the survival of culture depends on the sublimation of infantile sexuality:

Civilization has been built up, under the pressure of the struggle for existence, by sacrifices in gratification of the primitive impulses, and it is to a great extent forever being recreated, as each individual, successively joining the community, repeats the sacrifice of his instinctive pleasures for the common good. The sexual are amongst the most important of the instinctive forces thus utilized; they are in this way sublimated, that is to say, their energy is turned aside from its sexual goal and diverted towards other ends, no longer sexual and socially more valuable.[13]

The formulation shows that the concept of sublimation is an attempt to relate not only body and spirit, but also individual and society. . . .

The reason why the concept of sublimation remains obscure in psychoanalytical theory is that it lays bare the antagonism between man and culture which Freud was not able to solve. Reich was right in arguing that to fulfill its own therapeutic promise, psychoanalysis has to envisage a social transformation. Reich was wrong in limiting the social transformation involved to the liberation of adult genital sexuality. The therapeutic task is far larger; how large, only a resolute facing of the problem of sublimation can tell. Freud, having no solution to the general problem, and as a therapist handling patients who had to live in the world as it was, could only continue to recommend sublimation. And, since he did not shut his

---

[12] *Collected Papers*, V, 132-33. Cf. *A General Introduction to Psycho-Analysis*, p. 354.
[13] *A General Introduction to Psycho-Analysis*, p. 27.

eyes to the limitations of sublimation, he could only envisage the continuation of the warfare between ego and id, and therefore had to make even the psychoanalytically reconstructed ego continue the function of instinctual repression, in the form of stoic self-control and stoic renunciation. But no psychoanalytical reason is given or can be given for believing that "ego-syntonic controls," as Freud calls them, can succeed where old-fashioned repression failed; or, to follow Freud's language in another passage, that secular motives for civilized behavior will succeed where religious motives have failed.[14] The festering antagonism between man and culture remains.

Intimately connected with the problem of therapy, and also involved in the theory of sublimation, is the problem of rationality. For just as sublimation has an ambiguous relation to repression, so it has also an equally ambiguous relation to neurosis. The problem was opened up by one of the most famous formulations in *Totem and Taboo:*[15]

The neuroses exhibit on the one hand striking and far-reaching points of agreement with . . . art, religion and philosophy. But on the other hand they seem like distortions of them. It might be maintained that a case of hysteria is a caricature of a work of art, that an obsessional neurosis is a caricature of religion and that a paranoic delusion is a caricature of a philosophical system.

Although Freud was personally most interested in developing the relation between religion and neurosis, consistency requires us to say that psychoanalysis postulates a far-reaching connection between all sublimation and neurosis— between culture as such and neurosis:[16]

A little reflection was bound to show that it would be impossible to restrict to the provinces of dreams and nervous disorders a view such as this of the life of the mind. If that view has hit upon a truth, it must apply equally to normal mental events, and even the highest achievements of the human spirit must bear a demonstrable relation to the factors found in pathology— to repression, to the efforts at mastering the unconscious and to the possibilities of satisfying the primitive instincts.

What distinction, then, if any, can be drawn between neurosis and culture? In these formulations Freud does not equate the two. He makes three distinctions between them: in a cultural formation the activity, though sexual in origin, is desexualized, socialized, and directed at reality in the form of work; in a neurosis the activity is resexualized, withdrawn from the social, and involves a flight from reality.[17] While the criterion of desexualization is obscure, the other two—sociality and reality-reference— provide a useful guide which psychoanalysis has adopted. Thus Róheim: "The difference between a neurosis and a sublimation is evidently in the social aspect of the phenomenon. A neurosis isolates; a sublimation unites. In a sublimation something new is created—a house, or a community, or a tool—and it is created in a group or for the use of a group."[18]

But this rough-and-ready distinction between culture and neurosis was undermined by other lines of thought in Freud himself. Freud was always torn between two aims, individual therapy and general theory. To distinguish between neurosis and culture by taking as the criterion the integration of the activity in the social labor process is to adopt the standpoint of individual therapy.

[14] *Collected Papers,* V, 126, 128, 329, 331; *An Outline of Psychoanalysis,* p. 44; *The Future of an Illusion,* p. 68.

[15] *Works (Totem and Taboo),* XIII, 73. Cf. *Collected Papers,* II, 25-35; *Collected Papers,* V, 92-97.

[16] *Collected Papers,* V, 94.

[17] *The Basic Writings of Sigmund Freud (Totem and Taboo),* p. 864.

[18] Róheim, *The Origin and Function of Culture,* p. 74.

A neurotic individual is distinguished by his alienation from a useful role in society, and the function of individual therapy is to restore the individual to society. Individual therapy must be culture-bound, and its motto must be adjustment. But while cultural activities may be distinguished from individual neurosis by their social character, it does not follow that all socially integrated activity is non-neurotic. For Freud as theoretician recognized that the distinction between "normal" and "neurotic" as applied in individual therapy had no theoretical validity;[19] and as social critic he proceeded to psychoanalyze the irrationality of such universal cultural sublimations as devotion to the church, the army and the state.[20] . . .

It became apparent that therapy by making conscious the unconscious could be attained only on the condition that the patient re-enact his repressed instinctual life during the analysis itself, giving expression to repressed emotions of love or hate by directing them against the real person of the analyst. The theoretical implications of this fact are twofold, and both are fully recognized by Freud himself. In the first place, repetition in real life is the precondition for reestablishing contact between consciousness and the unconscious: "This revision of the process of repression can only partially be effected by means of the memory-traces of the processes which led up to repression. The decisive part of the work is carried through by creating—in the relationship to the physician, in the 'transference'—new editions of those early conflicts." [21] . . .

Orthodox psychoanalytical therapy fails to direct the libido back to the external world in the form of a project to change the world; by the same token it fails to provide a solution to the problem of aggression. Psychoanalytical consciousness, by returning to the microcosm of the inner world, puts at the disposal of the ego large quantities of libido that were previously in a state of repression. The result—in so far as psychoanalytical consciousness gets through words to reality—is to make us aware for the first time of the scope and nature of our real desires—in Rilke's beautiful phrase, the unlived lines of our body. And then what is the psychoanalytically conscious ego going to do with its newly discovered desires? Once the limitations of sublimation and the impossibility of "rising above the crude life of the instincts" are recognized,[22] orthodox psychoanalysis, as a result of its inability to transform itself into social criticism, has to send human desire back into repression again. Freud's earlier optimistic hopes of precluding repression through psychoanalytical consciousness are replaced by the theorem that psychoanalytical consciousness "reconstructs the repressions from more solid material." [23] In other words psychoanalysis, after showing us the unlived lines of our body, tells us to forget them, presumably because they are not compatible with "the processes of Nature" or "the aims of human society." And of course the institution of these new "ego-syntonic controls," if we take Freud's theory of aggression seriously, means the internalization of the aggression released by all instinctual renunciation.[24]

Thus Freud found no way of avoiding the internalization of aggression, the accumulation of guilt, which he himself showed to be a prime factor in the individual and in the social neurosis

[19] See above, note 9.

[20] *Group Psychology and the Analysis of the Ego*, pp. 41-51.

[21] *A General Introduction to Psycho-Analysis*, p. 462. Cf. *Delusion and Dream and Other Essays*, p. 115.

[22] See *Collected Papers*, V, chap. X.

[23] *Collected Papers*, V, 329. Cf. *An Outline of Psychoanalysis*, p. 44; contrast *A General Introduction to Psycho-Analysis*, p. 463.

[24] *Collected Papers*, V, 331; *Civilization and Its Discontents*, pp. 114-22.

of mankind. These sad consequences for therapy follow because Freud accepted the inevitability of culture as it is, with its two characteristics—"a strengthening of the intellect, which is beginning to govern instinctual life, and an internalization of the aggressive impulses, with all its consequent advantages and perils." [25]

The only alternative, the only way of avoiding "the intensification of the sense of guilt . . . until perhaps . . . it may swell to a magnitude that individuals can hardly support," [26] is to turn the aggression outward to the external world, as the energy working to change the world. . . .

Human culture exists in order to project the infantile complexes into concrete reality, where they can be seen and mastered. The essence of totemism, which Freud regarded as the primal model of human culture, is the projection of the Oedipus complex onto a real (animal) substitute-object in the external world, and the establishment of the social group by complicity in this symbolic solution to the Oedipal problem.

Human history, as neurosis subject to the law of the increasing return of the repressed, through its long evolution from totemism to monotheism on the one hand and the modern state on the other, has projected more and more of the Oedipus complex into the external world, where it can be seen and mastered. Human culture is thus one vast arena in which the logic of the transference works itself out; the infantile fantasies which create the universal human neurosis cannot themselves be directly apprehended or mastered, but their derivatives in human culture can. Human consciousness can be liberated from the parental (Oedipal) complex only by being liberated from its cultural derivatives, the paternalistic state and the patriarchal God. Thus culture actually does for all mankind what the transference phenomena were supposed to do for the individual. In Freud's words, "They and only they render the invaluable service of making the patient's buried and forgotten love-emotions actual and manifest; for in the last resort no one can be slain *in absentia* or *in effigie*." [27] In the last resort, no one exists *in absentia* or *in effigie;* in the last resort the Oedipus complex exists only in its cultural derivatives; it exists only as long as the life in culture in the present perpetuates the infantile flight from death. . . .

The life instinct, or sexual instinct, demands activity of a kind that, in contrast to our current mode of activity, can only be called play. The life instinct also demands a union with others and with the world around us based not on anxiety and aggression but on narcissism and erotic exuberance.

But the death instinct also demands satisfaction; as Hegel says in the *Phenomenology,* "The life and knowledge of God may doubtless be described as love playing with itself; but this idea sinks into triviality, if the seriousness, the pain, the patience and the labor of the Negative are omitted." [28] The death instinct is reconciled with the life instinct only in a life which is not repressed, which leaves no "unlived lines" in the human body, the death instinct then being affirmed in a body which is willing to die. And, because the body is satisfied, the death instinct no longer drives it to change itself and make history, and therefore, as Christian theology divined, its activity is in eternity.

At the same time—and here again Christian theology and psychoanalysis agree—the resurrected body is the transfigured body. The abolition of repression

[25] *Collected Papers,* V, 286.
[26] *Civilization and Its Discontents,* pp. 121-22.
[27] *Collected Papers,* II, 322.
[28] Hegel, *Phenomenology of Mind,* p. 81.

would abolish the unnatural concentrations of libido in certain particular bodily organs—concentrations engineered by the negativity of the morbid death instinct, and constituting the bodily base of the neurotic character disorders in the human ego. In the words of Thoreau: "We need pray for no higher heaven than the pure senses can furnish, a purely sensuous life. Our present senses are but rudiments of what they are destined to become." [29] The human body would become polymorphously perverse, delighting in that full life of all the body which it now fears. The consciousness strong enough to endure full life would be no longer Apollonian but Dionysian —consciousness which does not observe the limit, but overflows; consciousness which *does not negate any more*.

If the question facing mankind is the abolition of repression, psychoanalysis is not the only point of view from which the question can and should be raised. We have already indicated that the question is intrinsic to Christian theology. The time has come to ask Christian theologians, especially the neo-orthodox, what they mean by the resurrection of the body and by eternal life. Is this a promise of immortality after death? In other words, is the psychological premise of Christianity the impossibility of reconciling life and death either in "this" world or the "next," so that flight from death—with all its morbid consequences —is our eternal fate in "this world" and in "the next"? For we have seen that the perfect body, promised by Christian theology, enjoying that perfect felicity promised by Christian theology, is a body reconciled with death.

SOURCES

Beyond the Pleasure Principle, tr. J. Strachey. (International Psycho-Analytical Library, ed. E. Jones, no. 4.) London: Hogarth Press, 1950.

The Basic Writings of Sigmund Freud, tr. & ed. A. A. Brill. New York: The Modern Library, 1938. Contains six major works, herein distinguished as follows:
> *The Psychopathology of Everyday Life*
> *The Interpretation of Dreams*
> *Three Contributions to the Theory of Sex*
> *Wit and Its Relation to the Unconscious*
> *Totem and Taboo*
> *The History of the Psychoanalytic Movement*

Civilization and Its Discontents, tr. J. Riviere. (International Psycho-Analytical Library, ed. E. Jones, no. 17.) London: Hogarth, 1930.

Collected Papers, ed. J. Riviere & J. Strachey. 5 vols. (International Psycho-Analytical Library, no. 7-10, 37.) New York, London: The International Psycho-Analytical Press, 1924-50.

Delusion and Dream and Other Essays, ed. P. Rieff. Boston: Beacon Press, 1956.

The Ego and the Id, tr. J. Riviere. (International Psycho-Analytical Library, no. 12.) London: Hogarth Press and The Institute of Psycho-Analysis, 1927.

The Future of an Illusion, tr. W. D. Robson-Scott. (International Psycho-Analytical Library, no. 15.) London: Hogarth Press and The Institute of Psycho-Analysis, 1928.

A General Introduction to Psycho-Analysis, tr. J. Riviere. New York: Perma Giants, 1953. Copyright 1935 by Edward L. Bernays. (Quotations from this source by permission of Liveright Publishers, New York, and G. Allen & Unwin Ltd., London.)

Group Psychology and the Analysis of the Ego, tr. J. Strachey. (International Psycho-Analytical Library, no. 6.) London, Vienna: The International Psycho-Analytical Press, 1922.

Inhibitions, Symptoms and Anxiety, tr. A. Strachey. (International Psycho-Analytical Library, no. 28). London: Hogarth Press and The Institute of Psycho-Analysis, 1936.

[29] Thoreau, *A Week on the Concord and Merrimack Rivers;* Cf. Read, *Icon and Idea,* p. 139.

Leonardo da Vinci: A Study in Psychosexuality, tr. A. A. Brill. New York: Random House, 1947.

Moses and Monotheism, tr. K. Jones. (International Psycho-Analytical Library, no. 33.) London: Hogarth Press and The Institute of Psycho-Analysis, 1939 (New York: Knopf, 1939).

New Introductory Lectures on Psychoanalysis, tr. W. J. H. Sprott. (International Psycho-Analytical Library, no. 24.) London: Hogarth Press and The Institute of Psycho-Analysis, 1933.

An Outline of Psychoanalysis, tr. J. Strachey. (International Psycho-Analytical Library, no. 35.) London: Hogarth Press, 1949.

The Standard Edition of the Complete Psychological Works of Sigmund Freud, ed. James Strachey, Anna Freud, Alix Strachey, & Alan Tyson. (24) vols. London: Hogarth Press and The Institute of Psycho-Analysis, 1954.

H. RICHARD NIEBUHR

Christ and Culture: Five Types of Interpretation[*]

PART I

Belief in Jesus Christ by men in their various cultures always means belief in God. No one can know the Son without acknowledging the Father. To be related in devotion and obedience to Jesus Christ is to be related to the One to whom he undeviatingly points. As Son of God he points away from the many values of man's social life to the One who is alone good; from the many powers which men use and on which they depend to the One who alone is powerful; from the many times and seasons of history with their hopes and fears to the One who is Lord of all times and is alone to be feared and hoped for; he points away from all that is conditioned to the Unconditioned. He does not direct attention away from this world to another; but from all worlds, present and future, material and spiritual, to the One who creates all worlds, who is the Other of all worlds.

Yet this is only half the meaning of Christ, considered morally. . . . [Sonship to God] involves the double movement —with men toward God, with God toward men; from the world to the Other, from the Other to the world; from work to Grace, from Grace to work; from time to the Eternal and from the Eternal to the temporal. In his moral sonship to God Jesus Christ is not a median figure, half God, half man; he is a single person wholly directed as man toward God and wholly directed in his unity with the Father toward men. He is mediatorial, not median. He is not a center from which radiates love of God and of men, obedience to God and to Caesar, trust in God and in nature, hope in divine and in human action. He exists rather as

---

[*] From *Christ and Culture,* H. Richard Niebuhr. Copyright 1951 by Harper and Brothers (now Harper & Row, Publishers, Inc.); used by permission; pp. 27-29, 32-44, 117-23, 149-58, 190-96.

the focusing point in the continuous alternation of movements from God to man and man to God; and these movements are qualitatively as different as are *agape* and *eros,* authority and obedience, promise and hope, humiliation and glorification, faithfulness and trust. . . .

Even when theologies fail to do justice to this fact, Christians living with Christ in their cultures are aware of it. For they are forever being challenged to abandon all things for the sake of God; and forever being sent back into the world to teach and practice all the things that have been commanded them. . . .

What we have in view when we deal with Christ and culture is that total process of human activity and that total result of such activity to which now the name *culture,* now the name *civilization,* is applied in common speech. Culture is the "artificial, secondary environment" which man superimposes on the natural. It comprises language, habits, ideas, beliefs, customs, social organization, inherited artifacts, technical processes, and values. This "social heritage," this "reality sui generis," which the New Testament writers frequently had in mind when they spoke of "the world," which is represented in many forms but to which Christians like other men are inevitably subject, is what we mean when we speak of culture.

Though we cannot venture to define the "essence" of this culture, we can describe some of its chief characteristics. For one thing, it is inextricably bound up with man's life in society; it is always *social.* "The essential fact of culture, as we live and experience it, as we can observe it scientifically," writes Malinowski, "is the organization of human beings into permanent groups." [1] Whether or not this is the essential fact, it is an essential part of the fact. Individuals may use culture in their own ways; they may change elements in their culture, yet what they use and change is social. Culture is the social heritage they receive and transmit. Whatever is purely private, so that it neither derives from nor enters into social life, is not a part of culture. Conversely, social life is always cultural. Anthropology, it seems, has completely scotched the romantic idea of a purely natural society, not characterized by highly distinct and acquired habits, customs, forms of social organization, etc. Culture and social existence go together.

Culture, secondly, is *human achievement.* We distinguish it from nature by noting the evidences of human purposiveness and effort. A river is nature, a canal culture; a raw piece of quartz is nature, an arrowhead culture; a moan is natural, a word cultural. Culture is the work of men's minds and hands. . . . Furthermore, if one of the marks of culture is that it is the result of past human achievements, another is that no one can possess it without effort and achievement on his own part. The gifts of nature are received as they are communicated without human intent or conscious effort; but the gifts of culture cannot be possessed without striving on the part of the recipient. Speech must be laboriously acquired; government cannot be maintained without constant effort; scientific method must be re-enacted and reintended with every generation. Even the material results of cultural activity are useless unless they are accompanied by a learning process that enables us to employ them as they were intended to be employed. . . .

These human achievements, in the third place, are all designed for an end or ends; the world of culture is a *world of values.* Whether or not we should ask value-questions about nature or pass value-judgments on natural occurrences is a moot question. But with respect to culture phenomena this problem never arises. What men have made and what they make, we must assume, is intended for a purpose; it is designed to serve a good. It can never be described without

[1] Bronislaw Malinowski, *A Scientific Theory of Culture and Other Essays,* 1944, p. 43.

48

reference to ends in minds of designers and users. . . .

Further, the values with which these human achievements are concerned are dominantly those of the *good for man*. Philosophers in cultural societies may argue whether the ends that are to be served by culture are ideal or natural, whether they are ideas of value given to spiritual vision or natural goods, that is, ends interesting man as biological being. In either case, however, they seem to agree that man must serve his own good, that he is the measure of all things. In defining the ends that his activities are to realize in culture, man begins with himself as the chief value and the source of all other values. What is good is what is good for him. It seems self-evident in culture that animals are to be domesticated or annihilated so far as these measures serve man's good, that God or the gods are to be worshiped so far as this is necessary or desirable for the sake of maintaining and advancing human life, that ideas and ideals are to be served for the sake of human self-realization. Though the search of the good-for-man is dominant in the work of culture, it is not only conceivable that men should undertake to labor and produce for the sake of some other being's good, but it seems true that they do indeed in their cultures often seek to serve causes transcending human existence. From totemic to modern societies they identify themselves with orders of being that include more than men. They regard themselves as representatives of life, so that social organization and laws as well as art and religion show some respect for life even in non-human beings. They define themselves as representatives of the order of rational beings, and seek to realize what is good-for-reason. They also serve the gods. And yet the pragmatic tendency to do all these things for the sake of man seems inconquerable. It must at once be added, however, that no culture is really humanistic in the broad sense,

for there are only particular cultures, and in each of them a particular society or a particular class in that society tends to regard itself as the center and source of value, seeking to achieve what is good for it, though justifying that endeavor by claiming for itself a special status as the representative of something universal.

Again, culture in all its forms and varieties is concerned with the *temporal and material realization of values*. This does not mean that the goods that human effort seeks to realize are necessarily temporal or material, however much the concern for these is a part of all cultural achievement. It is fallacious to think of culture as materialistic in the sense that what men labor to achieve is always the satisfaction of their needs as physical and temporal beings. Even the economic interpretations of culture recognize that beyond material goods— that is, values relative to man's physical existence, beyond food, drink, clothing, progeny, and economic order—men in culture seek to gain less tangible values. But even the immaterial goods must be realized in temporal and material form; even the good-for-man as mind and person must be given "a local habitation and a name." Prestige and glory on the one hand, beauty, truth, and goodness on the other—to use the unsatisfactory symbols of spiritual-value theory—are presented to feeling, imagination, or intellectual vision; and human effort presses on to embody in concrete, tangible, visible, and audible forms what has been imaginatively discerned. The harmony and proportion, the form, order and rhythm, the meanings and ideas that men intuit and trace out as they confront nature, social events, and the world of dreams, these by infinite labor they must paint on wall or canvas, print on paper as systems of philosophy and science, outline in carved stone or cast in bronze, sing in ballad, ode, or symphony. Visions of order and justice, hopes of glory, must at the cost of much suffering be embodied in written laws, dramatic rites, structures of government, empires, ascetic lives.

Because all these actualizations of purpose are accomplished in transient and perishing stuff, cultural activity is almost as much concerned with the *conservation of values* as with their realization. Much of the energy which men in their societies expend at any time is given to this complicated task of preserving what they have inherited and made. Their houses, schools, and temples, their roads and machines, stand in constant need of repair. The desert and the jungle threaten every cultivated acre. Even greater are the dangers of decay that surround the less material achievements of the past. The systems of laws and liberties, the customs of social intercourse, the methods of thought, the institutions of learning and religion, the techniques of art, of language, and of morality itself —these cannot be conserved by keeping in repair the walls and documents that are their symbols. They need to be written afresh generation by generation "on the tables of the heart." Let education and training lapse for one generation, and the whole grand structure of past achievements falls into ruin. Culture is social tradition which must be conserved by painful struggle not so much against nonhuman natural forces as against revolutionary and critical powers in human life and reason. But whether customs or artifacts are in question, culture cannot be maintained unless men devote a large part of their efforts to the work of conservation.

Finally, attention must be directed to the *pluralism* that is characteristic of all culture. The values a culture seeks to realize in any time or place are many in number. No society can ever try to realize all its manifold possibilities; each is highly complex, made up of many institutions with many goals and interweaving interests. The values are many, partly because men are many. Culture is concerned with what is good for male

and female, child and adult, rulers and ruled; with what is good for men in special vocations and groups, according to the customary notions of such good. Moreover, all the individuals have their special claims and interests; and everyone in his individuality is a complex being with desires of body and mind, with self-regarding and other-regarding motives, with relations to other men, nature and supernatural beings. Even if economic or biological interpretations of culture are maintained, still all that can be claimed is that economic or biologic values are fundamental, while the vast superstructure of other interests must be recognized. But in culture as we meet it and live it not even such unity as these interpretations claim is recognizable. The values we seek in our societies and find represented in their institutional behavior are many, disparate, and often incomparable, so that these societies are always involved in a more or less laborious effort to hold together in tolerable conflict the many efforts of many men in many groups to achieve and conserve many goods. The cultures are forever seeking to combine peace with prosperity, justice with order, freedom with welfare, truth with beauty, scientific truth with moral good, technical proficiency with practical wisdom, holiness with life, and all these with all the rest. Among the many values the kingdom of God may be included—though scarcely as the one pearl of great price. Jesus Christ and God the Father, the gospel, the church, and eternal life may find places in the cultural complex, but only as elements in the great pluralism.

These are some of the obvious characteristics of that culture which lays its claim on every Christian, and under the authority of which he also lives when he lives under the authority of Jesus Christ. Though sometimes we state the fundamental human problem as that of grace and nature, in human existence we do not know a nature apart from culture. In any case we cannot escape culture any more readily than we can escape nature, for "the man of nature, the *Naturmensch*, does not exist,"[2] and "no man ever looks at the world with pristine eyes."[3]

Given these two complex realities—Christ and culture—an infinite dialogue must develop in the Christian conscience and the Christian community. In his single-minded direction toward God, Christ leads men away from the temporality and pluralism of culture. In its concern for the conservation of the many values of the past, culture rejects the Christ who bids men rely on grace. Yet the Son of God is himself child of a religious culture, and sends his disciples to tend his lambs and sheep, who cannot be guarded without cultural work. The dialogue proceeds with denials and affirmations, reconstructions, compromises, and new denials. Neither individual nor church can come to a stopping-place in the endless search for an answer which will not provoke a new rejoinder.

Yet it is possible to discern some order in this multiplicity, to stop the dialogue, as it were, at certain points; and to define typical partial answers that recur so often in different eras and societies that they seem to be less the product of historical conditioning than of the nature of the problem itself and the meanings of its terms. . . . Five sorts of answers are distinguished, of which three are closely related to each other as belonging to that median type in which both Christ and culture are distinguished and affirmed; yet strange family resemblances may be found along the whole scale.

Answers of the first type emphasize the *opposition* between Christ and culture. Whatever may be the customs of the society in which the Christian lives, and whatever the human achievements it conserves, Christ is seen as opposed to them, so that he confronts men with the challenge of an "either-or" decision.

In the early period of church history Jewish rejection of Jesus, defended by Klausner, found its counterpart in Christian antagonism to Jewish culture, while Roman outlawry of the new faith was accompanied by Christian flight from or attack upon Graeco-Roman civilization. In medieval times monastic orders and sectarian movements called on believers living in what purported to be a Christian culture to abandon the "world" and to "come out from among them and be separate." In the modern period answers of this kind are being given by missionaries who require their converts to abandon wholly the customs and institutions of so-called "heathen" societies, by little groups of withdrawing Christians in Western or "Christianized" civilization, and in partial manner, by those who emphasize the antagonism of Christian faith to capitalism and communism, to industrialism and nationalism, to Catholicism and Protestantism.

Recognition of a fundamental *agreement* between Christ and culture is typical of the answers offered by a second group. In them Jesus often appears as a great hero of human culture history; his life and teachings are regarded as the greatest human achievement; in him, it is believed, the aspirations of men toward their values are brought to a point of culmination; he confirms what is best in the past, and guides the process of civilization to its proper goal. Moreover, he is a part of culture in the sense that he himself is part of the social heritage that must be transmitted and conserved. In our time answers of this kind are given by Christians who note the close relation between Christianity and Western civilization, between Jesus' teachings or the teachings about him and democratic institutions; yet there are occasional interpretations that emphasize the agreement between Christ and Eastern culture as well as some that tend to identify him with the spirit of Marxian

[2] Bronislaw Malinowski in *Encyclopedia of Social Sciences,* Vol. IV, p. 621.
[3] Ruth Benedict, *Patterns of Culture,* 1934, p. 2.

society. In earlier times solutions of the problem along these lines were being offered simultaneously with the solutions of the first or "Christ-against-culture" type.

Three other typical answers agree with each other in seeking to maintain the great differences between the two principles and in undertaking to hold them together in some unity. They are distinguished from each other by the manner in which each attempts to combine the two authorities. One of them, our third type, understands Christ's relation to culture somewhat as the men of the second group do: he is the fulfillment of cultural aspirations and the restorer of the institutions of true society. Yet there is in him something that neither arises out of culture nor contributes directly to it. He is discontinuous as well as continuous with social life and its culture. The latter, indeed, leads men to Christ, yet only in so preliminary a fashion that a great leap is necessary if men are to reach him or, better, true culture is not possible unless beyond all human achievement, all human search for values, all human society, Christ enters into life from above with gifts which human aspiration has not envisioned and which human effort cannot attain unless he relates men to a supernatural society and a new value-center. Christ is, indeed, a Christ of culture, but he is also a *Christ above culture*. This *synthetic* type is best represented by Thomas Aquinas and his followers, but it has many other representatives in both early and modern times.

Another group of median answers constitutes our fourth type. In these the duality and inescapable authority of both Christ and culture are recognized, but the opposition between them is also accepted. To those who answer the question in this way it appears that Christians throughout life are subject to the tension that accompanies obedience to two authorities who do not agree yet must both be obeyed. They refuse to accommodate the claims of Christ to those of secular society, as, in their estimation, men in the second and third groups do. So they are like the "Christ-against-culture" believers, yet differ from them in the conviction that obedience to God requires obedience to the institutions of society and loyalty to its members as well as obedience to a Christ who sits in judgment on that society. Hence man is seen as subject to two moralities, and as a citizen of two worlds that are not only discontinuous with each other but largely opposed. In the *polarity* and *tension* of Christ and culture life must be lived precariously and sinfully in the hope of a justification which lies beyond history. Luther may be regarded as the greatest representative of this type, yet many a Christian who is not otherwise a Lutheran finds himself compelled to solve the problem in this way.

Finally, as the fifth type in the general series and as the third of the mediating answers, there is the *conversionist* solution. Those who offer it understand with the members of the first and the fourth groups that human nature is fallen or perverted, and that this perversion not only appears in culture but is transmitted by it. Hence the opposition between Christ and all human institutions and customs is to be recognized. Yet the antithesis does not lead either to Christian separation from the world as with the first group, or to mere endurance in the expectation of a transhistorical salvation, as with the fourth. Christ is seen as the converter of man in his culture and society, not apart from these, for there is no nature without culture and no turning of men from self and idols to God save in society. It is in Augustine that the great outlines of this answer seem to be offered; John Calvin makes it explicit; many others are associated with these two.

When the answers to the enduring problem are stated in this manner it is apparent that a construction has been set up that is partly artificial. A type is always something of a construct, even when it has not been constructed prior to long study of many historic individuals and movements. When one returns from the hypothetical scheme to the rich complexity of individual events, it is evident at once that no person or group ever conforms completely to a type. Each historical figure will show characteristics that are more reminiscent of some other family than the one by whose name he has been called, or traits will appear that seem wholly unique and individual. The method of typology, however, though historically inadequate, has the advantage of calling to attention the continuity and significance of the great *motifs* that appear and reappear in the long wrestling of Christians with their enduring problem. Hence also it may help us to gain orientation as we in our own time seek to answer the question of Christ and culture. . . .

The great majority movement in Christianity, which we may call the church of the center, has refused to take either the position of the anticultural radicals or that of the accommodators of Christ to culture. Yet it has not regarded its efforts at solution of the Christ-culture problem as compromising, however sinful it knows all human efforts to be. For it the fundamental issue does not lie between Christ and the world important as that issue is, but between God and man. The Christ-culture problem is approached from this point of view and with this conviction. Hence, wide as are the divergences among various groups in the church of the center they agree on certain points when they ask about their responsibility in the social life. The agreement is formulated in theological terms, and the relevance of such formulae to the practical questions of Christian life is often obscure both to radical critics and to uncritical followers. It is as great, however, as that of relativity and quantum theories to inventions, to medical and even political practice, in which millions participate who have no understanding of the theories. One of the theologically stated convictions with which the church of the center approaches the cultural problem is that Jesus Christ is the Son of God, the Father Almighty who created heaven and earth. With that formulation it introduces into the discussion about Christ and culture the conception of nature on which all culture is founded, and which is good and rightly ordered by the One to whom Jesus Christ is obedient and with whom he is inseparably united. Where this conviction rules, Christ and the world cannot be simply opposed to each other. Neither can the "world" as culture be simply regarded as the realm of godlessness; since it is at least founded on the "world" as nature, and cannot exist save as it is upheld by the Creator and Governor of nature.

There is agreement, too, among all the central groups that man is obligated in the nature of his being to be obedient to God—not to a Jesus separated from the Almighty Creator, nor to an author of nature separate from Jesus Christ, but to God-in-Christ and Christ-in-God—and that this obedience must be rendered in the concrete, actual life of natural, cultural man. In his sex life, in eating and drinking, in commanding and obeying other men, he is in the realm of God by divine ordering under divine orders. Since none of these activities can be carried on without the use of human intelligence and will, on a purely instinctive level, since man as created is endowed and burdened with freedom as he moves among necessities, culture is itself a divine requirement. As created and ordered by God, man must achieve what has not been given him; in obedience to God he must seek many values. There is agreement on this in the central church; though there are varieties of conviction about the extent of asceticism

53

which is to be mated with such living of the cultural life.

The main movement of the church is also characterized by a certain harmony of conviction about the universality and radical nature of sin. We have noted that radical Christians are tempted to exclude their holy commonwealths from the dominion of sin, and that cultural Christians tend to deny that it reaches into the depths of human personality. The Christians of the center are convinced that men cannot find in themselves, as persons or as communities, a holiness which can be possessed. Their agreement on the point is difficult to state, for Catholics and Protestants, Thomists and Lutherans, debate endlessly about it with each other—and doubtless misunderstand each other also. Yet the common use of the sacraments, and the common hope for redemption by grace, and the common attitude toward the institutions of culture, point to a fundamental agreement of conviction about sin's universality and radical character, even when express statements are somewhat difficult to reconcile.

These believers who reject both of the extreme positions also hold in common a conviction about grace and law that distinguishes them from legalists of any sort. Once more there are differences; so that Catholics are accused by Protestants of practicing "works-righteousness," and Catholics regard modern Protestants as independent men who think they can build the kingdom of God with the aid of good social engineering. But these are the criticisms they direct against each others' Abelards and Ritschls. In their central positions there is greater agreement. Thomas and Luther are closer to each other on the subject of grace than either is to the Gnostics or the modernists of the social movements to which they belong. The Christians of the center all recognize the primacy of grace and the necessity of works of obedience; though their analyses vary of the relation of man's

love of the brothers to that action of divine love which is always first. They cannot separate the works of human culture from the grace of God, for all those works are possible only by grace. But neither can they separate the experience of grace from cultural activity; for how can men love the unseen God in response to His love without serving the visible brother in human society?

Despite such common characteristics, the Christians of the center do not constitute one ordered group in their attack on the Christ-culture problem. There are at least three distinguishable families among them; and each of them may at special times or on certain specific issues find itself more closely allied to one of the extreme parties than to other movements in the central church. We have named them synthesists, dualists, and conversionists; and shall now try to give meaning to these terms by examining typical representatives of each. As we venture on this task, we warn ourselves once more against the danger of confusing hypothetical types with the rich variety and the colorful individuality of historical persons. These men with whom we are now to be concerned do not allow themselves to be forced into our typical molds any more than did Tertullian, Abelard, Tolstoy, and Ritschl. Yet the simplification our procedure calls for does serve to call attention to prominent features and to guiding motivations.

PART II

When Christians deal with the problem of Christ and culture, there are at all times some who see that they are not dealing with an "either-or" but with a "both-and" relation. Yet they cannot affirm both Christ and culture after the fashion of the culture Christians, since these achieve reconciliation between the spirit of Jesus Christ and the climate of current opinion by simplifying the nature of the Lord in a manner not

54

justified by the New Testament record. As Gnostics living in a society that regards the visible world more or less unreal or deceptive, they make him a wholly other-worldly being; as modernists adjusted to a society that in thought and action discounts what eye has not seen and ear has not heard, they portray him as man of this world. But the synthesist affirms both Christ and culture, as one who confesses a Lord who is both of this world and of the other. The accommodator of Christ to the views of the time erases the distinction between God and man by divinizing man or humanizing God, and worships either a divine or a human Jesus Christ. The synthesist maintains the distinction, and with it the paradoxical conviction, that Jesus, his Lord, is both God and man, one person with two "natures" that are neither to be confused nor separated. For the cultural Christian reconciliation of the gospel with the spirit of the times is made possible by its presentation either as a revelation of speculative truth about being, or of practical knowledge of value; but the true synthesist will have nothing to do with easy subordinations of value to being or being to value. He sees Jesus Christ as both Logos and Lord. Hence, when he affirms both Christ and culture, he does so as one who knows that the Christ who requires his loyalty is greater and more complex in character than the easier reconciliations envisage. Something of the same sort is true of his understanding of culture; which is both divine and human in its origin, both holy and sinful, a realm of both necessity and freedom, and one to which both reason and revelation apply. As his understanding of the meaning of Christ separates him from the cultural believer, so his appreciation of culture divides him from the radical.

There is in the synthesist's view a gap between Christ and culture that accommodation Christianity never takes seriously enough, and that radicalism does not try to overcome. The goal of other-worldly salvation to which Christ points cannot be indicated in the oratorio of the gospel by means of a few grace notes, as modernism does with its hard-to-find paragraphs on immortality or personal religion; it is a major theme. Neither may God's demand for present action, relevant to the crises of social life and to the establishment of just right relations between men, be put on a par with the tithing of anise and mint, as something also to be done. The commandments of Christ to sell everything for the sake of following him, to give up judging our fellows, to turn the other cheek to the violent, to humble ourselves and become the servants of all, to abandon family and to forget tomorrow, cannot, the synthesist sees, be made to rhyme with the requirements of human life in civilized society by allegorizing them or by projecting them into the future, when changed conditions will make them possible, or by relegating them to the sphere of personal disposition and good intention. They are too explicit for that. Yet, because he knows that God is the creator, he cannot evade responsibility for meeting requirements that are given in the nature of man, and which his reason discerns as commandments to his free will. He must procreate children, not because the sex urge is unconquerable by reason alone, but because he was made for this end among others, and cannot be disobedient to the requirement given with nature prior to any culture without denying what nature affirms and he affirms by living. He must organize social relations, because he is created social, intelligent, and free, inescapably a member of a group yet never an ant in its hill or a molecule in the crystal. There are other laws besides the laws of Jesus Christ; and they are also imperative, and also from God. To deal with this duality, as cultural Christianity or radical faith do, is to take neither Christ nor culture seriously

55

enough; for they fail to do justice either to the earnestness of Christ or to the constancy of the Creator, and each failure involves the other. We cannot say, "Either Christ or culture," in full awareness of the dual nature of our law, our end, and our situation.

So far the synthesist agrees in large part with other types of central Christian faith. His distinction from them arises as he analyzes the nature of the duality in Christian life, and combines in a single structure of thought and conduct the distinctly different elements. Some description of examples of the type may help to clarify its methods. Illustrations may be found in many periods and many groups—in the early church, the medieval and the modern, in Roman and in Anglican Catholicism, and even, though less plainly, in Protestantism. The New Testament contains no document that clearly expresses the synthetic view; but there are many statements in gospels and epistles which sound the *motif* or which can be interpreted, without violence to the text, as containing this solution of the Christ-and-culture problem. Among them are the following: "Think not that I have come to abolish the law and the prophets; I have not come to abolish them but to fulfill them. For truly, I say to you, till heaven and earth pass away, not an iota, not a dot, will pass from the law until all is accomplished. Whoever then relaxes one of the least of these commandments and teaches men so, shall be called least in the kingdom of heaven; but he who does them and teaches them shall be called great in the kingdom of heaven." [4] "Render to Caesar the things that are Caesar's and to God the things that are God's." [5] "Let every person be subject to the governing authorities. For there is no authority except from God, and those that exist have

been instituted by God. . . .The authorities are ministers of God." [6] . . .

Efforts to synthesize Christ and culture have been subject to sharp attacks throughout Christian history. Radicals have protested that these attempts are disguised versions of cultural accommodation of the rigorous gospel, and that they broaden the narrow way of life into an easy highway. Cultural Christians have objected that synthesists retain as evangelical truth vestigial remnants of old, immature ways of thought. The strongest opposition, however, has been voiced by neither left- nor right-wing parties but by another central group, that is to say, by one which also seeks to answer the Christ and culture question with a "both-and." This is the group which, for want of a better name, we have called *dualist,* though it is by no means dualistic in the sense that it divides the world in Manichaean fashion into realms of light and darkness, of kingdoms of God and Satan. Though the members of this group dissent from the synthesists' definitions and combinations of Christ and culture they also seek to do justice to the need for holding together as well as for distinguishing between loyalty to Christ and responsibility for culture.

If we would understand the dualists, we must note the place where they stand and take up our position with them as they deal with our problem. For them the fundamental issue in life is not the one which radical Christians face as they draw the line between Christian community and pagan world. Neither is it the issue which cultural Christianity discerns as it sees man everywhere in conflict with nature and locates Christ on the side of the spiritual forces of culture. Yet, like both of these and unlike the synthesist in his more irenic and developing world, the dualist lives in conflict, and in the presence of one

---

[4] Matthew 5:17-19; cf. 23:2.

[5] Matthew 22:21.

[6] Romans 13:1, 6.

great issue. That conflict is between God and man, or better—since the dualist is an existential thinker—between God and us; the issue lies between the righteousness of God and the righteousness of self. On the one side are we with all of our activities, our states and our churches, our pagan and our Christian works; on the other side is God in Christ and Christ in God. The question about Christ and culture in this situation is not one which man puts to himself, but one that God asks him; it is not a question about Christians and pagans, but a question about God and man.

No matter what the dualist's psychological history may have been, his logical starting point in dealing with the cultural problem is the great act of reconciliation and forgiveness that has occurred in the divine-human battle—the act we call Jesus Christ. From this beginning the fact that there was and is a conflict, the facts of God's grace and human sin are understood. No dualist has found it easy to arrive at this starting point. Each is quick to point out that he was on the wrong road until he was stopped and turned round in his tracks by another will than his own. The knowledge of the grace of God was not given him, and he does not believe it is given to any, as a self-evident truth of reason—as certain cultural Christians, the Deists for instance, believe. What these regard as the sin to be forgiven and as the grace that forgives are far removed from the depths and heights of wickedness and goodness revealed in the cross of Christ. The faith in grace and the correlate knowledge of sin that come through the cross are of another order from that easy acceptance of kindliness in the deity and of moral error in mankind of which those speak who have never faced up to the horror of a world in which men blaspheme and try to destroy the very image of Truth and Goodness, God himself. The miracle with which the dualist begins is the miracle of God's grace, which forgives these men without any merit on their part, receives them as children of the Father, gives them repentance, hope, and assurance of salvation from the dark powers that rule in their lives, especially death, and makes them companions of the one they willed to kill. Though His demands on them are so high that they daily deny them and Him, still He remains their savior, lifting them up after every fall and setting them on the road to life.

The fact that the new beginning has been made with the revelation of God's grace does not change the fundamental situation as far as grace and sin are concerned. Grace is in God, and sin is in man. The grace of God is not a substance, a *mana*-like power, which is mediated to men through human acts. Grace is always in God's action; it is God's attribute. It is the action of reconciliation that reaches out across the no-man's land of the historic war of men against God. If something of the graciousness of Christ is reflected in the thankful responses of a Paul or a Luther to the gracious action of Christ, they themselves cannot be aware of it; and those who behold it cannot but see that it is only reflection. As soon as man tries to locate it in himself it disappears, as gratitude disappears in the moment when I turn from my benefactor to the contemplation of this beneficial virtue in me. The faith also with which man acknowledges and turns in trust to the gracious Lord is nothing that he can bring forth out of his native capacities. It is the reflection of the faithfulness of God. We trust because he is faithful. Therefore in the divine-human encounter, in the situation in which man is after as well as before he hears the word of reconciliation, grace is all on God's side. And Jesus Christ is the grace of God and the God of grace.

But sin is in man and man is in sin. In the presence of the crucified Lord of glory, men see that all their works and their work are not only pitifully inadequate, measured by that standard of goodness, but sordid and depraved. The dualist Christians differ considerably from the synthesists in their understanding of both the extent and the thoroughness of human depravity. As to extent: Clement, Thomas, and their associates note that man's reason may be darkened, but is not in its nature misdirected; for them the cure of bad reasoning lies in better reasoning, and in the aid of the divine teacher. Moreover, they regard man's religious culture in its Christian form—the institutions and doctrines of the holy church—as beyond the range of sinful corruption, however many minor evils calling for reform may now and again appear in the sacred precincts. But the dualist of Luther's type discerns corruption and degradation in all man's work. *Before the holiness of God* as disclosed in the grace of Jesus Christ there is no distinction between the wisdom of the philosopher and the folly of the simpleton, between the crime of the murderer and his chastisement by the magistrate, between the profaning of sanctuaries by blasphemers and their hallowing by priests, between the carnal sins and the spiritual aspirations of men. The dualist does not say that there are no differences between these things, but that before the holiness of God there are no significant differences; as one might say that comparisons between the highest skyscrapers and the meanest hovels are meaningless in the presence of Betelgeuse. Human culture is corrupt; and it includes all human work, not simply the achievements of men outside the church but also those in it, not only philosophy so far as it is human achievement but theology also, not only Jewish defence of Jewish law but also Christian defence of Christian precept. If we would understand the dualist here, we must keep two things in mind. He

is not passing judgment on other men —save as in the sinfulness to which he is subject he abandons his position before God—but testifies rather to the judgment that is being passed on him and on the whole of mankind, with which he is inseparably united not only by nature but in culture. When he speaks of the sinfulness of the law-abiding man he does so as a Paul who has been zealous in observance of the law, and as a Luther who has rigorously sought to keep the letter and the spirit of the monastic vows. When he speaks about the corruption of reason, he does so as a reasoner who has tried ardently to ascend to the knowledge of truth. What is said about the depravity of man is said therefore from the standpoint and in the situation of cultured, sinful man confronting the holiness of divine grace. The other thing that must be kept in mind is that for these believers the attitude of man before God is not an attitude man takes in addition to other positions, after he has confronted nature, or his fellow men, or the concepts of reason. It is the fundamental and ever-present situation; though man is forever trying to ignore the fact that he is up against God, or that what he is up against when he is "up against it" is God.

The dualist differs from the synthesist also in his conception of the nature of corruption in culture. Perhaps the two schools share that religious sense of sin that can never be translated into moral or intellectual terms, and the dualist only feels more profoundly the sordidness of everything that is creaturely, human, and earthly when it is in the presence of the holy.[7] Having contended like Job for his own goodness, he also joins in the confession: "I had heard of thee by the hearing of the ear; but now mine eye seeth thee: wherefore I abhor myself and repent in dust and

---

[7] Cf. Rudolf Otto, *The Idea of the Holy* (1924), pp. 9 ff.; also A. E. Taylor, *The Faith of a Moralist* (1930), I, 163 ff.

ashes." Yet the holiness of God as presented in the grace of Jesus Christ has too precise a character to permit definition of its negative counterpart, human sin, in the vague terms of primitive feeling. The sense of sordidness, of shame, dirtiness, and pollution is the effective accompaniment of an objective moral judgment on the nature of the self and its society. Here is man before God, deriving his life from God, being sustained and forgiven by God, being loved and being lived; and this man is engaged in an attack on the One who is his life and his being. He is denying what he must assert in the very act of denial; he is rebelling against the One without whose loyalty he could not even rebel. All human action, all culture, is infected with godlessness, which is the essence of sin. Godlessness appears as the will to live without God, to ignore Him, to be one's own source and beginning, to live without being indebted and forgiven, to be independent and secure in one's self, to be godlike in oneself. It has a thousand forms and expresses itself in the most devious ways. It appears in the complacency of self-righteously moral and of self-authenticatedly rational men, but also in the despair of those for whom all is vanity. It manifests itself in irreligion, in atheism and antitheism; but also in the piety of those who consciously carry God around with them wherever they go. It issues in desperate acts of passion, by which men assert themselves against the social law with its claims to divine sanction; but also in the zealous obedience of the law-abiding, who desperately need the assurance that they are superior to the lesser breeds without the law. Thwarted in its efforts to found divine, enduring empires, the desire to be independent of God's grace expresses itself in attempts to establish godlike churches that have stored up all necessary truth and grace in doctrines and sacraments. Unable to impose its will on others through the morality of masters, the will to be god tries the methods of slave morality. When man cannot any longer assure himself that he is the master of his physical fate, he turns to the things he believes are really under his control, such things as sincerity and integrity, and tries to shelter himself under his honesty; in this domain, at least, he thinks he can get along without grace, an independent good man, needing nothing he cannot himself supply. The dualist likes to point out that the will to live as gods, hence without God, appears in man's noblest endeavors, that is, those that are noblest according to human standards. Men whose business it is to reason exalt reason to the position of judge and ruler of all things; they call it the divine element in man. Those who have the vocation of maintaining order in society deify law—and partly themselves. The independent, democratic citizen has a little god inside himself in an authoritative conscience that is not under authority. As Christians we want to be the forgivers of sins, the lovers of men, new incarnations of Christ, saviors rather than saved; secure in our own possession of the true religion, rather than dependent on a Lord who possesses us, chooses us, forgives us. If we do not try to have God under our control, then at least we try to give ourselves the assurance that we are on His side facing the rest of the world; not with that world facing Him in infinite dependence, with no security save in Him.

Thus in the dualist's view the whole edifice of culture is cracked and madly askew; the work of self-contradicting builders, erecting towers that aspire to heaven on a fault in the earth's crust. Where the synthesist rejoices in the rational content of law and social institutions, the dualist, with the skepticism of the Sophist and positivist, calls attention to the lust for power and the will of the strong which rationalizes itself in all these social arrangements. In monarchies, aristocracies, and de-

RELIGION AND CONTEMPORARY WESTERN CULTURE

mocracies, in middle-class and proletarian rules, in episcopal, presbyterian, and congregational polities, the hand of power is never wholly disguised by its soft glove of reason. In the work of science itself reason is confounded; as on the one hand it humbly surrenders itself to the given in disinterested questioning, and on the other hand seeks knowledge for power. In all the synthesists' defences of rational elements in culture the dualist sees this fatal flaw, that reason in human affairs is never separable from its egoistic, godless, perversion. The institution of property, he points out, not only guards against theft but also sanctions the great seizures of alien possessions, as when it protects the settler in his rights over lands taken by force or deceit from Indians. The reasonable institution rests on a great irrationality. Institutions of celibacy and marriage prevent and also cover a multitude of sins. Hence the dualist joins the radical Christian in pronouncing the whole world of human culture to be godless and sick unto death. But there is this difference between them: the dualist knows that he belongs to that culture and cannot get out of it, that God indeed sustains him in it and by it; for if God in His grace did not sustain the world in its sin it would not exist for a moment.

In this situation the dualist cannot speak otherwise than in what sound like paradoxes; for he is standing on the side of man in the encounter with God, yet seeks to interpret the Word of God which he has heard coming from the other side. In this tension he must speak of revelation and reason, of law and grace, of the Creator and Redeemer. Not only his speech is paradoxical under these circumstances, but his conduct also. He is under law, and yet not under law but grace; he is sinner, and yet righteous; he believes, as a doubter; he has assurance of salvation, yet walks along the knife-edge of insecurity. In Christ all things have

become new, and yet everything remains as it was from the beginning. God has revealed Himself in Christ, but hidden Himself in His revelation; the believer knows the One in whom he has believed, yet walks by faith, not sight.

Among these paradoxes two are of particular importance in the dualists' answer to the Christ-culture problem: those of law and grace, and of divine wrath and mercy. The dualist joins the radical Christian in maintaining the authority of the law of Christ over all men, and in stating it in its plain literal sense, objecting to the attenuations of the gospel precepts by cultural or synthetic Christians. The law of Christ is not, in his understanding, an addition to the law of man's nature but its true statement, a code for the average, normal man, and not a special rule for spiritual supermen. Yet he also insists that no human self-culture, in obedience to that law or any other, can avail to extricate man out of his sinful dilemma. Nor are institutions that claim this law as their basis—monastic orders or pacifist customs or communistic communities— less subject to the sin of godlessness and self-love than are the cruder forms of custom and society. The law of God in the hands of men is an instrument of sin. Yet as coming from God and heard from His lips it is a means of grace. But, again, it is a kind of negative means, driving man to despair of himself and so preparing him to turn away from himself to God. When, however, the sinner throws himself on the divine mercy and lives by that mercy alone, the law is reinstated in a new form, as something written on the heart—a law of nature, not an external commandment. Still, it is the law of God which the forgiven receives as the will of the Other rather than as his own. Thus the dialogue about law proceeds. It sounds paradoxical, because the effort is being made to state in a monologue a meaning that is clear only in the dramatic encounters and re-encounters of God and the souls of men. In his shorthand synopsis of the great action, the dualist seems to be saying that the law of life is not law but grace; that grace is not grace but law, an infinite demand made on man; that love is an impossible possibility and hope of salvation an improbable assurance. These are the abstractions; the reality is the continuing dialogue and struggle of man with God, with its questions and answers, its divine victories that look like defeats, its human defeats that turn into victories. . . .

The conversionists' understanding of the relations of Christ and culture is most closely akin to dualism, but it also has affinities with the other great Christian attitudes. That it represents a distinct *motif*, however, becomes apparent when one moves from the Gospel of Matthew and the Letter of James through Paul's epistles to the Fourth Gospel, or proceeds from Tertullian, the Gnostics, and Clement to Augustine, or from Tolstoy, Ritschl, and Kierkegaard to F. D. Maurice. The men who offer what we are calling the conversionist answer to the problem of Christ and culture evidently belong to the great central tradition of the church. Though they hold fast to the radical distinction between God's work in Christ and man's work in culture, they do not take the road of exclusive Christianity into isolation from civilization, or reject its institutions with Tolstoyan bitterness. Though they accept their station in society with its duties in obedience to their Lord, they do not seek to modify Jesus Christ's sharp judgment of the world and all its ways. In their Christology they are like synthesists and dualists; they refer to the Redeemer more than to the giver of a new law, and to the God whom men encounter more than to the representative of the best spiritual resources in humanity. They understand that his work is concerned not with the specious, external aspects of human behavior in the first

place, but that he tries the hearts and judges the subconscious life; that he deals with what is deepest and most fundamental in man. He heals the most stubborn and virulent human disease, the phthisis of the spirit, the sickness unto death; he forgives the most hidden and proliferous sin, the distrust, lovelessness, and hopelessness of man in his relation to God. And this he does not simply by offering ideas, counsel, and laws; but by living with men in great humility, enduring death for their sakes, and rising again from the grave in a demonstration of God's grace rather than an argument about it. In their understanding of sin the conversionists are more like dualists than synthesists. They note that it is deeply rooted in the human soul, that it pervades all man's work, and that there are no gradations of corruption, however various its symptoms. Hence they also discern how all cultural work in which men promote their own glory, whether individualistically or socially, whether as members of the nation or of humanity, lies under the judgment of God—who does not seek His own profit. They see the self-destructiveness in its self-contradictoriness. Yet they believe also that such culture is under God's sovereign rule, and that the Christian must carry on cultural work in obedience to the Lord.

What distinguishes conversionists from dualists is their more positive and hopeful attitude toward culture. Their more affirmative stand seems to be closely connected with three theological convictions. The first of these relates to creation. The dualist tends so to concentrate on redemption through Christ's cross and resurrection that creation becomes for him a kind of prologue to the one mighty deed of atonement. Though with Paul he affirms that in Christ "all things were created, in heaven and on earth, visible and invisible, whether thrones or dominions or principalities or authorities—all things were created

61

through him and for him," [8] yet this is a relatively unemphasized idea, used mostly to introduce the great theme of reconciliation. For the conversionist, however, the creative activity of God and of Christ-in-God is a major theme, neither overpowered by nor overpowering the idea of atonement. Hence man the creature, working in a created world, lives, as the conversionist sees it, under the rule of Christ and by the creative power and ordering of the divine Word, even though in his unredeemed mind he may believe that he lives among vain things under divine wrath. To be sure, the dualist often also says something like this; but he tends to qualify it so much by references to God's anger as peculiarly manifest in the physical world that the beneficence of the Ruler of nature becomes somewhat doubtful. The effect of the conversionist's theory of culture on his positive thought about creation is considerable. He finds room for affirmative and ordered response on the part of created man to the creative, ordering work of God; even though the creature may go about his work unwillingly as he tills the ground, cultivates his mind, and organizes his society, and though he may administer perversely the order given him with his existence. In connection with this interest in creation, the conversionist tends to develop a phase of Christology neglected by the dualist. On the one hand he emphasizes the participation of the Word, the Son of God, in creation, not as this took place once upon a time but as it occurs in the immediate origin, the logical and momentary beginning of everything, in the mind and power of God. On the other hand he is concerned with the redemptive work of God in the incarnation of the Son, and not merely with redemption in his death, resurrection, and return in power. Not that the conversionist turns from the historical Jesus

to the Logos that was in the beginning, or that he denies the wonder of the cross in marvelling at the birth in a barn; he seeks to hold together in one movement the various themes of creation and redemption, of incarnation and atonement. The effect of this understanding of the work of Christ in incarnation as well as creation on conversionist thought about culture is unmistakable. The Word that became flesh and dwelt among us, the Son who does the work of the Father in the world of creation, has entered into a human culture that has never been without his ordering action.

The second theological conviction that modifies the conversionist view of human work and custom is its understanding of the nature of man's fall from his created goodness. As we have noted, dualism often brings creation and fall into such close proximity that it is tempted to speak in almost Gnostic terms, as if creation of finite selfhood or matter involved fall. To be in the body is to be away from Christ; nothing good dwells in the flesh; to be carnal is to be sold under sin. All this is true for a Paul and a Luther not only because the spirit of man that dwells in his body is sinful but because the body offers unconquerable temptation to sin. [9] Hence such Christians tend to think of the institutions of culture as having largely a negative function in a temporal and corrupt world. They are orders for corruption, preventatives of anarchy, directives for the physical life, concerned wholly with temporal matters. The conversionist agrees with the dualist in asserting a doctrine of a radical fall of man. But he distinguishes the fall very sharply from creation, and from the conditions of life in the body. It is a kind of reversal of creation for him, and in no sense its continuation. It is entirely the action of man, and in no

[8] Colossians 1:16.

[9] On this much disputed point cf. Lietzmann, Hans, *An die Roemer* (*Handbuch zum Neuen Testament,* Vol. VIII) , pp. 75 ff.

way an action of God's. It is moral and personal, not physical and metaphysical, though it does have physical consequences. The results of man's defection from God, moreover, all occur on man's side and not on God's. The word that must be used here to designate the consequences of the fall is "corruption." Man's good nature has become corrupted; it is not bad, as something that ought not to exist, but warped, twisted, and misdirected. He loves with the love that is given him in his creation, but loves beings wrongly, in the wrong order; he desires good with the desire given him by his Maker, but aims at goods that are not good for him and misses his true good; he produces fruit, but it is misshapen and bitter; he organizes society with the aid of his practical reason, but works against the grain of things in self-willed forcing of his reason into irrational paths, and thus disorganizes things in his very acts of organization. Hence his culture is all corrupted order rather than order for corruption, as it is for dualists. It is perverted good, not evil; or it is evil as perversion, and not as badness of being. The problem of culture is therefore the problem of its conversion, not of its replacement by a new creation; though the conversion is so radical that it amounts to a kind of rebirth.

With these convictions about creation and fall the conversionists combine a third: a view of history that holds that to God all things are possible in a history that is fundamentally not a course of merely human events but always a dramatic interaction between God and men. For the exclusive Christian, history is the story of a rising church or Christian culture and a dying pagan civilization; for the cultural Christian, it is the story of the spirit's encounter with nature; for the synthesist, it is a period of preparation under law, reason, gospel, and church for an ultimate communion of the soul with God; for the dualist, history is the time of struggle between faith and unbelief, a period between the giving of the promise of life and its fulfillment. For the conversionist, history is the story of God's mighty deeds and of man's responses to them. He lives somewhat less "between the times" and somewhat more in the divine "Now" than do his brother Christians. The eschatological future has become for him an eschatological present. Eternity means for him less the action of God before time and less the life with God after time, and more the presence of God in time. Eternal life is a quality of existence in the here and now. Hence the conversionist is less concerned with conservation of what has been given in creation, less with preparation for what will be given in a final redemption, than with the divine possibility of a present renewal. Such differences of orientation in time are not to be defined with nice precision. There is a strain toward the future in every Christian life, as well as a reliance upon the God of Abraham, Isaac, and Jacob and the recognition that this is the day of salvation. But there is a difference between Paul's expectation of the time when the last enemy, death, will have been destroyed by Christ, and John's understanding of Christ's last words upon the cross, "It is finished." The conversionist, with his view of history as the present encounter with God in Christ, does not live so much in expectation of a final ending of the world of creation and culture as in awareness of the power of the Lord to transform all things by lifting them up to himself. His imagery is spatial and not temporal; and the movement of life he finds to be issuing from Jesus Christ is an upward movement, the rising of men's souls and deeds and thoughts in a mighty surge of adoration and glorification of the One who draws them to himself. This is what human culture can be—a transformed human life in

63

and to the glory of God. For man it is impossible, but all things are possible to God, who has created man, body and soul, for Himself, and sent his Son into the world that the world through him might be saved.

CHRISTOPHER DAWSON

Culture as a Window to the Supernatural*

There is still a certain amount of distrust of the sociological concept of culture among historians and men of letters, owing to the feeling that it is an alien importation into our language. Since the days when Tylor wrote his book on Primitive Culture, however, it has been adopted so widely by anthropologists and ethnologists, that it seems pedantic to object to a word which has acquired a scientific status as a specific term for which there is no satisfactory alternative.

A social culture is an organized way of life which is based on a common tradition and conditioned by a common environment. It is therefore not identical with the concept of civilization which involves a high degree of conscious rationalization nor with society itself, since a culture normally includes a number of independent social units.

The fact that a culture is a way of life adapted to a particular environment involves a certain degree of social specialization and the canalization of social energies along certain lines. We see this most clearly in the case of isolated marginal cultures, like that of the Esquimaux in the Arctic or that of the Bushmen in South Africa. In these cases the inter-relation of social organism, economic function and geographical environment is so complete that culture becomes inseparable from race.

But this does not mean, as the racialists believe, that culture is the result of predetermined racial inheritance. On the contrary it would be more true to say that race is the product of culture, and that the differentiation of racial types represents the culmination of an age-long process of cultural segregation and specialization at a very primitive level, just as in modern times nationality and the differentiation of national types is the result of the growth of special cultural traditions rather than vice versa.

It is indeed remarkable how rapidly the human type is modified or transformed by a new way of life or a new environment. Take a few hundred thousand nineteenth century English and Irish, transplant them to Australia and let them adapt their social habits and organization to this new environment, and in a century you find a new human type which is both physically and psychologically different from that of the parent society.

Nevertheless in spite of these far-

* From *Religion and Culture* by Christopher Dawson. Copyright 1948, Sheed & Ward, Inc., New York. Used by permission of the Society of Authors, Mr. Christopher Dawson, and Sheed & Ward; pp. 47-62.

64

reaching changes, the factor of cultural tradition remains predominant. The new Australian type is not a variety of the native Australian type but of the British type, so that to an Australian aboriginal the two will probably appear so similar as to be indistinguishable. For the way of life of any particular society exerts so powerful an influence on its individual members that hereditary differences of character and predisposition are worked into the pattern of culture as the multi-coloured threads are woven into the design of a fabric. Thus culture is the form of society. The society without culture is a formless society—a crowd or a collection of individuals brought together by the needs of the moment—while the stronger a culture is, the more completely does it inform and transform the diverse human material of which it is composed.

What then is the relation of culture to religion? It is clear that a common way of life involves a common view of life, common standards of behaviour and common standards of value, and consequently a culture is a spiritual community which owes its unity to common beliefs and common ways of thought far more than to any uniformity of physical type. Now it is easy for a modern man living in a highly secularized society to conceive this common view of life as a purely secular thing which has no necessary connection with religious beliefs. But in the past, it was not so. From the beginning man has already regarded his life and the life of society as intimately dependent on forces that lie outside his own control —on superhuman powers which rule both the world and the life of man. "No man," said an Indian hunter, "can succeed in life alone, and he cannot get the help he needs from men."

This conviction that "the way of man is not in himself", that it is not for man to walk and direct his own steps, is as old as humanity itself. We can find most clear and moving expressions

of this belief among the primitive peoples—most of all perhaps among the hunting peoples like the North American Indians whose conception of dependence on spiritual powers has been described with exceptional fullness by a series of excellent scholars and observers, like I. O. Dorsey, F. Boas and Ruth Benedict. But it is also found amongst much more primitive races, and needless to say in all the higher religions.

Therefore from the beginning the social way of life which is culture has been deliberately ordered and directed in accordance with the higher laws of life which are religion. As the powers of heaven rule the seasons, so the divine powers rule the life of man and society, and for a community to conduct its affairs without reference to these powers, seems as irrational as for a community to cultivate the earth without paying any attention to the course of the seasons. The complete secularization of social life is a relatively modern and anomalous phenomenon. Throughout the greater part of mankind's history, in all ages and states of society, religion has been the great central unifying force in culture. It has been the guardian of tradition, the preserver of the moral law, the educator and the teacher of wisdom.

And in addition to this conservative function, religion has also had a creative, conative, dynamic function, as energizer and life giver. Religion holds society in its fixed culture pattern, as in Plato's Laws, or as in the hierarchic order of Sumerian and Egyptian culture; but it also leads the people through the wilderness and brings them back from captivity and inspires them with the hope of future deliverance.

Religion is the key of history. We cannot understand the inner form of a society unless we understand its religion. We cannot understand its cultural achievements unless we understand the religious beliefs that lie behind them. In all ages the first creative works of a culture are due to a religious inspiration and dedicated to a religious end. The temples of the gods are the most enduring works of man. Religion stands at the threshold of all the great literatures of the world. Philosophy is its offspring and is a child which constantly returns to its parent.

And the same is true of social institutions. Kingship and law are religious institutions and even to-day they have not entirely divested themselves of their numinous character, as we can see in the English coronation rite and in the formulas of our law courts.

All the institutions of family and marriage and kinship have a religious background and have been maintained and are still maintained by formidable religious sanctions. The earliest social differentiation and the one that has had the most potent influence on culture has been due to the development of specialized social classes and institutions, charged with the function of maintaining relations between society and the divine powers. The fact that this class has almost invariably been responsible in whole or in part for the education of the community and the preservation of sacred tradition and learning gives it an exceptional importance in the history of culture; and we must study the specific form it takes in any particular culture or religion before we can begin to understand it. The Sumerian and Egyptian temple priesthoods, the Brahmin caste in ancient India, the clergy and the monastic orders in medieval Christendom are not merely religious institutions, they are also vital social organs in their respective cultures. And the same is true of the Shamans, the medicine men and witch doctors among primitive peoples although our current terminology often blurs the distinction between the sorcerer, whose function is non-social or anti-social, and the priest, who is the recognized religious organ of the community—a confusion which has been increased by the attempt to draw a rigid and exclusive line of division between religion and magic.

The more primitive a culture is, of course, the less room there is for an explicit differentiation of social functions, but on the other hand, the more directly is its religion bound up with the elementary needs of life, so that the social and economic way of life is more clearly interpenetrated by and fused with religion than is the case in the higher cultures.

Thus among the Australians there was no true priesthood, and the leadership in religion as in other matters fell to the old men who were the natural leaders of the tribe and the guardians of tradition. Nevertheless they possessed a most elaborate and highly organized system of religious rites to ensure the continuity of the life of the tribe and the maintenance of its food supply—a regular liturgy, which in some instances, as described by Spencer and Gillen, occupied the community almost continuously for three or four months at a time. In this case the way of life of the community is conceived as dependent on another and a sacred world— the world of the divine totemic ancestors —from which the spirit comes and to which it returns, and the totemic ceremonies provide the way of access and communion between the life of the tribe and the other world of the sacred *alcheringa* age.

It is difficult for a civilized man to understand either the religious significance or the cultural importance of such ceremonies. But to the primitive the dance or mime is at once the highest form of social activity and the most powerful kind of religious action. Through it the community participates in a mystery which confers supernatural efficacy upon its action. How this may affect social life and change the course of historical events may be seen in the rise of the Ghost Dance religion among the Indians of the Plains at the end of the nineteenth century. Here we have a well attested case of how a dance may become the medium by which the religious experience of an individual may be socialized and transmitted from one people to another with revolutionary political effects. Wovoka, an Indian of a little known and unimportant tribe in Nevada, received in a vision a dance the performance of which would bring back the spirits of their dead ancestors and the vanished herds of buffalo and the good times that were past. The dance cult spread like wildfire eastward across the mountains to the Indians of the great plains and finally stimulated the Sioux to their last desperate rising against the United States government.

The most remarkable thing about this movement was the extreme rapidity with which it communicated itself from people to people across half the continent, so that if it had not been defeated by a hopeless inequality of material power, the Ghost Dance might have changed not only the religion but also the social existence of the Indians of the Middle West in the course of a few years. Such revolutionary changes are in fact by no means rare in history. We have an example of it on the higher religious level and on a vast historical scale in the case of the rise of Islam. Here we see in full clearness and detail how a new religion may create a new culture. A single individual living in a cultural backwater originates a movement which in a comparatively short time sweeps across the world, destroying historic empires and civilizations and creating a new way of life which still moulds the thought and behaviour of millions from Senegal to Borneo. And in this case there is no common geographical environment or racial inheritance to form a basis for the spiritual community. A common faith has imposed its stamp on the most diverse human material so that the resultant product is even physically recognizable. The Arab of the desert, the West African negro, the Malay pirate, the Persian philosopher, the Turkish soldier,

the Indian merchant all speak the same religious language, profess the same theological dogmas and possess the same moral values and the same social conventions. Just as Moslem architecture is different in every country but is everywhere unmistakably Moslem, so it is with this literature and speech and behaviour.

No doubt modern nationalism and secularism have altered all this, but they have done so only recently and superficially and incompletely. Islam still exists as a living culture as well as a world religion.

Thus Islam provides a classic example of how culture—the social way of life—may be transformed by a new view of life and a new religious doctrine, and how as a result social forms and institutions may be created which transcend racial and geographical limits and remain fixed for centuries. And on the other hand we have countless examples —especially among primitive peoples— of religions which are so bound up with the culture of the community that they seem to be mere psychological reflections of the way of life of a particular people in a particular environment and to possess no religious significance apart from their social background. But however earthbound and socially conditioned these religions appear to be, they always look beyond society to some trans-social and superhuman reality towards which their worship is directed.

And conversely, however universal and spiritual a religion may be, it can never escape the necessity of becoming incarnated in culture and clothing itself in social institutions and traditions, if it is to exert a permanent influence on human life and behaviour.

For every historic religion from the lowest to the highest agrees on two fundamental points;—first in the belief in the existence of divine or supernatural powers whose nature is mysterious but which control the world and the life of man; and secondly in the association

67

of these powers with particular men, or things, or places or ceremonies, which act as channels of communication or means of access between the human and the divine worlds. Thus on the lowest levels of culture we find the Shaman, the fetish, the holy place and the sacred dance, while on the higher level we have the prophet and priest, the image or sacred symbol, the temple and the sacramental liturgy. Thus every great historic culture, viewed from within through the eyes of its members, represents a theogamy, a coming together of the divine and the human within the limits of a sacred tradition.

As a rule the creative role in the formation of culture is assigned to divine or semi-divine mythical figures—culture heroes or divine ancestors—who have delivered to their descendants or followers not only the sacred myths and sacred rites of religion but the arts of life and the principles of social organization.

Sometimes these figures are themselves the creators of man, like the totemic ancestors who, as the tribes of Central Australia believe, had in the beginning journeyed through their country, performing ceremonies and leaving spirit children behind them. Sometimes they are heroic human figures which have become the centres of a cycle of myths; while the great historic cultures for the most part look back to the personality of some historical prophet or lawgiver as the source of sacred tradition or the mediator of divine revelation. And there seems to be no reason why we should exclude *a priori* the possibility of such figures arising in very primitive cultures, in the same way that Wovoka arose among the Paviotso in the nineteenth century. We must never forget that existing or recorded primitive culture is, no less than any higher civilization, the result of a long process of historical change and development, in the course of which there may have been periods of advance and regression in thought as

68

well as in action. And though primitive culture is more communal and anonymous than the higher civilizations, it is never so communal as to exclude the creative action and influence of individual personalities. Hence the mythical figure of the first man, the culture hero, the firebearer, the teacher of the arts of life and the rites of religion is the archetype of the many forgotten or half-remembered figures which have played a decisive role in the formation or transformation of culture. In classical and oriental archaeology the progress of modern research has discovered again and again a solid bedrock of historical truth underlying the myths and legends that tradition has preserved, and in the same way behind primitive culture there is a lost world of history which is still more deeply submerged beneath the surface of consciousness.

In this twilight world history and religion are inextricably interwoven and confused, as we can see in the legends of our own past, where lost gods like Bran and Pwyll appear side by side with half-remembered historical figures like Arthur and Maxim Wledig and with the creatures of poetic legend. In fact culture is like a palimpsest in which the new characters never entirely efface the old, or a patchwork in which fragments of different age and material are brought together in a single social pattern.

To the outside observer the most striking feature of primitive culture is its extreme conservatism. Society follows the same path of custom and convention with the irrational persistence of animal life.

But in reality all living culture is intensely dynamic. It is dominated by the necessity of maintaining the common life, and it is possible to ward off the forces of evil and death and gain life and good fortune and prosperity only by a continuous effort of individual and social discipline. Hence the ascetic element is prominent in primitive culture and in both primitive and advanced religions. The law of life is the law of sacrifice and discipline. If the hunter is to capture his prey, if the warrior is to overcome his enemies, if the cultivator is to receive the fruits of the earth, he must give as well as take. And he does not think of this giving in terms of manure, or drill, or athletic exercise, he views it in religious terms as sacrifice and penance and ritual acts paid to the powers above. This is the meaning of the fertility rites of the peasant culture, of the ascetic practices of the Indians of the Plains and the cult of the animal guardians among primitive hunters, all of which are keys to the understanding of their respective cultures.

So too the initiation rites, which hold so large a place in every form of culture, represent an intensive effort of social discipline directed towards the incorporation of the individual into the community under the sanction of religious powers. These are not merely ordeals of social fitness to prepare the candidate for adult life as a full member of the community, they are even more an initiation into sacred mysteries which confer new powers upon him. In some cases these initiations involve supernormal psychological experiences so that a youth's future social career may depend on the nature of his visionary experience. "Your young men shall see visions and your old men shall dream dreams." This is no more than the common experience of many an uncivilized people, and it shows how, even in lower forms of culture, religion tends to transcend the social way of life and seeks to open a path of direct access to the world above.

Thus while a culture is essentially an organized way of life, it is never conceived as a purely man-made order. The social way of life is founded on a religious law of life, and this law in turn depends on non-human powers towards which man looks with hope and fear, powers which can be known in some fashion but which remain essentially mysterious, since they are superhuman and supernatural.

Hence the relation between religion and culture is always a two-sided one. The way of life influences the approach to religion, and the religious attitude influences the way of life. Whatever is felt to be of vital importance in the life of people is brought into close relation with religion and surrounded by religious sanctions, so that every economic and social way of life has its corresponding form of religion. In so far as this is so, it is possible to construct a classification of religions based on the main sociological and economic types of culture. Thus we can distinguish the religion of the hunter, the religion of the peasant, and the religion of the warrior. Or again the religion of the tribe, the religion of the city, and the religion of the empire. These types are, of course, abstractions and cannot be applied in an exclusive or wholesale manner to the historical actuality of a particular culture. Nevertheless they are valid and useful within their proper limits and it is hardly possible to understand a particular religion without reference to them. For example the religion of the hunter is characterized by the existence of Shamans or prophets, by the dream-vision and by the cult of animal spirits, and much that appears at first sight inexplicable in the culture and religion of a people of hunters can be understood when we view it in the context of these practises and ideas. In the same way, the religion of the peasant is characterized by the worship of the Earth Mother and the cult of fertility which recur with remarkable similarities all over the world wherever the peasant culture is to be found. And since the peasant way of life underlies the higher civilizations, even when the latter are controlled by a conquering warrior people, and consciously identified with its life, we cannot understand the development of the higher religions unless we take account of the underlying stratum of peasant religion which survives as a submerged and half-forgotten element in the spiritual tradition of the culture.

All this may seem to suggest that religion is so conditioned by culture and economics that it is itself a product of culture. But however far this process of cultural conditioning goes—and it certainly may go very far—we can never exclude the alternative relation—that culture is moulded and changed by religion. It is obvious that a man's way of life is the way by which he apprehends reality—and consequently the way in which he approaches religion. Nevertheless the object of religion essentially transcends human life and the human way of life. Over against the world of human experience and social behaviour there stands the world of divine power and mystery, which is conceived by the primitive no less than by the advanced theist as essentially creative and the ultimate source of all power.

Therefore while in practice the religion of a people is limited and conditioned by its culture, in theory—and even in the theory of the primitive himself—culture is a deliberate effort to bring human life into relation with divine reality and into subordination to divine power.

Thus the culture process is open to change from either direction. Any material change which transforms the external conditions of life will also change the cultural way of life and thus produce a new religious attitude. And likewise any spiritual change which transforms men's views of reality will tend to change their way of life and thus produce a new form of culture.

Great cultural changes are extremely complex processes in which it is often difficult to decide the relative importance of the spiritual and material factors. But it is no more possible to deny the creative influence of new religious beliefs and doctrines, than that of new political ideas or new scientific inven-

tions. And where the new religious influence is embodied in the personality of a great prophet or lawgiver, this creative influence of religion in cultural change is immediately evident.

No doubt great changes would have occurred in the culture of the Near East about the seventh century A.D. in any case, but that they should have taken the form they did can be explained only by the personality of Mohammed and by the doctrine he taught.

For religion, though it normally exerts a conservative influence on culture, also provides the most dynamic means of social change. Indeed one might almost go so far as to say that it is only by religion that a religious culture can be changed. The fact that a way of life has been consecrated by tradition and myth renders it singularly resistant to external change, even when the change seems obviously advantageous from a practical point of view. But if the impulse to change comes from above, from the organs of the sacred tradition itself or from some other source which claims superhuman authority, the elements in society which are most sensitive to religious impulses and most resistant to secular influences themselves become the willing agents of change.

And the creative role taken by religion in regard to culture is also to be seen in the case of those religions which at first sight seem entirely indifferent to cultural considerations. To the Western mind, for example, Buddhism has no obvious relation to culture. It appears to represent a turning of the mind away from life, in a victory of the death instinct and a denial of all the values of human culture. Nevertheless, Buddhism was emphatically a way of life, which created communities and institutions and had a more far-reaching influence on the culture of Eastern and Southern Asia than any other movement. Even to-day the Buddhist theocracy of Tibet is the most complete and imposing example of a purely religious culture existing in the modern world. And this is a remarkably interesting case, since it shows how a highly specialized way of life adapted to an exceptional environment can become fused with a very highly developed religious culture, which arose in an entirely different milieu and was imported ready-made into the utterly different social and geographical world of mediaeval Tibet. Not only was the extremely subtle and elaborate structure of Buddhist metaphysics transferred intact from Sanskrit to Tibetan, but it was later retransferred *en bloc* from Tibetan to Mongolian, so that the whole of Eastern Central Asia from the Himalayas to Lake Baikhal and Manchuria is dominated by this secondary derivative Buddhist culture which has its centre in the great monasteries of Lhasa and Tashi Llumpo and Urga. Thus by a strange irony of history the most aggressive warrior people of Asia—the Mongols—came to adopt a religion of non-aggression and universal compassion; and if, as seems probable, this event gradually led to a change in the character and habits of the people which contributed to the cessation of the age-long drive of the peoples of the steppes to East and West, it may be reckoned one of the turning points in world history.

On the other hand it is equally, or even more, clear that the native traditions of culture in Tibet and Mongolia had a powerful influence on the higher religion, so that the gods of the steppes have become members of the Buddhist pantheon and the Tibetan or Mongolian Lama is half or three-quarters a Shaman.

Here we see displayed on a colossal scale in time and space the processes of mutual interaction which are to be found everywhere at work in the relations between religion and culture. A new religion comes into contact with an old culture: it changes it and is changed by it; or a religion which has already found cultural expression in an old

advanced civilization comes into contact with a primitive culture which it assimilates by communicating its own higher tradition of culture. These patterns are repeated in an endless series of variations so that they form an immense labyrinth of cultural change in which every historic culture is involved. It has been the task of the modern science of religion to unravel this tangled web and reveal the simple patterns that underly its complexities. But this rational simplification is not enough; we also need the help of a true Natural Theology to interpret the supercultural and purely religious elements that are contained in the hieroglyphs of ritual and myth. This was the older tradition of the science of religion—the tradition of the philosophers and the Fathers—and although it was discredited by the absence of a true method of historical enquiry and a lack of psychological and philological techniques, it was more true in principle than the rationalism of nineteenth century comparative religion, since it did attempt to explain religious phenomena in terms of religion —theologically, not anthropologically.

From the point of view of the theologian who studies the nature of the divine as such, there is no insuperable difficulty in the cultural differentiation of religion and the development of types of religion corresponding to the nature of the primitive cultural types. For in so far as a culture represents a natural way of life, it reflects a distinct aspect of reality and has its own particular truth and its own scale of values which provide a way of approach to transcendent truths and values, and open, as it were, a new window to heaven as well as to earth. Every way of life is therefore a potential way to God, since the life that it seeks is not confined to material satisfaction and animal activities but reaches out beyond itself towards eternal life.

The theologian teaches that every being of its nature possesses an innate tendency towards God—the natural in-

71

clination to what is absolutely universal good.

Therefore the particular goods of particular cultures are not dead ends; they are the media by which the universal good is apprehended and through which these cultures are orientated towards the good that transcends their own power and knowledge.

And thus every culture, even the most primitive, seeks, like the old Roman civic religion, to establish a *jus divinum* which will maintain the *pax deorum,* a religious order which will relate the life of the community to the transcen-dent powers that rule the universe. The way of life must be a way of the service of God. Otherwise it will become a way of death. This is the lesson alike of the most primitive cultures and of the highest religions, and in this agreement we find, so it seems to me, a point at which the old Natural Theology and the new scientific study of comparative religion can establish contact and find a basis of mutual understanding. Without this the study of comparative religion becomes lost in the maze of sociological relativity, and Natural Theology loses contact with religion as an historical fact.

EMIL BRUNNER

The Christian Idea of Culture*

We have spoken so far, in the first series of these lectures, about the foundation of civilisation, and in the earlier lectures of this series about some spheres of civilised or cultural life. We now go back to the question with which we started: what is a Christian civilisation? We have seen how problematic this concept is. We have stated that there never was in a strict sense a Christian civilisation, and that what is usually called by that name is a compromise between Christian and non-Christian forces. We have now come to the point where it may be possible to sketch something like the Christian idea of civilisation or culture. By the two terms civilisation and culture, we understand something typically and exclusively human; man alone is capable of producing it. Whatever astonishing analogies may be found in the life of animals—the beaver-dam, the state of the ants, the so-called language and games of the animals—they are mere analogies and not beginnings of cultured and civilised life because they are all tied to biological necessities, as nourishment, procreation and shelter. Man alone can transcend these necessities by his creative imagination, and by the idea of something which is not yet but ought to be; by the ideas of the good, of justice, beauty, perfection, holiness and infinitude. It is true that even human civilisation and culture are related to biological necessity and have their basis within natural organic life which is common to us and the

* Reprinted with permission of Charles Scribner's Sons and James Nisbet and Company from *Christianity and Civilisation,* Volume II, pages 127-39, by Emil Brunner. Copyright 1949, Charles Scribner's Sons.

animals. But even where man is tied to biological necessity he acts in a way which transcends mere utility and gives his doings a human stamp. He does not "feed" like the animals, he eats; he ornaments his vessels, his instruments, his house, he establishes and observes fine customs, he explores truth irrespective of utility, he creates beautiful things for the sheer joy of beauty. He orders his relations according to ideas of justice and liberty. He masters power by law, he sacrifices time, energy and life for ideas and ideals. All this is civilisation and culture. Therefore we can define them as that formation of human life which has its origin not in mere biological necessity but in spiritual impulses. Wherever spirit, transcending the physical urge, enters the scene of life as a formative force, there civilisation and culture comes into existence.

These spiritual impulses and formative forces are of the most varied kinds. The impulse to create the beautiful, to realise justice, to know the truth, to preserve the past, to enter into spiritual communications, to invent the new, to extend the range of human intercommunion, to share the sufferings and joys of others; the impulse to submit the totality of life to ultimate directives and give it a meaning, unity and intelligibility, and finally to place everything under the divine will and receive it from the hands of God—all these are impulses out of which culture and civilisation arise.

All the same, we should not idealise culture and civilisation, as is done so often. These spiritual motives, although transcending biological necessity, are mixed with egoism, lust for power, and ambition. They are in competition with each other, one motive trying to displace the others and to monopolise life. Artistic or scientific impulses can be mixed with irresponsibility, inhuman hardness and brutality. The scientist can be blind to art, the artist to science, and both can be indifferent to moral or religious truth. Religion can become fanatical and cruel, it can hamper or even cripple art, science, technics, community, by its prejudices. Although all these spiritual elements transcend the biological urge, none of them as such is a guarantee of true, full humanity. Everyone of them can become a parasite in relation to the others, or an idol, or a caricature. The intensity and height of cultural achievement therefore is no sure mark of a truly human life. Intensity can be in conflict with harmony or totality. And this conflict can assume the most evil and ugliest forms of the struggle for life. Spiritual energy, combined with lust for power and egoism, gives the animal instincts a demoniac power unknown in the animal realm. The means which technics and organisation, planning and association, give to the human will, can produce a kind of civilisation which, although it is still characteristic of man, can lead into catastrophes that may amount to a suicide of humanity.

All these dark aspects belong to the character of human civilisation, which is the civilisation of sinful men. Civilisation and culture, then, are not in themselves the opposite of evil and depravity. They can become the very instruments of evil and negative forces, as they have always been to a certain extent. Culture and civilisation, although they belong exclusively to man, are not in themselves *the* truly human. True, without culture and civilisation man cannot be human, but in themselves they do not guarantee the truly human character of life. That is what we have called, in a previous connection, the formal character of civilisation. Wherever spirit expresses itself, there is civilised life; but what kind of a spirit creates that civilisation or culture is another question. Culture is an expression of the spirit, a formation by spiritual impulse, but this spiritual impulse can originate from the most different sources, and therefore is no guarantee of inner unity.

The question then arises whether

there exists a spiritual impulse capable of relating all the other impulses in the right proportions and unifying them in such a way as to produce a truly human life. Does there exist an understanding of man which gives to all the elements of human life—the biological, economic, technical, scientific, artistic, individual, social and communal—their full chance, and which at the same time subdues all of them to that which guarantees true humanity? Furthermore, is this understanding of man, if it exists, of such a kind that it is capable of functioning as an organising dynamic, so that it is not a mere idea but a directing power? As a result of our investigations we can give a positive answer to these questions. This conception of man is implicit in the Christian faith in its New Testament purity and dynamic.

The Christian faith alone views man as a spiritual-bodily unit whose powers and impulses, originating from his physical nature and from his spiritual disposition, are all co-ordinated in such a way that they are subordinated to a human destiny which transcends both the natural and the spiritual life, and is directive of both. "All are yours, and ye are Christ's, and Christ is God's." "Of every tree of the garden thou mayest freely eat"—only from the tree in the middle of the garden, the tree of the divine mystery, by reservation of the holy God, man shall not eat. All that is creature is in a specific way subordinated to man, but he himself with all his life and powers is subordinated to God who is holy love and who destines men for communion with Himself and with each other. Man is created to subdue and have dominion over all creation, but "whether you eat or drink or whatsoever you do, do all to the glory of God." This is the programme of life given to men by the Creator: free development of all their powers, free use of all the means under the dominion of the One who gives all and ordains all to Himself.

74

Now, before we go on to enlarge this Biblical idea of culture, some questions have to be taken up which obtrude themselves from the standpoint of history. As we have seen, in our first lecture, the New Testament shows very little interest in the specific tasks of civilisation and culture. How then can faith, which seems so indifferent to culture, be its basis? Our answer is twofold. First, it is true that the main concern of the New Testament message is not culture or civilisation, not the temporal but the eternal, not the earthly but the heavenly life. The Gospel is not focused on culture, but on the world-to-come. "This world passes away," and with it civilisation. Christian faith, indeed, is alive only where the life with God in Christ and the eternal kingdom of God is the centre of interest. "Seek ye first His kingdom and His righteousness." The kingdom of God is not human civilisation. It stands above both the physical and the cultural life. That is the first thing which has to be said. The second point, however, which must be repeated, is that this perspective of the kingdom of God does not alienate men from their temporal life. Faith in the kingdom and in eternal life does not make men indifferent to the tasks which earthly existence lays upon them. On the contrary, the Christian is summoned to tackle them with special energy, and his faith gives him the power to solve these problems better than he could without faith. "Seek ye first the kingdom of God . . . and these things shall be added unto you." It is precisely the man whose first concern is not culture but the kingdom of God that has the necessary distance from cultural aims and the necessary perspective to serve them in freedom, and to grasp that order which prevents the various sections of civilisation from monopolising the totality of life. Only from beyond civilisation can its order and harmony come.

It is a humanistic superstition to believe that the man to whom culture is everything is the true bearer of culture. The opposite is true. Culture necessarily degenerates where it is made God. Culture-idolatry is the sure road to cultural decay. If culture is to become and to remain truly human, it must have a culture-transcending centre. Man is more than his culture. Culture is means and tool, but not the essence of human life. It is not culture that gives man his humanity, but it is the human man that creates a human culture. That is why it is a grave error to think that the Christian faith is the enemy of culture, or at least indifferent to it, because it so emphatically accentuates the culture-transcending centre of life.

But what is the verdict of history? I think that, correctly interpreted, it confirms what has just been said. It is true that there have been Christian movements showing a kind of cultural asceticism, that there have been times when faith and theological interest absorbed men to such a degree that they neglected their cultural obligations. It is true that the Christian Church has sometimes obstructed the development of science or other cultural functions. While we are not justified in taking these negative facts too lightly, we are obliged on the other hand to beware of rash inferences. We have always to make sure first whether it is really Christian faith that acts, and secondly whether it is really cultural values that are at stake. In Occidental history so many things have usurped the name of "Christian" which were only half Christian or pseudo-Christian. On the other hand, so many things have been postulated in the name of cultural necessity that were pseudo-cultural. Because it is of the nature of sin that one branch of life wants to develop at the cost of another equally important, and because it is a temptation for the cultured man to idolise culture and thereby deprive it of its truly human character, it must always be the foremost interest of the Christian to proclaim faith and love as the source and norm of all true humanity. By doing this, he does, in the long run, the best service to culture.

Finally, there is always a certain tendency in cultural humanity to understand spirit and culture in such a way that so-called "higher" culture becomes detached from every-day life, from marriage and family, from civic order and from social obligations. Such a humanism is inclined to forget that the soundness of family life is the basis of all true civilisation, that justice and freedom in public life are necessary presuppositions of all higher culture. There is a certain aristocracy of spirit which has little interest in popular education, or in the task of giving a real meaning to the work of the ordinary man, and which focusses all its interest on science, art and so-called higher culture. Such an attitude proves detrimental to real culture. It is at this point that the importance of the Christian view of life becomes particularly obvious. All this makes the question of the relations between historical Christianity and civilisation so complicated that it is hardly possible to reach a final judgment. On one point, however, we can speak without reserve: the history of civilisation during the last hundred years has made clear beyond any doubt that the progressive decline of Christian influence has caused a progressive decay of civilisation. But even that may remain doubtful to one who personally has no understanding of what Christian faith means.

These preliminaries being settled, we can now proceed to develop a little further the Christian idea of culture and civilisation. We start from the statement that human culture presupposes human man. It is not culture that makes man human, but it is human man who makes culture human. This order of things is given with the Christian faith. Man comes first, not civilised life. Man becomes human, not by culture and civilisation, but by understanding his human destiny. In the Christian revelation the destiny of man is love. The measure of culture is personality; more exactly, person-in-communion. Creative individuality is no equivalent of personal life in community. God is love—that is the centre of the Christian message, and this doctrine is exclusively Christian. Love is the first and the last, the ultimate reality, being the very essence of God. Love is not one amongst others, not one virtue alongside other virtues; love is no virtue at all: it is true humanity, as it is the essence of God. This love, *agapé* in the New Testament sense, is no natural disposition. It is acquired by faith. Man is created for this love: that is why he has a longing for it. But in spite of this natural longing, man does not have it by birth, he has to receive it as a supernatural gift. By this, his eternal destiny, man is culture-transcending. The meaning of his life is not in culture; on the contrary, it is his task to express and to realise this culture-transcending destiny in his cultural life. Culture then is means, expression, tool of true humanity, but not its origin and aim.

The first consequence of this conception of life is that the most important thing in life is the relation between man and man. Therefore it is not impersonal spiritual activity, it is not spiritual creation as such, but it is the formation of truly personal social relationships, which is the basis of true culture. There is more real culture in a truly human family life without art and science than in the highest achievements of art and science on the basis of neglected family life and degenerate sex-relations.

The second consequence of Christian anthropology is the acknowledgment of man's bodily-spiritual unity. In contrast with idealistic humanism, Christian faith does not despise the body and the bodily needs. The Christian doctrine of incarnation obliges the Christian to take the body and its needs seriously, and gives him the double task of incorporating the spirit and spiritualising the bodily life. Spirituality detached from the concerns of the body contradicts the Biblical doctrine of creation and produces an abstract kind of culture. The Christian understanding of corporal-spiritual unity has two consequences. First, it places the body under the direction of the spirit. Second, it takes seriously the problems of manual work, economy and material property. From this point of view a decent and meaningful order of every-day life and healthy economic conditions are important criteria of true civilisation. A well-ordered estate, with dignified houses of simple beauty and a carefully-managed farm, is a surer indication of true culture than a marvellous university, a famous academy of art, in the midst of a peasant or industrial proletariat. The Christian ethos has—paradoxical as this may appear—a strongly *bourgeois* trait, if we understand this word in its original sense of well-ordered citizenship. In the New Testament, eschatology—which certainly is the very opposite of anything *bourgeois*—is combined with a sober and earnest ethic of work and an intention to equalise social conditions. One might say with Kierkegaard, that this *bourgeois* element is the necessary outward incognito of the essentially anti-bourgeois heart and mind of the Christian.

The primacy of personal relations, as distinguished from purely abstract spiritual creativity, has another important consequence. In the Christian conception of sin it is not sensuality but egoism and pride which hold the first place. That is why those dangers which come from lust of power are taken most seriously, and why a high premium is placed upon good government and public justice. Social relations cannot be in accordance with human dignity if this lust for power is not kept within firm barriers in economic as well as in political life. To lead a truly human life, man must have an intangible sphere of freedom guaranteed by law. For this reason the

76

Christian must regard civic order, security, and a certain homogeneity in the sphere of economics, as an important criterion of cultural soundness. Wherever public institutions give evidence of the will to form human life as a community of free personalities, there is culture.

From the same source derives the high valuation of tradition and social custom. These conservative forces, which limit the freedom of the individual, however, are not without strong counterweights, originating from the Christian hope of a new world. It may be said, perhaps, that in the Christian view of a good life the conservative elements are stressed so much because otherwise the eschatological perspective of the Christian faith might lead to an illusionist revolutionary attitude. On the other hand, tradition and social custom are an expression of the sense of responsibility and mutual obligation. They represent the element of solidarity and loyalty, helping the individual—if they are not stressed too much—to acquire mature independence.

One of the most obvious contributions of Christianity to civilised life is its pre-eminent interest in education and instruction. Again, the Christian view of education is characterised by its personalism. It is not knowledge and ability which stand in the first rank, but education of responsible personality and social training. Wherever Christian tradition has been alive, it has influenced the educational life of the nations in this direction. In contrast with it, the de-christianisation of Continental Europe, as the result first of an abstract spiritualism of a humanistic type and later on of materialistic utilitarianism, have resulted in an almost complete neglect of the personal and social element in education, and in the preponderance of abstract educational aims, such as knowledge and professional ability. Pestalozzi's idea of education, deeply rooted in the Christian understanding of life, and therefore putting responsible personality and love in the first place, has been entirely misunderstood or neglected, in spite of its fame.

It is only in the last place in a Christian programme of civilisation that we find what in the humanistic programme comes first: the so-called higher culture, embracing the purely spiritual elements, such as science and art. The expression, "higher culture," is justified in so far as in this realm the activity of the spirit is most remote from animalic urge and biological necessity. It is also, and for the same reason, the field of a spiritual *élite*. It is the realm of spiritual creativity. While in principle everyone can be good, only a few can be creative; the creative genius is the exception, and it is he who produces the works of which we mostly think when speaking of culture. It is, however, characteristic of the Christian conception of culture and civilisation to give these peak manifestations less importance than does idealistic humanism, for it is not science, art and spiritual activity which give life its truly human content, but love.

This specific order of values, however, does not prevent the Christian from giving art and science, as well as so-called higher education, a characteristic aim and meaning. Science as the search for truth, and art as the creation of the beautiful, are given the highest possible meaning: divine service. Wherever truth is known, something of the mystery of creation is revealed. The true scientist is a servant of God. To know and to acknowledge God is not a hindrance but, on the contrary, a help, in the search for truth. It keeps us from false absolutism and relativism, from idolatry of reason, and from sceptical despair. The scientist working, like Kepler, under highest command and for the honour of God is free from mean ambition and jealousy. The same is true of the artist. There is nothing which ennobles and purifies his creative powers so much as the conviction that he is a servant of God, called to praise the Creator and to manifest the secret which unites spirit and nature. It need not be proved, because it is proved already by history, that art can never rise higher than the point where the artist takes his highest inspiration devoutly as a gift of the Creator. There alone art is safeguarded from false aestheticism and idolatry of genius, as well as from that formalism and barbarism which lead to the ruin of art.

The second direction which Christian faith gives to the higher culture is service of man. To be sure, science remains sound only where it is not dominated by the principle of utility. Art degenerates if it becomes subservient to any aim outside of itself. Purpose-free science and purpose-free art are identical with true science and true art. All the same, if this is taken as the last word, a perilous dualism results; somewhere there must be a unity between truth and beauty on the one side and the good life on the other. This connection, however, must be very high if it is not to degrade art and science. This highest unity is God. God is the origin of truth and beauty, as well as the Creator of nature and the body, and the source of the moral order. Apart from God there is no possibility of uniting the principle of service with the principle of disinterested search for truth and beauty. God alone, theonomy, is the guarantee that such disinterested quest, such "autonomy" of science and art, does not contradict ethical standards.

It is not at all necessary that art, in order to honour God, must be "religious" art or Church art; neither is it necessary that science should be subordinated to theology. Science and art serve men best if they remain true to their own laws. They must be "autonomous". But if this autonomy is ultimate, final, it cannot but degenerate into sterile inhuman intellectualist "scientism" and into *l'art pour l'art* aestheticism. If, however, their autonomy is understood as theonomy, they keep their independence and yet are united to natural life and ethical principles by a unity standing above all of them. This is not mere theory but historical experience. It is what we have learnt from the greatest men of science and of art. Filled with reverence for God, the ultimate source of truth and beauty, they remained true to the immanent law of truth and beauty. And in doing so, they served their fellow men much better than by any direct sub-ordination to moral or utilitarian requirements. That is to say, the different spheres of higher culture have their autonomy, but at the same time they are linked with each other, not directly, not horizontally, but vertically, communicating with each other only by reference to the same source of their autonomy.

One last characteristic trait of the Christian idea of civilisation and culture relates to these two words as such. Why do we need two words, and which should take precedence? As everyone knows, there is a remarkable difference, again, between the German use of the words, on the one hand, and the English and French use on the other. In German it has become customary to think of *Zivilisation* as something much lower than *Kultur,* meaning primarily the technical aspect of what the English and French call civilisation. This degradation of "civilisation" is the result of that onesided idealistic spiritualisation which puts the purely spiritual things in the first place, calling them "higher" culture. The French and particularly the English use of words, however, is based on the high estimate of the civic element in all civilisation, the social and political element of justice and freedom, without which no true culture can exist. We need not repeat what has already been said in favour of this latter conception. It is a Christian heritage. Because in the Christian conception of man the relation between man and man is more important than the so-called "higher" culture, the problems of social and political order and, above all, those of marriage, family, and education, are basic in the Christian conception of civilisation and culture. We cannot put so-called higher culture in the first place, and therefore we cannot agree that civilisation be subordinated to culture. If we had to use one word only, we would rather use the word civilisation than the word culture, as we have done so far.

Having thus sketched the Christian idea of civilisation in rough outline, we can now, in conclusion, turn back to the very beginning of our lectures, to the question: What are the chances of a Christian civilisation in our age? The prospect seems to be very bad indeed, and we should not in closing make ourselves guilty of a false and facile optimism. Yet pessimism cannot be our attitude either. There is a German proverb: *Des Menschen Verlegenheiten sind Gottes Gelegenheiten* [Man's extremity, God's opportunity]. The terrible perspectives which are placed before us by the dechristianisation of the world during the past two centuries have opened the eyes of many of our contemporaries to the true foundations of civilisation and to the importance of the Christian tradition. It is not only the physicists and technicians, terrified by their latest results, that have become conscious of the imminent peril of human civilisation and are looking out for a new spiritual basis of life, but also the jurists, the sociologists, the psychologists, and—last, not least—the artists and poets. The lowest point of secularisation seems to be behind us. In all spheres of civilised life there is a new search for the foundation of a really human civilisation, and in this search the Christian tradition is rediscovered. I do not prophesy an epoch of general return to Christianity, any more than I accept the myth of the Christian culture of the past. If I did, I should be guilty of a new kind of determinism, mistaking for predictable necessity what is a matter of decision. Mankind is confronted with a decision of incomparable consequence. All we can say is this: the decision *may* be made in the right sense, there is nothing impossible about it; but whether it *will* be taken in the right sense, nobody can know. It is sufficient that everyone who sees it should do what is required of him.

CHARLES KEAN

Culture as the Arch-Enemy of Christian Faith*

I. THE SYMPTOMS OF THE CRISIS

An apparent contradiction exists in the modern world between political peace and economic stability. The result is the turning of normal social expectancies upside down, as war seems to bring chaos. One of the two major symptoms

* From "The Contemporary Cultural Crisis" by Charles D. Kean, reprinted with the permission of Charles Scribner's Sons from *Christian Faith and Social Action*, edited by John A. Hutchison. Copyright 1953, Charles Scribner's Sons; pp. 37-51.

of the cultural crisis of our time is the seeming inability of modern nations to conceive practically of peace and economic stability at the same time.

The observation about this contradiction is certainly an over-simplification of the real situation, but noticeable symptoms tend to be such exaggerated phenomena. It can be argued that the order brought to the economic scene by war, both "hot" and "cold," is illusory, and that the chaos brought by peace is largely the result of readjustment in a world which has never had a working peace long enough for the process to be completed. But even with recognition given to the partial truth of such comments, the general impression of contradiction remains as a terribly confusing cultural force in our day.

The contradiction has existed since before 1914, so that a majority of today's adults have never known anything else. The problem has grown more acute year after year. It is not that a majority of people do not desire simultaneously both peace and prosperity, but rather that when it comes to formulating public policy, they are unable to see their political and economic problems in such a perspective that both peace and stability appear to be simultaneously possible.

The background of this contradiction can be worked out easily in terms of simple cause and effect. But there is a more basic interpretation which must be made. This is illustrated by the fact that peace without general economic stability soon ceases to be peaceful because internal political tensions in the various nations become accentuated and international rivalries are increased, while, on the other hand, economic stability without a general atmosphere of political peace is only speciously prosperous.

The antithesis between peace and economic stability is the first major symptom of the cultural crisis of our times. It does not require very much perspicacity to recognize its existence. The other major symptom is equally serious but a little more subtle. It lacks dramatic manifestations. But it is just as real and presents just as serious a dilemma.

This second symptom is that freedom and an adequate standard of living likewise appear to be antithetical in our day. At first glance this does not appear to be so. But freedom to be an understandable concept must be explored beneath the surface of political configurations, so that in some real sense it can describe man's relative mastery of his own historical destiny. In this context it can be easily seen that modern man is becoming more and more the prisoner of his own technological enterprise.

While legitimate and important distinctions may be drawn between the various political economies of our day, the fact remains that collectivization as an engineering process—rather than as a political philosophy—is the concomitant of that standard of living which western man has come to regard as desirable. Transportation, communications, the production and marketing of all the necessities of life require a high organization both of capital and personnel. Therefore, the ability of any individual to affect the process, or even to handle his own affairs with any real independence of the process, becomes relatively impossible.

In the western world, man has paid the price of becoming an interchangeable part in the technological structure for the high standard of living he enjoys. Yet the observation must be made that collectivization in itself does not produce a high standard of living. Nazi Germany was one proof of that fact, and Soviet Russia today is an even more tragic example of what happens when the logic of the contradiction is reversed. But on the other hand, the result in the western world of relatively cheap and available automobiles, telephones in most homes, standard brands of clothing, food, and equipment has been to cause a standardization and regimentation of human as well as material resources. One has only to remember the "Great Depression" to have the truth of this contradiction brought home.

Since freedom and economic well-being are apparently opposed to each other, neither has any practical meaning by itself. Freedom at the expense of economic security and the appurtenances of what *Life* magazine calls "modern living," loses its glamor for the average western man; while a high standard of living without any real control over individual destiny leaves the individual, as Karen Horney has put it, likely to acquire "the neurotic personality of our time."

Here are the two symptoms of cultural crisis—the contradiction between peace and prosperity, and the contradiction between freedom and an adequate standard of living. When these are explained simply in terms of sociological or economic causation, their real significance is lost. They are symptoms of a breakdown in western culture. Modern man in the western world—for that matter in the communist-dominated countries, too—is unable to visualize and interpret his predicament, so that he can never attempt with general confidence a creative approach to the problems which beset him.

Individuals may propose attacks upon the results of these two contradictions. Indeed, fascism was in large measure a general reaction to this crisis situation by means of widespread group psychosis. Communism is a demonic attempt to cancel out the contradictions by an all-embracing political and economic program which is supposed to remove every possibility of unpredictable variations from the social scene, as well as to eliminate political and economic tensions. Fascism might be compared culturally to a paranoid lashing out at all and sundry in destructive frenzy, while Communism appears to be a reaction to the cultural crisis in which man turns to eating himself and forcing his neighbors to do likewise.

The fact remains that men are unable to account for the very pressures with which they must contend by the categories they are accustomed to use, and this means that western culture itself is called in question.

II. THE MEANING OF CULTURAL CRISIS

We live in an age of cultural crisis. This expression is used to describe a pervasive anxiety which makes many people feel that not only are they unable to deal adequately with their immediate problems, but even more seriously, they are uncertain as to the actual nature of what disturbs them. Therefore, they are continually prone to vent their hostility on groups and things which cannot be regarded in reality as fully responsible for the threatened nature of their existence.

Whatever political reality there may be to the threat of Communism in America, the widespread fear of Communism appears to be rather a matter of attempting to nail a free-floating general anxiety to a concrete object, rather than a serious attempt to deal with a political problem. Because world Communism is a deliberate attack upon the results of the cultural crisis without an adequate facing of the underlying nature of the problems of our age, it must be opposed. It cannot be regarded as the cause of our difficulties, but rather as one of the more serious results of our failure to appreciate the real causes.

To say we live in an age of cultural crisis does not mean that there are not analyses and proposed solutions being offered. We know the contrary to be true. It does not refer to the wide differences of opinion as to what we ought to do—except as these differences reveal a fundamental moral uncertainty. On the tactical level, differences of opinion may indicate cultural health rather than sickness.

Again, to say that we live in an age of cultural crisis does not mean that there is no health at all in western civilization. There is plenty of evidence to the contrary, and one of the most hopeful signs of it is the continued ability of both the United States and England to work out pragmatically mixed approaches to complicated political and economic questions. What cultural crisis does mean in this reference is that it is terribly difficult today to capitalize on the elements of health because the framework within which civilization is understood appears to be either so ambiguous or so inadequate as to make clear decisions in practical affairs impossible.

The threats of a third world war and of widespread economic confusion seem to indicate that our problems cannot be handled simply by the re-adjustment of the political and economic details. When the cultural framework can be taken for granted, men do meet their problems of social change by rearranging the details of their political and economic life. But when the underlying intellectual, emotional and institutional structure itself is involved as part of the problem with which we have to deal, then the situation becomes serious.

Culture is this structure in its totality. It includes not only the explicit intellectual rationale of civilization at particular times, but also the ideological factors which weight most normal decisions by individuals and groups in some specific direction. It includes the whole interlocking pattern of assumptions and both conscious and unconscious premises which men take for granted in seeking to understand an issue, to communicate with each other and to take practical action. Culture is summed up in a general individual and group sense of self-fulfillment.

Cultural stability is the most significant yardstick available for determining the relative health of a civilization. When the culture is fulfilling its functions, men can think, relate themselves to each other, and act with some real confidence that these processes can be congruent with things as they are—even if this is not the case in actual practice. When the culture is shaky, men's thoughts, relationships and actions have no sure foundation of confidence, even though they may appear to be pragmatically satisfactory. The expectancy which focuses social life is blurred, and anxiety inevitably results.

To say that we live in an age of cultural crisis, then, is to recognize that this sense of expectancy, by which the institutions and political and economic fabric of western civilization have been built, is hard to connect meaningfully with the historical decisions we have to make. Whether it is a question of American foreign policy, or of the role of the family in an urban technological society, there is no sufficiently clear perspective to enable men to make accurate decisions and to take purposeful action.

Historical issues continue to arise, but in the absence of an adequate perspective, consistent policies are difficult to make. The result is that there is a widespread free-floating anxiety regarding the past and the future, while the present remains confused. Satisfactions tend to become hysterical, while disappointments become either depressing or paranoid.

Western culture for the past two and a half centuries (and indeed for a much longer period if one wishes to go back to the roots) has been built upon two parallel and interlocking sets of presuppositions. These do not appear sufficient today to enable men to interpret their experience adequately. The two presuppositions are, (a) that by an objective relationship to whatever concerns him, man is able to control, manipulate or at least to adjust to, circumstances satisfactorily; and (b) that individual self-fulfillment through economic acquisitiveness is the means whereby a healthy society lives.

These two presuppositions have been

82

analyzed by many writers for a long time. While they may be stated in various ways, and while recognition must be given to shadings of emphasis between the classes in any nation or region, they are still the dominant characteristics of western society. But modern man is losing confidence in them without realizing it. They are not opposed by a live alternative, since even Communism is just a very systematic rationalization of western culture. The problem is that modern man is slipping into a position in which he has no cultural presuppositions which make decisive action meaningful.

The general evolution of western society since the Industrial Revolution —to say nothing of the evolution since the Renaissance—has been a long series of technological and scientific victories at the expense of the structure which made possible the winning of these victories. Three developments illustrate this point: (1) the popularity of what might be called "the peace of mind" school of religious thought; (2) the vogue of literary existentialism; and (3) atomic science. None of these can be explored fully in an essay of this size, but each is important.

The "peace of mind" school, as exemplified by Norman Vincent Peale's *Guide to Confident Living* and Joshua Loth Liebman's *Peace of Mind,* and including work by as widely divergent people as Fulton J. Sheen and Dale Carnegie, is an attempt to enable men to escape the results of the cultural crisis without facing the fact that the crisis arises out of an historical situation where real problems demand solution.

On the other hand, these searches for personal confidence presuppose the continued relevance of both premises and use a popularized version of the depth psychology and a Ritschlian understanding of the function of religion to authenticate it. They proclaim in various ways the possibility of individualistic self-fulfillment in nineteenth-century terms.

On the other hand, they suggest that the tensions which threaten men can be eliminated by the use of a proper technique, again derived from a combination of psychiatry with Christianity understood, not as Cross, but as euphoria.

Literary existentialism is another phenomenon which helps to illuminate the crisis of our culture. This is the school of thought associated with the names of Martin Heidegger in philosophy and Jean-Paul Sartre in the field of the novel and the drama, and must be distinguished from "existentialism" as the name for the influence of Soren Kierkegaard upon modern Protestant theology.

Any treatment of literary existentialism in short compass is bound to be inadequate, yet the existence of the school as such has significance for understanding the crisis of our culture. It is important to realize that this school arose during the unstable years of the decade prior to World War II and came to flower during the war itself. There are wide differences of interest and orientation within it, ranking from the attempt to make a synthesis with Roman Catholicism—as with Gabriel Marcel— to the frank nihilism of Sartre.

Literary existentialism on the whole, however, denies the significance of culture at all. It concentrates on knowledge through decisive action. The effect of this is not unlike the grin of the Cheshire Cat, as if decision without content and content without context were possible. As a matter of fact, both Marcel and Jaspers are quite aware of this problem. For our purpose in this essay, this school serves to dramatize by its rejection of western culture the seriousness of the breakdown because no one feels compelled to reject that which he can take for granted in the normal course of living.

The rise of atomic science as the present high point of both western science and technology illuminates still another facet of the cultural problem.

A direct corollary of the two presuppositions of our age is the general conviction that science—primarily the physical sciences—and ethics blend with each other as part and parcel of the same thing. The bomb dropped on Hiroshima brought an end to this miscegenation which the modern world had condoned. But it did not relate science and ethics in an alternative way. Instead, it left a question mark, which society only partly recognizes and about which it finds little to do.

These three manifestations of the cultural crisis, each in its own way, illuminates the fact that people do not find it easy to meet their practical problems of home, business, community, and world responsibility in the light of their inherited expectancy. This is because men cannot grasp the full significance of the difficulties they encounter, and when these are not clarified so as to be dealt with, their persistence causes increased confusion. Yet the three illustrations also point to the fact that men are not as yet prepared to analyze their culture critically, but that they either try to continue affirming it, or seek to reject it, or find it a frustrating problem.

At its inception, the communist movement purported to be the creation of a new culture, but its formulators did not go far enough in their analysis of that which they criticized. While the criticism made a positive contribution in its illumination of unfaced evils in western civilization, its own acceptance of the fundamental basis of that which it attacked made it peculiarly dangerous. Its attack on evils which men found hurting them had considerable appeal in spite of its assurance that it alone could provide an adequate foundation for social reconstruction.

As events have worked out in the past half-century, that which was theoretically dangerous in Communism became a terrible destructive force since one of the two greatest national powers in the world became the bearer of the communist promise. The combination of the tendency to cynical self-justification, found in all nations and enhanced in proportion to the actual power at that nation's disposal, with the messianism of a communist theory, which was actually a rationalization of a false alternative to that which it criticized, has made Russian Communism the menace that it is.

While the western world as a whole does not recognize this aspect of Communism for what it is, it is true that the movement as a desirable alternative to the traditional methods of handling political and economic affairs has lost most of its appeal. Its illumination of social injustice has become part of the general heritage, but its program now appears to be a way of embalming rather than reconstructing the culture as a whole.

Communism will not be accepted in the western world except where Russian military interference is sufficient to allow communist minorities to seize political control. In the Far East, it still has the appeal of a creative force. The political and economic ineptitude of the western powers makes the ambiguity of its Far Eastern appeal relatively unnoticeable, even though it appears to combine a blatant nineteenth-century nationalism requiring an individualistic basis with the mechanistic social approach of orthodox Leninism.

Yet the search for some kind of political and economic formula which will annul the tensions which distress us continues. In the United States there is still considerable faith, as evidenced by the right-wing Republican, that the "trickle-down" theory must still be tried. From this point of view to that of the radical anti-communist left, there are a number of differing faiths. But probably the most significant aspect of the cultural crisis is that the vast majority of people seem to have little confidence whatsoever, no awareness of the nature of their difficulties and no hope capable of practical expression, that anything will be done to change the situation.

III. THE CHRISTIAN FAITH AND THE CRISIS

For the Christian faith, here is challenge and judgment. Here also is the grace of God. The crisis of western culture is not by itself redemptive, but it affords a special opportunity for proclaiming the Gospel so that man can hear it and respond.

In one real sense, the very existence of culture is the arch-enemy of Christian faith. While it is impossible for man to live without culture of some kind in that he must have a framework for interpretation of the total setting of his life within history, he is always tempted to place his real confidence in that interpretation. When the current of affairs appears to flow quietly, the culture itself is given the role of God to all practical purposes. When the cultural situation is confused, men still tend to seek for a stable order as if that were an end in itself.

All cultures presuppose the possibility of man constructing an adequate man-centered frame of reference, even though they may use theological verbiage to describe this setting. What is really significant is that within such a frame of reference, men take it for granted that they have an institutional structure within which the problems of life not only can be met but ought to be met. For instance, during the depression of the 1930's, one of the more serious problems to be faced was the tendency of men, even whole families, to devalue themselves as they encountered unemployment, rather than question the rightness of an institutional framework which operated as if men were things.

While every culture, by its inherent tendency to pretension, is the arch-enemy of Christian faith, man cannot live without culture. A New Testament Christianity appraising the predicament of this middle period of the twentieth century cannot be naive enough to suppose that because we are in a period of cultural breakdown—and possibly of radical revision—we can eliminate having to deal with culture as such. Man must devise some generally acceptable set of categories, given concreteness by social institutions, or he cannot deal with life at all.

For Christianity, the challenge is to approach the problem of cultural reconstruction on an understanding that culture must be subordinate to faith. Yet there must also be an awareness, which Roman Catholic thinkers, no matter how profound in other areas, do not understand, that faith itself can become so involved in culture as to cease to be faith in the New Testament sense. This was the tragedy of the Middle Ages, where culture and faith became so identified with each other that the culture itself could not be analyzed and criticized.

The challenge, if it is to be accepted with realism, involves judgment. The Christian Church in its practical operations is as much involved in the culture of our times as any other social institution. It cannot face the problem of cultural crisis as if its organized life were not part of the problem. It cannot really claim to have understood the two great symptomatic contradictions of our day any more accurately, in its official teaching and institutional program, than the rest of the civilization of which it is a part.

A Christianity, which sees the challenge and accepts the judgment as being upon its own corporate life along with the total culture of our times, may make a profound contribution to the way in which men come to terms with their more serious dilemmas. Christianity will not serve in this as if it were a political-economic-social alternative. Christianity, as such, is not a different kind of engineering to be substituted in the world of technology, nor is it another way of organizing cities and handling international affairs. But Christianity can provide the basis for a new hope, as through faith in Christ it gives men a sense of "citizenship in heaven" along with a profound sense of responsibility on earth where they dare to admit their actual sin. And Christianity can make possible a creative attack upon social tensions, as through faith in Christ it gives men an awareness that "we are all one in Christ Jesus," even though the divisions of history are not cancelled.

Western culture understands peace to consist of the elimination of international tension, either through the suppression of all major difficulties or through the achievement of an equilibrium secure enough to withstand all conceivable shocks and strains. The modern cultural problem raises the question as to whether such an understanding of peace is either broad or deep enough to have any long-range significance. Certainly, peace as understood in the New Testament is neither monolithic nor judicial in essence, but rather it is an underlying harmony resting upon faith in Christ Jesus. But this harmony is not to be thought of as a political alternative to the various schemes attempted or proposed in the international scene. Rather, it stands in judgment on all political achievements, yet at the same time it is also a continual inspiration to those seeking more adequate political adjustments.

Western culture understands economic prosperity to consist either of continually full employment or of an everexpanding productive industry or both. Whether or not prosperity is understood in terms of production or consumption or in some balance between them, the premise that economic prosperity, however conceived, is self-authenticating continues. It is a fundamental good. It is an end in itself. The crisis of modern culture raises the question as to whether economic activity in any form can be regarded as the ultimate index of social health. As understood in the New Testament, the community—which certainly involves political action and economic enterprise—is not to be understood primarily in these terms, but rather as the "colony of heaven." But this is an entirely different thing from the "Christian social order" imagined by the Social Gospel movement of three decades ago. It is both a judgment on all social orders, since none can be the *politeuma* fully, and it is also the inspiration for those who work for better social conditions.

Western culture understands freedom to be the absence either of political coercion or of economic pressures, but in both cases its reference is to the "rights" of individuals to be self-determining. The contemporary crisis cannot but raise the question as to whether this understanding of freedom has the kind of dimensions which make it a meaningful category for the description of human existence. The New Testament sees freedom as the result of adoption into the family of the sons of God.

Western culture understands an adequate standard of living to be measured primarily by its material components. It is in this sense largely that the charges of "materialism" so often levelled against our age have any pertinence. People may vary greatly in what they regard to be necessary—as against simply desirable, but nobody wants to discard the opportunities for easier living made available by technological advance. The cultural crisis raises the question not whether our material accomplishments are in themselves wrong, but whether we understand that an adequate standard of living must have three dimensions: opportunity, environment, and appreciation. In the light of the New Testament, the setting for the good life is to be understood qualitatively not quantitatively, but the quantitative issue is not ignored.

When the historian of the future writes the story of the middle period of the twentieth century, he will be in a position to see more accurately than we can see now the significance of the contradictions between peace and prosperity, between freedom and an adequate standard of living. Certainly he will be able to appreciate more fully the various causes of that general lack of sureness with which we face our various political, economic, and social issues, which is the most distinctive characteristic of our age. But while we cannot have the advantages of afterthought in the course of dealing with immediacies, the Christian faith is rooted in an appreciation of the grace of God which frees us for creative action now.

Every age has its problems, and while those of this mid-century period are very serious indeed in their own right, our confused relationship to them is even more significant than the problems themselves. It is in this particular setting that the Christian doctrine of the grace of God is most important, and we become receptive to it as we make our own the Psalmist's insight, "The Lord is king, be the people never so impatient; He sitteth between the Cherubim, be the earth never so unquiet"; and likewise Paul's understanding in the Second Epistle to the Corinthians, "My grace is sufficient for thee: for my strength is made perfect in weakness."

The history of Christianity has seen continual attempts to synthesize it with whatever culture was prevailing in order that it might be used as cement for the social structure or as re-inforcement for the particular ethical standards of a society, and above all as the means whereby men may find justification within the social process. The Age of Justinian saw one form of such an attempt and the Middle Ages another. Kierkegaard felt that Gruntvig and Martensen were doing just this kind of thing in the Denmark of their day a century ago. The point is that Christianity is never a means to something else without ceasing to be fully Christian.

In our twentieth-century crisis, the distinctive contribution of a New Testament point of view has not been made very well. This is because the Christian Churches are still seeking to justify themselves in terms of the prevailing social structure. And tragically, the leadership of the Christian Churches co-operates more often than not, as in the various attempts to sell organized Christianity to the American people as a bulwark against Communism.

The general understanding of the relationship of the Christian Church to modern culture has continued to be much the same for a long time, but a peculiar advantage for the proclamation of the Gospel arises from this very fact. Within the increased tempo of social change in the past two centuries, the usefulness of Christianity for these auxiliary purposes has become less and less significant. A large element of modern society has come to believe that it can satisfy the same essential purposes without having to bother with the impedimenta of Christian traditions and statements. Therefore, the Gospel has become relatively useless for secondary purposes auxiliary to aims regarded as more important, and the opportunity exists for its proclamation in a primary sense.

We proclaim the Christian Gospel, not as the means of saving western society nor as the means of building the new order as the old one falls to pieces, but as the will of God for man. There is no such thing, in the New Testament sense, as a Christian culture—a Christian social order. God alone is Lord of history, and all human achievements are weighed in his hand as nothing. The Cross, taken seriously, both affirms and denies what men may accomplish, and this includes all culture.

As long as men have societies, they will have to use presuppositions in doing business with each other. The Cross recognizes this as the way life works since so much of its symbolism is concretely related to first-century Palestinian culture, and through its very congruence with the understandings of its own historical age is also available for the self-interpretation of other ages. But the Cross also denies the perennial titanism of all cultures, and thus enables us to see the pretensions of our inherited presuppositions. Man can never be in a purely subjective relationship to an otherwise objective world (in which other men are also objects) because he exists as the image of God, not as God himself. Man can never use any kind of self-fulfillment, economic or political, individualistic or socialistic, as the basis of society, because fulfillment is the free gift of God alone and is available only by faith and not through human accomplishment.

Yet our practical tasks continue and must be met. And the process of dealing with them requires the formulation of new presuppositions or the modification of the old ones so as to allow people to take into account the realities of life.

This means the continuation in some form of culture as the framework in which men deal with their historical problems. The difference, from the Christian point of view, is in the light in which these are faced.

Our expectancy is not in the achievement of a society without tension, a peace in which all conflicts of individuals and groups are annulled, nor a prosperity which is automatic, nor a freedom without demands. Our expectancy is rather that we may continue to seek both political peace and economic prosperity, both individual freedom and an adequate standard of living for everybody, not as ends in themselves, but as practical occasions in which we may see the love of God taking concrete form in human society. We know that the judgment of God must be pronounced on what we achieve as well as on what we oppose, and we pray that we may be given the grace to recognize it and accept it.

PAUL TILLICH

Culture as the Expression of Ultimate Concern*

PART I

If we abstract the concept of religion from the great commandment, we can say that religion is being ultimately concerned about that which is and should be our ultimate concern. This means

that faith is the state of being grasped by an ultimate concern, and God is the name for the content of the concern. Such a concept of religion has little in common with the description of religion as the belief in the existence of a highest being called God, and the theoretical

* Part I is from "Aspects of a Religious Analysis of Culture" by Paul Tillich in *World Christian Education* (2nd quarter, 1956). Reprinted by permission of World Council of Christian Education.

   Part II is reprinted from *The Protestant Era* by Paul Tillich by permission of The University of Chicago Press. Copyright 1948 by The University of Chicago; pp. 55-61.

and practical consequences of such a belief. Instead, we are pointing to an existential, not a theoretical, understanding of religion.

Christianity claims that the God who is manifest in Jesus the Christ is the true God, the true subject of an ultimate and unconditional concern. Judged by him, all other gods are less than valid objects of an ultimate concern, and if they are made into one, become idols. Christianity can claim this extraordinary character because of the extraordinary character of the events on which it is based, namely, the creation of a new reality within and under the conditions of man's predicament. Jesus as the bringer of this new reality is subject to those conditions, to finitude and anxiety, to law and tragedy, to conflicts and death. But he victoriously keeps the unity with God, sacrificing himself as Jesus to himself as the Christ. In doing so he creates the new reality of which the Church is the communal and historical embodiment.

From this it follows that the unconditional claim made by Christianity is not related to the Christian Church, but to the event on which the Church is based. If the Church does not subject itself to the judgment which is pronounced by the Church, it becomes idolatrous towards itself. Such idolatry is its permanent temptation, just because it is the bearer of the New Being in history. As such it judges the world by its very presence. But the Church is also of the world and included under the judgment with which it judges the world. A Church which tries to exclude itself from such a judgment loses its right to judge the world and is rightly judged by the world. This is the tragedy of the Roman Catholic Church. Its way of dealing with culture is dependent upon its unwillingness to subject itself to the judgment pronounced by itself. Protestantism, at least in principle, resists this temptation, though actually it falls into it in many ways, again and again.

A second consequence of the existential concept of religion is the disappearance of the gap between the sacred and secular realm. If religion is the state of being grasped by an ultimate concern, this state cannot be restricted to a special realm. The unconditional character of this concern implies that it refers to every moment of our life, to every space and every realm. The universe is God's sanctuary. Every work day is a day of the Lord, every supper a Lord's supper, every work the fulfillment of a divine task, every joy a joy in God. In all preliminary concerns, ultimate concern is present, consecrating them. Essentially the religious and the secular are not separated realms. Rather they are within each other.

But this is not the way things actually are. In actuality, the secular element tends to make itself independent and to establish a realm of its own. And in opposition to this, the religious element tends to establish itself also as a special realm. Man's predicament is determined by this situation. It is the situation of the estrangement of man from his true being. One could rightly say that the existence of religion as a special realm is the most conspicuous proof of man's fallen state. This does not mean that under the conditions of estrangement which determine our destiny the religious should be swallowed by the secular, as secularism desires, nor that the secular should be swallowed by the religious, as ecclesiastic imperialism desires. But it does mean that the inseparable division is a witness to our human predicament.

The third consequence following from the existential concept of religion refers to the relation of religion and culture. Religion as ultimate concern is the meaning-giving substance of culture, and culture is the totality of forms in which the basic concern of religion expresses itself. In abbreviation: religion is the substance of culture, culture is the form of religion. Such a consideration

89

definitely prevents the establishment of a dualism of religion and culture. Every religious act, not only in organized religion, but also in the most intimate movement of the soul, is culturally formed.

The fact that every act of man's spiritual life is carried by language, spoken or silent, is proof enough for this assertion. For language is the basic cultural creation. On the other hand, there is no cultural creation without an ultimate concern expressed in it. This is true of the theoretical functions of man's spiritual life, e.g. artistic intuition and cognitive reception of reality, and it is true of the practical functions of man's spiritual life, e.g. personal and social transformation of reality. In each of these functions in the whole of man's cultural creativity, an ultimate concern is present. Its immediate expression is the style of a culture. He who can read the style of a culture can discover its ultimate concern, its religious substance. This we will now try to do in relation to our present culture.

The Special Character of Contemporary Culture

Our present culture must be described in terms of one predominant movement and an increasing powerful protest against this movement. The spirit of the predominant movement is the spirit of industrial society. The spirit of the protest is the spirit of the existentialist analysis of man's actual predicament. The actual style of our life, as it was shaped in the 18th and 19th centuries, expresses the still unbroken power of the spirit of industrial society. There are numerous analyses of this style of thought, life, and artistic expression. One of the difficulties in analyzing it is its dynamic character, its continuous change, and the influence the protest against it has already had upon it. We may nevertheless elaborate two main characteristics of man in industrial society.

The first of these is the concentration of man's activities upon the methodical investigation and technical transformation of his world, including himself, and the consequent loss of the dimension of depth in his encounter with reality. Reality has lost its inner transcendence or, in another metaphor, its transparency for the eternal. The system of finite interrelations which we call the universe has become self-sufficient. It is calculable and manageable and can be improved from the point of view of man's needs and desires. Since the beginning of the 18th century God has been removed from the power field of man's activities. He has been put alongside the world without permission to interfere with it because every interference would disturb man's technical and business calculations. The result is that God has become superfluous and the universe left to man as its master. This situation leads to the second characteristic of industrial society.

In order to fulfill his destiny, man must be in possession of creative powers, analogous to those previously attributed to God, and so creativity must become a human quality. The conflict between what man essentially is and what he actually is, his estrangement, or in traditional terms his fallen state, is disregarded. Death and guilt disappear even in the preaching of early industrial society. Their acknowledgment would interfere with man's progressive conquest of nature, outside and inside himself. Man has shortcomings, but there is no sin and certainly no universal sinfulness. The bondage of the will, of which the Reformer spoke, the demonic powers which are central for the New Testament, the structures of destruction in personal and communal life, are ignored or denied. Educational processes are able to adjust the large majority of men to the demands of the system of production and consumption. Man's actual state is hence mistakenly regarded as his essential state, and he is pictured

90

in a position of progressive fulfillment of his potentialities.

This is supposed to be true not only of man as an individual personality, but also of man as community. The scientific and technical conquest of time and space is considered as the road to the reunion of mankind. The demonic structures of history, the conflicts of power in every realization of life are seen as preliminary impediments. Their tragic and inescapable character is denied. As the universe replaces God, as man in the center of the universe replaces Christ, so the expectation of peace and justice in history replaces the expectation of the Kingdom of God. The dimension of depth in the divine and demonic has disappeared. This is the spirit of industrial society manifest in the style of its creations.

The attitude of the churches toward this situation was contradictory. Partly they defended themselves by retiring to their traditional past in doctrine, cult, and life. But in so doing, they used the categories created by the industrial spirit against which they were fighting. They drew the symbols in which the depth of being expressed itself down to the level of ordinary, so to speak, two-dimensional experiences. They understood them literally and defended their validity by establishing a supranatural above the natural realm. But supranaturalism is only the counterpart of naturalism and vice versa. They produce each other in never-ending fights against each other. Neither could live without its opposite.

The impossibility of this kind of defense of the tradition was recognized by the other way in which the churches reached to the spirit of industrial society. They accepted the new situation and tried to adapt themselves to it by re-interpreting the traditional symbols in contemporary terms. This is the justification and even the glory of what we call today "liberal theology." But it must also be stated that in its theological understanding of God and man, liberal theology paid the price of adjustment by losing the message of the new reality which was preserved by its supranaturalistic defenders. Both ways in which the churches dealt with the spirit of industrial society proved to be inadequate.

While naturalism and supranaturalism, liberalism and orthodoxy were involved in undecisive struggles, historical providence prepared another way of relating religion to contemporary culture. This preparation was done in the depth of industrial civilization, sometimes by people who represented it in its most anti-religious implications. This is the large movement known as existentialism which started with Pascal, was carried on by a few prophetic minds in the 19th century and came to a full victory in the 20th century.

Existentialism, in the largest sense, is the protest against the spirit of industrial society within the framework of industrial society. The protest is directed against the position of man in the system of production and consumption of our society. Man is supposed to be the master of his world and of himself. But actually he has become a part of the reality he has created, an object among objects, a thing among things, a cog within a universal machine to which he must adapt himself in order not to be smashed by it. But this adaptation makes him a means for ends which are means themselves, and in which an ultimate end is lacking. Out of this predicament of man in the industrial society the experiences of emptiness and meaninglessness, of dehumanization and estrangement have resulted. Man has ceased to encounter reality as meaningful. Reality in its ordinary forms and structures does not speak to him any longer.

One way out is that man restricts himself to a limited section of reality and defends it against the intrusion of the world into his castle. This is the neurotic way out which becomes psychotic if reality disappears completely. It involves subjection to the demands

91

of culture and repression of the question of meaning. Or some may have the strength to take anxiety and meaninglessness courageously upon themselves and live creatively, expressing the predicament of the most sensitive people in our time in cultural production. It is the latter way to which we owe the artistic and philosophical works of culture in the first half of the 20th century. They are creative expressions of the destructive trends in contemporary culture. The great works of the visual arts, of music, of poetry, of literature, of architecture, of dance, of philosophy, show in their style both the encounter with non-being, and the strength which can stand this encounter and shape it creatively. Without this key, contemporary culture is a closed door. With this key, it can be understood as the revelation of man's predicament, both in the present world and in the world universally. This makes the protesting element in contemporary culture theologically significant.

The Cultural Forms in Which Religion Actualizes Itself

The form of religion is culture. This is especially obvious in the language used by religion. Every language, including that of the Bible, is the result of innumerable acts of cultural creativity. All functions of man's spiritual life are based on man's power to speak vocally or silently. Language is the expression of man's freedom from the given situation and its concrete demands. It gives him universals in whose power he can create worlds above the given world of technical civilization and spiritual content.

Conversely, the development of these worlds determines the development of language. There is no sacred language which has fallen from a supranatural heaven and been put between the covers of a book. But there is human language, based on man's encounter with reality, changing through the millenia, used for the needs of daily life, for expression and communication, for literature and poetry, and used also for the expression and communication of our ultimate concern. In each of these cases the language is different. Religious language is ordinary language, changed under the power of what it expresses, the ultimate of being and meaning. The expression of it can be narrative (mythological, legendary, historical), or it can be prophetic, poetic, liturgical. It becomes holy for those to whom it expresses their ultimate concern from generation to generation. But there is no holy language in itself, as translations, retranslations and revisions show.

This leads to a second example of the use of cultural creations within religion: religious art. One principle which must be emphasized again and again in religious art is the principle of artistic honesty. There is no sacred artistic style in Protestant, in contrast, for example, to Greek-Orthodox doctrine. An artistic style is honest only if it expresses the real situation of the artist and the cultural period to which he belongs. We can participate in the artistic styles of the past in so far as they were honestly expressing the encounter which they had with God, man, and world. But we cannot honestly imitate them and produce for the cult of the Church works which are not the result of a creating ecstasy, but which are learned reproductions of creative ecstasies of the past. It was a religiously significant achievement of modern architecture that it liberated itself from traditional forms which, in the context of our period, were nothing but trimmings without meaning and, therefore, neither aesthetically valuable nor religiously expressive.

A third example is taken from the cognitive realm. It is the question: what elements of the contemporary philosophical consciousness can be used for the theological interpretation of the Christian symbols? If we take the existentialist protest against the spirit of industrial society seriously, we must reject both naturalism and idealism as tools for theological self-expression. Both of them are creations of that spirit against which the protest of our century is directed. Both of them have been used by our theology in sharply conflicting methods, but neither of them expresses the contemporary culture.

Instead, theology must use the immense and profound material of the existential analysis in all cultural realms, including therapeutic psychology. But theology cannot use it by simply accepting it. Theology must confront it with the answer implied in the Christian message. The confrontation of the existential analysis with the symbol in which Christianity has expressed its ultimate concern is the method which is adequate both to the message of Jesus as the Christ and to the human predicament as rediscovered in contemporary culture. The answer cannot be derived from the question. It is said *to* him who asks, but it is not taken *from* him. Existentialism cannot give answers. It can determine the form of the answer, but whenever an existentialist artist or philosopher answers, he does so through the power of another tradition which has revelatory sources. To give such answers is the function of the Church not only to itself, but also to those outside the Church.

The Influences of the Church on Contemporary Culture

The Church has the function of answering the question implied in man's very existence, the question of the meaning of this existence. One of the ways in which the Church does this is evangelism. The principle of evangelism must be to show to the people outside the Church that the symbols in which the life of the Church expresses itself are answers to the question implied in their very existence as human beings. Because the Christian message is the message of salvation and because salvation means healing, the message of heal-ing in every sense of the word is appropriate to our situation. This is the reason why movements at the fringe of the Church, sectarian and evangelistic movements of a most primitive and unsound character, have such great success. Anxiety and despair about existence itself induces millions of people to look out for any kind of healing that promises success.

The Church cannot take this way. But it must understand that the average kind of preaching is unable to reach the people of our time. They must feel that Christianity is not a set of doctrinal or ritual or moral laws, but is rather the good news of the conquest of the law by the appearance of a new healing reality. They must feel that the Christian symbols are not absurdities, unacceptable for the questioning mind of our period, but that they point to that which alone is of ultimate concern, the ground and meaning of our existence and of existence generally.

There remains a last question, namely, the question of how the Church should deal with the spirit of our society which is responsible for much of what must be healed by the Christian message. Has the Church the task and the power to attack and to transform the spirit of industrial society? It certainly cannot try to replace the present social reality by another one, in terms of a progress to the realized Kingdom of God. It cannot sketch perfect social structures or suggest concrete reforms. Cultural changes occur by the inner dynamics of culture itself. The Church participates in them, sometimes in a leading role, but then it is a cultural force beside others and not the representative of a new reality in history.

In its prophetic role the Church is the guardian who reveals dynamic structures in society and undercuts their demonic power by revealing them, even within the Church itself. In so doing the Church listens to prophetic voices outside itself, judging both the culture and the Church in so far as it is a part of the culture. We have referred to such prophetic voices in our culture. Most of them are not active members of the manifest Church. But perhaps one could call them participants of a "latent Church," a Church in which the ultimate concern which drives the manifest Church is hidden under cultural forms and deformations.

Sometimes this latent Church comes into the open. Then the manifest Church should recognize in these voices what its own spirit should be and accept them even if they appear hostile to the Church. But the Church should also stand as a guardian against the demonic distortions into which attacks must fall if they are not grasped by the right subject of our ultimate concern. This was the fate of the communist movement. The Church was not sufficiently aware of its function as guardian when this movement was still undecided about its way. The Church did not hear the prophetic voice in communism and therefore did not recognize its demonic possibilities.

Judging means seeing both sides. The Church judges culture, including the Church's own forms of life. For its forms are created by culture, as its religious substance makes culture possible. The Church and culture are within, not alongside, each other. And the Kingdom of God includes both while transcending both.

PART II

The technical problem of a lecture on religion and secular culture is the implicit demand to give in one paper the content of at least two volumes, namely, that of a philosophy of religion and that of a philosophy of culture. Since this cannot be done except in terms of an abstract and unconvincing summary, I intend to limit myself to one central concept, namely, that of a "theonomous" culture, and to develop this concept in a kind of autobiographical retrospect from the end of the first World War to the

94

end of the second, adding some systematic analysis of the theonomous character of symbols.

When we returned from the first World War, we found a deep gap between the cultural revolution and the religious tradition in central and eastern Europe. The Lutheran and the Roman and Greek Catholic churches rejected the cultural and—with some exceptions on the part of Roman Catholicism—the political revolutions. They rejected them as the rebellious expression of a secular autonomy. The revolutionary movements, on the other hand, repudiated the churches as the expression of a transcendent heteronomy. It was very obvious to those of us who had spiritual ties with both sides that this situation was intolerable and, in the long run, disastrous for religion as well as for culture. We believed that it was possible to close the gap, partly by creating movements such as religious socialism, partly by a fresh interpretation of the mutual immanence of religion and culture within each other. History, however, has shown that it was too late for such an attempt to be successful at that time. It proved impossible to break down the secular ideology and the mechanistic (non-Marxist) materialism of the labor parties. The Old Guard prevailed against us and against the youth of their own movement. In the religious realm not only the conservative representatives of "ruling-class Christianity" (the European counterpart to American "suburban Christianity") ostracized us; we were also attacked by that dynamic theology which in this country is called "neo-orthodoxy" and which united prophetic powers with a non-prophetic detachment from culture, thus confirming and deepening the gap. Our attempt was frustrated; but we did not and do not accept defeat in so far as the truth of our conception is concerned; for we do not accept the idea, which a consistent pragmatism can hardly avoid, that victory is a method of pragmatic verification.

The first of my attempts to analyze the mutual immanence of religion and culture was made in a lecture which I read in Berlin immediately after the end of the war, entitled "The Idea of a Theology of Culture." It was written with the enthusiasm of those years in which we believed that a new beginning, a period of radical transformation, a fulfillment of time, or, as we called it with a New Testament term, a kairos had come upon us, in spite of breakdown and misery. We did *not,* however, share the feeling of many American religious and secular humanists of the twenties; we did *not* believe that the Kingdom of God, consisting in peace, justice, and democracy, had been established. Very early we saw those demonic structures of reality which during the past months have been recognized by all thoughtful people in this country. But we also saw a new chance, a moment pregnant with creative possibilities. The breakdown of bourgeois civilization in central and eastern Europe could pave the way for a reunion of religion and secular culture. That was what we hoped for and what religious socialism fought for, and to it we tried to give a philosophical and theological basis. The idea of a "theonomous culture" seemed to be adequate for this aim; it became the principle of philosophies of religion and of culture which proposed to fill the gap from both sides.

The churches had rejected the secularized autonomy of modern culture; the revolutionary movements had rejected the transcendent heteronomy of the churches. Both had rejected something from which, in the last analysis, they themselves lived; and this something is theonomy. The words "autonomy," "heteronomy," and "theonomy" answer the question of the *nomos* or the law of life in three different ways: Autonomy asserts that man as the bearer of universal reason is the source and measure of culture and religion—that he is his own law. Heteronomy asserts that man, being unable to act according to universal reason, must be subjected to a law, strange and superior to him. Theonomy asserts that the superior law is, at the same time, the innermost law of man himself, rooted in the divine ground which is man's own ground: the law of life transcends man, although it is, at the same time, his own. Applying these concepts to the relation between religion and culture, we called an autonomous culture the attempt to create the forms of personal and social life without any reference to something ultimate and unconditional, following only the demands of theoretical and practical rationality. A heteronomous culture, on the other hand, subjects the forms and laws of thinking and acting to authoritative criteria of an ecclesiastical religion or a political quasi-religion, even at the price of destroying the structures of rationality. A theonomous culture expresses in its creations an ultimate concern and a transcending meaning not as something strange but as its own spiritual ground. "Religion is the substance of culture and culture the form of religion." This was the most precise statement of theonomy.

With these distinctions it was possible to create a theonomous analysis of culture, a "theology of culture," so to speak, which shows its theonomous ground not only where it is clearly indicated, as in the archaic periods of the great cultures and the early and high Middle Ages of our Western civilization, but also in those periods in which heteronomy was victorious, as in the later Middle Ages and in Arabic and Protestant orthodoxy, and even in autonomous or secular epochs, such as classical Greece, the Renaissance, the Enlightenment, and the nineteenth century. No cultural creation can hide its religious ground or its rational formation. Against ecclesiastical heteronomy it is always possible to show that all the rites, doctrines, institutions, and symbols of a religious system constitute a religious cul-

95

ture which is derived from the surrounding general culture—from its social and economic structure, its character traits, its opinions and philosophy, its linguistic and artistic expressions, its complexes, its traumas, and its longings. It is possible to show that, if such a special religious culture be imposed on dissenters or foreign cultures, it is not the ultimate, with its justified claim to grasp the hearts of men, but something provisional and conditioned which uses the religious ultimacy for *its* claims. The Thomistic philosophy, as well as the Protestant ideal of personality, is a transitory form of religious culture, but neither has any claim to ultimacy and finality; and the same holds true of the Greek concepts in the dogma of the church, of the feudal pattern of the Roman hierarchy, of the patriarchalistic ethics of Lutheranism, of the democratic ideals of sectarian Protestantism, and even of the cultural traditions which, for instance, are embodied in the biblical language and world view. Theonomous thinking sides with autonomous criticism, if such forms of religious culture present themselves as absolutes.

But more important in our situation was and is the other task of a theonomous analysis of culture: to show that in the depth of every autonomous culture an ultimate concern, something unconditional and holy, is implied. It is the task of deciphering the style of an autonomous culture in all its characteristic expressions and of finding their hidden religious significance. This we did with all possible tools of historical research and comparative interpretation and empathic understanding and with a special effort in regard to such stages of civilization as were utterly secular, as, for instance, the later nineteenth century. Autonomous culture is secularized in the degree to which it has lost its ultimate reference, its center of meaning, its spiritual substance. The Renaissance was a step toward autonomy, but

still in the spiritual power of an unwasted medieval heritage. The Enlightenment quickly lost its Protestant and sectarian substance and became in some —though not in many—of its expressions completely secular. The later nineteenth century, with its subjection to the technical pattern of thought and action, shows the character of an extremely emptied and secularized autonomy in an advanced stage of disintegration. But even here the religious substance, a remnant of something ultimate, was noticeable and made the transitory existence of such a culture possible. However, more than in the disintegrating bourgeois autonomy, the religious reference was effective in the movements which protested—often with a prophetic passion—against this situation. Theonomous analysis was able to decipher puzzling experiences, such as the visionary destruction of bourgeois idealism and naturalism in art and literature by expressionism and surrealism; it was able to show the religious background of the rebellion of the vital and unconscious side of man's personality against the moral and intellectual tyranny of consciousness; it was able to interpret the quasi-religious, fanatical, and absolutistic character of the reactions of the twentieth century as against the nineteenth. It was able to do all this without special reference to organized religion, the churches being only a part of the whole picture, but with a decisive reference to the religious element which was and is hidden in all these anti-religious and anti-Christian movements. In all of them there is an ultimate, unconditional, and all-determining concern, something absolutely serious and therefore holy, even if expressed in secular terms.

So the gap between religion and culture is filled: religion is more than a system of special symbols, rites, and emotions, directed toward a highest being; religion is ultimate concern; it is the state of being grasped by something unconditional, holy, absolute. As such it gives meaning, seriousness, and depth to all culture and creates out of the cultural material a religious culture of its own. The contrast between religion and culture is reduced to the duality of religious and secular culture with innumerable transitions between them. The revolutionary movements, for instance, represent an ultimate concern, a religious principle, hidden but effective within them. The Lutheran churches for example, represent a special cultural period in which an ultimate concern, a religious principle, has embodied itself manifestly and directly. Both are religious and both are cultural at the same time. Why, then, the difference? The answer can only be that the Kingdom of God has not yet come, that God is not yet all in all, whatever this "not yet" may mean. Asked what the proof is for the fall of the world, I like to answer: religion itself, namely a religious culture beside a secular culture, a temple beside a town hall, a Lord's Supper beside a daily supper, prayer beside work, meditation beside research, *caritas* beside *eros*. But although this duality can never be overcome in time, space, and history, it makes a difference whether the duality is deepened into a bridgeless gap, as in periods in which autonomy and heteronomy fight with each other, or whether the duality is recognized as something which should not be and which is overcome fragmentarily by anticipation, so to speak, in a theonomous period. The kairos which we believed to be at hand was the coming of a new theonomous age, conquering the destructive gap between religion and secular culture.

But history took another path, and the question of religion and culture cannot be answered simply in those terms. A new element has come into the picture, the experience of the "end." Something of it appeared after the first World War; but we did not feel it in its horrible depth and its incredible thorough-ness. We looked at the beginning of the new more than at the end of the old. We did not realize the price that mankind has to pay for the coming of a new theonomy; we still believed in transitions without catastrophes. We did not see the possibility of final catastrophes as the true prophets, the prophets of doom, announced them. Therefore, our theonomous interpretation of history had a slight tinge of romanticism, though it tried to avoid any kind of utopianism. This has come to an end because the end itself has appeared like a flash of lightning before our eyes; and not only among the ruins of central and eastern Europe but also within the abundance of this country has it been seen. While after the first World War the mood of a new beginning prevailed, after the second World War a mood of the end prevails. A present theology of culture is, above all, a theology of the end of culture, not in general terms but in a concrete analysis of the inner void of most of our cultural expressions. Little is left in our present civilization which does not indicate to a sensitive mind the presence of this vacuum, this lack of ultimacy and substantial power in language and education, in politics and philosophy, in the development of personalities, and in the life of communities. Who of us has never been shocked by this void when he has used traditional or untraditional secular or religious language to make himself understandable and has not succeeded and has then made a vow of silence to himself, only to break it a few hours later? This is symbolic of our whole civilization. Often one gets the impression that only those cultural creations have greatness in which the experience of the void is expressed; for it can be expressed powerfully only on the basis of a foundation which is deeper than culture, which is ultimate concern, even if it accepts the void, even in respect to religious culture. Where this happens, the vacuum of disintegration can become a vacuum out of which creation is possible, a "sacred void," so to speak, which brings a quality of waiting, of "not yet," of a being broken from above, into all our cultural creativity. It is not an empty criticism, however radical and justified such criticism may be. It is not an indulgence in paradoxes that prevents the coming-down to concreteness. It is not cynical detachment, with its ultimate spiritual dishonesty. It is simple cultural work out of, and qualified by, the experience of the sacred void. This is the way—perhaps the only way—in which our time can reach a theonomous union between religion and culture.

One thing is clear: the experience of the end by no means undermines the idea of theonomy. On the contrary, it is its strongest confirmation. Two events may illustrate this. The first is the turn of Karl Barth from a theology of radical detachment from culture, religious as well as secular, to an equally radical attachment to the fight against a demonically distorted cultural system. Barth suddenly realized that culture can never be indifferent toward the ultimate. It ceases to be theonomous, it first becomes empty, and then it falls, at least for a time, under demonic control. The demand for a merely matter-of-fact culture is dishonesty or illusion, and a catastrophic illusion at that. This leads to the second event to which I want to refer: the change of attitude toward culture in this country. It was truly symbolic for the collapse of our secular autonomy when the atom scientists raised their voices and preached the end, not unconditionally but with conditions of salvation which present-day humanity is hardly willing to fulfil. It was and is a symptom of a changed mood when some of these men and others with them, statesmen, educators, psychologists, physicians, sociologists, not to speak of artists and poets, whose visions anticipated our cultural predicament long ago—when these people cry for religion as the saving power of our culture. They do it often in the ugly and false phraseology which demands the undergirding of culture by religion, as if religion were a tool for a higher purpose. But even in this inadequate form the ideal of a theonomous culture is transparent.

BERNARD MELAND

God's Creative Work in the Cultural Process*

Without exception, I should say, recent studies of faith and myth see the problem as being, in some sense, involved in the issue of faith and culture. Among anthropologically minded philosophers such as Cassirer[1] and Langer,[2] this issue is given prominence; for it is clear to them that religious expression is, itself,

* Abridged from *Faith and Culture* by Bernard Eugene Meland. Copyright 1953 by Oxford University Press, Inc. Reprinted by permission of Oxford University Press and Allen and Unwin, Ltd.; pp. 83-87, 96-110.

[1] Cf. his *Language and Myth,* Harper, 1946; *An Essay on Man,* Yale University Press, 1944; and *The Myth of the State,* Yale University Press, 1946.

[2] Cf. her *The Practice of Philosophy* (1930); *Introduction to Symbolic Logic* (1937), and *Philosophy in a New Key* (1942).

a cultural occurrence, not only in the sense of partaking of a cultural colouring but in the deeper sense of giving voice to human hungers, anxieties, and appreciations which, in turn, exemplify and articulate the cultural psyche in so far as religious utterances achieve a consensus. Even theological interpreters such as Brunner[3] are compelled to acknowledge the relevance of the cultural issue in dealing with the total content of the myth and its corporate witness; although Brunner's insistence upon restricting the Christian meaning of myth to revelation in the decisive, Christological sense causes him to take the problem out of its cultural context and to treat it as a concern to be beyond history and to speak with dogmatic assurance from a point outside history. From such a vantage point, Brunner is able to dissociate Christian myth in its decisive sense from all non-Christian (what he calls pagan) myths. For the latter, from his point of view, are clearly immersed in the stream of history and thus bear all the limitations of the human mind and the human psyche. They are, in the last analysis, according to Brunner, the precursors of metaphysics.[4]

This distinction bears analysis because, upon its issue, both the meaning and the relevance of myth as a theological tool turns. If myth in the Christian sense is so wholly different from myth in the long range of human response to mystery, then the literature in cultural anthropology has no contribution to make to the theological use of myth. And if myth is to be equated with revelation in the radically super-historical sense in which Brunner uses the term, the bearing of the cultural context or of cultural history in general, to say nothing of the cultural pattern of response, is of no consequence to theological inquiry. I should argue, however, contrary to Brunner, that we have no choice but to acknowledge some continuity between mythical thinking within a Christian context and mythical thinking as it has occurred in non-Christian cultures. This is not to equate Christian and non-Christian myths; nor to relate them in any serial sense. It is simply to recognize that comparable human responses in the way of being expressive and creative lie back of the cultural motifs to which the various myths have given form.

Such an observation places myth at the psychical core of culture and generalizes it as a common feature of every historical experience within a geographical and ethnical frame. It makes of myth a characteristic human response in any situation where the human psyche is awakened to a disturbing realization of an otherness, either in the form of a single object or power, or in the form of a total datum, affecting or determining man's present existence as well as his future destiny.

The cultural conditioning of the mythical response, however, is inescapable. That is to say, the human psyche, being inwardly formed by the valuational responses arising from numerous events within experience, assumes a characteristic probability of response in keeping with these serial events. Psychic life, like vegetable life, thus partakes of a regional character which can never be completely obscured or cancelled out.

This observation would suggest that the culture is always an exemplification of the structures of consciousness which are available within the region to initiate psychical responses as well as to express and to assimilate meanings. Sensitivity evidenced in creative imagination, in concern over human relations, or in the qualitative attainment of individual lives

[3] See esp. his chapter on 'Christian Mythology' in *The Mediator*.
[4] The conception of myth as a precursor of metaphysics was developed by Hegel. A restatement of this point of view has been given with extensive elaboration by W. M. Urban in *Language and Reality*.

and in the group life, reflects the operation of processes within these human structures. The culture can rise to heights of sensitive creation and to sensibility in relations only to the degree that there are structures of consciousness available to carry and exemplify these happenings. Culture, I should say, is the creative work of God, made possible through his prior creation of these structures of consciousness, articulating the full psycho-physical organism.

Given these cultural determinants, we shall see that the character of the psychical response, its quality, its degree of sensitivity, both in the realm of feeling and in the area of expression, varies from region to region; culture to culture. There is no universal human psyche; hence no universal human mythos. There is no common level of human, psychical response; hence no common level of mythical thinking, any more than there is a common level of creative expression. All cultures have historically manifested some capacity to be expressive in sensitive and creative ways; but there are marked variations among them, and in some instances the range of variation is vast indeed. It follows that no culture deserves to be neglected in the search for a full grasp of the psychical depth and outreach of the human spirit; for each culture exemplifies the concrete nature of God's working within the range of its available structures. But it is clear that some cultures deserve more serious attention than others when the concern is to focus upon the fullness of God's working within human structures.

Without attempting to appraise the degree of psychical superiority which can be ascribed to the Christian culture of the West, it can certainly be said that it reveals a range and reach of sensitivity and of creative imagination which must place it high in the human venture wherein God's creative working is exemplified. The pivotal point, or the summit of this cultural creation of

the West is Jesus Christ. But Jesus Christ as a structure of consciousness in which God's intent and creative working are concretely exemplified is not an isolated datum. Behind the Christ lies the long history of the Jewish people. Their moral consciousness which had been processed and refined throughout the centuries of devotion to the Law became as a seed bed for a more sensitive and appreciative consciousness in response to the working of God. The prophets, we might say, were intimations of this emergent in so far as they were in some sense sporadic efforts to transcend the rigid mechanisms of the legal tradition. Yet, the prophets were in a very real sense the fruition of the legal tradition; and must ultimately be interpreted in the light of its claim upon the Jewish people.

Christ stands to the moral culture of the Jews as love transcends the law. As over against the moral and the rational consciousness, the Christ exemplifies the appreciative consciousness in which love is regulative. His structure of consciousness is the ground from which spirit emerges as a novel event. The Christ is at once the exemplar of the human consciousness at the level of spirit and the innovation of spirit within the conscious structure of man. He is the clear exemplification of the concrete work of God in history, possibly the clearest; the clearest within Western history without any doubt. Christ as the innovation of spirit and the exemplar of man at the level of spirit constitutes a redemptive consciousness among the structures of human consciousness which are motivated and, in large measure, bound by the moral and the rational consciousness.

Christ as the summit of the cultural creation of the West is the focal point of the Christian myth. This should not be interpreted to mean that the Christian myth is to be equated with revelation in the trans-historical sense described by Brunner. On the contrary,

I should say, this summit vision points not beyond history but back to the formative events of history which have issued in this redemptive act; and to a further range of history which is to be seen, understood, and judged in the light of this redemptive act.

The Christian myth, then, is not one, decisive, isolated event; it is a pattern of events which has its luminous centre in the Christ, but which begins in the earliest vivid awareness of God's creative work in history. The full pattern of the myth is to be found in the Biblical account wherein the drama of creation and redemption is delineated. This drama conveys the feeling tone of the culture with regard to its ultimate dimensions. Its details consist of apprehensions concerning God's intent for creation, the nature of God's creative activity in history, the nature and destiny of man, the interplay of tragedy and hope in human history, the facts of good and evil, and the attending operations of judgment, grace, forgiveness, and redemption.

These details of the myth have been variously analyzed and elaborated into Christian doctrine. They have been applied in liturgy, Christian art and architecture. They have been subtly woven into the literature and musical epics of the West. To some extent, their motifs have shaped the philosophy and ethic of the West. To a degree not commonly recognized they have influenced the political expressions of Western man. Deeper than we can discern, these primal notions permeate the feeling context of the culture in this present moment of history, giving the structure of Western experience its distinctive character.

THE NATURE OF THE RELIGIOUS RESPONSE OUT OF WHICH THE MYTH OF THE CULTURE TAKES FORM

The myth of a culture is a symbolic utterance of long standing, attesting to a persistent outreach in man toward what is ultimate in that which is other than man. This outreach varies in depth and in clarity of procedure. The clarity of the response is often in reverse proportion to the degree of depth which is achieved. . . .

Myth gains ascendancy where the appreciative moods of wonder, adoration, or praise are in dominance in recognition of an unmanageable datum in the objective event. Here the religious response is less a direct effort to use or to control the ultimate power discerned in the Reality not oneself, and more a readiness to encounter the fullness of the mystery as an Event of Grace and Beneficence, or as Judgment. . . .

STRUCTURE OF EXPERIENCE

The myth of a culture, which rises to the surface in song and poetry, and is retained from age to age through these mediums, always points to a deeper, less articulate, emotional context. We might speak of it as a *feeling context*. We can speak of it also as a structure of experience, even though this term attributes too much form and definitiveness to the cohesion of feeling.

The structure of experience, or feeling context, is the most elemental level of meaning in any culture. I hesitate to call it a level of meaning because immediately it assumes a cognitive character. Obviously there is awareness of some sort, but it is an awareness comparable to that of nature's mindless creatures, moving in a familiar environment.

The structure of experience gives form to our repeated valuations. It is impossible to get at the details of this accumulative valuation response, though of course certain memorable events or observations stand out in any period. And the history of events presumes to tell the story of this growth of the psychical structure. But compared with the actual process of evolving structure of experience, recorded history is a relatively superficial account.

It must be said, too, that the evolving structure of experience is not to be equated with the passage of events. Somehow all events enter into this emerging structure of experience; but something of all events partakes of a perpetual perishing that accompanies emergence.

The structure of experience is not just accumulative. That is, it is not just a blind appropriation of heterogeneous valuations; rather, it simulates an organic unity at every stage of history. The struggles and crises of concrete events, the dedications and the betrayals, the discoveries, creations, and intellectual triumphs, become the formative stuff out of which rises the persisting structure of experience. Great insight at any one point becomes creative in its influence beyond calculation. Stretches of insensitivity, with its consequent brutality and evil, likewise affect the accumulative valuations, not only in an additive sense but in a transformative one. Within any given geographical environment, then, where human history has been in process, the present movement of time is laden with qualitative meaning so complex in character (being the accumulative decisions and resolutions of ages), so profound in implication for all existence and for all present events, that no living consciousness is equal to discerning its burden and its opportunity.

Now generations come into an organic inheritance that is greater in depth and range than the perceptions of any living persons. Thus they live in a context of feeling and awareness that is always beyond their grasp, emotionally or cognitively. They are not automatically bound by this inheritance; for they, too, are creative of its yet emerging structure in the way that all concrete events have influenced it. Nevertheless, all living persons carry within their conscious existence and in their perceptual nature something of the hidden drives and aspirations which rise out of this accumulative structure of experience.

Within our culture, the Christian faith is mediated in this structure of experience, rising out of the accumulative valuations of the culture in which its prophets and poets, its hopes and aspirations, its destructive and redemptive forces, have been persuasively at work. It is an oversimplification to say that this is the structure of experience that has arisen out of the dedications and betrayals of Jesus Christ, but this is one way of saying it. The process is much more complex, but clearly, Christ is the focal point of the pattern. . . .

Any dissociation from the structure of experience, in the sense of distrust in its valuations as revelations of the enduring good, places faith on an individual basis. When this occurs there is a loss of cultural orientation or such conscious extrication from the feeling context of the culture as to lose the sense of a saving continuity with it. We may then arbitrarily select out of the cultural history some event in history or some record of events, as an alternative norm or authority, thus placing some one element of the culture awkwardly in opposition to the structure of experience. . . .

Protestantism, it must be said, opened the way for a presentation of the Christian faith as a formula isolated from the structure of experience. Transcendence thus came to mean more than a valuational corrective of the autonomous tendencies within the culture; it meant discontinuity with the structure of experience itself. The Protestant corrective of Roman Catholic institutionalism, together with the persisting acidual cleansing which it provided, and its recognition of the illusion of rationality, justify it as a re-creative force in Christianity. In so far as it fostered a particularistic and schismatic faith, however, in rivalry with the structure of experience which communicates the living faith as a context of feeling, Protestantism precipitated two tragedies: a venture in faith that tends to be culturally impotent, and a culture, wherever Protestant influence prevails, that is meagerly nurtured in its spiritual aim.

Since the emerging structure of experience is the work of a creative happening in which the events of men become the focal point of brute force and God's sensitive working, this structure of experience, bearing its present fulfilments, can no more be dissociated from God's working than it can be dissociated from man's working. The creative process in which this structure of experience emerges is a highly complex pattern of events, accompanied by this undefinable, even undesignable, something which is not actuality and which is therefore not event, hovering over existence as possibility and as yet unrealized meaning. It will be seen from this characterization that no easy contrasting of God and culture is possible. What is possible is the designation of those events within the cultural process that pyramid in power when unrestrained by God's sensitive working, and which thus imperil the creative good that is in God. This is often so enormous in proportion to the sensitivities in men that carry the working of God in concrete form that it is readily identified with culture as a whole; hence the culture is seen as being antithetical to God. . . .

Preoccupation with history may have the further danger of isolating the past from the present in a normative sense, setting up some formal authority of the past as controlling, thus dissipating trust in the attachment to life. All forms of orthodoxies commit this folly. If none of these authorities can be accepted as sovereign by some individuals, then these individuals, uprooted from the existential faith, are thrown back solely upon intellectual resources. The fate of the modernist has been precisely this. . . .

The truth is that modernism in every one of its manifestations gave evidence of a faulty perspective upon man as regards the feeling orientation of his existence—that is, the orientation in which depths of past valuations persist in present experience. Henry Ford's much-quoted remark, 'History is bunk!' gives one clue to its defect. Ford represented modernism in its industrial role. Industry is radically modernistic. The past, we might say, literally has no meaning for it, except as a realm of spent ideas and processes. . . .

Creativeness does not imply that the future event is necessarily a preferred value. It implies, to be sure, that on-goingness is a basic feature of reality; and the advance into novelty is the inevitable consequence of this on-goingness. Yet there is no need to do homage to the reproductive process, saying this is the chief value in events; nor is there any point in saying that this process must be preserved above all else. . . .

That the burden of past attainment shall be transmitted to emerging events is a far more precarious matter than that this on-goingness shall be kept operative. The latter is not a matter for concern since it is *given*. The former is never assured because of the perpetual perishing on the one hand, and the impulse toward novelty on the other. It is assured in the sense that it is God's working that fulfils such qualitative attainment; but it is not assured in the sense that God works through the structures of events in which emergence and qualitative attainment must simultaneously take place. God's fulfilment of actualized good clearly depends upon the opportunities of history. . . .

It can be said, then, that the structure of experience in any age is the context of feeling in which past valuations persist by reason of God's creative working. It is, as it were, the reservoir of inherited wisdom, awaiting renewal in cognitive form whenever the impulse toward qualitative attainment shall motivate experience. . . .

The full, actual valuational content of the structure of experience, which is our immediate possession, no human consciousness can know. It is a depth in our natures that connects all that we are with all that has been within the context of actuality that defines our culture. It is a depth in our nature that relates us as events to all existent events. It is a depth that relates us to God, a sensitive nature within the vast context of nature, winning the creative passage for qualitative attainment. The actual content of all this, I say, we cannot know. Each man lives within his limitations. All men as a total system of conscious events live within limitations that characterize the human emergent. Beyond the perceptual powers of the human creature, vast, meaningful processes of creativity and qualitative creation transpire. Man picks up intimations of this vast working with such instruments of perception, conscious awareness, imagination and feeling, as he may be able to employ. The degree to which men apprehend this vast working depends greatly upon the sensibilities with which they are able to receive what is more than their self-conscious, self-attentive person.

The actual content of this we do not know. Yet, like the faint glimmerings of distant stars, there comes to us a perennial witness to the valuations that have been of the stuff of experience in this creative process out of which we have come. Such a witness comes to us through the mediums of access which we possess in memory, in recorded history, in the surviving creations of other days, in music, poetry and prose, in architecture, in numerous evidences of actual events long since gone into oblivion, except as they survive in the motivating structure of experience.

Of this witness there are many levels, reflecting the variegated colouring of life itself. In the continuing account of costume design, recreation, music, the dance, architecture; in the wealth of detail describing the customs of diet and dress, in all these we have one level of witness. One may call it a superficial level. It is nevertheless part of the concrete fullness of human existence, exhibiting men's valuations. At the deepest level of witness we encounter the themes of the myth, wherever they occur: in the written Word, in the stained glass window, in poetry and drama, in chorale and cantata, the Mass; in the symphony, in sermon and prayer, song and litany; in theology and in conversation that discusses its problems, in all of the numerous occasions where the myth or some theme of the myth is articulated, a witness is borne to what is deepest in our natures, and in the structure of experience which sustains us.

What is deepest in our natures and in actuality itself is defined by the creative act of God—a sensitive working that transmutes sheer process into qualitative attainment. The Christian myth is the drama of redemption that portrays this creative act of God in the destiny of human nature. Thus every communication of this tender regard—what Whitehead characterized as 'the tendernesses of life'—bears witness to this work of God in human history and in the world. . . .

Now the Christian faith, as it operates through the human psyche in the overt actions of people and institutions within Western culture, is the articulation of this shaping in conscious experience. Deeper than the faith, serving as a spatial medium for all that occurs under its motivation, is the structure of experience. And within the structure of experience, persisting like a protoplasm to shape the valuations and hopes which give rise to expressions of faith, are the seminal ideas of the mythos, articulating, as in a parable, the perceptions which point to the re-creative and redemptive resources of living.

HARVEY COX

Nonreligious Culture as the Work of God*

On April 30, 1944, Dietrich Bonhoeffer wrote to one of his friends from his prison cell words that have both tempted and tormented theologians ever since. "We are proceeding toward a time," he wrote, "of no religion at all. . . . How do we speak of God without religion. . . . How do we speak in a secular fashion of God?"[1] . . .

So Bonhoeffer's query has three parts. It is first of all a *sociological problem*. We say problem because it can be answered at that level with relatively little difficulty. It is also a *political issue*. An issue is a somewhat more demanding challenge. It requires us to take some risks and make some choices, to take sides. It necessitates our indicating where that same reality whom the Hebrews called Yahweh, whom the disciples saw in Jesus, is breaking in today. But finally, Bonhoeffer presents us with what is a *theological question*. He makes us answer for ourselves whether the God of the Bible is real or is just a rich and imaginative way man has fashioned to talk about himself. No amount of verbal clarification can set this disagreement aside. In the last analysis it is not a matter of clear thinking at all but a matter of personal decision. Luther was right: deciding on this question is a matter which, like dying, every man must do for himself.

SPEAKING OF GOD AS A SOCIOLOGICAL PROBLEM

The reason speaking about God in the secular city is in part a sociological problem is that all words, including the word *God,* emerge from a particular sociocultural setting. No language was ever handed down from heaven. When words change their meanings and become problematical, there is always some social dislocation or cultural breakdown which lies beneath the confusion. There are basically two types of such equivocality. One is caused by historical change, the other by social differentiation.

Equivocation through historical change means that the same word carries different connotations in different historical periods of a given language. The English word *let,* for example, has reversed its meaning since Shakespeare's day. When Hamlet, lunging for his father's ghost, says "I'll slay the man that *lets* me!," he means he will slay whoever tries to stop him. Equivocation through social differentiation means that in a complex society, the same word means different things in different settings. It may even mean different things for the same person, depending on where it is used. Take the word *operation.* It means something very different for the surgeon, the general, the business executive. Often equivocation through historical change and equivocation through social differentiation combine to confound the confusion. Thus groups within a society who retain cultural ties to some previous historical stage retain ways of speaking which to the larger culture sound like jargon. In the jargon, words will have a meaning they do not have for the culture at large. The ebb and flow of word meanings rides on the floods of social conflict and

* Reprinted with permission of The Macmillan Company from *The Secular City* by Harvey Cox. Copyright © Harvey Cox, 1965; pp. 241-48, 255-62.

[1] Dietrich Bonhoeffer, *Prisoner for God* (New York: Macmillan, 1959), p. 123.

change. Thus the cultural power of certain groups and the weakness of others can often be charted by noticing which meaning of a given word predominates.

Social change alters the meaning of words. French sociologist Antoine Meillet once wrote that ". . . the essential principle of change in meaning is to be found in the existence of social groupings in the milieu where a language is spoken—in short, in a fact of social structure." [2] Bearing this rule in mind, let us consider what has happened to the three-letter English word *God* and why it has become a virtually useless vocable today.

Historians of language indicate that the word *God* has a pre-Christian origin in the Germanic language group. During the centuries of the Christian era it was used to translate a number of different terms, including the *theos* of Greek philosophy, the *Deus* of Western metaphysics, and the *Yahweh* of the Hebrew Bible. This use of the word *God* (and its predecessors in Early and Middle English) was possible because the various cultural streams the other terms represented were more or less unified in a society where no decisive historical changes interrupted the cultural continuity. In fact, the word *God* and its modern-language equivalents served as the linguistic and conceptual linchpin by which these three traditions were fastened together in that cultural synthesis called "Christendom."

But this is just the trouble. Though it is rarely noticed by theologians, this sociocultural synthesis is now coming apart. Christendom is disappearing. We now find that the various uses of the word *God,* once conveniently fused, are now coming unstuck. Historical change and social differentiation have combined to make the word the most equivocal term in the English language. Theolo-

gians are fond of saying that the word is "empty." Its emptiness, however, is merely the symptom of a much more basic disorder, its equivocality. It is not true that no one uses the word *God* anymore. It is used all the time—by swearing sailors, impassioned preachers, and dedicated dialecticians intent on proving the nonexistence of the being or the meaninglessness of the word. The social basis for the fatal equivocality of the word *God* and its equivalents is the passing of Christendom and the emergence of a highly differentiated secular civilization.

In an important book on the problem of the existence of God in contemporary theology, Helmut Gollwitzer discusses the bewildering equivocality of the term. First we use it sometimes to refer to a category of beings, as when we talk about "the Greeks and their gods." Second, we use it for the supreme being of metaphysics. Third, we use it to *name* the One who discloses Himself through the biblical witness.[3]

Though the usages have always been mixed, the first two correspond in part to the two epochs we have designated as tribal and town. Tribal man experienced God as one of the "gods." The Old Testament, incorporating elements of this tribal mentality, is in no sense "monotheistic." Yahweh is the ruler of the gods. Similarly, in the epoch of town life, the great transition from magic through metaphysics to science, man perceived God as a part of one unified structure including both God and man. Urban-secular man, for whom tribal and town usages make no sense, is left with only the third usage, and that is made difficult because the other two uses are still in circulation, corrupting the currency. This does not mean that the people of the tribal and town epochs did not encounter the "true God"

---

[2] In Talcott Parsons, *et al.* (eds.), *Theories of Personality* (Glencoe, Ill.: The Free Press, 1961), p. 1018.

[3] Helmut Gollwitzer, *Die Existenz Gottes im Bekenntnis des Glaubens* (Munich: C. Kaiser Verlag, 1963), p 11, n. 2. English tr., London: SCM Press, 1965.

of the Bible. It does mean, however, that when they did encounter Him, it was within the world-views and meaning-images of their respective eras. It is for this reason that if urban-secular man is to meet Him, the God of the Bible must be carefully distinguished from the cultural avenues of perception through which presecular man met Him.

Gollwitzer's three usages of *God* correspond not only to historical periods. They also correspond to disparate groups within the present culture which still retain ties to tribal and town patterns of perception. The tribal use survives in profanity, folklore, and maxims. It survives also wherever the deity is perceived as the protector of one particular group. The metaphysical deity survives in those quarters where vestiges of the classical ontologies still hold out, where the stream of secularization has temporarily been escaped. Paradoxically, God also survives among philosophers intent on denying his existence. They seem to know, at least, what it is whose existence they are denying.

Where in all this do theologians and preachers fit? Sociologically speaking, they represent the victims *both* of historical change *and* of social differentiation. Most people perceive them as cultural antiques and may have the same fondness for them they have for *deuxième empire* furniture. Especially when they dress up and strut about occasionally in their vivid ecclesiastical regalia, clergymen give people a welcome sense of historical continuity, much like old soldiers in the dress uniform of some forgotten war. Or clergy are perceived as the custodians of a particular in-group lore, and as such are usually granted an expansive deference in a culture which has been taught to be meticulously tolerant of the beliefs of others, however quaint. But this dual role of personification of the past and preserver of a subcultural ethos, a role clergymen play quite avidly, takes its toll when they speak of God. Because of the role

they have been willing to play, when they use the word *God* it is heard in a certain way. It is heard, often with deference and usually with courtesy, as a word referring to the linchpin of the era of Christendom (past) or as the totem of one of the tribal subcultures (irrelevant). The only way clergy can ever change the way in which the word they use is perceived is to refuse to play the role of antiquarian and medicine man in which the society casts them, but this is difficult, because it is what they are paid for.

This close correlation between the meaning assigned a word by its hearer and the role of the person voicing the word can be illustrated by a parable Kierkegaard once used. A traveling circus once broke into flames just after it had encamped outside a Danish village. The manager turned to the performers who were already dressed for their acts and sent the clown to call the villagers to help put out the fire, which could not only destroy the circus but might race through the dry fields and envelop the town itself. Dashing pell-mell to the village square, the painted clown shouted to everyone to come to the circus and help put out the fire. The villagers laughed and applauded this novel way of tricking them into coming to the big top. The clown wept and pleaded. He insisted that he was not putting on an act but that the town really was in mortal danger. The more he implored the more the villagers howled . . . until the fire leaped across the fields and spread to the town itself. Before the villagers knew it, their homes had been destroyed.

The sociological problem of speaking about God is that the roles of the people who try to do so places them immediately in a perceptual context where what they say can be safely ignored. Of course there remain some people who can still understand what theologians mean when they use the word *God* and other religious terms. These include not only "religious" people but also people whose occupations or family histories have given them a visitor's pass, if not a membership card, to the meaning-world in which theologians and preachers live. Such people can often be found in church laymen's organizations. Academically trained people who specialize in the humanities also qualify. As a group, all these people retain part of the cultural residue of Christendom. However indispensable the service they render in the modern world, many of them nevertheless retain a "style" which is clearly held over from a previous historical epoch. They cherish customs, rituals, and mannerisms obviously derived from that period of Western history in which metaphysical discourse made some sense. But this subculture of humanistic academia holds a place of relatively reduced importance, in the university world itself as well as in the whole of society. Its importance for purposes of the present discussion is that it constitutes the *Sitz im Leben* of the academic theologian. It provides the context in which he perceives reality, and this goes a long way in explaining why academic theologians often fail to see the issues raised by the disappearance of the metaphysical era. Academic theologians pass their days among church people and scholarly humanists, insulated by career patterns, personal schedules, and professional obligations from the emerging technical and political era. The task of learning how to speak about God without a metaphysical system seems relatively unimportant.

But it is an important issue nonetheless. Cornelis van Peursen writes:

The word "God" can no longer function as a metaphysical entity. It can no longer be used to fill the gaps in our knowledge. . . . Christianity is in danger of becoming supernatural when it remains within the realm of . . . metaphysical and substantial thinking. . . . [It] becomes only a metaphysical escape. . . . The Biblical message is something quite different from . . . a doctrine of the highest Being.[4]

If van Peursen is right, then the first move to be made in answering Bonhoeffer's question would be to alter the social context in which "speaking of God" occurs and to refuse to play out the cultural roles which trivialize whatever the speaker says. If metaphysical talk of God has been made equivocal both by historical change and by social differentiation, then it cannot be discarded until the break with Christendom is accepted and the subcultural enclave is left behind. . . .

SPEAKING OF GOD AS A POLITICAL ISSUE

We speak of God politically whenever we give occasion to our neighbor to become the responsible, adult agent, the fully post-town and post-tribal man God expects him to be today. We speak to him of God whenever we cause him to realize consciously the web of inter-human reciprocity in which he is brought into being and sustained in it as a man. We speak to him of God whenever our words cause him to shed some of the blindness and prejudice of immaturity and to accept a larger and freer role in fashioning the instrumentalities of human justice and cultural vision. We do not speak to him of God by trying to make him religious but, on the contrary, by encouraging him to come fully of age, putting away childish things. . . .

To say that speaking of God must be political means that it must engage people at particular points, not just "in general." It must be a word about their own lives—their children, their jobs, their hopes or disappointments. It must be a word to the bewildering crises within which our personal troubles arise

[4] Cornelis van Peursen, "Man and Reality, the History of Human Thought," *Student World,* No. 1 (1963), pp. 19, 20.

—a word which builds peace in a nuclear world, which contributes to justice in an age stalked by hunger, which hastens the day of freedom in a society stifled by segregation. If the word is not a word which arises from a concrete involvement of the speaker in these realities, then it is not a Word of God at all but empty twaddle.

We speak of God to secular man by speaking about man, by talking about man as he is seen in the biblical perspective. Secular talk of God occurs only when we are away from the ghetto and out of costume, when we are participants in that political action by which He restores men to each other in mutual concern and responsibility. We speak of God in a secular fashion when we recognize man as His partner, as the one charged with the task of bestowing meaning and order in human history.

Speaking of God in a secular fashion is thus a political issue. It entails our discerning where God is working and then joining His work. Standing in a picket line is a way of speaking. By doing it a Christian speaks of God. He helps alter the word "God" by changing the society in which it has been trivialized, by moving away from the context where "God-talk" usually occurs, and by shedding the stereotyped roles in which God's name is usually intoned.

SPEAKING OF GOD AS A
THEOLOGICAL QUESTION

When all the preliminary work has been done and the ground has been cleared, the question Bonhoeffer poses is still a *theological* one. In the present theological climate it is especially important to remember this, since where theologians are not busily trying to dress God in tribal costume or enlist him in their existentialist histrionics, they may be just as avidly whittling down the fact that God does make a difference in the way men live. Their opportunity to do this arises from a new situation in theology. There have always been important similarities between biblical faith and atheism, as contrasted, for example, to belief in demons and spirits. But in our time this similarity has produced a rather novel heresy. It is a kind of atheism expressed in Christian theological terminology. This curious phenomenon is made possible by the fact that the biblical doctrine of the hiddenness of God comports so very well, at one level at least, with contemporary atheism or, better, "nontheism." The two can easily be confused unless real care is used. Thus the hidden God or *deus absconditus* of biblical theology may be mistaken for the no-god-at-all of nontheism. Though He is very different from Godot in Samuel Beckett's play, like Godot He has the similar habit of not appearing at the times and places men appoint. Because the two have often been jumbled, it is important that we distinguish them here.

Carl Michalson describes the biblical doctrine of the hiddenness of God in these terms:

> . . . it is God's way of life to be hidden. He is *ex officio* hidden. Hiddenness is intrinsic to his nature as God. . . . The doctrine of the hiddenness of God . . . is not a counsel of despair or a concession to human finitude, but a positive description of God himself which performs a merciful service. *It prevents man both from looking for God in the wrong place* and from esteeming God's role in reality with *less than ultimate seriousness.*[5]

This biblical God's hiddenness stands at the very center of the doctrine of God. It is so commanding that Pascal was echoing its intention when he said, "Every religion which does not affirm that God is hidden is not true."[6] It means that God discloses himself at those places and in those ways he chooses

[5] Carl Michalson, "The Real Presence of the Hidden God," in Paul Ramsey (ed.), *Faith and Ethics* (New York: Harper, 1957), p. 259. Emphasis added.

[6] Quoted by Michalson, *ibid.*, p. 245.

and not as man would want. And he always discloses himself as one who is at once different *from* man, unconditionally *for* man, and entirely *unavailable* for coercion and manipulation *by* man. It is his utter hiddenness which distinguishes God from the tribal deities man coaxes and expiates, and from the metaphysical deity man grandly includes in a rounded system of thought. Using God for the kingpin in an ontological system is not much different from wheedling Him into watering my corn. The hidden God of the Bible will not be utilized in either way.

But what part does Jesus of Nazareth play in this hiddenness of God? If Jesus were a theophany, an "appearance of God" in the customary religious sense, then in Jesus the hiddenness of God would be abrogated. But this is not the case. God does not "appear" in Jesus; He hides himself in the stable of human history. He hides himself in the sense that we have just mentioned, showing that He is not anything like what religions have wanted or expected from their gods. In Jesus God does not stop being hidden; rather He meets man as the unavailable "other." He does not "appear" but shows man that He acts, in His hiddenness, in human history.

No wonder the religious compulsion of man, whether in its mythological or in its metaphysical form, has never been too happy with Jesus. In Jesus, God refuses to fulfill either tribal expectations or philosophical quandaries. As Bonhoeffer says, in Jesus God is teaching man to get along without Him, to become mature, freed from infantile dependencies, fully human. Hence the act of God in Jesus offers slim pickings for those in hope of clues for the erection of some final system. God will not be used in this way. He will not perpetuate human adolescence, but insists on turning the world over to man as his responsibility.

The summons to accountability before God also precludes, however, the verbal byplay in which theologians sometimes try to convince contemporary nontheists that the differences among men today over the reality of God are merely verbal. They are not. Although to the neutral observer there may appear to be no difference between the God who absents himself, who refuses to bark at man's whistle, and the no-god-at-all; there is all the difference in the world. Given the fact that man in dialogue fashions the meanings by which history proceeds, that he is free to take responsibility for history, one utterly crucial question remains: Is this responsibility something which man himself has conjured, or is it *given* to him?

The biblical answer, of course, is that it is given to him. For the Bible after mythological and metaphysical overlay has been scraped away, God is not simply a different way of talking about man. God is not man, and man can only be really "*response*-able" when he *responds*. One must be responsible *for* something *before* someone. Man, in order to be free and responsible, which means to be *man*, must answer to that which is not man. Professor Ronald Gregor Smith sums it up when he says that theology, in order to be theology, has to do with what men "are not themselves"; it concerns

what they do not and never can possess at all as part of their self-equipment or as material for their self-mastery, but with what comes to them at all times from beyond themselves.[7]
. . .

The difference between men of biblical faith and serious nontheists is not that we do not encounter the same reality. The difference is that we give that reality a different *name*, and in naming it differently, we differ seriously in the way we respond. . . .

[7] Ronald Gregor Smith, "A Theological Perspective on the Secular," *The Christian Scholar,* **XLIII** (March 1960) , 15.

We have already suggested that God comes to us today in events of social change, in what theologians have often called *history*, what we call *politics*. But events of social change need not mean upheavals and revolutions. The events of everyday life are also events of social change. The smallest unit of society is two, and the relationship between two people never remains just the same. God meets us there, too. He meets us not just in the freedom revolution in America but also in a client, a customer, a patient, a co-worker.

But how? God is free and hidden. He cannot be expected to appear when we designate the place and time. This means that God is neither close nor far *as such*, but is able to be present in a situation without identifying with it, and He is always present to liberate man. This does not mean that He is there to be walked over. God frees us by supplying that framework of limitation within which alone freedom has any meaning. The freedom of man depends on the prior freedom of God, and man would be a prisoner of his own past if it were not for God who comes in that future-becoming-present where human freedom functions.

Thus we meet God at those places in life where we come up against that which is not pliable and disposable, at those hard edges where we are both stopped and challenged to move ahead. God meets us as the transcendent, at those aspects of our experience which can never be transmuted into extensions of ourselves. He meets us, in the wholly other.

Religion and Culture: Bibliography

Arendt, Hannah. *The Human Condition.* Chicago: University of Chicago Press, 1958. Paper (Anchor ed.) , New York: Doubleday & Company, 1959.

Barth, Karl. "Church and Culture" in *Theology and Church.* New York: Harper & Row, 1962.

Benedict, Ruth. *Patterns of Culture.* New York: Houghton Mifflin Company, 1934. Paper (Sentry ed.) , 1961.

Blakeley, T. J. *Soviet Philosophy.* New York: Humanities Press, n.d.

Eliot, T. S. *Notes Toward the Definition of Culture.* New York: Harcourt, Brace & World, 1949.

Freud, Sigmund. *Civilization and Its Discontents.* Ed. and trans. J. Strachey. New York: W. W. Norton & Company, 1962.

Kroner, Richard. *Culture and Faith.* Chicago: University of Chicago Press, 1951.

Malinowski, Bronislaw. *The Foundations of Faith and Morals.* London: Oxford University Press, 1936.

Maritain, Jacques. *True Humanism.* New York: Charles Scribner's Sons, 1938.

Pieper, Josef. *Leisure: The Basis of Culture.* Rev. ed. New York: Pantheon Books, 1964.

Thielicke, Helmut. *Nihilism, Its Origin and Nature, with a Christian Answer.* New York: Harper & Row, 1961.

Thomas, George Finger, ed. *The Vitality of the Christian Tradition.* New York: Harper & Brothers, 1944.

III

Religion
and Modern Art

Introduction

There are two poles in art, the realistic and the abstract. A painting may be called "realistic" if its form seems fairly similar to the form that its subject matter is experienced to have in nature. It may be termed "abstract" if there seems to be little or perhaps no similarity of this sort. At the realistic end of this continuum, one finds realism and impressionism, while the more abstract forms include expressionism, cubism, and surrealism.

Modern art typically has emphasized the abstract side, and thus we are concerned to ask both what this says about contemporary culture generally and in what ways other aspects of our culture are expressing something similar. (These same questions may be asked concerning the bewildering variety of form to be found in modern art.) Forms of this more abstract nature are seen by Read as the expression of both deep anxiety and "the creative freedom of the human mind in such a situation"; by Dixon as the attempt to develop greater expressive power; by Brunner as the unfortunate result of the "disappearance of religious content"; and by Tillich as belonging to an existential style which is fundamentally religious.[1]

Although the first two readings presenting Marxist and Freudian interpretations do not deal directly with modern art, they do provide significant comparisons with the other readings at a more general level.

In the reading by Read art and religion are seen to have the same function as do several other aspects of culture, that of "intensifying the life process." This raises the question whether and in what sense this function may itself be regarded as religious.

Brunner, it may be remembered, emphasizes the importance of the practical rather than the theoretical functions of culture. His ability to give an adequate account of the latter, in view of the secondary role assigned to them, would seem to be an important test of his position. Since his treatment of art is really based on his distinction between autonomy and theonomy, it may be helpful to review briefly his use of these terms in the reading in section one. This distinction is also fundamental to Tillich's approach to culture. Thus one may wish to ask whether—in view of his greater emphasis on the transcendence of God—Brunner's use of these terms differs at all from Tillich's. One might

---

[1] Elsewhere Dixon criticizes Tillich's theory, claiming that it applies fairly well to German expressionism and some related works but cannot be applied to many other areas of modern art, such as those represented by the work of Braque and Cézanne. To this is added the more fundamental criticism that "only an understanding of painting that begins with subject matter can see a painting as *essentially* disruptive. . . . The painting in its basic act is constructive, not destructive or disruptive." See "Is Tragedy Essential to Knowing? A Critique of Dr. Tillich's Aesthetic" in *The Journal of Religion,* XLIII (October, 1963) , 276-77.

ask this question, for example, in connection with their different interpretations of abstraction in modern art.

In reading Tillich it could be illuminating to bear in mind the positive and negative principles which he seeks to employ in his cultural analyses. It will also be helpful to know that by "symbol" Tillich means anything which points to something else in such a way that we not only become aware of this something else, but also "participate" in it; we experience ourselves as personally involved with it.

F. D. KLINGENDER

Marxism and Art*

Whatever its limitations, Chernyshevski's approach with its resolute rejection of all forms of philosophical idealism and mysticism clears the ground for a conception which regards art as a means of expressing the interests and aspirations of the people.

It is important to stress that it is not a theory of *formal* naturalism (although it may well have been interpreted as such in the mid-nineteenth century, at any rate as far as the visual arts are concerned). Chernyshevski explicitly differentiates his conception of "reproduction" from the ancient view of art as the "imitation" of nature which applies the test of "correctness or incorrectness" to the arts. His own demand for realism—the demand that art should reproduce and interpret what interests man in life—refers, on the contrary, exclusively to the *content* of art, and not to its form. All he claims regarding the *form* of art is, in the first place, that it should fully express what the artist means to convey and, secondly, that it should impart general significance to the artist's image of a particular aspect of reality.

This restriction of the meaning of realism to the content of art, which leaves the artist free to express his vision of reality in whatever manner he deems best, corresponds to the evidence of history. There has always been a realist current in art, in the sense that certain artists have endeavored to depict the actual conditions of life and not its idealization, although for centuries at a time this trend was submerged in the neglected undercurrent of folk-art or popular satire. But whether one takes the ancient mime or fifteenth-century misericords, the paintings of Bruegel or those of Goya, Gargantua or Don Quixote, Gulliver or the Drapier's Letters, Robinson Crusoe or Moll Flanders —the great tradition of realism has at all times been distinguished by a combination, or else by the alternate use, of quite distinct forms of expression. . . .

Nevertheless, to be useful for us today, Chernyshevski's broad formulations need to be refined and amplified. We want

* From *Marxism and Modern Art* by F. D. Klingender (New York: International Publishers Co., 1945). Reprinted by permission of the publishers; pp. 22-45, 47-49.

116

to know more fully how the artist has succeeded in the past and can succeed today in giving general significance to his particular image of reality; and we also need to know precisely how the test of truth can be applied to the evaluation of different kinds of images.

Chernyshevski's theory is particularly interesting for Marxists, because this great forerunner of Russian revolutionary socialism, who spent many years in exile in Siberia, adopted the materialist point of view of Feuerbach[1] for his attack on the Hegelian conception of art. Indeed, he claimed no more than to have applied Feuerbach's methods of analysis to the special sphere of aesthetics. Chernyshevski's thesis can therefore be regarded as the immediate predecessor of the Marxist theory of art, and its limitations can be discovered by turning to Marx's and Engels' critique of its philosophical basis, the materialism of Feuerbach.

In the first of his famous *Theses on Feuerbach* Marx wrote:

"The chief defect of all materialism up to now (including Feuerbach's) is, that the object, reality, what we apprehend through our senses, is understood only in the form of the *object* or *contemplation;* but not as *sensuous human activity,* as *practice;* not subjectively."

This statement is of great significance for evaluating Chernyshevski's conception of "reproduction." Chernyshevski follows Feuerbach in regarding reality as an isolated sphere, distinct from "man," an "object" which the artist reproduces for "man" to contemplate. Marx, on the other hand, insists that humanity is an inseparable part of reality, and that our consciousness is but the reflection in our minds of our own *practical activity* in changing reality. Art, too, is part of this practical activity of changing the world. Far from reproducing an eter-

nally unvarying "Nature" for the contemplation of "man," it reflects the unceasing struggle of humanity to master the forces of Nature. Indeed, the artist is in the vanguard of that struggle, for by virtue of his sensibility he is continually discovering new aspects of reality of which his fellow men are not as yet aware. Thus "beauty" is not eternally the same; its ever-changing substance must be continually discovered and rediscovered by the artist and transmitted by him to his fellow men. As Marx puts it: "The work of art—like any other product—*produces* a public conscious of its own peculiar beauty and capable of enjoying it."

Another fundamental limitation of Feuerbach's approach which is shared by Chernyshevski is defined in the sixth thesis of Marx:

"Feuerbach resolves the essence of religion into the essence of *man.* But the essence of man is no abstraction inherent in each separate individual. In its reality it is the *ensemble* (aggregate) of social relations.

"Feuerbach, who does not enter more deeply into the criticism of this real essence, is therefore forced to abstract from the process of history . . . and to postulate an abstract—*isolated*—human individual."

There are passages in Chernyshevski's essay which show that he was not unaware of the inadequacy of the abstraction "man"—thus he points out that the peasant's conception of life and hence of beauty differs from that of the aristocrat and that there are similar differences between the standards of taste prevailing at different historical periods —but it was left to Marx and Engels to point out the full significance of such differences. "Man" in the abstract is a fiction. "The essence of man" can have no meaning other than the social rela-

---

[1] The revolutionary significance of this point of view is evident from the fact that the Tsarist censor did not allow Chernyshevski even to mention Feuerbach's name either in the first edition or in the edition of 1888. It was not until 1906 that the original preface which mentions the names of Hegel and Feuerbach was allowed to appear.

tions of men in their struggle with Nature. Consciousness is the reflection in the minds of men of these social relations.

"Language," wrote Marx, "is as old as consciousness, language is practical consciousness, as it exists for other men, and for that reason is really beginning to exist for me personally as well; for language, like consciousness, only arises from the need, the necessity of intercourse with other men. . . . Consciousness is therefore from the beginning a social product, and remains so as long as men exist at all."

"Life is not determined by consciousness, but consciousness by life." Consequently, to understand consciousness, or any particular manifestation of consciousness, such as a work of art, one must start from the "real living individuals themselves, as they are in actual life" and consider "consciousness solely as *their* consciousness."

"Morality, religion, metaphysics, all the rest of ideology and their corresponding forms of consciousness, thus no longer retain the semblance of independence. They have no history, no development; but men, developing their material production and their material intercourse, alter, along with their real existence, their thinking and the products of their thinking." [2]

Nevertheless, there is a modicum of truth in Roger Fry's claim "that the usual assumption of a direct and decisive connection between art and life is by no means correct" (even if we take "life" in the broad meaning of the term and not in Fry's sense of the self-consciousness of the elect). But Fry's conception of what constitutes a "direct and decisive connection" is purely mechanical. In the "violently foreshortened view of history and art" which forms the first part of his Fabian lecture he shows that there have been many periods in history when there was "progress" in life while art stagnated or even declined, and *vice versa*. This is, of course, perfectly true; but it never seems to have occurred to Fry that an inverse relationship may also be due to a "direct and decisive connection." Indeed, as early as 1846 Marx and Engels had proved that a contradiction between consciousness (including art) and life was not only possible but under certain circumstances even inevitable. In the *German Ideology* they point out that this contradiction is inherent in the division of labor with its resulting stratification of society into classes which arose at a certain stage in the development of the material forces of production:

"Division of labor only becomes truly such from the moment when a division of material and mental labor appears. From this moment onwards consciousness *can* really flatter itself that it is something other than consciousness of existing practice, that it is *really* conceiving something without conceiving something *real;* from now on consciousness is in a position to emancipate itself from the world and to proceed to the formation of 'pure' theory, theology, philosophy, ethics, etc. But even if this theory, theology, philosophy, ethics, etc., comes into contradiction with the existing relations, this can only occur as a result of the fact that existing social relations have come into contradiction with existing forces of production. . . ." and further:

"The forces of production, the state of society, and consciousness, can and must come into contradiction with one another, because the division of labor implies the possibility, nay the fact that intellectual and material activity

<hr/>

[2] *German Ideology*, p 14. To forestall misinterpretation it is useful to remember Engels' statement: "Political, legal, philosophical, religious, literary, artistic, etc., development is grounded upon economic development. But all of them react, conjointly and separately, one upon another, and upon the economic foundation." Letter to Starkenburg, 25 January 1894. Marx-Engels, Selected Correspondence, p. 517.

—enjoyment and labor, production and consumption—devolve on different individuals, and that the only possibility of their not coming into contradiction lies in the negation in its turn of the division of labor."

In the second part of the same work the authors show more explicitly how the division of labor and its final negation affect the arts:

"The exclusive concentration of artistic talent in certain individuals, and its consequent suppression in the broad masses of the people, is an effect of the division of labor. Even if in certain social relations everyone could become an excellent painter, that would not prevent everyone from being also an original painter. . . . With a communist organization of society, the artist is not confined by the local and national seclusion which ensues solely from the division of labor, nor is the individual confined to one specific art, so that he becomes exclusively a painter, a sculptor, etc.; these very names express sufficiently the narrowness of his professional development, and his dependence on the division of labor. In a communist society there are no painters, but at most men who, among other things, also paint."

Marx and Engels believed that of all forms of society that of fully developed industrial capitalism, in which the division between material and mental labor reaches the extreme point, was most hostile to art. The consequent decline of art, so palpable in the nineteenth century, manifested itself on the one hand in the disappearance of craftsmanship and of beauty in the sense of fitness for its purpose from all the practical arts, and on the other hand in the ever increasing specialization of the fine arts and in their ever greater remoteness from life. Yet at the same time this decline was accompanied by spectacular advances in the technique of production, including the technique of artistic production. This contradiction was expressed in the remarkable speech which

Marx delivered on the occasion of the anniversary of the Chartist "People's Paper" in April 1856:

"There is one great fact characteristic of this our nineteenth century; a fact which no party dares deny. On the one hand there have started into life industrial and scientific forces which no epoch of former human history had ever suspected. On the other hand there exist symptoms of decay, far surpassing the horrors of the latter times of the Roman Empire. In our days, everything seems pregnant with its contrary: Machinery, gifted with the wonderful power of shortening and fructifying human labor, we behold starving and overworking it. The new-fangled sources of wealth, by some strange, weird spell, are turned into sources of want. *The victories of art are bought by the loss of character.* At the same pace that mankind masters nature, man seems to become enslaved to other men or to his own infamy. Even the pure light of science seems unable to shine but on the dark background of ignorance. All our inventions and progress seem to result in endowing material forces with intellectual life, and in stultifying human life into a material force. This antagonism between modern industry and science, on the one hand, and modern misery and dissolution, on the other; this antagonism between the productive forces and the social relations of our epoch is a fact, palpable, overwhelming, and not to be controverted. Some may wail over it; others may wish to get rid of modern arts in order to get rid of modern conflicts. Or they may imagine that so signal a progress in industry wants to be completed by as signal a regress in politics. For our part, we do not mistake the shape of the shrewd spirit that continues to mark all these contradictions. We know that to work well the new-fangled forces of society, they only want to be mastered by new-fangled men—and such are the working men. . . ."

It is evident from these quotations

that Marx's explanation of the temporary estrangement of art from life had nothing in common with Hegel's view of the irredeemable decline of art; for Marx pointed out that the very factors which lead to a temporary decline of art at the same time create the conditions for its resurrection once men have freed themselves from their enslavement "to other men or to their own infamy."

But Marx's resolution of the abstraction "man" into the concrete, historically conditioned and ever changing relations of men in society, and his method of explaining all forms of consciousness in terms of those relations, also laid the foundations for a scientific history of art which attempts more than a mere *description* of its ever changing forms. Just as Marx was able to explain the characteristic trend of nineteenth century art—the trend which culminated in the formalism of today—in terms of the contradictions of nineteenth century life, so historical materialism can accomplish what Fry's mechanical conception of "progress" could never do: namely to disclose the social roots of the entire, complex, history of styles.

It is a measure of Chernyshevski's profound insight that, in spite of the limitations of his approach, he recognized *why* the peasant's conception of beauty differs from that of the courtier. The peasant cannot live without work, Chernyshevski writes, therefore "the country beauty cannot have small hands and feet . . . and folksongs do not mention such features. . . . The description of beauty in folksongs will not contain a single tribute of beauty which would not be a sign of flourishing health and balanced strength of body, the consequences always of a life of plenty with constant, hard, though not excessive work." But precisely those features which are a sign of fitness for work in the peasant—the ruddy complexion, the sturdy figure, the strong hands—are considered "vulgar" by the sophisticated man of leisure who despises work. Instead of these he admires the languid pallor, the fragile form, the delicate extremities of the town-bred lady of fashion whose ancestors have lived for generations "without putting their hands to work." The ideals of beauty of the peasant and the nobleman are thus determined by their respective positions in the process of production and by their resulting conceptions of a "good life." What is true of their ideals of personal beauty is equally true of their artistic tastes. The aesthetic standards of the different classes differ, because their conditions of life differ; and the artist who wishes to please his public must conform to one or other of these standards. The same applies to different periods in history; differences in the conditions of life are reflected by corresponding differences in the standards of art.

This has important implications for the critical evaluation of art. While the courtier despises peasant art as crude and vulgar (unless, of course, he is a modern enthusiast for the "naïve"), the peasant on his part is no less contemptuous of sophisticated art. If a member of one class applies his own standards of appreciation to a work produced in another class or period, he does no more than express his own subjective, class- and time-conditioned preferences. He cannot do justice to the particular work, unless he *also* attempts to appreciate it in terms of *its* own standards.

But if it is true that all art must be judged in terms of its own *relative,* class- and time-conditioned standard of appreciation, does it necessarily follow that there is no *absolute,* objectively binding standard of value which can in turn be applied to these various relative standards?

Furthermore, if all art reflects the standards of a given class and period, does it follow that the artist is inevitably and rigidly bound to the standards of one particular class and period? Is Plekhanov right when he states: "Apple trees must give forth apples, pear trees, pears. . . . The art of a decadent epoch *'must'* be decadent; this is inevitable; and it would be futile to become indignant about it"? [3]

It will be appreciated that the answers to these questions are of fundamental importance for all artists at the present time, but especially for those who are striving to express the interests and aspirations of the people.

RELATIVISM

. . . Plekhanov agrees with Taine that it is impossible to compare the relative merits of different periods and styles in art. But that Marx maintained the opposite point of view is evident from his references to the decline of art under capitalism, i.e. during an entire era which produced a whole series of styles. . . .

Marx's own views concerning the relation of artists, and ideologists in general, to the class they represent is perfectly unambiguous:

One must not imagine, he writes, that the theoretical representatives of the democratic lower middle class "are all shopkeepers or enthusiastic champions of shopkeepers. According to their education and their individual position they may be separated from them as widely as heaven from earth. What makes them representatives of the petty bourgeoisie is the fact that in their minds they do not go beyond the limits which the latter do not go beyond in life, that they are consequently driven theoretically to the same tasks and solutions to which material interest and social position practically drive the latter. This is in general the relation of the political and literary representatives of a class to the class that they represent."

Hence it is a distortion of Marxism to assert that the content of an artist's work is rigidly determined by his own economic and social position. The artist inherits a particular conception of the world, because it corresponds to the practical attitude of the class into which he was born; if that is also the class to which his patrons belong he will, as a rule, be perfectly satisfied with that conception and express it in his work. But under certain circumstances he *may* adopt a position which is opposed to the interest of his own class, and there are even times when he *must* do so, if he is to preserve his integrity as an artist.

Consciousness, including art, is not therefore an automatic reflex of the individual's own position seen in isolation; it is the reflection in his mind, and consequently in his scientific or artistic work, of the sum-total of his social relations.

"The consciousness of the masses of the workers cannot be genuine class consciousness," wrote Lenin, "unless the workers learn to observe from concrete, and above all from topical, political facts and events, *every* other social class and *all* the manifestations of the intellectual, ethical life of these classes; unless they learn to apply practically the materialist analysis and the materialist estimate of *all* aspects of life and activity of *all* classes, strata and groups of the population. Those who concentrate the attention, observation and the consciousness of the working class exclusively, or even mainly, upon itself alone are not Social-Democrats; because for its self-realization the working class must . . . have a practical understanding . . . of the

---

[3] G. V. Plekhanov: *Art and Society*. Critics Group Series, No. 3, p. 93. Plekhanov is, of course, perfectly aware of the fact, and indeed he expressly goes on to state that "in times when the class struggle nears the decisive hour" certain bourgeois artists join the revolutionary camp. But, as we shall presently see, he never resolved the contradiction between these two sets of ideas. It is not my intention to belittle the profound importance of Plekhanov's contributions to the history of art and to Marxist thought in general. If the negative elements in his theory are emphasized in the present essay, this is solely due to the fact that they come to the surface precisely in this treatment of the problems which concern us here.

relationship between *all* the various classes of modern society."

This idea which Lenin expressed in 1902 had been applied by Marx in 1846 to the interpretation of art:

"If he will compare Raphael with Leonardo da Vinci and Titian, he will see to what extent the works of art of the first were conditioned by the flourishing of Rome, then under the influence of Florence; how the works of Leonardo were conditioned by the social milieu of Florence, and later those of Titian by the altogether different development of Venice. Raphael, like any other artist, was conditioned by the technical advances made in art before him, by the organization of society and the division of labor in his locality, and finally, by the division of labor *in all the countries with which his locality maintained relations.*"

In other words, the sum-total of relations which conditions the artist's work is coextensive with the practical contacts of his own society. Thus Dvořák was undoubtedly right when he asserted, in conscious opposition to the narrow, mechanistic approach of the "sociological" interpreters of art, that the great artist is always abreast of the most advanced spiritual (i.e. religious, philosophical, scientific, aesthetic) tendencies of his time, whatever their country of origin. It is clearly inadequate to interpret, say, the art of Bruegel purely in terms of the Flemish tradition. His work became the mirror of his people's great struggle for political and spiritual liberty precisely because he had mastered the outstanding intellectual and aesthetic achievements of his Italian, Spanish, French, German, English contemporaries, as well as his native heritage. But we cannot agree with Dvořák and his followers in divorcing the spiritual tendencies of an age from their material roots; hence we shall not fail to give due weight also to the tremendous influence which the discovery of the new world and the consequent extension of the

relations of Europe exerted on Bruegel's interpretation of reality. Today the complex of social relations which conditions the outlook and the work of every artist embraces the entire globe; and the fact that an entirely new type of social relation has been established over one-sixth of the earth's surface cannot but have the most profound influence, either directly or indirectly, on the work of every artist in this country at the present time.

Seen in this light, the statement "the art of a decadent epoch must be decadent" is a fatalistic perversion of the truth. There is no such thing in history as a period of decline which is not also at the same time a period of growth. While the old forms are declining, the conditions for the emergence of the new society are maturing. Hence the description of a given period as a "period of decline" can only mean that the old, declining forces still predominate over the growing forces which will eventually replace them. As long as the declining forces predominate, their decadence will, it is true, be reflected in the *dominating* trend of art (and if these forces are themselves inimical to art, as they are in capitalist society, that decadence will be expressed in the ever-increasing estrangement of art from life); but the dominating trend is never the only trend in the art of a "period of decline," nor is it even the most significant trend. The most significant art in a decadent epoch will be as much in opposition to the dominant trend of decadent art, as the growing forces are to the declining, but still dominating, forces in all other spheres of life. "Mankind," wrote Marx, "always takes up only such problems as it can solve; since, looking at the matter more closely, we will always find that the problem itself arises only when the material conditions necessary for its solution already exist or are at least in the process of formation." And Stalin adds: "New social ideas and theories arise precisely because they are necessary to

society, because it is *impossible* to carry out the urgent tasks of development of the material life of society without their organizing, mobilizing and transforming action." "Theory becomes a material force as soon as it has gripped the masses," and it grips the masses if it goes "to the roots of things." The artist, too, must go to the roots of things, if he spurns to reflect the decadence of a declining age: "To invent," wrote Gorky, "means to extract from the sum of a given reality its cardinal idea and embody it in imagery—that is how we got realism. But if to the idea extracted from the given reality we add . . . the desired, the possible, and thus supplement the image, we obtain that romanticism which is . . . highly beneficial in that it tends to provoke a revolutionary attitude to reality, an attitude that changes the world in a practical way."
. . .

A work of art is satisfying because in it the artist has fixed that fleeting, conditional and relative unity of opposites in which the particular is identical with the general. But a work of art is significant only if that relative unity of opposites at the same time contains and reflects the struggle of those same, mutually exclusive, opposites which is absolute, as movement, evolution and life are. Hence a work of art must stimulate at the same time as it satisfies. While revealing the unity of opposites, it must at the same time reveal the transient and merely relative nature of that unity, thus driving the spectator onward in the ceaseless struggle for an even greater, more profound and comprehensive unity. A work of art which lulls the creative faculties, which drugs and deflects men from the struggle of life, is unconditionally bad. . . .

Marxist theory applies a dual standard to the evaluation of art; it first appreciates a given work in terms of its own relative standard which is conditioned by its period and by the social class whose outlook it reflects; but it also applies to that work the absolute test whether its relative value contains a kernel of objective truth.

How this dual standard works may be illustrated by applying it to some of the artists mentioned in the course of this essay. The poems in which Tennyson transported the Victorians from the 'cankering cares of daily life' and the 'confusion of their philosophies' 'to some entirely new field of existence, some place of rest', are perfect, if judged by the relative standard of Victorian middle class taste. They are far better, in terms of that standard, than most of the poems which his less distinguished contemporaries contributed to the Victorian 'keepsakes' and 'annuals'. But they have ceased to have any meaning for us today, indeed they arouse our antipathy, because they are the complete expression of Victorian cant. Judged by the standard of objective truth they are unconditionally bad, because they evade the issues which were set to the poet by life.

This is not true, however, of those other poems in which Tennyson's true emotions break through the surface of assumed complacency. Judged by their own relative standard these poems seem to us today as perfect as the former type (although a careful study of contemporary criticism may reveal that the Victorians themselves were by no means always of the same opinion). Yet these poems can still stir us today, because the haunting fear and the perplexities focussed in them are a genuine, if confused, reflection of the realities which Tennyson's other poems ignore. . . .

If the history of art is examined from this point of view, it will be found that there is a continuous tradition of realism which started with the dawn of art (e.g. in the palaeolithic cave paintings) and which will survive to its end, for it reflects the productive intercourse between man and nature which is the basis of life. At that important phase in the development of society, when mental labour was divided from material

123

labour, there emerged another, secondary tradition of spiritualistic, religious or idealistic art. This, too, is continuous until it will vanish with the final negation of the division of labour—i.e. in a Communist world. During this entire period of development, i.e. as long as society is divided into classes, the history of art is the history of the ceaseless struggle and mutual inter-penetration of these two traditions. At successive, though widely overlapping phases corresponding to the specific stages in the development of society, both these traditions, and also the results of their inter-play, assume the historical forms which we call the 'Classical', 'Gothic', 'Baroque', etc., styles. A Marxist history of art should describe, first, the struggle which is absolute between these two opposite and mutually exclusive trends, and secondly, their fleeting, conditional and relative union, as manifested in the different styles and in each work of art, and it should explain both these aspects of art in terms of the social processes which they reflect. Marxist criticism consists in discovering the specific weight within each style, each artist and each single work of those elements which reflect objective truth in powerful and convincing imagery. But it should always be remembered that, un-

like science which reduces reality to a blue-print or formula, the images of art reveal reality in its infinite diversity and many-sided richness. And it is in its infinite diversity and many-sided richness that art, too, must be appreciated.

CONCLUSION

Realism, the attitude of the artist who strives to reflect some essential aspect of reality and to face the problems set by life, is from its very nature popular. It reflects the outlook of those men and women who produce the means of life. It is the only standard which can bring art back to the people today. For, as Lenin told Clara Zetkin: 'it does not greatly matter what we ourselves think about art. Nor does it matter what art means to some hundreds or even thousands in a nation, like our own, of many millions. Art belongs to the people. Its roots should penetrate deeply into the very thick of the masses of the people. It should be comprehensible to these masses and loved by them. It should unite the emotions, the thoughts, and the will of these masses and raise them to a higher level. It should awaken artists in these masses and foster their development.'

SIGMUND FREUD

Art as Sublimation*

... Consider ... the origin and meaning of that mental activity called "phantasy-

making." In general, as you know, it enjoys high esteem, although its place in

*Acknowledgment is made to Sigmund Freud Copyrights, Ltd., Mr. James Strachey, Allen & Unwin, Ltd., The Hogarth Press, Ltd., and Liveright Publishers to quote from *Introductory Lectures on Psychoanalysis* (1917), Vol. XVI of the Standard Edition of the *Complete Psychological Works of Sigmund Freud*. Liveright copyright © renewed, 1963, by Joan Riviere.

mental life has not been clearly understood. I can tell you as much as this about it. You know that the ego in man is gradually trained by the influence of external necessity to appreciate reality and to pursue the reality-principle, and that in so doing it must renounce temporarily or permanently various of the objects and aims—not only sexual—of its desire for pleasure. But renunciation of pleasure has always been very hard to man; he cannot accomplish it without some kind of compensation. Accordingly he has evolved for himself a mental activity in which all these relinquished sources of pleasure and abandoned paths of gratification are permitted to continue their existence, a form of existence in which they are free from the demands of reality and from what we call the exercise of "testing reality." Every longing is soon transformed into the idea of its fulfilment; there is no doubt that dwelling upon a wish-fulfilment in phantasy brings satisfaction, although the knowledge that it is not reality remains thereby unobscured. In phantasy, therefore, man can continue to enjoy a freedom from the grip of the external world, one which he has long relinquished in actuality. He has contrived to be alternately a pleasure-seeking animal and a reasonable being; for the meager satisfaction that he can extract from reality leaves him starving. "There is no doing without accessory constructions," said Fontane. The creation of the mental domain of phantasy has a complete counterpart in the establishment of "reservations" and "nature-parks" in places where the inroads of agriculture, traffic, or industry threaten to change the original face of the earth rapidly into something unrecognizable. The "reservation" is to maintain the old condition of things which has been regretfully sacrificed to necessity everywhere else; there everything may grow and spread as it pleases, including what is useless and even what

is harmful. The mental realm of phantasy is also such a reservation reclaimed from the encroachments of the reality-principle.

The best-known productions of phantasy have already been met by us; they are called day-dreams, and are imaginary gratifications of ambitious, grandiose, erotic wishes, dilating the more extravagantly the more reality admonishes humility and patience. In them is shown unmistakably the essence of imaginary happiness, the return of gratification to a condition in which it is independent of reality's sanction. We know that these day-dreams are the kernels and models of night-dreams; fundamentally the night-dream is nothing but a day-dream distorted by the nocturnal form of mental activity and made possible by the nocturnal freedom of instinctual excitations. We are already familiar with the idea that a day-dream is not necessarily conscious, that unconscious day-dreams also exist; such unconscious day-dreams are therefore just as much the source of night-dreams as of neurotic symptoms. . . .

The return of the libido[1] . . . to phantasy is an intermediate step on the way to symptom-formation which well deserves a special designation. C. G. Jung has coined for it the very appropriate name of *Introversion,* but inappropriately he uses it also to describe other things. We will adhere to the position that *introversion* describes the deflection of the libido away from the possibilities of real satisfaction and its excessive accumulation upon phantasies previously tolerated as harmless. An introverted person is not yet neurotic, but he is in an unstable condition; the next disturbance of the shifting forces will cause symptoms to develop, unless he can yet find other outlets for his pent-up libido. The unreal character of neurotic satisfaction and the disregard of the difference between phantasy and reality are

[1] Freud means by "libido" the psychic energy of the sexual instinct. [Editor's note.]

already determined by the arrest at this stage of introversion. . . .

Before you leave to-day I should like to direct your attention for a moment to a side of phantasy-life of very general interest. There is, in fact, a path from phantasy back again to reality, and that is—art. The artist has also an introverted disposition and has not far to go to become neurotic. He is one who is urged on by instinctual needs which are too clamorous; he longs to attain to honor, power, riches, fame, and the love of women; but he lacks the means of achieving these gratifications. So, like any other with an unsatisfied longing, he turns away from reality and transfers all his interest, and all his libido too, on to the creation of his wishes in the life of phantasy, from which the way might readily lead to neurosis. There must be many factors in combination to prevent this becoming the whole outcome of his development; it is well known how often artists in particular suffer from partial inhibition of their capacities through neurosis. Probably their constitution is endowed with a powerful capacity for sublimation and with a certain flexibility in the repressions determining the conflict. But the way back to reality is found by the artist thus: He is not the only one who has a life of phantasy; the intermediate world of phantasy is sanctioned by general human consent, and every hungry soul looks to it for comfort and consolation. But to those who are not artists the gratification that can be drawn from the springs of phantasy is very limited; their inexorable repressions prevent the enjoyment of all but the meager day-dreams which can become conscious. A true artist has more at his disposal. First of all he understands how to elaborate his day-dreams, so that they lose that personal note which grates upon strange ears and become enjoyable to others; he knows too how to modify them sufficiently so that their origin in prohibited sources is not easily detected. Further, he possesses the mysterious ability to mold his particular material until it expresses the ideas of his phantasy faithfully; and then he knows how to attach to this reflection of his phantasy-life so strong a stream of pleasure that, for a time at least, the repressions are outbalanced and dispelled by it. When he can do all this, he opens out to others the way back to the comfort and consolation of their own unconscious sources of pleasure, and so reaps their gratitude and admiration; then he has won—through his phantasy —what before he could only win in phantasy: honor, power, and the love of women.

HERBERT READ

Art as an Intensification of the Life Process*

Modern art offers a confusing variety of movements and mannerisms, and it would be a bold critic who attempted a comprehensive definition of them all. But if we were to arrange all the prevailing styles in an orderly sequence,

* Reprinted by permission of the publishers, Horizon Press (copyright 1952), and Faber and Faber, Ltd., from *The Philosophy of Modern Art* by Herbert Read; pp. 90, 96-109.

we should find at one extreme a style which without hesitation we should call 'realistic', and at the other extreme another style which, perhaps not quite so confidently, we should call 'abstract'. We might use other terms to describe these same extremes—terms like 'naturalistic' and 'geometric', 'organic' and 'conventional', 'vitalistic' and 'formalistic', but all these words indicate the same opposed tendencies. If in this essay I adopt 'realistic' and 'abstract', it is because they are in most general use. In addition, they seem to me to be based on common sense, and to have a descriptive aptness which explains their persistence. By *realism* we mean fidelity of representation, truth to nature. By *abstraction* we mean what is derived or disengaged from nature, the pure or essential form abstracted from the concrete details. . . .

We might begin by asking what wider philosophical significance can be claimed for the contrasted styles of realism and abstraction. The explanation which has hitherto prevailed, and which I myself have accepted, sees in realism an expression of confidence in, and sympathy for, the organic processes of life. In other words, realism is an affirmative mode of expression, by which we do not necessarily mean the expression of an optimistic mood—there is such a thing as affirmation of the tragic element in life. But abstraction is the reaction of man confronted with the abyss of nothingness, the expression of an *Angst* which distrusts or renounces the organic principle, and affirms the creative freedom of the human mind in such a situation. An interesting correlation could thus be made between the development of existential philosophy and of abstract art, and certain abstract artists with a philosophical insight have not hesitated to express themselves in phraseology that recalls Heidegger or Sartre. This is particularly true of a constructivist like Gabo, who demands for the artist the right to construct a visible image of that reality which is being created by the contemporary human spirit. 'It is evident', writes Gabo,[1] 'that no such demand could be warranted if I should accept the view prevalent in our philosophies that human thought is striving to discover an eternal truth which is embodied in some stable and universal reality outside us; or that in our striving for knowledge we are pursuing the discovery of that reality which is constant and pure. . . . I maintain that knowledge is nothing else but a construction of ours and that what we discover with our knowledge is not something outside us or a part of a constant and higher reality, in the absolute sense of the word; but that we discover exactly that which we put into the place where we make the discoveries. . . .' After making some further remarks—posing questions very much in the existentialist vein—Gabo continues: 'We know only what we do, what we make, what we construct; and all that we make, all that we construct, are realities. I call them *images,* not in Plato's sense (namely, that they are only reflections of reality), but I hold that these images are the reality itself and that there is no reality beyond this reality except when in our creative process we change the images: then we have created new realities.'

It will be seen that we have come full circle in our terminology. By subjecting the phenomenal world to logical criticism, we are left with a clean existential slate; we then create a new and logically consistent reality, and the images which the artist projects to make this reality concrete, the constructions of his imagination and his hands, are the only forms of art which can properly be called realistic.

[1] In a letter to an author; but the same point of view is developed in his lecture, 'A Retrospective View of Constructive Art', published in *Three Lectures on Modern Art*. (New York, Philosophical Library, 1949.)

This philosophy of Constructive Realism, as Gabo calls it, clearly defines the place of the artist in this society of ours. 'If I were an academician', Gabo explains, 'or a believer in a higher reality outside me, as most people are (lucky creatures!), I would have no need for any justification for painting landscapes, or portraits, or social realism. I would rely on my so-called common sense, on which I see and feel, and I would enjoy it. Or I would fix one point in the distant haze of that unknown reality, would try to approach it as nearly as I could, and would find solace in the fanatical belief that I am the only one who is portraying that reality which is the only truth. I would give myself to intolerance, obscurantism and prejudice, and would be one of those who decry and deride the fellow artist who is seeing things otherwise. But I am an artist who is doing so-called abstract work, and as you so rightly put it, few people know that you have to be another man to penetrate into this world of so-called abstractions which we are painting. I never forget that constructive art is a medium of expression still in its very tender age—it cannot live and grow exposed to all winds and weather. It has to strengthen its roots in the more solid soil of the whole human mind—it has to fit in with all that is troubling and exalting the creative spirit of our age. It also has to have its place not only sociologically but also mentally and spiritually. It has also to have an aim, a direction. . . . If this art is to survive for any length of time at all, or if it is to grow into something at least equivalent in importance to the coming ages as the old arts were for theirs, it can achieve this only if the artist of the future is capable of manifesting in this medium . . . a new image, pictorial or sculptural, which will, in its whole organization, express the very spirit of what the contemporary mind is trying to create and which will become the accepted image of life in the Universe.'

128

I have quoted so extensively from this private correspondence with Gabo because the ideas he is expressing have been expressed nowhere else; just as the type of art he is advocating has never been so uncompromisingly carried to plastic realization. He is virtually creating a new language, a symbolic language of concrete visual images. This language is necessary because our philosophical enquiries have brought us to a point where the old symbols no longer suffice. Philosophy itself has reached an impasse—an impasse of verbal expression—at which it hands over its task to the poets and painters, the sculptors and other creators of concrete images. It is for this reason that Heidegger turns to the poetry of Hölderlin, and that Sartre the philosopher becomes Sartre the novelist. It is not, I think, thereby implied that the only images of reality we can create are the artist's images; rather, no distinction is made between the images of the artist and the images of the scientist. 'In such a philosophy', says Gabo, 'there is no difference between art and science—they are both art; between technique and knowledge—they are both skill; and in such a philosophy the image of the world of the primitive is just as true and real as the image of the world of Thomas Aquinas and Einstein. It is up to us to choose one or the other according to which of those images appear to me or to you more coherent, more harmonious and more cogent, above all, more acceptable as a means for our orientation in this life of ours.'

By now the position we have reached in our argument is this: that which we call reality is a chain of images invented by man, whose personal existence must be affirmed before he proceeds with his invention. Reality is manmade, and the maker is the image-maker, the poet. Reality accords with the images the artist makes, and derives its validity from such values as integrity, self-consistency, viability, pragmatic satisfaction, aesthetic satisfaction, etc.

An age, a civilization, may accept a particular series of images as concordant, as expressive of its needs. In that way— for images, which are personal images, beget reflections and imitations in other minds—in that way a style is created; in that way a religion is created; in that way a science is created. A style, a religion, a science—each is a self-consistent, coherent image-series. The mistake—a mistake which mankind makes with tragic frequency—is to assume that a particular series of images is eternally real. The reality changes with our circumstances.

We can therefore now express our questions in another way, and as only one question: in the circumstances of our time is there any particular reason why the artist should adopt one or the other of the types of imagery or symbolism represented by the terms realism and abstraction?

In the Soviet Union there is, of course, the very good reason that realism is enforced, with extinction as an artist as the alternative. I do not think that this prejudice in favour of socialist realism is quite so stupid as the Russians themselves make it seem. There must be a vague realization of the existential dilemma of modern man, and a fear that the solutions which seek the creation of a reality in Art or God, offer an escape from the reality which should be Stalin, or the State. It is not a style of art that the communist dictatorship fears: it is art itself, in any form forceful enough to compel the allegiance of man's minds; and they have succeeded in reducing art to insignificance.

I believe that the same iconoclastic tendency is present in certain phases of modern thought not confined to the Soviet Union. There is always the recurrent fear among theologians that Art might in some sense replace God, and ever since Kierkegaard formulated his Either/Or, these religious philosophers have been busy telling us that a reliance on the reality created by the artist leads ultimately to despair. That, as I see it, is the attitude of an age that has lost all contact with the actuality of art—an age that can only conceive art as idea, and is utterly divorced from the creative experience, even in the humble form of handicraft.

Personally I find it hard to accept any ontology or theory of life which insists on a single and exclusive reaction to experience. There are various modes of understanding and various constructions to express this understanding. Why must we assume that life, which has evolved into such a diversity of creatures, should be expressed in a single category of understanding? The way of art and the way of religion, and equally the way of science or dialectical materialism, are equally valid alternatives, and the only question, in any comparative evaluation, is whether a particular construction furthers the continuance and intensification of the life-process itself. It follows that the imposition of any particular system of reality on any particular society, or the mere prejudice in favour of any particular system, is due to a kind of stupidity, to a lack of tolerance in the presence of life itself. Any construction which has positive meaning for the individual, or for the community, or for life as a whole, has value, has meaning, has relevance. It is what Woltereck calls a 'mode of resonance' in face of the incomprehensibility of existence, and there is certainly more than one such mode of resonance—not only 'dread' (as Heidegger supposes), but also amazement, joy, curiosity, affirmation, what Nietzsche called a yea-saying.

Various as the forms of these resonances are, they may perhaps be arranged along a polar axis, with transcendental metaphysics at one end and an intense self-awareness of physical vitality at the other end. It is along the same axis that we can place abstraction and realism in art. But again the choice is not imposed

129

on the individual artist. The axis exists *within* the individual artist, if only he can become conscious of it.

This fact I shall attempt to demonstrate by reference to the work of two or three English artists with whom I happen to have been intimately associated. All are artists who have developed alternate phases of realism and abstraction—not, in general, attempting to combine them, as Juan Gris did, and never seeking a dogmatic fixity in one or the other extreme.

The first example is Henry Moore. The greater part of his work could, I think, be described as an 'inward intensification' of subjective feeling, a discovery and an affirmation of the organic life-process. But at the extremes we have, on the one hand, direct transcripts of the human figures such as we find in his *Madonna and Child;* and, at the other extreme, his *String Figure* (No. 3), a composition which has only an indirect reference to the phenomenal world. At the one extreme, therefore, realism; at the other, abstraction.

The contrast in the work of Ben Nicholson is not so clear because, like Juan Gris, when he introduces a realistic motive, it is generally within an abstract architectural design. But both early and late in his career he has expressed himself in a purely realistic style; and at other times, with equal decisiveness, he has created pure abstractions of this uncompromising type.

A still more striking contrast is provided by Barbara Hepworth, for the contrast is embodied in the different media of sculpture and painting. Sometimes the drive to abstraction is carried to its farthest extreme in a construction of greatest purity and harmony. But the same artist, moved by a chance contact with life at a moment of crisis—for example, life hanging in the balance on a surgical operation table—has produced paintings in the style of the realistic art of the early Renaissance.

The point to notice about these cases

is the perfect ambivalence of the process. The change-over from one style to the other, from realism to abstraction or from abstraction to realism, is not accompanied by any deep psychological revolution. It is merely a change of direction, of destination. What is constant is the desire to create a reality, the will to form. At one extreme that will is expressed in the creation of new forms, of what might be called *free* form, so long as we do not assume that freedom implies any lack of aesthetic discipline; and at the other extreme, the will to form is expressed in a selective affirmation of some aspect of the organic world —notably a heightened awareness of the vitality or grace of the human form. In one of her letters to me (6.3.48) Barbara Hepworth describes this ambivalent process with perfect clarity: 'I don't feel any difference of intention or of mood when I paint (or carve) realistically and when I make abstract carvings. It all feels the same—the same happiness and pain, the same joy in a line, a form, a colour—the same feeling of being lost in pursuit of something. The same feeling at the end. The two ways of working flow into each other without effort . . . [The two methods of working] enhance each other by giving an absolute freedom —a freedom to complete the circle. . . . Working realistically replenishes one's *love* for life, humanity and the earth. Working abstractly seems to release one's personality and sharpen the perceptions, so that in the observation of life it is the wholeness or inner intention which moves one so profoundly: the components fall into place, the detail is significant of unity.'

That, it seems to me, is a very revealing explanation of the creative process within the artist, and it suggests a theory of reciprocal tensions, which, whether we call them realism-abstraction, conscious-unconscious, life-death, are expressive of the total world-process. The consciousness of the artist alternates between the two poles of this tension. One pole may be left unexpressed, and then the artist is wholly realistic, or wholly abstract. But it seems reasonable to suppose that a better balance, if only in the mental personality of the artist, will be achieved by the open expression of both polar extremes of tension.

Somewhere in this psychic shuttle, this alternation of the positive and negative forces of life, freedom intervenes —the freedom to create a new reality. Only on that assumption can we explain any form of evolutionary development in human consciousness, any kind of spiritual growth. A novelty-creating freedom exists by virtue of the intensity generated by aesthetic awareness; an evolutionary advance emerges from the act of expression.

What wider philosophical implications of these facts of aesthetic experience may have is a question for open discussion. But if I may conclude with a personal point of view, I would confess that it has always seemed to me that the opposition which we make in critical theory between reason and romanticism, and in wider philosophic terms between pragmatism and idealism, cannot be resolved and should not be resolved. It is merely the difference of the particular resonance expressed in that moment when, naked and comfortless on the abyss of nothingness, we question the meaning and the nature of existence. We answer as answer we can—that is to say, according to our particular psycho-physical constitution. We answer with wonder or we answer with dread; and for each answer there is a separate language. But the poetry is in the freedom with which we answer; the art is the affirmation, the acceptance and the intensification of the life. . . .

The specifically 'modern' movement in art, which began with the first cubistic experiments of Picasso and Braque, is now forty years old. Its vagaries, its violence, its sudden transitions and frequent schisms, suggest that it has developed haphazardly, without premedita-tion, justifying itself from day to day, pragmatically. But the briefest consideration of the historical facts shows that the philosophical foundations of the modern movements were already established in logical completeness before the creation of any parallel manifestations in plastic form. A spiritual situation existed, and had already been described by the philosophers, before the artists became conscious of the style, or of the choice of styles, implicit in that situation.

The psychological analysis of Lipps, the historical generalizations of Riegl and Wölfflin, and many other works in the wider field of general philosophy, had contributed to the intellectual clarification in question. For the purposes of my present argument there is no need to review such a vast field because, at the critical moment, a brilliant synthesis was made by Wilhelm Worringer, and the dates are not in question. Worringer's dissertation on *Abstraction and Empathy* was completed in 1906 and published in 1908. I doubt if any work of art which deserves the name of *abstraction* was created before 1910. Picasso's *Demoiselles D'Avignon,* which was painted in 1907, is sometimes cited as the first work in the cubist style, but its cubistic elements are very slight, and are taken over from negro sculpture without any fundamental feeling for abstraction as such. Picasso may have been conscious of the stylistic integrity represented by the African sculpture which at the moment influenced him, but he was equally inspired in this composition by Cézanne's late bathing groups, and the attempt to combine two such antagonistic styles in one picture cannot be described as aesthetically satisfying, however important as an historical document. The landscapes painted at Horta de Ebro in the summer of 1909 are the first compositions thoroughly penetrated by a geometrical principle, and it is only in 1910 with such paintings as the *Portrait of Kahnweiler* that the will to abstraction has succeeded in completely

131

dominating the organic elements of the subject-matter.

The position in Germany does not seem to have been any different. Kandinsky settled in Munich in 1908, the year in which Worringer's book was published in that city. His paintings began to show a tendency towards abstraction, but it was not until 1910 that he painted anything of a completely abstract character. Was Kandinsky prompted by the philosophical discussions which Worringer's book had provoked in Munich? It is significant that when he himself, two years later, wrote his book *On the Spiritual In Art*, it was published by the same house (the Piper Verlag) that had published Worringer's dissertation. All the members of the *Blaue Reiter* group, which was founded in Munich by Kandinsky and Franz Marc in 1912, were philosophically minded. The extent to which they were philosophically instructed is not known to me, but I am persuaded that a conscious integration of art and philosophy took place at this time. I would even like to suggest that the comparatively consistent development of the art of Kandinsky and Klee is due to their early acquisition of a philosophical background.

The philosophical situation at the beginning of the twentieth century was the result of a long development of which artists, during the preceding century, had remained serenely unconscious. It is not to be denied, of course, that a close correspondence of feeling and of development exists between transcendentalism and romanticism, but when philosophy began to question the very basis of existence, it was leading in a direction in which art, for the moment, was not willing to follow. The philosophical development which leads from Schelling through Kierkegaard, Nietzsche, and Husserl to Heidegger and Jaspers has no parallel in the plastic arts until we reach Picasso, Kandinsky, Klee, Mondrian and Gabo. Art, even

132

in the extremes of Fauvism, remains positively naturalistic, sympathetically realistic. There is, no doubt, a certain degree of metaphysical *fear* (*Angst*) in a painter like Van Gogh, but one has only to read his letters to discover how strongly he was resisting this feeling of doom, plunging into a state of apprehension which was crudely vitalistic. The particular kind of 'nullity' which becomes the starting-point of modern philosophy can only be represented in art by an attitude which leaves the artist for the moment independent of nature. The possibility of creating a reality through the means of art becomes, indeed, an important aspect of philosophy, for here at any rate is one positive method of vindicating the individuality of the person. Art in this sense becomes the most precious evidence of *freedom*.

The abstract movement in art awaits, therefore, a justification which is already present in the philosophy of existentialism. But existentialism itself is not a coherent body of doctrine, and apart from the distinct varieties represented by such names as Heidegger, Jaspers, Marcel and Sartre, all of which are erected on a basic mood of fear, there is a dialectically opposed reaction to the existential situation which is affirmative, eudemonistic, optimistic. In its historical development this philosophical attitude is closely intertwined with the other, and a philosopher like Nietzsche, for example, embraces both attitudes in tragic dualism. At this point science intervenes, and the biological metaphysics of Bergson constitutes a challenge to the excessive intellectualism of Husserl and Heidegger. Finally it becomes possible (for example, in Woltereck's *Ontology of the Vital*), to oppose a 'natural' ontology to the existential ontology, both acknowledging the same ground, but reacting with opposite feelings. To the dread (*Angst*) of the existentialists Woltereck opposes cheerfulness (*Freudigkeit*), and he claims that this other resonance, which was already known to Aristotle, has no less importance, humanly and ontically speaking, than the Kierkegaard-Heidegger-Jaspers dread born of the consciousness of nothing and the feeling of shipwreck. He goes further and claims that this amazement in face of the world's wonders lacks the narrow self-preoccupation of world 'dread': instead, something positive, lacking in dread, attaches to it, the joyfulness and inner impulse to assimilate, examine, understand, create. And according to Woltereck the sciences as well as the arts are born of this impulse:

'Out of this, even for the single life, genuine and lofty values may arise, for amazement may be heightened until it becomes that which moves and overpowers the whole being. In the experiencing of pure expression in the form of great art, great scenes in Nature, of great—or beloved—individuals, transcendent summits of existence may be attained, as certainly as in the immediate appeal of the transcendent. It depends on the profundity of the experience that falls to a person's lot. The Parthenon, the Eroica, the Moses of Michelangelo may constitute such experiences, but they may also be given to us by a single tree, a single hawk, a single human individual, or by the recognition of a single truth.'

The tendency of *Kunstwissenschaft* has been to recognize contrasted attitudes to nature as period phenomena —abstraction and empathy alternating with, and being determined by, environmental and historical circumstances. We now seem to have reached a stage of intellectual development where an individual choice is possible. That is to say, once we have completed our analysis of the existential problem, then the particular resonance we adopt (fear or joyfulness) is determined by a free exercise of the will. It cannot, I think, be argued that only the positive resonance has any significance for the future of humanity—even Woltereck admits that existential dread undoubtedly possesses, for many of us, a deep ontic significance.

He even describes it as 'an especially human mode of resonance', but it is not the only resonance, nor the fundamental mood of man.

We can now turn to modern art which illustrates in its development and scope the philosophical problems which confront the contemporary artist. It would be a too-simple interpretation of the complexity of the situation to make a direct correlation between fear and abstraction and between cheerfulness and empathy. That would be a purely logical *schema*. We must remember that the artist is a human being and not an automaton. He has moods and feelings, and these are not fixed or constant: It is quite possible for the individual artist to alternate between fear and cheerfulness, and to express himself in forms appropriate to each attitude. This has happened, as in the case of Hans Erni, as a change of total-attitude: in the case of other artists, Henry Moore or Picasso, a frequent alternation of style takes place, much to the surprise and confusion of the naïve public, who expect an artist to be 'consistent'. Such ambivalence in the artist proves that the human will can intervene as a process in the existential dialectic. The freedom to create is thus to be interpreted as a freedom to affirm and intensify the life-process itself (which would imply a naturalistic art) or as a freedom to create a new order of reality, distinct from the life-process, but enhancing the independent spiritual powers of man's isolated consciousness (which would imply an abstract and transcendental art.) The choice will be made according to the disposition of any particular artist, and the choice might be for an inclusive ambivalent attitude, a taking-into-oneself of the complete dialectical process. Some words of Schelling's seem to anticipate such a poetic monism: 'To be drunk and sober not in different moments but at one and the same moment—this is the secret of true poetry. Thus is the Apollonian different from

133

the merely Dionysian ecstasy. To represent an infinite content, therefore, a content which really resists form, which seems to destroy any form—to represent such an infinite content in the most perfect, that is, in the most finite form, that is the highest task of art.'[2] The definition of 'the most finite form' can only be accomplished by endless research and experiment, and therein lies the best justification of the vagaries of modern art.

JOHN W. DIXON

Religious Interpretations of Art[*]

PAINTING IS MAN'S IMAGE OF HIMSELF IN THE WORLD

My way of expressing my Ego is by painting; there are, of course, other means to this end—such as literature, philosophy or music—but as a painter, cursed or blessed with a terrible and vital sensuality, I must look for wisdom with my eyes. I repeat, with my eyes, for nothing could be more ridiculous, or irrelevant than a "philosophical conception" painted purely intellectually without the terrible fury of the senses, grasping each visible form of beauty and ugliness. If, from those forms which I have found in the Visible, literary subjects result—such as portraits, landscapes or recognizable compositions—they have all originated from the senses—in this case, from the eyes, and each intellectual subject has been transformed again into form, color and space.
—Extract from Max Beckmann's lecture given at the New Burlington Galleries, July 21, 1938.

Two types of categories for approaching a work of art have been offered. In Chapter IV it was things like space and mass, color, light, line. These are categories of analysis of form, therefore of style. They are qualities of the thing itself, objective, open to sensitivity of vision. This is the language by which art is understood, the means of entering into the world of art.

In the Prologue it was creation, the image, the fall and redemption. These are categories of interpretation. They are more subjective, derived from faith, linking the art work to faith. They are qualities of the art work if this interpretation of the Christian faith is true, and if the analysis is sound. This is vital. To impose such categories on a work without thorough and careful and sensitive analysis is to force it into a quality that is not its own. Yet to leave aside such categories is to leave art isolated in a world of its own, unrelated to the rest of man's life.

INTERPRETATION MUST FOLLOW ANALYSIS

Therefore, these categories can be used only after the categories of analysis have

[2] Sämmtliche Werke, Pt. II, Vol. IV, p. 25.

[*] From *Form and Reality: Art as Communication*, copyright 1957. Reprinted by permission of the author and the Board of Education of The Methodist Church; pp. 63-84.

been mastered. The categories of analysis derive from and relate to the common experience. They cannot be mastered by a short course fifteen minutes a day for they require years of discipline. Yet they can be begun by anyone for it is doubtful if anyone is wholly blind to the language of art. . . .

LEONARDO AND TINTORETTO

Let us begin with two paintings of the same religious subject—"The Last Supper"—one by Leonardo da Vinci [**Plate 1**], the other by Tintoretto [**Plate 2**]. The first is one of the most popular and universally loved of all great paintings. . . .

Leonardo's painting was done in 1495-98, Tintoretto's in 1592-94. This is more than just a difference in date for during this period there occurred a shift from one historical period to another (Renaissance to Baroque). . . .

Both of these paintings are properly entitled "The Last Supper." Yet the supper itself was long and a number of significant events took place. The particular event a man chooses to emphasize reveals a great deal about his attitude.

In this case two distinctly different moments have been chosen. Leonardo has chosen the moment when Jesus has just announced, "One of you will betray me," and shows the disciples' reaction to this announcement. Tintoretto, on the other hand, has chosen the moment when Christ actually institutes the Communion service, or the Eucharist, as the church has always known it, saying, "Take, eat, this is my body."

These represent more than just two different events. Choosing them means two different attitudes. Leonardo's is not specifically Christian in its essence, at all. Such a moment could take place in the life of any great human leader who knew that one of his followers was about to betray him. Tintoretto's, on the other hand, is very specifically Christian, for the moment chosen could have

happened at no other time or place and with no other leader. The first is a great human drama, the second a great spiritual drama.

Now, let us examine briefly the form, the way the pictures are made. The first thing that strikes the attention (in the black-and-white reproduction) is the space. What does the word "space" mean?

Space is that which we occupy or that contains us, that which extends in all directions. This is a general definition. But art is built with particulars, not general definitions. At any given moment space is something specific. In architecture the space is formed and contained by the walls of the building. It is real, palpable, sensible.

A painting has no space of itself for it is basically a two-dimensional surface. Space must be created by the artist and so the artist has complete control of the space. Both Leonardo and Tintoretto have used the same means of creating a sense of space—perspective. (This is the commonly understood effect that makes railroad tracks or an avenue of trees seem to come together in the distance.)

But compare the use of perspective. Leonardo clearly indicates the lines of perspective by the ceiling, the tapestries and the floor. All these lines come together in the exact center of the picture, the head of Christ. All this is perfectly clear, easily understood and grasped by the mind. Everything is balanced, harmonious.

Tintoretto uses the same sort of lines but instead of leading the eye to the center he has the lines shooting off precipitately to the upper right-hand corner, meeting just below the wing of the angel. This meeting point is shadowy, unclear, mysterious. The picture is unbalanced, restless, unharmonious.

Compare the position of the tables. Leonardo has placed his across the front of the picture. Everything takes place

135

on the other side of the table so the table acts as a kind of barrier, like the edge of a stage. The spectator is cut off from the drama which he watches.

Tintoretto has turned his table and placed it along, rather than across, the perspective lines. Thus the space is opened up and the spectator is not cut off from the scene but, rather, he is drawn into it, becomes part of it.

Notice how these different characteristics fit into each other. The one is a human drama cut off from the spectator, who watches from the outside. The other is a spiritual drama which draws in the spectator as one of the participants.

Now, compare the way the people are represented, for the representation of man is as important a clue as the representation of space. Leonardo has lined up his figures so that each one is clearly seen. Each is reacting as a distinct individual. The study of these clearly defined individuals is one of the abiding sources of the interest in Leonardo's painting. It might be safe to say that Leonardo was primarily interested in this aspect of the subject. The words of Jesus provide the stimulus and the focus for these individual reactions which make up a magnificent study in personality and individual psychology.

Tintoretto, on the other hand, has so turned and twisted his figures, and sunk them in shadow that they do not stand out as individuals. They do not react as individuals for they are all caught up in the sweep of movement leading into the picture. They are not separate individuals, added together to make the whole. They are part of a whole which is more than themselves and which is definable as an overwhelming religious experience.

What about the matter of "realism"? Both are about equally realistic and unrealistic. Leonardo's is clearer, more precise, carefully drawn in details. Yet the room is abstract, the figures are impossibly jammed together (for con-

centration) and everything is made to serve his dramatic purpose. Tintoretto's is an unreal room, full of mysterious light, apparitions, shadows. Yet the figures and objects are solid, full and vigorous. The question of realism is quite irrelevant for each artist manipulates what he sees to make it a part of a painting which is, in turn, his interpretation of the deeper meaning of the event.

So far the analysis has made it appear that Leonardo's painting, one of the most popular religious paintings ever made, is not really very religious and is primarily a study in human psychology while Tintoretto's concentrates on the religious experience. This, however, is a little too simple. Basic to Christianity is the belief in the importance of the individual. This Leonardo clearly recognizes, while Tintoretto subordinates the individual to the group. It is no accident that Tintoretto's work was done not long after the founding of the Roman Catholic Church as we know it today. The individual is part of a whole which is created by the liturgical act.

Leonardo's is not, certainly, a Protestant painting nor even a strongly Christian painting, but it does recognize the central Protestant principle of the importance of the individual. Yet the emphasis is on the single individual added to others to make the whole. Tintoretto has a much firmer grasp of the sense of community created by that which is outside the individual.

Both are dramatic and the essence of drama is interaction of persons in time. Each interrupts a continuous action at a particular moment. The chosen moment reveals much of the interests and concerns of the artist. The formal means for establishing the chosen moment is equally revealing.

Leonardo portrays his figures at the crucial moment of their most revealing gesture. (As an art term, "gesture" refers to a significantly expressive act or movement. It can be exploited equally by dramatist, dancer and artist. One of the heaviest prices paid by the modern artist for his directly expressive form is the loss of gesture.) The act is suspended like a pendulum that pauses at the top of the swing. The act is complete in its essence and the only movement would be away from gesture to formlessness. The picture is a cross section of time, and the important thing is not the flowing movement of time but the revelation of existence.

Tintoretto, on the other hand, concentrates on the flow of movement and of time. Part of the restless effect of the picture comes from the sense of watching a continuous movement that is observed but not slowed down, much less suspended as Leonardo's. Where Leonardo uses drama for the revelation of significant character, Tintoretto uses drama for the unfolding of significant event, where the end and beginning are equally important and equally part of the whole. Space and time, light and darkness serve to elicit the creative event that is the focus and meaning of all.

Let us turn now to a secular subject —the portrait, a crucial occasion for the demonstration of art's ability to analyze and communicate its interpretation of the nature of man through the language of form.

What do we mean by "the nature of man"? Can we just take for granted that man is what he is? Can the artist do more than record what man is? But the situation is not quite so simple. In the first place, there are all kinds of people all the time, not only good people and bad people but people who act well or badly for all sorts of reasons. Man is made up of all sorts of complicated feelings and emotions, desires and urges. Part of the reason he acts as he does lies in the dominance of one or another combination of these elements which all men share. The artist can explore these characteristics but it is rather the literary than the visual artist who can do so. A novel can examine

the intricate combination of good and evil found in all men. But the painter can present only one moment in time, and since he can paint only physical forms there are many things he cannot bring into his painting.

What is relevant to painting, and can be communicated by painting, is the conception of what man is essentially. This is another basic determinative factor in conduct and life as well. If a man believes he is basically an animal, that his mind and spirit are insignificant additions to an animal nature, then it is easy to see how radically his conduct will be affected. If, on the other hand, the man thinks he is essentially a spirit, that his body is an evil force to be suppressed or an insignificant part to be ignored, his conduct will be seriously affected in a different direction. These are just two possibilities but both have been important in the affairs of man in the past. There are other basic attitudes that are equally influential. In fact, all people at all times hold some basic attitude, whether they know it or not. Usually they hold it unconsciously, take it for granted. This is one of the good reasons for studying works of art. We can see what other men have believed, how they tried to interpret themselves in the light of their faith. Thus we can begin to hold our faith consciously, not accept it blindly.

We have already touched briefly on two interpretations of the nature of man as seen in painting. Leonardo saw man as a distinct, separate individual, living his own life, reacting in his own way to the event at the immediate center of his experience. Tintoretto saw man as basically part of a larger whole.

Does this sound distant from the ordinary affairs of men? Just look at the consequences of this for the life of the church. If Leonardo's understanding of the nature of man is followed to its logical conclusion there really is not any effective church. There might be a club, a sort of organization which these free

137

and independent individuals enter or leave as it pleases them. There is no such thing as a church with a life of its own.

Under Tintoretto's doctrine the church is everything rather than nothing. Man has reality only as he is a part of the church and the church focuses on a particular act of worship. In other words, we have here the beginning of the modern Roman Catholic idea of the church. So different can be the interpretation of the nature of man in a painting!

It might be added here that we are not at the moment dealing with difference of value. It is possible not to agree with the interpretation of the nature of man in either painting but recognize each as a great painting.

TITIAN AND REMBRANDT

Now let us turn to the two portraits and see what they say about the nature of man. The first is a portrait of a man named Pietro Aretino by Titian, the other is a self-portrait by Rembrandt. Readers in New York can see the originals of each of these paintings for both are in the Frick Gallery.

First, a mention of the relevant facts. Titian was an older contemporary of Tintoretto. He was a Venetian of the sixteenth century. This time the comparison spans a larger distance for Rembrandt was from Holland and lived in the seventeenth century.

Here the point of beginning cannot be the different conception of the subject matter for each has for a subject the single human figure. So we can begin with the more usual beginning, the important differences in form, the way the pictures are made.

There are three important formal differences: space, line and light. These are by no means separate but are inseparable parts of a whole. However, we analyze in pieces and, since the idea of space has been introduced, let us look at line. Again, the notion is not obscure

or esoteric. A line, for our purposes, is an edge or a boundary, the sort of thing that can be drawn with a pencil. There are all degrees of emphasis on line but the two extremes—which are represented here—heavy emphasis on line and the suppression of line, represent fundamental differences of attitude toward the world. Emphasizing a line separates and divides; subordinating lines unites.

There are paintings that emphasize line more than Titian does, paintings that could almost be called drawings with the areas between the lines filled in with color. Titian does not go that far but he does go far. Every object, every feature is clearly outlined, distinct and solid. Eyes, nose, mouth, the whole head, the chain, the robe, the whole figure are specific and distinct.

Compare Rembrandt. Here there are virtually no lines at all. Objects and features fade out at the edges. Shadows obscure the separation between different details. Stand back from the picture and it looks very detailed. In truth, it is an admirably exact portrait. It is as easy to imagine meeting this man in actuality as it is the clear and solid Aretino. Yet approach closely and the details fade out into areas of light and shadow.

What does this mean? What is the effect and purpose of this difference? See how this treatment affects and relates to the background. Titian's background is a clear area of color, not solid color but still forming something of an impenetrable wall. Against this wall the figure stands, clear and solid. He is weighty and impressive. His rich clothes indicate his social status (in fact, Titian never painted anyone of a social class other than the wealthy and powerful). Their texture is clear and precise and enjoyed, metal chain, heavy silk, thick fur. The eyes are clearly drawn and look out arrogantly from the figure.

Again [consider] Rembrandt's picture. Here the background is not solid but is a mysterious depth of shadow, shot through with flashes of red and gold. . . . Neither the figure nor the background is separate but the one dissolves into the other. See now the relevance of the lack of lines. There is no clear line setting the figure off from the background, but the figure fades out at the edge and is absorbed into the background. Similarly, the eyes are deep pools of shadow gazing out steadily and reflectively.

Titian's figure is powerful, assertive, vigorous and above all self-contained, independent, self-sufficient. This is a clearly defined doctrine of man, man as master, man as sufficient unto himself. This man is no part of and is not dependent on anything beyond himself. This is a statement of the nature of man that is not Christian but secular and pagan.

Rembrandt's figure, on the other hand, does not stand out from a positive background wall but is immersed in the immensity of a mysterious space. He is not weighty and assertive, he is isolated and lonely in the infinity of the space around him.

He does not lose his bodily form. The wholeness of the figure is presented, accurately and lovingly. Yet, again, the figure and its dress are not presented simply for delight in their physical texture as in Titian but are transfigured into light.

This is a statement on the complex nature of man, that man is both body and spirit. A spirit or the spiritual cannot be painted, but the presence of something more than the physical can be suggested by transforming the material into light.

Without losing his hold on the natural world, he saw man in the world and built his greatest art on the revelation of men caught at the intersection of the timeless with time. The word to him was never the rational concept but the word of God which is "living and active, sharper than any two-edged sword, piercing to the division of soul and spirit,

of joints and marrow, and discerning the thoughts and intentions of the heart. And before him no creature is hidden, but all are open and laid bare to the eyes of him with whom we have to do." (Hebrews 4:12-13)

It is not possible to demonstrate the details of Rembrandt's doctrine of man from this one painting, but from a study of his whole life and work it is possible to say we have here Rembrandt expressing the Protestant doctrine of man. It is not the self-assertion and self-sufficiency of Titian's Aretino, nor the independence of Leonardo's apostles. It is not Tintoretto's dependence on the church but the loneliness of man faced with the infinite majesty of God. Man does not stand apart from God nor does he approach God only through and by means of the institution but is man (a real man, not a cipher) standing in awful loneliness before God. . . .

PIERO DELLA FRANCESCA AND EL GRECO

. . . The first picture of the Resurrection [**Plate** 4] was painted in 1462 by Piero in his home village of Borgo San Sepoloero. At first glance it seems to reproduce just what the artist might have thought the Resurrection actually looked like. It does not appear to be "abstract" in the sense of much modern art. Everything is easily recognized for what it is. The figure of Jesus stands up out of the tomb, the soldiers sleep and the whole landscape is filled with the glory of dawn. The same glory and beauty of the rising day become equally the glory and beauty of the rising Christ.

But closer examination shows that the picture isn't quite so realistic. The tomb that Christ actually came from was a cavelike excavation in a hill with a stone in front of the entrance. Here the tomb is an Italian sarcophagus. The uniforms of the soldiers are one-third Roman, one-third Italian and one-third imagination. They are closer together than they could possibly be in reality, their poses are definitely not those of natural sleep.

The landscape is not really natural but is petrified, solemn, quiet, under its light. Trees are stiff, unmoving. Perhaps unmovable is not too strong a word.

What does all this mean, in the language of art?

Let us begin the answer by looking at another change of reality. Look at the point of view, the point from which the spectator seems to see the scene. In the lower part of the picture the point of view is low. The spectator looks up at the soldiers from below. He looks up at the edge of the tomb. But he looks at Christ from directly in front, at the same level! The point of view has risen so that the sense of the physical action of the Resurrection is reproduced in the spectator himself.

This fits in well with the rest of the picture. The soldiers crowded together at the bottom of the picture fit into the space of the tomb and make a solid base for a pyramid that rises to its peak at the head of Christ. Again the upward movement is made immediately apparent.

The rigid landscape flows back away from the tomb and so does not contain the figures but serves only as a kind of "backdrop" for them. Thus the figure of Christ stands apart from nature, greater than nature, dominant over all. Not a movement distracts attention from this great figure. The whole world is steeped in stillness before its Lord.

The only movement is the suggestion of a movement completed—the leg of Jesus lifted up out of the tomb, accenting the driving force that has overcome the grave.

Everything adds up, not to a "picture" of the resurrection, but an interpretation of it. This he achieves in the language of the form. He creates in the spectator the sense of the ascending movement —but in the painting itself this is a statement translated into spatial terms.

The movement is less of an action, as in Tintoretto, than a fact, a thing, an object almost, that can be related into the spatial structure.

The picture is full of carefully detailed objects, yet they serve chiefly to define the space by the precision of their spacing. The picture is suffused with a limpid light but it is the space that contains it.

This is expression through pure geometry. Stillness and light, not the darkness of drama, are dominant here. Time is translated into timelessness. It is the transfiguration of time into the eternal. . . .

Few artists could be more unlike Piero than El Greco. His "Resurrection" [**Plate 3**] has no space, the light is unreal, overcoming darkness, the whole composition is dominated by movement. Yet each in its way is an authentic Christian interpretation of the Resurrection. Any human view, even great ones of this character, is partial and fragmentary and there is room for each.

One element that brings El Greco so close to the modern idiom is the virtual denial of space. In Leonardo and Piero alike the space goes away from the spectator. The frame of the picture is like the frame of a window through which the spectator looks into another world. This is a world apart from himself which moves him first by analogy with his own experience. It moves him, too, in the work of a master such as Piero, by the direct language of form, the pure geometry of forms in space. Yet the imagination is largely influenced by the fact that the picture space is away from the spectator.

Tintoretto sought a closer involvement of the spectator with the space of the picture. So he turned the direction of the action and the composition, overlapped edges and generally established a continuity between the spectator and the picture. There is an obvious difference in the conception, not only of art, but of man in these works: man as an independent unit in an additive whole or man as a component part of a continuous whole.

El Greco goes further, however, and with considerable force projects the picture out from the canvas. This doesn't go nearly so far as many contemporary painters whose pictures exist as forms in front of the canvas, but the picture doesn't exist behind the imaginary picture plane but is more like a hollow, shallow space opening emphatically forward. The bottom figure sprawls back, seemingly into the world of the spectator.

No little of the picture's disturbing quality, however, comes from the discontinuity of the picture with the world into which it is thrust. Leonardo's world or Piero's is a different world into which we look. Its difference does not disturb us because we are outsiders, spectators. Tintoretto's is like enough to our world to maintain a continuity, unlike enough to make things interesting. It is not discordant. El Greco, on the other hand, disturbs and upsets. He clashes with the ordinary world, he is discordant; not strident but piercing.

The compact space of the picture is jammed full of figures who do not depend on space for their reality but derive their formal existence from the flickering play of light and dark and color over the picture. The figure of Christ sets the tone and unites the light on which the other figures subsist. There is no attempt at representation of nature (although the essential motif of a figure in action is caught with precision in a different kind of gesture language). Rather the figures are like notes in a piece of visual music. They flame up within a pattern of colored shapes and lights that have a distinct and highly expressive pattern of their own.

This is not an attempt to recreate an event but to give a mystical vision of the event or rather the event's meaning under the category of eternity rather than time. Time is here not transformed but transcended. This is the inter-section of time with the timeless, quite the opposite movement from Rembrandt.

As Piero's style links with the modern in the expressive geometry of forms in space, so the decisive quality in El Greco is the direct expression of emotional states through forms that have a kind of distinctive and individual existence apart from the human forms they evoke. . . .

MODERN "ART" USES THE SAME LANGUAGE

. . . Even with these hints of the nature of the language of the older art, this account could not be considered complete without showing how modern art is a part [of] the language of Western painting. It appears to be different but it is actually a different way of using the same language.

For example, [consider] two "nonobjective" paintings (meaning there is no reference to an objective reality, no subject in the painting), one by the Russian Kandinsky, the other by the Dutchman Mondrian. Each has isolated a single strand that has always been a part of the language of Western painting.

Mondrian has concentrated exclusively on the language of pure geometric form, the relation of colored shapes. Kandinsky has concentrated exclusively on the direct expression of emotional states through the interaction of color. Both styles are developed in a highly personal fashion, yet neither was invented by these painters. Even in the samples shown in this chapter both have been seen as essential parts in a more complex style.

Each is a limited style but explored with great intelligence and subtlety. These two men had much to do with clarifying the vision of modern man, making it possible for the artist to develop his style without subservience to the subject. Since the style has been developed, artists should be able to return to subject matter with greater penetration to its essence rather than the bare reproduction of its surface appearance.

Most modern art shares one quality with these painters—a mistrust for space effects. So many modern paintings act from the surface of the painting outward. They crowd the spectator and when, as they often do, they use strong primary colors and distort or eliminate the appearance of the familiar world it is small wonder the average spectator is disturbed by the paintings. Yet none of this is capricious. It is all part of the necessity of artistic communication out of the life of modern man.

In the course of the nineteenth century, painting for the most part lost touch completely with any kind of reality. Making a painting was no longer a matter of interacting with reality, attaining a creative relation to reality in a given material. It became a matter of applying rules, and technical skill was the only thing that mattered.

The life of art, as the life of man, is in relation; the creative relation of the artist to reality by means of his material. These paintings were as lacking in life as it is possible for art works to be. They were skillfully executed, highly finished, closely imitative and completely dead.

To live the artist had to rebel. The myth of the artist as rebel is a recent one, imposed on him by a world that required him to do nothing but the slick imitations and the prurient, semi-respectable sex that characterized nineteenth-century painting. Many artists may continue the pose after it is unnecessary but originally rebellion against the authority of false standards was the only way he could survive as an artist.

The rebellion generally took the form of a concentrated, systematic development in depth of a limited aspect of the formal language. This gives modern art the aspect of variety that appears chaotic to the untrained observer.

The first to break free from the com-

pulsion of the academic were Manet and the Impressionists. Manet finally liberated the painting to live by its own nature. The Impressionist developed the single aspect of light effects, the "impression" made on the eye by light reflecting from objects. Monet was described as "Only an eye—but what an eye"!

Van Gogh sought the direct expression of emotional states through forms distorted and violently colored. Surrealism developed the imaginative side of the language, producing paintings that both express and evoke the world of dreams, visions, nightmares, terror and longing. The cubists reduced objects to their elemental geometric form and recombined these into highly decorative and revealing patterns.

Others sought to explore color as a language as unrelated to objective reality as music, and so produced painting with violently discordant color arrangements or with gently muted melodies in soft pastel colors. These are often combined with abstract shapes to add another dimension to painting or with scenes from the natural world to evoke the terror and horror that can be in life or else peace and order and serenity.

A similar attempt is often made with shapes in space or lines or texture (hence the incorporation of materials unfamiliar to art in the painting).

A significant indication of a possible return to a creative relation between the artist and the church can be seen in Matisse. Matisse, an unbeliever, had spent a lifetime exploring the harmony of colored shapes in as pure a style as modern art has produced. (When a spectator reproached him, saying, "That doesn't look like any woman I ever saw," Matisse placidly replied, "It isn't a woman. It's a painting.") In his late years he was asked to do a chapel at Vence in southern France. With the simplest of color schemes (mostly yellow, green and white), he produced a work of singular purity, clarity and simplicity.

It is only one aspect of the whole gospel but it is valid for all of that.

A comment on content and subject matter is worth adding. The dominant element in the chapel is the glass and the vestments and these are pure form, with no subject matter. Yet there is content communicated: a tender glory that is authentic to the Christian faith.

CEZANNE AND PICASSO

Only two modern artists, Cezanne and Picasso, have attempted a much more comprehensive style than the more narrowly concentrated development that is the rule among the moderns. They have done this in quite different ways. Cezanne faced the major formal problem of painting—the reconciliation of the essential two-dimensional character of the painting with the three-dimensional character of the represented objects. Some styles (e.g., Leonardo) destroy the two-dimensionality. Other styles (Byzantine and much of modern painting) are completely subservient to it. Cezanne sought to preserve the tension with fidelity to each, to translate three-dimensionality into two-dimensionality without loss. To this purpose he brought his tremendous command of color and mass. With a limited range of subject (landscape and still life, and occasionally figures) he created a style of coherence and strength that has established much of the order of modern art.

Cezanne's search for structure (structure in nature translated into the structure of painting) is paralleled by Picasso's search for expression. This search has led Picasso through a bewildering, almost fantastic, variety of styles, yet each apparent change in style develops from the common center of this concern by expressing the condition of modern man in the language of art.

In an early work, "The Acrobat's Family," Picasso made one of the great paintings of the century. It is significant in many ways, not least for its penetrating analysis of the real state of modern man when (1906) man's optimism about himself was as high as it has ever been.

Picasso chose as a subject a group from a circus. A circus is a little world in itself that can serve as an image of the large world and therefore had a special attraction for many artists. Many aspects of the circus could be chosen for the artist's purpose, but Picasso chooses the fact of their common life. The group of costumed performers, obviously a family, stand in a curving line. The mother is apart from the group, seated, closer to the earth. The persons are dressed for the performance but stand motionless, apart even from the equipment of their action. They are a family, the primal social unit, yet no person looks at another, all look blankly into emptiness. The earth is sterile, dead, empty.

If this is an image of the twentieth century, it is an image of a desolate loneliness, isolation, discontinuity. The relatedness of persons, of person to the fruitfulness of earth, is broken and without relation there is no life.

Picasso has continued to make the image of modern man even in his thrashing about from style to style. In the thirties, for example, he spent years in a work that culminated in his "Guernica" [Plate 5], a kind of final image of the destruction of humanness. At other times he explores decorative construction in his cubism, brutal primitiveness in his "African period," bizarre imagination in his "bone period" and many another twist and turn in the modern mind. His wartime pictures have a desolate and deformed deadness, and since the war his work has been characterized by a capricious lyricism. Rarely does an artist so precisely reflect his age and, at the same time, pursue the development of his formal language with such integrity.

ROUAULT AND MODERN CHRISTIAN ART

Picasso, however, does not make the only image of his age. Rouault [Plate 7],

143

the only great Christian artist of the century, is at the same time one of the great Christian artists of the Christian era. His formal language is worth comment. It is a commonplace of writing on Rouault that he once worked in a stained-glass factory and this influenced his style. Certainly there is a resemblance, for he uses heavy black lines within which are areas of glowing, rich colors. Yet, after the manner of the true artist, he has transmuted his influences. The line is not simply a support for the color areas but a powerful contour which in his case does not simply determine the meaningful edge but the expressive gesture of the figure reduced to its essential simplicity. Within this vigorous contour he has packed strong color in compact areas. These almost strain against the restraint of the lines and this interaction of line and color establishes so much of the dramatic structure of the picture. This quality of the dramatic (a literary term which is here made truly applicable to painting) gives Rouault his sensitive and powerful tool for penetrating the reality of the modern world but does not lose the sense of all that is common to the human condition. Contemporary painting in asserting its independence and, in fact, creating an art of real freedom and power, too often goes off an isolate subjectivity that evades the issues of man's humanity. Rouault seeks out the engagement but never lets his formal language decay.

Contemporary American painting is an art of considerable power and promise. The most publicized and influential of the numerous "schools" is abstract expressionism. Here an art that began as an interesting and potentially significant essay in technical means became a direct statement of subjective emotion. It is a limited art that quickly becomes repetitive.

Less exciting but probably more solid are the "abstract realists" such as Lyonel Feininger, John Marin, B. J. Nordfeldt, and Lamar Dodd. These men never lose touch with objective reality and so their abstractions are more solidly built and more individual.

A number of contemporary artists are turning to Christian subjects. Of these Rico Lebrun's "Crucifixion" is perhaps the best example. It is of very considerable significance that the modern artist, who has spent so much time in a veritable jungle of forms, should begin to see the Christian history as more than a pleasant story but as containing images significant of the modern condition.

So far most of these are humanistic renderings. The tragic dimensions of Christ's humanity are expressed with real sensitivity and perceptiveness. But it is his humanity alone and there is no sense of transcendence or redemption.

CHRISTIAN CATEGORIES AND THE INTERPRETATION OF ART

So far the analysis has, within human competence, concerned itself with factors based on objective instruments of criticism. The specifically Christian categories suggested in the Prologue are more subjective and rest on standards that could have little acceptability beyond the Christian community. Yet the judicious use of them may have something to do with the place of art in the general experience of the Christian.

It is a difficult thing to designate the arts of creation. Man is no longer in the Garden and can never quite see the world in the joyous freshness of its creation. He is always touched by the fall. Yet the artist above all cultivates the innocence and directness of vision that are associated with unfallen nature.

Much of the music of Mozart has this quality of joy in the things that are simply because they are.

In the visual arts this category can be found in much of Gothic art where nature and wit are found together even in noble and austere monuments. In the Northern Renaissance (Italy was nearly always too preoccupied with

Plate 1. Leonardo da Vinci, THE LAST SUPPER.

Plate 2. Tintoretto, THE LAST SUPPER.

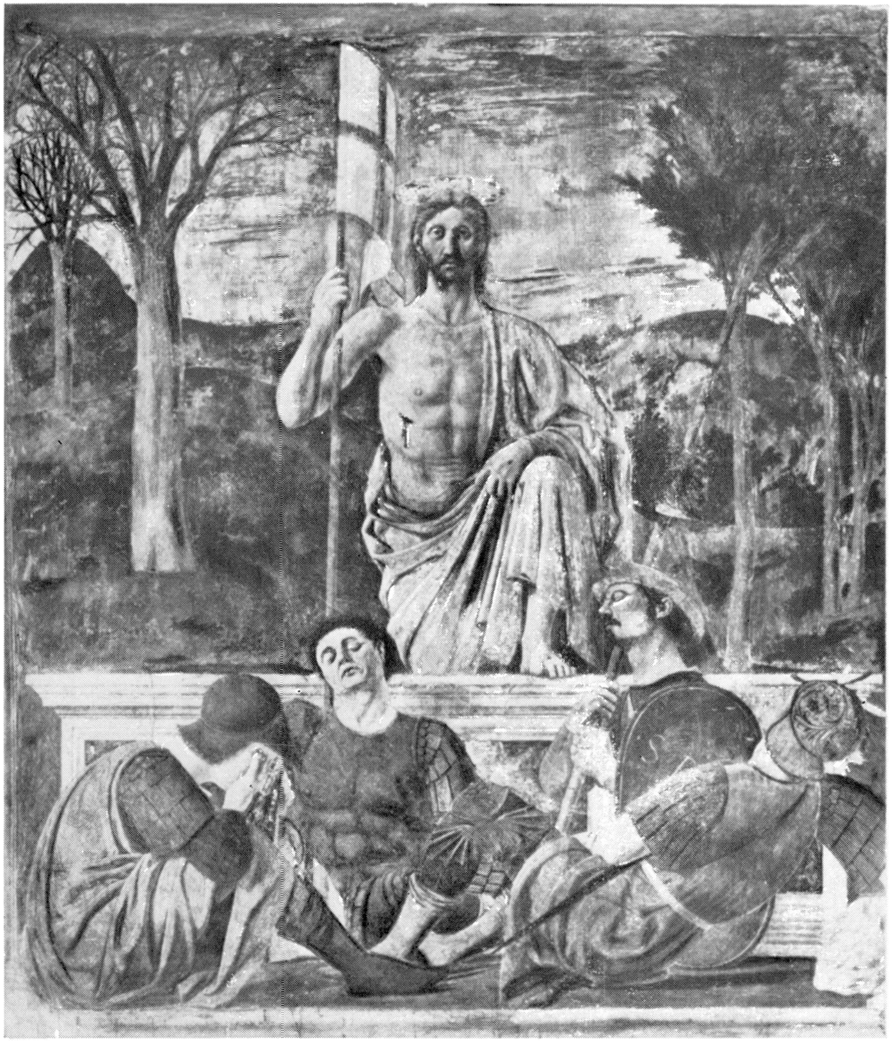

Courtesy of Alinari-Art Reference Bureau.

Plate 4. Piero della Francesca, THE RESURRECTION.

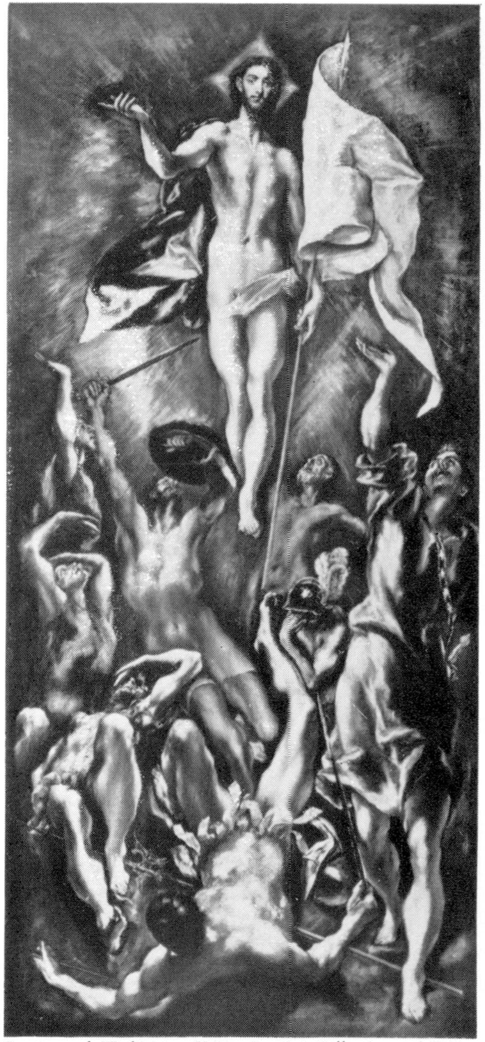

Courtesy of Washington University Art Collection and Piaget, St. Louis.

Plate 3. El Greco, THE RESURRECTION.

Plate 5. Pablo Picasso, GUERNICA (mural), 1937.

Plate 6. Peter Paul Rubens, LANDSCAPE WITH AN AVENUE OF TREES.

Plate 7. Georges Rouault, "The just, like sandalwood, perfume the axe that strikes them." Plate 46 from MISERERE, 1926.

intellect and structure) the whole of nature and the works of man seem to vibrate with a light from the face of the creator God.

A humbler form of it is found in seventeenth-century Holland where the things man has made are seen in their singular thingness under the glowing light of the sky. Much of this painting is ostentatious display and exhibited skill but much is an astonished loving of the things that are.

In our own day an ancient innocent like Grandma Moses catches the fresh innocence that a child sees but only an adult can state.

In a less simple way Rouault transcended the tragedy of his early work and his late landscapes glow with the sense of a new earth. Yet it is less the earth of the Garden of Eden than it is the garden where the tomb was on Easter morning and thus these works belong in a later category.

Those arts that proceed from man's character, as created in the image of God, are both larger in number and easier to find. They include much of those discussed in this book, man with his sovereign intelligence searching the mystery of life and imposing this determined order on the disorder of his material. Cezanne and Piero are distinctive examples of this quality but, in their way, all the others show it.

The arts of the fall present a different problem. There are those who explore the fall of man. These are not the works that simply acknowledge the existence of sinners as a detective story uses the fact of criminals as something that is mechanically a part of life yet not affecting the substance of it. Properly the artist in this category is the one who sees sin as part of the substance of the heart of man, built into his being. They are the men who engage the very stuff of life, the tragic poets and music makers. In the visual arts there were the late Gothic sculptors, some of the great Renaissance artists who could see beyond the simple humanism (Michelangelo in the Medici chapel, for example). Then, for another example, Goya, and in our own day Picasso and Rouault of the Miserere and the early works showing prostitutes and judges.

Yet art cannot only analyze the sin of man. As a human enterprise it manifests that sin. All that man does tends to some extreme that would destroy him if it comes into existence. Examples of this can be seen in the consuming sexuality of much Indian art that sees man as only a process in nature. Or some Roman art that asserts the pure brutality of power. Or again some forms of modern art that would make the artist as God creating from nothing.

God in his infinite wisdom can use what he will as an instrument of redemption, and it is not necessarily what man would suggest. Yet in his categories man can set certain standards. It isn't sufficient for a man to describe the redemptive acts. His work must embody the structure of events out of which the work of redemption could proceed. This means encompassing the great tensions that are the Christian description of the order of things: matter and soul or, better, enspirited matter; sin and sanctity; tragedy and triumph. No purely tragic work can be in the order of redemption for it is only tragedy redeemed that can be fully loyal to the redeeming Lord.

Of these are the great dramas like "King Lear" and the music like Bach's "St. Matthew Passion." It includes certain sculptures on Chartres cathedral, Donatello's "Pulpits" and Michelangelo's "Rondanini Pieta," Titian's "Flagellation and Pieta"; all of Rembrandt's late work and Grünewald's "Crucifixion."

In our own day it is only Rouault's late work, especially the great landscapes of the fifties. Here the tragedy has become a "peace out of pain," and all

145

nature glows in the light out of darkness of the rebirth of Creation at Easter. These are not just landscapes recording

nature. They are hymns to the glory of the God who could say, "Behold I make all things new."

EMIL BRUNNER

The Religious Soil Necessary to Art*

Human activity is not merely working, producing useful things which are necessary for the preservation of life. The human spirit transcends this sphere of vital necessity. Man decorates his home, he adorns his garment and his garden, he builds not only a solid, but a beautiful house, he carves, he draws, he paints without any useful purpose, merely from the inner drive for beauty and self-expression. He makes poetry, he sings, he invents stories, he acts plays. If we ask for a word embracing all that, it seems to be again, as in the case of science, the German language alone which dares to form this all-comprehensive concept of *Kunst,* whilst the English and French, following the Latin tradition, speak of the liberal arts in the plural, including in them also what the German calls *Geisteswissenschaften.* This daring, comprehending conception, which combines the arts of the eye with those of the ear, has the great merit of leading our attention to something common in them all, the element of creativity, which is detached from all usefulness and intent merely upon creating beautiful work for the enjoyment of its beauty.

Many attempts have been made to solve the riddle why men do all this.

It cannot be our task to add one more to a hundred existing theories of art, but merely to see how, from the Christian faith, this most mysterious and at the same time most enjoyable phenomenon of culture is to be understood and what its relation is to the Christian faith.

At first sight, art seems to be wholly independent of religion. *Kunst* comes from *können;* a *Künstler* is a man who can do something that others cannot. Similarly we use the word artist, sometimes in a very general sense. We speak of the art of riding, of skating, of tailoring, and so on. But we are conscious that by art in the proper sense we mean something higher. Mere virtuosity is not yet art, although the transition may be gradual. We speak of art in the proper sense where works of permanent value are created. Often art has been defined as the production of the beautiful, and therefore the secret of art has been identified with the secret of beauty. But the idea of beauty seems inadequate to indicate the mystery of art. What has Hamlet or King Lear, what has Goya's "Bull Fight", what has Strauss' "Eulenspiegel" to do with beauty? Beauty is a

* Reprinted with the permission of Charles Scribner's Sons and James Nisbet Company from *Christianity and Civilisation,* Volume II, pages 72-85, by Emil Brunner. Copyright 1949, Charles Scribner's Sons.

fascinating mystery, but art is more mysterious than beauty.

Why do men create works of art? We put aside all accidental motives, such as gaining one's living, love of fame and power. The work of art is so much the greater as these motives are less prominent. Art is surrender to something supra-personal. It originates from an inner urge. It is pledged to a spiritual "ought" which is almost as severe as the moral one; we speak of artistic conscience. We honour Rembrandt who, in his early days a spoilt and prosperous favourite of society, in his later years lost the favour of the public because he painted according to his artistic conscience without any compromise with the taste of the public, so that he died in poverty.

We know that the Aristotelian theory, which gives first place to the imitation of nature, is inadequate, even for the explanation of painting, whilst in all other arts the model of nature hardly plays any role. In any case, whether it be in poetry, painting or music, the work of art is the expression of something inward, passing on that inwardness to the one who enjoys it. Art therefore, in all its branches, is expression capable of impressing. But in distinction from speech, it is without direct reference to the "receiver". It has an objective intention, making it, to a certain degree, independent and indifferent as to whether there is somebody who might enjoy it or not. In medieval glass paintings there are parts which can normally hardly be seen by anybody but which are just as carefully designed and painted as the visible parts. The artistic expression is so united with the inward feeling, that both cannot be detached from each other. The artistic form is externalised inwardness. The true artist does not like to speak of an "idea" of his work, he is—emphatically—not a double of the philosopher. Form and inwardness are one. The artist creating his work creates a second reality distinguished from nature by its anthropomorphism. It is materialised soul and exalted nature. The work of art is the product of imagination. The German word for imagination, *Einbildung,* is an aesthetics in a nutshell. The power of imagination is the capacity to externalise inwardness or to spiritualise matter. Once more we ask: Why do men do this? And why do others enjoy the results? A negative reason is obvious: They want to transcend existing reality because for some reason it does not satisfy. Artistic creation is somehow a correction and completion of reality. The dramas of Shakespeare show us people like ourselves. Why then this duplication of the human tragedy and comedy? The persons of Shakespeare's tragedies are no duplicates of those of every-day experience, they are the products of a sifting enhancement which cuts away what is casual and enlarges the essential. Art is condensation, omitting the unimportant and magnifying the important; art intensifies and elates, it brings order to the chaotic, gives form to the casual and shape to the shapeless, it exalts and ennobles the material reality to which it gives form.

What, for instance, is the meaning of the verse in poetry? If man wants to say something important, he tries to make as great a distance as possible between that and mere talk. He wants to liberate his speech from every-day casualness, he gives it *gebundene Form.* The free submission under a law, the mounting of springing life in a self-chosen discipline, the firm shape of that which otherwise is shapeless, gives his speech lasting form, nobility.

Art, then, is the attempt of man to raise himself out of the casualness, lowness, transitoriness of every-day life to a higher existence. This is the elevating effect of all art whatever its content may be. There is nothing elevating in the content of Othello, but in its form, which gives to human passion a purity, a necessity and an intensity by which

147

it represents a higher form of existence. All art strives with more or less success after perfection which cannot be found in reality. *Art is an imaginary elevation of life in the direction of the perfect.*

Imaginary indeed! Of course a Greek temple or a Gothic cathedral are not imaginary, but very real, built of massive blocks. But the beauty of this work is an imaginary elevation of life, a perfection which does not belong to ordinary existence but stands apart. Art does not change our life. The aesthetic solution of a problem by which a poet gets rid of it is no real solution, no real liberation. Art originates from and lives within imagination; it is an imaginary reality, similar to the dream. As long as we dream happily, happiness is real, but when we awake this happiness is gone. It cannot be integrated into our reality; it stands outside of that continuity which we call reality. Reality is the same to-day and to-morrow, but the dream of to-night will not be the dream of to-morrow. When the sound of Bach's Double Violin Concerto, which filled me with heavenly joy, has faded away, it still somehow remains with me for a while, like a beautiful dream when I awake. But then comes reality which is not heavenly joy, but sorrow and conflict, which the beauty of Bach's Concerto cannot alter.

This is the limit of art. It is imaginary, *playing perfection.* It is the greatness and the delight of art to be perfection; it is its limitation to be merely imaginary perfection. It is the danger of art that it is so powerful although imaginary. Is there really a danger in art? Is art not that one thing in our life for which we can be thankful and which we can enjoy without reserve? This indeed is our first response: as Christians we say: art is one of the great gifts of God the Creator. Works of art are not produced as a matter of course. Talent or genius is the decisive element, and this is a gift of the Creator. It is not in vain that the word "talent" is taken from the

Biblical parable which speaks of trustee-ship. What then is its danger? It lies close to its very essence. Its essence is to be imaginary, its danger is that imaginary perfection may be confounded with real perfection. Art then becomes a substitute for religion. One looks for something in art, which it is not able to give: real elevation, real perfection. This confusion is what we call aestheticism. Art is not to be blamed for it, and it can be said that the great artists have rarely become victims of this temptation. This confusion of imagination with reality happens more often to those who enjoy art than to the productive genius.

Furthermore, it must be said that art does not really displace religion, but rather fills a vacuum in the soul which ought to be filled by faith. But we cannot evade the question whether there is not a fundamental opposition between art and faith, as expressed in the second commandment of the Decalogue. "Thou shalt not make unto Thee a graven image, nor the likeness of anything that is in heaven above, or that is in the earth beneath, or that is in the water under the earth." Can the believer in face of this unambiguous prohibition enjoy art without reserve? One might reply that the divine prohibition is not referred to art as such but to idolatry, that is, to pantheistic confusion of Creator and creation. The question, however, remains whether art as the work of imagination and as imaginary perfection does not involve a fundamental conflict with faith in the invisible perfect One from whom alone comes real perfection. Is there not a secret opposition between the enjoyment of heavenly beauty in the imaginary world of art and the hope in the real heavenly redemption? Is not art, at its best, some kind of parallel to pantheistic mysticism, both being an anticipation of heavenly bliss here and now?

It seems to me, we must not be extreme on either side. The true artist is no ecstatic who forgets about reality.

Great art has always been rather tragic than happy, just as we can say that tragedy is the highest form of art. In tragedy and in all tragic art, man is conscious of his predicament and of his need for redemption. It is only the artist of the second rank who wants to deceive men and himself with the belief that art itself can solve the contradictions of human reality. One great poet, defining the origin and essence of his art, says: *und wo der Mensch in seiner Qual verstummt, gab mir ein Gott zu sagen, was ich leide*. We need not therefore take too seriously that mystical or pantheistic danger, great as it may be, but we must take account of the opposite possibility that art can, by its capacity to intensify and to emphasise the essential, show to man with particular impressiveness his real situation as a creature needing redemption.

We have to face the problem of Christian art. First of all, Christian art is not merely a possibility, but a historical reality. Since the decay of the Roman Empire during more than a thousand years, European art has been "Christian". At first, this does not mean more than that the majority of the works of architecture in this era were Christian churches, from the Byzantine basilicas of Ravenna and Monreale to St. Peter's in Rome and the baroque churches of Germany and Austria. It means, furthermore, that the sculpture of these centuries is primarily Church decoration, that the subject-matter of painting, too, is drawn mostly from Biblical stories of Christian legends, that poetry and music, up to the time of Bach, are dedicated to the service of Church life. It is, then, an indubitable fact—although a fact which needs interpretation—that during more than ten centuries art in all its aspects was an expression primarily Christian in essence and served the Christian Church. The question remains, however, in what sense we can speak of Christian art.

We should beware from the outset of two extreme views: the one is a naïve confusion of Christian art with art, the contents of which or the themes of which are Christian. When certain painters of the 16th century Renaissance treat Biblical themes or Christian legend, it is obvious that this connection between Art and Christianity is merely an outward and casual one. Sometimes, as in the case of the great Peter Breughel, one might even call this relation ironical. Even if we allow for the fact that the religious expression of an Italian is, in any case, more declamatory and dramatic than that of a North European, and even if we grant that Roman Catholic Christianity in itself is more externalised than Protestant, still we must confess that there is a kind of Renaissance art which, in spite of its Christian content, cannot really be called Christian. On the other hand, we cannot acknowledge the formalist theory that it is of no importance for art to have a Christian content or indeed any content at all. Here, then, we are up against the difficult problem of form and content in art.

First, it cannot be denied that in art form and not content is primary. It is great art, when van Gogh paints a sunflower, when Daumier paints a boulevard scene. It is not great art when Kaulbach, in an enormous picture, interprets the Reformation. One might say, then, the content is nothing and form everything. Furthermore, what should "content" mean in pure music? But, on the other hand, could you seriously contend that it does not matter whether Michelangelo chooses as his object the Biblical story of Creation and the Fall or treats some scene of every-day life? Do you think that Bach could express his deepest feelings, as in his B Minor Mass, just as well by using some banal worldly text? Or that it was by chance that Rembrandt in his later years turned more and more exclusively to Biblical stories? What, after all, is form and content when an inward world has to be visibly or audibly incarnated? The relation between art and religion, between art and Christian faith, cannot be accidental, even though there exists supreme art without any noticeable relation to religion. There must be some deep connection between art and religion and, in particular, between art and Christian faith. What is it?

Let us start with Greek tragedy. It may not be of decisive importance that the Greek theatre grew out of a religious ceremony, just as the great manifestation of Greek architecture and sculpture originated from religious life. But tragedy as such—the phenomenon of the tragic—cannot be understood without man's relation to the moral order of the world. Without tragic guilt, no tragedy. It is not by chance that a Christian tragedy does not exist. Not because there was not enough dramatic talent to form a tragedy, but because Christian faith and the tragic understanding of life are irreconcilable. This form of art then, tragedy, has a definitely religious but certainly no Christian basis. How could you separate here form and content? Take a parallel from within Christian times: the Biblical oratorio and the musical mass, where the text supplies incomparable musical possibilities. Certainly, there do exist oratoria of an entirely secular character; the musical form of an oratorio is not necessarily tied to the Christian content. But it cannot be a matter of chance that so many of the greatest works of music are those in which Christian texts are interpreted by music.

Even if we understand musical art merely from the point of view of dynamic expression, we would still have to take account of the fact that there are emotions of the soul, tensions and contrasts, and therefore a dynamism which cannot be found apart from religious, nay, even Christian faith. If you think of the "Sanctus" or the "Kyrie eleison" of Bach's Mass, you can hardly deny that such music could not be created but by a deeply Christian composer.

Take another example: It is hardly to be denied that the Roman Catholic faith has a closer relation to the arts of the eye than the Protestant, that, on the other hand, Protestant church music has reached heights which no Catholic composition has attained to. Roman Catholic faith tends to the visual, its relation to the visible is essentially positive, whilst Evangelical faith clings to the Word and has only an indirect and uncertain relation to the visible. That is why painting disappears in the Protestant Church, whilst church music acquires an importance which it never had before.

The relation between art and religion, art and Biblical faith, must not be studied merely to answer the question as to what importance the religious element has for art; but also from the other viewpoint, to answer the question whether religion and Christian faith do not in themselves tend towards artistic expression. The Christian community through the ages has been a singing community. Christian worship is hardly thinkable without a hymn, psalm, chorale or anthem. The praise of God, joyful thanks, and passionate supplication of the congregation almost necessarily take shape in singing. There is hardly a more alarming, though infallible criterion of the decline of Christian community life than the decadence of Christian church music in the last two centuries. The Christian hymns that have been invented and sung during the last century have little to do with art, whilst the choral melodies which abounded in the first two centuries of the Reformation churches were works of art of the first order; even Bach, who did not himself produce one, showed almost envious admiration of them.

Not every live Christian is *ipso facto* also a church musician, but where musical talent comes within the life-stream of faith and within the magnetic field of a true Christian community, church music is born inevitably. The same can

150

be said with regard to the relation of faith and poetic form. All the great prophets of Israel, from Amos to the anonymous writer of the exile, were also great poets. The weakening of poetic power goes hand in hand with the weakening of prophetic originality in the later Old Testament prophets. There is hardly a word of Jesus which is not a little poem and some of His parables are poetry of the highest order. We can hardly imagine Luther's prophetic genius apart from the powerful rhythm of his hymn, "A mighty fortress is our God". That is Luther! Who is able to delimit here prophetic faith and poetic expression? Both are so united in this hymn that the power of faith and the power of expression cannot be distinguished.

A similar relation is to be observed conversely: in respect of *im*pression. The religious hymn is not merely a necessary expression of faith, but also an effective means of faith. It is as if sacred music "turned the soul" for faith. As the Marseillaise was a powerful factor in spreading the spirit of the French Revolution, in a similar way really Christian music can kindle faith. The music of Bach and Schütz has this effect, but not that of Wagner. There are works of Bach to which, though they are pure music without any text, one could add the adequate Biblical words. We know by now that his most abstract composition, *Die Kunst der Fuge,* is Christian theology expressed in the form of immensely complicated fugues.

Something similar is a common experience in the sphere of architecture. A Gothic cathedral generates a certain kind of reverent feeling, without there being any direct indications of the cultus. The very structure of the Gothic church, being an expression of medieval religion and theology, impresses the mind with that same spirit from which it originates. It is utterly inept to build a modern bank in Gothic style. If the so-called Gothic civil architecture of the Middle Ages does not have this character of dissonance, it is because in that era all life was permeated by the spirit of its theology and piety. How far, however, this Gothic structure is Christian, and how far neoplatonic mysticism is its root, is another question.

If then there exists an indubitable relation between faith and art on the side of expression as well as on that of impression, we cannot avoid the question what the fate of art will be in a thoroughly secularised society where faith has ceased to be a formative factor. Indeed, this question is not merely academic in our time. It would not be historically correct to claim, on the basis of what has been said before, that the decline of religion must necessarily carry with it the decay of art. History gives many clear examples to the contrary. Greek art reached its zenith at a time when religion had already begun to decay. The same is true of Renaissance art in the 16th century, and French painting was at its best in the age where positivist and even materialist philosophy dominated. Again; a similar observation can be made about German music from the time of Mozart onwards, the only exception, confirming the rule, being Bruckner. And if instead of speaking of epochs we think in terms of individual artists, it would be hard to discover any definite proportion between artistic power and perfection on the one hand, and religious intensity on the other. Alongside Michelangelo and Fra Angelico, we have Raphael, Leonardo and Titian; alongside Rembrandt, we have Peter Breughel and Vermeer; alongside Bach, we have Gluck and Strauss, not to speak of certain schools of first-rate art with a decidedly frivolous conception of life as background.

Let us remember once more that *Kunst* comes from *können,* that artistic genius is a natural disposition, and as such indifferent to religion or any philosophy of life. Whether a man who is born with creative genius is deeply religious or indifferent to religion, does not in itself increase or diminish his creative capacity. But in spite of this we venture to contend that in a society where religious faith is dead, or has been dead for a while, art also decays. It is difficult to prove this assertion from history, because, whilst there have been times of religious decline, there never has been an epoch of predominant atheism. There may be one exception to this rule: our own age, as far as certain countries are concerned. But this period has not yet lasted long enough for us to draw definite conclusions. All the same our assertion does not hang in the air, for there are strong reasons for its validity.

Whilst it cannot be said that faith or religious power is a necessary presupposition of art, two statements can hardly be denied. First, that creative genius combined with religious depth produces ultimate artistic possibilities which otherwise do not exist. Secondly, no artistic life can thrive on dehumanised soil. Where men are no longer capable of deep and great feelings, where the spiritual horizon has lost infinity, where the understanding of life is devoid of all metaphysical or religious depth, art cannot but degenerate to mere virtuosity, and creative originality exhausts itself in inventions which may be witty, striking or pleasant, but which cannot move the depth of the heart. The grand passions, which are the source of all genuine art, are not a phenomenon of merely psychological dynamic. Grand passions are not merely a matter of temperament or instinct. Their greatness originates not from natural dispositions but from spiritual tensions which do not exist any more where thinking clings to the surface of things.

We touched on this point when we spoke about tragedy. Christian faith in itself cannot accept the tragic view; but being in itself the victory over tragedy, it presupposes the understanding of the tragic. Where there is neither understanding of the tragic nor Christian

faith, where all relation to something transcendent and absolute has disappeared, where crude naturalism and materialism have taken the place of religion and metaphysics, great passions, deep feelings and those mysterious longings of the soul out of which great art is born, disappear also. The decay of the truly human necessarily brings with it the decay of beauty and mystery. This decay of the truly human, however, cannot be avoided in a materialistic world. When man is cut off from the third dimension of depth, when he lives on the surface of mere utility, animal instinct and economic rationality, the element of humanity vanishes. This assertion, I think, has been sufficiently proved in the first series of these lectures.

We now are in a position to see the dual fact: art in its dependence on, and its independence of, religion. The dependence is absolute only in an indirect sense, relative and partial in the direct sense. In so far as the depth of human existence is founded ultimately in the "third dimension", in religion and metaphysics, and in so far as the Christian faith produces the deepest and most human kind of existence, art is dependent on it. In so far, however, as in the individual case and for a certain time this deep humanity can exist after the faith which has produced it has disappeared, like an evening light after sunset, like the marvellous *Abendrot* in our Swiss Alps, art can persist for a certain while in individuals or during a whole generation after the sunset of faith. But this *Abendrot* cannot be of long duration. The stock of human values created in a time of faith is soon exhausted in a time of faithlessness and with it the possibility of real art. The humanity of man is much more historical than we usually think, and that is true of art.

I think we are justified in applying this general observation to our time, although we have to do it with great caution. If what I have just said is correct, we should expect that the secularisation of modern mankind—which, although fortunately not complete, is the characteristic feature of the modern age—must have its effects on art. And we should guess that this effect must be a certain loss of depth and at the same time a tendency in two directions: barbarism or crudeness as a result of the lost distinction between man and animal nature on the one hand, and a certain abstractness as a result of formalism, because of the disappearance of metaphysical and religious content. Now, with all the reserve which my little knowledge of contemporary art puts upon me, I think that these tendencies are indeed quite obvious in the artistic production of our time, although the reaction against them is also to be felt, and in a quite remarkable degree. But this reaction against barbarism and formalism is at the same time also a reaction against secularism and to this extent proves our thesis.

Let me point out another feature of modern art which is a necessary result of what I called the loss of the third dimension of depth. Where men lose their religious faith, art is apt to take the place of religion. That danger, which as we have just seen is immanent in all art, becomes real. Art itself becomes the highest value, aestheticism becomes the religion of the time. It can hardly be denied that this is true for a good many of our contemporaries. The imaginary perfection and elevation of life which art gives them becomes a substitute for real salvation. They live in their imaginary world of artistic creation as in a sort of earthly heaven or paradise, measuring all life by their art and artistic genius. If I am not wrong, this is one of the elements which account for the sad condition of the French nation. The prevalent aestheticism of French cultural life has broken or at least seriously damaged its moral backbone. The religion of art is a poor substitute for true religion as a basis of civilisation.

Still, real faith has not vanished. On the contrary, it is just in the sphere of modern art that we find, along with barbarism and formalism, most impressive signs of a spiritual awakening parallel to the reawakening of Christian theology and religious philosophy. Perhaps we may venture to say that the art of our time confirms what we have seen happening in other fields, that the low point of the secularist movement is already passed. At any rate, the battle is on and all of us are engaged in it.

To close—let me take up once more the question raised in the beginning. Why do men create works of art? What is the function of art in the human household? For the creative artist himself this question hardly exists. To him art is a "calling". To some of the greatest artists it is a divine calling. They follow an inward "must" which permits no further derivation except the religious one. For most men, however, who are not artists, but mere lovers of art, the answer is, from the Christian point of view: art is the noblest form of resting from the struggle of life, closely related with the quiet of the Sabbath in the Biblical sense. All work, even the highest spiritual work, produces a kind of hardness and cramp. The man who knows nothing but work becomes soulless. Art is the noblest means of re-creation. It cannot redeem our soul, but it can "tune the heart", even for the highest: for communion with God. It never produces or creates faith, but it can support the Word of the Gospel, which creates faith. It can open the closed soul and help it to relax in the most human way from the stress of every-day life. That is why we sing in our church services and why we should not underestimate the function of real church music. But apart from this highest function, man needs relaxation, especially if he is engaged in intellectual work. Art is the beneficent mediator between spirit and sensuality. It is a spiritualisation of the sensual and the sensualisation of the spiritual. It is a necessity primarily for those who do not live in immediate contact with nature. Art is therefore, before all, a necessity for the city man. What

Luther and Bach have said of music is true of all art: it is the servant of God to help his sorrowful creatures, to give them joy worthy of their destiny.

PAUL TILLICH

The Religious Style of Modern Art*

To do justice to my subject I should really write three books—one on existentialism, one on art, and one on religion. Then I should relate these three to each other. Here, however, all this has to be done in the narrow space of a single chapter.

MEANING AND HISTORY OF EXISTENTIALISM

Let me start with the first "book." First, I want to devote a few words to what I believe existentialism is, just as the other contributors to this volume have given some description or definition of what they understand by existentialism. I distinguish three meanings of this term: existentialism as an element in all important human thinking, existentialism as a revolt against some features of the industrial society of the nineteenth century, and existentialism as a mirror of the situation of sensitive human beings in our twentieth century. Of course the main emphasis will be on the last meaning of this term. I believe that most creative art, literature and

philosophy in the twentieth century is in its very essence existentialist. And this is the reason why I have proposed to address myself to existentialist elements in recent visual art. I believe that the people for whom visual impressions are important will perhaps understand what existentialism means better by looking at modern art than by reading recent philosophers.

Existentialism as a universal element in all thinking is the attempt of man to describe his existence and its conflicts, the origin of these conflicts, and the anticipations of overcoming them. In this sense, the first classical philosopher who had many existentialist elements in his thinking was Plato. I refer here especially to those instances where he employs mythology, for existence, in distinction from essence (from what man essentially is), cannot be derived in terms of necessity from his essential nature. Existence is that which stands against essence although it is dependent on essence. Plato uses existentialist terms when he speaks of the transition from existence to essence or from essence to

* From "Existential Aspects of Modern Art" by Paul Tillich, reprinted with the permission of Charles Scribner's Sons from *Christianity and the Existentialists,* edited by Carl Michalson. Copyright © 1956 Charles Scribner's Sons; pp. 128-47.

existence; when he speaks of the fall of the souls; when he speaks of the seeming but not true character of the world of appearances and opinions; or when he speaks of the bondage of the soul in the cave of shadows. In many other cases he brings into his philosophy existentialist elements, and he is wise enough to know that this cannot be done in terms of essentialist analysis.

There are existentialist elements in early Christian theology—very outspoken elements for instance in Augustine and his doctrine of man's estrangement from his true essence, from his union with God as his creative ground. There are existentialist elements in classical theology, in the Middle Ages, and in Protestantism. Wherever man's predicament is described either theologically or philosophically, either poetically or artistically, there we have existentialist elements. This is the first meaning of this word.

The second meaning is existentialism as a revolt. It is a revolt which started almost at the moment when modern industrial society found its fundamental concepts, in the seventeenth century. The man who first expressed these elements as a revolt was Pascal, although at the same time he made great contributions to the development of modern thinking by his mathematical discoveries. From Pascal on, we have had an uninterrupted series of men who repeated this protest against the attitude of industrial society. Man was considered to be only a part, an element in the great machine of the Newtonian World, and, later on, an element in the great social process of production and consumption in which we all are now living. The protest against this view was a protest of the existing man, of man in his estrangement, his finitude, in his feeling of guilt and meaninglessness. It was a protest against the world view in which man is nothing but a piece of an all-embracing mechanical reality, be it in physical terms, be it in economic or sociological terms, or even be it in psychological terms. This protest was continued in the nineteenth century by the founders of existentialism (in the special sense of the word). Schelling, in his old age, realized that he had to protest not only against his former pupil and friend, Hegel, but also against the Schelling of his earlier years, and introduced most of the categories in which present day existentialism is thinking. From him, people like Kierkegaard, Engels, and Feuerbach took concepts of anti-essentialist philosophy. These protesting men—Kierkegaard, Marx, Feuerbach, Trendelenburg, later Nietzsche, and at the end of the century people like Bergson and Whitehead—these are people who wanted to save human existence from being swallowed by the essential structure of industrial society in which man was in danger of becoming a thing.

With the beginning of the twentieth century this feeling became much more universal. The people whom I have just cited were lonely prophets, often in despair, often at the boundary line of insanity in their desperate and futile fight against the over-powering forms of modern industrial society. In the twentieth century the outcry of existentialism became universal. It became the subject matter of some great philosophers, such as Heidegger, Jaspers, Sartre, Marcel, and many others; it became a topic of the drama; it became effective in poetry. After some predecessors like Baudelaire and Rimbaud in the nineteenth century it has become widespread, and men like Eliot and Auden are widely known. It was expressed especially powerfully in the novel. In two of Kafka's main novels, *The Castle* and *The Trial,* we have descriptions. of the two fundamental anxieties. The anxiety of meaninglessness is described in *The Castle*. He himself, Mr. K., tries in vain to reach the sources of meaning which direct all life in the village in which he lives, and he never reaches them. The anxiety of guilt is described in *The*

Trial, where guilt is an objective factor. The protagonist does not know why he is accused, or who accuses him, he only knows he is accused. He is on trial, he cannot do anything against it, and finally the guilt overcomes him and brings him to judgment and death.

I believe that developments similar to these have taken place in the realm of art. And out of the different visual arts I want to take, not on principle, but for reasons of expediency, painting alone. Painting will reveal some of the innermost motives of existentialism if we are able to analyze the creations since the turn of the century in the right way. In order to do this I want to go immediately to the second "book" and say a few words about religion and about the relationship of religion and art.

LEVELS OF RELATION BETWEEN
RELIGION AND ART

Religion means being ultimately concerned, asking the question of "to be or not to be" with respect to the meaning of one's existence, and having symbols in which this question is answered. This is the largest and most basic concept of religion. And the whole development, not only of modern art but also of existentialism in all its realms —and that means of the culture of the twentieth century—is only possible if we understand that this is fundamentally what religion means: being ultimately concerned about one's own being, about one's self and one's world, about its meaning and its estrangement and its finitude. If this is religion, we must distinguish from it religion in a narrower sense, namely, religion as having a set of symbols, normally of divine beings or a divine being, having symbolic statements about activities of these gods or this god, having ritual activities and doctrinal formulations about their relationship to us. This is religion in the narrower sense, where religion is

156

identified first of all as a belief in the existence of a God, and then with intellectual and practical activities following out of this belief. When we speak about religion and art, we must speak in terms of both concepts.

When we hear the words, "religious art," we usually believe that one refers to particular religious symbols like pictures of Christ, pictures of the Holy Virgin and Child, pictures of Saints and their stories, and many other religious symbols. Now this is one meaning of religious art; but there is another following from the larger concept of religion, namely, art as an expression of an ultimate concern. Naturally, it will be an esthetic expression, an artistic expression, but it will be an expression of ultimate concern. And if we distinguish these two ways in which art can express religion, and religion can appear in art, then it is perhaps expedient to distinguish four levels of the relation of religion and art.

The first level is a style in which ultimate concern is not directly but only indirectly expressed. It is what we usually call secular art, and it has no religious content. It does not deal with the religious symbols and rites of any special religion. This first level deals with landscapes, with human scenes, with portraits, with events, with all kinds of things on the level of secular human existence.

Neither on the second level do we have religious contents—pictures of saints, or of Christ, or of the Holy Virgin. There are no sacred scenes, but there is a style, and the style is the form which expresses the meaning of the period. If you want to know what is the ultimate self-interpretation of an historical period, you must ask, "What kind of style is present in the artistic creations of this period." Style is the over-all form which, in the particular forms of every particular artist and of every particular school, is still visible as the over-all form; and this over-all form is the expression of that which unconsciously is present in this period as its self-interpretation, as the answer to the question of the ultimate meaning of its existence. Now the characteristic of this style is that there is something always breaking through out of the depths to the surface. Wherever this happens we have a style that is religious even if there is no religious content whatsoever depicted. I will come back to this again since it will be the center of our consideration. But first let me proceed to the third level.

The third level is the level of secular forms of non-religious style which nevertheless deals with religious content. These are pictures of Christ, pictures of the saints, of the Holy Virgin and the Holy Child. When we think of this third realm we immediately think of the art of the High Renaissance. It is a non-religious style dealing with religious content.

The fourth level is mainly the level on which religious style and religious content are united. That is an art which, in the most concrete sense, can be called religious art. It can be used for liturgical purposes or for private devotion. In it style and content agree. However, I must conclude this description of the fourth level with the question, "Is such a religious art possible today?" And with this question I return to the four levels and call to your attention a few examples.

1. *Non-religious Style, Non-religious Content.* For the first level I could cite two examples. The first is a picture by Jan Steen, "The World Upside Down." I recall another picture, very similar to this one. It also is an interior, with play, dance, drunkenness, love, and everything together—very dynamic, very vital, as was the old Dutch way at that time. I saw that picture in the National Gallery, two or three years ago, when I first started to think about a study on religion and art. I had wanted to look at religious pictures or at least the pictures where religious style is visible. But it so happened that I could not look away from that picture very similar to this one by Steen. I asked myself, "What does this picture express in terms of an ultimate interpretation of human existence?" And my answer was, "It too expresses power of being in terms of an unrestricted vitality in which the self-affirmation of life becomes almost ecstatic." Now one may say that this has nothing to do with religion. I cannot accept this. I may accept that it is only indirectly religious. It has neither a religious style, nor a completely secular style, nor has it any religious content. Nevertheless—and this is a Protestant principle—God is present in secular existence as much as he is present in sacred existence. There is no greater nearness to Him in the one than in the other, and using this as a yardstick for understanding pictures like this, I would say that this is the first level of the relation of religion and art, namely that level in which, in secular style and without religious content, power of being is visible, not directly, but indirectly. There is another example, a picture by Rubens with animals and landscape, "Return of the Prodigal." The landscapes of Rubens, for some mystical reasons, have always interested me philosophically. What is the matter with them? You are in them somehow, they take you in, you live in them, they give you a feeling for the cosmos in a rather dynamic way, though completely on the surface of colors and forms [**Plate 6**]. There is something in this landscape which you never would see without the painter, and that is what art has to do, anyway. Here another entire volume could start: namely, to show in symbols, taken from ordinary experience, a level of reality which cannot be grasped in any other way. If this were not the case, art would be unnecessary from the very beginning and should be abolished. But art is necessary. It is as necessary as knowledge and other forms of human spiritual life. It is necessary for it reveals

levels of reality, even in such secular objects which are, neither in style nor in content, religious.

2. *Religious Style, Non-religious Content: The Existentialist Level.* I come now to the second level, and this level is the existentialist level. The movement of modern existentialism in visual art starts with Cézanne in France. Let me relate one experience I had two years ago when I was in Paris. There was an exhibit of still lifes, starting with works from the sixteenth and seventeenth century and continuing through to the present day. Progressing in chronological order I noticed a strong trend towards the still life. In some way it became apparent that most modern art has transformed all of reality into forms of still life. What does this mean? It means that organic forms have disappeared, and with them has disappeared idealism which always is connected with the description of the organic forms. The forms of our existence are no more organic. They are atomistic, disrupted. These disrupted forms of our existence are taken by themselves by modern artists as the real elements of reality, and now these artists do a tremendous job with them. They reduce the colorful world of the impressionists and of the beautifying idealists of the past to more and more cubic forms. This treatment begins with Cézanne. Cubic forms are the unorganic forms out of which the world is constituted. But the artists do not accept the statement that these forms are only unorganic. Embodied in this very unorganic form is the power of being itself. In this way the disruptedness of expressionism, surrealism, and all the other recent forms of styles, such as cubism and futurism, is nothing else than an attempt to look into the depths of reality, below any surface and any beautification of the surface and any organic unity. It is the attempt to see the elements of reality as fundamental powers of being out of which reality is constructed.

158

Or, consider another artist, Van Gogh, and, for instance, his "Starry Night." Here again we have the character of going below the surface. It is a description of the creative powers of nature. It goes into the depths of reality where the forms are dynamically created. He does not accept the surface alone. Therefore he goes into those depths in which the tension of the forces creates nature. The same is expressed from the point of view of human society in Van Gogh's "Night Cafe." Here you see something I call late emptiness—only one figure. The waiter has left, and just one man is sitting there, and that is all. He represents, in all the beautiful colors you see, the horror of emptiness.

The Norwegian Munch could be added here. He has painted pictures not so much of emptiness—although this factor is also in them, but of horror, crime, shock, that which is uncanny, that which you cannot grasp. In this way, this Nordic man also became one of the existentialists, at the same time in which Strindberg wrote his great existentialist dramas with all the terrible tensions, sufferings, and anxieties.

Then there is Picasso. One of Picasso's most important pictures bears the title, "Guernica" [Plate 5]. Guernica was a place in Northern Spain where the Fascist countries, Germany and Italy, helped the Fascist Spaniards to overthrow the Loyalist government, the official government, because it was leftist. This place, Guernica, a small town in the country of the Basques, was completely destroyed by a combined air attack by the Italians and Germans. It was the first exercise of what is called, "saturation bombing," a terrible word. That means bombing in such a way that nothing is left. Now Picasso has painted this immense horror —the pieces of reality, men and animals and unorganic pieces of houses all together—in a way in which the "piece" character of our reality is perhaps more horribly visible than in any other of the modern pictures. During one of my lectures I once was asked, "What would you think is the best present-day Protestant religious picture?" I answered almost without hesitating, "Guernica." I named this picture, because it shows the human situation without any cover. It shows what very soon followed in most European countries in terms of the second World War, and it shows what is now in the souls of many Americans as disruptiveness, existential doubt, emptiness and meaninglessness. And if Protestantism means that, first of all, we do not have to cover up anything, but have to look at the human situation in its depths of estrangement and despair, then this is one of the most powerful religious pictures. And, although it has no religious content, it does have religious style in a very deep and profound sense.

Now I come to a man named Braque in France who, in his style, is one of Picasso's followers. The picture to which I wish to refer has the name, "Table." Here you have the dissolution of the organic realities which we usually think of when we speak of a table with things on top of it. Everything is dissolved into planes, lines and colors, elements of reality, but not reality itself. We call this "cubism"; this term naturally demands an explanation. It means that the essence of reality is contained in these original forms. What modern art tries to do is to move away from the surface which had nothing to say any more to men of the twentieth century, and to move to the *Urelemente,* the original elements of reality which in the physical realm are cubes, planes, colors, lines and shadows. From this point of view, such a picture can have a tremendous religious power, and I want to say a few words about this later.

In Germany towards the end of the nineteenth century, and in America with the building of Riverside Church in New York, many pictures were produced by two men, Oude and Hoffman. These pictures all portray Jesus either in terms of a sentimental, religious man, as does the Hoffman work in Riverside Church, or in terms of a rheumatic or otherwise sick, dull school teacher walking through little villages. Now, this kind of picture was supposed to be very religious at that time. I would say that for me, however, religious art must show something of God and the basic structures out of which He has made His reality, and not these sentimentalisms. This, of course, does not exclude occasional romantic expressions within these genuine forms.

As another illustration of the second level I refer to Chagall's picture, "River without Edges." Here again we have nothing which can be understood from the naturalistic point of view. It is strongly symbolistic, and perhaps this is the limit of the picture. However, everybody feels here the metaphysics of time in the wild moving clock and the animal above it and the whole constellation of colors and forms. Here the artist tries to use some elements of the encountered world in order to go beyond the surface into the depths of the phenomenon of time. Time is a river without edges.

Or, take another picture by Chagall, named "Lovers." Notice how the fantastic element comes in, how the forms are taken out of the possibility of natural relationships. The lover comes from the clouds because he is probably in her imagination much more than in her reality.

Then there is a surrealist, Chirico. One of his pictures is called "Toys of a Prince." It is characteristic for existentialist art. I would even say it is surrealistic. What does surrealistic mean? It means the elements of reality are brought into a context which has nothing to do with reality. Surrealism points to special dimensions and qualities of the reality as we encounter it. In some of Chirico's pictures it is infinite space into which we look or it is the loneliness, or the blinding power of the sun;

159

or it is the occasional coming together of elements of reality which have nothing whatsoever to do with each other.

Let me deal now a little bit more systematically with this whole second realm which is the center of our interest. I would call this, in the sense of my basic definition, religious style, although I have alluded to no picture whatsoever which had a religious content. And why is it a religious style? Because it puts the religious question radically, and has the power, the courage, to face the situation out of which this question comes, namely the human predicament. In earlier centuries we have painters who did very similar things. We have it in the mannerist period, after Michelangelo. We have it in some of the Baroque pictures. We find it in people like Goya. We have it in those great demonic pictures by Brueghel and Bosch where elements of the psychological as well as the natural reality are brought into the picture without a naturalistic connection with each other, without a system of categories into which they are put. This is the all-important element in existentialism. The essential categories, time, space, causality, substance, have lost their ultimate power. They give meaning to our world. With their help we can understand things. We can understand that one thing follows the other, one causes the other, one is distinguished from the other, each has its space and its time and so on. But all this no longer applies. Mankind does not feel at home in this world any more. The categories have lost their embracing and over-whelming and asserting power. There is no safety in the world.

We have Psalms in this spirit in the Old Testament, especially in the Book of Job, where it is said of man, "and his place does not know him anymore," and this is repeated in the 90th Psalm. Those are very profound words. The things in these pictures are displaced. Displaced persons are a symbol of our time, and displaced souls can be found in all countries. This large scale displacement of our existence is expressed in these pictures. All this is no positive answer to the question of our existence, and therefore I would agree that there is no Christian existentialism. There are many Christian existentialists; but insofar as they are existentialists they ask the question, show the estrangement, show the finitude, show the meaninglessness. Insofar as they are Christian, they answer these questions as Christians, but not as existentialists. For this reason, I do not believe that the ordinary distinction between atheistic and theistic existentialism makes any sense. As long as an existentialist is theistic he is either not existentialist or he is not really theistic. As far as people like Jaspers, like Kierkegaard, like Heidegger in his last mystical period, like Marcel, are Christians, or at least religious, or at least mystics, they are not existentialists but they answer their own existentialism, and that must be clearly distinguished. Existentialism describes the human situation, and as such it is a decisive element in present day religious thinking and Christian theology.

3. Non-religious Style, Religious Content. Now, before coming back to this, I wish to indicate a few examples of the two other levels for a complete picture of the whole situation. A picture which is extremely beautiful, which has a religious subject, is a Raphael Madonna and Child. It is religious neither in substance nor in style. This is one difference between the Raphael and the Chirico picture. In the Chirico, the disruptiveness of reality is visible; in the Raphael, we have a harmonious humanity which of course is indirectly religious, but is not religious in style. Or take another picture, a Madonna by the French painter Fouquet. The Madonna is a court lady of not too good a reputation. You know who she was, yet she is depicted as a Madonna. That shows that here the religious symbol in the Madonna and Child is not combined with the religious style but is reduced to the mother-child relationship of a great lady of the court of France. Or consider another, a Rubens "Madonna and Child." Here is another type of beautiful lady and another type of child. It is wonderful to look at, but nobody would think that this is the mother of God in the Catholic symbolism of this relationship. This is enough to show that religious content in itself does not give a religious picture, and many of those pictures which you find in the magazines of the churches, in the little Sunday papers in the churches themselves or, even worse, in the assembly rooms of the churches or the offices of the ministers are of this same character. They have religious content but no religious style. In this sense they are dangerously irreligious, and they are something against which everybody who understands the situation of our time has to fight.

4. *Religious Style, Religious Content.* Now I come to the fourth level, namely, pictures in which the religious form is combined with the religious content. This form is generally called expressionistic, because it is a form in which the surface is disrupted in order to express something. I have already stated that there have been such pictures long before modern times. Take, for instance, Greco's "Crucifixion." Here you have an absolutely unnatural form of the body. It is an expression of the esthetic form of the counter-reformation in which a small tenuous line goes up in ecstatic self-elevation towards the Divine with asceticism and often self-destruction. Or, an even earlier picture of the late gothic period, Mathäus Grünewald's famous "Crucifixion" on the Isenheim Altar. I believe it is the greatest German picture ever painted, and it shows you that expressionism is by no means a modern invention.

Then there is a modern "Crucifixion" by Sutherland. There you have very similar expression but in modern forms.

This is a recent expressionism using forms similar to Grünewald's, but with all the elements of disrupted style which modern art has created. In this context I put a question which I cannot answer: Is it possible to have this fourth level today? Is it possible to use these elements of expressionist visual art in dealing with the traditional symbols of Christianity? Sometimes, as for instance in the work by Sutherland, I am willing to say that it is possible. Sometimes I am not willing to say so.

Nolde, an expressionist of the German school which started in 1905, like other German expressionists tried to renew, by means of the expressionistic forms which they had created, the religious symbols of the past. Sometimes I am impressed by them—but in most cases I feel that they did not succeed. To illustrate this I refer you to Rouault's works, "Christ mocked by the soldiers," and plate 46 from the series called "Miserere" [**Plate 7**]: attempts to use his expressionist forms in order to make Christ's story present and contemporaneous to us. The last illustration I will cite is a "Crucifixion" by Rouault. I must repeat, sometimes I have the feeling that these are solutions, at least better ones than anything we have in the traditional "junk" of religious art today. But on the other hand, I ask myself, "Is the present day man really able to answer the question put before us by existentialism?"

EXISTENTIALISM AND IDEALIZED NATURALISM

Idealized naturalism still is the favorite form of art for many people. What does this favorite form mean from an existentialist point of view? It means the unwillingness to see and to face our real situation; therefore the relationship to modern art and its existentialist elements is a very serious affair. Let me tell you of an experience from my past after I had come out of the first World War, and the German Republic had been established. I was teaching at the University of Berlin, opposite the Museum of Modern Art just established by the newly formed republic. I myself used pictures in my lectures in order to show in other realms of life, especially philosophy, the relationship of form and substance, the possibility of breaking the surface form of reality in order to dig into its depths; and I must confess that I have not learned from any theological book as much as I learned from these pictures of the great modern artists who broke through into the realm out of which symbols are born. And you cannot understand theology without understanding symbols. In this museum something happened every day. The petty bourgeoisie of Germany also went to these exhibitions and I will never forget the smiling and laughing, or hostile and malignant faces in front of these pictures. What they expected in a museum was idealized naturalism. These pictures, however, had neither nature in the surface sense of the word in them, nor idealizing beauty. Instead of this they had shocking disruptions, distortions, elements of reality brought out of the depths to the surface by the painter. These petty people fought against this. This was, in the realm of art, the fight between the coming Nazism, produced by the same petty bourgeoisie, against the progressive intelligentsia which realized the dangerous situation in the industrial society. The petty bourgeoisie did not want to see that its situation had fundamentally changed, and Fascism was the attempt to maintain the old situation by means of suppression and terror. Now this shows that in artistic problems, and especially in the problems of existentialism in art, all realms are somehow present. However, let me go back to the religious realm. What has this situation to tell us about the religious realm and about our human situation? It has to tell us, first of all, that there are moments in individual life and in the life of society

when something cannot be hidden, cannot be covered any more. If the surface is maintained, then this can be done only at the price of honesty, of realism, of looking into the depths of our situation, and this price always includes fanaticism, repressing elements of truth, and self-destruction. We must be able—and that was the great work of these artists—to face our present reality as what it is. These artists were accused by many of having only negative characteristics. Hitler piled up their works in a museum of decadent art, a museum which contained some of the greatest treasures which later were brought to this country as great works of art. But as for Hitler, as a representative of the desperate petty bourgeoisie which wanted to keep itself in existence, he called this distorted, degenerated art. As long as we remove from our sight what we cannot help facing, we become dishonest; then that kind of art which he favored, that kind of beautifying realism, is what covers reality. These artists, therefore, who took away the cover from our situation, had a prophetic function in our time. I do not like all of them, either. But I know they created revealing works of art to look at which is the joy of participating in a level of reality which we otherwise can never reach.

And now finally about the relationship of the churches to all of this. The churches followed in most cases the petty bourgeoisie resistance against modern art and against existentialism generally. The churches believed they had all the answers. But in believing that they had all the answers they deprived the answers of their meaning. These answers were no longer understood because the questions were no longer understood, and this was the churches' fault. They did not do what the existentialist artist did. They did not ask the questions over again as they should have out of the experience of despair in industrial society. The churches did not ask the question, and therefore their answers, all the religious answers Christianity has in its creeds, became empty. Nobody knew what to do with them because the questions were not vivid any more as they were in the periods in which these answers were given. This, then, is my last statement about the whole thing. I believe that existentialist art has a tremendous religious function, in visual art as well as in all other realms of art, namely, to rediscover the basic questions to which the Christian symbols are the answers in a way which is understandable to our time. These symbols can then become again understandable to our time.

Religion and Modern Art: Bibliography

Barr, Alfred H., Jr., ed. *What Is Modern Painting?* New York: The Museum of Modern Art, 1946. Paper, New York: Doubleday & Company, 1958.

Berdyaev, Nicolas. *The Meaning of the Creative Act.* New York: Harper & Brothers, 1955.

Christian Scholar, The. December, 1957.

Dixon, John W., Jr. *Nature and Grace in Art.* Chapel Hill: University of North Carolina Press, 1964.

Eversole, Finley, ed. *Christian Faith and the Contemporary Arts.* Nashville: Abingdon Press, 1957.

Fallico, Arturo. *Art and Existentialism.* Englewood Cliffs, N. J.: Prentice-Hall, 1962.

Gilson, Étienne. *Painting and Reality.* New York: Pantheon Books, 1957. Paper, New York: Meridian Books.

Hazelton, Roger. *New Accents in Contemporary Theology.* New York: Harper & Row, 1960.

Kandinsky, Wassily. *Concerning the Spiritual in Art and Painting in Particular.* New York: George Wittenborn, 1964.

Malraux, André. *The Psychology of Art.* Trans. Stuart Gilbert. New York: Pantheon Books, 1949.

Maritain, Jacques. *Creative Intuition in Art and Poetry.* New York: Pantheon Books, 1953.

Sayers, Dorothy L. *The Mind of the Maker.* New York: Meridian Books, 1954.

IV
Religion
and Modern Literature

Introduction

Literature is intended here in the broad sense of the verbal arts, so that drama and poetry are included.

Three of the readings are basically concerned with a theme that is quite prominent in the interpretation of modern literature, namely, the absence or death of God: Esslin in terms of the absurd, Killinger in terms of Faulkner's world of the demonic, and Berger in terms of Camus' world of joy. Note the difference between Killinger and Berger on secularization.

One might compare Esslin's treatment of the Theatre of the Absurd with the previous discussions of abstractionism in modern art. Note, too, his treatment of the spiritual significance of modern science.

Scott addresses himself to a characteristic of our culture which is a by-product of our concern with science and which stands in tension with the concerns of art, literature, and religion. This is the conviction that all knowledge is, in the final analysis, scientific knowledge, so that there is nothing to be said about our world which is distinctive to literature—or to art or religion.

The last two readings concern the work of Albert Camus. It would be helpful to prepare for them by reading his rather short confessional narrative *The Fall* and perhaps also *The Stranger* and *The Plague*. Camus was chosen because he was a leading interpreter of our cultural situation and because of the interesting questions which are involved in Christian interpretations of a non-Christian—in some respects anti-Christian—writer. Some see in *The Fall* (and *The Plague*) signs of a turn toward Christianity while others strongly reject any such interpretations and point to Camus' own comments on this work, such as the following: "Europeans are no longer believers. . . . But they have retained their sense of sin. They can't unburden themselves by going to confession. So they feel the need to act. They start passing severe judgments, putting people in concentration camps, killing. My 'hero' is the exact illustration of a guilty conscience." [1]

---

[1] Quoted by Charles Rollo in "Albert Camus: A Good Man," *The Atlantic* (May, 1958), p. 32.

MARTIN ESSLIN

The Religious Function of the Theatre of the Absurd *

When Nietzsche's Zarathustra descended from his mountains to preach to mankind, he met a saintly hermit in the forest. This old man invited him to stay in the wilderness rather than go into the cities of men. When Zarathustra asked the hermit how he passed his time in his solitude, he replied:

I make up songs and sing them; and when I make up songs I laugh, I weep, and I growl; thus do I praise God.

Zarathustra declined the old man's offer and continued on his journey:

But when he was alone, he spoke thus to his heart: "Can it be possible! This old saint in the forest has not yet heard that God is dead!"[1]

Zarathustra was first published in 1883. The number of people for whom God is dead has greatly increased since Nietzsche's day, and mankind has learned the bitter lesson of the falseness and evil nature of some of the cheap and vulgar substitutes that have been set up to take His place. And so, after two terrible wars, there are still many who are trying to come to terms with the implications of Zarathustra's message, searching for a way in which they can, with dignity, confront a universe deprived of what was once its center and its living purpose, a world deprived of a generally accepted integrating principle, which has become disjointed, purposeless—absurd.

The Theatre of the Absurd is one of the expressions of this search. It bravely faces up to the fact that for those to whom the world has lost its central explanation and meaning, it is no longer possible to accept art forms still based on the continuation of standards and concepts that have lost their validity; that is, the possibility of knowing the laws of conduct and ultimate values, as deducible from a firm foundation of revealed certainty about the purpose of man in the universe.

In expressing the tragic sense of loss at the disappearance of ultimate certainties the Theatre of the Absurd, by a strange paradox, is also a symptom of what probably comes nearest to being a genuine religious quest in our age: an effort, however timid and tentative, to sing, to laugh, to weep—and to growl—if not in praise of God (whose name, in Adamov's phrase, has for so long been degraded by usage that it has lost its meaning), at least in search of a dimension of the Ineffable; an effort to make man aware of the ultimate realities of his condition, to instill in him again the lost sense of cosmic wonder and primeval anguish, to shock him out of an existence that has become trite, mechanical, complacent, and deprived of the dignity that comes of awareness. For God is dead, above all, to the masses who live from day to day and have lost all contact with the basic facts—and mysteries—of the human condition with which, in former times, they were kept in touch through the living ritual of their religion, which made them parts of a real community and not just atoms in an atomized society.

The Theatre of the Absurd forms part of the unceasing endeavor of the

[1] Nietzsche, *Also Sprach Zarathustra*, in *Werke,* Vol. II (Munich: Hanser, 1955), p. 297.

true artists of our time to breach this dead wall of complacency and automatism and to re-establish an awareness of man's situation when confronted with the ultimate reality of his condition. As such, the Theatre of the Absurd fulfills a dual purpose and presents its audience with a two-fold absurdity.

On the one hand, it castigates, satirically, the absurdity of lives lived unaware and unconscious of ultimate reality. This is the feeling of the deadness and mechanical senselessness of half-unconscious lives, the feeling of "human beings secreting inhumanity," which Camus describes in *The Myth of Sisyphus:*

In certain hours of lucidity, the mechanical aspect of their gestures, their senseless pantomime, makes stupid everything around them. A man speaking on the telephone behind a glass partition—one cannot hear him but observes his trivial gesturing. One asks oneself, why is he alive? This malaise in front of man's own inhumanity, this incalculable letdown when faced with the image of what we are, this "nausea," as a contemporary writer calls it, also is the Absurd.[2]

This is the experience that Ionesco expresses in plays like *The Bald Soprano* or *The Chairs,* Adamov in *La Parodie,* or N. F. Simpson in *A Resounding Tinkle.* It represents the satirical, parodistic aspect of the Theatre of the Absurd, its social criticism, its pillorying of an inauthentic, petty society. This may be the most easily accessible, and therefore most widely recognized, message of the Theatre of the Absurd, but it is far from being its most essential or most significant feature.

Behind the satirical exposure of the absurdity of inauthentic ways of life, the Theatre of the Absurd is facing up to a deeper layer of absurdity—the absurdity of the human condition itself in a world where the decline of religious belief has deprived man of certainties.

When it is no longer possible to accept simple and complete systems of values and revelations of divine purpose, life must be faced in its ultimate, stark reality. That is why, in the analysis of the dramatists of the Absurd in this book, we have always seen man stripped of the accidental circumstances of social position or historical context, confronted with the basic choices, the basic situations of his existence: man faced with time and therefore waiting, in Beckett's plays or Gelber's, waiting between birth and death; man running away from death, climbing higher and higher, in Vian's play, or passively sinking down toward death, in Buzzati's; man rebelling against death, confronting and accepting it, in Ionesco's *Tueur Sans Gages;* man inextricably entangled in a mirage of illusions, mirrors reflecting mirrors, and forever hiding ultimate reality, in the plays of Genet; man trying to establish his position, or to break out into freedom, only to find himself newly imprisoned, in the parables of Manuel de Pedrolo; man trying to stake out a modest place for himself in the cold and darkness that envelop him, in Pinter's plays; man vainly striving to grasp the moral law forever beyond his comprehension, in Arrabal's; man caught in the inescapable dilemma that strenuous effort leads to the same result as passive indolence—complete futility and ultimate death—in the earlier work of Adamov; man forever lonely, immured in the prison of his subjectivity, unable to reach his fellow man, in the vast majority of these plays.

Concerned as it is with the ultimate realities of the human condition, the relatively few fundamental problems of life and death, isolation and communication, the Theatre of the Absurd, however grotesque, frivolous, and irreverent it may appear, represents a return to the original, religious function of the theatre —the confrontation of man with the

[2] Camus, *Le Mythe de Sisyphe* (Paris: Gallimard, 1942), p. 29.

spheres of myth and religious reality. Like ancient Greek tragedy and the medieval mystery plays and baroque allegories, the Theatre of the Absurd is intent on making its audience aware of man's precarious and mysterious position in the universe.

The difference is merely that in ancient Greek tragedy—and comedy—as well as in the medieval mystery play and the baroque *auto sacramental,* the ultimate realities concerned were generally known and universally accepted metaphysical systems, while the Theatre of the Absurd expresses the absence of any such generally accepted cosmic system of values. Hence, much more modestly, the Theatre of the Absurd makes no pretense at explaining the ways of God to man. It can merely present, in anxiety or with derision, an individual human being's intuition of the ultimate realities as he experiences them; the fruits of one man's descent into the depths of his personality, his dreams, fantasies, and nightmares.

While former attempts at confronting man with the ultimate realities of his condition projected a coherent and generally recognized version of the truth, the Theatre of the Absurd merely communicates one poet's most intimate and personal intuition of the human situation, his own *sense of being,* his individual vision of the world. This is the *subject matter* of the Theatre of the Absurd, and it determines its *form,* which must, of necessity, represent a convention of the stage basically different from the "realistic" theatre of our time.

As the Theatre of the Absurd is not concerned with conveying information or presenting the problems or destinies of characters that exist outside the author's inner world, as it does not expound a thesis or debate ideological propositions, it is not concerned with the representation of events, the narration of the fate or the adventures of characters, but instead with the presenta-

tion of one individual's basic situation. It is a theatre of situation as against a theatre of events in sequence, and therefore it uses a language based on patterns of concrete images rather than argument and discursive speech. And since it is trying to present a sense of being, it can neither investigate nor solve problems of conduct or morals.

Because the Theatre of the Absurd projects its author's personal world, it lacks objectively valid characters. It cannot show the clash of opposing temperaments or study human passions locked in conflict, and is therefore not dramatic in the accepted sense of the term. Nor is it concerned with telling a story in order to communicate some moral or social lesson, as is the aim of Brecht's narrative, "epic" theatre. The action in a play of the Theatre of the Absurd is not intended to tell a story but to communicate a pattern of poetic images. To give but one example: Things happen in *Waiting for Godot,* but these happenings do not constitute a plot or story; they are an image of Beckett's intuition that *nothing really ever happens* in man's existence. The whole play is a complex poetic image made up of a complicated pattern of subsidiary images and themes, which are interwoven like the themes of a musical composition, not, as in most well-made plays, to present a line of development, but to make in the spectator's mind a total, complex impression of a basic, and static, situation. In this, the Theatre of the Absurd is analogous to a Symbolist or Imagist poem, which also presents a pattern of images and associations in a mutually interdependent structure.

While the Brechtian epic theatre tries to widen the range of drama by introducing narrative, epic elements, the Theatre of the Absurd aims at concentration and depth in an essentially lyrical, poetic pattern. Of course, dramatic, narrative, and lyrical elements are present in all drama. Brecht's own theatre, like Shakespeare's, contains lyrical inserts in the form of songs; even at their most didactic, Ibsen and Shaw are rich in purely poetic moments. The Theatre of the Absurd, however, in abandoning psychology, subtlety of characterization, and plot in the conventional sense, gives the poetical element an incomparably greater emphasis. While the play with a linear plot describes a development in time, in a dramatic form that presents a concretized poetic image the play's extension in time is purely incidental. Expressing an *intuition in depth,* it should ideally be apprehended *in a single moment,* and only because it is physically impossible to present so complex an image in an instant does it have to be spread over a period of time. The formal structure of such a play is, therefore, merely a device to express a complex total image by unfolding it in a sequence of interacting elements. . . .

And it is in this striving to communicate a basic and as yet undissolved totality of perception, an intuition of being, that we can find a key to the devaluation and disintegration of language in the Theatre of the Absurd. For if it is the translation of the total intuition of being into the logical and temporal sequence of conceptual thought that deprives it of its pristine complexity and poetic truth, it is understandable that the artist should try to find ways to circumvent this influence of discursive speech and logic. Here lies the chief difference between poetry and prose: Poetry is ambiguous and associative, striving to approximate the wholly unconceptual language of music. The Theatre of the Absurd, in carrying the same poetic endeavor into the concrete imagery of the stage, can go further than pure poetry in dispensing with logic, discursive thought, and language. The stage is a multidimensional medium; it allows the simultaneous use of visual elements, movement, light, and language. It is, therefore, particularly suited to the communication of complex images consisting of the contrapuntal interaction of all these elements. . . .

Exposed to the incessant, and inexorably loquacious, onslaught of the mass media, the press, and advertising, the man in the street becomes more and more skeptical toward the language he is exposed to. The citizens of totalitarian countries know full well that most of what they are told is double-talk, devoid of real meaning. They become adept at reading between the lines; that is, at guessing at the reality the language conceals rather than reveals. In the West, euphemisms and circumlocutions fill the press or resound from the pulpits. And advertising, by its constant use of superlatives, has succeeded in devaluing language to a point where it is a generally accepted axiom that most of the words one sees displayed on billboards or in the colored pages of magazine advertising are as meaningless as the jingles of television commercials. A yawning gulf has opened between language and reality. . . .

That is why communication between human beings is so often shown in a state of breakdown in the Theatre of the Absurd. It is merely a satirical magnification of the existing state of affairs. Language has run riot in an age of mass communication. It must be reduced to its proper function—the expression of authentic content, rather than its concealment. But this will be possible only if man's reverence toward the spoken or written word as a means of communication is restored and the ossified clichés that dominate thought (as they do in the limericks of Edward Lear or the world of Humpty Dumpty) are replaced by a living language that serves it. And this, in turn, can be achieved only if the limitations of logic and discursive language are recognized and respected, and the uses of poetic language acknowledged. . . .

As the reality with which the Theatre of the Absurd is concerned is a psychological reality expressed in images that are the outward projection of states of mind, fears, dreams, nightmares, and conflicts within the personality of the author, the dramatic tension produced by this kind of play differs fundamentally from the suspense created in a theatre concerned mainly with the revelation of objective characters through the unfolding of a narrative plot. The pattern of exposition, conflict, and final solution mirrors a view of the world in which solutions are possible, a view based on a recognizable and generally accepted pattern of an objective reality that can be apprehended so that the purpose of man's existence and the rules of conduct it entails can be deduced from it.

This is true even of the lightest type of drawing-room comedy, in which the action proceeds on a deliberately restricted view of the world—that the sole purpose of the characters involved is for each boy to get his girl. And even in the darkest pessimistic tragedies of the naturalistic or Expressionist theatres, the final curtain enables the audience to go home with a formulated message or philosophy in their minds: the solution may have been a sad one, but it was a rationally formulated conclusion nevertheless. This, as I pointed out in the introduction, applies even to the theatre of Sartre and Camus, which is based on a philosophy of the absurdity of human existence. Even plays like *Huis Clos (No Exit)*, *Le Diable et le Bon Dieu (Lucifer and the Lord)*, and *Caligula* allow the audience to take home an intellectually formulated philosophical lesson.

The Theatre of the Absurd, however, which proceeds not by intellectual concepts but by poetic images, neither poses an intellectual problem in its exposition nor provides any clear-cut solution that would be reducible to a lesson or an apothegm. Many of the plays of the Theatre of the Absurd have a circular structure, ending exactly as they began; others progress merely by a growing intensification of the initial situation. And

as the Theatre of the Absurd rejects the idea that it is possible to motivate all human behavior, or that human character is based on an immutable essence, it is impossible for it to base its effect on the suspense that in other dramatic conventions springs from awaiting the solution of a dramatic equation based on the working out of a problem involving clearly defined quantities introduced in the opening scenes. In most dramatic conventions, the audience is constantly asking itself the question "What is going to happen next?"

In the Theatre of the Absurd, the audience is confronted with actions that lack apparent motivation, characters that are in constant flux, and often happenings that are clearly outside the realm of rational experience. Here, too, the audience can ask, "What is going to happen next?" But then *anything* may happen next, so that the answer to this question cannot be worked out according to the rules of ordinary probability based on motives and characterizations that will remain constant throughout the play. The relevant question here is not so much what is going to happen next but what *is* happening. "What does the action of the play represent?" . . .

It is *not* true that it is infinitely more difficult to construct a rational plot than to summon up the irrational imagery of a play of the Theatre of the Absurd, just as it is quite untrue that any child could draw as well as Klee or Picasso. There is an immense difference between artistically and dramatically valid nonsense and just nonsense. Anyone who has seriously tried to write nonsense verse or to devise a nonsense play will confirm the truth of this assertion. In constructing a realistic plot, as in painting from a model, there is always reality itself and the writer's own experience and observation to fall back on—characters one has known, events one has witnessed. Writing in a medium in which there is complete freedom of invention, on the other hand, requires the ability to *create* images and situations that have no counterpart in nature while, at the same time, establishing a world of its own, with its own inherent logic and consistency, which will be instantly acceptable to the audience. Mere combinations of incongruities produce mere banality. Anyone attempting to work in this medium simply by writing down what comes into his mind will find that the supposed flights of spontaneous invention have never left the ground, that they consist of incoherent fragments of reality that have not been transposed into a valid imaginative whole. Unsuccessful examples of the Theatre of the Absurd, like unsuccessful abstract painting, are usually characterized by the transparent way in which they still bear the mark of the fragments of reality from which they are made up. They have not undergone that sea change through which the merely *negative* quality of *lack* of logic or verisimilitude is transmuted into the *positive* quality of a new world that makes imaginative sense in its own right.

Here we have one of the real hallmarks of excellence in the Theatre of the Absurd. Only when its invention springs from deep layers of profoundly experienced emotion, only when it mirrors real obsessions, dreams, and valid images in the subconscious mind of its author, will such a work of art have that quality of truth, of instantly recognized general, as distinct from merely private, validity that distinguishes the vision of a poet from the delusions of the mentally afflicted. . . .

The criteria of achievement in the Theatre of the Absurd are not only the quality of invention, the complexity of the poetic images evoked, and the skill with which they are combined and sustained but also, and even more essentially, the *reality* and *truth* of the vision these images embody. For all its freedom of invention and spontaneity, the Theatre of the Absurd is concerned with

communicating an experience of being, and in doing so it is trying to be uncompromisingly honest and fearless in exposing the reality of the human condition. . . .

In trying to deal with the ultimates of the human condition not in terms of intellectual understanding but in terms of communicating a metaphysical truth through a living experience, the Theatre of the Absurd touches the religious sphere. There is a vast difference between *knowing* something to be the case in the conceptual sphere and *experiencing* it as a living reality. It is the mark of all great religions that they not only possess a body of knowledge that can be taught in the form of cosmological information or ethical rules but that they also communicate the essence of this body of doctrine in the living, recurring poetic imagery of ritual. It is the loss of the latter sphere, which responds to a deep inner need in all human beings, that the decline of religion has left as a deeply felt deficiency in our civilization. We possess at least an approximation to a coherent philosophy in the scientific method, but we lack the means to make it a living reality, an experienced focus of men's lives. That is why the theatre, a place where men congregate to experience poetic or artistic insights, has in many ways assumed the function of a substitute church. Hence the immense importance placed upon the theatre by totalitarian creeds, which are fully aware of the need to make their doctrines a living, experienced reality to their followers.

The Theatre of the Absurd, paradoxical though this may appear at first sight, can be seen as an attempt to communicate the metaphysical experience behind the scientific attitude and, at the same time, to supplement it by rounding off the partial view of the world it presents, and integrating it in a wider vision of the world and its mystery.

For if the Theatre of the Absurd

presents the world as senseless and lacking a unifying principle, it does so merely in the terms of those philosophies that start from the idea that human thought *can* reduce the totality of the universe to a complete, unified, coherent system. It is only from the point of view of those who cannot bear a world where it is impossible to know why it was created, what part man has been assigned in it, and what constitutes right actions and wrong actions that a picture of the universe lacking all these clear-cut definitions appears deprived of sense and sanity, and tragically absurd. The modern scientific attitude, however, rejects the postulate of a wholly coherent and simplified explanation that must account for all the phenomena, purposes, and moral rules of the world. In concentrating on the slow, painstaking exploration of limited areas of reality by trial and error—by the construction, testing, and discarding of hypotheses—the scientific attitude cheerfully accepts the view that we must be able to live with the realization that large segments of knowledge and experience will remain for a long time, perhaps forever, outside our ken; that ultimate purposes cannot, and never will be, known; and that we must therefore be able to accept the fact that much that earlier metaphysical systems, mythical, religious, or philosophical, sought to explain must forever remain unexplained. From this point of view, any clinging to systems of thought that provide, or purport to provide, complete explanations of the world and man's place in it must appear childish and immature, a flight from reality into illusion and self-deception.

The Theatre of the Absurd expresses the anxiety and despair that spring from the recognition that man is surrounded by areas of impenetrable darkness, that he can never know his true nature and purpose, and that no one will provide him with ready-made rules of conduct. As Camus says in *The Myth of Sisyphus:*

The certainty of the existence of a God who would give meaning to life has a far greater attraction than the knowledge that without him one could do evil without being punished. The choice between these alternatives would not be difficult. But there is no choice, and that is where the bitterness begins.[3]

But by facing up to anxiety and despair and the absence of divinely revealed alternatives, anxiety and despair can be overcome. The sense of loss at the disintegration of facile solutions and the disappearance of cherished illusions retains its sting only while the mind still clings to the illusions concerned. Once they are given up, we have to readjust ourselves to the new situation and face reality itself. And because the illusions we suffered from made it more difficult for us to deal with reality, their loss will ultimately be felt as exhilarating. In the words of Democritus that Beckett is fond of quoting, "Nothing is more real than Nothing."

To confront the limits of the human condition is not only equivalent to facing up to the philosophical basis of the scientific attitude, it is also a profound mystical experience. It is precisely this experience of the ineffability, the emptiness, the nothingness at the basis of the universe that forms the content of Eastern as well as Christian mystical experience. For if Lao-tzu says, "It was from the nameless that Heaven and Earth sprang, the named is but the mother that rears the ten thousand creatures, each after its kind,"[4] St. John of the Cross speaks of the soul's intuition "that it cannot comprehend God at all,"[5] and Meister Eckhart expresses the same experience in the words, "The Godhead

[3] *Le Mythe de Sisyphe,* p. 94.

[4] Lao-tzu, quoted by Aldous Huxley, *The Perennial Philosophy* (London: Chatto & Windus, 1946), p. 33.

[5] St. John of the Cross, quoted by Huxley, *op. cit.*

is poor, naked, and empty, as though it were not; it has not, wills not, wants not, works not, gets not. . . . The Godhead is as void as though it were not." [6] In other words, in facing man's inability ever to comprehend the meaning of the universe, in recognizing the Godhead's total transcendence, His total otherness from all we can understand with our senses, the great mystics experienced a sense of exhilaration and liberation. This exhilaration also springs from the recognition that the language and logic of cognitive thought cannot do justice to the ultimate nature of reality. Hence a profoundly mystical philosophy like Zen Buddhism bases itself on the rejection of conceptual thinking itself:

The denying of reality is the asserting of it, And the asserting of emptiness is the denying of it. [7]

The recent rise of interest in Zen in Western countries is an expression of the same tendencies that explain the success of the Theatre of the Absurd—a preoccupation with ultimate realities and a recognition that they are not approachable through conceptual thought alone. Ionesco has been quoted as drawing a parallel between the method of the Zen Buddhists and the Theatre of the Absurd,[8] and in fact the teaching methods of the Zen masters, their use of kicks and blows in reply to questions about the nature of enlightenment and their setting of nonsense problems, closely resemble some of the procedures of the Theatre of the Absurd.

Seen from this angle the dethronement of language and logic forms part of an essentially mystical attitude toward the basis of reality as being too complex and at the same time too unified, too much of one piece, to be validly expressed by the analytical means of orderly syntax and conceptual thought. As the mystics resort to poetic images, so does the Theatre of the Absurd. But if the Theatre of the Absurd presents analogies with the methods and imagery of mysticism, how can it, at the same time, be regarded as expressing the skepticism, the humble refusal to provide an explanation of absolutes, that characterize the scientific attitude?

The answer is simply that there is no contradiction between the recognition of the limitations of man's ability to comprehend all of reality by integrating it in a single system of values and the recognition of the mysterious and ineffable oneness, beyond all rational comprehension, that, once experienced, gives serenity of mind and the strength to face the human condition. These are in fact two sides of the same medal—the mystical experience of the absolute otherness and ineffability of ultimate reality is the religious, poetic counterpart to the rational recognition of the limitation of man's senses and intellect, which reduces him to exploring the world slowly by trial and error. Both these attitudes are in basic contradiction to systems of thought, religious or ideological (e.g., Marxism), that claim to provide complete answers to all questions of ultimate purpose and day-to-day conduct.

The realization that thinking in poetic images has its validity side by side with conceptual thought and the insistence on a clear recognition of the function and possibilities of each mode does not amount to a return to irrationalism; on the contrary, it opens the way to a truly rational attitude.

Ultimately, a phenomenon like the Theatre of the Absurd does not reflect despair or a return to dark irrational

---

[6] Meister Eckhart, quoted by Huxley, *op. cit.*

[7] Seng-t'san, "On Believing in Mind," quoted by Suzuki, *Manual of Zen Buddhism* (London: Rider, 1950), p. 77.

[8] Ionesco, quoted by Towarnicki, *Spectacles*, No. 2, July, 1958.

forces but expresses modern man's endeavor to come to terms with the world in which he lives. It attempts to make him face up to the human condition as it really is, to free him from illusions that are bound to cause constant maladjustment and disappointment. There are enormous pressures in our world that seek to induce mankind to bear the loss of faith and moral certainties by being drugged into oblivion—by mass entertainments, shallow material satisfactions, pseudo-explanations of reality, and cheap ideologies. At the end of that road lies Huxley's Brave New World of senseless euphoric automata. Today, when death and old age are increasingly concealed behind euphemisms and comforting baby talk, and life is threatened with being smothered in the mass consumption of hypnotic mechanized vulgarity, the need to confront man with the reality of his situation is greater than ever. For the dignity of man lies in his ability to face reality in all its senselessness; to accept it freely, without fear, without illusions—and to laugh at it.

That is the cause to which, in their various individual, modest, and quixotic ways, the dramatists of the Absurd are dedicated.

JOHN KILLINGER

The Absence of God in Modern Literature*

What has happened, both in the world of fiction and in the real life it is supposed to body forth, to convince men of God's absence? Hosts of answers have been given: the Copernican revolution; the Renaissance and the rebirth of humanism; the scientific spirit of Newton and Bacon and Hobbes and Descartes; deism; Darwinism; higher criticism; progressivism; two world wars and the onset of twentieth-century pessimism. Certainly all these have been involved, one way or another, in the debacle of faith. But beyond all of them, or perhaps through them and involved in them, there is a more direct answer—one given from a theological point of view.

What, after all, is the primary mode of relationship between God and the world? Nature has of course always been one mode of relationship. Paul began the argument of Romans there: God's self-revelation in nature has left all men without excuse. But beyond nature is God's ultimate revelation of himself in the Incarnation. That which Tillich calls the "Christ-event" has always, for the Christian faith, been the real ground of interaction between God and man. "God was, in Christ, reconciling the world unto himself."

Here is the reason the world has lost God: it has first lost Christ, and the loss of Christ means the loss of relation.

Not that Christ does not appear in

* From *The Failure of Theology in Modern Literature* by John Killinger. Copyright © 1963 by Abingdon Press; pp. 44-58.

contemporary writing. One does not obliterate him and his effects upon history simply by saying to him, as Dostoevski's Grand Inquisitor did, "Go, and come no more." Jeffers was right when he said,

His personal anguish and insane solution
Have stained an age; nearly two thousand
  years are one vast poem drunk with the
  wine of his blood.[1]

There are numerous references to Christ in modern literature—countless symbols, analogues on his ministry and passion, even direct references.

But the majority of the better-known Christ figures are ineffectual ones, like Jeffers' "young Jew writhing on the doomed hill in the earthquake." [2] Alan Paton and Liston Pope, discussing the prevalent ideas of the Christ symbol in an article on "The Novelist and Christ," said that "apparently any fictional character qualifies who is innocent, selfless, and strange, even if he is banal or amoral or utterly humanist." [3] Herman Melville's Billy Budd, according to critic James Baird,[4] is merely the apotheosis of the *puer aeternus*. Steinbeck's Casy, in *Grapes of Wrath*, is a holiness preacher who gets his head smashed by a pick handle during an attempt to organize a fruit pickers' union. George Brush, in Thornton Wilder's *Heaven's My Destination*, is a fundamentalist textbook salesman who is given a kind of Christ-before-Pilate trial for trying to break a thief from stealing by giving him money. Hemingway's Santiago, in *The Old Man and the Sea*, loses his fish to the galanos and falls wearily under the weight of his ship's mast as he bears it up the hill. Faulkner's Benjy, in *The Sound and the Fury*, is a thirty-three-year-old idiot who has been gelded to keep him from molesting little girls; and Joe Christmas, in *Light in August,* is a half-breed who is murdered and mutilated for killing a spinster woman to whom he has made love.

This is not to say that there have not been some beautiful and inspiring uses of the Christ image. F. W. Dillistone has discussed several of them in *The Novelist and the Passion Story:* Mauriac's *The Lamb* and *A Woman of the Pharisees*, Melville's *Billy Budd,* Kazantzakis' *The Greek Passion,* and Faulkner's *A Fable.* There is absolutely no doubt of Mauriac's intention of making Xavier Dartigelongue, in *The Lamb,* a Christ figure. His life is surrendered in one great passion for other persons; again and again he gives himself that they might have life. Especially poignant is the scene in which he carries a ladder through the dark night to put against the window where the boy Roland is imprisoned. He has put off his shoes in order to make no noise when passing out of the house, and the furze bushes and pine cones are giving him excruciating pain as he half carries, half drags, the ladder along. Mauriac says,

It was the very flesh of his body now that was being torn and mangled. In the past he had talked endlessly of the Cross, had fed his meditations on the thought of it, but only here, in the loneliness of a cold, dark night, was it born [sic] in upon him that he had never understood its full meaning, had never truly merged himself with the experience. The Cross was not, as he had once believed, a love withdrawn, an agonized bending of the spirit, an humiliation, an obstacle; it was, quite simply, a crushing weight of timber, a bruised and tortured shoulder, carried on feet flayed by stones and earth.[5]

---

[1] "Dear Judas." Copyright 1929 and renewed 1957 by Robinson Jeffers. Reprinted from *Dear Judas and Other Poems,* by Robinson Jeffers, by permission of Random House, Inc.

[2] "Meditation on Saviors." Copyright 1928 and renewed 1956 by Robinson Jeffers. Reprinted from *The Selected Poetry of Robinson Jeffers,* by permission of Random House, Inc.

[3] In the *Saturday Review,* December 4, 1954, p. 15.

[4] *Ishmael: A Study of the Symbolic Mode of Primitivism* (New York: Harper & Row, 1960), p. 205.

[5] Tr. Gerard Hopkins (New York: Farrar, Straus & Company, 1956), p. 104.

In the end, Xavier dies a ridiculous death—he is struck by an automobile while riding a bicycle. But the driver of the vehicle, Jean de Mirbel, is strangely "redeemed" by the death.

Faulkner's *A Fable* is probably the most intricate refashioning of the Passion narrative to appear in the last half century. It is a "big" novel, capturing innumerable facets of life along the wavering battlefronts of Europe in the First World War. In my opinion, it is the finest novel Faulkner ever wrote and the nearest thing the English-speaking world has ever had to put against the grandeur of Tolstoi and Dostoevski. The plot centers in upon an act of passive resistance by a regiment of soldiers in the Allied trenches. An old general holds the power of life and death over them. At the center of the resistance is a little band of thirteen men, of whom a certain corporal (*corpus:* incarnation!) is the leader. Ironically, the corporal is discovered to be the illegitimate son of the general. In a private interview, the general offers him a limousine to escape to the coast, but the corporal refuses; he will not desert his men. The old man reminds him that one of them has already deserted him and that the others will probably do likewise when given the chance, but he is obdurate. The order is given and the corporal is executed —on a post between a thief and a murderer. His body is taken away by friends and buried on French farmland. When the bombardment has fallen on the farm again, leaving it pockmarked with craters, the peasants rush to the place where they had entombed him, only to find a crater there, and some fragments of the unpainted wood of the coffin. They search the area and find a few more shards and pieces of the coffin; but the body itself is gone.

The unfortunate ingredient in the novel, from the Christian viewpoint, is Faulkner's known humanism, which he puts eloquently into the words of the old general during his interview with the son he is trying to save. The son tells him not to be afraid. "Afraid?" he says.

> No no, it's not I but you who are afraid of man; not I but you who believe that nothing but a death can save him. I know better. I know that he has that in him which will enable him to outlast even his wars; that in him more durable than all his vices, even that last and most fearsome one; to outlast even this next avatar of his servitude which he now faces: his enslavement to the demonic progeny of his own mechanical curiosity, from which he will emancipate himself by that one ancient tried-and-true method by which slaves have always freed themselves: by inculcating their masters with the slaves' own vices—in this case the vice of war and that other one which is no vice at all but instead is the quality-mark and warrant of man's immortality: his deathless folly.[6]

In words Faulkner himself repeated when he accepted the Nobel Prize for Literature, the old general says that man and his folly "will prevail."

Dillistone is probably correct when he says that any attempt to present Christ again in fiction is sure to involve the artist in heresy of one kind or another, for the *work* of a Christ figure must always fall short of the work of Christ. As Paton and Pope remind us in "The Novelist and Christ," the plot involving a Christ figure is prescribed at the outset, and the writer's failure to bring it off theologically is unavoidable:

> The end is inevitable from the beginning, whatever form the crucifixion may take. Hence he can write only tragedy if he is faithful. He does not have the consolation of the Gospels, which transcend tragedy in the Resurrection. Most often in modern fiction the Christ figure is lost "in the gathering fog" or exiled or executed; we know of no novelist who has undertaken to depict the ultimate triumph. Hence the

[6] (New York: Random House, 1954), p. 352.

reader is compelled to behold the agony again without the promise; the Christ figure is reduced to a victim of history, largely without hope other than a vague appeal to the future.[7]

Perhaps the triumph Faulkner reveals in *A Fable* is penultimate; but it can hardly be said to be ultimate. What is impossible for fiction is probably not so impossible for poetry: one thinks of Hopkins' "The Windhover," for example, or Auden's *For the Time Being*. But fiction, as a rule, when it attempts to present the figure of Christ, is limited to the presentation of a kind of spiritually scented humanism in which the most it can say is little more than was said of the Crucified by one of the soldiers in Hemingway's "Today is Friday"; "He was good in there today." It is good humanism, but it is truncated Christianity. It is the earth's-side version as told by the buzzard in Robert Penn Warren's "Pondy Woods": "The Jew-boy died."

Perhaps some authors sincerely believe they are doing Christ a service by rescuing him from the gray supernaturalism that tended to enshroud him in the pietistic literature of earlier generations. But the real result is that they have depicted him as an ineffectual, as a Revelation who does not reveal and a Redeemer who cannot redeem. Consequently the doctrine of God is obscured at a vital point, for the Christian faith has always placed a premium upon the indivisibility of Father and Son, God and Incarnation. As Gabriel Vahanian has suggested,

While the literary effects, even the religious ones, can be tremendous, the theological implication is disastrous. The Christ-figure is a result of the process of leveling down. If all is grace, any man can take on the marks of Christ; and Christ, the unique, according to Christian theology, becomes a

mere mask, suitable to any man. The Christ-figure is but another devaluation of Christianity. It is expressive of the broad secularization of Christian concepts, whose content has been hollowed out. The humanization of God—or the deification of man which takes place in many ideologies, from communism to some forms of existentialism—indeed goes hand in hand with the secularization of Christ and the assimilation of Christianity with a culture which *ipso facto* is less and less Christian.[8]

Nor has the doctrine of the Holy Spirit fared much better in contemporary writing, unless lack of treatment could itself be called better. Hopkins, Eliot, and Auden allude to the Spirit in several places, but I can remember very few such allusions in the prose of our time. One that I do remember vividly is in Camus' *The Fall*. Clamence is discoursing to his *"cher compatriote"* about the "beautiful negative landscape" of Amsterdam. He observes how horizontal, how colorless and lifeless it is—a soggy kind of hell. His friend apparently observes in return that the sky seems to be alive. "You are right, *cher ami*," says Clamence.

It thickens, becomes concave, opens up air shafts and closes cloudy doors. Those are the doves. Haven't you noticed that the sky of Holland is filled with millions of doves, invisible because of their altitude, which flap their wings, rise or fall in unison, filling the heavenly space with dense multitudes of grayish feathers carried hither and thither by the wind? The doves wait up there all year round. They wheel above the earth, look down, and would like to come down. But there is nothing but the sea and the canals, roofs covered with shop signs, and never a head on which to light.[9]

The reference is clearly to the descent of the dove upon Christ at his baptism and to the traditional identification of the dove as the Holy Spirit. But in the

[7] P. 59.
[8] *The Death of God* (New York: George Braziller, 1961), p. 131.
[9] Albert Camus, *The Fall*, tr. Justin O'Brien (New York: Alfred A. Knopf, 1957), p. 73.

flat and colorless modern world there is no head on which the dove may light. Without the Second Person of the Trinity, there can be no Third Person. Without the Third Person, there can be no true community; and therefore man in the contemporary world is condemned to Clamence's existential hell of introspection and monological discourse. It is a dreary prospect.

Admittedly it is a difficult thing to refer directly to the Holy Spirit in a piece of fiction. The New Testament itself does not fully articulate a doctrine of the Spirit. That task was left to the church councils. But if, as most contemporary theologians insist, the doctrine of the Trinity is the Church's reference to her *experience* with God, to the manner in which she has known him, then it seems reasonable to expect the "Christian" writer to do more writing as John of the Apocalypse did, "in the Spirit," or as Milton did in *Paradise Lost,* under an invocation to the Spirit.

How does one recognize a literary composition that has been written "in the Spirit"? I am not sure that there are any suitable criteria. But I think it is something that the reflective Christian can intuit. Charles Williams' *War in Heaven* and *Descent into Hell,* for example, exude a kind of spiritual quality that strongly suggests such composition. On a different level, James Street's *The High Calling* gives me such a feeling. I cannot put my finger precisely on the thing that evokes this feeling. Sometimes I think it is a happy combination of *knowledge* and *love:* a kind of doctrinally informed compassion. It is not precisely what Arnold meant by "sweetness and light," but they are the words, when set in the reverse order, I should like to use. Perhaps it is a case of our spirits bearing witness with his spirit that we are the sons of God.

Even with such a generous criterion as this, though, there seem to be few writers on the contemporary scene bearing such a witness. The doves simply do not light.

George Santayana once wrote, in an essay about Dante:

If any similar adequacy is attained again by any poet, it will not be, presumably, by a poet of the supernatural. Henceforth, for any wide and honest imagination, the supernatural must figure as an idea in the human mind—a part of the natural. To conceive otherwise would be to fall short of the insight of this age, not to express or to complete it.[10]

In a similar vein, Charles Glicksberg says that

No writer of our time who has been exposed to the teachings of Darwin, Freud, Dewey, Russell, Carnap, and Einstein can hope to recapture the medieval intensity of faith in the supernatural. The revival of interest in the work of Kierkegaard serves but to reinforce the impression that doubt in our age is universal. The strenuous attempts of Christian apologists to revive the faith so that it will once more impregnate the body of modern literature have not borne much fruit.[11]

Literary realism devoid of supernaturalism was probably an inevitable corollary of the loss of God. It is worth noting that there was an incipient "realism," a strain of vulgarity, in some of the best literature of the neoclassical period, when the influence of deism was most strongly felt; and that naturalism *per se* was the product of the latter half of the nineteenth century, when the real erosion of faith was under way. One of the main tenets of the naturalism of Zola, Gissing, Hardy, Norris, and Dreiser was the certainty that there is an inexorable mechanism or determinism at work in man. It is this secret and baleful force that accounts in many instances for the degradation of a worthy

---

[10] *Three Philosophical Poets* (Cambridge: Harvard University Press, 1935), p. 134.
[11] *Literature and Religion,* p. 92.

character or the rewarding of an unworthy one. Considered from the moral aspect, then, naturalism is a literary revolt against the traditional belief that God is a rewarder of those who "do justly and walk uprightly." It preaches with relentless dogmatism the blindness of justice—and the absence of God.

At the *fin de siècle,* the primary aim of naturalism was to provide a kind of photographic realism in writing; it was espoused by writers reacting strongly against the saccharinity of most late-Victorian prose and melodrama. Had the movement remained merely a corrective, we should owe it much. But soon the literary "photographers" were enthusiastically arranging their own scenes. Setting up their cameras in the kitchen or the bathroom, they left the dirty dishes in the sink, even added a few more for good measure, strewed a month's collection of moldy garbage and cigarette butts on the floor, and arranged a couple of cadavers in a suggestive position somewhere in the sideground with a mangy cat eating on them. The whole effect was as far from real life on one side as sentimentalism had been on the other. But whereas in earlier literature God had stood around like some embarrassed entrepreneur waiting to reward virtue and punish vice, now he was nowhere around. He had simply been written out of the plot.

And although the passionate naturalism of Zola's generation has by and large given way to the more casual sort of naturalism discoverable in the works of such men as John Steinbeck and Erskine Caldwell and Mickey Spillane, it requires but the mention of these names to remind us of how completely a modified naturalism dominates the literary scene in our day. It takes but a glance at the contents of the average newsstand bookrack to see how far we

have come from William Dean Howells' "smiling" aspects of life or Henry James's incisive gentility. I cannot help thinking there is a fortuitous—though perhaps unintentional—description of the present literary malaise in the opening lines of Robert Penn Warren's "Pondy Woods":

The buzzards over Pondy Woods
Achieve the blue tense altitudes,
Black figments that the woods release,
Obscenity in form and grace,
Drifting high through the pure sunshine
Till the sun in gold decline.[12]

The buzzards could symbolize the triumph of the predatory spirit in contemporary writing. Woods have long suggested darkness and evil—as witness the first lines of the *Inferno* and the secret meetings of Hester and Arthur in *The Scarlet Letter.* The "black figments that the woods release" might then be the compositions of the naturalists— "obscenity in form and grace." Much of the literature of the naturalists does have form and grace, to be sure; but like the buzzards it is also dark, menacing, and associated with death. And "the sun in gold decline": could this not be Dante's "profound and shining being," the God who has gone from the scene?

But I have spoken of the Paradox of the *Manifest* Absence. It seems to me that we must distinguish between that literature from which God is *merely* absent and that from which he is plainly, or manifestly, absent. And it may well be the fact that we have always made this distinction, whether consciously or unconsciously, that has caused us to respect some works of realistic literature over others and to apply to them the adjective "serious." Why else would a critic like Hyatt Waggoner write an article about Hemingway's contribution to Christian thinking in our time,[13]

---

[12] From *Selected Poems 1923-1943* (New York: Harcourt, Brace & Co., 1944). Copyright © 1944 by Robert Penn Warren.
[13] "Ernest Hemingway," *The Christian Scholar,* XXXVIII (June, 1955), 114-20.

when Hemingway was rather obviously something of a nihilist? Or why do we return again and again to Faulkner's Latinate, mesmeric descriptions of the decadent South? Why indeed, unless we find there is something in the way these writers depict the godless world that actually speaks to us of God, that makes plain to us what is missing from the picture?

As I try to discover what it is that makes such writers different from other competent writers, I find myself coming back repeatedly to the feeling I find in them for the demonic. Is it not precisely this—the sense of the demonic—that haunts the pages of a writer for whom God is manifestly absent? Certainly it was very strong in Melville and Hawthorne and Dostoevski, the very figures who had most to say in their time about a coming age of apostasy from the Christian faith. Ivan Karamazov even said that he found it easier to believe in the devil than to believe in God.

Hemingway's world may lack the depth and the height of a good supernaturalism, but where in his world does the supernatural come closest to appearing? Where but in the light-and-dark symbolism of which we have spoken earlier? An acute sensitivity to darkness informs scenes in many of his stories and novels, culminating, probably, in "A Clean, Well-Lighted Place," where the darkness surrounding the neat little bar is almost animated. It is not simply a matter of a childish fear of the dark. With Hemingway it is something much more sinister. The darkness threatens. It menaces. It breathes annihilation—or at least *nada*.

Or take the works of Thomas Wolfe. The demonism there is far less subtle. The starched and decent Presbyterianism of Altamont, in *Look Homeward, Angel,* is too tame and orderly for Eugene Gant's wildish centaur heart, but he does believe in the dark beings of the air. When his brother Ben is dying, he begins suddenly, "under the mastering surge of his wild Celtic superstition," to pray. "He did not believe in God," says Wolfe, "nor in Heaven or Hell, but he was afraid they might be true. He did not believe in angels with soft faces and bright wings, but he believed in the dark spirits that hovered above the heads of lonely men." [14] After Ben's death he continues for a long time to pray at night—

not from devout belief, but from the superstition of habit and number, muttering a set formula over sixteen times, while he held his breath . . . not to propitiate God, but to fulfil a mysterious harmonic relation with the universe, or to pay worship to the demonic force that brooded over him. He could not sleep of nights until he did this.[15]

But it is Faulkner's world that is most truly demonic—the world of the Compsons and Sartorises and Snopeses. At first this strikes us as being a strangely incongruous fact in light of the strong tinge of Calvinism we find also in his writing. Some inexorable predestination seems to manipulate his characters, lending to his fiction the sense that something far larger than man is just behind the veil of history. But then we remember Hawthorne and Melville and the same strange blend of darkness and doctrine in them. The combination has even prompted Randall Stewart to suggest that the two greatest corpora of American literature have come from the two special loci of Puritanism—Hawthorne and Melville in New England, and Warren and Faulkner in the South.

If it is God who is behind the veil of Faulkner's world—and his repeated use of Christian imagery would argue that it is—then he is evidently the *deus in absentia,* and the absence is what accounts for the radical dementia of

---

[14] (New York: Charles Scribner's Sons, 1929) , p. 556.
[15] *Ibid.,* p. 611.

that freakish world. God is not far away, to be sure—if he were, some kind of order might be achieved on the human level. But neither is he very near, or he would introduce his own order, the order of his presence. It is the nearness and the farness together that confound Faulkner's South and hurl it into the most profound agitation. The propinquity of the holy, when it fails to become articulated into explicit terms or relationships, throws life into twistedness and torment.

Consider, for example, the plot of *Sanctuary*,[16] all of which takes place during a four-week period ten years after the violent death of young Bayard Sartoris in the novel *Sartoris*. For ten years Horace Benbow has been living with his wife Belle in Kinston. Every Friday afternoon he has met the train and carried a package of fresh shrimp home for her; he is repulsed to think that for ten years his life has been represented in those faint-smelling blotches of shrimp drippings on the pavement between the depot and his home. Now, at the beginning of *Sanctuary*, he has left Belle and is on his way home to Jefferson. He stops for a drink at a spring somewhere in Yoknapatawpha County, and looks up from the water's edge to see standing before him an undersized man with a colorless face and eyes like "two knobs of soft black rubber." Thus begins a story of almost incredible windings and turnings, with episodes where the strands cross that are even more incredible.

Popeye—that is the name of the man at the spring—is a petty despot in a nest of moonshiners that includes an idiot named Tommy, a truck driver named Van, an ex-convict named Lee Goodwin, and Lee's wife Ruby, who carries about a baby that has never come more than half alive.

One night a man named Gowan Stevens and a co-ed named Temple Drake are driving drunkenly through the country and crash into a tree lying across the road at a point adjacent to Popeye's domain. They are made prisoners of the bootleggers. Stevens manages to sneak off the next day. Temple, apparently pleased with her role as main temptress in the camp, sets man against man until Popeye finally shoots the idiot Tommy. After the murder, he flees to Memphis, taking Temple with him. Lee sends Ruby for the sheriff. When the sheriff arrives, he arrests Lee and takes him to Jefferson, because everyone else has fled.

In Memphis, Popeye establishes Temple in a house run by a fat, asthmatic woman named Reba Rivers. He showers her with expensive clothes and perfumes and makes love to her by proxy—he brings a man named Red who lies in bed with her while he himself bends over the bed without so much as his cap off, whinnying and making other strange noises. But when Temple and Red try to run off together, he shoots Red and flees to Pensacola, where, of all things, he annually visits his mother.

Red's funeral is held in a speakeasy, where a jazz band plays "Nearer, My God, to Thee" while the crowd gets high on illegal booze. At one point, a drunk lurches at the orchestra and tips over the coffin so that Red's body rolls out and the wax plug in the forehead where the bullet entered is knocked out and lost.

Horace Benbow, who has assumed the job of defending Lee Goodwin against a murder charge, hears that Temple is in Memphis and has her brought to Jefferson as a witness for the defense. Evidently fearful of Popeye's vengeance if she should incriminate him, she testifies that Lee really did murder Tommy. The D.A. holds up a corncob with some muddy brown stains on it, makes some muted references to a gynecologist's having connected the stains

[16] (New York: Modern Library, 1931).

183

with the sacredness of womanhood, and leaves the court assured that Lee has abused Temple's body. The jury is out only eight minutes, and returns the verdict of guilty.

Sick at the outcome, Horace prepares to return to Kinston. He is waiting at the station for his train when he hears the cry of "Fire!" He joins the crowd rushing toward the alley by the jail. Lee Goodwin has been dragged outside by a mob and burned alive in coal oil.

Popeye is picked up by the police in a southern city on the charge of having killed a policeman on the very night when he had actually murdered Red. For some unknown reason, he sullenly declines to combat the accusation, refusing even the entreaties of a sharp Memphis lawyer who has got him off on worse charges several times before. As the minister's voice drones quietly, the sheriff throws the trap of the gallows floor and Popeye swings silently at the end of a rope.

In the Luxembourg Gardens, Temple Drake strolls with her father, Judge Drake. Fall, "the season of rain and death," is in the air.

What an intense spectrum of horror! Faulkner has seemed to ignore deliberately the more genteel aspects of life in favor of the ugly and the perverted and the grotesque. The result is a world of monstrous distortion and terror. Halford Luccock has said that Faulkner revolted "against the predominance of honeysuckle and magnolia in the Southern vegetation" and "planted his own garden with thistles and skunk cabbage." But it is more than that. The very title of *Sanctuary*—a word that once meant a refuge given under religious auspices—implies that there is more than that.

Here is a world that is a kinetoscope of terror because it is a world without God. It is the outcome of Goodman Brown's apostasy in Hawthorne and Ahab's sky-hurled defiance in Melville, and it is terrifying to behold. Its twisted-

ness is so ultimate that even Christ is represented as an idiot in *The Sound and the Fury*, and as a half-Negro murderer in *Light in August*. Nothing is safe from distortion. The truancy of God has thrown everything into convulsion.

It was Luther who first formulated the paradoxical statement that where God is revealed, there he is also hidden, and where he is hidden, there he is also revealed—the *deus revelatus* is always *deus absconditus*, and vice versa. Is there some sense in which this is true also of God in modern literature? Is not his very hiddenness there charged with the tension of his presence? We should like to think that this is so—for the works of some authors, at least. When a writer is as sensitive and serious about life as Faulkner, for instance, it is probably safe to assume that many readers are able to see the God behind his world, revealed *as through torment*. Or, when a poet like Jeffers is so bitter about humanity and so lavish in his praise of jagged rocks and turbulent waters and strong animals, he doubtless inadvertently tells us something about God and his relationship to the created sphere. Or even when a playwright like Beckett confronts us with the nihilism and despair of a *Waiting for Godot*, we think that we can discern the subtle, oh-so-subtle overtones of the *mysterium tremendum* that does not blush to reveal itself even in negativity.

But again, these are only the *implications* for theology from contemporary writing—*they do not necessarily proceed from the Christian faith*. They are not, like Dante's *Commedia*, a direct product of the faith. Some of them are not even by-products. They are not kerygmatic or didactic in their orientation, but incidental, and there is a vast difference in that. Literature that reflects only the loss of God is not Christian literature, any more than a pamphlet on anarchy is pro-government because it

184

happens to use the word government in every other sentence. Its real shortcoming is that it fails to reflect fully, if at all, the mighty facts that are central to the Christian faith—the Incarnation of God and the resurrection of Jesus Christ. In the face of the true gospel, it might almost be said to be blasphemous.

NATHAN A. SCOTT, JR.

Poetic Vision as an Expression of Ultimate Concern*

When we seek for the principal motives that underlie the general movement of criticism in our period, we cannot, of course, for long escape the recognition that, among them at least, has been the intention of many of its most distinguished representatives to offer some resistance to the reductionist tendency of modern scientism, particularly when it broaches upon those transactions with reality that are peculiar to the humanistic imagination. I can think of no single doctrine or emphasis that is subscribed to by all those writers who at one time or another have been held accountable for "the new criticism," but certainly by far a greater number of them are of a single mind in their apprehensiveness about the deeper cultural implications of the reigning positivism than they are on any other single point. And it has been their unwillingness to give their suffrage to the absolute hegemony of empirical science which has been a decisive influence upon their approach to the fundamental issues in theory of literature. Ours has been a time in which it has been generally supposed that the only responsible versions of experience that can be had are those afforded us by the empirical sciences and in which, therefore, the common impulse has been to trivialize the arts by regarding them as merely a kind of harmless play which, at best, is to be tolerated for the sedative effect that it has upon the nervous system. But even this assignment hardly constitutes a satisfactory charter for the artist, since, in the ministry of health to the nervous system, he is not likely to compete successfully with our modern doctors of psychology. So, in the last analysis, our culture has been incapable of finding for the arts, and especially for literature, a valuable or an irreplaceable function. And the result has been that the major strategists of modern criticism have felt it incumbent upon themselves to revindicate the poetic enterprise by doing what the culture was unable to do—namely, by seeking to define that unique and indispensable role in the human economy that is played by imaginative literature and that can be preempted by nothing else.

This contemporary effort to specify the nature of the autonomy which a work of literary art possesses has involved a careful analysis of what is special in the linguistic strategies of

* From *Modern Literature and the Religious Frontier,* Nathan A. Scott. Copyrighted 1958 by Nathan A. Scott; used by permission of the publisher, Harper & Row, Publishers, Inc.; pp. 23-38, 42-45.

the poet. And the aim has been to establish that poetry is poetry and not another thing. . . . Which is to say that the contemporary critic has come to see poetic meaning not as a function of the relationships between the terms of the poem and some reality which is extrinsic to them, but rather as a function of the interrelationships that knit the terms together into the total pattern that forms the unity of the work. Our way of stating this distinctive character of poetic language is to say that its terms function not ostensively but reflexively, not semantically but syntactically—by which we mean that, unlike the situation that obtains in logical discourse in which the terms "retain their distinctive characters despite the relationship into which they have been brought," in poetic discourse they lose their distinctive characters, as they fuse into one another and are modified by what Mr. Cleanth Brooks calls "the pressure of the context." . . .

Now it is in terms of this organic character of poetic structure that our generation has come to understand the resistance of literary art to the discursive paraphrase. It does not yield a series of paraphrasable abstractions because no set of terms of which a poetic work is constituted refers to anything extrinsic to the work: they refer, rather, to the other terms to which they are related within the work. And thus the perception of the meaning of the work awaits not an act of comparison between the component terms and the external objects or events which they may be taken to symbolize, but, rather, an act of imaginative prehension that will focus upon "the entire pattern of internal reference . . . apprehended as a unity." The coherence of a work of imaginative literature is to be sought, in other words, not in any set of logically manageable propositions into which it may be paraphrased but rather in the living pattern of interrelated themes and "resolved stresses" that the work contains. . . .

Now this redefinition in modern criticism of "the mode of existence of a literary work of art" has in turn led to a redefinition of the creative process. For so rigorous has been the stress that has been put upon the autonomy of poetic language till language itself has often very nearly been regarded as the enabling cause of literary art. It is assumed that art is a virtue of the practical intellect and that the poet's vision is not fully formed until it has become objectified in language. Indeed, the executive principle of the creative process is considered really to derive not from the poet's metaphysic or his special perspective upon the human story but rather from the medium to which his vision is submitted and by which it is controlled. It is regarded as a truism that whatever it is that the poet "says" about reality in a given work is something the content of which he himself did not fully possess until the completion of the work. For, as Mr. Murray Krieger has recently put it, "the poet's original idea for his work, no matter how clearly thought out and complete he thinks it is, undergoes such radical transformations as language goes creatively to work upon it that the finished poem, in its full internal relations, is far removed from what the author thought he had when he began." [1] The medium alone, in other words, objectifies the poet's materials and gives them their implications. This axiom of the contemporary movement in criticism is expressed with especial directness by Mr. R. P. Blackmur, when he remarks in his essay on Melville:

Words, and their intimate arrangements, must be the ultimate as well as the immediate source of every effect in the written or spoken arts. Words bring meaning to birth and themselves contained the meaning

---

[1] Murray Krieger, *The New Apologists for Poetry* (Minneapolis: University of Minnesota Press, 1956), p. 23.

as an imminent possibility before the pangs of junction. To the individual artist the use of words is an adventure in discovery; the imagination is heuristic among the words it manipulates. The reality you labour desperately or luckily to put into your words . . . you will actually have found there, deeply ready and innately formed to give an objective being and specific idiom to what you knew and did not know that you knew.[2]

Whatever it is, in other words, that is in the completed work is there by virtue of the language which controls the creative process and which produces the "new word" that Mr. Yvor Winters declares the authentic work of literary art to be. The poet does not have a version of the human situation to express, some imperious preoccupation to voice, or some difficult report to make; no, he has none of this: indeed, as Mr. Eliot tells us, there is no good reason for supposing that he does "any thinking on his own" at all, for it is not his business to think—not even poets as great as Dante and Shakespeare. No, all the writer need have is his medium, and, if he knows how to trust it and how to submit to it, it will do his work for him: it will, as Mr. Blackmur says, bring the "meaning to birth."

Now, to be sure, what I have offered thus far is patently an abridgment of the advanced poetics of our time, but perhaps this account is at least sufficiently complex to provide some indication of the sources of the crisis that I earlier remarked as having arisen in contemporary criticism. It is clear certainly that we are being asked by many of the most distinguished theorists of our day to regard the work of literary art as a linguistic artifact that exists in complete detachment from any other independently existent reality. The fully achieved work of art, as the argument runs, is a discrete and closed system of mutually interrelated terms: the organic character of the structure prevents the constituent terms from being atomistically wrenched out of their context and made to perform a simple referential function, and it also succeeds in so segregating the total structure from the circumambient world as to prevent its entering into any extramural affiliation. "A poem should not mean but be," says Mr. MacLeish, and thereby, in this famous line from his poem "Ars Poetica," he summarizes, with a beautiful concision, the mind of a generation.

But, then, if the work of literary art exists in complete isolation from all those contexts that lie beyond the one established by the work itself, if it neither points outward toward the world nor inward toward the poet's subjectivity, if it is wholly self-contained and cut off from the general world of meaning, why then it would seem that nothing really can be said about it at all. And in this unpromising strait are we not all chargeable with "the heresy of paraphrase"? . . .

The English critic Mr. D. S. Savage . . . suggests in the Preface to his book *The Withered Branch* that this "dizzy elevation" of the medium in contemporary criticism clearly leaves something important out of account. And there is, I believe, no finer recent statement of what is unaccounted for than that which M. Jacques Maritain gives us in his great book *Creative Intuition in Art and Poetry.* . . .

"As to the great artists," [Maritain] says, "who take pleasure in describing themselves as mere engineers in the manufacturing of an artifact of words or sounds, as Paul Valéry did, and as Stravinsky does, I think that they purposely do not tell the truth, at least completely. In reality the spiritual content of a creative intuition, with the poetic or melodic sense it conveys, animates their artifact, despite their grudge

[2] R. P. Blackmur, "The Craft of Herman Melville: A Putative Statement," in *The Lion and the Honeycomb* (New York: Harcourt, Brace and Co., 1955), p. 138.

against inspiration." [3] And this must be so, because, as M. Maritain insists, the activity which produces poetic art does not begin until the poet permits himself to be invaded by the reality of "Things" and until he himself seeks to invade the deepest recesses of his own subjectivity—the two movements of the spirit being performed together, as though one, "in a moment of affective union." When the soul thus comes into profound spiritual contact with itself and when it also enters into the silent and mysterious depths of Being, it is brought back to "the single root" of its powers, "where the entire subjectivity is, as it were, gathered in a state of expectation and virtual creativity." [4] And the whole experience becomes "a state of obscure . . . and sapid knowing." Then

after the silent gathering a breath arises, coming not from the outside, but from the center of the soul—sometimes a breath which is almost imperceptible, but compelling and powerful, through which everything is given in easiness and happy expansion; sometimes a gale bursting all of a sudden, through which everything is given in violence and rapture; sometimes the gift of the beginning of a song; sometimes an outburst of unstoppable words. [5]

And only when this point in the artistic process has been reached may *operation* begin. For the artist to initiate the processes of *operation* at any earlier point is for him "to put the instrumental and secondary before the principal and primary, and to search for an escape through the discovery of a new external approach and new technical revolutions, instead of passing first through the creative source. . . ." [6] Then what is produced is but "a corpse of a work of art—a product of academicism." "If creative

intuition is lacking," he says, "a work can be perfectly made, and it is nothing; the artist has nothing to say. If creative intuition is present, and passes, to some extent, into the work, the work exists and speaks to us, even if it is imperfectly made and proceeds from a man who has the habit of art and a hand which shakes." [7] . . .

At a time when it is too much our habit to regard the medium as the single factor controlling the poetic process, M. Maritain's formulation of the problem has the very great merit of eloquently reminding us again of the actual primacy in the process of *poetic vision*. He discloses to us, that is, a stratagem for declaring once again that it is not language which brings "meaning to birth" and which enables the mind "to order itself"—not language, but *vision*.

Mr. Eliseo Vivas also helps us to some extent, I believe, with our difficulties when he reminds us that what is in part distinctive about the artist is his "passion for order." "Really, universally," said Henry James, "relations stop nowhere, and the exquisite problem of the artist is eternally but to draw, by a geometry of his own, the circle within which they shall happily *appear* to do so." [8] That is to say, the artist wants to give a shape and a significance to what Mr. Vivas calls "the primary data of experience." He wants to contain the rich plenitude of experience within a pattern that will illumine and give meaning to its multifarious detail and its bewildering contingency. But, of course, he cannot discover such a pattern unless he has a vantage point from which to view experience and by means of which his insights may be given order and proportion. Which is to say that he can

[3] Jacques Maritain, *Creative Intuition in Art and Poetry* (New York: Pantheon Books, 1953), p. 62.

[4] *Ibid.*, p. 239.

[5] *Ibid.*, p. 243.

[6] *Ibid.*, p. 223.

[7] *Ibid.*, p. 60.

[8] Henry James, *The Art of the Novel: Critical Prefaces* (New York: Charles Scribner's Sons, 1934), p. 5.

transmute the viscous stuff of existential reality into the order of significant form only in accordance with what are his most fundamental beliefs about what is radically significant in life, and these beliefs he will have arrived at as a result of all the dealings that he has had with the religious and philosophical and moral and social issues that the adventure of living has brought his way. The imaginative writer's beliefs, to be sure, are very rarely highly propositional in character: they do not generally involve a highly schematized set of ideas or a fully integrated philosophic system. He customarily has something much less abstract—namely, a number of sharp and deeply felt insights into the meaning of the human story that control all his transactions with the world that lies before him. And it is by means of these insights that he discovers "the figure in the carpet."

Mr. Graham Greene, in his criticism, has often liked to observe that "Every creative writer worth our consideration, every writer who can be called in the wide eighteenth-century use of the term a poet, is a victim: a man given to an obsession," [9] or to what he sometimes calls a "ruling passion." And I take it that when he speaks in this way he has in mind the poet's habit of loyalty to some discovered method of construing experience, to some way of seeing things, by means of which he grapples and comes to terms with the tumultuous and fragmentary world that presses in upon him. That is to say, I assume that Mr. Greene has in mind the act of consent which the poet gives to some fundamental hypothesis about the nature of existence which itself in turn introduces structure and coherence for him into the formless stuff of life itself. And it is indeed, I believe, this act that constitutes

the real beginning of the poetic process: the rest is simply a matter of the kind of knowledgeable experimentation within the limits of his medium that the expert craftsman engages in till he discovers what he wants to say gaining incarnation within a given form. . . .

What I am now insisting upon principally is the precedence and the primacy of the act by which the poet searches experience and finds therein an ultimate concern that gives him then a perspective upon the flux and the flow.

Now whatever it is that concerns the poet ultimately, that constitutes his "ruling passion" and the substance of his *vision,* is something to which the critic can be attentive only as it is discoverable in the work. By now surely we have all taken to heart the lesson of Messrs. Wimsatt and Beardsley on "The Intentional Fallacy," and we understand the irrelevance of any essay in literary criticism that is based upon some process of armchair psychoanalysis which seeks to elevate the biographical category of the artist's conscious intention into a category of aesthetic discrimination. But the designation of "intentionalism" as fallacious becomes itself a fallacy if it is made to support the view that a work of literary art is "a merely formal structure devoid of embodied meanings and values." [10] For such aesthetic objects, though "they may be found in the realm of pure design or pure music," [11] simply do not exist in the realm of literature where surely a main part of the critic's task involves the discovery of "the actual operative intention which, as telic cause, accounts for the finished work" [12] and which can be defined only in terms of the vision of the world which it serves. The authentic work of literary art, says M. de Rougemont, is a trap for the attention, but he also says that it is an

---

[9] Graham Greene, *The Lost Childhood* (New York: Viking Press, 1952), p. 79.

[10] *Vide* Eliseo Vivas, "A Definition of the Esthetic Experience," in *The Problems of Aesthetics,* ed. Eliseo Vivas and Murray Krieger (New York: Rinehart and Co., 1953), p. 172.

[11] *Ibid.*

[12] *Ibid.,* p. 164.

"oriented trap." It is a trap, in the sense that, having the kind of autonomy that modern criticism has claimed for it, it "has for its specific function . . . the magnetizing of the sensibility, the fascinating of the meditation";[13] as Mr. Vivas would put it, it can command upon itself an act of "intransitive attention." But the trap is "oriented": it *focuses* the attention, that is, upon something which transcends the verbal structure itself, this simply being the circumambient world of human experience, in those of its aspects that have claimed the poet's concern. . . .

The work is not wholly self-contained and utterly cut off from the reader, because, in the creative process, the aesthetic intentions of the artist are not segregated from all that most vitally concerns him as a human being but are, on the contrary, formed by these concerns and are thus empowered to orient the work toward the common human experience. This experience has, of course, to be grasped in and through the structures by means of which it is aesthetically rendered. But to stress the fact that poetic art signifies *by means of its structure* need not, I think, commit us to a formalism so purist as to require the view that the autonomy of the work is absolute. For, as I have been insisting, great literature does, in point of fact, always open outward toward the world, and that which keeps the universe of poetry from being hermetically sealed off from the universe of man is the poet's vision that it incarnates, of spaces and horizons, of cities and men, of time and eternity. This is why those modern theorists who tell us that the literary work is merely a verbal structure and that its analysis therefore involves merely a study of grammar and syntax—this is why they so completely miss the mark. They forget that writers use language with reference to what they know and feel and believe and that we can therefore understand their poems and novels only if we have some appreciation of how their beliefs have operated in enriching the meaning of the words that they employ. The poem-in-itself, in other words, as merely a structure of language, is simply a naked abstraction, for the real poem, the real novel, is something that we begin to appropriate only as we seek some knowledge of the context of belief and the quality of vision out of which it springs and with reference to which the words on the printed page have their fullest and richest meaning.

Now we have, I think, arrived at the point in our argument at which it is finally possible for me to turn to the generality of my subject, as it is formulated in the title of this chapter. For what I can now say is that the aspect of poetic art to which I have been referring by the terms *vision* and *belief* is precisely the element which we ought to regard as constituting the religious dimension of imaginative literature. When I speak of the religious dimension of literary art, in other words, I do not have in mind any special iconic materials stemming from a tradition of orthodoxy which may or may not appear in a given work. For were it to be so conceived, it might indeed then be something peripheral and inorganic to the nature of literature itself; whereas the way of regarding our problem that I now want to recommend is one that involves the proposal that the religious dimension is something intrinsic to and constitutive of the nature of literature as such. And I am here guided in my understanding of what is religious in the orders of cultural expression by the conception of the matter that has been so ably advanced by the distinguished Protestant theologian Paul Tillich. In all the work that he has done in the philosophy of culture over the past thirty years the persistent strain that is to be noted is one that arises out of his in-

[13] Denis de Rougemont, "Religion and the Mission of the Artist," in *Spiritual Problems in Contemporary Literature,* ed. Stanley R. Hopper (New York: Harper & Brothers, 1952), p. 176.

sistence upon what might be called the coinherence of religion and culture. He likes to say that "Religion is the substance of culture and culture the form of religion." [14] He has remarked, for example:

If any one, being impressed by the mosaics of Ravenna or the ceiling paintings of the Sistine Chapel, or by the portraits of the older Rembrandt, should be asked whether his experience was religious or cultural, he would find the answer difficult. Perhaps it would be correct to say that his experience was cultural as to form, and religious as to substance. It is cultural because it is not attached to a specific ritual-activity; and religious, because it evokes questioning as to the Absolute or the limits of human existence. This is equally true of painting, of music and poetry, of philosophy and science. . . . Wherever human existence in thought or action becomes a subject of doubts and questions, wherever unconditioned meaning becomes visible in works which only have conditioned meaning in themselves, there culture is religious.[15]

And professor Tillich has acknowledged that it is to the theoretical comprehension of this "mutual immanence of religion and culture" that his philosophy of religion is primarily dedicated. "No cultural creation," he says, "can hide its religious ground," and its religious ground is formed by the "ultimate concern" to which it bears witness; for that, he insists, is what religion is: it "is ultimate concern." And since it is religion, in this sense, that is truly substantive in the various symbolic expressions of a culture, the task of criticism, in whatever medium it may be conducted, is, at bottom, that of deciphering the given work at hand in such a way

as to reveal the ultimate concern which it implies. For, as he says, in the depth of every culture creation "there is an ultimate . . . and [an] all-determining concern, something absolutely serious," [16] even if it is expressed in what are conventionally regarded as secular terms.

It should, of course, be said that, in these definitions, Professor Tillich is not seeking to *identify* religion and culture; but he does want to avoid the error that Mr. T. S. Eliot has cautioned us against "of regarding religion and culture as two separate things between which there is a relation." [17] For what he recognizes is that the whole cultural process by which man expresses and realizes his rational humanity is actually governed by what are his most ultimate concerns—his concerns, that is, "with the meaning of life and with all the forces that threaten or support that meaning. . . ." [18] And, in passing, it is, I think, worth remarking that it is this profoundly realistic approach to the problem of cultural interpretation that enables Professor Tillich to see that in our own period the most radically religious movements in literature and painting and music may gain expression in strangely uncanonical terms—in despairing maledictions and in apocalyptic visions of "the abyss" of disintegration that threatens the world today. For, as he would say, in the very profundity with which *Wozzeck* and the *Guernica* and *The Waste Land* express the disorder of the times there is an equally profound witness to the spiritual order that has been lost, so that these great expressions of the modern movement in art are rather like a confused and uncertain prayer that corresponds to the

[14] Paul Tillich, *The Protestant Era* (Chicago: University of Chicago Press, 1948), p. 57.

[15] Paul Tillich, *The Interpretation of History* (New York: Charles Scribner's Sons, 1936), p. 49.

[16] Tillich, *The Protestant Era*, pp. 58-59.

[17] T. S. Eliot, *Notes Towards the Definition of Culture* (New York: Harcourt, Brace and Co., 1949), pp. 31-32.

[18] James Luther Adams, "Tillich's Concept of the Protestant Era," Editor's Appendix, *The Protestant Era*, p. 273.

second petition of the *Our Father*.[19] . . .

The great effort of the Christian critic in our day should have as its ultimate aim a reconciliation between the modern arts and the Church, between the creative imagination and the Christian faith. The immense obstacles on the side of art and on the side of the Church that hinder this achievement are, however, not to be minimized. The great misfortune is that those modern writers who have experienced most profoundly the intellectual and spiritual predicaments of the time and whose return to Christianity would therefore be most arresting are often those who are most acutely sensible of the failure of institutional Christianity—and especially of Protestantism—to give due place to "the yea-saying impulse of the biblical faith and its moment of creative play."[20] It is felt "that a Christian so sterilizes his heart that there is no concern left for art and the rich play, the riot and fecundity of life."[21] It is the rejection of a Christianity (and generally a Protestant Christianity) that is felt to be ascetical and world-denying which forms the rule among modern writers rather than the exception: Yeats and Joyce and Wallace Stevens and many others have refused the Gospel, very largely, one feels, because of the failure of its interpreters to express what Professor Wilder feels to be the genuine element of antinomianism in the Gospel itself.[22] He puts the issue with great clarity in his book *The Spiritual Aspects of the New Poetry:*

For the poets the scandal of Christ is his asceticism. The very medium of their art as poets; indeed, the very element of their experience as men, is the gamut of human living, emotions, drama. "Man's resinous heart" and the loves, loyalties, the pride, the grief it feels—these are the stuff of poetry and the sense of life. And the Cross lays its shadow on this; it draws away all the blood from the glowing body of existence and leaves it mutilated and charred in the hope of some thin ethereal felicity. The wine of life is changed to water. . . . The "dramatic caves" of the human heart and imagination are renounced for some wan empyrean of spiritual revery. The very word "spiritual" has come to signify inanity and vacuity. The refusal of religion by the modern poet, and by more than moderns and by more than poets, goes back to the apparent denial of human living by religion, to the supposed incompatibility of life with Life and of art with faith.[23]

That this is the major hindrance on the side of art to a reconciliation between the creative imagination and the Church one may very quickly discover by a perusal of one of the most interesting spiritual documents of our period, the *Partisan Review* symposium, *Religion and the Intellectuals* (1950), in which the general testimony of many of the most influential literary figures of our day tends to confirm Professor Wilder's assessment.

There are also serious hindrances on the side of the Church to a *rapprochement* between art and faith. There are many religious people who suppose their own conservative and unaroused attitudes toward modern life to be based upon valid Christian principles, when they really derive from a protected social situation in which it has been possible for them to shut their eyes to the dislocations of the age to which history

[19] M. de Rougemont says that "art would appear to be like an invocation (more often than not unconscious) to the lost harmony, like a prayer (more often than not confused), corresponding to the second petition of the Lord's Prayer—'Thy Kingdom come.'" *Vide op. cit.*, p. 186.

[20] Amos N. Wilder, *Modern Poetry and the Christian Tradition* (New York: Charles Scribner's Sons, 1952), p. 243.

[21] Amos N. Wilder, *The Spiritual Aspects of the New Poetry* (New York: Harper & Brothers, 1940), pp. 197-198.

[22] *Vide* Wilder, *Modern Poetry and the Christian Tradition*, Chapter X.

[23] Wilder, *The Spiritual Aspects of the New Poetry*, p. 196.

192

has committed both them and ourselves. They face with defensiveness and hostility much of modern literature in which these stresses and strains are reflected, and they insist upon the excessiveness of its alarmism and its irrelevance to the world in which they choose to believe that they live. It is their habit to speak of many of the major writers of this century—Pound and Gide, Joyce and Lawrence, Kafka and Faulkner—as if the difficulties presented by their work were merely frivolous and as if the inclination of their vision toward a tragic perspective were a consequence merely of their morbidity or even of the disorder in their personal lives. And they mistake their censoriousness with respect to the modern artist for a genuinely Christian position. A more sophisticated version of the same unfriendliness to the modern arts arises out of the extreme disjunctions between the natural order and the order of revelation that are insisted upon in those currents of Protestant thought stemming from Crisis Theology.[24] In this theological framework the arts, as a department of human culture, are comprehended in terms of their issuance from the natural order, all of whose fruits are, of course, to be viewed, as a matter of principle, with a deep suspicion and skepticism. . . .

Now Professor Tillich's excellent point is that the way of heteronomy can never be the way of Protestantism. A truly Protestant orientation to culture must, to be sure, also involve a criticism of "self-complacent autonomy," but always, he insists, the Protestant community, when it is true to its own informing principle, will remember that "in the depth of every autonomous culture an ultimate concern, something unconditional and holy, is implied." And the genius of Protestant Christianity is most truly expressed when, in its dealings with what is called "secular culture," it so takes this body of witness up into itself that the distinction between the sacred and the secular ceases to exist.

It will, I believe, be along this way—the way of "theonomy"—that a reunion of art and religion, if it is to occur at all, will be achieved. But, of course, what will be chiefly required is an infinite degree of tact and humility in the Christian critic, and thus a reconciliation between art and faith in our day would be, as Professor Weidlé has said,

the symptom of a renewal of the religious life itself. When frozen faith melts again, when it is once more love and freedom, then will be the time that art will light up again at the new kindling of the fire of the spirit. There seem to be many indications that such a future is possible; and in any case it is the only future still open to art. There is one way alone—and there is no other—because artistic experience is, deep down, a religious experience, because the world art lives in cannot be made habitable save by religion alone.[25]

[24] "Crisis Theology" refers to neo-orthodoxy. The positions of Brunner and Kean are representative. (Editor's note.)

[25] Weidlé, *The Dilemma of the Arts,* trans. by Martin Jarrett-Kerr (London: S.C.M. Press Ltd., 1948), p. 125.

PETER L. BERGER

Camus, Bonhöffer, and the World Come of Age*

Dietrich Bonhöffer, the promising young Lutheran theologian who was hanged by the nazis in 1945 for his part in the German resistance movement, spoke of our time as that of "the world come of age"; and in the last years of his life it was a main concern of his to clarify the implications of that phrase for the Christian church. No better representative of the "world come of age" can be found than the Algerian-born French writer Albert Camus—perhaps the most read contemporary author in the noncommunist sphere. Camus's popularity points to the representative character of this thought. The Nobel Prize committee cited him as one who "illuminates the problems of the human conscience in our time." Yet Camus is more than a moralist of peculiar relevance to our generation. He offers a novel perspective on man's being in the world, represents a specifically contemporary form of consciousness which is likely to be more significant in the future than the pseudo-religiosity of the Communists.

TWO CAMUS THEMES

One of Camus's heroes describes his problem as that of becoming a saint without God. There were many such troubled heroes in the European resistance movements against nazism. It was in the midst of their struggle that Camus's moral positions were worked out. These men turned away from Christianity as much as from the para-Christian ideology of the Communists. The Christian church has had little difficulty in clarifying its position with reference to the latter. Every eschatology, after all,

faces similar problems of interpretation. But the form of consciousness that Camus represents still baffles Christian thought. His challenge to Christianity is most sharply apparent in two themes that recur in his work: a radical affirmation of this-worldliness and rejection of the Christian theodicy (the vindication of God's justice in permitting evil to exist).

At one point in his development Camus came close to Sartre's analysis of the human condition. This was the period of *The Stranger, The Myth of Sisyphus* and *Caligula,* when he was concerned with the absurd as a dimension of existence. But the absurd was for Camus a starting point, not by any means the culmination of his thought. Moreover, even during this period he sounded a strong affirmation of life, the simple life of this world and this world only (for example, in his prewar book of essays *Nuptials*). This affirmation is a continuing theme. Camus passionately defends the ultimate validity of the joys which he associates with his childhood and youth in North Africa. Friendship and conversations, an open sensuality without guilt, swimming in the sea, the touch of the evening's cool breeze when the day's work is done— these are joys that all men can share, the joys of this life, the only real joys. Supernatural hopes are a betrayal of this common world of men and thus of humanity itself.

Camus lags behind no contemporary writer in describing the "extreme situations" of human existence. But over and over again in his work the experiences of anguish, terror, guilt and the absurd are transcended in an affirmation of joy. This is the "invincible summer" that Camus says he has found within himself, a peculiarly Mediterranean lucidity which disdains those who take refuge in either faith or despair. It is precisely *The Plague,* the book in which he deals most directly with the "extreme situation," that ends with the declaration that "there are more things to admire in men than to despise."

Christian thought and preaching ordinarily hold that Christian hope is the only alternative to despair. Camus not only regards this position as in error, but identifies the error with a lack of human decency. Yet the bitterest pill for Christians probably is not Camus's this-worldliness but his condemnation of Christianity, along with communism, as an apologist for injustice. This theme, developed most fully in *The Plague* and *The Rebel,* reveals Camus's indebtedness to the Russian anarchists of the 19th century (to whom he devotes his play *The Just Assassins*). In *The Plague* Camus, like Dostoevsky in *The Brothers Karamazov,* takes us to the bedside of a dying child. Thus the problem of God is narrowed down to the problem of the innocent suffering. The Christian theodicy is understood as essentially an acceptance of this suffering as in some way part of an ultimate harmony. Christianity, then, is a betrayal of suffering humanity. The same is true of Communism. The Christian eschatology accepts injustice by pointing to eternity and to the suffering God on the cross. The Communist eschatology points to a this-worldly redemption. Both, Camus tells us, make men accessories to murder.

In his recurring discussion of capital punishment Camus brings the problem into sharp focus. One is reminded here of the remark of the 19th century Russian anarchist Mikhail Bakunin that all religions had a bloodthirsty notion of sacrifice as their basis and that it is not surprising that the clergy are usually defenders of capital punishment. Arthur Koestler, in his *Reflections on Hanging,* recently gave us a good case history of the role of the Anglican Church in capital punishment in England. There is an awful affinity between priest and hangman. That the symbol waved by Christian priest before countless victims of Christian torture is itself an instrument of execution may be ground for reflection.

THE ATHEISM OF CAMUS

In *The Rebel* Camus relates this conception of religion, especially the Christian religion, as requiring sacrifice to a political creed. Rebellion against injustice is possible only after the God who silenced Job has been removed from the scene. Abolition of the kingdom of grace precedes establishment of the republic of justice. The anti-Christian overtones of the French revolution heralded a process which continues into our own time with increasing momentum. Far from being the basis of democracy (another favorite statement of preachers), Camus maintains the Christian religion is the chief obstacle to human liberation. In its central myth it accepts the sacrifice of the innocent. Again and again, as the innocent of this world are slaughtered, this myth provides the divine alibi.

The French Jesuit Henri de Lubac has given us a brilliant analysis of the atheistic humanism of our time. It is based, he says, not so much on rationalistic skepticism but on ethics: God is rejected not because he is improbable but because he is unjust. Voltaire's famous "If God did not exist, we should have to invent Him" might be taken to mark him as a late Christian thinker. The temper of the post-Christian era in which we find ourselves is well expressed in Bakunin's paraphrase of Voltaire's statement "If God *did* exist, we should have to abolish Him." It is this version of atheism that we encounter in Camus. Its starting point is the problem of

195

theodicy and rejection of its Christian solution.

There is remarkably little discussion of this problem in contemporary theology. P. T. Forsyth is perhaps the only modern theologian who took it very seriously. If the problem is not rejected outright as blasphemous, it is sidetracked into a discussion of human sin. Religious psychology makes this maneuver quite understandable. It is more bearable to the religious consciousness to think of God even as the terrible judge than to question his goodness. We are dealing here with a kind of metaphysical masochism.

HIS CHALLENGE TO CHRISTIANS

This sidetracking of the problem from God's justice to man's guilt shows the weakness of the Christian position in the face of the new atheism. The question of human guilt is not at issue here. Camus, like the existentialists, would willingly grant that human action is enmeshed in guilt. But the problem of human guilt is overshadowed by the problem of the guilt of God. There is irony in the fact that, of all his works, Camus's *The Fall* should have been hailed as a step in the direction of Christianity. For it is in this work that the searching paragraph occurs which asks why such a melancholy air hangs over the Jesus of the Gospel narratives. The melancholy, Camus says, is explained by guilt. Jesus is guilty of the massacre of the innocents; because of him the children of Bethlehem are dead, while he goes on living. It might be added that Jesus is guilty also of the death of the Christian martyrs, and of all those martyred in turn by the new religion. The bystander is guilty, says the implacable morality of Camus. And God is the eternal bystander.

Camus's challenge to Christianity could be summed up in one question: Can a Christian be a decent human being? This question may not only

196

sound shocking but be quite incomprehensible to Americans. In many ways American religion still lives under an *ancien regime,* in what may well be intellectually the least modern of Western countries. Atheists are even rarer among us than Communists. If history has any lessons, however, we may expect an end to this state of innocence. It may be well, then, for American Christians to look at the manner in which Dietrich Bonhöffer grappled with the problem of the church in the post-Christian era. . . .

BONHÖFFER

The names of Albert Camus and Dietrich Bonhöffer are not linked arbitrarily. Indeed it can be said that our situation in history compels a choice between the two positions they represent. Like Camus, . . . Bonhöffer developed his political ethics in the midst of revolutionary action. He found himself forced to face his relationship to the "saints without God" at whose side he fought against nazism. His thoughts on the "world come of age" date from the last years of his life, and are known to us through letters he wrote in prison (published in America under the title *Prisoner for God*).

The German pastor's analysis of this "world come of age" is a complete reversal of the perennial complaint of the church about the secularization of Western civilization. Bonhöffer welcomes that secularization and rightly sees that Christianity itself helped bring it about. The "world come of age" is one in which the "religious hypothesis" is no longer needed by man; he can get along very well without it. Nietzsche's prophecy has been fulfilled. God *is* dead, and more and more men are beginning to grasp the fact. We must not be misled by miscellaneous "religious revivals," by new mythologies, indigenous or imported, or by the massive pseudo-religiosity of the communist world.

CHRISTIANS IN RETREAT

The process of religion's disappearance is irreversible, Bonhöffer declares. We are dealing now with a new form of consciousness, from which Christians have been on the retreat for well over a hundred years. One position after another has been surrendered. Little by little, God has been relegated to the remote reaches of human knowledge and experience, has been turned into a *deus ex machina*. Thus God has been called to the scene on the frontiers that physics is now pushing against. The undignified scramble with which Christians have pounced on the utterances of men like Sir James Jeans is a case in point. As the frontiers of knowledge expanded, God receded farther into the realms of mystery that remained. On the other hand, God has been called to the scene in the "extreme situations" of human existence. There the religious hypothesis is presented as necessary in dealing with pain and guilt and death. The sympathy of many Christian theologians for the murkier depths of psychoanalysis and existentialism illustrates the point. Bonhöffer aptly calls this activity a "rummaging in garbage cans."

IMAGE OF JOY

Camus . . . presents to us an image of modern man quite different from the Freudian or Sartrian figure of gloom which Christians have capitalized on. It is an image of joy: man has attained the capacity for freedom, including the freedom to get along without the old *deus ex machina* even in the face of mystery and anguish. Bonhöffer tells us that it is indecent for Christians to convince men that they are not free, *not* happy, and are therefore in need of the religious medicine. If, he says, the church can be no more in the modern world than a sort of "religious drugstore," or "religious comfort station," as he more vulgarly calls it, then its fate is already sealed.

An analysis of the historical relationship between the biblical tradition and the secularization process is crucial here. The essence of religion is its dichotomization of the world into the spheres of the sacred and the profane. In the mythologies of religion the two spheres interpenetrate. The religious era in this sense, Bonhöffer would agree with Nietzsche, is coming to an end. Rudolf Bultmann, who seeks to "demythologize" Christianity, does not go far enough. Not only is the mythological view of the world "finished"; religion as such is "finished." But the disintegration of religion as the dichotomous view of the world begins with the transcendent God of the Old Testament. There is a historical line from the strange, unnatural Yahweh of the desert to the universe of modern science, which is altogether devoid of divinity. The old Hebrew knife of circumcision is still cutting. It began by cutting man off from the religious security of the mythological cosmos and driving him out into the desert. It has now cut off the cosmos itself, leaving the sky empty of gods, requiring a study of astronautics instead of angelology. The incarnation of God in the New Testament is the redemptive side of this same destruction of religion. By coming into the cosmos in the human being Jesus Christ, God forever puts his seal of acceptance upon it. Never again can there be sacred places, sacred refuges within the world. The entire world is empty of God; and the entire world is redeemed by God in Jesus Christ. And Christianity is not concerned with religion; it is concerned with Jesus Christ.

Thus Bonhöffer sees the problem of the contemporary church as that of witnessing to the living Christ in a world in which God is dead. Atheism is suddenly seen to be closer to Christianity than religion. Atheism is wrong, of course, in denying the transcendent God, but it constitutes the negative witness to this transcendence. Religion, on the other hand, seeks to deny the transcen-

197

dence, to reduce God in some way to immanence, to return to the divine cosmos in which man was once safe. As Karl Kraus has so beautifully put it: "The true believers are those who miss God."

A SECULAR CHRISTIANITY

It is in this sense that we must understand Bonhöffer's call for a secular or "religionless" Christianity. It is foolish to seek for God in the remote boundaries of darkness, in far-away nebulae or in the depths of human anguish. It is certainly part of the Christian's faith that the risen Lord is present on all possible boundaries, but no more there than in the center of life. Perhaps Protestants especially need a little more of the "Easter jubilation" of the Greek church, when all the creatures of the world and the distant stars join in the liturgy of the resurrected Savior. Christianity is not meant primarily for the "extreme situations" of human existence. It embraces *all* existence in its meaning, and perhaps is to be found above all in the experience of joy. It is not so much repentance which calls out for God but gratitude. Such a eucharistic faith rediscovers God in the midst of the world —not a world that has to be magically or mystically transformed, but the real world as created and redeemed, the real world which all men share.

Bonhöffer would have us stop thinking of secularization as primarily a turning away from God. He would have us think of it as revealing God's gift of freedom and of the world to man. Here we may use the Jewish concept known as *tsimtsum* or contraction: God created the world by contracting so that there was room for it. The act of creation was an act of renunciation on God's part. We can understand secularization as part of God's *tsimtsum*.

The Christian, then, Bonhöffer tells us, is not a special kind of man, a saint or a *homo religiosus*. To be a Christian means to be a *man*. The Christian life is lived entirely in the world. Christian love is not a religious exercise, a "spiritual concern." It is responsible action in the world, exercised in the mandates of political life, of work and friendship and marriage, of human solidarity against evil.

CHEAP GRACE

With the problem of theodicy Bonhöffer does not deal directly. However, in his search for a political ethic he repeatedly attacks those to whom religion becomes an alibi for standing by when the innocent are slaughtered. Even in the pre-war years he spoke scathingly of the "cheap grace" proclaimed from Protestant pulpits. Later he seriously questioned the Confessing Church of Germany, for he believed that its resistance to Hitler had been mainly a matter of self-defense rather than a struggle for justice. In his own words, "only he who cries out for the Jews has the right to sing Gregorian chants." Like Camus, it would seem, he considers the bystander guilty.

But if religion is "finished," so are all the functions of religion that sociologists would call "social control." The cross of Jesus Christ, erected jointly by church and state, is the ultimate condemnation of religion as the basis of social order. Before the cross, all talk of religion as the basis of Western civilization or democracy or morality is silenced. The Christian cannot be on the side of the orders that set up the crosses of history. His place is with the victim— and with the rebel. Thus Bonhöffer's fragmentary formulations not only open up the possibility of a new Christian political ethic but let us glimpse the outlines of a new Christian humanism.

Bonhöffer's radical doctrine of the world—the point at which he confronts Camus—carries far-reaching implications regarding a doctrine of the church. A conception seems to emerge here which breaks the bounds of the traditional formulations, Protestant *or* Catholic. Any idea of the church as a sacred institution, set apart from the world, is ruled out. Bonhöffer tried to express as much in his concept of "secret discipline"—a concept strikingly close to Simone Weil's "implicit love of God." Christian faith here becomes almost a secret, as the hidden Christ walks secretly through the byways of history. There is no secure position from which we can look out over the world and be safe. There is no ground for us to stand on except Jesus Christ, the Christ of the cross and the resurrection. But this ground is not in the places where men say "Lord, Lord!"—in the sacred precincts, in the realm of religion. Both crucifixion and resurrection took place outside the sacred city. Perhaps we are now being called to a new exodus, except that our fleshpots (especially in America) are not those of Egypt but of Zion. God still waits for us in the wilderness.

BONHÖFFER'S SIGNIFICANCE

Bonhöffer is not the only contemporary who has given expression to these conceptions. Simone Weil expressed the same when she refused to be baptized and chose to remain outside the religious community. And this concern makes understandable the refusal of Catholic prisoners in Spain to take the sacrament, lest they impair their solidarity with their non-Christian fellow revolutionaries. Bonhöffer himself, called to conduct his last worship service in prison shortly before his execution, held back, for he did not want to offend his neighbor, a Soviet officer. But what makes Bonhöffer most significant for us is that to the end his thoughts are related to the mainstream of the Protestant tradition. We find in him the challenging application to our contemporary situation of what Paul Tillich has called the "Protestant principle." Let us remind ourselves that it was religion, not the world, against which the Protestant witness was first directed.

Today most Americans still live in a country that is intact. So are its religious structures, as our religious revival shows. There is an uncanny similarity between this revival and the religious boom in Victorian England, which was followed by a rapid disintegration of religion. When the religious collapse comes on this side of the globe, the voices of Camus and Bonhöffer may turn out to be of vital urgency for the Christian church in America.

THOMAS HANNA

The Religious Significance of Camus' *The Fall**

It seems that Camus "feels" his way into philosophy. His thought takes on form in the gradual manner of a growing art-work. He moves forward through a kind of lyrical intuition which first finds its reality and validation in

* From *The Thought and Art of Albert Camus* by Thomas Hanna. Copyright 1958. Reprinted by permission of Henry Regnery Company, Chicago; pp. 214-37.

dramatic form. He thinks existentially before he thinks rationally, and this is the mark of an artistic temperament. This could be called a lyrical method in philosophy, even as Camus himself can be most clearly described as a lyrical existentialist. . . . And the wonder of his art works is that they are structured on a rationale of thought which carries beyond the confines of the work's immediate drama and points to an immensely wider realm in which this drama finds an ultimate meaning and universality.

It is because of this quality of Albert Camus as thinker and artist that his novels have tended to be harbingers of some coming extension or enrichment of his thought. The work, *The Fall*, is just such a harbinger. It could hardly be called a novel, nor does Camus himself do so; for him it is a *récit*, a narrative. And in order to fix the work clearly we need only to add the remark that *The Fall* is a confessional narrative. . . .

The confessor in this instance is Jean-Baptiste Clamence, noted Paris defense lawyer who had attained fame, some fortune, and considerable happiness as defender of society's unfortunate criminals and helpless oppressed. He was a pleader of unusual lyrical and persuasive powers who played the role of protector, interceding for the accused before the heartless machinery of justice. Clamence was one of those blessed individuals for whom virtue was its own ample reward. Life offered itself to him without restraint: he had position, respect, the love of women, and the affection of friends. He was, by all standards, not only a supremely happy man but an astonishingly good man. But then, without apparent warning, he began to change; quite deliberately he folded up the serenity of his life and disappeared from Paris, from France, from all that he had known and loved. He became of his own free will an exile, a man

200

withdrawn and set apart from the world that we know.

Clamence turns up in Amsterdam, and it is only by accident that the reader, while slumming, meets him in one of those bars with which European port towns are dotted: a motley consort of world transients mixed with local thieves, prostitutes, and procurers. Having forsaken all, he has taken refuge with the accused and rejected of the world; he has come home to the criminals and lost souls which he once defended. If not of publicans, he is at least the friend of sinners. It is here that we hear his narrative and come to appreciate the background of what has happened. Clamence tells us why it was that he has fallen from the paradise he once knew.

Jean-Baptiste Clamence and his story constitute a remarkable event in the career of Camus. . . . Camus has for the first time dealt directly and seriously not only with religious symbols and myths but with religious problems themselves. The ideas and problems of immortality, guilt, innocence, judgment, christology, duty, and hope have, from the beginning, played a necessary yet subdued role in Camus' works; they were problems which remained in the background while Camus turned his attention to immediate problems of a social nature. . . .

In no other work has Camus so enjoyed playing with his readers, alternately speaking rather obviously about himself and abruptly shoving the mask of Clamence between himself and the reader without so much as a comma or period of warning. . . . He admits that

. . . I adapt my words to my listener and lead him to go me one better. I mingle what concerns me and what concerns others. I choose features we have in common, the experiences we have endured together, the failings we share—good form, in other words, the man of the hour as he is rife in me and in others. With all that I construct a portrait which is the image of all and of no one. A mask, in short, rather like those carnival masks which are both lifelike and stylized, so that they make people say: "Why surely, I've met him!" When the portrait is finished, as it is this evening, I show it with great sorrow: "This, alas, is what I am!" The prosecutor's charge is finished. But at the same time the portrait I hold out to my contemporaries becomes a mirror.[1]

. . . The crucial event in Clamence's life in his Parisian "paradise" was the night when, returning home over the Pont Royal, he passed a girl who was leaning over the railing, staring into the river. It was one o'clock, and a drizzling rain assured the presence of no one else on the streets. There were but two people there: Clamence and the girl who stared into the Seine. When Clamence had crossed over the bridge and strolled eastward toward St. Michel he heard a splash and then a series of cries as the body was swept downstream. Clamence stopped and listened, knowing he should do something, yet realizing he wouldn't do anything. There was only himself and a being's cry of help. He listened there in the rain and the night, aware of the great distance between himself and the drowning girl, the swift current of the river, the coldness of the water, and the effort required for an almost impossible attempt to rescue the girl. He was dimly aware of these things: they were in the back of a mind which was pleasantly becalmed by the exertions of an evening's love-making. The cry of the girl did not quite penetrate through the lethargy of Clamence's lingering self-enjoyment. He stopped, listened, and then walked on. It was too late then, too late for anything, for this was the beginning of his fall. When he ignored the cry and walked on he had given the lie to his entire life of virtue: here he was, completely alone and uncompelled before this distressed cry; he was, in that moment, perfectly free; and when

his love for others was tested in that moment he discovered that he loved only himself, that his life of virtue and service to others was a sham, was nothing more than a means of buttressing his self-importance and sense of superiority. The distant splash of a young body into the night-filled waters of the Seine has, without his realizing it, commenced the destruction of Clamence. He will never again be the same.

The other central moment in Clamence's narrative is simply derived from this crucial event just recounted. It is the moment, two or three years later, when Clamence first becomes aware of his fall, and it occurs, quite understandably, on a bridge over the Seine. It is night, and Clamence again stands alone, this time gazing out over the river and sensing within him an overwhelming feeling of power and personal completion in this paradise which he has made so fully his own. At this moment he hears laughter behind him. He turns, but no one is there. The laughter breaks out once again, this time as if drifting downstream. But there is no one on the river; there is no one anywhere: there is just Clamence alone with the laughter. And it is this happening, which follows so naturally from the earlier incident on the Seine, which precipitates Clamence's fall, transforming him into the figure we meet in the Amsterdam bar, the judge-penitent who, by condemning his own life in the most general terms, is simultaneously condemning the life of his listener, is, in fact, provoking in his listener a process of self-judgment. Only by judging himself can he escape the judgment and mocking laughter of others and at the same time earn the right of judging others. Only in proclaiming the inescapable guilt of all men can Clamence lighten the burden of judgment which has weighed upon him. What is at stake in all this is man's freedom. Clamence is telling us

[1] Albert Camus, *The Fall*, trans. Justin O'Brien (New York: Alfred A. Knopf, 1957), pp. 138-40.

that men are free but that no man wants to bear the guilt which freedom must entail. The heart of his confession is that "on the bridges of Paris I, too, learned that I was afraid of freedom." [2] He had freely chosen to ignore the cry of distress but in the end he was unable to endure the personal guilt which this free choice brought with it. He was caught between social virtue and personal freedom, and his guilt showed him that in his inner being he was free even from morality. Clamence had neither God, nor confessor, nor master to whom he could give up his burden of freedom: no such messiah had yet come along. And in this interim period the one thing possible for this latter day John the Baptist was at least to proclaim the guilt of all men, thereby compromising the freedom which he knew he could never escape.

A very real question to interpose at this juncture is this: Which way has Clamence fallen, down or up? A man who has lost a paradise is presumably a man who has fallen "downward" and away from a higher state. But it so happens that the paradise of Clamence was not lost but was rejected, indeed, fled from. The prelapsarian Clamence was a man of blithesome, unconscious wholeness. His virtue gave direction to his being, sufficed for all, protected him from shock, reflection, or doubt. Clamence was indistinguishable from his habitual virtues until that crucial moment when the plaint of a drowning woman inserted itself between Clamence and his virtue. In that instant Clamence chose himself and not his virtue, he suddenly acted as a completely free individual and, in this very act, took upon himself the enormous, inescapable responsibility for his act. He was no longer safe or unconscious; he was in trouble. His virtue could not justify his action; he alone had to be its justification. From this point onward, Clamence moved toward consciousness and the agony of decision. In this respect Clamence did not fall downward but upward; he fell into a higher state: that of self-conscious freedom. All things told, he is morally more solid than he was previously. But the difficulty is that no matter how we view it Clamence has gone from one state to another neither through his own choice nor through the choice of another being. Whether one considers it a better or worse state is indifferent inasmuch as Clamence had suffered an experience which made his transformation unavoidable. Clamence forsook his "paradise" for the simple reason that he could do no other. He had discovered the burden of freedom, and this was his fall.

And in what way is Jean-Baptiste Clamence "the image of all and of no one"? In what way is he you or I, the picture of his times? We need only ask ourselves: In what way are we, children of the 20th century, like someone who could once act simply and innocently, never knowing the agony of moral uncertainty or the deep gnawing of freedom, because we were protected from this gnawing and this agony by the impassibility of the heavens, the assurance of revelation, the reassurance of providence, the divinely inspired rule of kings, and the divinely given word of the law? and in what way are we, children of the 20th century, like someone who has, through inexplicable events, lost this simplicity and innocence, having awakened to the consciousness of a freedom which gives lie to the pretension of providence and divine rule and leaves us heir to moral uncertainty and the gnawing of freedom? Clamence is a man in serious trouble, and the suggestion is that a whole age is in serious trouble. Clamence, as well as an entire age, has fallen out of one state and into another; both states of mind have their advantages and both have their drawbacks; it

[2] *Ibid.*, p. 136.

was neither an advance nor a decline. It was unavoidable: neither Clamence nor his age could help themselves.

This confessional narrative never goes beyond the point of being a confession: the rich anguish of Clamence and his age is methodically if playfully laid out before us and then left there. The narrative progressively charges the air with the weight of trouble and allows it to remain, trembling, without the dissipating breath of the ready answer that makes all things right. Camus has brought us trouble, a whole vision of trouble, and he has given us little more with which to deal with it than a certain irony and cynicism, and a searing honesty.

We have said that *The Fall* is a foretoken of some sea-change in Camus' thought, and the truth of this appears obvious enough in just the manner in which Camus ends his narrative in an unresolved cynicism. The implacable lucidity of *The Myth* is not here to lead us into the open, nor do we find the impassioned argument of *The Rebel*, which gives us a balanced perspective beyond the tangle of history. These previous high points of Camus' thought have no application here; he is no longer dealing with the romanticized individual facing a fragmented universe or the rebellious individual facing an oppressive metaphysical or political system. For the first time Camus is concerned with the individual as he faces himself, the reflective individual attempting to bring his personal history and destiny into accord with his understanding of himself and his world. And this is what was meant in pointing out the novel religious and psychological qualities of *The Fall*. But, having noted this religious character of the work, we still cannot help being troubled by the unresolved quality of the narrative. One feels that "it is not quite Camus," that "it doesn't conform to type." The un-

relieved tension and irony of *The Fall* appear bewildering and unaccountable to the admirer of Camus. And yet, what we wish to do from this point onward is to make it very clear that the genius and beauty of this work resides in the charged atmosphere which is left above us like a pall. To understand this peculiarity is to understand the narrative as a whole.

The first thing to note is that this unprecedented air of tense cynicism is not entirely unprecedented. Three years previously, in a short, sketchy shipboard diary, Camus had already unveiled this curious attitude with the cryptic remark that there is

no homeland for the despairer and me, I know that the sea goes before me and follows me, I have a ready made folly. Those who love one another and are separated can live in pain, but this is not despair: they know that love exists. This is why, with dry eyes, I suffer exile. I am still waiting. A day will come, finally. . . .[3]

And, almost as if in continuing, he writes later,

Thus a day will come which will bring the completion of everything; hence it is necessary to let oneself go on and on like those who swim until exhaustion. The completion of what? From the beginning I have refused to reveal it to myself. Oh bitter bed, princely couch, the crown is in the depths of the waters.[4]

These are, of course, highly personal remarks and at the same time rather unusual words to have come from the pen of Camus. Yet it is significant enough that Camus wished to see such passages made public. The notions of exile, waiting, and an unknown, still unfulfilled destiny are woven about the central image of the sea and portray both here and throughout much of the shipboard diary the thinking of a man who chafes against his past and present

[3] Albert Camus, "La Mer au plus près," *L'Eté* (Paris: Gallimard, 1954), p. 170.
[4] *Ibid.*, p. 181.

and views the future with a strange and visionary hope. For Camus, the sea is always more than the sea; his love for it has brought with it a vaster love for that which is innocent, young, cleansing and, in a wider sense, redemptive. If Camus feels himself alienated from these qualities, it is not that he feels himself entirely alone in this. For him, an entire age is in exile from the beauty of the sea, and he has been content as a child of this age to reflect the anguish of that exile more sensitively perhaps than any other. And the difficulty is that this is not an exile which can be ended simply by wishing it. The exile from the redeeming beauties of life is not self-imposed either by Camus or his age. It simply happened. They "fell" into it, and now they must live it through. To deny it would be to deny the one reality that was given them: their present history. And yet to forget or ignore that state of youth in which the world's beauty is enjoyed innocently and fully, to forget this would be to take away that which makes this exile bearable and somehow filled with hope. If we understand the dialectic of anguish which flows from such exile, then we can appreciate the awful poignancy of that moment in *The Fall* when Clamence, feeling the misery of his exile, allows the seams of this dialectic to stretch wide and almost burst:

On the Damrak the first streetcar sounds its bell in the damp air and marks the awakening of life at the extremity of this Europe where, at the same moment, hundreds of millions of men, my subjects, painfully slip out of bed, a bitter taste in their mouths, to go to a joyless work. Then, soaring over this whole continent which is under my sway without knowing it, drinking in the absinthe-colored light of breaking day, intoxicated with evil words, I am happy—I am happy, I tell you, I won't let you think I'm not happy, I am happy unto death! Oh, sun, beaches, and the islands in the path of the trade winds, youth whose memory drives one to despair!

I'm going back to bed; forgive me. I fear I got worked up; yet I'm not weeping. At times one wanders, doubting the facts, even when one has discovered the secrets of the good life.[5]

No, Clamence is not weeping; he is Europe's shaggy John the Baptist "with dry eyes," who, in the wilderness of a city's gray stones and stagnant canals, makes straight the way for a non-existent messiah. In this moment Clamence lays bare the *déchirement* of what is more than the soul of an individual; the anguish should find its response in every man. But the cardinal fact is that there is nothing tragic here: the tension is not broken as if before an irremediable loss of "islands in the path of the trade winds." Nor is Clamence pathetic: there is no suggestion of his being caught in a situation to which he cannot reply and in which he cannot insert some distant hope. To the very end Clamence plods on in his role of judge-penitent. The tension never lapses.

We said that *The Fall,* in marking a return to self by Camus, actually constituted a reversal of his previous concerns with revolt. We can now make clear just how sharp a reversal this is. It should be remembered that the theme which rings through the works of Camus from the very beginning is the innocence of men; Camus, from *Noces* onward, has defended the innocence of men against those theologies, ideologies, and regimes which would treat mankind as guilty. The whole call to revolt is a call to an innocent state in which all that is of value is within a man and all that is evil is outside him. This constant proclamation of the rebel's inner innocence and goodness and the outside world's oppressive evil has been the lyrical touchstone for much of Camus' writings and is given its fullest development in *L'Homme révolté.* But the question

[5] Camus, *The Fall,* op. cit., p. 144.

which must eventually be put to Camus, and which he must put to himself, is this: If, in revolt, man is innocent before the evil with which he is afflicted, then how do you account for the origin of this evil against which man revolts? Are all men innocent? Obviously not, inasmuch as it is men who create the oppressive conditions against which the rebel revolts. How, then, do you explain the guilt and evil of the men whom the rebel opposes? The theme of human innocence running through Camus' works is, finally, a one-sided theme, a conviction which only emphasizes the incomplete nature of Camus' message. Whence human guilt and evil?

The problem which Camus creates for himself out of his philosophy of revolt is inescapable: It is all very well to speak of the evil outside of men in "others," but to every other man I *am* an "other," and thus how is it that I am a man of guilt and evil as well as of innocence and goodness? To the sensitive reader Camus' almost continual emphasis on the guilt of the external "other" is the prime fault haunting the philosophy of revolt, but in justice to Camus we should note that *The Fall* is not the first indication of his awareness of this other side of the problem. It is in *The Plague* that we first see this aspect of revolt in its full complexity. Here we find Rieux and Tarrou struggling against the external evil of the plague; in relation to the plague they are innocent, they are proponents of goodness. But it is Tarrou who is aware of all that is involved in this; it is he who suggests that the plague is not simply something outside of men but is within them as well, as evil against which they must struggle. Tarrou is keenly aware that in relation to the plague which afflicts him he is innocent. But, simultaneously, in relation to the plague within him he is guilty. This is the contradiction in which he is caught, and it is beyond this that he yearns. It is just this yearning which is carried over

into *The Fall,* and *The Fall* constitutes a reversal of Camus' concerns precisely because he is no longer dealing with "I, the innocent rebel" but rather with "I, the guilty 'other.'" This is an entirely new exploration for Camus, the rounding out of the neglected other half of his position. And it is because of its newness as an exploration that Camus has turned up with new tools of a religious, psychological, and introspective nature. The decisiveness of this reversal is nowhere reflected more strikingly than in the way in which, in obvious reference to himself, he looks at himself as the innocent and virtuous defender of the oppressed and charges that this defender is actually the evil "other" which he is constantly reviling. The true moral stature of Albert Camus comes into focus in this moment when he confesses, "I am an innocent rebel, but I am much more than this: I am also a guilty evildoer." At this point Camus' philosophy of revolt becomes both complex and profound. And at this point Camus submits his thought to a tension which it has never before known and a yearning which was never before so anguished.

In *The Fall* we discover more sharply than in any other of his works the Camusian scene of a single individual given over to a lucid acceptance of "his times"—an acceptance which lives in this conflict, allowing the social anguish of an historical moment to become the personal anguish of an individual moment. Jean-Baptiste Clamence is a mirror of his times, but not simply this alone: he is the existential embodiment of his times. In a very real sense he *is* the times. There are those philosophers who think of God as being involved in the total historical process while yet standing above it, like a conscience, judging and suffering it. Clamence is, in a sense, this kind of being; he is playing the role of such a God by accepting within himself the rich and conflicting currents of a whole age and not simply living this but suffering it, because a conscience, a sense of rightness and proportion, has been brought into this acceptance. In consciousness of his guilt Clamence suffers the wrongs committed in his paradise. Yet beyond these two conflicting realms of paradise and penitence, he envisions those islands on the high seas which mean innocence and redemption. Without these islands he would not suffer, for there would be nothing finally at stake. What we see here is an illustration of Nietzsche's dictum: If the old tablets of the law have been broken, then we must make new ones. No man can live in absolute freedom. Clamence is a man who forsook his virtue and became free, but complete freedom is an unbearable condition: a new "virtue," a new law had to be found. But there was no such law, and Clamence is left in an interim period, attempting, as a judge-penitent, at least to make it clear to all men exactly what it is in which they are caught. And perhaps by clarifying the problem he has taken the first step toward the creation of the "new law." In Clamence we do not see the "rebel" who has discovered his innate value by virtue of a threat which is external to him; rather we find a man who, not being involved in a social situation of external threat, discovers that no innate value is forthcoming; taken alone, without being in conflict with the world, Clamence's soul reveals only the unbearable emptiness of freedom. And this is why he longs for the innocence he once knew, while rejecting the virtue he once practiced. Clamence, the mirror of his times, hints that the life of rebellion is not all-sufficing, that it must finally create something out of itself which makes possible an ongoing civilization that can guarantee a certain innocence and peace without being ceaselessly revolted against. Clamence and his age seek an old innocence and a new law.

It is in this way that Clamence suffers: his is the suffering of history. Certainly there is no suffering of history except as it is embodied in an individual. But there is more to this: simply in being what he is, Clamence suffers not just history but *our* history; he suffers it for us. Here we come to his unusual significance: he is essentially a Christ-like figure who accepts the common sins and ills of every man while holding them in tension with the common longing of every man. Like Christ, he suffers for us. And perhaps this is the only kind of Christ that Camus could ever conceive: one who suffered for us without hope or final assurance. Perhaps this is the only Christ possible for an age which has suffered the fall: a poor and stumbling Christ who, in an age before the fall, would be nothing more than a preparer of the way, not worthy to tie the thongs on the sandals of a true Christ. Clamence, whose effort it is to lead men to a certain penitence and a certain righteousness, is clearing a path which becomes overgrown almost as soon as he has finished. He recognizes the situation he is in, knows that "It's too late now. It will always be too late. Fortunately!" He knows himself and his age and knows the difficulty of his task, and yet he plods on. He can do no other. He lives in a time when there can be only a preparation and never a completion. But it is the duty of a man to remain true to those things he knows to be true: his own searing conflict and a yearning for the islands. If history forbids hope and if human nature withholds promise, this is no matter. The essential task is to hold fast to one's truth and one's reality. All else will take care of itself.

In Clamence's narrative the profoundly religious concern of Camus comes into the thick confusion of our history like light filtering through the tangle of a jungle. This religious concern is "profound" precisely because it is at grips not with religious doctrines and practices but rather with the fundamental human condition out of which religions arise. Clamence may be a kind of Christ in our times, but to say this is not to imply that Camus has given over to Christian faith. No, Camus is at grips with the abiding human problems out of which the Christian faith sprang and to which it responded. *The Fall* goes far toward reopening a debate to which the Christian faith has given the last and best rejoinder. The question seems to be roughly this: Given the inescapability of personal guilt and judgment, how may one go beyond guilt and judgment to attain the blessedness of innocence? Put even more traditionally, the question is: How can my existence find justification? In this strange monologue of a troubled modern conscience an ancient question has somehow been struck and tossed up. Clamence is a man who has absorbed all the blows that a modern man can absorb, yet he stands beyond either a tragic end or a pathetic ongoing. He stands burdened and tense, troubled by the yearning which has already found voice in other of Camus' pages: How can one become a saint without God? It seems that ultimately this is the only question worth asking. There is no answer given, and Clamence must go on holding out the question and preserving his tension unflinchingly.

Much of Camus' genius and power comes from the way in which he competes with the Christian faith on its own ground. His concerns are not so much Christian as pre-Christian in nature, and he stands alongside Kierkegaard and Nietzsche as a thinker who is convinced that the advent of the "modern world" has brought with it novel problems and novel insights which force us to look again at the abiding condition of men in a way which was not fully possible for the first Christians. Without any doubt this is the reason for the profound and disturbing appeal which Camus, as well as his two forebears, has for our time. In challenging the Jewish-Christian heritage and in taking up again the problems to which it responded, he has touched upon that painfully suppressed conviction that the Jewish-Christian heritage can no longer inspire or support individuals and their culture, and that hence we must turn our thoughts once more to the fundamental reality of a world in which men are born, find suffering and happiness, and die. In *The Fall* Camus has put his finger on the anguish of an age. And we see that Clamence and the tension in which he lives and waits is not something unusual in the world of Camus; rather, it is typical of this world and essential to it, for, after all, Clamence can only be described in the same terms in which we have originally characterized Camus himself when it was said that he was "the most acute conscience of the contradictions of our times between the nihilism of destruction and the nostalgia for peace."

Religion and Modern Literature: Bibliography

Barnes, Hazel E. *Humanistic Existentialism: The Literature of Possibility*. Lincoln: University of Nebraska Press, 1959.

Barrett, William. *Irrational Man*. New York: Doubleday & Company, 1958.

Hopper, Stanley R., ed. *Spiritual Problems in Contemporary Literature*. New York: Harper & Row, 1957.

Lynch, William F. *Christ and Apollo*. New York: Sheed & Ward, 1960. Paper, New York: The New American Library.

Mueller, William R. *The Prophetic Voice in Modern Fiction.* New York: Association Press, 1959.

Scott, Nathan A., Jr. *Rehearsals of Discomposure.* New York: Columbia University Press, 1952.

————, ed. *Forms of Extremity in the Modern Novel.* Richmond, Va.: John Knox Press, 1965.

————, ed. *Man in the Modern Theatre.* Richmond, Va.: John Knox Press, 1965.

Stewart, Randall. *American Literature and Christian Doctrine.* Baton Rouge: Louisiana State University Press, 1958.

Vahanian, Gabriel. *The Death of God.* New York: George Braziller, 1961.

————. *Wait Without Idols.* New York: George Braziller, 1964.

Wilder, Amos N. *Modern Poetry and the Christian Tradition.* New York: Charles Scribner's Sons, 1952.

Camus

Brée, Germaine. *Camus.* Rev. ed. New Brunswick, N. J.: Rutgers University Press, 1961.

————, ed. *Camus.* Englewood Cliffs, N. J.: Prentice-Hall, 1962.

Camus, Albert. *The Myth of Sisyphus.* New York: Alfred A. Knopf, 1955. Paper (Vintage ed.), 1955.

————. *The Rebel.* New York: Random House, 1954. Paper (Vintage ed.), 1954.

Cruickshank, John. *Albert Camus and the Literature of Revolt.* New York: Oxford University Press, 1959.

Scott, Nathan A., Jr. *Camus.* New York: Hillary House Publishers, n.d.

208

V

Religion
and Philosophy

Introduction

The question of the relation of religion to philosophy will mean something different depending upon whether one has in mind metaphysics or analytic philosophy or existential philosophy.

The readings on metaphysics may be compared to the discussion of the same subject to be found in the selections from Ayer and Gilson in the "Religion and Science" section. Note in Brunner the conflict between faith, on the one hand, and that "general cultural consciousness" which finds expression in philosophy, on the other. Does Tillich see any conflict between "the truth of faith" and "the truth of philosophy"?

The next two readings are concerned with the linguistic side of analytic philosophy, which is based on the belief that the meaning of a sentence is the use that men give it and that it is the job of philosophy—or a large part of that job —to analyze those uses in which important concepts are involved. In order to analyze the meaning of the term "God" Wisdom finds it necessary to deal with the same problem that Scott was concerned with, namely, that of showing that knowledge is not limited to what can be gained by scientific or experimental (and logical) procedures—as

Ayer will later be found insisting that it is.

A helpful focal point for the selections on existentialism may perhaps be found in the use of psychological concepts (such as anxiety) as metaphysical or ontological concepts—i.e., as concepts by which to describe the basic structure of being. Bultmann argues that these are the most adequate ontological concepts we have for understanding the possibility of human existence presented in the Bible, while Williams sees them as in basic conflict with the biblical message. Sartre uses these concepts to explore a different possibility of human existence —one based on the premise of atheism. Cox rejects their use because he believes that metaphysics as such belongs to the style of the previous cultural period and is not an expression of the authentic style of our culture. (Compare Cox and Bultmann on secularization) Tillich takes the opposite point of view in maintaining that the authentic style of our culture is existentialist and that this style is expressed in metaphysics in the use of these concepts.[1] Tillich discusses existentialism in his selection in the "Religion and Psychotherapy" section.

[1] See "Existential Philosophy: Its Historical Meaning" in the *Journal of the History of Ideas* (January, 1944), reprinted in *Theology of Culture*, pp. 94-96.

EMIL BRUNNER

The Priority of Revelation over Metaphysics*

Philosophy consists in reflection on the connection between all particular facts, and the means it employs to this end is thought investigating the way in which the facts are intellectually founded.[1] . . . Such an inquiry will include that into the meaning of all science, all civilization and indeed human life in general. But when any school of philosophy surveys the more significant expressions of human life, it will discover among them a form of life which on the one hand is in the closest connection with the set of problems peculiar to philosophy, while on the other it has characteristic differences from every school of philosophy, or is even actually opposed to philosophy. This form of life is religion. The kinship between the two rests on the fact that religion as well as philosophy has in view the whole of existence and life; the opposition between them consists in the fact that religion itself claims to supply an answer to the crucial question about reality. It gives this answer in the shape of revelation, and not as the result of the methodical reflection of the intellect, i.e. of an activity within the bounds of reason. Thus philosophy is brought face to face with a most difficult problem, that of showing the meaning and justification of religion within the mental ground known to philosophy. In this way philosophy of religion arises as a part, and perhaps indeed as the culminating point, of philosophy in general.

Provided, however, that the philosopher is serious in his concern about the truth of religion, he cannot avoid listening in the first place to the affirmations of religion about itself—and this always means the affirmations of some specific form of religion. It might of course be the case that religion will have to reject altogether any such classification under philosophy on the plea that it would involve a misinterpretation of religion. In that case the relation between the two would have to be determined conversely, i.e. by starting from religion. Then religion would not have its basis assigned within the bounds of philosophy, but conversely, viz. philosophy, being a special department of man's activity as a reasonable creature, would take its place within the bounds of revealed truth. If such an assertion is not meant to forego every connection with the mind of science, civilization, and philosophy, we must of course make several requirements: that religion should find in her own presuppositions the grounds for thus inverting the relationship between ground and consequence; that it should also report on its mode of supplying these grounds; and once more, that, on the second presupposition, it should make plain the possibility of science, civilization, and philosophy. That would be the way in which, starting from the side of religion, the discussion would have to be carried on with a philosophy originating in the general cultural consciousness. But such an undertaking could be called philosophy of religion only in a secondary sense, and the name as just defined could merely serve to designate the sphere of the discussion.

[1] . . . [Philosophy] inquires how far a mental ground is discoverable for the connection between particular facts.

The state of the case only becomes really clear when, as is incumbent upon us, we look from the stand-point of general possibilities at the special situation that faces us. There are two reasons why we can speak only in a secondary sense of a Christian, and more particularly of a Protestant, philosophy of religion. First, Christian faith, especially in the particular form given to it in Protestant theology, is a fundamentally different thing from every philosophy. To philosophize is to reflect on the mental grounds, with the assumption that ultimate validity belongs to the complex of grounds and consequences developed by natural reason. Christian faith on the other hand involves recognizing that this complex has been broken into by revelation. It is on this revelation that the affirmations of Christian faith are grounded. Theology, which is Christian faith in scientific form, could only lay claim to a scientific character provided it gave clear and exact expression to the fact that its complex of grounds and consequences differs from that of all other sciences as to the final authority it recognizes; provided further that it developed all its affirmations purely out of its own presuppositions and thus founded them on that complex; and provided finally, that on this basis it investigated the relations, whether positive or negative, between revealed faith and rational knowledge. Thus theology is on common ground with philosophy in showing the existence of an intelligible connection embracing all things; but this is not, as it is for philosophy, the logos of the natural reasoning process, but the logos of revelation. Hence Christian theology can never be required to make faith rational by giving it scientific form; on the contrary, it has to keep revelation and religion duly apart by means of clearly defined concepts. . . .

Neither can there be philosophy of religion in the strict sense of the term in the realm of Christian theology, for the further reason that theology has to do not with religion but with revelation. Whatever else religion may be, it is a mode of human life, whereas revelation is a self-disclosure of God. While the philosopher of religion is concerned with historical phenomena, i.e. with the historical religions and their "nature", the theologian is concerned with the ground of all phenomena.

To the philosopher as to the theologian, religion is not the ultimate fact but something that roots in the ultimate. In the former case it is reason that supplies the ultimate ground, while in the latter it is revelation. The aim of theology is thus something quite different from religion, and at bottom is no more closely related to religion than it is to any other department of human life. This conclusion, moreover, follows directly from the fundamental presupposition of theology: its ground, its content, and its standard alike are found not in any consciousness of man's, but in God's self-disclosure.

Christian faith, to which theology gives the form of scientific conceptions, is the knowledge and acknowledgment of God's self-revelation in Jesus Christ. He, the incarnate logos, is the ground, content, and standard of all the affirmations of faith. That is where faith differs from every religion as well as from every philosophy. By Christian faith is meant, not some universal truth, nor yet some universal religious experience, but a definite fact which as such is opposed to every universal, be it religion or philosophy. Not that it denies the existence of a certain universal knowledge of God, religious as well as philosophical: rather it presupposes this. But it does deny that the personal and living God can be generally known from possibilities that lie either in the world or in man's spirit as such. It contends that the living and personal God can be known only by a personal meeting, through His personal word, through that special event to which the Bible, and the Bible alone, bears witness, and the content of which

213

is Jesus Christ. Hence this definite fact is not to be understood merely as an illustration, or an embodiment, or even a symbol; where such language is used concerning this matter it is not Christian faith with which we have to do. On the contrary, the definite fact of revelation takes the place of what is universal, of truth in general, or of the final criterion of valid assertions; the incarnate logos here occupies the position otherwise held by the logos of reason, the essential idea of truth. This is the case because the personal God, who is the ground of all truth, cannot be known as personal by means of idea, but only by personal, concrete revelation; only when He no longer hides Himself, but issues forth and discloses Himself as the ground of all being, all values, and all thought.

This particular fact, this miracle of divine revelation, which by its very particularity is a stumbling block to thinking in universals, is the presupposition of Christian theology. Christian faith consists precisely in taking this peculiar view of ultimate truth. It would cease to be faith, it would indeed give the lie to its own affirmation, if it wanted to ground the truth of this affirmation on a universal truth. Either revelation supplies its own grounds or else it is not revelation. . . . Only by perceiving in scripture the utterance of God does a man become a believer; and only as such, i.e. as a member of the community of believers, is the thinker in a position to think theologically. Theology is in place only in the church, just as in the same way its ground and content are to be found in the scriptural revelation.

This again is the starting point for a Protestant philosophy of religion, using this term now in the modified or secondary sense. Such a philosophy must come from theology and, further back still, from faith. It is not the case that it leads towards faith. It is a part of Christian theology as such, i.e. that part in which it carries on the discussion with the common consciousness of truth, i.e.

with philosophy; it is that chapter of Christian theology whose business is to start from definitely Christian presuppositions, and give a well-founded description of the relations between revelation and rational knowledge on the one hand, and between revelation and religion on the other. Hence it is not a universal science, of which Christian theology would form a subdivision as being the doctrine of a particular religion. This erroneous view was largely followed in the nineteenth century. The very nature of revealed faith involves reversing the classification of universal and special in this case, because here a particular, viz. revelation, is regarded as ranking above every universal. . . .

At bottom, the philosopher of religion knows no more than any plain Christian: he merely knows it in the more exact form of abstract conceptions and in connection with the rational knowledge of his age. The reverse side of this advantage is that the abstract nature of his knowledge imperils the personal character of his faith—which ought to penetrate the said knowledge—even more than does the abstract nature of theology in general.

There is no fundamental difference between a theological and a nontheological expression of Christian faith. All utterance about God, no matter how much of personal earnestness it may have, has always the abstractness of theology. Even the parables of Jesus are theology. And conversely, the very earnestness of a personal, vital faith may lead it in certain circumstances, e.g. in its discussion and contention with the thought of one's age, to avail itself of the most abstract forms conceivable. Yet the primary interest of Christianity is not systematic knowledge, but the relation of a personal faith to revelation. Hence of course faith is constantly directed towards overcoming abstract concepts as completely as possible; and therefore the philosophy of religion must be judged as lying at best on the edge of

214

Christian doctrine and never at its centre.

Revelation meets and fits human consciousness. It is not a matter of indifference that this consciousness should be defined as human, although on the other hand it is not essential to know in what more specific way it is so defined. Faith is indeed bound up with humanity but not with any particular grade of humanity. Of course it presupposes man as man, but not a particular type of humanity, nor yet any particular feature in man. It takes man in his totality, not in some special locus that can be fixed by psychology. The locus in which revelation and the spirit of man meet each other cannot be assigned positively but only negatively: it consists in receptivity. If in place of this we would rather put a particular form of consciousness, we might say that it is "inquiry" when this has assumed the form of a vital need. But although this is a presupposition for faith, it does not designate a particular psychological quality, but, on the contrary, what is universally human. In fact, we can indicate the locus yet more definitely without thereby abandoning what is universally human: the negative point of contact is a consciousness of vital need which is at the same time a consciousness of guilt. Therefore we might fittingly express our meaning as follows: any account of the faith evoked by revelation should be preceded by another account giving the results of man's investigation of universal mental characteristics, which investigation would lead up to the afore-mentioned point of contact. Lack of space obliges us to omit such an account. Ultimately, however, this makes no difference because in every case faith appropriate to revelation must be understood entirely by itself and not by means of any common consciousness of man's. Faith appropriate to revelation can be understood only by revelation, just in the same way as any rational thought can only be understood by its ground in reason, or a sensation of light only by the light-stimulus. Therefore it is necessary to start from revelation as known to faith; in doing so we have only to bear in mind that revelation is always the answer to a question on man's part. But whether man's question, and indeed humanity itself, have their ground in revelation, and only in it can attain their proper meaning; and therefore whether man's question has not its *prius* in God's address to him—these are matters that can be discussed only in connection with the knowledge appropriate to revelation. At all events faith is certain that revelation alone enables us rightly to apprehend that need, that vital incapacity, which is the presupposition of faith; and that thereby revelation itself begets its own presupposition in the crucial sense.

According to the testimony of the apostles, what took place in Christ took place once for all. There was no historical continuity of revelation but only a paradoxical unity between that unique event and the present time, the contemporaneity of faith with revelation which is immediate and independent of intermediary criteria. Between Christ as the mediator and the believer there is no intermediation, because this could come about only by means of a continually renewed incarnation of the logos, thus contradicting the apostolic dictum "once for all." Only God, as the Holy Spirit, can speak again the word which was spoken at that time once for all, and speak it in the heart of the believer at any later moment in history. God as identical with Himself in His historically unique revelation, and in the "subjective" knowledge that appropriates it, God as the ground, object, and subject of knowledge, the triune God, is the content of Christian faith, a content incomprehensible to reason. The norm of that faith was formulated in the creed of the early church. With it corresponds, as the doctrine of the formal norm, the

Reformation principle of Scripture, viz. the word of God in Scripture which is identical with the word of God in the soul, or in brief, Scripture and spirit in their paradoxical and incomprehensible identity.

In this way the Christian normative principle is marked off on two sides: from realistic heteronomy or authority, and from idealistic autonomy or freedom. Realism makes us dependent on a given fact, and thus on something which, as itself relative, has a place in the flux of relative phenomena. At the same time, it makes us dependent upon something external which seems foreign to us. By the former dependence the bond is made uncertain, by the latter, "dark" or "blind", because it does not take inward possession of the spirit. Hence a protest must be raised against it in the name of idealism. Idealism will recognize as binding only what comes from within and not what comes from without: accordingly what it recognizes cannot be a datum but must be a non-temporal entity located in the spirit itself and therefore to be found in oneself in advance. That is the nature of its extraordinarily

significant principle of autonomy. But it overstrains freedom as surely as realism denies it. Idealism does not recognize any irrational element either in the sphere of knowledge or in that of the will, i.e. it recognizes neither the incomprehensible data of reality nor the fact of evil. If we deal seriously with the question of evil, the deepest ego is not identical with, but in contradiction to, its idea of itself. Therefore genuine freedom, which resolves the contradiction, cannot originate in the deepest ego as if it belonged to that ego, but must be bestowed on it as something foreign that is at the same time truly its own. That is the divine challenge, the word of God, by which at the same time we recognize our self-contradiction, sin, and by which we are adopted again into union with Himself, and thereby into the divine purpose. But this word does not arise from our deepest self; it is not an innate truth which has merely to be aroused or discovered. Rather it must come to us as a datum from without, a word of revelation which subjects us to itself as authority and yet, at the same time, lays hold of our spirits inwardly as truth.

PAUL TILLICH

Metaphysics as an Expression of Ultimate Concern*

The difficulty of every discussion concerning philosophy as such is the fact that every definition of philosophy is an expression of the point of view of the

philosopher who gives the definition. Nevertheless, there is a kind of pre-philosophical agreement about the meaning of philosophy, and the only

* From *Dynamics of Faith* by Paul Tillich. Copyright © 1957 by Paul Tillich. Reprinted by permission of Harper & Row, Publishers; pp. 90-95.

thing one can do in a discussion like the present one is to use this prephilosophical notion of what philosophy is. In this sense philosophy is the attempt to answer the most general questions about the nature of reality and human existence. Most general are those questions which do not ask about the nature of a specific sphere of reality (as the physical or the historical realms) but about the nature of reality, which is effective in all realms. Philosophy tries to find the universal categories in which being is experienced.

If such a notion of philosophy is presupposed, the relation of philosophical truth to the truth of faith can be determined. Philosophical truth is truth about the structure of being; the truth of faith is truth about one's ultimate concern. Up to this point the relation seems to be very similar to that between the truth of faith and scientific truth. But the difference is that there is a point of identity between the ultimate of the philosophical question and the ultimate of the religious concern. In both cases ultimate reality is sought and expressed —conceptually in philosophy, symbolically in religion. Philosophical truth consists in true concepts concerning the ultimate; the truth of faith consists in true symbols concerning the ultimate. The relation between these two is the problem with which we have to deal.

The question will certainly be raised: Why does philosophy use concepts and why does faith use symbols if both try to express the same ultimate? The answer, of course, is that the relation to the ultimate is not the same in each case. The philosophical relation is in principle a detached description of the basic structure in which the ultimate manifests itself. The relation of faith is in principle an involved expression of concern about the meaning of the ultimate for the faithful. The difference is obvious and fundamental. But it is, as the phrase "in principle" indicates, a difference which is not maintained in the actual life of philosophy and of faith. It cannot be maintained, because the philosopher is a human being with an ultimate concern, hidden or open. And the faithful one is a human being with the power of thought and the need for conceptual understanding. This is not only a biographical fact. It has consequences for the life of philosophy in the philosopher and for the life of faith in the faithful.

An analysis of philosophical systems, essays or fragments of all kinds shows that the direction in which the philosopher asks the question and the preference he gives to special types of answers is determined by cognitive consideration and by a state of ultimate concern. The historically most significant philosophies show not only the greatest power of thought but the most passionate concern about the meaning of the ultimate whose manifestations they describe. One needs only to be reminded of the Indian and Greek philosophers, almost without exception, and the modern philosophers from Leibnitz and Spinoza to Kant and Hegel. If it seems that the positivistic line of philosophers from Locke and Hume to present-day logical positivism is an exception to this rule, one must consider that the tasks to which these philosophers restricted themselves were special problems of the doctrine of knowledge and, in our time especially, analyses of the linguistic tools of scientific knowledge. This certainly is a justified and very important endeavor, but is not philosophy in the traditional sense.

Philosophy, in its genuine meaning, is carried on by people in whom the passion of an ultimate concern is united with a clear and detached observation of the way ultimate reality manifests itself in the processes of the universe. It is this element of ultimate concern behind philosophical ideas which supplies the truth of faith in them. Their vision of the universe and of man's predicament within it unites faith and conceptual work. Philosophy is not only the mother's womb out of which science and history have come, it is also an ever-present element in actual scientific and historical work. The frame of reference within which the great physicists have seen and are seeing the universe of their inquiries is philosophical, even if their actual inquiries verify it. In no case is it a result of their discoveries. It is always a vision of the totality of being which consciously or unconsciously determines the frame of their thought. Because this is so one is justified in saying that even in the scientific view of reality an element of faith is effective. Scientists rightly try to prevent these elements of faith and philosophical truth from interfering with their actual research. This is possible to a great extent; but even the most protected experiment is not absolutely "pure"—pure in the sense of the exclusion of interfering factors such as the observer, and as the interest which determines the kind of question asked of nature in an experiment. What we said about the philosopher must also be said about the scientist. Even in his scientific work he is a human being, grasped by an ultimate concern, and he asks the question of the universe as such, the philosophical question.

In the same way the historian is consciously or unconsciously a philosopher. It is quite obvious that every task of the historian beyond the finding of facts is dependent on evaluations of historical factors, especially the nature of man, his freedom, his determination, his development out of nature, etc. It is less obvious but also true that even in the act of finding historical facts philosophical presuppositions are involved. This is especially true in deciding, out of the infinite number of happenings in every infinitely small moment of time, which facts shall be called historically relevant facts. The historian is further forced to give his evaluation of sources and their reliability, a task which is not independent of his interpretation of human nature. Finally, in the moment in which a historical work gives implicit or explicit assertions about the meaning of historical events for human existence, the philosophical presuppositions of history are evident. Where there is philosophy there is expression of an ultimate concern; there is an element of faith, however hidden it may be by the passion of the historian for pure facts.

All these considerations show that, in spite of their essential difference, there is an actual union of philosophical truth and the truth of faith in every philosophy and that this union is significant for the work of the scientist and the historian. This union has been called "philosophical faith." [1] The term is misleading, because it seems to confuse the two elements, philosophical truth and the truth of faith. Further, the term seems to indicate that there is *one* philosophical faith, a "philosophia perennis," as it has been termed. But only the philosophical question is perennial, not the answers. There is a continuous process of interpretation of philosophical elements and elements of faith, not *one* philosophical faith.

There is truth of faith in philosophical truth. And there is philosophical truth in the truth of faith. In order to see the latter point we must confront the conceptual expression of philosophical truth with the symbolical expression of the truth of faith. Now, one can say that most philosophical concepts have mythological ancestors and that most mythological symbols have conceptual elements which can and must be developed as soon as the philosophical consciousness has appeared. In the idea of God the concepts of being, life, spirit, unity and diversity are implied. In the symbol of the creation concepts of finitude, anxiety, freedom and time are

[1] In the book of this name by Jaspers.

218

implied. The symbol of the "fall of Adam" implies a concept of man's essential nature, of his conflict with himself, of his estrangement from himself. Only because every religious symbol has conceptual potentialities is "theo-logy" possible. There is a philosophy implied in every symbol of faith. But faith does not determine the movement of the philosophical thought, just as philosophy does not determine the character of one's ultimate concern. Symbols of faith can open the eyes of the philosopher to qualities of the universe which otherwise would not have been recognized by him. But faith does not command a definite philosophy, although churches and theological movements have claimed and used Platonic, Aristotelian, Kantian or Humean philosophies. The philosophical implications of the symbols of faith can be developed in many ways, but the truth of faith and the truth of philosophy have no authority over each other.

JOHN WISDOM

Conceptual Analysis and the Religious Pattern in Human Behavior*

1. *The existence of God is not an experimental issue in the way it was.* An atheist or agnostic might say to a theist 'You still think there are spirits in the trees, nymphs in the streams, a God of the world.' He might say this because he noticed the theist in time of drought pray for rain and make a sacrifice and in the morning look for rain. But disagreement about whether there are gods is now less of this experimental or betting sort than it used to be. This is due in part, if not wholly, to our better knowledge of why things happen as they do.

It is true that even in these days it is seldom that one who believes in God has no hopes or fears which an atheist has not. Few believers now expect prayer to still the waves, but some think it makes a difference to people and not merely in ways the atheist would admit. Of course with people, as opposed to waves and machines, one never knows what they won't do next, so that expecting prayer to make a difference to them is not so definite a thing as believing in its mechanical efficacy. Still, just as primitive people pray in a business-like way for rain so some people still pray for others with a real feeling of doing something to help. However, in spite of this persistence of an experimental element in some theistic belief, it remains true that Elijah's method on Mount Carmel of settling the matter of what god or gods exist would be far less appropriate to-day than it was then.

* From "Gods" by John Wisdom in *Proceedings of the Aristotelian Society* (1944-45). Reprinted by permission of the Editor of The Aristotelian Society; pp. 185-206.

2. *Belief in gods is not merely a matter of expectation of a world to come.* Someone may say 'The fact that a theist no more than an atheist expects prayer to bring down fire from heaven or cure the sick does not mean that there is no difference between them as to the facts, it does not mean that the theist has no expectations different from the atheist's. For very often those who believe in God believe in another world and believe that God is there and that we shall go to that world when we die.'

This is true, but I do not want to consider here expectations as to what one will see and feel after death nor what sort of reasons these logically unique expectations could have. So I want to consider those theists who do not believe in a future life, or rather, I want to consider the differences between atheists and theists in so far as these differences are not a matter of belief in a future life.

3. *What are these differences? And is it that theists are superstitious or that atheists are blind?* A child may wish to sit a while with his father and he may, when he has done what his father dislikes fear punishment and feel distress at causing vexation, and while his father is alive he may feel sure of help when danger threatens and feel that there is sympathy for him when disaster has come. When his father is dead he will no longer expect punishment or help. Maybe for a moment an old fear will come or a cry for help escape him, but he will at once remember that this is no good now. He may feel that his father is no more until perhaps someone says to him that his father is still alive though he lives now in another world and one so far away that there is no hope of seeing him or hearing his voice again. The child may be told that nevertheless his father can see him and hear all he says. When he has been told this the child will still fear no punishment nor expect any sign of his father, but now, even more than he did when his

father was alive, he will feel that his father sees him all the time and will dread distressing him and when he has done something wrong he will feel separated from his father until he has felt sorry for what he has done. Maybe when he himself comes to die he will be like a man who expects to find a friend in the strange country where he is going, but even when this is so, it is by no means all of what makes the difference between a child who believes that his father lives still in another world and one who does not.

Likewise one who believes in God may face death differently from one who does not, but there is another difference between them besides this. This other difference may still be described as belief in another world, only this belief is not a matter of expecting one thing rather than another here or hereafter, it is not a matter of a world to come but of a world that now is, though beyond our senses.

We are at once reminded of those other unseen worlds which some philosophers 'believe in' and others 'deny', while non-philosophers unconsciously 'accept' them by using them as models with which to 'get the hang of' the patterns in the flux of experience. We recall the timeless entities whose changeless connections we seek to represent in symbols, and the values which stand firm amidst our flickering satisfaction and remorse, and the physical things which, though not beyond the corruption of moth and rust, are yet more permanent than the shadows they throw upon the screen before our minds. We recall, too, our talk of souls and of what lies in their depths and is manifested to us partially and intermittently in our own feelings and the behaviour of others. The hypothesis of mind, of other human minds and of animal minds, is reasonable because it explains for each of us why certain things behave so cunningly all by themselves unlike even the most ingenious machines. Is the hypothesis of minds in flowers and trees reasonable for like reasons? Is the hypothesis of a world mind reasonable for like reasons—someone who adjusts the blossom to the bees, someone whose presence may at times be felt—in a garden in high summer, in the hills when clouds are gathering, but not, perhaps, in a cholera epidemic?

4. *The question 'Is belief in gods reasonable?' has more than one source.* It is clear now that in order to grasp fully the logic of belief in divine minds we need to examine the logic of belief in animal and human minds. But we cannot do that here and so for the purposes of this discussion about divine minds let us acknowledge the reasonableness of our belief in human minds without troubling ourselves about its logic. The question of the reasonableness of belief in divine minds then becomes a matter of whether there are facts in nature which support claims about divine minds in the way facts in nature support our claims about human minds.

In this way we resolve the force behind the problem of the existence of gods into two components, one metaphysical and the same which prompts the question 'Is there *ever any* behaviour which gives reason to believe in *any* sort of mind?' and one which finds expression in 'Are there other mind-patterns in nature beside the human and animal patterns which we can all easily detect, and are these other mind-patterns super-human?'

Such over-determination of a question syndrome is common. Thus, the puzzling questions 'Do dogs think?', 'Do animals feel?' are partly metaphysical puzzles and partly scientific questions. They are not purely metaphysical; for the reports of scientists about the poor performances of cats in cages and old ladies' stories about the remarkable performances of their pets are not irrelevant. But nor are these questions purely scientific; for the stories never settle them and therefore they have other sources. One other source is the metaphysical source we have already noticed, namely, the difficulty about getting behind an animal's behaviour to its mind, whether it is a non-human animal or a human one.

But there's a third component in the force behind these questions, these disputes have a third source, and it is one which is important in the dispute which finds expression in the words 'I believe in God', 'I do not'. This source comes out well if we consider the question 'Do flowers feel?' Like the questions about dogs and animals this question about flowers comes partly from the difficulty we sometimes feel over inference from *any* behaviour to thought or feeling and partly from ignorance as to what behaviour is to be found. But these questions, as opposed to a like question about human beings, come also from hesitation as to whether the behaviour in question is *enough* mind-like, that is, is it enough similar to or superior to human behaviour to be called 'mind-proving'? Likewise, even when we are satisfied that human behaviour shows mind and even when we have learned whatever mind-suggesting things there are in nature which are not explained by human and animal minds, we may still ask 'But are these things sufficiently striking to be called a mind-pattern? Can we fairly call them manifestations of a divine being?'

'The question', someone may say, 'has then become merely a matter of the application of a name. And "What's in a name?" '

5. *But the line between a question of fact and a question or decision as to the application of a name is not so simple as this way of putting things suggests.* The question 'What's in a name?' is engaging because we are inclined to answer both 'Nothing' and 'Very much'. And this 'Very much' has more than one source. We might have tried to comfort Heloise by saying 'It isn't that Abelard no longer loves you,

for this man isn't Abelard'; we might have said to poor Mr. Tebrick in Mr. Garnet's *Lady into Fox* 'But this is no longer Silvia'. But if Mr. Tebrick replied 'Ah, but it is!' this might come not at all from observing facts about the fox which we have not observed, but from noticing facts about the fox which we had missed, although we had in a sense observed all that Mr. Tebrick had observed. It is possible to have before one's eyes all the items of a pattern and still to miss the pattern. Consider the following conversation:

"And I think Kay and I are pretty happy. We've always been happy."
Bill lifted up his glass and put it down without drinking.
"Would you mind saying that again?" he asked.
"I don't see what's so queer about it. Taken all in all, Kay and I have really been happy."
"All right," Bill said gently, "Just tell me how you and Kay have been happy."
Bill had a way of being amused by things which I could not understand.
"It's a little hard to explain," I said. "It's like taking a lot of numbers that don't look alike and that don't mean anything until you add them all together."
I stopped, because I hadn't meant to talk to him about Kay and me.
"Go ahead," Bill said. "What about the numbers." And he began to smile.
"I don't know why you think it's so funny," I said. "All the things that two people do together, two people like Kay and me, add up to something. There are the kids and the house and the dog and all the people we have known and all the times we've been out to dinner. Of course, Kay and I do quarrel sometimes but when you add it all together, all of it isn't as bad as the parts of it seem. I mean, maybe that's all there is to anybody's life."
Bill poured himself another drink. He seemed about to say something and checked himself. He kept looking at me.[1]

Or again, suppose two people are speaking of two characters in a story which both have read[2] or of two friends which both have known, and one says 'Really she hated him', and the other says 'She didn't, she loved him'. Then the first may have noticed what the other has not although he knows no incident in the lives of the people they are talking about which the other doesn't know too, and the second speaker may say 'She didn't, she loved him' because he hasn't noticed what the first noticed, although he can remember every incident the first can remember. But then again he may say 'She didn't, she loved him' not because he hasn't noticed the patterns in time which the first has noticed but because though he has noticed them he doesn't feel he still needs to emphasize them with 'Really she hated him'. The line between using a name because of how we feel and because of what we have noticed isn't sharp. 'A difference as to the facts', 'a discovery', 'a revelation', these phrases cover many things. Discoveries have been made not only by Christopher Columbus and Pasteur, but also by Tolstoy and Dostoievsky and Freud. Things are revealed to us not only by the scientists with microscopes, but also by the poets, the prophets, and the painters. What is so isn't merely a matter of 'the facts'. For sometimes when there is agreement as to the facts there is still argument as to whether defendant did or did not 'exercise reasonable care', was or was not 'negligent'.

And though we shall need to emphasize how much 'There is a God' evinces an attitude to the familiar[3] we shall find in the end that it also evinces some recognition of patterns in time easily missed and that, therefore, difference as to there being any gods is in part a difference as to what is so and therefore

---

[1] *H. M. Pulham, Esq.*, p. 320, by John P. Marquand.
[2] e.g. Havelock Ellis's autobiography.
[3] 'Persuasive Definitions', *Mind*, July, 1938, by Charles Leslie Stevenson, should be read here. It is very good.

as to the facts, though not in the simple ways which first occurred to us.

6. *Let us now approach these same points by a different road.*

6.1. *How it is that an explanatory hypothesis, such as the existence of God, may start by being experimental and gradually become something quite different can be seen from the following story:*

Two people return to their long neglected garden and find among the weeds a few old plants surprisingly vigorous. One says to the other 'It must be that a gardener has been coming and doing something about these plants'. Upon inquiry they find that no neighbour has ever seen anyone at work in their garden. The first man says to the other 'He must have worked while people slept'. The other says 'No, someone would have heard him and besides, anybody who cared about the plants would have kept down these weeds'. The first man says 'Look at the way these are arranged. There is purpose and a feeling for beauty here. I believe that someone comes, someone invisible to mortal eyes. I believe that the more carefully we look the more we shall find confirmation of this.' They examine the garden ever so carefully and sometimes they come on new things suggesting that a gardener comes and sometimes they come on new things suggesting the contrary and even that a malicious person has been at work. Besides examining the garden carefully they also study what happens to gardens left without attention. Each learns all the other learns about this and about the garden. Consequently, when after all this, one says 'I still believe a gardener comes' while the other says 'I don't' their different words now reflect no difference as to what they have found in the garden, no difference as to what they would find in the garden if they looked further and no difference about how fast untended gardens fall into disorder. At this stage, in this context, the gardener hypothesis has ceased to be experimental, the differ-ence between one who accepts and one who rejects it is now not a matter of the one expecting something the other does not expect. What is the difference between them? The one says 'A gardener comes unseen and unheard. He is manifested only in his works with which we are all familiar', the other says 'There is no gardener' and with this difference in what they say about the gardener goes a difference in how they feel towards the garden, in spite of the fact that neither expects anything of it which the other does not expect.

But is this the whole difference between them—that the one calls the garden by one name and feels one way towards it, while the other calls it by another name and feels in another way towards it? And if this is what the difference has become then is it any longer appropriate to ask 'Which is right?' or 'Which is reasonable?'

And yet surely such questions *are* appropriate when one person says to another 'You still think the world's a garden and not a wilderness, and that the gardener has not forsaken it' or 'You still think there are nymphs of the streams, a presence in the hills, a spirit of the world'. Perhaps when a man sings 'God's in His heaven' we need not take this as more than an expression of how he feels. But when Bishop Gore or Dr. Joad write about belief in God and young men read them in order to settle their religious doubts the impression is not simply that of persons choosing exclamations with which to face nature and the 'changes and chances of this mortal life'. The disputants speak as if they are concerned with a matter of scientific fact, or of trans-sensual, trans-scientific and metaphysical fact, but still of fact and still a matter about which reasons for and against may be offered, although no scientific reasons in the sense of field surveys for fossils or experiments on delinquents are to the point.

6.2 *Now can an interjection have a logic?* Can the manifestation of an attitude in the utterance of a word, in the application of a name, have a logic? When all the facts are known how can there still be a question of fact? How can there still be a question? Surely as Hume says '. . . after every circumstance, every relation is known, the understanding has no further room to operate'? [4]

6.3 When the madness of these questions leaves us for a moment *we can all easily recollect disputes which though they cannot be settled by experiment are yet disputes in which one party may be right and the other wrong* and in which both parties may offer reasons and the one better reasons than the other. *This may happen in pure and applied mathematics and logic.* Two accountants or two engineers provided with the same data may reach different results and this difference is resolved not by collecting further data but by going over the calculations again. Such differences indeed share with differences as to what will win a race, the honour of being among the most 'settlable' disputes in the language.

6.4 *But it won't do to describe the theistic issue as one settlable by such calculation,* or as one about what can be deduced in this *vertical* fashion from the facts we know. No doubt dispute about **God** has sometimes, perhaps especially in mediaeval times, been carried on in this fashion. But nowadays it is not and we must look for some other analogy, some other case in which a dispute is settled but not by experiment.

6.5 *In courts of law* it sometimes happens that opposing counsel are agreed as to the facts and are not trying to settle a question of further fact, are not trying to settle whether the man who admittedly had quarrelled with the deceased did nor did not murder him, but are concerned with whether Mr. A who admittedly handed his long-trusted clerk signed blank cheques did or did not exercise reasonable care, whether a ledger is or is not a document, whether a certain body was or was not a public authority.

In such cases we notice that the process of argument is not a *chain* of demonstrative reasoning. It is a presenting and re-presenting of those features of the case which *severally co-operate* in favour of the conclusion, in favour of saying what the reasoner wishes said, in favour of calling the situation by the name by which he wishes to call it. The reasons are like the legs of a chair, not the links of a chain. Consequently although the discussion is *a priori* and the steps are not a matter of experience, the procedure resembles scientific argument in that the reasoning is not *vertically* extensive but *horizontally* extensive—it is a matter of the cumulative effect of several independent premises, not of the repeated transformation of one or two. And because the premises are severally inconclusive the process of deciding the issue becomes a matter of weighing the cumulative effect of one group of severally inconclusive items against the cumulative effect of another group of severally inconclusive items, and thus lends itself to description in terms of conflicting 'probabilities'. This encourages the feeling that the issue is one of fact—that it is a matter of guessing from the premises at a further fact, at what is to come. But this is a muddle. *The dispute does not cease to be* a priori *because it is a matter of the cumulative effect of severally inconclusive premises.* The logic of the dispute is not that of a chain of deductive reasoning as in a mathematical calculation. But nor is it a matter of collecting from several inconclusive items of information an expectation as to something further, as when a doctor from a patient's symptoms guesses at what is wrong, or a detective from many clues guesses the criminal. It has its own sort of logic and its own sort of end—the solution of the question at

[4] Hume, *An Enquiry concerning the Principles of Morals.* Appendix I.

issue is a decision, a ruling by the judge. But it is not an arbitrary decision though the rational connections are neither quite like those in vertical deductions nor like those in inductions in which from many signs we guess at what is to come; and though the decision manifests itself in the application of a name it is no more merely the application of a name than is the pinning on of a medal merely the pinning on of a bit of metal. Whether a lion with stripes is a tiger or a lion is, if you like, merely a matter of the application of a name. Whether Mr. So-and-So of whose conduct we have so complete a record did or did not exercise reasonable care is not merely a matter of the application of a name or, if we choose to say it is, then we must remember that with this name a game is lost and won and a game with very heavy stakes. With the judges' choice of a name for the facts goes an attitude, and the declaration, the ruling, is an exclamation evincing that attitude. But *it is an exclamation which not only has a purpose but also has a logic,* a logic surprisingly like that of 'futile', 'deplorable', 'graceful', 'grand', 'divine'.

6.6 *Suppose two people are looking at a picture or natural scene.* One says 'Excellent' or 'Beautiful' or 'Divine'; the other says 'I don't see it'. He means he doesn't see the beauty. And this reminds us of how we felt the theist accuse the atheist of blindness and the atheist accuse the theist of seeing what isn't there. And yet surely each sees what the other sees. It isn't that one can see part of the picture which the other can't see. So the difference is in a sense not one as to the facts. And so it cannot be removed by the one disputant discovering to the other what so far he hasn't seen. It isn't that the one sees the picture in a different light and so, as we might say, sees a different picture. Consequently the difference between them cannot be resolved by putting the picture in a different light. And yet surely this is just what can be done in such a case—

not by moving the picture but by talk perhaps. To settle a dispute as to whether a piece of music is good or better than another we listen again, with a picture we look again. Someone perhaps points to emphasize certain features and we see it in a different light. Shall we call this 'field work' and 'the last of observation' or shall we call it 'reviewing the premises' and 'the beginning of deduction (horizontal)'?

If in spite of all this we choose to say that a difference as to whether a thing is beautiful is not a factual difference we must be careful to remember that there is a procedure for settling these differences and that this consists not only in reasoning and redescription as in the legal case, but also in a more literal re-setting-before with re-looking or re-listening.

6.7 *And if we say as we did at the beginning that when a difference as to the existence of a God is not one as to future happenings then it is not experimental and therefore not as to the facts, we must not forthwith assume that there is no right and wrong about it,* no rationality or irrationality, no appropriateness or inappropriateness, no procedure which tends to settle it, *nor even that this procedure is in no sense a discovery of new facts.* After all even in science this is not so. Our two gardeners even when they had reached the stage when neither expected any experimental result which the other did not, might yet have continued the dispute, each presenting and representing the features of the garden favouring his hypothesis, that is fitting his model for describing the accepted fact; each emphasizing the pattern he wishes to emphasize. True, in science, there is seldom or never a pure instance of this sort of dispute, for nearly always with difference of hypothesis goes some difference of expectation as to the facts. But scientists argue about rival hypotheses with a vigour which is not exactly proportioned to difference in expectations of experimental results.

The difference as to whether a God exists involves our feelings more than most scientific disputes and in this respect is more like a difference as to whether there is beauty in a thing.

7. *The Connecting Technique*. Let us consider again the technique used in revealing or proving beauty, in removing a blindness, in inducing an attitude which is lacking, in reducing a reaction that is inappropriate. Besides running over in a special way the features of the picture, tracing the rhythms, making sure that this and that are not only seen but noticed, and their relation to each other—besides all this—there are other things we can do to justify our attitude and alter that of the man who cannot see. For features of the picture may be brought out by setting beside it other pictures; just as the merits of an argument may be brought out, proved, by setting beside it other arguments, in which striking but irrelevant features of the original are changed and relevant features emphasized; just as the merits and demerits of a line of action may be brought out by setting beside it other actions. To use Susan Stebbing's example: Nathan brought out for David certain features of what David had done in the matter of Uriah the Hittite by telling him a story about two sheep-owners. This is the kind of thing we very often do when someone is "inconsistent' or 'unreasonable'. This is what we do in referring to other cases in law. The paths we need to trace from other cases to the case in question are often numerous and difficult to detect and the person with whom we are discussing the matter may well draw attention to connections which, while not incompatible with those we have tried to emphasize, are of an opposite inclination. A may have noticed in B subtle and hidden likenesses to an angel and reveal these to C, while C has noticed in B subtle and hidden likenesses to a devil which he reveals to A.

Imagine that a man picks up some flowers that lie half withered on a table and gently puts them in water. Another man says to him 'You believe flowers feel'. He says this although he knows that the man who helps the flowers doesn't expect anything of them which he himself doesn't expect; for he himself expects the flowers to be 'refreshed' and to be easily hurt, injured, I mean, by rough handling, while the man who puts them in water does not expect them to whisper 'Thank you'. The Sceptic says 'You believe flowers feel' because something about the way the other man lifts the flowers and puts them in water suggests an attitude to the flowers which he feels inappropriate although perhaps he would not feel it inappropriate to butterflies. He feels that this attitude to flowers is somewhat crazy *just as it is sometimes felt that a lover's attitude is somewhat crazy even when this is not a matter of his having false hopes about how the person he is in love with will act.* It is often said in such cases that reasoning is useless. But the very person who says this feels that the lover's attitude is crazy, is inappropriate like some dreads and hatreds, such as some horrors of enclosed places. And often one who says 'It is useless to reason' proceeds at once to reason with the lover, nor is this reasoning always quite without effect. We may draw the lover's attention to certain things done by her he is in love with and trace for him a path to these from things done by others at other times[5] which have disgusted and infuriated him. And by this means we may weaken his admiration and confidence, make him feel it unjustified and arouse his suspicion and contempt and make him feel our suspicion and contempt reasonable. It is possible, of course, that he has already noticed the analogies, the connections, we point out and that

[5] Thus, like the scientist, the critic is concerned to show up the irrelevance of time and space.

he has accepted them—that is, he has not denied them nor passed them off. He has recognized them and they have altered his attitude, altered his love, but he still loves. We then feel that perhaps it is we who are blind and cannot see what he can see.

8. *Connecting and Disconnecting.* But before we confess ourselves thus inadequate there are other fires his admiration must pass through. For when a man has an attitude which it seems to us he should not have or lacks one which it seems to us he should have then, not only do we suspect that he is not influenced by connections which we feel should influence him and draw his attention to these, but also we suspect he is influenced by connections which should not influence him and draw his attention to these. It may, for a moment, seem strange that we should draw his attention to connections which we feel should not influence him, and which, since they do influence him, he has in a sense already noticed. But we do—such is our confidence in 'the light of reason'.

Sometimes the power of these connections comes mainly from a man's mismanagement of the language he is using. This is what happens in the Monte Carlo fallacy, where by mismanaging the laws of chance a man passes from noticing that a certain colour or number has not turned up for a long while to an improper confidence that now it soon will turn up. In such cases our showing up of the false connections is a process we call 'explaining a fallacy in reasoning'. To remove fallacies in reasoning we urge a man to call a spade a spade, ask him what he means by 'the State' and having pointed out ambiguities and vagueness ask him to reconsider the steps in his argument.

9. *Unspoken Connections. Usually, however, wrongheadedness or wrongheartedness in a situation, blindness to* *what is there or seeing what is not, does not arise merely from mismanagement of language but is more due to connections which are not mishandled in language, for the reason that they are not put into language at all.* And often these misconnections too, weaken in the light of reason, if only we can guess where they lie and turn it on them. In so far as these connections are not presented in language the process of removing their power is not a process of correcting the mismanagement of language. But it is still akin to such a process; for though it is not a process of setting out fairly what has been set out unfairly, it is a process of setting out fairly what has not been set out at all. And we must remember that the line between connections ill-presented or half-presented in language and connections operative but not presented in language, or only hinted at, is not a sharp one.

Whether or not we call the process of showing up these connections 'reasoning to remove bad unconscious reasoning', it is certain that in order to settle in ourselves what weight we shall attach to someone's confidence or attitude we not only ask him for his reasons but also look for unconscious reasons both good and bad; that is, for reasons which he can't put into words, isn't explicitly aware of, is hardly aware of, isn't aware of at all—perhaps it's long experience which he *doesn't* recall which lets him know a squall is coming, perhaps it's old experience which he *can't* recall which makes the cake in the tea mean so much and makes Odette so fascinating.[6]

I am well aware of the distinction between the question 'What reasons are there for the belief that S is P?' and the question 'What are the sources of beliefs that S is P?' There are cases where investigation of the rationality of a claim which certain persons make is done with

---

[6] Proust: *Swann's Way*, Vol. I, p. 58, Vol. II. Phoenix Edition.

very little inquiry into why they say what they do, into the causes of their beliefs. This is so when we have very definite ideas about what is really logically relevant to their claim and what is not. Offered a mathematical theorem we ask for the proof; offered the generalization that parental discord causes crime we ask for the correlation co-efficients. But even in this last case, if we fancy that only the figures are reasons we underestimate the complexity of the logic of our conclusion; and yet it is difficult to describe the other features of the evidence which have weight and there is apt to be disagreement about the weight they should have. In criticizing other conclusions and especially conclusions which are largely the expression of an attitude, we have not only to ascertain what reasons there are for them but also to decide what things are reasons and how much. This latter process of sifting reasons from causes is part of the critical process for every belief, but in some spheres it has been done pretty fully already. In these spheres we don't need to examine the actual processes to belief and distil from them a logic. But in other spheres this remains to be done. Even in science or on the stock exchange or in ordinary life we sometimes hesitate to condemn a belief or a hunch merely because those who believe it cannot offer the sort of reasons we had hoped for. And now suppose Miss Gertrude Stein finds excellent the work of a new artist while we see nothing in it. We nervously recall, perhaps, how pictures by Picasso, which Miss Stein admired and others rejected, later came to be admired by many who gave attention to them, and we wonder whether the case is not a new instance of her perspicacity and our blindness. But if, upon giving all our attention to the work in question, we still do not respond to it, and we notice that the subject matter of the

new pictures is perhaps birds in wild places and learn that Miss Stein is a bird-watcher, then we begin to trouble ourselves less about her admiration.

It must not be forgotten that our attempt to show up misconnections in Miss Stein may have an opposite result and reveal to us connections we had missed. Thinking to remove the spell exercised upon his patient by the old stories of the Greeks, the psycho-analyst may himself fall under that spell and find in them what his patient has found and, incidentally, what made the Greeks tell those tales.

10. *Now what happens, what should happen, when we inquire in this way into the reasonableness, the propriety of belief in gods?* The answer is: A double and opposite-phased change. Wordsworth writes:

. . . And I have felt
A presence that disturbs me with the joy
Of elevated thoughts; a sense sublime
Of something far more deeply interfused,
Whose dwelling is the light of setting suns,
And the round ocean and the living air,
And the blue sky, and in the mind of
    man:
A motion and a spirit, that impels
All thinking things, all objects of all
    thought,
And rolls through all things. . . .[7]

We most of us know this feeling. But is it well placed like the feeling that here is first-rate work, which we sometimes rightly have even before we have fully grasped the picture we are looking at or the book we are reading? Or is it misplaced like the feeling in a house that has long been empty that someone secretly lives there still. Wordsworth's feeling *is* the feeling that the world is haunted, that something watches in the hills and manages the stars. The child feels that the stone tripped him when he stumbled, that the bough struck him when it flew back in his face. He has to learn that the wind isn't buffeting him,

[7] Tintern Abbey.

that there is not a devil in it, that he was wrong, that his attitude was inappropriate. And as he learns that the wind wasn't hindering him so he also learns it wasn't helping him. But we know how, though he learns, his attitude lingers. It is plain that Wordsworth's feeling is of this family.

Belief in gods, it is true, is often very different from belief that stones are spiteful, the sun kindly. For the gods appear in human form and from the waves and control these things and by so doing reward and punish us. But varied as are the stories of the gods they have a family likeness and we have only to recall them to feel sure of the other main sources which co-operate with animism to produce them.

What are the stories of the gods? What are our feelings when we believe in God? They are feelings of awe before power, dread of the thunderbolts of Zeus, confidence in the everlasting arms, unease beneath the all-seeing eye. They are feelings of guilt and inescapable vengeance, of smothered hate and of a security we can hardly do without. We have only to remind ourselves of these feelings and the stories of the gods and goddesses and heroes in which these feelings find expression, to be reminded of how we felt as children to our parents and the big people of our childhood. Writing of a first telephone call from his grandmother, Proust says: '. . . it was rather that this isolation of the voice was like a symbol, a presentation, a direct consequence of another isolation, that of my grandmother, separated for the first time in my life, from myself. The orders or prohibitions which she addressed to me at every moment in the ordinary course of my life, the tedium of obedience or the fire of rebellion which neutralized the affection that I felt for her were at this moment eliminated. . . . "Granny!" I cried to her

. . . but I had beside me only that voice, a phantom, as unpalpable as that which would come to revisit me when my grandmother was dead. "Speak to me!" but then it happened that, left more solitary still, I ceased to catch the sound of her voice. My grandmother could no longer hear me . . . I continued to call her, sounding the empty night, in which I felt that her appeals also must be straying. I was shaken by the same anguish which, in the distant past, I had felt once before, one day when, a little child, in a crowd, I had lost her.'

Giorgio de Chirico, writing of Courbet, says: 'The word yesterday envelops us with its yearning echo, just as, on waking, when the sense of time and the logic of things remain a while confused, the memory of a happy hour we spent the day before may sometimes linger reverberating within us. At times we think of Courbet and his work as we do of our own father's youth.'

When a man's father fails him by death or weakness how much he needs another father, one in the heavens with whom is 'no variableness nor shadow of turning'.

We understood Mr. Kenneth Graham when he wrote of the Golden Age we feel we have lived in under the Olympians. Freud says: 'The ordinary man cannot imagine this Providence in any other form but that of a greatly exalted father, for only such a one could understand the needs of the sons of men, or be softened by their prayers and be placated by the signs of their remorse. The whole thing is so patently infantile, so incongruous with reality. . . .' 'So incongruous with reality'! It cannot be denied.

But here a new aspect of the matter may strike us.[8] For the very facts which make us feel that now we can recognize systems of superhuman, sub-human, elusive, beings for what they are —the persistent projections of infantile

---

[8] I owe to the late Dr. Susan Isaacs the thought of this different aspect of the matter, of this connection between the heavenly Father and 'the good father' spoken of in psychoanalysis.

phantasies—include facts which make these systems less fantastic. What are these facts? They are patterns in human reactions which are well described by saying that we are as if there were hidden within us powers, persons, not ourselves and stronger than ourselves. That this is so may perhaps be said to have been common knowledge yielded by ordinary observation of people,[9] but we did not know the degree in which this is so until recent study of extra-ordinary cases in extraordinary conditions had revealed it. I refer, of course, to the study of multiple personalities and the wider studies of psycho-analysts. Even when the results of this work are reported to us that is not the same as tracing the patterns in the details of the cases on which the results are based; and even that is not the same as taking part in the studies oneself. One thing not sufficiently realized is that some of the things shut within us are good.

Now the gods, good and evil and mixed, have always been mysterious powers outside us rather than within. But they have also been within. It is not a modern theory but an old saying that in each of us a devil sleeps. Eve said: 'The serpent beguiled me.' Helen says to Menelaus:

. . . And yet how strange it is!
I ask not thee; I ask my own sad thought,
What was there in my heart, that I forgot
My home and land and all I loved, to fly
With a strange man? Surely it was not I,
But Cypris there! [10]

Elijah found that God was not in the wind, not in the thunder, but in a still small voice. The kingdom of Heaven is within us, Christ insisted, though usually about the size of a grain of mustard seed, and he prayed that we should become one with the Father in Heaven.

New knowledge made it necessary either to give up saying 'The sun is sinking' or to give the words a new meaning. In many contexts we preferred to stick to the old words and give them a new meaning which was not entirely new but, on the contrary, *practically* the same as the old. The Greeks did not speak of the dangers of repressing instincts but they did speak of the dangers of thwarting Dionysos, of neglecting Cypris for Diana, of forgetting Poseidon for Athena. We have eaten of the fruit of a garden we can't forget though we were never there, a garden we still look for though we can never find it. Maybe we look for too simple a likeness to what we dreamed. Maybe we are not as free as we fancy from the old idea that Heaven is a happy hunting ground, or a city with streets of gold. Lately Mr. Aldous Huxley has recommended our seeking not somewhere beyond the sky or late in time but a timeless state not made of the stuff of this world, which he rejects, picking it into worthless pieces. But this sounds to me still too much a looking for another place, not indeed one filled with sweets but instead so empty that some of us would rather remain in the Lamb or the Elephant, where, as we know, they stop whimper-

[9] Consider Tolstoy and Dostoievsky—I do not mean, of course, that their observation was ordinary.

[10] Euripides: *The Trojan Women*, Gilbert Murray's translation. Roger Hinks in *Myth and Allegory in Ancient Art* writes (p. 108) : 'Personifications made their appearance very early in Greek poetry. . . . It is out of the question to call these terrible beings "abstractions". . . . They are real daemons to be worshipped and propitiated. . . . These beings we observe correspond to states of mind. The experience of man teaches him that from time to time his composure is invaded and overturned by some power from outside, panic, intoxication, sexual desire.'

'What use to shoot off guns at unicorns?
Where one horn's hit another fierce horn grows.
These beasts are fabulous, and none were born
Of woman who could lay a fable low,'—
The Glass Tower, NICHOLAS MOORE, p. 100.

ing with another bitter and so far from sneering at all things, hang pictures of winners at Kempton and stars of the 'nineties. Something good we have for each other is freed there, and in some degree and for a while the miasma of time is rolled back without obliging us to deny the present. The artists who do most for us don't tell us only of fairylands. Proust, Manet, Breughel, even Botticelli and Vermeer show us reality. And yet they give us for a moment exhilaration without anxiety, peace without boredom. And those who, like Freud, work in a different way against that which too often comes over us and forces us into deadness or despair,[11] also deserve critical, patient and courageous attention. For they, too, work to release us from human bondage into human freedom.

Many have tried to find ways of salvation. The reports they bring back are always incomplete and apt to mislead even when they are not in words but in music or paint. But they are by no means useless; and not the worst of them are those which speak of oneness with God. But in so far as we become one with Him He becomes one with us. St. John says he is in us as we love one another.

This love, I suppose, is not benevolence but something that comes of the oneness with one another of which Christ spoke.[12] Sometimes it momentarily gains strength.[13] Hate and the Devil do too. And what is oneness without otherness?

MICHAEL FOSTER

The Theological Elements in Conceptual Analysis[*]

I wish to discuss the significance of sentences in the first person plural as they occur in the writings of modern philosophers, especially of those who represent the philosophy of Analysis.

The following are examples of these sentences:

'The philosopher, as an analyst, is not directly concerned with the physical properties of things. He is concerned only with the way in which *we speak* about them.' [1]

'In ordinary language *we call* a person 'rational' if he is capable of learning from experience.' [2]

'A full understanding of the logic of

---

[11] Matthew Arnold: *Summer Night*.

[12] St. John xvi, 21.

[13] 'The Harvesters' in *The Golden Age*, Kenneth Graham.

[*] From "'We' in Modern Philosophy" by Michael Foster in *Faith and Logic*, ed. Basil Mitchell. Reprinted by permission of the Beacon Press. First published in 1957 and copyright under the Berne Convention; pp. 194-97, 199-204, 210-20.

[1] A. J. Ayer, *Language, Truth and Logic*, Ch. II. My italics.

[2] H. Feigl in 'Logical Empiricism', *Readings in Philosophical Analysis*, ed. Feigl and Sellars, p. 15. My italics.

231

value-terms can only be achieved by continual and sensitive attention to the way *we use* them.' [3]

'The primary task of philosophy is to describe the *use* of words and expressions. . . . One part, albeit the root part, of this task is to give a logical account of the way in which *all of us employ* certain key expressions, like "know", "cause", "see" and others.' [4]

'*We do not know* what to reply to "Do shadows exist?" in the way *we do* to "are there shadows on the moon?" and the reason is plain. *We do not in fact use* the word "exist" in talk about shadows.' [5]

'Philosophers' arguments have frequently turned on references to what *we* do and do not say, or, more strongly, on what *we* can or cannot say.' [6] . . .

When a philosopher says, e.g. 'We do not use the word "exist" in talk about shadows,' what kind of sentence is this? It seems clear that it is not an empirical statement. The philosopher is not reporting a usage which he has observed in himself and among his associates. The utterance seems more like those which Professor Austin has taught us to call 'performatory'. In using the first person plural I am not merely describing a usage but am subscribing to it, or expressing my own adhesion to it. I am *owning* the usage, and this is an avowal rather than a statement. I am not merely stating that a certain group uses language in this way, but am ranking myself in that group as a member of it, and this ranking is not a description but an act. Sentences in the third person do not exhibit this performatory character.

The performatory element of these sentences is comparable to the evaluative element which Mr. Hare discerns in all genuine moral judgments.[7] This element, on Hare's account of it, may be mixed in varying proportions with a descriptive element, and the descriptive element increases in proportion as the judgment loses vitality and becomes ossified. Thus 'You ought to do so and so' can degenerate until it is *hardly* more than the descriptive statement that so-and-so is required by the customary standards of a certain society. 'It is wrong to do so and so' can become *almost* equivalent to the factual report that I have certain psychological inhibitions in regard to it. But if this process is completed, so that the judgment becomes wholly factual, then it has lost the essential character of a value-judgment. The evaluative element involves something more than a description, namely the speaker's adhesion to the standard which he enunciates. 'The test, whether someone is using the judgment "I ought to do X" as a value-judgment or not is, 'Does he or does he not recognize that if he assents to the judgment he must also assent to the command "Let me do X"?'? [8]

Mutatis mutandis, I suggest that a corresponding element is present in sentences enunciating a linguistic usage in the first person. No doubt in these sentences also a descriptive element is present in varying proportions. It is a fact that the usage is prevalent among a certain human group which is capable of historical or sociological definition. But if the sentence became wholly descriptive, so that it could be adequately expressed in the third person instead of in the first: if, in other words, it became a report upon linguistic usage of the kind which might be established by empirical (e.g. statisti-

---

[3] R. M. Hare, *Language of Morals,* p. 126. My italics.

[4] Morris Weitz (expounding G. Ryle) in 'Oxford Philosophy,' *Philosophical Review,* 1953, p. 229. 'Use' author's italics; other italics mine.

[5] Weitz, *ibid.,* p. 226, quoting G. J. Warnock from *Proceedings of the Aristotelian Society,* 1951. My italics.

[6] G. Ryle, 'Ordinary Language' in *Philosophical Review,* 1953. My italics.

[7] *The Language of Morals,* Ch. II.

[8] *Ibid.,* pp. 168-9.

cal) enquiry, then (like Hare's degenerate value-judgments), it would have lost an essential element.

Would it have lost thereby the element which makes it capable of serving as the datum (the analysandum) of logical analysis? In order for analysis to be philosophical is it necessary that it should begin with sentences in which meanings are not only reported, but are also *owned?* . . .

In order to gain a starting-point for philosophical analysis we need a . . . criterion of proper use. What is this criterion? This is the crux.

Let us illustrate the problem by considering an ethical term such as 'right'. How does the beginner learn its proper use? The beginner will normally be a child, and he will learn, as children do, by imitation and by trial and error, the correct ways of using moral as well as other terms. We may say that the child is learning the use of language, and this is true: but in order to use moral language correctly, a moral as well as linguistic training is required. With a child, these two trainings take place side by side, and without clear separation one from another. But we can see how separate they are if we suppose a man who sets himself in adult years to acquire a correct use of an unfamiliar language. He will achieve linguistic mastery by the familiar methods of language-study —learning the grammar, taking lessons from language-masters, use of gramophone records, attendance at language-institutes, and conversation with anyone who knows the language. But in order to apply the moral terms of the language with propriety he will need also something quite different from this. He will need to be initiated into the basic moral attitudes by which the use of the language is determined.[9] What a man needs to learn in order to use words correctly in *this* sense (not purely linguistic fa-

cility) —this is what provides the basis of philosophical analysis.

I have illustrated the difference with moral terms, but it holds also of other terms. Think for example, of the terms 'reasonable' or 'real'.

The contexts in which they are properly to be applied are not determined solely by linguistic considerations. You cannot learn what is to be deemed reasonable behaviour and what unreasonable merely by taking language-lessons. By what lessons, then? Whatever it is that these other lessons teach, will be the starting-point of philosophy.

Propriety in the use of language, in the sense of propriety which is other than merely linguistic, is relative to the basic attitude which the speaker assumes. Imagine, for example, a Hindu, a Marxist and a scientific humanist, who have all acquired a mastery of the English language, but without surrendering their fundamental beliefs. Then they will agree in their standards of linguistic correctitude, but will differ in the other standards which determine propriety in the use of moral and other terms.

Among different possible standards of propriety how is the proper standard to be selected? Granted that there is an accepted standard of linguistic propriety ('standard English usage') can this determine not only linguistic, but also (so to speak) moral and metaphysical correctitude in the use of language? Perhaps we must admit that, to a certain point, it can even do this. Languages have been informed by the basic attitudes of those who have used them, and so the mere use of a language may have a powerful effect in inducing a congruous attitude. (Thus a German writer who fled from Hitler's Germany to America—or his publisher—writes of his efforts to master the English language, 'that wonderful exercise in reason and sanity'[10]). But though this is true, it does not answer

---

[9] For this and what follows cf. H. A. Hodges 'Languages, Standpoints and Attitudes'. Especially Ch. III.

[10] Frederic Lilge, *The Abuse of Learning,* Dust Cover.

our question. We may say of an attitude that it is congruous to the genius of a given language, our own or another, but this is in itself no more than an historical statement, and it does not mark this attitude out from others which may be congruous to other languages.

How, then, is the *use* (in the philosophically important sense) of a word decided? If I am right, there is not an external standard which the thinker can first recognize and then adopt. On the contrary, the adoption is primary. The correct use, that is the philosophically important use, for him is that which he can adopt. The act of adoption, making his statement more than an historical one, is the source from which philosophical analysis can flow.

Hence the importance of the 'we' sentences. They are the expressions of this act of adoption. Let us consider these sentences a little further.

An older logic would have assumed that we can discover the proper meaning of a word by analysing the concept. Modern analysis discards this assumption. Words do not mean but people mean things by words. 'To mean' thus becomes an active, personal verb, no longer an impersonal one. It is possible to repeat forms of words without meaning them, or only half-meaning them. When this happens, thought lacks authenticity (if I may borrow a word from the Existentialists). The starting-point of philosophy is there when I have the courage (as Ayer had) to discard what is unauthentic, and to restate only that which I can commit myself to meaning in good faith, thereby *revalidating* it. Such a commitment is expressed in a linguistic 'we' sentence. The philosophical activity of analysing which then succeeds is not discontinuous from the initial act of affirmation. It makes clearer what the initial affirmation involved; indeed it will be only after the analysis

that the speaker fully realizes what it was that he was affirming.

If this is true, it gives a somewhat different appearance to disagreements between philosophers (especially to disagreements between contemporary philosophers and those of previous ages) from that which is often assumed. A common assumption is that the meaning of the expression to be analysed is fixed independently of the analysis, and identically for all philosophers. The philosophical differences have to be held to arise wholly from the process of the analysis, and to be due to logical errors committed by one of the parties. Hence the difference of theory is ascribed to a technical defect in the earlier philosopher, which has now been exposed and corrected. Thus, for example, Plato's 'theory of Ideas' is ascribed to a logical naiveté on his part, which caused him to construe general words as though they were proper names. Descartes is said to have based his metaphysics of mind upon a 'category mistake', which deluded him into thinking that the word 'mind' must stand for a thing, and that in consequence, since it was clearly not a material thing, it must be a non-material thing.[11]

But if what I have said is right, we shall not be able to adopt this attitude towards the philosophers of the past. Even if we regard them as having been themselves engaged unconsciously in the analysis of linguistic use (I think it legitimate up to a certain point to think of them like this), we shall not be able to attribute all the divergences of their results to faults of analysis unless we assume that we have independent knowledge of their analysandum. But this, it seems clear, we have not got. On the contrary, the result of their analysis is part of the evidence which reveals to us what their analysandum was.[12]

This does not commit us to an histori-

---

[11] G. Ryle, *Concept of Mind*, Ch. I.

[12] I think this notion is borrowed ultimately from Professor É. Gilson: I owe it proximately to Dr. E. L. Mascall. Professor H. H. Price suggests that the traditional proofs of the existence of God

cal relativism, as though we could only say different philosophies are the outcome of different 'absolute presuppositions',[13] and must renounce all criticism of them in the light of our own. But the criticism will take a different form. It will require us to reveal our own presuppositions and to confront the others with them, committing ourselves in witness. We shall not be able to confine ourselves to refutation from the vantage-point of a technical superiority.[14]

The linguistic philosopher commits himself in his selection of those expressions of which he is prepared to say 'we' use them. It may be instructive to compare his 'we' sentences with first-personal utterances occurring in other, non-linguistic philosophies.

It is characteristic of G. E. Moore to use 'we' sentences in stating the views of Common Sense about the nature of the Universe. I will quote examples at some length from his lectures recently published (but originally delivered in 1910-11) on 'Some Main Problems of Philosophy'.

'There are, it seems to me, certain views about the nature of the Universe which are held nowadays by almost everybody. They are so universally held that they may, I think, fairly be called the views of Common Sense. . . . I wish therefore to begin by describing what I take to be the most important view of Common Sense: things which *we* all commonly assume to be true about the Universe, and which *we* are sure that we know to be true about it.' [15]

Moore then sketches the generally accepted modern picture of the universe —physical, biological and human, and concludes: 'All this *we now believe* about the material universe: it is surely Common Sense to believe it all'.[16]

The Common Sense picture of the Universe is shown to exclude some beliefs which have previously been held —animism, and the belief in disembodied acts of consciousness.[17] It is later found to be incompatible with the philosophical theory of Idealism in regard to material objects, and is Moore's ground, as is well known, for rejecting that theory. 'It seems to me that these views' [Idealist views, namely] 'are utterly different from what *we all commonly believe*, when *we believe* in the existence of material objects. . . . *We believe—we all cannot help believing*, even though we may hold philosophical views to the contrary—that this something which exists now or existed a moment ago, is not merely a something which may or may not have shape or be situated in space . . .' [but that it really has the characteristics of a material object].[18]

These statements of Moore, which I have italicized, are instructive because they form a link between two things which I wish to bring into comparison with one another.

(a) They seem clearly akin to the 'we' sentences of linguistic philosophers. Moore's characteristic appeal to Common Sense can pass by imperceptible gradations into an appeal to linguistic use. . . .

(b) Secondly, they are like credal affirmations. . . .

'We,' . . . in the mouth of a modern

---

ought to be regarded not as proofs, in the sense that they 'would follow logically from premises which every reasonable man is bound to accept', but rather 'as analyses or clarifications of propositions which religious persons antecedently believe' (*Some Aspects of the Conflict between Science and Religion*, Eddington Memorial Lecture, 1953, p. 18). In a somewhat similar manner linguistic analysis clarifies a meaning which the analyst owns.

[13] R. G. Collingwood's term. See his *Essay on Metaphysics*, Pt. I. I think that Collingwood's position *is* one of historical relativism.

[14] See Hodges, *op. cit.*

[15] *Op. cit.,* p. 2. My italics.

[16] P. 3. My italics.

[17] Pp. 7-8.

[18] P. 115. My italics.

philosopher, seems to mean 'we men'. The kind of philosopher he is will depend upon what he believes a man to be. Thus 'we' for Kant meant 'we rational beings, who are bound by our human condition to a physical nature'. To say 'we' in Kant's sense is to affirm ourselves to be members of the intelligible world. But when Moore speaks of 'human beings with human bodies' who 'have lived upon the earth', this expresses a different conception of what man is. 'We' now commits me to membership of a differently conceived society, and involves me in a different affirmation of my own being. Is not this new anthropological affirmation really what is basic to Moore's philosophy? Other philosophers had gone on talking the language of a spiritual anthropology which no longer resonated with what they or their hearers were prepared to affirm existentially. Moore refused to say what he could not authentically affirm.[19]

'We' sentences of the type which is under consideration affirm an anthropology, but not a descriptive anthropology, they do not express my adhesion to an anthropological theory. Nor do they exactly express a decision of policy. It is not that I am giving notice of my intention *in future* to be such and such or to do so and so. Or so far as they can be said to express such a decision, this must be thought of as a decision to be what I am. In the previous paragraph I used the word 'existential' to describe such affirmations. I am tempted to use another word and to call them 'theological'.

It is worth while to distinguish two forms which a humanist anthropology has taken. To recognize myself as man may mean (i) the affirmation that I share in manhood by exhibiting a certain universal character (human nature),

or (ii) an affirmation of my solidarity with mankind conceived not now as an abstract class-concept, but as a race fulfilling its destiny in history.

(i) Humanism of the former sort was characteristic of the great British Empiricists of the seventeenth and eighteenth centuries. They thought of man as exhibiting human nature, this being a timeless and universal character.

(ii) But the nineteenth century began to think of man as belonging to the human race, which is an historical entity. To affirm myself as man in this sense seems to be characteristically modern, and this affirmation seems to be involved in some analytical philosophy.

It is revealed by the use of tensed verbs in place of the timeless present, as in the following examples:

'All this we *now* believe about the material universe. It is surely common sense to believe it all' (Moore).[20]

'Ordinary languages and calculi like logic, geometry and arithmetic are devices which *we have invented*' (T. D. Weldon).[21]

'There was a real Jesus Christ who preached to the Jews and was crucified; but *we do not now believe* that he was the son of God and of a virgin, or that he rose from the dead.'[22]

There is a similar implication in the use of the phrase 'We now know', in cases where the context makes clear that what is referred to is an increase of human knowledge (e.g. that the earth goes round the sun).

But although 'we' sentences of the latter type are about mankind as an historical entity, they are not simply historical, any more than sentences of the former kind are empirical. The following passage may illustrate this point:

[19] Cf. his repudiation of belief in immortality and in the divine creation of the world in his *Defense of Common Sense*.

[20] Quoted above. My italics.

[21] *Vocabulary of Politics,* p. 191. My italics.

[22] From a broadcast talk. My italics, I think.

H. Reichenbach is speaking of the supersession of Euclidean geometry and of Newtonian physics which has formed part of the experience of our age. He writes:

'Such experience has made us wise enough to anticipate the breaking down of any system. It has not discouraged us though. The new physics has shown that we can have knowledge outside the frame of the Kantian principles, that the human mind is not a rigid system of categories into which it packs all experience, but that the principles of knowledge change with its content and can be adapted to a much more complicated world than that of Newtonian mechanics. We hope that in any future situation our minds will be flexible enough to supply methods of logical organization that can cope with the given observational material. That is a hope, not a belief for which we pretend to have a philosophical proof. We can do without certainty.' [23]

The 'we' who are not discouraged, who can have knowledge outside the frame of the Kantian principles, who can do without certainty, are surely mankind; yet what kind of statements are these which are being made?

Such assertions as these are logically homogeneous with theological statements; I mean by this that they can contradict theological statements and be contradicted by them. Two further passages from Reichenbach will illustrate this:

'As we have discovered that . . . the feeling of obligation cannot be transformed into a source of the validity of ethics, let us forget about the appeal to obligation. Let us throw away the crutches we needed for walking, let us stand on our own feet and trust our volitions, not because they are secondary ones but because they are our own volitions. Only a distorted morality can argue that our will is bad if it is not the response to a command from another source.' [24]

What is asserted here is surely logically homogeneous with the doctrine of Original Sin, which is confessedly theological.

Again:

'Speculative philosophy strove to establish moral directives in the same way that it constructed absolute knowledge. Reason was considered the giver of the moral law as well as of the cognitive law; ethical rules were to be discovered by an act of vision, analogous to the vision revealing the ultimate rules of the cosmos. Scientific philosophy has abandoned completely the plan of advancing moral rules. It regards moral aims as products of acts of volition, not of cognition; only the relations between aims, or between aims and means, are accessible to cognitive knowledge. The fundamental ethical rules are not justifiable through knowledge, but are adhered to because human beings want these rules and want other persons to follow the same rules. Volition is not derivable from cognition. Human will is its own progenitor and its own judge.' [25]

Compare statements in the Bible that human will is judged by Jesus Christ.[26]

Mr. P. F. Strawson writes: 'What makes predicates incompatible? . . . I want to answer . . . It is we, the makers of language, who make predicates incompatible. . . . It is we who decide where the boundaries are to be drawn.' [27] This 'we' can refer only to mankind, and to mankind as an historical body. But it is not an historical statement. Logically, does it not belong to the same realm as the statement in Genesis ii., that Adam gave names to the living creatures? ('Adam' means man).

Contemporary British philosophy is often described as Empiricist, and its representatives regard themselves as heirs

[23] *Rise of Scientific Philosophy*, p. 49.
[24] *Ibid.*, pp. 291-2.
[25] *Ibid.*, p. 304.
[26] Cf. perhaps especially John v. 27: the Father has given the Son authority to execute judgment 'because he is the Son of man'.
[27] *Introduction to Logical Theory*, p. 5.

of the classical tradition of British Empiricism. From this point of view it is natural to think of the opposition between this philosophy and the philosophy of the Continent (Descartes, Spinoza, Kant and his Idealist successors) as being that between a metaphysical (the latter) and an unmetaphysical philosophy. I do not deny truth to this contrast, but I have suggested a different one. I have suggested that the Empiricists (the moderns as well as their Seventeenth and Eighteenth Century predecessors) are based on an affirmation of humanism which is not empirical. From this point of view, the contrast between British and Continentals will be that they affirm different anthropologies. To what I have read was Plotinus' question, 'Who are we?', the latter answer, 'We are mind (or spirit, or mind linked with matter, or spirit linked with nature)', the former answer, 'We are men'.[28] I wish to pursue this contrast a little more at length.

Descartes began not with a 'we' sentence but with an 'I' sentence. 'I thence concluded that I was a substance, whose whole essence or nature consists only in thinking.'[29] This is of course no more an empirical statement than are the 'we' sentences hitherto considered. It, like them, is an existential affirmation, but a different one. Descartes is not affirming himself to be a man, nor claiming solidarity with mankind, but is affirming himself to be mind or spirit, naturally immortal, and claiming solidarity with the timeless and infinite substance of mind as such.

Kant's philosophy was still spiritual and not human. In his ethics he insists that we are subject to the moral law not *qua* human but *qua* rational; this means *qua* spiritual. The capacity of determining his will by the moral law gives man 'dignity (or prerogative) . . . above all the mere things of nature'.[30] Our 'will as intelligence' which gives us this capacity is 'our proper self',[31] (whereas man 'as a human being . . . is merely an appearance of himself').[32] In affirming ourselves as spirits, we affirm our membership of a spiritual world. 'When we think of ourselves as free, we transfer ourselves into the intelligible world as members.'[33] The concept of an intelligible world is that of 'the totality of rational beings as ends in themselves'.[34] Kant speaks elsewhere of a *corpus mysticum* of the rational beings in the sensible world, 'in so far as the free will of each being is, under moral laws, in complete systematic unity with itself and with the freedom of every other'.[35]

The basis of Kant's ethics is thus that I should recognize myself as spirit and affirm my membership of a spiritual world. When we turn to Mill, we find that this spiritualism has given place to humanism. I am to recognize myself as man, and to affirm my solidarity with mankind—mankind being now conceived not as an abstract class-concept but as a race fulfilling its destiny in history.

In his epistemology Kant's metaphysics takes a different form. The self knowing nature affirms itself as spirit

---

[28] 'Men are not machines, not even ghost-ridden machines. They are men—a tautology which is sometimes worth remembering.' Ryle, *The Concept of Mind*, p. 88.

[29] *Discourse on Method*, Pt. IV, Everyman Edition, p. 27. Contrast Moore's statement 'I am a human being' (*Some Main Problems of Philosophy*, p. 195).

[30] *Foundation of the Metaphysic of Morals,* Paton's translation *The Moral Law,* p. 105.

[31] 'The law interests us because it is valid for us as men in virtue of having sprung from our will as intelligence and so from our proper self.' *Ibid.,* p. 129.

[32] 'In [the intelligible world] reason alone, and indeed pure reason independent of sensibility, is the source of law; and . . . since he is there his proper self only as intelligence (while as a human being he is merely an appearance of himself), these laws apply to him immediately and categorically.' *Ibid.,* p. 125.

[33] *Ibid.,* p. 121.

[34] *Ibid.,* p. 126.

[35] *Critique of Pure Reason,* A. 808, B. 836. Kemp Smith's translation, pp. 637-8.

distinct from nature and giving laws to it: but it is not thought of here as affirming its membership in a society of spirits. Instead it affirms its solidarity with 'consciousness as such'; this is like Descartes' identification of himself with 'mind' or 'mental substance'. Hence it would not be surprising, though I have not confirmed this by inspection, if in Kant's epistemology and in the epistemologies bearing a Kantian impress which held the academical field for so long after his death, 'we' sentences are not prominent or characteristic. What is spoken of is 'the mind'.

An early document of the philosophy of Analysis, a paper of 1922 by C. I. Lewis, entitled 'The Pragmatic Conception of the a Priori',[36] illustrates the transition from the Kantian to the humanist basis.

Lewis maintains the thesis that 'the a priori represents an attitude in some sense freely taken, a stipulation of the mind itself, and a stipulation which might be taken in some other way if it suited our bent or need'.[37] He maintains this against anticipated resistance from 'those who would conceive the a priori in terms of an absolute mind or an absolutely universal human nature'.[38] The point which Lewis is making is that we must think of the categories through which we perceive things as being chosen, not necessitated. This is a departure from what we have come to regard as the traditional 'metaphysical' language; but notice that what it substitutes is not more positive or empirical than what it rejects. The acts of free choice attributed to mind are not datable acts performed by individual minds. They are more like the acts of decision which the social contract theo-

rists postulated as the origin of the state; or like the decisions which Professor Toulmin postulates as the origin of everyday language.[39] These are not decisions which anyone can be supposed ever to have actually *taken*, or the taking of which could be verified by empirical evidence in the ordinary sense.

A consequence of the alteration is that one must think of the chosen categories as being subject to variation, not as fixed once for all by the nature of mind. The conceptions and principles with which we are concerned 'have altered in human history'.[40] (We should think, for example, of the displacement of Newtonian ways of looking at nature by Einsteinian ones.) Yet it is not simply empirical proof or disproof which has caused the substitution. Rather, they 'represent the uncompelled initiative of human thought,' without which no 'growth of science, nor any science at all, would be conceivable'. *Logical* laws have a permanence in human thought which is relatively greater than that of physical principles, but this is a difference only of degree.

'The difference between such conceptions as are, for example, concerned in the decision of relativity *versus* absolute space and time, and those more permanent attitudes such as are vested in the Laws of Logic, there is only a difference of degree. The dividing line between the *a priori* and the *a posteriori* is that between principles and definitive concepts which *can* be maintained in the face of all experience and those genuinely empirical generalizations which *might* be proven flatly false. The thought which both rationalism and empiricism have missed is that there are principles, representing the initiative of mind, which impose upon experience no limitations whatever, but that such conceptions are still

---

[36] Reprinted in *Readings in Philosophical Analysis,* ed. Feigl and Sellars, pp. 286-94.

[37] *Op. cit.,* p. 286.

[38] P. 292.

[39] 'If the decisions on which our physical theories rest are easy to forget, those which have gone to the making of every-day speech are yet more easily forgotten.' S. E. Toulmin, *The Philosophy of Science,* p. 129.

[40] P. 293.

subject to alteration on pragmatic grounds when the expanding boundaries of experience reveal their infelicity as intellectual instruments.' [41]

The transition which we are witnessing in these passages is that from a timeless deduction to a temporal story, and from a spiritualist metaphysics to humanism. The categories of thought are not eternal, but are subject to change, the changes take place in history, and this history is human history.

We are witnessing the disappearance of metaphysics and its replacement by —what? It is not true that nothing has stepped into the place which metaphysics has vacated. What has stepped in is what I have called by the vague name of 'humanism'. This is not an empirical matter, as we have seen. The choices and stipulations with which it is concerned are not datable acts of individual human beings. To call it a humanist *metaphysics* would stress the fact that the old metaphysics has been replaced by something which is, so to speak, on the same level as itself, but it would be misleading, because we do not use the name 'metaphysics' to describe the kind of thing which it is.

In some ways 'humanist myth' would be a better description, since it indicates both its temporal character and the fact that it is not susceptible of empirical verification or falsification in the ordinary sense. But myth is unsuitable, too, because it suggests something unrelated to history, whereas humanism supplies a key for the understanding of history (it is metahistory, in the sense illustrated above).

Besides 'myth' suggests something which is poetical in character and not to be taken seriously, whereas humanism tells a history which we recognize and adopt as our own. Hence the characteristic 'we' appears in Lewis's article.

'The law of excluded middle formulates our decision that whatever is not designated by a certain term shall be designated by its negative. It declares our purpose to make, for every term, a complete dichotomy of experience, instead as we might choose of classifying on the basis of a tripartite division into opposites (as black and white) and the middle ground between the two. Our rejection of such tripartite division represents only our penchant for simplicity.' [42]

We have seen that these assertions are logically homogeneous with theological assertions. There would be something to be said for calling them themselves theological, and describing what they express as a theological anthropology: though it would be a paradoxical use, since it would involve us in speaking of a theology without God.

---

[41] P. 293.
[42] P. 287

JEAN-PAUL SARTRE

Atheistic Existentialism: Man Creates Himself*

. . .There are two kinds of existentialist; first, those who are Christian, among whom I would include Jaspers and Gabriel Marcel, both Catholic; and on the other hand the atheistic existentialists, among whom I class Heidegger, and then the French existentialists and myself. What they have in common is that they think that existence precedes essence, or, if you prefer, that subjectivity must be the starting point.

Just what does that mean? Let us consider some object that is manufactured, for example, a book or a paper-cutter: here is an object which has been made by an artisan whose inspiration came from a concept. He referred to the concept of what a paper-cutter is and likewise to a known method of production, which is part of the concept, something which is, by and large, a routine. Thus, the paper-cutter is at once an object produced in a certain way and, on the other hand, one having a specific use; and one can not postulate a man who produces a paper-cutter but does not know what it is used for. Therefore, let us say that, for the paper-cutter, essence —that is, the ensemble of both the production routines and the properties which enable it to be both produced and defined—precedes existence. Thus, the presence of the paper-cutter or book in front of me is determined. Therefore, we have here a technical view of the world whereby it can be said that production precedes existence.

When we conceive God as the Creator, He is generally thought of as a superior sort of artisan. Whatever doctrine we may be considering, whether one like that of Descartes or that of Leibnitz, we always grant that will more or less follows understanding or, at the very least, accompanies it, and that when God creates He knows exactly what He is creating. Thus, the concept of man in the mind of God is comparable to the concept of paper-cutter in the mind of the manufacturer, and, following certain techniques and a conception, God produces man, just as the artisan, following a definition and a technique, makes a paper-cutter. Thus, the individual man is the realisation of a certain concept in the divine intelligence.

In the eighteenth century, the atheism of the *philosophes* discarded the idea of God, but not so much for the notion that essence precedes existence. To a certain extent, this idea is found everywhere; we find it in Diderot, in Voltaire, and even in Kant. Man has a human nature; this human nature, which is the concept of the human, is found in all men, which means that each man is a particular example of a universal concept, man. In Kant, the result of this universality is that the wild-man, the natural man, as well as the bourgeois, are circumscribed by the same definition and have the same basic qualities. Thus, here too the essence of man precedes the historical existence that we find in nature.

Atheistic existentialism, which I represent, is more coherent. It states that if God does not exist, there is at least one being in whom existence precedes essence, a being who exists before he can be defined by a concept, and that this being is man, or, as Heidegger says, human reality. What is meant here by saying that existence precedes essence?

* From *Existentialism* by Jean-Paul Sartre. Copyright 1947 by the Philosophical Library; pp. 15-27, 34-37, 60-61.

It means that, first of all, man exists, turns up, appears on the scene, and, only afterwards, defines himself. If man, as the existentialist conceives him, is indefinable, it is because at first he is nothing. Only afterward will he be something, and he himself will have made what he will be. Thus, there is no human nature, since there is no God to conceive it. Not only is man what he conceives himself to be, but he is also only what he wills himself to be after this thrust toward existence.

Man is nothing else but what he makes of himself. Such is the first principle of existentialism. It is also what is called subjectivity, the name we are labeled with when charges are brought against us. But what do we mean by this, if not that man has a greater dignity than a stone or table? For we mean that man first exists, that is, that man first of all is the being who hurls himself toward a future and who is conscious of imagining himself as being in the future. Man is at the start a plan which is aware of itself, rather than a patch of moss, a piece of garbage, or a cauliflower; nothing exists prior to this plan; there is nothing in heaven; man will be what he will have planned to be. Not what he will want to be. Because by the word "will" we generally mean a conscious decision, which is subsequent to what we have already made of ourselves. I may want to belong to a political party, write a book, get married; but all that is only a manifestation of an earlier, more spontaneous choice that is called "will." But if existence really does precede essence, man is responsible for what he is. Thus, existentialism's first move is to make every man aware of what he is and to make the full responsibility of his existence rest on him. And when we say that a man is responsible for himself, we do not only mean that he is responsible for his own individuality, but that he is responsible for all men.

The word subjectivism has two meanings, and our opponents play on the two. Subjectivism means, on the one hand, that an individual chooses and makes himself; and, on the other, that it is impossible for man to transcend human subjectivity. The second of these is the essential meaning of existentialism. When we say that man chooses his own self, we mean that every one of us does likewise; but we also mean by that that in making this choice he also chooses all men. In fact, in creating the man that we want to be, there is not a single one of our acts which does not at the same time create an image of man as we think he ought to be. To choose to be this or that is to affirm at the same time the value of what we choose, because we can never choose evil. We always choose the good, and nothing can be good for us without being good for all.

If, on the other hand, existence precedes essence, and if we grant that we exist and fashion our image at one and the same time, the image is valid for everybody and for our whole age. Thus, our responsibility is much greater than we might have supposed, because it involves all mankind. If I am a workingman and choose to join a Christian trade-union rather than be a communist, and if by being a member I want to show that the best thing for man is resignation, that the kingdom of man is not of this world, I am not only involving my own case—I want to be resigned for everyone. As a result, my action has involved all humanity. To take a more individual matter, if I want to marry, to have children; even if this marriage depends solely on my own circumstances or passion or wish, I am involving all humanity in monogamy and not merely myself. Therefore, I am responsible for myself and for everyone else. I am creating a certain image of man of my own choosing. In choosing myself, I choose man.

This helps us understand what the actual content is of such rather grandiloquent words as anguish, forlornness, despair. As you will see, it's all quite simple.

First, what is meant by anguish? The existentialists say at once that man is anguish. What that means is this: the man who involves himself and who realizes that he is not only the person he chooses to be, but also a law-maker who is, at the same time, choosing all mankind as well as himself, can not help escape the feeling of his total and deep responsibility. Of course, there are many people who are not anxious; but we claim that they are hiding their anxiety, that they are fleeing from it. Certainly, many people believe that when they do something, they themselves are the only ones involved, and when someone says to them, "What if everyone acted that way?" they shrug their shoulders and answer, "Everyone doesn't act that way." But really, one should always ask himself, "What would happen if everybody looked at things that way?" There is no escaping this disturbing thought except by a kind of double-dealing. A man who lies and makes excuses for himself by saying "not everybody does that," is someone with an uneasy conscience, because the act of lying implies that a universal value is conferred upon the lie.

Anguish is evident even when it conceals itself. This is the anguish that Kierkegaard called the anguish of Abraham. You know the story: an angel has ordered Abraham to sacrifice his son; if it really were an angel who has come and said, "You are Abraham, you shall sacrifice your son," everything would be all right. But everyone might first wonder, "Is it really an angel, and am I really Abraham? What proof do I have?"

There was a madwoman who had hallucinations; someone used to speak to her on the telephone and give her orders. Her doctor asked her, "Who is it who talks to you?" She answered, "He says it's God." What proof did she really have that it was God? If an angel comes to me, what proof is there that it's an angel? And if I hear voices, what proof is there that they come from heaven and not from hell, or from the subconscious, or a pathological condition? What proves that they are addressed to me? What proof is there that I have been appointed to impose my choice and my conception of man on humanity? I'll never find any proof or sign to convince me of that. If a voice addresses me, it is always for me to decide that this is the angel's voice; if I consider that such an act is a good one, it is I who will choose to say that it is good rather than bad.

Now, I'm not being singled out as an Abraham, and yet at every moment I'm obliged to perform exemplary acts. For every man, everything happens as if all mankind had its eyes fixed on him and were guiding itself by what he does. And every man ought to say to himself, "Am I really the kind of man who has the right to act in such a way that humanity might guide itself by my action?" And if he does not say that to himself, he is masking his anguish.

There is no question here of the kind of anguish which would lead to quietism, to inaction. It is a matter of a simple sort of anguish that anybody who has had responsibilities is familiar with. For example, when a military officer takes the responsibility for an attack and sends a certain number of men to death, he chooses to do so, and in the main he alone makes the choice. Doubtless, orders come from above, but they are too broad; he interprets them, and on this interpretation depend the lives of ten or fourteen or twenty men. In making a decision he can not help having a certain anguish. All leaders know this anguish. That doesn't keep them from acting; on the contrary, it is the very condition of their action. For it implies that they envisage a number of possibilities, and when they choose one, they realize that it has value only because it is chosen. We shall see that this kind

243

of anguish, which is the kind that existentialism describes, is explained, in addition, by a direct responsibility to the other men whom it involves. It is not a curtain separating us from action, but is part of action itself.

When we speak of forlornness, a term Heidegger was fond of, we mean only that God does not exist and that we have to face all the consequences of this. The existentialist is strongly opposed to a certain kind of secular ethics which would like to abolish God with the least possible expense. About 1880, some French teachers tried to set up a secular ethics which went something like this: God is a useless and costly hypothesis; we are discarding it; but, meanwhile, in order for there to be an ethics, a society, a civilization, it is essential that certain values be taken seriously and that they be considered as having an *a priori* existence. It must be obligatory, *a priori*, to be honest, not to lie, not to beat your wife, to have children, etc., etc. So we're going to try a little device which will make it possible to show that values exist all the same, inscribed in a heaven of ideas, though otherwise God does not exist. In other words—and this, I believe, is the tendency of everything called reformism in France—nothing will be changed if God does not exist. We shall find ourselves with the same norms of honesty, progress, and humanism, and we shall have made of God an outdated hypothesis which will peacefully die off by itself.

The existentialist, on the contrary, thinks it very distressing that God does not exist, because all possibility of finding values in a heaven of ideas disappears along with Him; there can no longer be an *a priori* Good, since there is no infinite and perfect consciousness to think it. Nowhere is it written that the Good exists, that we must be honest, that we must not lie; because the fact is we are on a plane where there are only men. Dostoievsky said, "If God didn't exist, everything would be possible."

That is the very starting point of existentialism. Indeed, everything is permissible if God does not exist, and as a result man is forlorn, because neither within him nor without does he find anything to cling to. He can't start making excuses for himself.

If existence really does precede essence, there is no explaining things away by reference to a fixed and given human nature. In other words, there is no determinism, man is free, man is freedom. On the other hand, if God does not exist, we find no values or commands to turn to which legitimize our conduct. So, in the bright realm of values, we have no excuse behind us, nor justification before us. We are alone, with no excuses.

That is the idea I shall try to convey when I say that man is condemned to be free. Condemned, because he did not create himself, yet, in other respects is free; because, once thrown into the world, he is responsible for everything he does. . . .

As for despair, the term has a very simple meaning. It means that we shall confine ourselves to reckoning only with what depends upon our will, or on the ensemble of probabilities which make our action possible. When we want something, we always have to reckon with probabilities. I may be counting on the arrival of a friend. The friend is coming by rail or street-car; this supposes that the train will arrive on schedule, or that the street-car will not jump the track. I am left in the realm of possibility; but possibilities are to be reckoned with only to the point where my action comports with the ensemble of these possibilities, and no further. The moment the possibilities I am considering are not rigorously involved by my action, I ought to disengage myself from them, because no God, no scheme, can adapt the world and its possibilities to my will. When Descartes said, "Conquer yourself rather than the world," he meant essentially the same thing.

The Marxists to whom I have spoken reply, "You can rely on the support of others in your action, which obviously has certain limits because you're not going to live forever. That means: rely on both what others are doing elsewhere to help you, in China, in Russia, and what they will do later on, after your death, to carry on the action and lead it to its fulfillment, which will be the revolution. You even *have* to rely upon that, otherwise you're immoral." I reply at once that I will always rely on fellow-fighters insofar as these comrades are involved with me in a common struggle, in the unity of a party or a group in which I can more or less make my weight felt; that is, one whose ranks I am in as a fighter and whose movements I am aware of at every moment. In such a situation, relying on the unity and will of the party is exactly like counting on the fact that the train will arrive on time or that the car won't jump the track. But, given that man is free and that there is no human nature for me to depend on, I can not count on men whom I do not know by relying on human goodness or man's concern for the good of society. I don't know what will become of the Russian revolution; I may make an example of it to the extent that at the present time it is apparent that the proletariat plays a part in Russia that it plays in no other nation. But I can't swear that this will inevitably lead to a triumph of the proletariat. I've got to limit myself to what I see.

Given that men are free and that tomorrow they will freely decide what man will be, I can not be sure that, after my death, fellow-fighters will carry on my work to bring it to its maximum perfection. . . .

Existentialism is nothing else than an attempt to draw all the consequences of a coherent atheistic position. It isn't trying to plunge man into despair at all. But if one calls every attitude of unbelief despair, like the Christians, then the word is not being used in its original sense. Existentialism isn't so atheistic that it wears itself out showing that God doesn't exist. Rather, it declares that even if God did exist, that would change nothing. There you've got our point of view. Not that we believe that God exists, but we think that the problem of His existence is not the issue. In this sense existentialism is optimistic, a doctrine of action, and it is plain dishonesty for Christians to make no distinction between their own despair and ours and then to call us despairing.

RUDOLF BULTMANN

Existentialism and Demythologizing the Biblical Message*

THE MYTHOLOGICAL WORLD VIEW

This hope of Jesus and of the early Christian community [that the Kingdom of God would come in the immediate future] was not fulfilled. The same world still exists and history continues. The course of history has refuted mythology. For the conception "Kingdom of God" is mythological, as is the conception of the eschatological drama. Just as mythological are the presuppositions of the expectation of the Kingdom of God, namely, the theory that the world, although created by God, is ruled by the devil, Satan, and that his army, the demons, is the cause of all evil, sin and disease. The whole conception of the world which is presupposed in the preaching of Jesus as in the New Testament generally is mythological; i.e., the conception of the world as being structured in three stories, heaven, earth and hell; the conception of the intervention of supernatural powers in the course of events; and the conception of miracles, especially the conception of the intervention of supernatural powers in the inner life of the soul, the conception that men can be tempted and corrupted by the devil and possessed by evil spirits. This conception of the world we call mythological because it is different from the conception of the world which has been formed and developed by science since its inception in ancient Greece and which has been accepted by all modern man. In this modern conception of the world the cause-and-effect nexus is fundamental. Although modern physi-cal theories take account of chance in the chain of cause and effect in sub-atomic phenomena, our daily living, purposes and actions are not affected. In any case, modern science does not believe that the course of nature can be interrupted or, so to speak, perforated, by supernatural powers. . . .

THE MODERN WORLD-VIEW

An objection often heard against the attempt to de-mythologize is that it takes the modern world-view as the criterion of the interpretation of the Scripture and the Christian message and that Scripture and Christian message are not allowed to say anything that is in contradiction with the modern world-view.

It is, of course, true that de-mythologizing takes the modern world-view as a criterion. To de-mythologize is to reject not Scripture or the Christian message as a whole, but the world-view of Scripture, which is the world-view of a past epoch, which all too often is retained in Christian dogmatics and in the preaching of the Church. To de-mythologize is to deny that the message of Scripture and of the Church is bound to an ancient world-view which is obsolete.

The attempt to de-mythologize begins with this important insight: Christian preaching, in so far as it is preaching of the Word of God by God's command and in His name, does not offer a doctrine which can be accepted either by reason or by a *sacrificium intellectus*. Christian preaching is *kerygma*, that is, a proclamation addressed not to the theoretical reason, but to the hearer as a self. In this manner Paul commends himself to every man's conscience in the sight of God (II Cor. 4:2). De-mythologizing will make clear this function of preaching as a personal message, and in doing so it will eliminate a false stumbling-block and bring into sharp focus the real stumbling-block, the word of the cross.

For the world-view of the Scripture is mythological and is therefore unacceptable to modern man whose thinking has been shaped by science and is therefore no longer mythological. Modern man always makes use of technical means which are the result of science. In case of illness modern man has recourse to physicians, to medical science. In case of economic and political affairs, he makes use of the results of psychological, social, economic and political sciences, and so on. Nobody reckons with direct intervention by transcendent powers.

Of course, there are today some survivals and revivals of primitive thinking and superstition. But the preaching of the Church would make a disastrous mistake if it looked to such revivals and conformed to them. The nature of man is to be seen in modern literature, as, for instance, in the novels of Thomas Mann, Ernst Jünger, Thornton Wilder, Ernest Hemingway, William Faulkner, Graham Greene and Albert Camus, or in the plays of Jean-Paul Sartre, Jean Anouilh, Jean Giraudoux, etc. Or let us think simply of the newspapers. Have you read anywhere in them that political or social or economic events are performed by supernatural powers such as God, angels or demons? Such events are always ascribed to natural powers, or to good or bad will on the part of men, or to human wisdom or stupidity.

The science of today is no longer the same as it was in the nineteenth century, and to be sure, all the results of science are relative, and no world-view of yesterday or today or tomorrow is definitive. The main point, however, is not the concrete results of scientific research and the contents of a world-view, but the method of thinking from which world-views follow. For example, it makes no difference in principle whether the earth rotates round the sun or the sun rotates round the earth, but it does make a decisive difference that modern man understands the motion of the universe as a motion which obeys a cosmic law, a law of nature which human reason can discover. Therefore, modern man acknowledges as reality only such phenomena or events as are comprehensible within the framework of the rational order of the universe. He does not acknowledge miracles because they do not fit into this lawful order. When a strange or marvelous accident occurs, he does not rest until he has found a rational cause.

The contrast between the ancient world-view of the Bible and the modern world-view is the contrast between two ways of thinking, the mythological and the scientific. The method of scientific thinking and inquiry is in principle the same today as it was at the beginning of methodical and critical science in ancient Greece. It begins with the question about the ἀρχή (origin) from which the world is conceivable as unity, as κόσμος, as systematic order and harmony. It begins therefore also with the attempt to give reasonable proofs for every statement (λόγον διδόναι). These principles are the same in modern science, and it does not matter that the results of scientific research are changing over and over again, since the change itself results from the permanent principles.

Certainly it is a philosophical problem whether the scientific world-view can perceive the whole reality of the world and of human life. There are reasons for doubting whether it can do so, and we shall have to say more about this problem in the following chapters. But for present purposes it is enough to say that the thinking of modern men is really shaped by the scientific world-view, and that modern men need it for their daily lives.

Therefore, it is mere wishful thinking to suppose that the ancient world-view of the Bible can be renewed. It is the radical abandonment and the conscious critique of the mythological world-view of the Bible which bring the real stumbling-block into sharp focus. This stumbling-block is that the Word of God calls man out of all man-made security. The scientific world-view engenders a great temptation, namely, that man strive for mastery over the world and over his own life. He knows the laws of nature and can use the powers of nature according to his plans and desires. He discovers more and more accurately the laws of social and of economic life, and thus organizes the life of the community more and more effectively—as Sophocles said in the famous chorus from *Antigone*

> Many wonders there be,
> but nought more wondrous than man.
> (332-333)

Thus modern man is in danger of forgetting two things: first, that his plans and undertakings should be guided not by his own desires for happiness and security, usefulness and profit, but rather by obedient response to the challenge of goodness, truth and love, by obedience to the commandment of God which man forgets in his selfishness and presumption; and secondly, that it is an illusion to suppose that real security can be gained by men organizing their own personal and community life. There are encounters and destinies which man cannot master. He cannot secure endurance for his works. His life is fleeting and its end is death. History goes on and pulls down all the towers of Babel again and again. There is no real, definitive security, and it is precisely this illusion to which men are prone to succumb in their yearning for security.

What is the underlying reason for this yearning? It is the sorrow, the secret anxiety which moves in the depths of the soul at the very moment when man thinks that he must obtain security for himself.

It is the Word of God which calls man away from his selfishness and from the illusory security which he has built up for himself. It calls him to God, who is beyond the world and beyond scientific thinking. At the same time, it calls man to his true self. For the self of man, his inner life, his personal existence is also beyond the visible world and beyond rational thinking. The Word of God addresses man in his personal existence and thereby it gives him freedom from the world and from the sorrow and anxiety which overwhelm him when he forgets the beyond. By means of science men try to take possession of the world, but in fact the world gets possession of men We can see in our times to what degree men are dependent on technology, and to what degree technology brings with it terrible consequences. To believe in the Word of God means to abandon all merely human security and thus to overcome the despair which arises from the attempt to find security, an attempt which is always vain. . . .

EXISTENTIALISM AND BIBLICAL INTERPRETATION

This is, then, the basic presupposition for every form of exegesis: that your own relation to the subject-matter prompts the question you bring to the text and elicits the answers you obtain from the text.

I have tried to analyze the situation of the interpreter by using the example of psychological interpretation. You can read and interpret a text with other interests, for example, with aesthetical or with historical interest, with the interest in political or cultural history of states, etc. With regard to historical interpretation there are two possibilities. First, your interest may be to give a picture of a past time, to reconstruct the past; second, your interest may be to learn from historical documents what you need for your present practical life. For example, you can interpret Plato as an interesting figure of the culture of fifth-century Athenian Greece, but you can also interpret Plato to learn through him the truth about human life. In the latter case your interpretation is not motivated by interest in a past epoch of history, but by your search for the truth.

Now, when we interpret the Bible, what is our interest? Certainly the Bible is an historical document and we must interpret the Bible by the methods of historical research. We must study the language of the Bible, the historical situation of the Biblical authors, etc. But what is our true and real interest? Are we to read the Bible only as an historical document in order to reconstruct an epoch of past history for which the Bible serves as a "source"? Or is it more than a source? I think our interest is really to hear what the Bible has to say for our actual present, to hear what is the truth about our life and about our soul.

Now the question arises as to which is the adequate method, which are the adequate conceptions? And also, which is the relation, the "life-relation," which we have in advance, to the theme (*Sache*) of the Bible from which our questions and our conceptions arise? Must we say that we do not have such relation in advance, since the theme of the Bible is the revelation of God, and we can gain a relation to God only by His revelation and not in advance of it?

Indeed, there are theologians who have argued in this manner, but it seems to me that they are in error. Man does have in advance a relation to God which has found its classical expression in the words of Augustine: "Tu nos fecisti ad te, et cor nostrum inquietum est, donec requioscat in te" (Thou hast made us for Thyself, and our heart is restless,

until it rests in Thee). Man has a knowledge of God in advance, though not of the revelation of God, that is, of His action in Christ. He has a relation to God in his search for God, conscious or unconscious. Man's life is moved, consciously or unconsciously, by the question about his own personal existence. The question of God and the question of myself are identical.

Now we have found the adequate way to put the question when we interpret the Bible. This question is, *how is man's existence understood in the Bible?* I approach the Biblical texts with this question for the same reason which supplies the deepest motive for all historical research and for all interpretation of historical documents. It is that by understanding history I can gain an understanding of the possibilities of human life and thereby of the possibilities of my own life. The ultimate reason for studying history is to become conscious of the possibilities of human existence.

The interpretation of the Biblical scriptures, however, has a special motive. The tradition and the preaching of the Church tells us that we are to hear in the Bible authoritative words about our existence. What distinguishes the Bible from other literature is that in the Bible a certain possibility of existence is shown to me not as something which I am free to choose or to refuse. Rather, the Bible becomes for me a word addressed personally to me, which not only informs me about existence in general, but gives me real existence. This, however, is a possibility on which I cannot count in advance. It is not a methodological presupposition by means of which I can understand the Bible. For this possibility can become a reality only when I understand the word.

Our task, therefore, is to discover the hermeneutical principle by which we can understand what is said in the Bible. It is not permissible to evade this question, since in principle every historical document raises it, namely, what possibility of understanding human existence is shown and offered in each document of the Bible? In critical study of the Bible I can do no more than search for an answer to this question. It is beyond the competence of critical study that I should hear the word of the Bible as a word addressed personally to me and that I should believe in it. This personal understanding, in traditional terminology, is imparted by the Holy Spirit, who is not at my disposal. On the other hand, we can discover the adequate hermeneutical principle, the right way to ask the right questions, only by objective, critical reflection. If it is true that the right questions are concerned with the possibilities of understanding human existence, then it is necessary to discover the adequate conceptions by which such understanding is to be expressed. To discover these conceptions is the task of philosophy.

But now the objection is brought forward that exegesis falls under the control of philosophy. This is the case indeed, but we must ask in what sense it is so. It is an illusion to hold that any exegesis can be independent of secular conceptions. Every interpreter is inescapably dependent on conceptions which he has inherited from a tradition, consciously or unconsciously, and every tradition is dependent on some philosophy or other. In this way, for example, much of the exegesis of the nineteenth century was dependent on idealistic philosophy and on its conceptions, on its understanding of human existence. Such idealistic conceptions still influence many interpreters today. It follows, then, that historical and exegetical study should not be practiced without reflection and without giving an account of the conceptions which guide the exegesis. In other words, the question of the "right" philosophy arises.

At this point we must realize that there will never be a right philosophy in the sense of an absolutely perfect system, a philosophy which could give answers to all questions and clear up all riddles of human existence. Our question is simply which philosophy today offers the most adequate perspective and conceptions for understanding human existence. Here it seems to me that we should learn from existentialist philosophy, because in this philosophical school human existence is directly the object of attention.

We would learn little if existential philosophy, as many people suppose, attempted to offer an ideal pattern of human existence. The concept of "truth of existence" (*Eigentlichkeit*) does not furnish such a pattern. Existentialist philosophy does not say to me "in such and such a way you must exist"; it says only "you must exist"; or, since even this claim may be too large, it shows me what it means to exist. Existentialist philosophy tries to show what it means to exist by distinguishing between man's being as "existence" and the being of all worldly beings which are not "existing" but only "extant" (*vorhanden*). (This technical use of the word "existence" goes back to Kierkegaard.) Only men can have an existence, because they are historical beings. That is to say, every man has his own history. Always his present comes out of his past and leads into his future. He realizes his existence if he is aware that each "now" is the moment of free decision: What element in his past is to retain value? What is his responsibility toward his future, since no one can take the place of another? No one can take another's place, since every man realizes his existence.

Of course, I cannot here carry out the existentialist analysis in detail. It may be enough to say that existentialist philosophy shows human existence to be true only in the act of existing. Existentialist philosophy is far from pretending that it secures for man a self-understanding of his own personal existence. For this self-understanding of my very personal existence can only be realized in the concrete moments of my "here" and "now." Existentialist philosophy, while it gives no answer to the question of my personal existence, makes personal existence my own personal responsibility, and by doing so it helps to make me open to the word of the Bible. It is clear, of course, that existentialist philosophy has its origin in the personal-existential question about existence and its possibilities. For how could it know about existence except from its own existential awareness, provided that existentialist philosophy is not identified with traditional anthropology? Thus it follows that existentialist philosophy can offer adequate conceptions for the interpretation of the Bible, since the interpretation of the Bible is concerned with the understanding of existence.

Once again we ask, does the existentialist understanding of existence and the existentialist analysis of that understanding already include a decision in favor of a particular understanding? Certainly such a decision is included, but what decision? Precisely the decision of which I have already spoken: "You must exist." Without this decision, without the readiness to be a human being, a person who in responsibility takes it upon himself to be, no one can understand a single word of the Bible as speaking to his own personal existence. While this decision does not require philosophical knowledge, scientific interpretation of the Bible does require the existentialist conceptions in order to explain the Biblical understanding of human existence. Thus only does it become clear that the hearing of the word of the Bible can take place only in personal decision.

That existentialist philosophy does not furnish a pattern of ideal existence may be illustrated by an example. Existentialist analysis describes particular phenomena of existence, for example, the phenomenon of love. It would be a misunderstanding to think that the existentialist analysis of love can lead me to understand how I must love here and now. The existentialist analysis can do nothing more than make it clear to me that I can understand love only by loving. No analysis can take the place of my duty to understand my love as an encounter in my own personal existence.

To be sure, philosophical analysis presupposes the judgment that it is possible to analyze human existence without reflection on the relation between man and God. But to understand human existence in its relation to God can only mean to understand my personal existence, and philosophical analysis does not claim to instruct me about my personal self-understanding. The purely formal analysis of existence does not take into account the relation between man and God, because it does not take into account the concrete events of the personal life, the concrete encounters which constitute personal existence. If it is true that the revelation of God is realized only in concrete events of life here and now, and that the analysis of existence is confined to man's temporal life with its series of here and now, then this analysis unveils a sphere which faith alone can understand as the sphere of the relation between man and God.

The judgment that man's existence can be analyzed without taking into account his relation with God may be called an existential decision, but the elimination is not a matter of subjective preference; it is grounded in the existential insight that the idea of God is not at our disposal when we construct a theory of man's existence. Moreover, the judgment points to the idea of absolute freedom, whether this idea be accepted as true or rejected as absurd. We can also put it this way: that the elimination of man's relation with God is the expression of my personal knowledge of myself, the acknowledgment that I cannot find God by looking at or into myself. Thus, this elimination itself gives to the analysis of existence its neutrality.

251

In the fact that existentialist philosophy does not take into account the relation between man and God, the confession is implied that I cannot speak of God as my God by looking into myself. My personal relation with God can be made real by God only, by the acting God who meets me in His Word.

J. RODMAN WILLIAMS

Christian Faith Against Existentialism *

Christian faith finds itself in basic disagreement [with existentialism]. The "awakened man" is *not* one whose fundamental attitude is that of anxiety, but rather that of faith and trust. He is one who has heeded the word, "Do not be anxious about your life . . ." (Matthew 6:25). A genuine awakening has occurred at the center of his being that has changed him from a creature of basic anxiety about life, death, the future —indeed anything that may come—to a person of essential freedom from fear and dread.[1] Again, anxiety is not laudable, as if to say it is the basic mood of a man who reflects on his freedom and has to make decisions. According to Christian faith, the truly free man is one who has been freed by Christ ("for freedom Christ has set us free" Galatians 5:1) ; consequently anxiety does not permeate the contemplation of his freedom. Rather, because it is a freedom *in* Christ, not in himself, anxiety is essentially nonexistent. To be sure, freedom points to infinite possibilities which, without a sense of direction, can only produce anxiety. But Christian man has this guidance and knows that of all the alternatives before him only quite specific ones are God's will, and those he will seek to do without anxiety. How is this possible? The answer is that he has appropriated the biblical injunction, "Have no anxiety about anything, but in every thing by prayer and supplication with thanksgiving let your requests be made known to God" (Philippians 4:6) . Through prayer, thanksgiving, and the accompanying trust in God, he is the man basically of "no anxiety." He is *truly* human and is *not* in anguish. Again, it is undoubtedly the case that anxiety "individualizes" a man and reveals something significant about his reality, but this very individualization becomes one of self-preoccupation; hence the self-disclosure is not that of basic

---

* From J. Rodman Williams, *Contemporary Existentialism and Christian Faith,* © 1965. Reprinted by permission of Prentice-Hall, Inc., Englewood Cliffs, New Jersey; pp. 125-32, 175-76.

[1] Jaspers' earlier statement to the effect that "ultimate anxiety" is the turning point leading to experience of being (or transcendence) is highly questionable. What assurance is there that through growth of anxiety to ultimate proportions one will experience reality? Why is it not more likely that the whole experience will only issue in further compounded anxiety, hopelessness, despair—with reality further away than ever? Hence according to Christian faith, there is urgent need for essential freedom from anxiety.

truth but of a departure therefrom, which the mood of anxiety signalizes. Anxiety does point to truth, but only in negative fashion. Finally, by no means does anxiety belong to creation or the creature as such. According to Christian faith, it belongs to creation only insofar as it does not heed the word of its Creator. (Disobedient man is the one filled with anxiety—see Genesis 3:8-10: "I was afraid. . . .") Anxiety, therefore, is the manifest sign that good has somehow been pervaded by evil. Existentialist thought fails to recognize that the very anxiety it approves is a deterrent to effective life and action. . . .

Christian faith [maintains] that, while fully agreeing with existentialism's recognition of the presence of anxiety in the situation of human freedom, the accompanying anxiety is not inevitable. For anxiety is not the natural corollary of freedom but the result of freedom's abuse; it is not simply the reverse side of freedom but the concomitant of lack of faith and obedience. The Christian faith holds that life truly lived is life without anxiety. The fulfillment of the New Testament injunction, "Do not be anxious," is to be found in a life of complete trust in God. To be sure, people are anxious—Christians included—this, however, is not due to their freedom but to their faithlessness. Jesus Christ, whose freedom is as much as a Sartre or Heidegger or Tillich could ever want, is the man of no anxiety;[2] therefore, those who have faith in Him are not satisfied to look on anxiety as part and parcel of being truly human.

It follows that Christian faith is no happier with the existentialist theme that "life's situations" inevitably produce anxiety. Jaspers, as we have noted, views all "ultimate situations"—guilt, suffering, struggle, death—as producing "ultimate anxiety"; Tillich sees anxiety as existentially bound up with fate and death, meaninglessness and emptiness, guilt and condemnation; so likewise the other existentialists in varying degrees. Anxiety, accordingly, belongs to all of life. Christian faith sharply dissents, for it views anxiety, in even the most trying of life's situations, not as a normal accompaniment but as abnormal. Anxiety belongs to sin and not to faith. There is no anxiety in suffering —even in "uninterpretable foundering" (Jaspers)—if borne in a spirit of trustful acceptance; there is no anxiety in guilt, if divine forgiveness is known and received; there is no anxiety in death, if one is able to say, "Father, into thy hands I commit my spirit" (Luke 23:46). Christian faith is not blind to the fact that all men, those of faith as well as unfaith, live in some degree of anxiety, but unlike existentialism's readiness to accept the situation, it seeks to purge men of anxiety as an evil.

A further word of disagreement concerns the existentialist premise of the inevitability of anxiety in the face of death. We may recall Jaspers' speaking about the "indeterminate anxiety" of being between beginning and end, Heidegger's description of anxiety as essential to human existence in its reality as "Being-towards-death," Tillich's statement that anxiety is grounded in the fact of our being "exposed to annihilation," and Bultmann's view about anxiety before "the void." All in all the assumption is that man is necessarily anxious because he is finite. As finite he must die; consequently his daily existence is ever threatened by nonbeing.

[2] It will be recalled that, according to Tillich, there is nonontological anxiety, *viz.*, pathological or neurotic, that can and should be removed. "Ontological anxiety" remains however as the "given" of being human. Hence even Christ was anxious (as noted earlier), since Christ represents true human nature. Tillich's view is hardly that of the New Testament, which invariably pictures Christ as one without anxiety and as calling others to the same freedom from care. One must admire Tillich's consistency in not hesitating to impute "ontological anxiety" to Christ while at the same time one must deplore the fractured view of Christ he presents.

There is no point in denying this anxiety, or in trying to forget it; it is there, and as long as one lives, it must be lived with. The only hope is to find some way of taking up this anxiety, making it creative, *etc.* Christian faith, on the other hand, urges that anxiety does not "belong"; it is a foreign ingredient; it is a blight upon man's existence as God's creature, and therefore ought to be removed. *Anxiety is due to man's sin, not to his being human; it is the result of his faithlessness, not of his finitude.* If man were not living contrary to God, there would be no anxiety in the face of death. In faith he would confront death not as the end of all things, but as the transition to the new, which God has prepared for all who love Him. The fact that men are anxious in the face of death is not, according to Christian faith, natural; it is unnatural. There is no "threat of nonbeing" creating anxiety for the man who knows in faith the power of God over death and the grave. Of course the man of faith may be anxious at times, but he can never justify it as natural or inevitable; he knows that his anxiety is due to his lack of faith.

Furthermore on this matter of anxiety in the face of death, Christian faith urges that existentialism does not really estimate the profound depths of the human situation. Man *is* anxious; however, the anxiety is not basically due to the "threat of nonbeing," but to the threat of "continued being." ...

Existentialism views anxiety as ontological. We may recall such statements as "we *are* anxiety" (Sartre); anxiety "belongs to the created character of being quite apart from estrangement and sin" (Tillich); and the " 'care'-structure of man's nature" is "an ontological structure of human existence" (Bultmann). It follows that not only is basic anxiety inevitable, as we have been noting, it is also unremovable. From the Christian perspective this existentialist viewpoint is doubly wrong. On the one hand, to say for example that "anxiety belongs to the created character of being" is to malign God's good creation (since, in the Christian view, this suggests a stigma or inadequacy in what comes from the Creator). On the other hand it makes man's condition a hopeless one; for if anxiety is ontological, there is utterly no possibility of its removal or elimination[3] (since it is structural, to remove it would be to destroy man). One must somehow learn to live with it, bear it, seek to make it creative, and so on. Thus, from the existentialist viewpoint, such a biblical word as "Do not be anxious" is either an impossible counsel or an admonition concerning only nonontological anxiety or "sinful" anxiety. Man is and remains structurally anxious; there is no hope for his cure. Christian faith can only see in such a view a failure to appreciate the power of faith that essentially changes man's anxious condition.

This affirmation of "ontological anxiety" in existentialism calls for further consideration of some earlier positive comments that underscored the genuine contribution existentialism has made in

---

[3] Recall that even Bultmann, who might be supposed to differ here, says that there can only be a "modification" of anxiety in faith. If anxiety is spoken of as "overcome," it is only so as "annulled and *preserved.*" Hence here again we see Bultmann caught between scriptural teaching ("overcome" and "annulled") and philosophical understanding ("preserved"), but with the ontological analysis the determinative factor. [Ed. note: Earlier Bultmann was quoted as saying "If *he* cannot free himself from the world and the past and himself, *God* can. And the way in which God does it is by the *forgiveness of sin.* That means simply the obliteration of man's past, and taking him to be what he is not—the man of the future; it means relieving him of dread and thereby making him free for the future." (*Essays: Philosophical and Theological,* trans. James C. G. Greig, London: SCM Press, 1955, p. 85.) To this Williams replied: "Anxiety thus is overcome. Man moves freely, no longer fleeing the nothing, but unreservedly facing toward it. Yet, despite man's freedom from the anxiety that inheres in attachments to the world, the "structure" of anxiety (or care) remains." (p. 121.)]

recognizing an anxiety that is deeper than "pathological." Christian faith, as before noted, agrees with existentialism that there is a pervasive anxiety in all men that is nonpathological and that it is *this* anxiety that is the universal human problem. But now the further, decisive, point that should be stressed, from the perspective of Christian faith, is that *existentialism misunderstands the very anxiety that it has uncovered: it sees what depth psychology often does not see, but it does not see it aright. . . .*

Why, we may finally ask, does existentialism slip into this dark and drear condition? Why does a philosophy that shares with Christianity a deep concern for man's anxious condition find itself moving toward despair? Why the sealing of man into a mold of "care" from which there is no real escape? Christian faith can only see in all this the inevitable results of a philosophy for which "truth is subjectivity," "man is central," "God is obscure," and "death is final." Man shut up to himself, with God in the shadows, and moving toward his assured end has no alternative but to accept anxiety and despair as the very fabric of existence.

Most of all, from the Christian perspective, existentialism fails here because it misunderstands the reality of God. God and man are so much identified that anxiety can have no resolution. Either man plays the role of God by presuming to create and maintain all values and meaning in life (Sartre) so that he becomes a creature of "pure anguish"; or man views God as the ground and depth of his own being (Tillich) so that there is no transcendent power radically to change his anxious lot. In the latter instance anxiety is grounded in God Himself, God becomes the ultimate and final threat, and man is doomed to "naked anxiety." When God is in the shadows, man is indeed a miserable creature.

To conclude: existentialism is rightly concerned about man's anxious reality, but with its own self-imposed limitations, it has no way of speaking a life-giving word. . . .

A final word by way of summing up: Christian faith discovers in existentialism many features gladly to be affirmed. The concern of the existentialists, philosophers and theologians alike, for truth that is inwardly experienced; the recognition that man is unique and must not be leveled down to object or animal; the realization that belief in God is not easy for many people today and that many gods ought to fall since they are little more than idols; the willingness to confront the fact of death rather than run from it or pretend that it is not there; the probing of man's condition of deep anxiety and the desire to meet it constructively; the recognition that the prevailing existence of mankind is far from authentic: these and many other existentialist convictions are genuinely consonant with Christian faith. Indeed in comparison with much speculative philosophy and empirical science, which seldom grapple with ultimate issues, existentialism would seem to be inside the Christian camp. Truly, for some people today who no longer can hear the genuine notes of Christian faith and are desperately searching for a living alternative existentialism seem to provide an authentic word.

However, having recognized much that is positive in value in existentialism, Christian faith must conclude that the existentialist philosophers and theologians, for all their contributions, are nonetheless missing the way. "Existentialism," as Sartre has frankly put it, "is a humanism," and the degree of belief or disbelief in God makes little difference: man is the center. For existentialism, truth must begin with man, existence must center in man, God (if admitted) must be the ground of man, and eternity (if recognized) must be confined to the present life of man. Furthermore anxiety must be accepted as a condition of man written into the very structure of his being, and man can have no other valid goal in life than that of his own self-fulfillment.

HARVEY COX

Man Come of Age Vs. Existentialism*

Despite its popularity with some intellectuals, existentialist theology is not an avenue into the world of urban-secular man. It is the religious branch of the larger existentialist movement. This movement, as Ernst Topitsch has shown in his essay on the sociology of existentialism, sprang from a particular social crisis in what he calls the European *Bildungsschicht*,[1] the educated middle classes who once discarded the aristocratic tradition of Throne and Altar and substituted their own prestigious combination of property and education. They ran Europe in the eighteenth and nineteenth centuries. Their monument can be found in the opera houses, museums, and educational institutions which still delight tourists.

But beginning in the early nineteenth century another type of person began to shoulder himself toward the center of the stage in European culture. He was the technician and scientist, the social planner and political revolutionary. It quickly became evident that in the world he was creating there was little room for the "cultivated personality" in the traditional sense. The response of the *Bildungsschicht* is not surprising. They decided that the whole world was going to the dogs. Humiliated by their own loss of prestige and by the disappearance of the secure little world in which they had exercised quiet but effective power, they concluded that a monumental decline of the whole culture had set in. They were convinced that *all* life had become meaningless, so they retreated into esthetic, spiritual, or religious detachment. It was in this heavy atmosphere of cultural *Weltschmerz* that existentialism was born.

Existentialism appeared just as the Western metaphysical tradition, whose social base was dismantled by revolution and technology, reached its end phase. It is the last child of a cultural epoch, born in its mother's senility. This is why existentialist writers seem so arcadian and antiurban. They represent an epoch marked for extinction. Consequently their thinking tends to be antitechnological, individualistic, romantic, and deeply suspicious of cities and of science.

Because the world had already moved beyond the pathos and narcissism of existentialism, such theological efforts to update the biblical message as that of

* Reprinted with permission of The Macmillan Company from *The Secular City* by Harvey Cox. Copyright © Harvey Cox, 1965; pp. 251-54.
[1] Ernst Topitsch, "Zur Soziologie des Existenzialismus. Kosmos-Existenz-Gesellschaft," *Sozialphilosophie zwischen Ideologie und Wissenschaft* (Neuwied: Hermann Luchterhand Verlag, 1961) , p. 87.

256

Rudolf Bultmann fall far short of the mark. They fail not because they are too radical but because they are not nearly radical enough. They deliver a nineteenth-century answer to a twentieth-century dilemma. Bultmann seems incapable of believing that God could be present in the urban-secular world of today rather than in the moldering sitting rooms of the turn-of-the-century bourgeois *Bildungsschicht*. He fails to reach the man of today because he translates the Bible from mythical language into yesterday's metaphysics rather than into today's post-metaphysical lexicon.

Naturally Bultmann would deny that existentialist categories are metaphysical, but they are. The ruling figures who stand at the fountainhead of existentialist thought still breathe the air of the presecular *Bildungsschicht*. They pen weighty tomes on traditional metaphysical questions. Except for Sartre, who has written some good plays, they employ a style which speaks mainly to their scholarly peers. Their thought, though it often puts on a fiercely antimetaphysical face, turns out to be a kind of fun-house mirror of metaphysics. Everything is grotesquely reversed, but it is all recognizable nonetheless. Thus nothingness replaces being, essence and existence are reversed, and man takes the place of God. The result is a kind of antitheism and antimetaphysic which fails utterly to make contact with the thought world of contemporary man. There is something immature about existentialism. Like classical theism, it needs some ultimate explanation for reality. In this sense it is closer to traditional theism than to the starting point of urban-secular man, who does not feel this compulsion to find some inclusive and overarching meaning.

Because they have been gullible enough to believe that the existentialist philosophers really spoke for modern man, theologians have found themselves in the awkward position of having first to lure people into existential vertigo as a kind of preparation for preaching. This has always been difficult, but especially so in pragmatic America, where the existentialist anxiety never really took root. It is now increasingly hard to do in Europe, where the younger generation no longer takes out its feelings of deprivation by projecting them into worldviews.

Religion and Philosophy: Bibliography

Metaphysics

Casserly, Julian V. Langmead. *The Christian in Philosophy.* New York: Charles Scribner's Sons, 1951.

Frank, Erich. *Philosophical Understanding and Religious Truth.* London: Oxford University Press, 1945.

Hook, Sidney, ed. *Religious Experience and Truth.* New York: New York University Press, 1961.

Maritain, Jacques. *An Introduction to Philosophy.* New York: Sheed & Ward.

Smith, John E. *Reason and God.* New Haven, Conn.: Yale University Press, 1961.

Conceptual Analysis

Flew, Antony and MacIntyre, A., eds. *New Essays in Philosophical Theology.* New York: The Macmillan Company, 1964.

Hepburn, Ronald W. *Christianity and Paradox.* London: A. P. Watt & Son, 1958.

Mitchell, Basil, ed. *Faith and Logic*. Boston: Beacon Press, 1957.

Smart, Ninian. *Reasons and Faiths*. New York: Humanities Press, 1959.

Zuurdeeg, Willem Frederick. *An Analytical Philosophy of Religion*. Nashville: Abingdon Press, 1958.

Existentialism

Barnes, Hazel E. *Humanistic Existentialism: The Literature of Possibility*. Lincoln: University of Nebraska Press, 1959.

Earle, William *et al. Christianity and Existentialism*. Evanston, Ill.: Northwestern University Press, 1963.

Marcel, Gabriel. *The Mystery of Being*. 2 vols. New York: Henry Regnery Company, 1960.

Michalson, Carl. *Rationality of Faith*. New York: Charles Scribner's Sons, 1963.

Roberts, David E. *Existentialism and Religious Belief*. New York: Oxford University Press, 1957.

VI
Religion
and Psychotherapy

Introduction

In this section one will find references to "psychiatry," "psychotherapy," and "psychoanalysis." For our purposes these terms may be regarded as interchangeable. Technically, however, "psychiatry" refers to any form of medical treatment of mental illness, while "psychotherapy" and "psychoanalysis" refer to one form of such treatment—"psychoanalysis" being further restricted, on the part of some, to the Freudian form of psychotherapy. Furthermore, psychiatrists must have the M.D. while psychotherapists need not.

The subject of psychotherapy lends itself particularly well to the study of religion and modern culture since both psychotherapy and religion are centrally concerned with the question of healing and since our ideas about health reveal with particular clarity our fundamental aspirations and the images which guide them. The relation between religious and psychological healing centers especially on the relation of religion to the unconscious since the latter is so basic to the concerns of psychotherapy. On this subject Vanderweldt and Odenwald maintain that "religion does not go deeper than the conscious level," while Tillich rejects the "philosophy of con-sciousness" underlying the Thomistic and other positions, and Roberts sees religious healing as intimately tied to the facing of the unconscious sources of unhealth. Fromm believes that by "uncovering those psychological processes within man which underlie his religious experience" psychoanalysis promotes humanistic religion and exposes authoritarian religion (including all belief in a transcendent God) as based on an unhealthy projection. In making these comparisons, one may also wish to bear in mind a special problem connected with the relation of religion to the unconscious: the unconscious is a deterministic side of the self, and this raises questions about the concepts of freedom and responsibility which have played such a significant part in Western religious thought.

In Fromm one finds a convergence of Marxist and Freudian thought, with emphasis on the former. He also uses Tillich's concept of "ultimate concern," which illustrates the question often raised about Tillich's position whether he really succeeds in distinguishing his thought from that of naturalistic humanism (such as Fromm's) .[1]

In reading Roberts, note particularly

---

[1] On this subject, Tillich has said: "When God is identified with an element in human nature, as in humanism, the terrifying and annihilating encounter with majesty becomes an impossibility"; and, elsewhere, "A man who has never tried to flee God has never experienced the God who is really God. . . . And there is no reason to flee from a god who is simply the universe, or the laws of nature, or the course of history. Why try to escape from a reality of which we are a part?" *The Shaking of the Foundations* (New York: Charles Scribner's Sons, 1955) , pp. 89-90, 42.

such references to process as the following: "the destiny of man cannot be conceived apart from his linkage with processes at every level in nature." One may wish to compare this selection with the reading from Meland in section one.

ERICH FROMM

Psychoanalysis and Humanistic Religion*

That early Christianity is humanistic and not authoritarian is evident from the spirit and text of all Jesus' teachings. Jesus' precept that "the kingdom of God is within you" is the simple and clear expression of nonauthoritarian thinking. But only a few hundred years later, after Christianity had ceased to be the religion of the poor and humble peasants, artisans, and slaves (the *Amhaarez*) and had become the religion of those ruling the Roman Empire, the authoritarian trend in Christianity became dominant. Even so, the conflict between the authoritarian and humanistic principles in Christianity never ceased. It was the conflict between Augustine and Pelagius, between the Catholic Church and the many "heretic" groups and between various sects within Protestantism. The humanistic, democratic element was never subdued in Christian or in Jewish history, and this element found one of its most potent expressions in the mystic thinking within both religions. The mystics have been deeply imbued with the experience of man's strength, his likeness to God, and with the idea that God needs man as much as man needs God; they have

understood the sentence that man is created in the image of God to mean the fundamental identity of God and man. Not fear and submission but love and the assertion of one's own powers are the basis of mystical experience. *God is not a symbol of power over man but of man's own powers.*

Thus far we have dealt with the distinctive features of authoritarian and humanistic religions mainly in descriptive terms. But the psychoanalyst must proceed from the description of attitudes to the analysis of their dynamics, and it is here that he can contribute to our discussion from an area not accessible to other fields of inquiry. The full understanding of an attitude requires an appreciation of those conscious and, in particular, unconscious processes occurring in the individual which provide the necessity for and the conditions of its development.

While in humanistic religion God is the image of man's higher self, a symbol of what man potentially is or ought to become, in authoritarian religion God becomes the sole possessor of what was originally man's: of his reason and his love. The more perfect God becomes,

* From Erich Fromm, *Psychoanalysis and Religion,* Copyright 1950. Reprinted by permission of Yale University Press; pp. 48-55, 88-89, 93-98.

the more imperfect becomes man. He *projects* the best he has onto God and thus impoverishes himself. Now God has all love, all wisdom, all justice—and man is deprived of these qualities, he is empty and poor. He had begun with the feeling of smallness, but he now has become completely powerless and without strength; all his powers have been projected onto God. This mechanism of projection is the very same which can be observed in interpersonal relationships of a masochistic, submissive character, where one person is awed by another and attributes his own powers and aspirations to the other person. It is the same mechanism that makes people endow the leaders of even the most inhuman systems with qualities of superwisdom and kindness.[1]

When man has thus projected his own most valuable powers onto God, what of his relationship to his own powers? They have become separated from him and in this process he has become *alienated* from himself. Everything he has is now God's and nothing is left in him. *His only access to himself is through God.* In worshiping God he tries to get in touch with that part of himself which he has lost through projection. After having given God all he has, he begs God to return to him some of what originally was his own. But having lost his own he is completely at God's mercy. He necessarily feels like a "sinner" since he has deprived himself of everything that is good, and it is only through God's mercy or grace that he can regain that which alone makes him human. And in order to persuade God to give him some of his love, he must prove to him how utterly deprived he is of love; in order to persuade God to guide him by his superior wisdom he must prove to him how deprived he is of wisdom when he is left to himself.

But this alienation from his own powers not only makes man feel slavishly dependent on God, it makes him bad too. He becomes a man without faith in his fellow men or in himself, without the experience of his own love, of his own power of reason. As a result the separation between the "holy" and the "secular" occurs. In his worldly activities man acts without love, in that sector of his life which is reserved to religion he feels himself to be a sinner (which he actually is, since to live without love is to live in sin) and tries to recover some of his lost humanity by being in touch with God. Simultaneously, he tries to win forgiveness by emphasizing his own helplessness and worthlessness. Thus the attempt to obtain forgiveness results in the activation of the very attitude from which his sins stem. He is caught in a painful dilemma. The more he praises God, the emptier he becomes. The emptier he becomes, the more sinful he feels. The more sinful he feels, the more he praises his God—and the less able is he to regain himself.

Analysis of religion must not stop at uncovering those psychological processes within man which underly his religious experience; it must proceed to discover the conditions which make for the development of authoritarian and humanistic character structures, respectively, from which different kinds of religious experience stem. Such a sociopsychological analysis goes far beyond the context of these chapters. However, the principal point can be made briefly. What people think and feel is rooted in their character and their character is molded by the total configuration of their practice of life—more precisely, by the socioeconomic and political structure of their society. In societies ruled by a powerful minority which holds the masses in subjection, the individual will be so imbued with fear, so incapable of

---

[1] Cf. the discussion about symbiotic relationship in *Escape from Freedom* (Farrar Rinehart, 1941), pp. 158 ff.

feeling strong or independent, that his religious experience will be authoritarian. Whether he worships a punishing, awesome God or a similarly conceived leader makes little difference. On the other hand, where the individual feels free and responsible for his own fate, or among minorities striving for freedom and independence, humanistic religious experience develops. The history of religion gives ample evidence of this correlation between social structure and kinds of religious experience. Early Christianity was a religion of the poor and downtrodden; the history of religious sects fighting against authoritarian political pressure shows the same principle again and again. Judaism, in which a strong anti-authoritarian tradition could grow up because secular authority never had much of a chance to govern and to build up a legend of its wisdom, therefore developed the humanistic aspect of religion to a remarkable degree. Whenever, on the other hand, religion allied itself with secular power, the religion had by necessity to become authoritarian. The real fall of man is his alienation from himself, his submission to power, his turning against himself even though under the guise of his worship of God.

From the spirit of authoritarian religion stem two fallacies of reasoning which have been used again and again as arguments for theistic religion. One argument runs as follows: How can you criticize the emphasis on dependence on a power transcending man; is not man dependent on forces outside himself which he cannot understand, much less control?

Indeed, man is dependent; he remains subject to death, age, illness, and even if he were to control nature and to make it wholly serviceable to him, he and his earth remain tiny specks in the universe. But it is one thing to recognize one's dependence and limitations, and it is something entirely different to indulge

in this dependence, to worship the forces on which one depends. To understand realistically and soberly how limited our power is is an essential part of wisdom and of maturity; to worship it is masochistic and self-destructive. The one is humility, the other self-humiliation. . . .

Another fallacy of theological thinking is closely related to the one concerning dependence. I mean here the argument that there must be a power or being outside of man because we find that man has an ineradicable longing to relate himself to something beyond himself. Indeed, any sane human being has a need to relate himself to others; a person who has lost that capacity completely is insane. No wonder that man has created figures outside of himself to which he relates himself, which he loves and cherishes because they are not subject to the vacillations and inconsistencies of human objects. That God is a symbol of man's need to love is simple enough to understand. But does it follow from the existence and intensity of this human need that there exists an outer being who corresponds to this need? Obviously that follows as little as our strongest desire to love someone proves that there is a person with whom we are in love. All it proves is our need and perhaps our capacity. . . .

There is no religion which does not deal in some fashion with sin and with methods for recognizing and overcoming it. The various concepts of sin differ of course with various types of religion. In primitive religions sin may be conceived essentially as the violation of a tabu and of little or no ethical implication. In authoritarian religion sin is primarily disobedience to authority and only secondarily a violation of ethical norms. In humanistic religion conscience is not the internalized voice of authority but man's own voice, the guardian of our integrity which recalls us to ourselves when we are in danger of losing

264

ourselves. Sin is not primarily sin against God but sin against ourselves.[2]

The reaction to sin depends on the particular concept and experience of sin. In the authoritarian attitude the recognition of one's sins is frightening because to have sinned means to have disobeyed powerful authorities who will punish the sinner. Moral failures are so many acts of rebellion which can be atoned only in a new orgy of submission. The reaction to one's feeling of guilt is that of being depraved and powerless, of throwing oneself completely at the mercy of the authority and thus hoping to be forgiven. The mood of this kind of contrition is one of fear and trembling.

The result of this contrition is that the sinner, having indulged in the feeling of depravity, is morally weakened, filled with hate and disgust for himself, and hence prone to sin again when he is over his orgy of self-flagellation. This reaction is less extreme when his religion offers him ritualistic atonement or the words of a priest who can absolve him from his guilt. But he pays for this alleviation of the pain of guilt by dependence on those who are privileged to dispense absolution.

In the humanistic trends in religions we find an entirely different reaction to sin. Lacking the spirit of hate and intolerance, which as compensation for submission is always present in authoritarian systems, man's tendency to violate the norms for living is looked upon with understanding and love, not with scorn and contempt. The reaction to the awareness of guilt is not self-hate but an active stimulation to do better. . . .

. . . The psychoanalytic cure of the soul aims at helping the patient to achieve an attitude which can be called religious in the humanistic though not in the authoritarian sense of the word. It seeks to enable him to gain the faculty to see the truth, to love, to become free and responsible, and to be sensitive to the voice of his conscience. But am I not, the reader may ask, describing here an attitude which is more rightly called ethical than religious? Am I not leaving out the very element which distinguishes the religious from the ethical realm? I believe that the difference between the religious and the ethical is to a large extent only an epistemological one, though not entirely so. Indeed, it seems that there is a factor common to certain kinds of religious experience which goes beyond the purely ethical.[3] But it is exceedingly difficult if not impossible to formulate this factor of religious experience. Only those who experience it will understand the formulation, and they do not need any formulation. This difficulty is greater but not different in kind from that of expressing any feeling experience in word symbols, and I want to make at least an attempt to indicate what I mean by this specifically religious experience and what its relation is to the psychoanalytic process.

One aspect of religious experience is the wondering, the marveling, the becoming aware of life and of one's own existence, and of the puzzling problem of one's relatedness to the world. Existence, one's own existence and that of one's fellow men, is not taken for granted but is felt as a problem, is not an answer but a question. Socrates' statement that wonder is the beginning of all wisdom is true not only for wisdom but for the religious experience. One who

---

[2] Cf. the discussion of authoritarian versus humanistic conscience in *Man for Himself* (Rinehart and Company, 1947), pp. 141 ff.

[3] The kind of religious experience which I have in mind in these remarks is the one characteristic of Indian religious experience, Christian and Jewish mysticism, and Spinoza's pantheism. I should like to note that, quite in contrast to a popular sentiment that mysticism is an irrational type of religious experience, it represents—like Hindu and Buddhistic thought and Spinozism—the highest development of rationality in religious thinking. As Albert Schweitzer has put it: "Rational thinking which is free from assumptions ends in mysticism." *Philosophy of Civilization* (Macmillan Company, 1949), p. 79.

has never been bewildered, who has never looked upon life and his own existence as phenomena which require answers and yet, paradoxically, for which the only answers are new questions, can hardly understand what religious experience is.

Another quality of religious experience is what Paul Tillich has called the "ultimate concern." It is not passionate concern with the fulfillment of our desires but the concern connected with the attitude of wonder I have been discussing: an ultimate concern with the meaning of life, with the self-realization of man, with the fulfillment of the task which life sets us. This ultimate concern gives all desires and aims, inasmuch as they do not contribute to the welfare of the soul and the realization of the self, a secondary importance; in fact they are made unimportant by comparison with the object of this ultimate concern. It necessarily excludes division between the holy and the secular because the secular is subordinated to and molded by it.

Beyond the attitude of wonder and of concern there is a third element in religious experience, the one which is most clearly exhibited and described by the mystics. It is an attitude of oneness not only in oneself, not only with one's fellow men, but with all life and, beyond that, with the universe. Some may think that this attitude is one in which the uniqueness and individuality of the self are denied and the experience of self weakened. That this is not so constitutes the paradoxical nature of this attitude. It comprises both the sharp and even painful awareness of one's self as a separate and unique entity and the longing to break through the confines of this individual organization and to be one with the All. The religious attitude in this sense is simultaneously the fullest experience of individuality and of its opposite; it is not so much a blending of the two as a polarity from whose tension religious experience springs. It

is an attitude of pride and integrity and at the same time of a humility which stems from experiencing oneself as but a thread in the texture of the universe.

Has the psychoanalytic process any bearing on this kind of religious experience?

That it presupposes an attitude of ultimate concern I have already indicated. It is no less true that it tends to awaken the patient's sense of wondering and questioning. Once this sense is awakened the patient will find answers which are his own. If it is not awakened, no answer the psychoanalyst can give, not even the best and truest one, will be of any use. This wondering is the most significant therapeutic factor in analysis. The patient has taken his reactions, his desires and anxieties for granted, has interpreted his troubles as the result of the actions of others, of bad luck, constitution, or what not. If the psychoanalysis is effective it is not because the patient accepts new theories about the reasons of his unhappiness but because he acquires a capacity for being genuinely bewildered; he marvels at the discovery of a part of himself whose existence he had never suspected.

It is this process of breaking through the confines of one's organized self—the ego—and of getting in touch with the excluded and disassociated part of oneself, the unconscious, which is closely related to the religious experience of breaking down individuation and feeling one with the All. The concept of the unconscious however, as I use it here, is neither quite that of Freud nor that of Jung.

In Freud's thinking the unconscious is essentially that in us which is bad, the repressed, that which is incompatible with the demands of our culture and of our higher self. In Jung's system the unconscious becomes a source of revelation, a symbol for that which in religious language is God himself. In his view the fact that we are subject to the dictates of our unconscious is in itself a religious phenomenon. I believe that both these concepts of the unconscious are one-sided distortions of the truth. Our unconscious—that is, that part of our self which is excluded from the organized ego which we identify with our self—contains both the lowest and the highest, the worst and the best. We must approach the unconscious not as if it were a God whom we must worship or a dragon we must slay but in humility, with a profound sense of humor, in which we see that other part of ourselves as it is, neither with horror nor with awe. We discover in ourselves desires, fears, ideas, insights which have been excluded from our conscious organization and we have seen in others but not in ourselves. It is true, by necessity we can realize only a limited part of all the potentialities within us. We have to exclude many others, since we could not live our short and limited life without such exclusion. But outside the confines of the particular organiza-

tion of ego are all human potentialities, in fact, the whole of humanity. When we get in touch with this disassociated part we retain the individuation of our ego structure but we experience this unique and individualized ego as only one of the infinite versions of life, just as a drop from the ocean is different from and yet the same as all other drops which are also only particularized modes of the same ocean.

In getting in touch with this disassociated world of the unconscious one replaces the principle of repression by that of permeation and integration. Repression is an act of force, of cutting off, of "law and order." It destroys the connection between our ego and the unorganized life from which it springs and makes our self into something finished, no longer growing but dead. In dissolving repression we permit ourselves to sense the living process and to have faith in life rather than in order.

JAMES H. VANDERVELDT
and ROBERT P. ODENWALD

Psychiatry and Catholicism*

The growing interest among psychiatrists as well as the general public in the therapeutic value of religion . . . goes to show that Freud's expectation about the "future of an illusion" has not come true and that, instead, one might well

speak of the illusion of what Freud predicted to be the future.

Freud considered religion to be the universal obsessional neurosis.[1] To the founder of psychoanalysis, religion was a pure fiction, an illusion having no

* From James H. Vanderveldt and Robert P. Odenwald, *Psychiatry and Catholicism*. (2nd ed.; copyright © 1957 by McGraw-Hill Book Company.) Used by permission of McGraw-Hill Book Company, pp. 211-33, with some modification.
[1] Freud, S., "Die Zukunft einer Illusion" (Vienna, 1927), p. 48.

real value and, therefore, an illusion from which mankind should liberate itself and for which psychoanalysis, supposed to be not an illusion but a reality, should be substituted. Freud came to his opinion about religion through his blind belief in the infallibility of his own method. His argument runs briefly as follows. Psychoanalysis has laid bare the real nature of religion by revealing the nature of its object, the divinity. Psychoanalysis has shown that God is nothing but the external projection of the early childhood image of the parent. But, if God does not really exist but is a figment of the mind, then religion is the worship of a fiction and, therefore, an illusion itself.

It is clear that the entire argument rests on the premise that psychoanalysis has once and for all solved the tremendous problem of the existence of God and the origin of religion—a premise that finds few believers outside psychoanalytic circles. The argument boils down to a very simple one. If God does not exist, psychoanalysis may possibly be a substitute for religion; but the fact that Freud and some of his followers make it a substitute for religion does not prove that God does not exist. Freud, of course, was well aware of the fact that mankind as a whole did not accept his dogmatic pronouncements, and his hostile attitude toward any kind of religion is probably explained by this awareness. If he believed that psychoanalysis meant a challenge to religion, he knew also that religion was the chief enemy of his system, for he said, "Of the three forces which can dispute the position of Science religion alone is a really serious enemy." [2] Freud considered this enemy a real danger because, in brief, to his mind religion makes weaklings out of people.

A very simple factual observation would show that Freud's fear of this danger was slightly exaggerated, to say the least. Long before Freud, millions of people professed one or another form of religion but were, on the whole, no more neurotic than Freud. It would be a somewhat gratuitous statement to maintain that all those millions who "survived" their belief in God were weaklings; their strength and powers did not seem to be paralyzed by their obedience to God.

After seeing that Freud and other analysts have made psychiatry an inextricable tangle of psychology, medicine, ethnology, history, pseudo-philosophy, pseudo-theology, comparative religion, etc., people asked themselves if it would not be more reasonable to stop arguing about philosophical and theological problems. They wondered if it were really necessary to make lectures about the existence of God and the origin of religion the prerequisites for psychiatric treatment. If some therapist feels obliged to contest religious beliefs, let him put on the cap and gown of a theologian and thus enter the theological arena. However, does he need these impressive paraphernalia also when he enters his psychiatric office in order to treat a poor anxiety patient? Why not put psychiatry back on a factual basis? If Paracelsus returned, he might, perhaps, find reason to repeat his old warning, "to forget words and manners and treat your patients."

Of course, religious problems may be at the root of the patient's condition. But is the psychiatrist requested to solve these problems on the theological level? The only thing that seems to be required is that the psychiatrist, regardless of what his own conviction about religion may be, do not brand his patient's religion as an illusion. At times, he can use the patient's religious experiences in such ways that they will be helpful for the treatment.

Freud's exaggerated position is contradicted by many psychiatrists including analysts, who no longer hold that belief

[2] Freud, S., "New Introductory Lectures on Psychoanalysis," p. 205.

in God is an illusion or a danger. One of the first to side with Freud's "really serious enemy" was his own pupil, Carl G. Jung. In his book "Modern Man in Search of a Soul," Jung makes the statement that he would have few patients if people, after passing the age of puberty, lived up to the tenets that the well-established religions have to offer.[3] And in an address delivered to a group of Protestant ministers at Strasbourg in 1932, he expressed an opinion directly opposite to Freud's: "It seems to me," he said, "that the considerable increase in the number of neuroses has paralleled the decrease of religious life."

Jung holds that the chief tenets of religious belief exist as "images" in the collective psyche or, as Klages expresses it, in mankind's primeval original consciousness.[4] The philosopher will ask, of course, how these "images" happen to be there, but for purposes of this book one may well dispense with the question and simply point out that to these authors religious beliefs are not a mere illusion but a fact—a fact, moreover, that may be used to great advantage in psychotherapy. . . .

However, a serious word of caution must be inserted. Although some analysts begin to recognize the therapeutic significance of dependency on what they call, rather vaguely, religion and morality and to consider "religion" as a powerful source of emotional security, the concept of religion as it seems to exist in the mind of many of them is simply that of a tool that they incorporate into their therapeutic devices. What is worse, many of them seem to

hope that psychoanalysis by incorporating religion will eventually be able to serve as a substitute for religion or at least to compete with it. In other words, psychoanalysis is to become the "new religion."

It seems, therefore, advisable to the authors to clarify their own position by defining the term "religion." . . . "Religion is the sum-total of beliefs, rules of conduct, and rites governing the relations of man with a Power or Powers looked upon as transcendent."[5] . . .

In recent times, the term "religion" has been used with a still broader meaning in certain ideological systems in which the state or the political party is supposed to control the individual's destiny and is, hence, elevated to the rank of Supreme Being. . . .

The usual consequence of the ideological or political type of religion is that people express their "belief" in one man, the leader, whose dictates they follow with some sort of religious fanaticism. Here, then, a man takes the position of central and supreme importance in the convictions of his followers, and if one still wishes to extend the term "religion" to such an authoritarian man-centered system, one might aptly call it humanistic religion. In other words, it would be perfectly arbitrary to see in humanistic religion the opposite of authoritarian religion.

Yet, this is precisely what some authors are doing at the present. They oppose humanistic to authoritarian religion, and in their eyes humanistic religion means that each individual takes the place of supreme importance, each becoming his

---

[3] Jung, C. G., "Modern Man in Search of a Soul" (New York: Harcourt, Brace and Company, Inc., 1936) , p. 264: "During the past thirty years, people from all the civilized countries of the earth have consulted me. I have treated many hundreds of patients, the larger number being Protestants, a smaller number Jews, and not more than five or six believing Catholics. Among all my patients in the second half of life—that is to say, over thirty-five—there has not been one person whose problem in the last resort was not that of finding a religious outlook on life. It is safe to say that every one of them fell ill because he had lost that which the living religions of every age have given to their followers, and none of them has been really healed who did not regain his religious outlook."

[4] Klages, L., "Vom kosmogenischen Eros" (Munich, 1922) .

[5] Grandmaison, L. de, "L'Étude des religions" in "Christus, Manuel d'histoire des religions," edited by J. Huby (Paris: Beauchesne, 1931) , pp. 6-7.

own god. The cultivation of his own personality, his self-realization, the development of his own strength and powers, is the objective of this kind of religion. This religion is the type advocated by Erich Fromm. But one might well ask if the term "religion" is still in order when used in this way. It might be called a philosophy of life, but the claim that it is religion seems to be as confusing as the claim of the Russians that they, too, have democracy. . . .

The above digression was necessary in order to point out the demarcation line between theistic and nontheistic religion. In this chapter the term "religion" is used to mean the theistic type, as it is practiced, for instance, by Catholics, orthodox Protestants, Jews, and Mohammedans—with, of course, special emphasis on the Catholic position.

Although Freud was antagonistic to all religions, it may well be that he would find little difficulty in accepting the nontheistic, humanistic kind of religion, for there seems to be little difference between this nontheistic religion and Freud's atheistic philosophy. But, regardless of what Freud would, or would not accept, the fact remains that Freud's chief enemy, theistic religion, is still very much alive—certainly the Catholic religion is.

The Catholic concept concerning the origin of religion is clear. Religion is not born out of fear or out of a need of security; it is neither the projection of a father-image nor a common denominator of the teachings of the so-called great religions of the world. Religion is twofold, natural and revealed. The human mind is able to arrive through logical reasoning at the conclusion that God, the Creator of the universe, exists and that, in consequence, He has a right to obedience and to certain forms of worship; this is natural religion. Revealed religion comprises the body of truths that God Himself has taught mankind, either directly or by means of those

who spoke in His name. These prophets who are God's mouthpiece are either men or, as Catholics and orthodox Protestants believe, God's own Son, Jesus Christ who took to Himself human nature, while remaining a Divine Person. In so far as that body of teachings contains truths which, theoretically speaking, the human mind could find out by itself, but which are so difficult and obscure that only a few would be able to do so, one may speak of revealed natural religion.

Blaise Pascal has written these profound words: . . . "There are only two kinds of people who may be called reasonable: those who serve God with all their heart, because they know Him, and those who seek God with all their heart, because they do not yet know Him."

Indeed, there are many people who have serious religious convictions, either of natural or revealed religion. Furthermore, many of them live up to their belief in such a way that their convictions regulate and dominate their moral conduct; as Pascal put it, they serve God with all their heart. Obviously, in these cases, religious experiences belong to the person's conscious sphere. To such people, religion is doubtless a strong anchor in life's emotional crises.

There are also people who apparently have no religion whatever; whose attitude toward God is, if not hostile, at least negative. And yet it may be found that, subconsciously or unconsciously, they are longing for "something higher" than what life seems to offer them. These are the ones who would command the interest of the depth psychologist.

If there are many people who belong to neither class, who lack religion and feel no desire to have any, not even unconsciously, it would ordinarily be a waste of time to "try religion" on them.

In the attitude of those "who serve God because they know Him," who not only have serious religious convictions but also try to live up to their belief in practice, there is certainly found a philosophy of life. For, when God holds the position of supreme importance in a person's life, that man has a purpose to live for and therefore understands the meaning of life and his own destiny. Such knowledge, based on deep conviction, is of immense value for mental health, both in the so-called ordinary days of life and in the times of acute emotional crisis. He knows that he is playing a role in the universal scheme of things as planned by the Creator. The role may seem insignificant, but it acquires worthwhile significance if one views it as part and parcel of God's plan. This knowledge gives the truly religious man a sense of submissiveness and resignation as well as satisfaction with his lot, peace of soul, and happiness. Modern psychiatry stresses the importance of creative activity. But if one is convinced that he is playing the role that God has assigned him, he will joyfully act his part, be he an artist or a banker or a bootblack.

Perhaps someone may say that non-theistic religion, too, is able to give a meaning to life and to outline for man his destiny. Indeed, a humanistic philosophy of life may well be beneficial to man's health, if it embodies a set of moral principles that are in accordance with the natural law. But again, one may well doubt the stability of a system that sees man's ultimate destiny in man himself. Moreover, that a humanistic philosophy may possess a positive value does not in the least mean that theistic religion has a negative value.

To speak of serving God implies, of course, that religion teaches dependency on God. Now, some psychoanalysts think that this is not a desirable attitude. In fact, one of Freud's objections to religion was precisely that it teaches dependency on an external power, for to Freud and his followers, the supreme good of psychiatry should be to make the patient a mature, independent, self-sufficient person. But this type of psychiatry seems to be decreasing in practice, since psychiatrists are beginning to realize that independence and self-sufficiency may be just as unhealthy and neurotic as some forms of dependency; they have learned by experience that the extremely independent individuals are not the most useful elements in society. To quote M. R. Sapirstein: "More and more, psychiatrists seem prepared to accept the dependencies of religion, social causes and group movements, as healthy, and needful, without labeling them 'sublimated homosexuality' to a father figure, or a desire to return to the mother's womb." [6] This is the opinion of a non-Catholic. Catholics hold that the dependency on God is a healthy one because it prevents the individual from becoming unduly attached to, and therefore dependent on, himself, other persons, and things. On the other hand, dependency on God, according to the Catholic doctrine, does not make a weakling out of man, for that doctrine teaches very emphatically that God helps those who help themselves (*"Facienti quod in se est, Deus non denegat gratiam"*). This conviction gives him strength, self-respect, and the proper evaluation of success.

In the light of his own destiny, religion teaches a person to accept frustrations and suffering, and thereby religion is able to dissipate unhappiness. The individual aware of life's basic meaning more readily endures sorrow, grief, the monotony of everyday routine, and emotional crises that otherwise might result in depression. He may see that even suffering serves a purpose, and thus it becomes a constructive element.

Does religion take away life's disappointments, difficulties, perplexities, drudgery, labor, duress, and pressure? Certainly not! But it teaches the indi-

[6] Sapirstein, M. R., "Emotional Security" (New York: Crown Publishers, 1948), p. 82.

vidual endurance and resignation, because religion—and religion alone—gives him the answer to the perennial problem of the nature of evil and sorrow. One who does not know why there is evil in the world and why so much hardship befalls him personally, is likely to collapse and fall into depression, and eventually he may be driven to suicide. For those who are tortured by the problem of good and evil there is only one alternative—an alternative strikingly illustrated in the life of the French writer Joris Karl Huysmans, who tried Satanism but finally returned to Catholicism, the faith of his childhood. His friend, Barbey d'Aurevilly, wrote of him: "Only one choice is left to Huysmans, the choice between the revolver and the crucifix." Huysmans chose the crucifix.

As for the duress or pressure that arises from exterior circumstances, it may easily happen that religious leaders, e.g., priests, are able to ease such pressure by modifying the environment; in this respect, they are better qualified than the psychiatrists. Religion, as such, cannot, of course, modify the environment, but it can modify the individual by helping him to adjust better to his environment. Psychiatry can do that, too, but it acknowledges defeat in the face of truly insuperable difficulties coming from without. Now, even in such cases religion may be of considerable help, for there are numerous examples of persons who find sufficient strength in their religion to face, and adjust themselves to, apparently insuperable difficulties. However, such cases can hardly be explained from the natural standpoint.

A theocentric plan of life teaches a person to surmount his egocentricity. An example is the notoriously self-centered hysteric, who is well on the road to mental health if he can be brought to an attitude of patiently enduring his sufferings for God's sake instead of making a show of them. The surmounting of one's egocentricity also provides a basis for satisfactory interpersonal relationship and charity toward his fellow man, because respect for persons is grounded in the fatherhood of God instead of in changing human sentiments.

Not infrequently one finds a certain confusion about the respective roles of ethics and religion. The two are not identical. An ethical system is not necessarily a religion, unless one wished to give to the term "religion" the far-fetched interpretation that was rejected in the discussion of nontheistic religion. Such a system easily breaks down when the stress of life becomes really serious, because it lacks a solid basis. On the other hand, every religion worthy of the name includes a body of moral principles which it presents to its followers as the rules that should govern their conduct. Religion is effective in the implementation of moral standards, which, if sincerely followed up, would prevent a great deal of mental and emotional grief. In addition, religion gives the individual the reasons why he should conform his conduct to those standards.

When the authors, in their discussions with psychiatrists, particularly analysts, have compared what the psychiatrists call desirable and undesirable habits with what Catholic ethics and theology call virtues and vices, they have repeatedly come to the conclusion that most psychiatrists lack a correct understanding of the latter. If psychiatrists would learn what Catholic moral theology means by virtues and vices, much misunderstanding could be prevented. For that purpose they would do well to read the clear-cut definitions set forth by St. Thomas Aquinas, particularly in the Second Part of the *Summa Theologica*.

An example of such misunderstanding may be found in connection with the virtue of humility. The reason why some psychiatrists appear to rate humility as of little value seems to be their erroneous definition of that virtue. They believe that the desire that they encourage in their patients to be successfully competitive as a part of their normal self-fulfillment violates humility, even when they insist that the desire be kept within limits, since they are well aware of the fact that the excessive drive for success may become pathological and endanger healthy human relationships. It is hard to see where psychiatry and religion differ concerning the strivings resulting from such a desire when they are considered from the purely natural standard. To be sure, religion forbids pride, the inordinate, excessive striving after one's own excellence and greatness, and vainglory, pride's resultant showing off of one's real, or imagined greatness. If this drive to appear more than one is, goes to excess, it may well become pathological and the source of neurosis, especially when the drive is frustrated. Now, the opposite of pride is humility, but humility is not what some seem to think it. It is not opposed to moderate self-respect. The humble man recognizes that all that he is and has, comes from God, but he is also convinced that he may use all the gifts and talents that God has given him, not for his own but for God's glory. Real humility does not prevent normal self-fulfillment. On the contrary, Catholic ethics encourages the full development of one's capacities, talents, and skills. In fact, it considers normal self-fulfillment here on earth for the rank and file of people their best preparation for eternal life. And in that sense, Catholic ethics does not prohibit the drive for success, even worldly success, as long as this drive does not become excessive and turn into pride, vainglory, ambition, or presumption. We said Catholic *ethics*, because Catholic asceticism may stress the renunciation of all worldly success; but this renunciation is not the general rule and is advised only to those who wish to strive after higher perfection and are spiritually equipped for such a life.

Another example of misunderstanding is found in the concept of hostility, of which there is so much talk in the more recent psychoanalytic literature. The thesis of the analytic school is that no close relationship exists without a certain amount of hostility, which then is traced back to some hurtful relationship in early childhood. And because the analysts believe that the release of such hostility feelings serves a useful therapeutic purpose, they feel that they should encourage the expression of such feelings during the analytical sessions. For the same reason they look somewhat askance at religion, which—so they suppose—suppresses all feelings of hostility. The supposition is incorrect, because religion does not merely take a negative attitude by suppressing these feelings, but it makes a positive attempt to resolve hostility by the exercise of the opposite virtue; i.e., religion teaches that hostility toward men should be met by exercising the virtue of charity, and hostility toward God by the virtue of religion. As to the latter, feelings of hostility toward God are by no means always evidence of the lack of faith, as some analysts seem to surmise. On the contrary, it happens that such feelings are found in believing and devout people. Another wrong notion found in the writings of psychoanalysts is that hostility toward God is forbidden because it implies retaliation. This is an erroneous idea. Such hostility is forbidden because it is evil. As a matter of fact, psychiatrists ought to be grateful that true religion tries to resolve hostility; for the more religion succeeds in doing so, the less work they have to do to analyze and release those feelings of hostility. On the other hand, it is understood that religion does not go deeper than the conscious level and does not reach or attack the unconscious source of certain forms of hostility.

Still another example of confusion is

found in the concepts of sin, guilt, and guilt feelings. It may, therefore, be valuable to set forth the correct distinctions. Sin and the feeling of guilt do not parallel each other. Sin is a violation of the moral law and, therefore, an offense against the Supreme Lawgiver. Sin supposes full consciousness. This is an important point, because it means that there is no such thing as an unconscious sin and that a purely material deviation from the law, not adverted to as such, is no sin in the formal sense.

Now, if one has committed a formal sin, he is guilty; yet, the feeling of guilt is a subjective phenomenon. As a feeling it is evidently conscious, although it may be vague or confused. But such a feeling may be the result of either conscious or unconscious factors. When a person commits a sin, he knows full well why he feels guilty. But the source of guilt feelings may also be unconscious; in other words, an individual may feel guilty where there does not seem to be any apparent sin. With these distinctions in mind, one is in a position to give an answer to a question that arose among a group of psychiatrists at whose meeting the authors were present: Are guilt feelings always undesirable? Some of those present were of the opinion that all guilt feelings are undesirable; others, that some guilt feelings could be put to constructive use. The authors' answer was that sin itself is always "undesirable," but that when it comes to feelings of guilt, one must distinguish among them. Guilt feelings caused by a formal, conscious sin are a natural phenomenon and desirable because they motivate a man to see his own inadequacy. The realization that he has committed a sin may well create in a person a feeling of humiliation; it shows him his imperfection and limitations, and in that manner, guilt feelings may have a constructive character. On the other hand, guilt feelings that stem from an unconscious source are always undesirable. Now, religion has little to do with the

latter, because it plays a role only with regard to those guilt feelings that are the result of a conscious sin.

A final question remains concerning sin. If the psychiatrist is not, and should not be, a moralist, what, then, should be his attitude toward sin? The question is important, because wrong ideas about it seem to exist, even among Catholics. Sin, in the sense of an offense against God, should be treated in the confessional, not in the office of the psychiatrist. A comparison may make this point clear. When a physician treats a syphilitic, he does so without moralizing about the patient's previous conduct that has caused the sickness. However, after the man has been cured, the physician might, perhaps, give him a bit of human advice for the future—at least he might, if he has at heart the patient's well-being and not his own pocketbook. A similar condition exists when the psychotherapist is treating a mental case. Suppose that certain activities which ethics calls sinful have made the patient what he is, a neurotic. During the treatment, there will be appraisal of the conflict and of the motivations underlying the man's actions, but it is not within the psychiatrist's scope to enter into a discussion about the morality of these actions. However, although the psychiatrist is not a moralist, this does not in the least imply that psychiatry is divorced from morality in the sense that it may advise or allow immoral practices if it considers them useful or needful for the "self-fulfillment" of the patient.

When the contributions of religion to mental health are compared with those of psychiatry, psychiatrists often make two remarks that deserve an answer. The first remark concerns the nature of the goals and aspirations of psychiatry and religion respectively. Some psychoanalysts hold that the goals and aspirations of psychiatry are usually quite high, and they believe that those set by religion are "much lower and easier of fulfillment." This is really an amazing statement—a statement that no one with even a superficial acquaintance with the teachings of Christian ethics, moral theology, and asceticism would ever make. Psychiatry may set itself various goals, but the all-embracing goal is, probably, to heighten the individual's aspirations for personal fulfillment—but, psychiatry wisely adds, within limits; it does not believe that a person achieves his fulfillment by aspiring at goals of a neurotic or infantile nature. What are religion's goals? The Catholic religion teaches that the ultimate end of man is, objectively, God's extrinsic glory, and subjectively, his own eternal happiness. How is he to attain this goal in his present life? By knowing and serving God to the best of his abilities; in a word, by striving after self-perfection. To be sure, this includes spiritual self-perfection, but it includes, too, the perfecting of his nature by the exercise of all its functions, physical as well as mental. The proximate end of a man is the self-realization of all his potentialities: he *must* strive to become a useful person in society, and he *may* strive after recognition, honor, riches, and pleasure. . . as long as [they] do not clash with his primary goal, the service of God, the observance of His commandments, and the welfare of his fellow man. In view of this statement, it would seem that the goals of serious psychiatry and religion may, at times, coincide. But it is false to believe that religion's aims are of a lower order. Since striving toward self-perfection requires an unwavering discipline throughout life, it is hard to understand how anyone would think that the goals and aspirations of religion are set "much lower" than those of psychiatry. As a matter of fact, religion sets them on a higher level.

The second remark, somewhat contradictory to the first, is that psychiatry can, after all, contribute all that religion has to offer. Apart from the simple, pragmatic observation that religion is for the millions and psychiatry is for the few who can pay a handsome fee, the Catholic psychiatrists' answer is that religion is not a substitute for psychiatry nor psychiatry a substitute for religion.

Psychiatry, including any type of depth therapy, offers methods and techniques for the treatment of the mentally ill. In that respect, religion is no substitute for psychiatry, for the simple reason that religion—at least the Catholic religion—is not a medical system. Religion primarily aims at bringing people closer to God, and by doing so, it may secondarily promote their mental health. And this secondary task is mostly of a protective, preventive, and safeguarding nature.

However, once a person has a serious mental breakdown, he may—if he so wishes—go to church and light a candle, but right after that it would be a sensible thing for him to visit the office of a psychiatrist. And then, while the psychotherapeutic treatment develops, the therapist may feel the need of assisting the patient to outline a better plan of life for the future. This plan of life may stress various values that may help to make the individual's life worth living; e.g., as we have seen, it may stress artistic or social values, or even economic or political values. The psychiatrist may also stress the value of religion, and by religion is meant—the demarcation line having been drawn in the beginning of our discussions—theistic religion.

Nevertheless, there are certain things that no psychiatry can ever give. Of these, two points may be considered here. Religion alone (again, theistic religion) can give what the Germans call the *"ruhenden Pol"*—the firmly fixed pole, the Absolute. When God holds the central place in one's life, life's perplexities and emotional crises become relatively unimportant. But no psychiatry can give God to a patient unless he already has serious religious convictions.

But there is more: people who have such serious convictions believe that God assists them in a very personal way. This belief is found among Catholics and Protestants alike and is far from uncommon among the adherents of non-Christian religions. This assistance is called divine grace. And no psychiatrist can give grace to his patients. Many a psychiatrist will shrug his shoulders and say that he does not know what that means. That may well be true, but ignorance gives no one the right to refer to grace as an illusion. It is well to remember occasionally Shakespeare's caustic words: "There are more things in heaven and earth, Horatio, than are dreamt of in your philosophy." Regardless of what grace may mean to the unbeliever, the fact is that it is a very real thing in the minds of the faithful and that it plays a real part in their lives.

Avoiding theological discussions and distinctions, a simple description of what Catholics mean by supernatural grace may help to make the concept at least understandable, if not acceptable. Grace is a supernatural gift of God to man, bestowed for the purpose of helping him to achieve his salvation. This divine assistance illumines a person's reason so that he may see more clearly what is good and expected of him, and it strengthens his will so that he may more readily fulfill his obligations.

Many Catholics may not have a very clear conception about grace, but every good Catholic possesses the basic concept that God helps him in a special way, particularly in times of need, stress, strain, and emotional trouble. This very idea that "God will help me to overcome even that" contributes greatly to producing in him a sense of trust, strength, resignation, and submission, and, if necessary, the capability of starting a change of life.

A few illustrations may clarify what might be called the psychodynamics of grace. It should be understood that supernatural grace does not substitute for, or destroy, the natural powers and functions of man, but, rather, builds

upon them. A person during or after prayer, when he "feels better," may see his difficulties in a different light; he may feel deeply sorry for his sins and thereby feel reconciled with God; he may feel a greater love for God; he may see the importance of things eternal and, by the same token, the relative insignificance of earthly things, including his sufferings; his hope may be strengthened so that the future looks brighter; he may feel resigned to accept whatever comes to him; etc. All these thoughts, desires, acts of the will, and aspirations have a reassuring, uplifting effect, even when we look upon them from the purely natural standpoint. But Catholics hold that God influences the soul of a person in prayer in such a way that he not only experiences these thoughts and aspirations, but does so to a higher and more efficacious degree. And everyone will agree that such aspirations have a beneficial effect on one's mental condition and, according to psychosomatics, on his physical well-being, too.

Another illustration is faith. The acceptance of the body of Catholic teachings is, in the final analysis, based on faith. Faith is an assent of the mind based on the authority—i.e., the wisdom and veracity—of another. If the "other" is God, we speak of divine faith. Now divine faith is a grace; i.e., without a gift from God of His enlightening and helping grace, no man can make an act of faith that is profitable for salvation. And this faith in God is, in the minds of the faithful, a powerful means for overriding doubt, fear, and anxiety.

True, faith also inspires hope; the faithful Catholic not only hopes that God will reward him with eternal life but also trusts that God will help him in the difficulties of his earthly life. But again, according to the Catholic doctrine, hope is not only a natural phenomenon, but also a supernatural gift, which the faithful acquire and develop through God's grace.

One of the main difficulties that every

person encounters in his present life is the fight to control his animal instincts. Of course, the Catholic Church rejects the "man is only an animal" theory, of certain groups of psychiatrists. As long as they adhere to this principle, any further discussion is perfectly useless. Catholic doctrine concedes that man is an animal, but adds that he is "endowed with reason." The aim of the Catholic religion, therefore, is not to kill the animal in man, but so to enlighten and strengthen his higher powers, intellect and will, that man may achieve the purpose for which he is created. And here is another illustration of what is meant by grace. Left to himself, a person would hardly be able to subdue his animal instincts, but if he asks for it, God will help him. A good example is found in the case of the alcoholic who asks the Lord every morning to help him to stay sober that day; he is convinced that, if he succeeds, he owes it to God's assistance, and to the alcoholic this assistance is not an illusion, but a very real thing.

The fact that grace is a reality does not mean that it must be tangible or visible. Except in extraordinary conditions, grace is usually known only by its effects. If one wishes to adopt analytical language, one might say that divine grace usually works on the unconscious level to produce very conscious effects, but that this is an unconscious sphere that is not accessible to psychoanalysis.

A psychiatrist may here remark that he cannot work with such a thing as grace. No, of course not. This is precisely the point that the authors wanted to make clear. In this respect, religion infinitely transcends any type of psychiatry. And it was necessary to make this point clear, because this chapter deals with the relationship between religion and psychiatry.

In a discussion of that relationship, one often encounters the trite objection that religion is, after all, not a perfect guide, because religious people may also become mentally ill. Indeed they do! Before taking up a more detailed discussion, it may be well to repeat the thesis of this chapter: the sincere observance of serious religious convictions and practices protects and safeguards mental health, but religion is not a panacea any more than psychiatric treatment is an infallible means for curing a patient.

This problem may now be considered from several angles. When one has to do with a mental disorder of an organogenic, or endogenous or constitutional, nature, such as certain forms of psychosis, religion can no more prevent its development than it can prevent or cure, e.g., hereditary ataxia. Hence, the problem dwindles down to a consideration of the exogenous and psychogenic disorders, particularly the psychoneuroses.

Now, it happens in some instances that, far from being preventive, the patient's religion is, on the contrary, conducive to the creation of mental disorders. We mean those types of religion that are based exclusively, or almost exclusively, on irrational, emotional elements. Examples in point would be voodooism, spiritism, and mediumism. The treatment of a patient who is the victim of his own religious practices seems to run into a dilemma. On the one hand, the patient's religion —not an interpretation of it, but his religion itself—is supposed to be the cause of his problems; on the other hand, the psychiatrist is bound to respect a person's conscience in the choice of religion. It is not for Catholic psychology to solve this dilemma, since Catholicism certainly does not belong to the irrational or highly emotional types of religion, but it would be interesting to see how a conscientious psychiatrist would solve it. Anyway, the example shows that not every type of religion is conducive to mental health.

It happens also that an individual may falsely interpret the precepts of his religion. Such a misinterpretation of otherwise perfectly sound rules may lead to such deplorable conditions as compulsions, fixed ideas, and scrupulosity. In that case, not religion, but the peculiar twist in the patient's mind (or, at times even a peculiar twist in the mind of the spiritual adviser) is to be blamed. In that case, the first thing a psychiatrist has to do is to give the patient a correct picture of his own religion. Therefore, the therapist ought to know the teachings of his patient's religion about objective and subjective sin as well as what the limitations of free will are in a mentally sick person. Naturally, there arises the question of how the psychiatrist is to approach his task if he has little knowledge of religion in general and of his patient's religion in particular. The ideal in such cases is usually that the psychiatrist and patient observe the same religion.

Moreover, while it may well be true that a conflict is at the root of most psychoneuroses, it is equally true that not all these conflicts are of a religious or moral nature. For instance, the seed of these conflicts may well be sowed in childhood, an age in which religious convictions are quite unstable or nonexistent. To ask religion to uproot in later life the evils planted in early life would be asking for a kind of miracle.

Finally, once more it must be repeated that the condition for the mental-health value of religion is that people truly live their religion. Perhaps not all people who are supposed to be religious and yet become neurotic have made their religious convictions an integral part of their lives. . . .

The reader may remember that the assumption underlying the discussion of . . . this . . . chapter is that the psychiatrist is looking for a plan of life to give the patient in order to secure his future. If the patient does not seem to show any religion, is the psychiatrist to renounce religious values and rely on some social, or vaguely moral, value as the basis of the patient's reorientation?

This is one of the most serious problems that confront a psychiatrist who is concerned about the future of his patient, as is evidenced by Jung's complaint that often he did not know what to do with patients who lacked religious ideals that might give meaning and direction to their lives.

At this point, a solution is offered by the existential analysts, whose remarkable work has done a great deal to break down false and prejudiced ideas and to revive very old ones. They maintain . . . that an analysis unbiased by any preconceived concepts reveals a longing for spiritual values in many individuals. These religious strivings may emerge from the deepest levels of an individual's unconscious, even in persons who reject all religion. Like other strivings, they demand release; in fact, the repression of these longings for something higher may be found to be the very reason for the patient's restlessness and depressions. This standpoint is, after all, nothing new, but it is very remote from Freud's.

The observations of the existential analysts, although expressed in the analytic language, are consistent with Pascal's observation that many of those who do not know God are at least seeking Him. They are consistent with St. Augustine's immortal words: *"Inquietum est cor nostrum, donec requiescat in te, Domine*—Restless is our heart, O Lord, until it rests in Thee." They are also consistent with the age-old adage that *"anima est naturaliter religiosa—* the soul is naturally religious," a truth that Tertullian expressed in an even stronger form. The observations of the existential analysts are, in fine, consistent with the teachings of Catholic philosophy concerning the "eternal quest"; i.e., in a rational human being there is a natural desire for God. Therefore, when treating their patients, the existential analysts do not hesitate to bring these spiritual strivings into the open. They act somewhat like St. Paul, who, after finding in the midst of the Areopagus

278

an altar with the inscription "To the unknown God," began to proclaim to the men of Athens what they worshiped in ignorance (Acts 17:22-31) .

But, supposing that the psychiatrist thinks that the revival of religious ideals might be beneficial for the patient, there recurs the same question that has already been presented with regard to the moral values. How is the analyst to approach his task? The existential analyst, like any other pyschiatrist, knows that he is not a priest; neither should he, as a physician, attempt to replace, or substitute himself for, the priest. Such an attempt would be beyond his task. What is more, it would serve no curative purpose were he to drive or to stimulate his patient in a religious direction, since an imposed religion is no real religion. Therefore, the patient must decide his ideals for himself. All that the therapist should do is to wait until the latent religious elements within his patient break through spontaneously. Sooner or later, as he knows by experience, they will appear, even with a manifestly irreligious person. When they do, the psychiatrist may help the patient to develop them.

This discussion of the mental-hygiene value of religion leaves little doubt that religion can be useful in preserving mental health or in giving a solid basis for its recovery should it be lost. However, it is wholly wrong to consider religion as the handmaid of psychiatry. Such a notion might arise in the minds of those who conceive of depth psychology as a new form of religion. If analysts wish to make use of religious experiences in the treatment of their patient, it may be all the better; but they should not presume that psychoanalysis is the yardstick by which these experiences must be measured, nor should they believe that religious and moral convictions and experiences have value only when they can be interpreted in analytical terms, as if that were the only language that counted. Religion

has a mental-health value all its own, and had it long before there was any professional depth therapy.

Although psychiatry and religion cannot be compared in many respects, it is quite possible for the psychiatrist and the pastor to work together for the well-being of the people. The work of one may supplement that of the other. The necessary condition to such cooperation is that the psychiatrist consider religion not as an illusion, but as a reality, for simple fairness would forbid him to use an illusion as a means of helping his patients. If religion were an illusion, Freud would have been right in suggesting that it should be stamped out. Since it is a reality, the therapist may make use of it; but, when doing so, he no longers adheres to the gospel of the Viennese master.

This evaluation of the analytical methodology may now be summarized briefly. Although in theory some depth psychologists may advocate a purely nondirective and neutral inner-release therapy, in practice the majority aim at educating their patients to be responsible individuals. Obviously, the term "responsible" makes little sense unless we know for what and to whom we are responsible. An increasing number of therapists consider the task of psychotherapy to be that of making their patients so aware of their responsibility for the fulfillment of certain positive values that purpose is given to their lives. Which values the patient chooses depends upon his own individual personality structure. It is precisely the task of the analyst to bring this individual disposition to the fore. How far the analyst wishes to go in guiding or correcting his patient's aspirations will greatly depend upon his own principles and personality and upon his own conscience.

Objectively speaking, not all values that a person considers worth living for are to be put on the same plane. Purely hedonistic values will scarcely

279

be found to be beneficial to the individual, and such other values as the social, economic, and political ones have only a relative significance; but moral values are of the greatest importance. To whom is an individual responsible? The demarcation line is here drawn by the individual's positive or negative attitude toward God. If he has a nonreligious philosophy of life, he may feel responsible to society or to his own conscience for whatever value he wishes to realize in his life; if his plan of life is religious, he knows that he is responsible to God. Again, the first attitude has only relative significance; the latter has absolute value.

The relationship between theistic religion and mental health may be summed up in the following statements:

1. Sincere religious convictions are a powerful therapeutic aid to the preservation of mental health, but they do not constitute an infallible panacea.

2. Religious convictions have no mental-health value for an individual unless he makes an honest attempt to regulate his conduct according to his belief.

3. Religion is no substitute for psychiatry: when a person's health has broken . . . pious exhortations alone will not restore it, but religion may well provide a better . . . life in the future.

4. Psychiatry is no substitute for religion, despite the attempts of some "new religionists."

5. Religion may be considered from the natural standpoint and, as such, helpful for mental health as it provides for a stable set of moral principles.

6. The Catholic religion is revealed, supernatural religion; being supernatural, it cannot be compared with psychiatry. However, this fact does not imply opposition; there need be no more opposition between the Catholic religion and psychiatry in the sense of treatment of the mentally ill than there is between the Catholic religion and general medicine.

7. Religion works on the conscious level; analytical psychology to a great extent, on the unconscious level. There need be no opposition between the Catholic religion and analytical psychiatry so long as the latter avoids smuggling into either its psychological theories or its therapy any philosophical principles that are unacceptable to the former. Freudian psychoanalysis is doing just that.

PAUL TILLICH

The Theological Significance of Existentialism and Psychoanalysis*

We shall be using the two words psychoanalysis and theology. By their very nature they pose semantic problems for us. Psychoanalysis can be a special term, and it is often usurped by the Freudian school, which declares that no other

* From *Faith and Freedom*, Vol. IX, No. 25 (Autumn, 1955). Reprinted by permission of the editor of *Faith and Freedom*; pp. 112-26.

school has a right to use the term. A recent conversation with a representative of this school moved cordially up to the moment when people like Horney, Fromm, Jung, and Rank were called psychoanalysts. At this moment the Freudian broke in and said, "They are dishonest in calling themselves psychoanalysts. They shouldn't do it. They do it only for purposes of profit."

This situation shows that we have to do something about this term. It is not used here as this psychoanalyst used it, but rather in the meaning into which this term has been transformed and enlarged during the last half-century. These developments surely are dependent on the basic Freudian discovery, namely, the role of the unconscious. However, there are two other words which indicate something about the matter itself and could be used here: "therapeutic psychology" is one term often used, and another is "depth psychology."

About the term theology, perhaps many of you know that in our theological seminaries and divinity schools, the word theology often is used exclusively for systematic theology, and that historical and practical theology are not considered theology at all. We will enlarge the concept of theology for our discussion of its relationship to depth psychology and include in it past religious movements and great religious figures, and also the New Testament writings. Also, we want to include practical theology, where the relationship to psychoanalysis has become most conspicuous, namely, in the function of the counsellor who gives counsel in religious and in psychoanalytic terms at the same time.

Then we must also discuss the gap that has developed in the relation of existentialism to psychoanalysis. This is a real gap, because existentialism is now taken in a much broader sense than it was a few years after the Second World War. At that time existentialism was identified with the philosophy of Sartre. But existentialism appears in decisive forms early in the 17th and in the 19th centuries, and it is incorporated in almost all great creations in all areas of life in the 20th century. If you understand existentialism in this broader sense, it suggests very definitely a relationship between existentialism and psychoanalysis. A basic assertion to be made about the relationship of theology and psychoanalysis is that psychoanalysis belongs fundamentally to the whole existentialist movement of the 20th century, and that as a part of this movement it must be understood in its relationship to theology in the same way in which the relationship of existentialism generally must be understood.

This factor reveals something about the philosophical implications of depth psychology, and also about the interdependence between this movement and the existentialist movement of the 19th and 20th centuries. It is a fact that psychoanalysis and existentialism have been connected with each other from the very beginning; they have mutually influenced each other in the most radical and profound ways. Everybody who has looked into the works of existentialist writers from Dostoyevsky on to the present will immediately agree that there is much depth-psychological material in the novels, the dramas, and the poems, as well as in the visual arts—modern art being the existentialist form of visual art. All this is understandable only if we see that there is a common root and intention in existentialism and psychoanalysis.

If these common roots are found, the question of the relationship of psychoanalysis and theology is brought into a larger and more fundamental framework. Then it is possible to reject the attempts of some theologians and some psychologists to divide these two realms carefully and give to each of them a special sphere. It is then possible to dis-

281

regard those people who tell us to stay in this or that field: here a system of theological doctrines and there congeries of psychological insights. This is not so. The relationship is not one of existing alongside each other; it is a relationship of mutual interpenetration.

The common root of existentialism and psychoanalysis is the protest against the increasing power of the philosophy of consciousness in modern industrial society. This conflict between the philosophy of consciousness and the protest against it is of course much older than modern industrial society. It appeared in the 13th century in the famous conflict between the primacy of the intellect in Thomas Aquinas and the primacy of the irrational will in Duns Scotus. Both of these men were theologians, and I mention them mainly in order to show how untenable theological positions are which want to exclude philosophical and psychological problems from theology. The struggle between these two basic attitudes towards not only the nature of man but also the nature of God and the world has continued ever since.

In the Renaissance, we have philosophers of consciousness, for instance, humanists of the type of Erasmus of Rotterdam or scientists of the type of Galileo. But against them stood others, as for instance, Paracelsus in the realm of medical philosophy who fought against the anatomical mechanization of medicine and against the separation of body and mind, or Jacob Boehme, who influenced the subsequent period very much, particularly by his description in mythological terms of the unconscious elements in the ground of the divine life itself and therefore of all life. We find the same conflict in the Reformation: on the one hand the victory of consciousness in reformers like Melanchthon, Zwingli, and Calvin, all of them dependent on humanists of the Erasmus type, while the irrational will was emphasized by Luther, on whom Jacob Boehme was largely dependent.

The history of industrial society, the end of which we are experiencing, represents the history of the victory of the philosophy of consciousness over the philosophy of the unconscious, irrational will. The symbolic name for the complete victory of the philosophy of consciousness is René Descartes; and the victory became complete, even in religion, at the moment when Protestant theology became the ally of the Cartesian emphasis on man as pure consciousness on the one hand, and a mechanical process called body on the other hand. In Lutheranism it was especially the cognitive side of man's consciousness which overwhelmed the early Luther's understanding of the irrational will. In Calvin it was the moral consciousness, the moral self-controlling center of consciousness that predominated. We have in America, which is mostly dependent on Calvinism and related outlooks, the moralistic and oppressive types of Protestantism which are the result of the complete victory of the philosophy of consciousness in modern Protestantism. But in spite of this victory, the protest was not silenced.

Pascal in the 17th century stood in conscious opposition to Descartes. His was the first existentialist analysis of the human situation, and he described it in ways very similar to those of later existentialist and non-existentialist philosophers, that is, in terms of anxiety, of finitude, of doubt, of guilt, of meaninglessness, of a world in which Newtonian atoms and cosmic bodies move according to mechanical laws; and as we know from many utterances, man decentralized, deprived of the earth as center, felt completely lost in this mechanized universe, in anxiety and meaninglessness. There were others in the 18th century; for example, Hamann, who is very little known outside of Germany, a kind of prophetic spirit anticipating many of the existentialist ideas. But the most radical protest came at the moment when the philosophy of consciousness reached its peak in the philosophy of Hegel. Against this victorious philosophy of consciousness Schelling arose, giving to Kierkegaard and many others the basic concepts of existentialism; then Schopenhauer's irrational will, Hartmann's philosophy of the unconscious, Nietzsche's analysis which anticipated most of the results of later depth-psychological inquiries. The protest appeared also in Kierkegaard's and Marx's description of the human predicament, in finitude, estrangement, and loss of subjectivity. And in Dostoyevsky we find the description of the demonic subconscious in man; we find it also in French poetry of the type of Rimbaud and Baudelaire. This was the preparation of the ground for what was to follow in the 20th century.

All the things which in these men were ontological intuition or theological analysis now through Freud became methodological scientific words. Freud, in his discovery of the unconscious, rediscovered something that was known long before, and had been used for many decades and even centuries to fight the victorious philosophy of consciousness. What Freud did was to give to this protest a scientific methodological foundation. In him we must see the old protest against the philosophy of consciousness. Especially in men like Heidegger and Sartre, and in the whole literature and art of the 20th century, the existentialist point of view became aware of itself. It now was expressed intentionally and directly, and not only as a suppressed element of protest.

This short survey shows the inseparability of depth psychology from philosophy, and of both of them from theology. It is also clear that they cannot be separated if we now compare depth psychology and existentialist philosophy in their differences and in their similarities. The basic point is that both existentialism and depth psychology are interested in the description of man's existential predicament—in time and space, in finitude and estrangement—in contrast to man's essential nature, for if you speak of man's existential predicament as opposite to his essential nature, you must in some way presuppose an idea of his essential nature. But this is not the purpose to which all existentialist literature is directed. Instead, the focus in both existentialism and depth psychology is man's estranged existence, the characteristics and symptoms of this estrangement, and the conditions of existence in time and space. The term "therapeutic psychology" shows clearly that here something that contradicts the norm, that must be healed, is expressed. It shows the relation between disease —mental, bodily, or psychosomatic—and man's existential predicament.

It is also clear that all existential utterances deal with the boundary line between healthy and sick and ask one question—you can reduce it to this— how is it possible that a being has a structure that produces psychosomatic diseases? Existentialism in order to answer these questions points to the possible experience of meaninglessness, to the continuous experience of loneliness, to the widespread feeling of emptiness. It derives them from finitude, from the awareness of finitude which is anxiety; it derives them from estrangement from oneself and one's world. It points to the possibility and the danger of freedom, and to the threat of non-being in all respects—from death to guilt. All these are characteristic of man's existential predicament, and in this, depth psychology and existentialism agree.

However, there is a basic difference between them. Existentialism as philosophy speaks of the universal human situation, which refers to everybody, healthy or sick. Depth psychology points to the ways in which people try to escape the situation by fleeing into neurosis and falling into psychosis. In existentialist literature, not only in novels and poems and dramas but even in philosophy, it is difficult to distinguish clearly the boundary line between man's universal existential situation based on finitude and estrangement on the one hand, and man's psychosomatic disease which is considered an attempt to escape from this situation and its anxieties by fleeing into a mental fortress.

Now how are theological judgments applied to depth psychology and existentialism (which are in reality one thing). The relation between man's essential nature and his existential predicament is the first and basic question that theology has asked whenever it encounters existentialist analyses and psychoanalytic material. In the Christian tradition, there are three fundamental concepts. First: *Esse qua esse bonum est.* This Latin phrase is a basic dogma of Christianity. It means "Being as being is good," or in the biblical mythological form: God saw everything that he had created, and behold, it was good. The second statement is the universal fall —fall meaning the transition from this essential goodness into existential estrangement from oneself, which happens in every living being and in every time. The third statement refers to the possibility of salvation. We should remember that salvation is derived from *salvus* or *salus* in Latin, which means "healed" or "whole," as opposed to disruptiveness.

These three considerations of human nature are present in all genuine theological thinking: essential goodness, existential estrangement, and the possibility of something, a "third," beyond essence and existence, through which the cleavage is overcome and healed. Now, in philosophical terms, this means that man's essential and existential nature points to his teleological nature (derived from *telos*, aim, that for which and towards which his life drives).

If you do not distinguish these three elements, which are always present in man, you will fall into innumerable confusions. Every criticism of existentialism and psychoanalysis on the basis

of this tripartite view of human nature is directed against the confusion of these three fundamental elements, which always must be distinguished although they always are together in all of us. Freud, in this respect, was unclear, namely, he was not able to distinguish man's essential and existential nature. This is a basic theological criticism, not of any special result of his thinking, but of his doctrine of man and the central intuition he has of man. His thought about libido makes this deficiency very obvious.

Man, according to him, is infinite libido which never can be satisfied and which therefore produces the desire to get rid of oneself, the desire he has called the death instinct. And this is not only true of the individual, it is also true of man's relation to culture as a whole. His dismay about culture shows that he is very consistent in his negative judgments about man as existentially distorted. Now if you see man only from the point of view of existence and not from the point of view of essence, only from the point of view of estrangement and not from the point of view of essential goodness, then this consequence is unavoidable. And it is true for Freud in this respect.

Let us make this clear by means of a theological concept which is very old, the classical concept of concupiscence. This concept is used in Christian theology exactly as libido is used by Freud, but it is used for man under the conditions of existence; it is the indefinite striving beyond any given satisfaction, to induce satisfaction beyond the given one. But according to theological doctrine, man in his essential goodness is not in the state of concupiscence or indefinite libido. Rather he is directed to a definite special subject, to content, to somebody, to something with which he is connected in love, or *eros,* or *agape,* whatever it may be. If this is the case, then the situation is quite different. Then you can have libido, but the fulfilled libido is real fulfillment, and you are not driven beyond this indefinitely. This means that Freud's description of libido is to be viewed theologically as the description of man in his existential self-estrangement. But Freud does not know any other man, and this is the basic criticism that theology would weigh against him on this point.

Now, fortunately, Freud, like most great men, was not consistent. With respect to the healing process, he knew something about the healed man, man in the third form, teleological man. And in so far as he was thus convinced of the possibility of healing, this contradicted profoundly his fundamental restriction to existential man. In popular terms, his pessimism about the nature of man and his optimism about the possibilities of healing were never reconciled in him or in his followers.

But some of his followers have done something else. They have rejected the profound insight of Freud about existential libido and the death instinct, and in so doing they have reduced and cut off from Freud what made him and still makes him the most profound of all the depth psychologists. This can be said even in relation to Jung, who is much more religiously interested than was Freud. But Freud, theologically speaking, saw more about human nature than all his followers who, when they lost the existentialist element in Freud, went more to an essentialist and optimistic view of man.

We can make the same criticism of Sartre's pure existentialism and his sensitive psychological analysis. The greatness of this man is that he is the psychological interpreter of Heidegger. He is perhaps misinterpreted on many points, but nevertheless his psychological insights are profound. But here we have the same thing that we have found before: Sartre says man's essence is his existence. In saying this he makes it impossible for man to be saved or to be healed. Sartre knows this, and every

one of his plays shows this too. But here also we have a happy inconsistency. He calls his existentialism humanism. But if he calls it humanism, that means he has an idea of what man essentially is, and he must consider the possibility that the essential being of man, his freedom, might be lost. And if this is a possibility, then he makes, against his own will, a distinction between man as he essentially is and man as he can be lost: man is to be free and to create himself.

We have the same problem in Heidegger. Heidegger talks also as if there were no norms whatsoever, no essential man, as if man makes himself. On the other hand, he speaks of the difference between authentic existence and unauthentic existence, [of man] falling into the average existence of conventional thought and nonsense—into an existence where he has lost himself. This is very interesting, because it shows that even the most radical existentialist, if he wants to say something, necessarily falls back to some essentialist statements because without them he cannot even speak.

Other psychoanalysts have described the human situation as correctible and amendable, as a weakness only. But we can ask: is man essentially healthy? If he is, only his basic anxiety has to be taken away; for example, if you save him from the evil influences of society, of competition and things like that, everything will be all right. Men like Fromm speak of the possibility of becoming an autonomous non-authoritarian personality who develops himself according to reason. And even Jung, who knows so much about the depths of the human soul and about the religious symbols, thinks that there are essential structures in the human soul and that it is possible (and one may be successful) to search for personality.

In all these representatives of contemporary depth psychology we miss the depths of Freud. We miss the feeling for the irrational element that we have in Freud and in much of the existentialist literature. Dostoyevsky has already been mentioned. We could also mention Kafka and many others.

Now we come to the third element, namely, the teleological, the element of fulfillment, the question of healing. Here we have the difference between the healing of an acute illness and the healing of the existential presuppositions of every disease and of every healthy existence. This is the basis for the healing of special acute illnesses; on this all groups agree. There are acute illnesses that produce psychosomatic irregularities and destruction. There are compulsive restrictions of man's potentialities which lead to neurosis and eventually to psychosis. But beyond this there are the existential presuppositions. Neither Freudianism nor any purely existentialist consideration can heal these fundamental presuppositions. Many psychoanalysts try to do it. They try with their methods to overcome existential negativity, anxiety, estrangement, meaninglessness, or guilt. They deny that they are universal, that they are existential in this sense. They call all anxiety, all guilt, all emptiness, illnesses which can be overcome as any illness can be, and they try to remove them. But this is impossible. The existential structures cannot be healed by the most refined techniques. They are objects of salvation. The analyst can be an instrument of salvation as every friend, every parent, every child can be an instrument of salvation. But as analyst he cannot bring salvation by means of his medical methods, for this requires the healing of the center of the personality. So much for the criticism.

Now how can theology deal with depth psychology? Certainly the growth of the two movements, existentialism and depth psychology, is of infinite value for theology. Both of them brought to theology something which it always should have known but which it had forgotten and covered up. They helped to rediscover the immense depth psychological material which we find in the religious literature of the last two thousand years and even beyond that. Almost every insight concerning the movement of the soul can be found in this literature, and the most classical example of all is perhaps Dante's *Divine Comedy*, especially in the description of hell and purgatory, and of the inner self-destructiveness of man in his estrangement from his essential being.

Second, it was a rediscovery of the meaning of the word "sin" which had become entirely unintelligible by the identification of sin with sins, and by the identification of sins with certain acts that are not conventional or not approvable. Sin is something quite different. It is universal, tragic estrangement, based on freedom and destiny in all human beings, and should never be used in the plural. Sin is separation, estrangement from one's essential being. That is what it means; and if this is the result of depth psychological work, then this of course is a great gift that depth psychology and existentialism have offered to theology.

Thirdly, depth psychology has helped theology to rediscover the demonic structures that determine our consciousness and our decisions. Again, this is very important. It means that if we believe we are free in terms of conscious decision, we can find that something has happened to us which directed these decisions before we made them. The illusion of freedom in the absolute sense in which it was used is included in this rediscovery. This is not determinism. Existentialism is certainly not determinism. But existentialism and especially psychoanalysis and the whole philosophy of the unconscious have rediscovered the totality of the personality in which not only the conscious elements are decisive.

The fourth point, connected with the previous one, is that moralism can be conquered to a great extent in Christian theology. The call for moralism was one of the great forms of self-estrangement of theology from its whole being. And it is indeed important to know that theology had to learn from the psychoanalytic method the meaning of grace, the meaning of forgiveness as acceptance of those who are unacceptable and not of those who are the good people. On the contrary, the non-good people are those who are accepted, or in religious language, forgiven, justified, whatever you wish to call it. The word grace, which had lost any meaning, has gained a new meaning by the way in which the analyst deals with his patient. He accepts him. He does not say, "You are acceptable," but he accepts him. And that is the way in which, according to religious symbolism, God deals with us; and it is the way every minister and every Christian should deal with the other person.

Before the rediscovery of confession and counselling (which were completely lost in Protestantism), everybody was asked to do something, and if he didn't do it he was reproached. Now he can go to somebody, can talk to him, and in talking he can objectify what is in him and get rid of it. If the counsellor or confessor is somebody who knows the human situation, he can be a medium of grace for him who comes to him, a medium for the feeling of overcoming the cleavage between essence and existence.

Finally, what is the influence of psychoanalysis on systematic theology? The interpretation of man's predicament by psychoanalysis raises the question that is implied in man's very existence. Systematic theology has to show that the religious symbols are answers to this question. Now, if you understand the relation of theology and depth psychology in this way, you have grasped the fundamental importance, the final and decisive importance, of all this for theology. There is no theistic and nontheistic existentialism or psychoanalysis. They analyze the human situation. Whenever the analysts or the philosophers give an answer, they do it not as existentialists. They do it from other traditions, whether it be Catholic, Protestant, Lutheran, humanist, or socialist. Traditions come from everywhere, but they do not come from the *question*.

In a long talk in London with T. S. Eliot, who is really considered to be an existentialist, we talked about just this problem. I told him, "I believe that you cannot answer the question you develop in your plays and your poems on the basis of your plays and poems, because they only develop the question—they describe human existence. But if there is an answer, it comes from somewhere else." He replied, "That is exactly what I am fighting for all the time. I am, as you know, an Episcopalian." And he is really a faithful Episcopalian; he answers as an Episcopalian but not as an existentialist. This means that the existentialist raises the question and analyzes the human situation to which the theologian can then give the answer, an answer given not from the question but from somewhere else, and not from the human situation itself.

Theology has received tremendous gifts from existentialism and psychoanalysis, gifts not dreamed of fifty years ago or even thirty years ago. We have these gifts. Existentialists and analysts themselves do not need to know that they have given to theology these great things. But the theologians should know it.

DAVID E. ROBERTS

Correcting Theological Doctrine in the Light of Psychotherapy*

THE IMAGE OF GOD

Ancient stories such as the Prometheus myth reflect the fact that man has viewed the autonomous exercise of his powers as dangerous. Yet failure to find outlets for his creativity is just as perilous as the irresponsible employment of it.

In this connection many versions of the doctrine [of the image of God] need to be corrected or expanded in the light of psychotherapy. Man's longing to exercise his creative powers should not be regarded necessarily as an indication of pride (*hybris*). And if his creativeness is to be "like God's," subject to ineradicable differences between Creator and creature, it can take forms which reflect man's affinity with the natural world which is God's handiwork. Both rigid moralism (operating all too often under the ægis of orthodox Christianity) and the doctrine of the transcendence of God have often been employed to repudiate elements of vitality and spontaneity in man which should be incorporated in the meaning of wholeness. A paralyzing conflict between arid virtue and wayward vitality should not be regarded as part and parcel of what it means to be limited and creaturely. On the contrary, it reflects failure on man's part to align himself aright with the divine vitality which moves through all growing, breathing things. The helplessness to which the doctrine of sin calls attention has far too often been conceived in such a way that the doctrine condemns, as an effort on man's part to "save himself," what is really indispensable to man's

"being himself." Despite its acceptance of the goodness of creation, Christian theology has frequently allowed the doctrine of sin virtually to obliterate the first affirmation. The result is that one scolds himself, not merely for egocentricity, but for being a self; he condemns not merely sexual excesses, but sexuality itself; he feels guilty, not merely for grasping at power unduly, but for asserting and maintaining his own existence at all. Repeatedly in the history of Christianity, the Church has sought to force artistic creativity, romantic love, intellectual inquiry and the venturing spirit into preconceived molds; it has used these talents insofar as they could be subjugated to the Church's own conception of obedience to God, but it has steadily opposed them insofar as they refused to capitulate.

The regrettable alienation of modern culture from Christianity must be understood, in part, as a reaction against ecclesiastical shackles which, if they had not been thrown off, really would have prevented man from carrying through important forms of progress, enlightenment and self-understanding. The failure of Christianity to furnish an organic center for culture has meant that many of these potentially creative powers have run riot. Modern society, armed with technology and dreaming of self-sufficiency, has been set adrift to fashion its own gods and ideologies. These dreams have indeed brought our civilization to the edge of the abyss. But part of the explanation (how large a part, it is impossible to guess) lies in the fact that the Church, by labeling "sinful" human resources which are potentially creative, has failed to provide a religious framework within which these potentialities could be expressed and guided; as a consequence of their repudiation they have been driven into revolt and aggressiveness.

Therefore theology should expand its conception of what is implied in man's creation in the image of God so as to make room for a thorough-going integration between natural vitality and rational order. It should expand its conception of those factors in human nature which can be used by God in overcoming sin; and, as we shall see, this may also involve some alterations in its conception of sin. Some of the derangement which goes into sin has been due, not to the fact that man has tried to save himself, but to the fact that his religion has taught him to regard as liabilities what are actually latent assets. A strategy which continues unqualifiedly to set the Church against the world will shut itself off from nurturing these resources for recovery and new life. If the Church is really interested in curing sin, instead of merely calling attention to its ineradicability, it will not despise the effective help which "worldly" agencies can offer, even though the agencies in question do not use the word "sin."

The image of integrity and innocence, wherein man lived in harmony with nature, his fellows and God, is nonsense if one tries to locate it literally in a primitive age at the dawn of history. But it is not nonsense if one takes it as indicative of every man's capacity and striving for such integrity and harmony. If it be true that man's finding of his place in the scheme of creation, so that he can be harmoniously related to nature, himself and his fellows, is contingent upon his being related harmoniously with God, then this fact is of paramount importance for the psychotherapist. For it implies that man's striving for psychic and spiritual health can be counted on, in the struggle against illness, insanity and evil, only because his essential nature is suited to an appropriate role in this scheme of creation, and because nature is suited to the emergence and sustenance of man. In a word, man need neither capitulate to nature nor defy it in order to be himself. The tragic struggle whereby he seeks to come to terms with life and destiny is not a lonely, transitory one, wherein for a brief period he creates *ex nihilo* whatever humane meaning existence can possess; for this struggle is an integral part of a cosmic creativity. The buried resources are "there," so that they can be drawn upon, only because of a divine strategy which reaches back beyond the appearance of man upon this planet. Man is in his own body and mind a compendium of every preceding "level" of evolution—physical, chemical, biological and psychological. The resources he draws upon, in seeking to become at one with himself, are not merely "his"; they are rooted in the whole creation, which is grounded in God. Therefore man can become at one with himself only by finding his place in a harmony much wider than himself; but this harmony is not "pre-established"; he has a share in winning, in actualizing, it. He cannot fulfill his own nature unless his capacities gain free expression; but neither can he fulfill his own nature unless his freedom is brought into right relationship with God.

MORALISM

The concept of responsibility has been a source of endless difficulties in psychology, philosophy and theology. Any one who has pondered the problem of freedom and determinism will probably sympathize with the sentiment which prompted Milton to assign discussion of this topic to some little devils in Satan's legions who liked to bandy it about during moments of relaxation—without getting anywhere. Nevertheless, psychotherapy has thrown light upon the problem by uncovering the manner in which we are determined by unconscious forces. Its findings point to a form of self-determinism. The self is not merely the passive resultant of inherited constitution plus environmental influences; it builds up an internal unity of its own which enters actively as well as passively into interplay with the surrounding world and other persons. Yet the character-structure being what it is at a given moment, the thoughts, feelings and actions of that moment follow necessarily. This does not imply that the character-structure cannot change, radically and fundamentally; but it does imply that such changes are "law-abiding" in the sense that they come about in response to specific conditions. Psychotherapy interprets particular responses, however, in the light of the whole self's striving to reach or maintain a workable balance between this internal structure and external events. As enriched by the discoveries of psychosomatic medicine, it sees each "level" within man's psycho-physical organism as affected by every other level. Therefore, it does not fall into the reductionist mistake of talking as though physiological processes or psychological mechanisms were isolable items, each possessing a specific gravity of its own, which, when arranged in a certain way, automatically produce thoughts and actions. Psychotherapy is one version of modern psychology which cannot get along without the "psyche." It sees physical, biological and unconscious processes as participating in the life of a self which is held together, in the end, by consciousness and purposiveness. Indeed, unless the therapist believed that conscious intention can influence events he could not carry on his work at all.

Because psychotherapy is committed to the increase of man's capacity to achieve responsibility, it must oppose those forms of psychology which, when taken seriously, spread the illusion that man is an automaton. Yet because it is determinist, it assumes that what is called "moral wrong," as well as mental and physical disease, must be regarded as the necessary consequence, in a given moment, of the interplay between a formed character-structure and an external situation. This does not mean that the distinction between what man can help and what he cannot help disappears entirely; but it does mean that some of our ideas concerning *how* man can alter conditions may have to be revised.

Christian theology has produced many theories, of course, concerning freedom and determinism; but we shall confine our attention to two major trends, discussing the first in this chapter and the second in the next. The first holds that each child comes into the world free from hereditary guilt, and that every man possesses free will in such a fashion that, whenever matters of right and wrong are at stake, he can make his own choice. The most famous advocate of this theory, Pelagius, was an earnest, practically minded moralist who was convinced that men could promote good ends if they tried hard enough; therefore, he sought to close off the "excuse" that they are compelled to do evil by sinful predispositions. He regarded the road to good character as marked by a steady effort of will whereby an individual makes the rational and ethical parts of himself dominant over his lower nature.

The second theory might be called "theological determinism," or "bondage to original sin." Variant forms of it can be found in St. Paul, Augustine, Luther and Calvin. Basically it holds that because human nature has been corrupted at the center, no effort of will can suffice to bring about a radical change of heart. Therefore, no man can save himself, no man can make himself righteous. He can be released from bondage to sin only by a power stronger than himself (God) ; and the transformation which comes about through being forgiven and redeemed by God is a gift, it cannot be earned. Christ, by taking human nature upon Himself and by conquering sin's power, has made available to all men who trust in Him a spiritual and ethical emancipation which they could not possibly achieve by themselves. In fairness to Pelagians we should add that they do not deny the need for divine grace through Christ; but they have regarded this assistance primarily as taking the form of an inspiring moral example. According to the second type of theology, however, the old, corrupt self, which was in bondage to sin, must be replaced by a "new creation"—that rectified human nature which has been instituted by Christ in perfect union with God. This new human nature remains, therefore, a gift, sustained by the indwelling Spirit of Christ working in the hearts of believers through the Christian community; it is not man's property.

One more distinction needs to be made. In the Pelagian view the individual is conceived atomistically; neither hereditary factors nor what we would now call "social conditioning" can rob him of free will. A person may be helped by following worthy examples or harmed by imitating unworthy ones; but nothing forces him to turn toward one or the other; the choice, in any instance, is at his own disposal. The second theory, on the other hand, is much more capable of taking into account the fateful way in which every child is influenced by both heredity and society before he has an opportunity to exercise moral discrimination.

We are now ready to appraise Pelagian moralism in the light of psychotherapy. It rests on the familiar conception of "will power" as something whereby the individual can force himself in any direction he wants to go. This conception underlies moralism generally, whether associated with religious beliefs or not. It assumes that man can live up to any ideal or law that is obligatory upon him. He fulfills what he ought to do by making the principles of reason and conscience triumph over the irrational and sensuous elements in his make-up. Psychotherapeutic findings indicate, however, that this sort of an organization of the self is not "free" at all. On the contrary, it represents a continual condition of internal division and strife. The moralistic individual has not made fully "his own" the ideals which he strives to promote, and they fail to satisfy important needs and capacities. The more he has to force himself by conscientious effort, the more something in him is obviously resisting. The attempt to become virtuous *against* one's "wants" instead of by transformation of them is foredoomed to failure, and the history of moralism illustrates the failure. Ethical standards are insecure so long as they can be enforced only through coercion and conflict-ridden conscientiousness. Resistance to them gathers momentum, underneath the surface; and the more pressure is exerted to hold these resistances in check, the more explosive and disruptive is their rebellion whenever they find an opportunity to break loose. In at least two ways, the ideals toward which a moralistic individual directs his will power are compulsive instead of free. First, they represent the internalization of authoritarian standards instead of his own responsible judgment. If they represented the latter, the forcing would not be necessary. Second, the strenuousness with which he imposes them upon himself reflects the amount of energy that must be expended in overcoming resistance. The "moral energy" which the individual may interpret as manifesting singleness of purpose is precisely correlated with the strength of the psychic forces ranged against his conscience. And moral effort can do nothing to reduce the pressure from the latter because the individual's consciousness is out of touch with them and wants to avoid recognizing their existence and power.

Once moralism gets established, a person feels quite sincerely that it is worth the price—especially in view of the fact that apparently he has no other alternative unless he wants to "go to pot." In return for holding himself in line, he receives a good opinion of himself, and a good reputation in the community. Almost everything he prizes, including his own sense of direction, would be jeopardized if he became seriously skeptical about the soundness of the methods and standards he uses. All of the advantages of moralism are immediately obvious, tangible and important; most of the price he is paying is hidden. The price may include a sacrifice in wholeheartedness, deep friendship, full experience of both the bodily and the spiritual riches of human love, steady joy in living, the unforced employment of talents he already possesses, and the development of interests which have never been given a chance. The price may also include psychosomatic ills which he does not remotely associate with his moralism.

The fact that there may be many inclinations which go counter to his virtuous actions (such as hostility accompanying the "generous" deed) can easily be discounted. Even if he is aware of them (and he usually is not), he can say to himself: "Well, I did the right thing, didn't I? I put the base motives aside, didn't I?" By such methods he can succeed indefinitely in avoiding the full truth about the condition of his "heart," because externally his actions remain so consistently correct. One of the disturbing things about Jesus was that he punctured moralism by looking behind the deed to the spirit in which it is done.

An important qualification must be added, however. Undeniably there are times in any one's life when carrying out a given line of duty, which one espouses as a whole, involves specific

292

segments that are extremely distasteful. One can promote the end-result only by performing tasks some of which are repugnant. Under such circumstances, one has to use "will power" to go ahead; but the ultimate aim is accepted freely, not compulsively. . . .

A DYNAMIC VIEW OF SALVATION

Over against the foregoing results, let us set a "dynamic" conception of salvation. Here the validity of an ethical or a religious ideal depends upon its power to *resolve* conflict. Insofar as a person finds organic harmony between his ideals and his unforced behavior, the resulting release and serenity provide a firm and stimulating basis for further development along the same lines. He becomes a "gracious" instead of a "moralistic" human being. So far as Christianity is concerned, this conception implies that its saving purpose is to give men a faith and a mode of life which will make them no longer ashamed of themselves. It cures guilt, not by putting forward ideas which assure men willy-nilly that they are "all right," but by releasing a power which removes the *causes* of guilt.

The stock objection is that, if one allows a man to be content with ideals he is actually able to reach, he will "accept himself" at an immoral or complacent level. But the clinical data of psychotherapy point to an opposite conclusion. Most emotional disorders and behavior problems reveal a pattern where the individual has *not* reached self-acceptance—which is functionally interrelated, incidentally, with his capacity to accept others. On the contrary, such personality problems go hand-in-hand with a sense of moral inferiority, unacceptability and estrangement, no matter how much these may be overlaid with a bold, defiant "front." Under present circumstances coercive methods have to be used in protecting society against the consequences that would ensue if moral evil were allowed to run rampant. These coercive methods range from punishment in home and school to imprisonment of criminals and resistance of aggressors in war. But such methods do not "cure" anything. A constructive transformation is not brought about merely by driving home upon either an individual or a nation an acknowledgment of moral inferiority and its consequences. Men can be frightened into abiding by certain restrictions, or otherwise compelled to abide by them; but these expedients do not alter motivation in a desirable direction. Whether we think of domestic crime or of international warfare, who can deny that the threat of punishment and the enforcement of retaliation are staggeringly inefficient as methods of preventing anti-social behavior? Permanent cures occur only insofar as a man finds forms of affection, respect and trust in which he can participate. Such values are "self-sustaining" in the sense that once they are experienced, a man wants them, affirms those things in himself which promote them, and voluntarily renounces those things in himself which would destroy them. Even if most human beings (past and present) are regarded as "incurable" because limitations in themselves or in their surroundings have excluded the fulfillment of these conditions, that does not invalidate the psychological principles involved.

None of this means, however, that an ideal must be *immediately* realizable in order to be dynamic. One can acknowledge the desirability of a style of life, a family relationship, or a social order which neither he nor any one else has yet achieved. He can retain belief in the worth of such ideals despite the fact that they remain in some measure unattainable in any foreseeable future. But his ideals are held in such a way that failure can be made a priceless source of deepening understanding and effective change—instead of a source of paralysis and despair. Admittedly it is exceedingly difficult to discriminate aright between the factors in any human problem that cannot be changed and those which can be. But so long as a norm is employed statically, all failure to fulfill it is condemned forthwith; hence discrimination cannot even get started. In general, most people who are caught in serious conflict blame themselves for things they cannot help, and fail to move toward procedures which are within their power. For example, they scold themselves for an outburst of rage, anxiety or eroticism which, at the existing level of self-understanding, was quite inevitable; but they feel sincerely that they "cannot" face what lies behind their problems.

If an ideal is dynamic, it provides positive guidance concerning the extent to which, and the methods by which, it can be effectively promoted. Insofar as obstacles are strictly irremediable, one operates within the limits they set; one does not cling to a vision of perfection in defiance of them, and one does not blame either himself or any one else for failing to do the impossible. Let us acknowledge again that often the line between the remediable and the irremediable cannot be drawn with certainty. We can be certain that man cannot slough off his body and live as pure spirit, so that any ethic which is applicable only to the latter condition may be disregarded. But we cannot be certain, for example, as to whether a specific endeavor toward lessening racial prejudice will evoke enough of a favorable response to outweigh the hatred it may stir up. The latter dilemma illustrates why well-intentioned persons can differ honestly concerning the best strategy for promoting the same end. It also illustrates why ideal norms should be alterable in the light of continual study of empirical data. A dynamic approach is our best available method for moving flexibly between the Scylla of impractical idealism (which underestimates the odds ranged against it), and the Charybdis of compromising cynicism (which underestimates the releasability of moral resources).

Similarly, in our religious conceptions of salvation there must be organic connection between the goal itself and the human conditions which are to be fulfilled in reaching it. Because the conditions on which human beatitude rests do not consist merely of external techniques and operations, theology must steadily resist those modes of thought which look upon the problem involved merely as a piece of psychological and sociological engineering. The "Brave New World" is a secular substitute for salvation, and many of our contemporaries worship at its shrine, either because they believe it is the best they can get, or because they have become so spiritually obtuse as actually to believe it is splendid. Yet Christianity's purpose of calling men to a higher destiny cannot be served if its manner of "facing the worst" about human nature prevents it from finding realistically and practically those areas in which significant changes are feasible. Where it is literally the case concerning a personal or social problem that nothing can be done about it, the only wise course involves accepting the restriction and focusing attention upon anything that can be accomplished despite its limits. Human beings have amazing capacities for morale and adjustment when they know definitely what they are up against. The circumstances that drive them into despair, insanity and suicide are mainly connected with man-made events. Strictly unpreventable evils can make life tragic; it is the preventable evils *which become* inexorable that make life intolerable.

Hence salvation should be thought of primarily in terms of a dynamic transformation that removes man-made evils at the source by changing the man. It should not be thought of in terms that would require a complete sloughing off of creatureliness. We have already suggested that the Theology of Crisis (in its most extreme version) [1] is wrong when it regards the conditions of salvation as fulfilled exclusively by God, apart from existing resources in human nature. We have also contended that humanism is wrong in claiming that the conditions of salvation (or "amelioration") must be fulfilled exclusively by man, because there is no God. The preceding discussion has led up to a conception of salvation as that condition of wholeness which comes about when human life is based in openness (*i.e.,* with "self-knowledge") upon the creative and redemptive power of God. This condition is reached *by means of* man's freedom, and constitutes an enhancement of that freedom. Its initiation, once or repeatedly, may involve "taking him captive"; but the "captivation" is releasing and the released person affirms it and desires to sustain it. The freedom of man, as we have conceived it, is directly related to acquaintance with his own depths; his assent cannot be unforced and wholehearted if it is opposed by unconscious motives and impulses. Yet the very process of widening acquaintance with the sources of human bondage leads to the release of healing power. . . . The structure of reality links misery and conflict to man's failure to reach a position where he can affirm his *whole* self; and it links beatitude to honesty and wholeness. Hence faith in God can rest upon actualities that function in human existence here and now; it need not be directed exclusively to something which utterly transcends our experience and our history.

In theological language, our conception of salvation definitely involves acceptance of the doctrine of divine immanence.[2] The drive toward integra-

---

[1] "Theology of Crisis" refers to Neo-orthodox Theology and "its most extreme version" refers to the position of Karl Barth as over against the positions of Brunner and of the Niebuhrs. (Ed.)

[2] I am concerned to stress this point because this doctrine has been strenuously attacked by Barthian theology. Affirmation of divine immanence does not here imply a denial of divine transcendence.

tion, which man can discern in himself, is not confined to him. It moves through all levels of creation; but in man the problem of how to reach integration-in-freedom gives rise to unparalleled difficulties and opportunities. Man's freedom shuts him off from reaching harmony by becoming an item in the routine and vitality of natural process —a harmony which animals enjoy. But it is equally impossible for man to reach wholeness by attempting to fulfill "divine" demands which transcend his status as a temporal creature in nature. The principles whereby man reaches harmony within himself are at once rational and "animal," spiritual and physical. The destiny of man cannot be conceived apart from his linkage with processes at every level in nature. In this sense God moves *through* His creation. As Fritz Kunkel has put it: "Creation continues." Moreover, the doctrine of the Resurrection issues from a (Jewish) view of man's psycho-physical wholeness which is congenial with the foregoing, while Platonic views of immortality are incompatible with it.

The identification of "the voice of conscience" with "the voice of God" leads to a dangerous half-truth so long as the voice of conscience perpetuates conflict instead of resolving it. As Berdyaev has suggested, the Gospel is "strange" not merely because it comes to us over a chasm of twenty centuries; it is "strange" because it is anti-legalistic. It is personal, whereas every culture's moral ideas—whether those of the first century or the twentieth century—tend to be collective and tyrannical. The relationship to God it envisages is spontaneous, whereas all ethical *law* is abstract and compulsive. If he is right, then the voice of God speaks and the creative power of God moves through forms of organic solidarity with nature and with fellow human beings which the condemning conscience rejects. Both moralism and rationalism, insofar as they estrange man from parts of himself,

prevent him from reaching wholeness. And a theology that denies or minimizes the immanence of God cannot use the full resources of the Gospel in counteracting the distortions of human nature which result.

We have already rejected the theory of revelation which regards man's likeness to God as so completely destroyed that nothing in him can participate in the achievement of salvation. We have also rejected views of salvation through Christ which impose upon men a norm they are not expected to appropriate through their own insight and through the emancipating consequences that flow from insight. Belief in Christ is compatible with a dynamic view of salvation, however, when it finds in Him the supreme disclosure of a universal fact—the fact that divine and human love cannot be fulfilled apart from each other. In such a conception His union with God is not used tyrannically as the basis for condemning other men because they are incapable of reproducing His unique endowments. Instead, He points to the redeemability of *our* human nature, and to the possibility of reaching self-acceptance in fellowship with God.

In the process of reaching maturity and autonomy most of us do strive for security by trying to organize the universe around ourselves. And most of us learn only through the suffering and estrangement which attend egocentricity that this way leads not to security, but to an endlessly precarious and ultimately fruitless attempt to twist reality into meeting our private specifications. Insofar as we are incapable of love, we are not only divided within ourselves and isolated from other human beings, we are violating the universal principle upon which human beatitude is based. Our defensive structures are broken through by healing power which is wider than ourselves; yet it is ours. We see—not merely intellectually, but with heart and soul—that what is made accessible to us in our "new" selves has been what we have yearned for all along. We have evaded it partly because the price in suffering seemed too high, especially when there was no guarantee of a satisfying outcome. We have also "evaded" it because we literally could not work toward it effectively so long as we were imprisoned within the old strategies of defensiveness, anxiety and the need to feel superior. The price in suffering is a facing and grasping, in feeling as well as in thought, of the deeply hidden causes of inner dividedness. This facing can be carried on healingly (*i.e.,* redemptively) only in a relationship of acceptance (*i.e.,* forgiveness).

We reach our highest freedom not by asserting our own interests against the world, but by devoting ourselves in fellowship to a way of life which reaches personal fulfillment along with, and partly *through,* the fulfillment of others. We reach security only by a trustful acceptance of the full truth about ourselves and others, not by evasion of it. Healing power is latent in men because it is latent "in the nature of things." Hence it is not surprising that men and women have found in Christ the supreme disclosure of what coincidence between human beatitude and divine love means. Christ is Savior as He opens, for each man, the way whereby that individual can move toward such coincidence. This involves moving forward into a deepened recognition of failure, impotence and need at many points. But the divine forgiveness which He discloses always has been and always will be accessible to men. We experience divine forgiveness as that "making right" of our lives which occurs when we turn away from fighting ourselves, and others, and the truth itself, and turn trustfully toward the divine power which surrounds us and can work through us. This experience of reconciliation, despite past failures and unsolved problems in the present, makes men actually more lovable, more discerning, more capable of devoting themselves to goods which enrich all humanity.

Religion and Psychotherapy: Bibliography

Academy of Religion and Mental Health (Symposia published annually since 1959 by New York University Press).

Allport, Gordon W. *The Individual and His Religion.* New York: The Macmillan Company, 1950.

Birmington, William and Cunneen, Joseph, eds. *Cross Currents of Psychiatry and Catholic Morality.* New York: Pantheon Books, 1964.

Freud, Sigmund. *The Future of an Illusion.* New York: Liveright Publishing Corp., 1949. Paper (Anchor ed.), New York: Doubleday & Company.

Guntrip, Henry J. S. *Psychotherapy and Religion.* New York: Harper & Brothers, 1957.

Johnson, Paul E. *The Psychology of Religion.* Rev. ed. Nashville: Abingdon Press, 1959.

Jung, Carl G. *Psychology and Religion.* New Haven, Conn.: Yale University Press [1938], 1960.

Mollegen, Albert T. *et al.* "Christianity and Psychoanalysis." Washington, D.C.: Henderson Services. Reprinted in *The Journal of Pastoral Care,* VI, 4 (Winter, 1952).

Mowrer, O. Hobart. *The Crisis in Psychiatry and Religion.* Princeton, N.J.: D. Van Nostrand Company, 1961.

Outler, Albert C. *Psychotherapy and the Christian Message.* New York: Charles Scribner's Sons, 1954.

Nelson, Benjamin, ed. *Freud and the Twentieth Century.* New York: Meridian Books, 1957.

Zilboorg, Gregory. *Freud and Religion.* Westminster, Md.: The Newman Press, 1964.

VII
Religion
and Science

Introduction

In this section there are two questions concerning the relation of religion and natural science which are especially prominent. First, is the whole of reality open to scientific method or are there dimensions of reality which can be known only in other ways? Second, what is the relation of science to the experiences of wonder and awe which play such an important part in religion?

Concerning the first question, Ayer believes that the world open to scientific study is the only reality there is—or, strictly speaking, the only reality we can know about. This is the implication of Ayer's claim that, aside from purely logical statements, the only utterances which give us information are those which lead us to expect certain sensory experiences in the future and not to expect others. All other sentences are simply emotive. This is true of metaphysical sentences, including talk about God, although their form makes them seem to be factual assertions, and they are often mistakenly treated as factual.

Heim is representative of the existentialist view which maintains that there are dimensions of reality which can be known only through a personal attitude and not through the detached, impersonal attitude required by scientific method. He borrows a usage from physics and speaks of different dimensions of reality as different spaces. (Instead of spaces, Gilson speaks of orders and Schilling of levels.)

According to Gilson, we go beyond the order of science to that of metaphysics whenever we ask the question "Why?" rather than the question "How?"

Concerning our second question, it is Ayer's contention that "science tends to destroy the feeling of awe with which men regard an alien world, by making them believe that they can . . . to some extent control it." According to Gilson, "the universe of science *qua* science exactly consists of that part of the total universe from which . . . mysteries have been removed." This universe of science, he believes, has seemed mysterious to some scientists only because they have confused scientific questions with metaphysical questions, and it is the latter which have to do with the mysterious. Schilling, on the other hand, denies that science is any longer such that "as its understanding grows the mystery dissolves." Rather, as he sees it, the world of science is increasingly discovered to be a mysterious world.

Gilson and Heim discuss two different ways in which science can become an obstacle to faith. Gilson is concerned with the metaphysical elements— typically materialistic—which creep into scientific thought. Heim believes that scientific concepts or principles may themselves become idols.

In reading Schilling, several comparisons might be kept in mind. His belief that "there are many aspects of the new science . . . that are destined to become useful, or even indispensable, to Christian thought" may be compared to Roberts' view of the relevance of psychotherapy to religious thought. This belief may be compared also to Heim's view that "the only way which really leads [from natural events] to God is the . . . negative way . . . marked by the collapse . . . of the Absolutes which stand as hindrances in the way of God's sole Lordship." Finally, Schilling's high estimate of the spiritual significance of turning from the "older scientific views of nature as shallow, closed and unmysterious" to the newer view of nature as deep, open, and mysterious might be compared to Cox's interpretation of secularization (as distinguished from secularism).

ALFRED JULES AYER

Science and Religion in Conflict*

The criterion which we use to test the genuineness of apparent statements of fact is the criterion of verifiability. We say that a sentence is factually significant to any given person, if, and only if, he knows how to verify the proposition which it purports to express—that is, if he knows what observations would lead him, under certain conditions, to accept the proposition as being true, or reject it as being false. If, on the other hand, the putative proposition is of such a character that the assumption of its truth, or falsehood, is consistent with any assumption whatsoever concerning the nature of his future experience, then, as far as he is concerned, it is, if not a tautology, a mere pseudo-proposition. The sentence expressing it may be emotionally significant to him; but it is not literally significant. And with regard to questions the procedure is the same. We enquire in every case what observations would lead us to an-

swer the question, one way or the other; and, if none can be discovered, we must conclude that the sentence under consideration does not, as far as we are concerned, express a genuine question, however strongly its grammatical appearance may suggest that it does. . . .

It is now generally admitted, at any rate by philosophers, that the existence of a being having the attributes which define the god of any non-animistic religion cannot be demonstratively proved. To see that this is so, we have only to ask ourselves what are the premises from which the existence of such a god could be deduced. If the conclusion that a god exists is to be demonstratively certain, then these premises must be certain; for, as the conclusion of a deductive argument is already contained in the premises, any uncertainty there may be about the truth of the premises is necessarily shared by it. But we know that no

* From Alfred Jules Ayer, *Language, Truth, and Logic* (2nd ed.; 1946). Reprinted by permission of Victor Gollancz, Ltd.; pp. 35, 114-20.

empirical proposition can ever be anything more than probable. It is only *a priori* propositions that are logically certain. But we cannot deduce the existence of a god from an *a priori* proposition. For we know that the reason why *a priori* propositions are certain is that they are tautologies.* And from a set of tautologies nothing but a further tautology can be validly deduced. It follows that there is no possibility of demonstrating the existence of a god.

What is not so generally recognized is that there can be no way of proving that the existence of a god, such as the God of Christianity, is even probable. Yet this also is easily shown. For if the existence of such a god were probable, then the proposition that he existed would be an empirical hypothesis. And in that case it would be possible to deduce from it, and other empirical hypotheses, certain experiential propositions which were not deducible from those other hypotheses alone. But in fact this is not possible. It is sometimes claimed, indeed, that the existence of a certain sort of regularity in nature constitutes sufficient evidence for the existence of a god. But if the sentence "God exists" entails no more than that certain types of phenomena occur in certain sequences, then to assert the existence of a god will be simply equivalent to asserting that there is the requisite regularity in nature; and no religious man would admit that this was all he intended to assert in asserting the existence of a god. He would say that in talking about God, he was talking about a transcendent being who might be known through certain empirical manifestations, but certainly could not be defined in terms of those manifestations. But in that case the term "god" is a metaphysical term. And if "god" is a

metaphysical term, then it cannot be even probable that a god exists. For to say that "God exists" is to make a metaphysical utterance† which cannot be either true or false. And by the same criterion, no sentence which purports to describe the nature of a transcendent god can possess any literal significance.

It is important not to confuse this view of religious assertions with the view that is adopted by atheists, or agnostics.[1] For it is characteristic of an agnostic to hold that the existence of a god is a possibility in which there is no good reason either to believe or disbelieve; and it is characteristic of an atheist to hold that it is at least probable that no god exists. And our view that all utterances about the nature of God are nonsensical, so far from being identical with, or even lending any support to, either of these familiar contentions, is actually incompatible with them. For if the assertion that there is a god is nonsensical, then the atheist's assertion that there is no god is equally nonsensical, since it is only a significant proposition that can be significantly contradicted. As for the agnostic, although he refrains from saying either that there is or that there is not a god, he does not deny that the question whether a transcendent god exists is a genuine question. He does not deny that the two sentences "There is a transcendent god" and "There is no transcendent god" express propositions one of which is actually true and the other false. All he says is that we have no means of telling which of them is true, and therefore ought not to commit ourselves to either. But we have seen that the sentences in question do not express propositions at all. And this means that agnosticism also is ruled out.

* [Editor's note]. A tautology is any proposition whose "validity depends solely on the definitions of the symbols it contains." See *Language, Truth, and Logic,* p. 78.

† [Editor's note]. A metaphysical utterance is any sentence "which purports to express a genuine proposition, but does, in fact, express neither a tautology nor an empirical hypothesis." See *Language, Truth, and Logic,* p. 41.

[1] This point was suggested to me by Professor H. H. Price.

Thus we offer the theist the same comfort as we gave to the moralist. His assertions cannot possibly be valid, but they cannot be invalid either. As he says nothing at all about the world, he cannot justly be accused of saying anything false, or anything for which he has insufficient grounds. It is only when the theist claims that in asserting the existence of a transcendent god he is expressing a genuine proposition that we are entitled to disagree with him.

It is to be remarked that in cases where deities are identified with natural objects, assertions concerning them may be allowed to be significant. If, for example, a man tells me that the occurrence of thunder is alone both necessary and sufficient to establish the truth of the proposition that Jehovah is angry, I may conclude that, in his usage of words, the sentence "Jehovah is angry" is equivalent to "It is thundering." But in sophisticated religions, though they may be to some extent based on men's awe of natural process which they cannot sufficiently understand, the "person" who is supposed to control the empirical world is not himself located in it; he is held to be superior to the empirical world, and so outside it; and he is endowed with super-empirical attributes. But the notion of a person whose essential attributes are non-empirical is not an intelligible notion at all. We may have a word which is used as if it named this "person," but, unless the sentences in which it occurs express propositions which are empirically verifiable, it cannot be said to symbolize anything. And this is the case with regard to the word "god," in the usage in which it is intended to refer to a transcendent object. The mere existence of the noun is enough to foster the illusion that there is a real, or at any rate a possible entity corresponding to it. It is only when we enquire what God's attributes are that we discover that "God," in this usage, is not a genuine name.

It is common to find belief in a transcendent god conjoined with belief in an after-life. But, in the form which it usually takes, the content of this belief is not a genuine hypothesis. To say that men do not ever die, or that the state of death is merely a state of prolonged insensibility, is indeed to express a significant proposition, though all the available evidence goes to show that it is false. But to say that there is something imperceptible inside a man, which is his soul or his real self, and that it goes on living after he is dead, is to make a metaphysical assertion which has no more factual content than the assertion that there is a transcendent god.

It is worth mentioning that, according to the account which we have given of religious assertions, there is no logical ground for antagonism between religion and natural science. As far as the question of truth or falsehood is concerned, there is no opposition between the natural scientist and the theist who believes in a transcendent god. For since the religious utterances of the theist are not genuine propositions at all, they cannot stand in any logical relation to the propositions of science. Such antagonism as there is between religion and science appears to consist in the fact that science takes away one of the motives which make men religious. For it is acknowledged that one of the ultimate sources of religious feeling lies in the inability of men to determine their own destiny; and science tends to destroy the feeling of awe with which men regard an alien world, by making them believe that they can understand and anticipate the course of natural phenomena, and even to some extent control it. The fact that it has recently become fashionable for physicists themselves to be sympathetic towards religion is a point in favour of this hypothesis. For this sympathy towards religion marks the physicists' own lack of confidence in the validity of their hypotheses, which is a reaction on their part from the anti-religious dogmatism of nineteenth-century scientists, and a natural outcome of the crisis through which physics has just passed.

It is not within the scope of this enquiry to enter more deeply into the causes of religious feeling, or to discuss the probability of the continuance of religious belief. We are concerned only to answer those questions which arise out of our discussion of the possibility of religious knowledge. The point which we wish to establish is that there cannot be any transcendent truths of religion. For the sentences which the theist uses to express such "truths" are not literally significant.

An interesting feature of this conclusion is that it accords with what many theists are accustomed to say themselves. For we are often told that the nature of God is a mystery which transcends the human understanding. But to say that something transcends the human understanding is to say that it is unintelligible. And what is unintelligible cannot significantly be described. Again, we are told that God is not an object of reason but an object of faith. This may be nothing more than an admission that the existence of God must be taken on trust, since it cannot be proved. But it may also be an assertion that God is the object of a purely mystical intuition, and cannot therefore be defined in terms which are intelligible to the reason. And I think there are many theists who would assert this. But if one allows that it is impossible to define God in intelligible terms, then one is allowing that it is impossible for a sentence both to be significant and to be about God. If a mystic admits that the object of his vision is something which cannot be described, then he must also admit that he is bound to talk nonsense when he describes it.

For his part, the mystic may protest that his intuition does reveal truths to him, even though he cannot explain to others what these truths are; and that we who do not possess this faculty of intuition can have no ground for denying that it is a cognitive faculty. For we can hardly maintain *a priori* that there are no ways of discovering true propositions except those which we ourselves employ. The answer is that we set no limit to the number of ways in which one may come to formulate a true proposition. We do not in any way deny that a synthetic truth may be discovered by purely intuitive methods as well as by the rational method of induction. But we do say that every synthetic proposition, however it may have been arrived at, must be subject to the test of actual experience. We do not deny *a priori* that the mystic is able to discover truths by his own special methods. We wait to hear what are the propositions which embody his discoveries, in order to see whether they are verified or confuted by our empirical observations. But the mystic, so far from producing propositions which are empirically verified, is unable to produce any intelligible propositions at all. And therefore we say that his intuition has not revealed to him any facts. It is no use his saying that he has apprehended facts but is unable to express them. For we know that if he really had acquired any information, he would be able to express it. He would be able to indicate in some way or other how the genuineness of his discovery might be empirically determined. The fact that he cannot reveal what he "knows," or even himself devise an empirical test to validate his "knowledge," shows that his state of mystical intuition is not a genuinely cognitive state. So that in describing his vision the mystic does not give us any information about the external world; he merely gives us indirect information about the condition of his own mind.

These considerations dispose of the argument from religious experience, which many philosophers still regard as a valid argument in favour of the existence of a god. They say that it is logically possible for men to be immediately acquainted with God, as they are immediately acquainted with a sense-content, and that there is no reason why one should be prepared to believe a man when he says that he is seeing a yellow patch, and refuse to believe him when he says that he is seeing God. The answer to this is that if the man who asserts that he is seeing God is merely asserting that he is experiencing a peculiar kind of sense-content, then we do not for a moment deny that his assertion may be true. But, ordinarily, the man who says that he is seeing God is saying not merely that he is experiencing a religious emotion, but also that there exists a transcendent being who is the object of this emotion; just as the man who says that he sees a yellow patch is ordinarily saying not merely that his visual sense-field contains a yellow sense-content, but also that there exists a yellow object to which the sense-content belongs. And it is not irrational to be prepared to believe a man when he asserts the existence of a yellow object, and to refuse to believe him when he asserts the existence of a transcendent god. For whereas the sentence "There exists here a yellow-coloured material thing" expresses a genuine synthetic proposition which could be empirically verified, the sentence "There exists a transcendent god" has, as we have seen, no literal significance.

We conclude, therefore, that the argument from religious experience is altogether fallacious. The fact that people have religious experiences is interesting from the psychological point of view, but it does not in any way imply that there is such a thing as religious knowledge, any more than our having moral experiences implies that there is such a thing as moral knowledge. The theist, like the moralist, may believe that his experiences are cognitive experiences, but, unless he can formulate his "knowledge" in propositions that are empirically verifiable, we may be sure that he is deceiving himself. It follows that those philosophers who fill their books with assertions that they intuitively "know" this or that moral or religious "truth" are merely providing material for the psychoanalyst. For no act of intuition can be said to reveal a truth about any matter of fact unless it issues in verifiable propositions. And all such propositions are to be incorporated in the system of empirical propositions which constitutes science.

ÉTIENNE GILSON

The God Beyond the World of Science*

The present-day position of the problem of God is wholly dominated by the thought of Immanuel Kant and of Auguste Comte. Their doctrines are about as widely different as two philosophical doctrines can possibly be. Yet

* From "God and Contemporary Thought" in *God and Philosophy* by Étienne Gilson (New Haven, Conn.: Yale University Press, 1941). Reprinted by permission of the publishers; pp. 109-44.

the Criticism of Kant and the Positivism of Comte have this in common, that in both doctrines the notion of knowledge is reduced to that of scientific knowledge, and the notion of scientific knowledge itself to the type of intelligibility provided by the physics of Newton. The verb "to know" then means to express observable relations between given facts in terms of mathematical relations. Now, however we look at it, no given fact answers to our notion of God. Since God is not an object of empirical knowledge, we have no concept of him. Consequently God is no object of knowledge, and what we call natural theology is just idle talking.

If we compare it with the Kantian revolution, the Cartesian revolution hardly deserved such a name. From Thomas Aquinas to Descartes the distance is assuredly a long one. Yet, although extremely far from each other, they are on comparable lines of thought. Between Kant and them, the line has been broken. Coming after the Greeks, the Christian philosophers had asked themselves the question: How obtain from Greek metaphysics an answer to the problems raised by the Christian God? After centuries of patient work, one of them had at last found the answer, and that is why we find Thomas Aquinas constantly using the language of Aristotle in order to say Christian things. Coming after the Christian philosophers, Descartes, Leibniz, Malebranche, and Spinoza found themselves confronted with this new problem: How find a metaphysical justification for the world of seventeenth-century science? As scientists, Descartes and Leibniz had no metaphysics of their own. Just as Augustine and Thomas Aquinas had had to borrow their technique from the Greeks, Descartes and Leibniz had to borrow their technique from the Christian philosophers who had preceded them. Hence the vast number of scholastic expressions which we meet in the works of Descartes, Leibniz, Spinoza, and even Locke. All of them freely use the language of the Schoolmen in order to express nonscholastic views of a nonscholastic world. Yet all of them appear to us as seeking in a more or less traditional metaphysics the ultimate justification of the mechanical world of modern science. In short, and this is true of Newton himself, the supreme principle of the intelligibility of nature remains, for all of them, the Author of Nature, that is, God.

With the Criticism of Kant and the Positivism of Comte, things become entirely different. Since God is not an object apprehended in the a priori forms of sensibility, space and time, he cannot be related to anything else by the category of causality. Hence, Kant concludes, God may well be a pure idea of reason, that is, a general principle of unification of our cognitions; he is not an object of cognition. Or we may have to posit his existence as required by the exigencies of practical reason; the existence of God then becomes a postulate, it is still not a cognition. In his own way, which was a much more radical one, Comte at once reached identically the same conclusion. Science, Comte says, has no use for the notion of cause. Scientists never ask themselves *why* things happen, but *how* they happen. Now as soon as you substitute the positivist's notion of relation for the metaphysical notion of cause, you at once lose all right to wonder *why* things are, and why they are what they are. To dismiss all such questions as irrelevant to the order of positive knowledge is, at the same time, to cut the very root of all speculation concerning the nature and existence of God.

It had taken Christian thinkers thirteen centuries to achieve a perfectly consistent philosophy of the universe of Christianity. It has taken modern scientists about two centuries to achieve a perfectly consistent philosophy of the mechanical universe of modern science. This is a fact which it is very important for us to realize, because it clearly shows where the pure philosophical positions are actually to be found.

If what we are after is a rational interpretation of the world of science given as an ultimate fact, either the Criticism of Kant himself or some edition of his Criticism revised to suit the demands of today's science should provide us with a satisfactory answer to our question. We might nevertheless prefer the Positivism of Comte, or some revised edition of it. A large number among our own contemporaries actually subscribe to one or the other of these two possible attitudes. The Neo-Criticism has been represented by such men as Paulsen and Vaihinger in Germany, by Renouvier in France; and it has found what will perhaps remain its purest formulation in the works of our own contemporary, Professor Leon Brunschvicg. As to Positivism, it has found important supporters in England, John Stuart Mill and Herbert Spencer, for instance; in France, Émile Littré, Émile Durkheim, and the whole French sociological school; and it has recently been revived, under a new form, by the Neo-Positivism of the Vienna school. Whatever their many differences, all these schools have at least this in common, that their ambition does not extend beyond achieving a rational interpretation of the world of science given as an irreducible and ultimate fact.

But if we do not think that science is adequate to rational knowledge, if we hold that other than scientifically answerable problems can still be rationally posed concerning the universe, then there is no use for us to stop at the eighteenth-century Author of Nature. Why should we content ourselves with the ghost of God when we can have God? But there is no reason either why we should waste our time in weighing the respective merits of the gods of Spinoza, of Leibniz, or of Descartes. We now know what these gods are: mere by-products born of the philosophical decomposition of the Christian living God. Today our only choice is not Kant or Descartes; it is rather Kant or Thomas Aquinas. All the other positions are but halfway houses on the roads which lead either to absolute religious agnosticism or to the natural theology of Christian metaphysics.

Philosophical halfway houses have always been pretty crowded, but never more than they are in our own times, especially in the field of natural theology. This fact is not a wholly inexplicable one. What makes it difficult for us to go back to Thomas Aquinas is Kant. Modern men are held spellbound by science, in some cases because they know it, but in an incomparably larger number of cases because they know that, to those who know science, the problem of God does not appear susceptible of a scientific formulation. But what makes it difficult for us to go as far as Kant is, if not Thomas Aquinas himself, at least the whole order of facts which provides a basis for his own natural theology. Quite apart from any philosophical demonstration of the existence of God, there is such a thing as a spontaneous natural theology. A quasi-instinctive tendency, observable in most men, seems to invite them to wonder from time to time if, after all, there is not such an unseen being as the one we call God. The current objection that such a feeling is but a survival in us of primitive myths, or of our own early religious education, is not a very strong one. Primitive myths do not account for the human belief in the existence of the Divinity; obviously, it is the reverse which is true. Early religious education is no sufficient explanation for the questions which sometimes arise in the minds of men concerning the reality or unreality of God. Some among us have received a decidedly antireligious education; others have had no religious education at all; and there are even quite a few who, having once received a religious education, fail to find in its memory any incentive to think too seriously of God. The natural invitations to apply his mind to the problem come to man from quite different sources. These are the very selfsame sources which once gave rise not only to Greek mythology but to all mythologies. God spontaneously offers himself to most of us, more as a confusedly felt presence than as an answer to any problem, when we find ourselves confronted with the vastness of the ocean, the still purity of mountains, or the mysterious life of a midsummer starry sky. Far from being social in essence, these fleeting temptations to think of God usually visit us in our moments of solitude. But there is no more solitary solitude than that of a man in deep sorrow or confronted with the tragic perspective of his own impending end. "One dies alone," Pascal says. That is perhaps the reason why so many men finally meet God waiting for them on the threshold of death.

What do such feelings prove? Absolutely nothing. They are not proofs but facts, the very facts which give philosophers occasion to ask themselves precise questions concerning the possible existence of God. Just as such personal experiences precede any attempt to prove that there is a God, they survive our failures to prove it. Pascal did not make much of the so-called proofs of God's existence. To him, it was incomprehensible that God should exist, and it was incomprehensible that God should not exist; then he would simply wager that God exist—a safe betting indeed, since there was much to gain and nothing to lose. Thus to bet is not to know, especially in a case when, if we lose, we cannot even hope to know it. Yet Pascal was still willing to bet on what he could not know. Similarly, after proving in his *Critique of Pure Reason* that the existence of God could not be demon-

strated, Kant still insisted on keeping God as at least a unifying idea in the order of speculative reason and as postulate in the moral order of practical reason. It may even appear to be true that, out of its own nature, the human mind is equally unable both to prove the existence of any God and "to escape its deep-seated instinct to personify its intellectual conceptions." [1] Whether we make it the result of spontaneous judgment of reason, with Thomas Aquinas; or an innate idea, with Descartes; or an intellectual intuition, with Malebranche; or an idea born of the unifying power of human reason, with Kant; or a phantasm of human imagination, with Thomas Henry Huxley, this common notion of God is there as a practically universal fact whose speculative value may well be disputed, but whose existence cannot be denied. The only problem is for us to determine the truth value of this notion.

At first sight, the shortest way to test it seems to judge it from the point of view of scientific knowledge. But the shortest way might not be the safest one. This method rests upon the assumption that nothing can be rationally known unless it be scientifically known, which is far from being an evident proposition. The names of Kant and of Comte have very little importance, if any, in the history of modern science; Descartes and Leibniz, two of the creators of modern science, have also been great metaphysicians. The simple truth may be that while human reason remains one and the same in dealing with different orders of problems, it nevertheless must approach these various orders of problems in as many different ways. Whatever our final answer to the problem of God may be, we all agree that God is not an empirically observable fact. Mystical experience itself is both unspeakable and intransmissible; hence, it cannot become an objective experience. If, speaking in the order of pure natural knowledge, the

[1] Thomas Henry Huxley, *The Evolution of Theology: an Anthropological Study,* as quoted in Julian Huxley, *Essays in Popular Science* (London, Pelican Books, 1937), p. 123.

proposition "God exists" makes any sense at all, it must be for its rational value as a philosophical answer to a metaphysical question.

When a man falls to wondering whether there is such a being as God, he is not conscious of raising a scientific problem, or hoping to give it a scientific solution. Scientific problems are all related to the knowledge of *what* given things actually are. An ideal scientific explanation of the world would be an exhaustive rational explanation of *what* the world actually is; but *why* nature exists is not a scientific problem, because its answer is not susceptible of empirical verification. The notion of God, on the contrary, always appears to us in history as an answer to some existential problem, that is, as the *why* of a certain existence. The Greek gods were constantly invoked in order to account for various "happenings" in the history of men as well as in that of things. A religious interpretation of nature never worries about what things are—that is a problem for scientists—but it is very much concerned with the questions why things happen to be precisely what they are, and why they happen to be at all. The Jewish-Christian God to whom we are introduced by the Bible is there at once posited as the ultimate explanation for the very existence of man, for the present condition of man upon earth, for all the successive events that make up the history of the Jewish people as well as for these momentous events: the Incarnation of Christ and the Redemption of man by Grace. Whatever their ultimate value, these are existential answers to existential questions. As such, they cannot possibly be transposed into terms of science, but only into terms of an existential metaphysics. Hence these two immediate consequences: that natural theology is in bondage not to the method of positive science but to the method of metaphysics, and that it can correctly ask its own problems only in the frame of an existential metaphysics.

Of these two conclusions, the first one is doomed to remain very unpopular. To tell the whole truth, it sounds perfectly absurd to say, and ridiculous to maintain, that the highest metaphysical problems in no way depend upon the answers given by science to its own questions. The most common view of this matter is best expressed by these words of a modern astronomer: "Before the philosophers have a right to speak, science ought first to be asked to tell all she can as to ascertain facts and provisional hypotheses. Then, and then only, may discussion legitimately pass into the realms of philosophy." [2] This, I quite agree, looks much more sensible than what I myself have said. But when people behave as if what I have said were false, what does happen? In 1696, John Toland decided to discuss religious problems by a method borrowed from natural philosophy. The result was his book, which I have already mentioned: *Christianity Not Mysterious*. Now, if Christianity is not mysterious, what is? In 1930, in his Rede Lecture delivered before the University of Cambridge, Sir James Jeans decided to deal with philosophical problems in the light of contemporary science. The upshot was his most popular book: *The Mysterious Universe*. Now, if the universe of science is mysterious, what is not? We do not need science to tell us that the universe is indeed mysterious. Men have known that since the very beginning of the human race. The true and proper function of science is, on the contrary, to make as much of the universe as possible grow less and less mysterious to us. Science does it, and she does it magnificently. Any sixteen-year-old boy, in any one of our schools, knows more today about the physical structure of the world than Thomas Aquinas, Aristotle, or Plato ever did. He can give rational

[2] Sir James Jeans, *The Mysterious Universe* (London, Pelican Books, 1937), Foreword, p. vii.

explanations of phenomena which once appeared to the greatest minds as puzzling mysteries. The universe of science *qua* science exactly consists of that part of the total universe from which, owing to human reason, mysteries have been removed.

How is it, then, that a scientist can feel well founded in calling this universe a "mysterious universe"? Is it because the very progress of science brings him face to face with phenomena that are more and more difficult to observe and whose laws are more and more difficult to formulate? But the unknown is not necessarily a mystery; and science naturally proceeds upon the assumption that it is not, because it is at least knowable, even though we do not yet know it. The true reason why this universe appears to some scientists as mysterious is that, mistaking existential, that is, metaphysical, questions for scientific ones, they ask science to answer them. Naturally, they get no answers. Then they are puzzled, and they say that the universe is mysterious.

The scientific cosmogony of Sir James Jeans himself exhibits an instructive collection of such perplexities. His starting point is the actual existence of innumerable stars "wandering about space" at such enormous distances from one another "that it is an event of almost unimaginable rarity for a star to come anywhere near to another star." Yet, we must "believe" that "some two thousand million years ago, this rare event took place, and that a second star, wandering blindly through space," happened to come so near the sun that it raised a huge tidal wave on its surface. This mountainous wave finally exploded, and its fragments, still "circulating around their parent sun . . . are the planets, great and small, of which our earth is one." These ejected fragments of the sun gradually cooled; "in course of time, we know not how, when, or why, one

of these cooling fragments gave birth to life." Hence, the emergence of a stream of life which has culminated in man. In a universe where empty space is deadly cold and most of the matter deadly hot, the emergence of life was highly improbable. Nevertheless, "into such a universe we have stumbled, if not exactly by mistake, at least as the result of what may properly be described as an accident." Such is, Sir James Jeans concludes, "the surprising manner in which, so far as science can at present inform us, we came into being." [3]

That all this is very mysterious everybody will agree, but the question then arises: Is this science? Even if we take them, as their author evidently does, for so many "provisional hypotheses," can we consider such hypotheses as being, in any sense of the word, scientific? Is it scientific to explain the existence of man by a series of accidents, each of which is more improbable than the other one? The truth of the case simply is that on the problem of the existence of man modern astronomy has strictly nothing to say. And the same conclusion holds good if, to modern astronomy, we add modern physics. When, after describing the physical world of Einstein, Heisenberg, Dirac, Lemaître, and Louis de Broglie, he at last takes a dive into what, this time at least, he knows to be "the deep waters" of metaphysics, what conclusion does Sir James Jeans ultimately reach? That although many scientists prefer the notion of a "cyclic universe, the more orthodox scientific view" is that this universe owes its present form to a "creation" and that "its creation must have been an act of thought." [4] Granted. But what have these answers to do with Einstein, Heisenberg, and the justly famous galaxy of modern physicists? The two doctrines of a "cyclical universe" and of a supreme Thought were formulated by pre-Socratic philosophers who knew nothing of what

[3] Sir James Jeans, *op. cit.*, chap. i, pp. 11-22.
[4] *Ibid.*, chap. v, p. 182.

Einstein would say twenty-six centuries after them. "Modern scientific theory," Jeans adds, "compels us to think of the creator as working outside time and space, which are part of his creation, just as the artist is outside his canvas." [5] Why should modern theory compel us to say what has already been said, not only by Saint Augustine, whom our scientist quotes, but by any and every one of countless Christian theologians who knew no other world than that of Ptolemy? Clearly enough, the philosophical answer of Sir James Jeans to the problem of the world order has absolutely nothing to do with modern science. And no wonder, since it has absolutely nothing to do with any scientific knowledge at all.

If we consider it more closely, the initial question asked by Jeans had taken him at once not only into deep waters but, scientifically speaking, out of soundings. To ask the question why, out of an infinity of possible combinations of physicochemical elements, there has arisen the living and thinking being we call man is to seek the cause why such a complex of physical energies as man actually is, or exists. In other words, it is to inquire into the possible causes for the *existence* of living and thinking organisms upon earth. The hypothesis that living substances may tomorrow be produced by biochemists in their laboratories is irrelevant to the question. If a chemist ever succeeds in turning out living cells, or some elementary sorts of organisms, nothing will be easier for him than to say why such organisms exist. His answer will be: I made them. Our own question is not at all: Are living and thinking beings made up of nothing else than physical elements? It rather is: Supposing they ultimately consist of nothing else, how can we account for the *existence* of the very order of molecules which produces what we call life, and thought?

Scientifically speaking, such problems do not make sense. If there were no living and thinking beings, there would be no science. Hence there would be no questions. Even the scientific universe of inorganic matter is a structural universe; as to the world of organic matter, it everywhere exhibits coordination, adaptation, functions. When asked why there are such organized beings, scientists answer: Chance. Now anybody may fluke a brilliant stroke at billiards; but when a billiard player makes a run of a hundred, to say that he fluked it is to offer a rather weak explanation. Some scientists know this so well that they substitute for the notion of chance the notion of mechanical laws, which is its very reverse. But when they come to explaining how these mechanical laws have given rise to living organized beings, they are driven back to chance as to the last reason it is possible to quote. "The powers operating in the cosmos," Julian Huxley says, "are, though unitary, yet subdivisible; and, though subdivisible, yet related. There are the vast powers of inorganic nature, neutral or hostile to man. Yet they gave birth to evolving life, whose development, though blind and fortuitous, has tended in the same general direction as our own conscious desires and ideals, and so gives us an external sanction for our directional activities. This again gave birth to human mind, which, in the race, is changing the course of evolution by acceleration," [6] and so on, ad infinitum. In other words, the only scientific reasons why our billiard player makes a run of a hundred are that he cannot play billiards and that all the chances are against it.

If scientists, speaking as scientists, have no intelligible answer to this problem, why are some of them so keen on talking

---

[5] *Ibid.*, chap. v, p. 183.

[6] Julian Huxley, "Rationalism and the Idea of God," in *Essays of a Biologist*, chap. vi (London, Pelican Books, 1939), p. 176.

nonsense about it? The reason is simple, and this time we can be sure that chance has nothing to do with their obstinacy. They prefer to say anything rather than to ascribe existence to God on the ground that a purpose exists in the universe. Now there is some justification for their attitude. Just as science can play havoc with metaphysics, metaphysics can play havoc with science. Coming before science in the past, it has often done so to the point of preventing its rise and of blocking its development. For centuries final causes have been mistaken for scientific explanations by so many generations of philosophers that today many scientists still consider the fear of final causes as the beginning of scientific wisdom. Science is thus making metaphysics suffer for its centuries-long meddling in matters of physics and biology.

In both cases, however, the real victim of this epistemological strife is one and the same: the human mind. Nobody denies that living organisms appear as though they had been designed, or intended, to fulfill the various functions related to life. Everybody agrees that this appearance may be but an illusion. We would be bound to hold it for an illusion if science could account for the rise of life by its usual explanations of mechanical type, where nothing more is involved than the relations of observable phenomena according to the geometrical properties of space and the physical laws of motion. What is most remarkable, on the contrary, is that many scientists obstinately maintain the illusory character of this appearance though they freely acknowledge their failure to imagine any scientific explanation for the organic constitution of living beings. As soon as modern physics had reached the structural problems raised by molecular physics, it found itself confronted with such difficulties. Yet scientists much preferred to introduce into physics the nonmechanical notions of discontinuity and indeterminacy rather than resort to anything like design. On a much larger scale, we have seen Julian Huxley boldly account for the existence of organized bodies by those very properties of matter which, according to himself, make it infinitely improbable that such bodies should ever exist. Why should those eminently rational beings, the scientists, deliberately prefer to the simple notions of design, or purposiveness, in nature, the arbitrary notions of blind force, chance, emergence, sudden variation, and similar ones? Simply because they much prefer a complete absence of intelligibility to the presence of a nonscientific intelligibility.

We seem to be here reaching at last the very core of this epistemological problem. Unintelligible as they are, these arbitrary notions are at least homogeneous with a chain of mechanical interpretations. Posited at the beginning of such a chain, or inserted in it where they are needed, they provide the scientist with the very existences which he needs in order to have something to know. Their very irrationality is expressive of the invincible resistance opposed by existence to any type of scientific explanation. By accepting design, or purposiveness, as a possible principle of explanation, a scientist would introduce into his system of laws a ring wholly heterogeneous with the rest of the chain. He would intertwine the metaphysical causes for the existence of organisms with the physical causes which he must assign to both their structure and their functioning. Still worse, he might feel tempted to mistake the existential causes of living organisms for their efficient and physical causes, thus coming back to the good old times when fishes had fins because they had been made to swim. Now it may well be true that fishes have been made to swim, but when we know it we know just as much about fishes as we know about airplanes when we know that they are made to fly. If they had not been made to fly, there would be no airplanes, since to be flying-machines is their very definition; but it takes us at least two sciences, aerodynamics and mechanics, in order to know how they do fly. A final cause has posited an existence whose science alone can posit the laws.

This heterogeneity of these two orders was strikingly expressed by Francis Bacon, when he said, speaking of final causes, that "in physics, they are impertinent, and as remoras to the ship, that hinder the sciences from holding their course of improvement." [7] Their scientific sterility is particularly complete in a world like that of modern science, where essences have been reduced to mere phenomena, themselves reduced to the order of that which can be observed. Modern scientists live, or they pretend to live, in a world of mere appearances, where that which appears is the appearance of nothing. Yet the fact that final causes are scientifically sterile does not entail their disqualification as metaphysical causes, and to reject metaphysical answers to a problem just because they are not scientific is deliberately to maim the knowing power of the human mind. If the only intelligible way to explain the existence of organized bodies is to admit that there is design, purposiveness, at their origin, then let us admit it, if not as scientists, at least as metaphysicians. And since the notions of design and of purpose are for us inseparable from the notion of thought, to posit the existence of a thought as cause of the purposiveness of organized bodies is also to posit an end of all ends, or an ultimate end, that is, God.

It goes without saying that this is the very consequence which the adversaries of final causes intend to deny. "Purpose," Julian Huxley says, "is a psychological term; and to ascribe purpose to a process merely because its results are somewhat similar to those of a true purposeful process is completely unjustified, and a mere projection of our own ideas into the economy of nature." [8] This is most certainly what we do, but why should we not do so? We do not need to *project* our own ideas into the economy of nature; they belong there in their own right. Our own ideas are in the economy of nature because we ourselves are in it. Any and every one of the things which a man does intelligently is done with a purpose and to a certain end which is the final cause why he does it. Whatever a worker, an engineer, an industrialist, a writer, or an artist makes is but the actualization, by intelligently selected means, of a certain end. There is no known example of a self-made machine spontaneously arising in virtue of the mechanical laws of matter. Through man, who is part and parcel of nature, purposiveness most certainly is part and parcel of nature. In what sense then is it arbitrary, knowing from within that where there is organization there always is a purpose, to conclude that there is a purpose wherever there is organization? I fully understand a scientist who turns down such an inference as wholly non-scientific. I also understand a scientist who tells me that, as a scientist, he has no business to draw any inference as to the possible cause why organized bodies actually exist. But I wholly fail to see in what sense my inference, if I choose to draw it, is "a common fallacy."

Why should there be a fallacy in inferring that there is purpose in the universe on the ground of biological progress? Because, Julian Huxley answers, this "can be shown to be as natural and inevitable a product of the struggle for existence as is adaptation, and to be no more mysterious than, for instance, the increase in effectiveness both of armour-piercing projectile and armour-plate during the last century." [9]

---

[7] Francis Bacon, *The Dignity and Advancement of Learning*, Bk. III, chap. iv, ed. J. E. Creighton (New York: The Colonial Press, 1900), p. 97.

[8] Julian Huxley, *op. cit.*, chap. vi, p. 173.

[9] *Ibid.*, p. 172.

Does Julian Huxley suggest that steel plates have spontaneously grown thicker as shells were growing heavier during the last century? In other words, does he maintain that purposiveness is as wholly absent from human industry as it is from the rest of the world? Or does he perhaps maintain that the rest of the world is as full of purposiveness as human industry obviously is? In the name of science he maintains both, namely, that adaptations in organisms are no more mysterious where there is no purposiveness to account for them, than is adaptation in human industry where purposiveness everywhere accounts for it. That adaptations due to a purpose*less* struggle for life are no more mysterious than adaptations due to a purpose*ful* struggle—whether this proposition is "a common fallacy," I do not know, but it certainly seems to be a fallacy. It is the fallacy of a scientist who, because he does not know how to ask metaphysical problems, obstinately refuses their correct metaphysical answers. In the *Inferno* of the world of knowledge, there is a special punishment for this sort of sin; it is the relapse into mythology. Better known as a distinguished zoologist, Julian Huxley must also be credited with having added the god Struggle to the already large family of Olympians.

A world which has lost the Christian God cannot but resemble a world which had not yet found him. Just like the world of Thales and of Plato, our own modern world is "full of gods." There are blind Evolution, clear-sighted Orthogenesis, benevolent Progress, and others which it is more advisable not to mention by name. Why unnecessarily hurt the feelings of men who, today, render them a cult? It is however important for us to realize that mankind is doomed to live more and more under the spell of a new scientific, social, and political mythology, unless we resolutely exorcise these befuddled notions whose influence on modern life is becoming appalling. Millions of men are starving and bleeding to death because two or three of these pseudo-scientific or pseudosocial deified abstractions are now at war. For when gods fight among themselves, men have to die. Could we not make an effort to realize that evolution is to be largely what we will make it to be? That Progress is not an automatically self-achieving law but something to be patiently achieved by the will of men? That Equality is not an actually given fact but an ideal to be progressively approached by means of justice? That Democracy is not the leading goddess of some societies but a magnificent promise to be fulfilled by all through their obstinate will for friendship, if they are strong enough to make it last for generations after generations?

I think we could, but a good deal of clear thinking should come first, and this is where, in spite of its proverbial helplessness, philosophy might be of some help. The trouble with so many of our contemporaries is not that they are agnostics but rather that they are misguided theologians. Real agnostics are exceedingly rare, and they harm nobody but themselves. Just as they have no God, these have no gods. Much more common, unfortunately, are those pseudo-agnostics who, because they combine scientific knowledge and social generosity with a complete lack of philosophical culture, substitute dangerous mythologies for the natural theology which they do not even understand.

The problem of final causes is perhaps the problem most commonly discussed by these modern agnostics. As such, it particularly recommended itself to our attention. It is nevertheless only one among the many aspects of the highest of all metaphysical problems, that of Being. Beyond the question: Why are there organized beings? lies this deeper one, which I am asking in Leibniz's own terms: Why is there something rather than nothing? Here again, I fully understand a scientist who refuses to ask it.

313

He is welcome to tell me that the question does not make sense. Scientifically speaking, it does not. Metaphysically speaking, however, it does. Science can account for many things in the world; it may some day account for all that which the world of phenomena actually is. But why anything at all is, or exists, science knows not, precisely because it cannot even ask the question.

To this supreme question, the only conceivable answer is that each and every particular existential energy, each and every particular existing thing, depends for its existence upon a pure Act of existence. In order to be the ultimate answer to all existential problems, this supreme cause has to be absolute existence. Being absolute, such a cause is self-sufficient; if it creates, its creative act must be free. Since it creates not only being but order, it must be something which at least eminently contains the only principle of order known to us in experience, namely, thought. Now an absolute, self-subsisting, and knowing cause is not an It but a He. In short, the first cause is the One in whom the cause of both nature and history coincide, a philosophical God who can also be the God of a religion.

To go one step further would be to match the mistake of some agnostics with a similar one. The failure of too many metaphysicians to distinguish between philosophy and religion has proved no less harmful to natural theology than have the encroachments of pseudometaphysical science. Metaphysics posits God as a pure Act of existence, but it does not provide us with any concept of His essence. We know that He is; we do not comprehend Him. Simple-minded metaphysicians have unwillingly led agnostics to believe that the God of natural theology was the "watchmaker" of Voltaire, or the "carpenter" of cheap apologetics. First of all, no watch has ever been made by any watchmaker; "watchmakers" as such simply do not exist; watches are made by men who know how to make watches. Similarly, to posit God as the supreme cause of that which is, is to know that He is He who can create, because He is "He who is"; but this tells us still less concerning what absolute existence can be than any piece of carpentry tells us about the man who made it. Being men, we can affirm God only on anthropomorphic grounds, but this does not oblige us to posit Him as an anthropomorphic God. As Saint Thomas Aquinas says:

The verb *to be* is used in two different ways: in a first one, it signifies the act of existing (*actu essendi*); in the second one it signifies the composition of those propositions which the soul invents by joining a predicate with a subject. Taking *to be* in the first way, we cannot know the "to be" of God (*esse Dei*), no more than we know His essence. We know it in the second way only. For, indeed, we know that the proposition we are forming about God, when we say: God is, is a true proposition, and we know this from His effects.[10]

If such be the God of natural theology, true metaphysics does not culminate in a concept, be it that of Thought, of Good, of One, or of Substance. It does not even culminate in an essence, be it that of Being itself. Its last word is not *ens*, but *esse;* not *being*, but *is*. The ultimate effort of true metaphysics is to posit an Act by an act, that is, to posit by an act of judging the supreme Act of existing whose very essence, because it is to be, passes human understanding. Where a man's metaphysics comes to an end, his religion begins. But the only path which can lead him to the point where the true religion begins must of necessity lead him beyond the contemplation of essences, up to the very mystery of existence. This path is not very hard to find, but few are those who dare to

---

[10] Saint Thomas Aquinas, *Summa theologica,* Pars I, qu. 3, art. 4, ad 2ᵐ.

follow it to the end. Seduced as they are by the intelligible beauty of science, many men lose all taste for metaphysics and religion. A few others, absorbed in the contemplation of some supreme cause, become aware that metaphysics and religion should ultimately meet, but they cannot tell how or where; hence they separate religion from philosophy, or else they renounce religion for philosophy, if they do not, like Pascal, renounce philosophy for religion. Why should not we keep truth, and keep it whole? It can be done. But only those can do it who realize that He Who is the God of the philosophers is HE WHO IS, the God of Abraham, of Isaac, and of Jacob.

KARL HEIM

Faith and the Idolatries of Science*

PART I

God and the Absolutes of Science

Some time ago, one of our leading scientists, Pascual Jordan, one of the first exponents of quantum mechanics, wrote as follows: 'We are not living in an age of religious fruitfulness—we have neither a Luther nor a Francis. Nor are we living in an age of artistic fruitfulness. In the outlook of modern man there is only one spiritual phenomenon characteristic of our age and at the same time of unqualified magnitude and power. Our epoch has found the authentic symbol of its inner struggle in the researches of natural science.' . . . We propose to look at this mighty spiritual phenomenon, of which Pascual Jordan spoke, exclusively in the light of the question about God.

If one asks what is the bearing on the question about God of the transformation of the scientific view of the world with which we are confronted today, one receives as a rule this kind of answer. Even in natural science, we are near the end of atheism, near to the 'liquidation of materialism' such as governed scientific thought in the days of Ernst Haeckel or Virchow. The collapse of a causal-mechanical world picture has again made room for God. Well-known scientists have committed themselves to the view that the marvelous constitution of the world's structure not only permits the inference of an intelligent Creator but invites such an inference. It is widely held, therefore, that the significance of the current transformation in the scientific world view is this: that the line of approach from nature to God which was pursued by men to the Enlightenment and Rationalism, but which was blocked in the age of causal mechanism, is now open again following upon the breakdown of the causal-mechanical world-view. Is this a true perception of the meaning of the prodigious events which concern us here?

* Part I is from *The Transformation of the Scientific World View,* pp. 16-26, 200-206, and Part II is from *Christian Faith and Natural Science,* pp. 163-64, 167, 169-71, both by Karl Heim and used by permission of Harper & Row and the SCM Press.

If we are to deal with this question with firm ground beneath our feet, not, that is to say, by trusting to our own insecure experience, but by attending to the Bible, we shall have to reckon with an impressive passage in the first chapter of the Epistle to the Romans, where we are told that we have no excuse if we repudiate a knowledge of God from His works. . . . 'For what can be known about God is plain to them, because God has shown it to them.' The question is this. Does Paul mean that since the creation of the world, God has made Himself so clearly known uninterruptedly in His created works, that we incur inexcusable guilt if we do not see the Creator, and therefore consider Him to be unreal? Is this passage dealing in fact with the denial of God as the intrinsic guilt of the heathen world? This exposition of the Pauline passage is the one adopted almost universally today among celebrated theologians (for instance, Paul Althaus, *Der Brief an die Römer,* p. 14, Göttingen, 1933). It is the one which naturally occurs to us on a first reading of verse 18. If, therefore, we venture to deviate from this customary interpretation, it will be necessary to establish carefully the ground for such deviation. The main reason for it is the only one to be advanced here. It is found in the context in which the sentence occurs. It so happens that what we call atheism is not mentioned again in the whole of the rest of the chapter, and therefore that the idea we expect is not further developed, namely that man is guilty of gross self-delusion if he represses a conclusion which his intellect is bound to draw when he studies nature, and thereby heedlessly ignores a manifest and obvious reality. This atheism, of which there were sporadic representatives among the philosophers even in the time of Paul, is certainly not the matter under discussion. The inexcusable guilt which Paul says the heathen have incurred is that of a tremendous confusion (note

the Greek words *allattein* and *metallattein*); the confusion or exchange of some part of the visible transient creation with the invisible intransient eternal God. The guilt of which Paul here accuses the heathen is that of making a confusion between two realities which are in conflict with one another and can never be brought into line, which confusion and interchange brings our whole thought and life into hopeless chaos. Paul subsequently illustrates this by reference to the fatal aberration in sexual life which comes to expression in homosexuality in the case of both men and women. Paul's use of this illustration shows precisely and clearly that the guilt of which he speaks consists in the confusion of things which may never be exchanged for one another without creating a chaotic situation.

The radical denial of God which is familiar to us today did indeed come to occasional expression in antiquity. Think, for instance, of Lucretius and his disciples. But this late product of classical culture could never have merited so explicit a refutation as is here deemed necessary by Paul. Atheism was as remote from the broad mass of men in that age as it is from the average citizen in India or Japan today. The men of that time were not atheists; they were religious to a degree. Paul says as much to them in Acts 17:23, where he is impressed by the wealth of temples and the costly cultus which Athens boasted at the Parthenon. . . .

The Old Testament does not range itself against doubt about God or against godlessness. This plays only a small part in the Old Testament. 'The fool,' it observes, 'says in his heart; there is no God.' But it does range itself with all passion against that Absolute which would put itself alongside God. Such an Absolute alongside God is, for instance, the human self, which puts itself on the throne and prescribes for itself autonomously the law of its conduct. Another Absolute is an absolute human ruler, not appointed by God. Every such Absolute takes away from God a measure of his own absoluteness. God, according to Luther's declaration, is that wherein we place our entire confidence, that which is our sole refuge in all our need, that which we should love with all our heart and soul and strength and all our powers. If there is a second Absolute, set alongside God, it takes out of our hearts some part of the sovereign power of God, some part of the unconditional confidence and entire love which we owe to God. According to Luther, therefore, to believe in such an Absolute is not mere godlessness, but a movement of rebellion against God, and therefore an alliance with an idol.

If this is correct, then we have to do with the question of God and of the opposition between him and every kind of idolatry which seeks to demolish His sole Lordship, not merely in the history of religion, but over all fields of experience and enquiry including philosophy and natural science. Thus there is not simply a direct way which leads up to God from natural events, the *via causalitatis* pursued by the older apologists. This direct way leads, not to God, but to a higher form of divinized creature. The only way which really leads to God is the indirect, or negative way. This indirect way is marked by the collapse, over all fields of life and thought, of the Absolutes which stand as hindrances in the way of God's sole Lordship. An illustration of what is involved can be drawn from the world powers which rise one after another out of the sea of world history, as the Book of Daniel indicates; each one, as it comes to the zenith of its power, is tempted to divinize its ruler. As soon as they reach this point, they stand in the way of God's sole Lordship. The road to faith in the true God proceeds then not only by the believing man seeing through this glorification of the ruler beforehand as the divinizing of a creature; God's sole Lordship and complete sovereignty may come

to expression in even stronger form, in the fact that these great powers rise one after another from the sea of history, and sink back into it just as quickly after their short flowering. This repeated collapse of every earthly imperialism is the most impressive demonstration of the fact that no divinization of any earthly power can stand, that every absolutizing of any earthly absolute always carries within itself the seeds of death. God sets up His throne on the wreckage of human earthly thrones, and the history of the world is strewn with the wreckage of demolished imperialisms and smashed altars, whose debris reveals impressively the sole Lordship of God.

We can carry over this law which obtains in world history in another form into the field of natural science. Wherever, in the description of nature, an absolute is posited; wherever a magnitude is postulated which needs no other magnitude through which it exists, but which exists only through itself, or wherever a form of existence is presupposed which needs no other form of existence to which it is relative, but which has validity solely through itself, there faith breaks into scientific description, though the word 'faith' or the word 'God' does not occur. For the subjective function fulfilled by such an absolute is that mentioned by Luther in the Large Catechism, when he speaks of that in which we trust unconditionally and to which we wholly commit ourselves. This function of unconditional trust is not only possible with respect to an indivisible personality whom we portray to ourselves as a Father enthroned in heaven. It can also come into play with respect to a magnitude which can only be expressed abstractly.

An illustration can be given of how such a mathematical magnitude can take on a religious character. The plan which an architect produces rests on the assumption that the axioms of Euclidean geometry, and of the statics which depend on it, are absolutely valid. If the validity of these axioms were to be shattered; if, for instance, the statement were open to question that the shortest distance between two points is the straight line joining them, and if in fact the shortest distance between them were a curved line (as is the case in spherical space), then the whole calculation of building materials necessary for the job would have to be altered, and the estimated cost would be different from what was originally planned. The architect, therefore, must include in his reckoning a factor which is not proved but has to be accepted in faith, if all his calculations are not to be based on mere chance. The geometrical axioms and the laws of statics bound up with them are not capable of further proof. They must, however, hold for the future which as yet we cannot see. Every proof of these fundamental assumptions is a vicious circle, assuming in the end the validity of what it purports to prove. Gifted but hypercritical master-builders, like the one who built the tower of Ulm Cathedral, have sometimes experienced a real struggle for faith by reason of the insecurity of these fundamentals. They have had sleepless nights, contemplating the catastrophe that must follow if their calculations contained an insecure factor. From this it is evident that wherever an absolute factor has to be accepted, in the description of nature or in calculations, what is fundamentally a religious faith breaks into scientific reckoning. It is necessary to put one's confidence in some absolute or other. The ultimate object of this confidence can only be either God, who is alone capable of giving us an eternal anchorage, or an idol, which tears us down into the abyss.

Now at last we are able to answer the question which has been in view through all these considerations. What is the significance of the inner transformation which has taken place in contemporary natural science, if that transformation be considered not merely from the point of view of scholarship, but in relation to the question of God? Wherein does the revolution consist which has taken place before our eyes in modern science, particularly in physics? Manifestly in a 'twilight of the gods', involving on a large scale one after another of the absolutes which have held their own unquestioned for centuries. They have collapsed together, and not by reason of any theoretical reflections of the kind which were advanced in the earlier period of scepticism and relativism, but rather through facts of experience verified experimentally and not to be denied, although they were in clear contradiction to dogmatic principles with which men had hitherto approached the study of nature, and although the experiments by which they were established were of an unlooked-for kind.

Three such absolutes are pre-eminently involved. The first is the *absolute object,* by which I mean the hypothesis that there is an objective matter of fact which has a completely determinate structure and constitution, completely independent of any other subject, and therefore independent of the point of view of an observer or experimenter.

The second is *absolute space* and *absolute time*. This was the ultimate hypothesis upon which the whole of classical physics was built according to Newton's fundamental work.

The third is the *absolute determination of the world process,* by which I mean the hypothesis that the course of world events is absolutely established because it is subject to the universally valid law of causality, according to which one event follows necessarily from preceding events. According to Laplace, an omniscient spirit, capable of seeing nature in its entirety at any moment, could argue backwards to everything which has ever happened, and predict exactly everything which is yet to happen.

We know instinctively that these three

absolutes are of decisive importance for the question of God. If any one of them were to be invalidated, it would seem to us at first glance as though the whole universe and all its ordinances had been imperilled as though by an earthquake. If there is no absolute object, and everything we see is conditioned by the subject, then there is nothing in which we can put our unconditional trust. We can never make a statement expressing something which is true of all things and can claim universal validity. Real life and dreams fuse together suddenly, and there is nothing constant to which we can hold fast.

The same is true of the second absolute, absolute space and absolute time. Only if we live in a space whose measure and regularities are fixed do we feel really safe in this world. It is not an accident that the medieval Church could accept the Copernican revolution without resistance, for that revolution only involved new courses for the stars within the same fixed universal space as before. Space and time themselves kept their measure and order. It was not until Giordano Bruno's attack on space itself, which implied that it had no centre and therefore no boundaries, that the Church felt the blow as of an earthquake which made its foundations tremble. The man who entertained this foolhardy notion must die at the stake, a danger to the Church and a menace to faith in God.

The destruction of the old conviction that the course of events is absolutely determined by the law of causality is equally serious. Oswald Spengler realized the strong religious importance of this fundamental conviction. He took it to be the profane expression of the elementary fact which faith intends to affirm when it clings to predestination in face of all possible doubts. This religious determinism is rendered precarious once the law of causation loses its unconditional significance. . . .

And in what has been said it has be-come clear that wherever the mysterious and comprehensive notion of the absolute is employed, whether in a theoretical or practical sense, we are confronted with the question of God. In the last resort there are only two kinds of men, two points of view, two kinds of conviction, which are opposed to one another: those for which there is an absolute, and those who know only relative values and realities. In respect of this ultimate Either/Or, all other antitheses are secondary. In respect of this fundamental antithesis which divides the spirits, all other differences in meaning have only a relative significance. . . .

"Beyond Scientific Space": The Space of Finite Consciousness

If we look back over the conclusions which have been reached in the three previous sections, we see how it has become clear to us from one side after another why natural science, at the highly developed stage which it has now reached, stands at a frontier of its theoretical possibilities. This awareness of a frontier does not arise from the fact that there are further regions which must still be regarded as *terra incognita* for whose illumination we need better microscopes and better telescopes, nor from the fact that future generations of specialized research workers must continue to collect observations and make experiments and draw conclusions. Such a frontier of knowledge would be purely relative, and with each year it would be broken through. The frontier of which we are now aware is an absolute frontier, imposed by the nature of the case. It arises from the fact that the whole of exact natural research, with all its appropriate methods, lies within the limits of a particular space, within which all being and all happening must be ordered and beyond which we cannot see and shall not be able to see, even though the mirror of the latest American telescope were capable of reflecting all the spiral nebulae in the universe or if

319

the latest electronic microscope should reach down to the as yet unattainable molecular dimensions. The only space which can be brought within our field of view is the space of objectivity. And our own existence, from which we cannot escape, reminds us every moment that the space of objectivity is only a partial aspect of the world and that reality has other sides of which we cannot give an objective representation. This other side of the world is too near to us for us to be able to stand away from it and bring it into focus on the photographic plate of our world-picture. And yet we know of its existence. We are entrusted with it as directly as we are with everything that enters into our intuitive picture. This non-intuitive space chiefly relates to the place where I myself stand, when the objective world in all its measureless expanse unfolds before my gaze like a brilliantly colored panorama or an exciting film. This place is, at the same time, the point of origin from which I am able to intervene responsibly in the small area of reality which is open to my influence. The objective space has thereby come to receive an invisible foreground, a region from which it is visible much as a lighted stage is visible from the auditorium. But to this invisible foreground of the objective world there is also added an invisible background. For, in dealing with my fellow men, I am driven, as we saw earlier, by inescapable analogical reasoning to the hypothesis that my fellow men are not soulless automata. It is plain, on the contrary, that behind the objective appearance of their bodies, which is all that I am able to perceive, there stands an 'I', which is no more perceptible than my own 'I', but which stands in the same relation to the body which is sitting before me and speaking as does my 'I' to my body. Thus, with all the techniques of natural science which are available to me, I cannot discover a single clue to the existence of this knowing and willing 'I' which

320

belongs to my fellow man's body. To take an X-ray of his body or to operate upon it and lay bare its inner constitution and submit all its parts to microscopic examination, would be of no avail. I should never be brought to entertain the idea that behind the cerebral cortex and the electric currents which it radiates through nerve channels to the muscles over a system which extends to the furthest parts of a flesh-covered skeleton there may be something other than all that is directly observed and that enters into an anatomical analysis. I have this notion because, at the one point where I can see directly into the invisible background of the world— the point at which I myself act and suffer—the invisible 'I' which eludes every category of medical research is given to me as a reality which is more real than all visible corporeality. Therefore, if I wish to avoid the 'toll-house point of view' of solipsism, which is so alien to reality, I am bound to conclude that behind the outward show offered to me by the body of my fellow man there is an inward spectacle analogous to my own 'I', even though it is hidden from my observing eye. Once I have drawn this analogical conclusion about my fellow men, I shall be further impelled, as we also saw earlier, to regard animals also, and indeed all organic beings, as something other than soulless automata whose existence is exhausted in their objective outward show. These beings would not be engaging in such a desperate battle for light and air and living space against their enemies, had they not been placed, as I have, by a necessity of destiny which arises out of nonperceptible depths, in a position which they are obliged to defend even as I am obliged to defend my own. I must therefore suppose that there is an inner life behind non-human organisms, one which is indeed utterly different from our human thinking and willing but which, when it comes to the crucial point, has something in common with us. But now because, as we shall see in a moment, it is suggested by the present state of research that there is an equivalence of structure between single-celled organisms and the molecules of the physicist, of a kind which eliminates the difference between the organic and the inorganic worlds, the 'principle of continuity' suggests the idea that an inner life may stand behind the elementary structures of inorganic reality, one which is still further removed from our human life of soul than is the inner life of plants, but one which we must assume to be there if the parallelism between an objective outward show and a non-objective inner spectacle is not to be broken at an entirely arbitrary point. If we follow this line of thought to its conclusion, we shall come to the hypothesis that the world of objective space, which is the object of attention in natural science, has not only an invisible foreground, viz. the unobjectifiable 'I' which observes the brightly lit film of objective reality as from a darkened seat in the stalls, but that it also has an invisible background. This will be the inner life which we are driven to postulate behind the outward show, which alone is visible, of both organic and inorganic processes. . . .

From this point of view the limits of natural science which have appeared in the course of the last three sections become intelligible. Research which is directed exclusively to what can be established objectively is bound to overlook two magnitudes which belong to the very substance of reality as a whole: the invisible foreground and the invisible background. All that it can take into account is the third magnitude, stretched between these two like a visible screen which carries projections from both sides. What comes into our field of view is thus an abstraction which holds together the two realities belonging necessarily to the total picture. This brings us at once to a frontier of knowledge at two distinct points. The first

point is revealed by the question: What is the object of natural knowledge? What is the essence of the world's substance? What is matter? If we abstract from the invisible background which manifests itself through the medium, the question about the deepest essence of the reality we have to do with can never be really answered. For always we see only the frontal aspect which this reality presents to us; the background remains hidden. We are sharply reminded of this when matter, the fundamental element to which we are led by objective contemplation of the world, itself becomes a problem for scientific theory, since it has been shown not to be something at rest in itself and existing through itself but rather to consist of fundamental particles whose continual transformations work out the effects of causes unknown to the particles themselves. At this point, therefore, we begin to feel that in matter something is manifesting itself which is not accessible to any objective observation. The second point where the limit of objective natural knowledge must be admitted, has to do with the relationship between the objective picture of nature and the invisible foreground across which it necessarily comes into our field of vision. Once the process of research destroyed the absoluteness of measurement and related motions, science was obliged to take seriously the mystery of 'placing' by 'destiny', whose origin lies in unknown depths, but apart from which all our measurements and calculations remain relative, and which serves to supply us with an origin or perspective for our world-picture. Thus both the foreground and the background . . . have come to be taken seriously. From these two points there arises a third where we know ourselves to stand on the frontier of objective study of nature. We feel the presence of the frontier when we regard reality not simply as a static picture but rather as . . . something which is happening. The question arises whether the course of events is fixed once for all by some determination, or whether it is an interplay between various possible tendencies which contribute to what shall be. As long as we remain unaware of the invisible background of reality, and therefore think that we have probed the world to its roots by getting down to fixed fundamental particles, what happens will seem to us to be a causal mechanism whose details can all be calculated and where the various parts move like wheels in a thoroughly intelligible clock. The Laplace picture of causal predictability expressed in the strongest possible form the sole sovereignty of the objective attitude to the world, in which both the invisible foreground and the magic glimpse into the invisible background were ruthlessly eliminated from the mind. But as soon as the firm bricks which had been taken to be the original components of the world-stuff dissolved into interchangeable systems, we found ourselves standing at a third point on the frontier of natural knowledge. For the fundamental processes, from whose cumulative effects the whole of macroscopic events are built, turned out to be something a-causal, something beyond the range of scientific explanation, arising from invisible origins and backgrounds.

PART II

"Beyond Scientific Space":
The Space of God

The men of the Old Testament, and, independently of them, primitive tribesmen becoming aware of the presence of God for the very first time, could always find only one form in which to express the mystery of the invisible divine omnipresence. This form is space. For only a space in which we are situated is really inescapable. We can escape from any reality, any person or any thing, which is contained within a space, simply by removing ourselves to another

part of the space, where this person or thing is not present. It is only the space itself that we cannot escape. Go where we may, we shall still run into it. That is why there is no other form of expression for the presence of the inescapable God than space.

But this cannot be the three-dimensional observable space in which for the time being we find ourselves situated. For, as it says in the Old Testament, we cannot see God and live. It follows that there must be some second space, just as all-present as the three-dimensional space but completely unobservable. If we become conscious of this fact, then a 'space-discovery' has occurred, still more fraught with consequences than was the quasi-Copernican revolution which had previously led to the discovery of the non-objective I-Thou space. . . .

[A space is] a *relation* into which a reality enters with respect to me, the percipient subject. In [an earlier] chapter we spoke of language as illustrating this relation, in that it is the means whereby a book enters into a relation with us, when, after appearing in a number of other languages, it is translated into our own. Just as the language is not the substance of the book itself, but the form in which this substance reveals itself to a certain group of readers, so too the suprapolar space, in which God is present for us, is not the reality of God itself. This ultimate reality remains that which is 'wholly other', totally incomprehensible and entirely inaccessible to our thought and observation. It confronts us neither as an object, in the way in which solid objects are disclosed to us, nor as a Thou, in the sense in which the I and the Thou confront one another in the polar space. When we speak of the suprapolar space, we cannot be referring to the eternal reality of God itself, but only to one aspect, a side which is turned towards us, the only side from which God can be accessible to us, to you and me, if

He is willing to disclose Himself to us at all. . . .

Each space possesses a structure which is fundamentally different from the structures of all other spaces. Consequently, any two spaces are separated from one another by an immense gulf. We need only consider the antithesis between the ego-space and the objective space. And yet these two spaces belong so closely together that they can only be distinguished by means of an abstraction.

It is only when this mysterious law which governs relations between spaces is applied to the connexion between the polar and the suprapolar space that we can understand the paradoxical fact, to which the Bible repeatedly refers, that God, whom no man can see, and who, as the Creator, is distinguished from all created things by an infinite qualitative dissimilarity, is nevertheless at the same time, everywhere and at every point in the world, inescapably near. If what we have here is two spaces, each of which embraces the whole universe but each in a quite different aspect, then a clear meaning is given to Max Planck's dictum: 'Our impulse to gain knowledge demands a unified view of the world and therefore requires that the two powers should be identified with one another which are everywhere effective and yet still mysterious, namely the world order of natural science and the God of religion. This would mean that the Deity, which the religious person endeavours to conceive with the aid of his outward and visible symbols, is essentially the same as the power which is present in the laws of nature, the power which the enquirer's sense impressions to some extent make known to him.'[1]

But it is not merely the paradoxical 'identifiability' of the two extremely different regions referred to here by Planck that becomes comprehensible only when we 'think in spaces'. The same is true of the fact from which we set out at the very beginning of this section, the fact which repeatedly troubles us in the present-day conflict of beliefs, namely that the world of God, the world in which he who believes and prays is rooted with every fibre of his heart, the world which alone remains when all earthly things fade away, 'the sweetest and the surest, the noblest of all treasures', the world which for the believer is infinitely more real than the whole visible world together, for secularist man this world is simply not there. For him it is no more than an empty phantom, and he could swear that there is nothing whatever behind it and never can be anything. One cannot help asking how it is possible that two human beings, both belonging to the same genus *homo sapiens*, should confront one another with such an absolute lack of mutual understanding. This too we can understand only if we 'think in spaces'. As we have seen, it is a peculiar characteristic of the relation between any two spaces that they belong inseparably together and yet each is hermetically sealed off from the other. Neither of the two spaces stands directly open with respect to the other in such a way that it can make itself immediately manifest within it.

It is true that we are all at every moment situated simultaneously in all the spaces which together constitute the 'universe of spaces' (das All der Räume); for whenever there is disclosed to us the existence of a space which had previously been concealed from us, we know from the very first moment that this space has not just come into being, but that it had always surrounded us without our noticing it. Yet, nevertheless, we are not ourselves able to force open the gate which leads to a space that has so far been closed to us. Whenever we experience the discovery of a space, this discovery always simply falls

[1] Max Planck, *Religion und Naturwissenschaft* (Religion and Science), 1947, p. 33.

into our laps as a gift. It is a transformation which takes place in the depths of our existence and which we cannot ourselves bring about by force. It is as when one who has been born blind receives the gift of sight, so that a world with quite new dimensions is suddenly accorded to him as a boon from heaven. This is true already of the first space-discovery, the disclosure of the non-observable world of the subjective encounters. Fichte once said that when a child pronounces the word 'I' for the first time, after always having spoken of itself only in the third person, this is a greater and more far-reaching event than its bodily birth had been. Until now it had been living only in the objective It-space. But now the gate has been forced open which leads to a new space, the world of the I. What is said here about the I-space is even truer with regard to the final and decisive space-discovery, the realization that, while we are encompassed on all sides by the temporal world, we stand at the same time even now in the midst of eternity and are enclosed within the archetypal space (*Urraum*) of God. We cannot free ourselves by means of our own reason or our own strength from the secularist state of mind in which we are blind to the space of eternity and live confined within the endless prison of the polar space. Some event must supervene which we cannot ourselves bring about, so that, as it were, the scales suddenly fall from our eyes.

HAROLD K. SCHILLING

The Significance of Science for Religious Thought*

I

Our question is whether or not contemporary science has any significance for religious thought, and more specifically, whether its world view may have any bearing on the problem of how we shall think of God.

Until rather recently this kind of question would have seemed superfluous, if not downright impertinent, to many people, for to anyone who "believed in God" it seemed obvious that since He created the world, many aspects of His nature must necessarily be discernible through His handiwork. Indeed, there flourished then a branch of Christian thought, called natural theology, devoted in large part to inferring or even "proving" God's existence, as well as His attributes, from man's knowledge of nature.

Today that approach is suspect. At least in Protestant circles it is widely regarded as inadequate and undesirable. For one thing, in retrospect its "proofs" now seem utterly unconvincing. For another, the God it conceived now looks more like the far distant, aloof, inactive God of deism than the near, living and loving God of the Bible. Moreover, from its point of view, the theology that

* From the monograph "On the Significance of Science for Religious Thought" by Harold K. Schilling, copyright 1964. Reprinted by permission of the author and the Board of Education of The Methodist Church.

took as its point of departure the revelatory event of the Christ often seemed incongruous and intellectually embarrassing. In turn from the point of view of "revelation theology" it seemed to miss the main point of the gospel and therefore to be largely irrelevant, or even erroneous.

So it came about that natural theology was banished almost completely from Protestant thought. It now begins to look, however, as though this has not turned out to be an unmixed blessing. For one consequence of it has been that many theologians seem to have lost interest in nature and its study, and have become so completely preoccupied with history as to give the impression that it is the only locus of God's self-revealing activities. Science has thus come to have virtually no theological significance for them. This seems to have been the situation for several decades.

In the meantime science has been marching on, and a remarkable new world view has come into being based on its recent findings. This has created some serious problems for theology. Fortunately this development has been accompanied by the appearance on the theological horizon of a relatively small but growing cloud of revived interest in these matters. While there is no disposition among Protestant theologians to return to anything like the old teleology-oriented *natural theology,* many of them are saying that we do need a *theology of nature* and of science. By this they seem to mean a theology that is based squarely on the revelation in Christ and God's "mighty deeds in history," and at the same time recognizes and seeks to understand God's "mighty deeds in nature" as these are related to history.

Now as a scientist who has had the opportunity of observing a considerable number of theologians in action as they have struggled with this problem, I have come to appreciate some of their difficulties. For one thing, I can understand why it is not at all obvious to them how natural science can have any relevance for them. It proceeds—as they grant that it must—quite without regard to any "hypothesis of a God." The term *God* does not, therefore, belong to its technical vocabulary. In this sense it is utterly godless or secular. How then can it have any value technically for theology, or contribute to its thought? Why then should theology be concerned with it? This is not an easy question. On the other hand, it is not the only question that is difficult. For this same secular science, with its new ways of thinking about the world is now characterized also by a new intellectual freedom and openness, by sharpened sensitivities and creativity in the humanistic sense, by genuine moral and ethical concerns, and it has deservedly become one of the most potent determinants of contemporary life not only in its physical aspects, but in its spiritual ones as well. How can theology possibly fail to profit from the emergence and flowering of such a science? How can it possibly function properly in terms of its own purposes, and make its contribution to the life and work of the world, unless its thinking is somehow related closely to those ideals, concerns, images and modes of thought of our times that are molded to so large an extent by science?

It is my belief that there are many aspects of the new science and its conception of the world that are destined to become useful, or even indispensable, to Christian thought. In support of this belief I should like to call attention at this time to three of these, namely its *depth,* its *unboundedness* or *openness,* and its *mystery.*[1] We shall begin with mystery.

---

[1] These three terms are not used widely in the technical discourse of scientists. They are used by some and I can claim no credit for originating them. In my opinion they accurately connote the newer views.

II

In a remarkably enlightening book about the nature of theology,[2] Karl Barth raises the interesting question of "how theology encounters a man—how it confronts him, and assumes concrete form in him." His answer may be surprising, for he asserts that it begins with wonder—not, as is commonly supposed, with the submissive acceptance of a set of presuppositions or established doctrinal beliefs. By wonder he means open-minded astonishment; and he discusses this in the following way. "Wonder occurs when someone encounters a spiritual or natural phenomenon that he has never met before—it is for the moment something uncommon and strange and novel to him." It is therefore the root of all true sciences, and theology is one of these. The amazement of science is provisional or temporary, for always, when it confronts a new phenomenon or mystery, science immediately seeks to explain it, and as its understanding grows the mystery dissolves and the wonder disappears. In theology, however, he says, it is different, for there one encounters the mystery of God, and therefore wonder never ceases.

Now it seems to me beyond doubt that what Barth says positively about theology itself is true, namely that its mystery is unfathomable and unbounded. But I wonder whether what he says negatively in this respect about science is equally true. May Barth not be missing something when he asserts that nature is such that all its mystery necessarily disappears under the prolonged gaze of science?

III

Perhaps those who, like Barth, insist on contrasting science and theology sharply with regard to wonder and mystery, do so because they hold to a conception of nature—and of science—that most scientists have abandoned.

There was a time when the reigning conception of nature was one of rather simple order. It was supposed that the apparent complexities of visible nature could be explained by appealing to hidden basic simplicities of substance and relationship. Thus according to the so-called Newtonian billiard ball conception of the world, as refined by Laplace, nature was thought to be explainable and its future completely predictable, at least in principle, in terms of very simple, unchanging elementary particles, and of abstract, synthesizing laws that described their motions.

In a sense this was a shallow, closed and unmysterious world. It was *shallow* in the analogical sense that science was expected to find its final explanations relatively close to the surface of things. Certainly no one would have dreamt then of the many depths of penetration into physical reality to which science has had to push its inquiry since then. It was a *closed* world in the sense that in principle it could have no surprises that could not have been predicted. For it was thought to be completely determined. And it was *unmysterious* in the sense that it was felt that eventually all questions about it could be answered—again, at least in principle. Final explanations were fully expected, certainly in their broad outline, if not in complete detail, and perhaps in the form of a grand all-inclusive equation. Later this extremely simple picture had to be modified for various reasons we can't go into now. Nevertheless, its general point of view, commonly referred to as mechanistic and deterministic, persisted until late in the 19th century, and had not completely disappeared early in the 20th.

The conception being espoused by scientists today is very different. It views nature as a *world of depth*, not as a

[2] Karl Barth: *Evangelical Theology: An Introduction*, Holt, Rinehart and Winston, 1953: see especially p. 63 ff.

shallow one; as an *open, unbounded world,* not a closed one; and as a *world of mystery* that is in the end not fathomable. How extensive the implications of this view are becomes apparent when one thinks about some of the most basic questions of science, such as what is matter? Or energy, or life, or mind? None of these can be answered adequately by appealing to the idea of a simple and closed world.

Consider, for example, the first of these: What is matter? Think how very much we mean by it today! To begin with, speaking quite unsophisticatedly, it is that primal stuff or reality that we become aware of through our senses, and is the physical basis of existence. It appears in various states, the solid, liquid, gaseous, and plasma states, that have remarkably different attributes. To describe its internal structure we must mention a whole hierarchy of building blocks, fields of force, and dynamic micro-structures. If we were to subject a bit of matter, such as animal tissue, to microscopic and submicroscopic analysis, our findings would have to refer to *at least* the following entities found at different depths of its interior: cells, protoplasm, cell nuclei, chromosomes, genes, crystals, chemical compounds, chemical elements, molecules, atoms, atomic nuclei, electrons, protons, neutrons, and still other subatomic particles.

Clearly this picture does not impress one with any shallow simplicity of the kind envisioned in either the early Newtonian conception or the later modified versions of it. Rather it is one of depths and of complexities, and the greater the depth, the greater the complexity. It indicates also rich qualitative variety.[3] This shows up in at least three ways. First, there is the large number of species of so-called particles that differ from one another in being heavy or light in mass; electrically positive, negative or

neutral; long- or short-lived; right- or left-handed in spin; and so on. Second, there is the variety indicated by the necessity of speaking of the subatomic entities as including not only particles, but waves and fields. The third aspect of variety is displayed by the fact that going deeper discloses other kinds of reality, so to speak. Thus the realities of the microworld are so different in kind from those of the macroworld as to require radically different language, modes of thought, and theories to deal with them. This is why we must say ambiguously that entities like molecules, atoms, and electrons are *somewhat like particles and somewhat like waves.* Nothing in the macroworld is like that. Then too there are in the microworld strange kinds of dynamic interactions and phenomena in which corpuscles of matter of various kinds appear or disappear; and to speak adequately of these we employ concepts like *fusion, fission,* and *transmutation,* and even the apparently paradoxical one of *anti-matter.* It is a most interesting situation when in discussing certain features of matter one must speak of anti-matter! And finally all this has led us to see that the ordinary laws of mechanics that apply to large bodies like stones and bullets, do not apply in the microworld, and this in turn has led us to invent a new kind of mechanics, namely quantum mechanics, to deal with its phenomena.

Now turning our attention in another direction, we note also that matter has the capacity for what I shall call aggregation. There is an endless hierarchy of aggregations of various sorts, e.g. aggregates called rocks, then those called planets, and then the stars, and at a higher level galaxies, and then even super galaxies. Here too we see a succession of depths and levels, this time as we penetrate "outward" and "up-

[3] David Bohm in his *Causality and Chance in Modern Physics,* Harper Torchbook, uses the concept of "the qualitative infinity of nature," p. 132 ff.

ward," rather than "inward" and "downward," into the depths of space.

Here too it must be noted that as we probe to greater depths, beyond the "surface appearance" of things, we do not find things to be simpler and simpler, as though converging toward some final simplicity, but more and more variegated, strange and complex. Beyond the so-called celestial sphere of nearby stars visible to the naked eye are depths of space and celestial expanse, each successively disclosed concentric shell of which reveals greater numbers and complexities than the preceding one. The description of the strange realities encountered by modern macro-astronomy has required the use of new ideas quite at variance with those of classical astrophysical theory.

There are also depths in time, so to speak. Here we see matter in its temporal, evolutionary unfolding, in its transformation of hidden possibilities and potentialities into ever newly manifest actualities. According to present conceptions matter was "at the beginning," several billions of years ago,[4] in the simple state of elementary particles which later aggregated to form atoms. Still later some of these came together to form molecules. Then very long molecules appeared, capable of reproduction, thus exhibiting characteristics we attribute to *life*. Later cells and still larger organisms came forth, then mind, and finally social aggregations. Here is a most remarkable dimension or attribute of matter: this capacity to change in time, to manifest utterly new properties, phenomena and structures. For a long time it was all inanimate, and then some of it became animate. According to contemporary conceptions life is not an entity added to matter, but one of the states in which matter can exist. And similar remarks apply to mind.

No doubt in the future science will devote more and more of its attention to the investigation of life and mind. Already the biologists and psychologists are probing them at great depths, and the deeper they go the more complex and unbounded things seem to be. Indeed the concept of depth seems to have come into scientific language first through the term *depth psychology*. Without a doubt these explorations will further confirm the general conclusions about nature that we have drawn thus far mostly from advances in the physical sciences.

IV

At this point it will be useful to bring together the ideas developed thus far by means of a few summarizing propositions.

P1. *Nature has extension not only in space and time, but also in depth, or interiority.* In support of this, it is necessary to point out only that science has always been an enterprise in probing beneath the surface appearance of things to discover more basic, constituent realities.[5]

P2. *In its depth the reality of nature has many recognizably different levels.*

P3. *Its depth is characterized by great complexity and rich variety.*

P4. *The degree of the complexity and variety does not decrease with depth, as though approaching a limit at some final boundary level, but seems rather to increase indefinitely.* The history of science has not unearthed any evidence that with increasing depth complexity dissolves into some sort of ultimate simplicity. The evidence actually points the other way.

P5. *Nature seems then to be unbounded not only in space and time, but also in depth.* It is not a closed, but

---

[4] There are scientists who speak also of a still earlier stage in the history of nature, i.e. when there was no matter at all, after which it then appeared.

[5] See my "Seeing the Unseen" in *Wesleyan Studies in Religion,* 1963-64 (West Virginia Wesleyan College); also in *motive,* October, 1963.

an open, world. The notion of unboundedness has been a familiar one in science for some time; for in physics ever since Einstein it has been common to speak of the space-time continuum as finite but unbounded. It should not then be too difficult to think of depth, or interiority, in similar fashion. What this means is that the series of successive levels is unlimited; that, analogically speaking, there is no "bottom" if we go "downward," and no "top" or "ceiling" if we go "upward," into the depths of the space-time-depth continuum of nature.[6] Apropos of this boundlessness of depth, David Bohm has made the exceedingly interesting suggestion, in harmony with his idea of the qualitative infinity of nature, that at great depths reality may be so very different that the concept of level itself may have to be abandoned for another, or be greatly modified or "enriched." [7]

P6. *Nature has not been fixed in time, but has been changing—"creatively," i.e. by the successive emergences of novelty. These have been characterized by increasing complexity and organization.* The evolutionary story of the long history of nature supports this generalization.

At this point of our summary let us introduce the term *mystery*. Many scientists have been saying recently that the process of scientific discovery has disclosed nature to be such that an answer to any given question opens up many new questions, and that the answer to each of these leads to still others, and so on in a diverging series of more and more, rather than a converging one of fewer and fewer, questions. Apparently increasing the known does not decrease the unknown. Here, it would seem, is genuine, unbounded openness and genuine unfathomable mystery. This conception enables us then to distinguish

between temporary and permanent mystery, or between the superficial mystery and the mystery of depth. The history of science is a remarkable success story of the finding and resolving of transient mysteries. And yet that very history has shown also that the resolving of each such mystery has led to innumerable others; and that as the questioning has been pushed to deeper levels and added to our knowledge and understanding, it has at the same time disclosed more complexity and diversity. It is then by way of partial definition that I offer the seventh proposition. (P7) *Genuine, permanent mystery marks that state of affairs, or that quality of reality, because of which each answer to a question about reality leads to indefinitely more questions, and so on and on—in a divergent rather than convergent series.* I submit that it refers not to a subjective state of affairs, but to a definitely objective one. It is not conjured up by our minds, but is imposed on them by the way things actually are.

There are at least four other aspects of the permanent mystery of nature that call for recognition here.

In terms of present knowledge it seems that, like the space-time-depth continuum, (P8) *the network of so-called cause-and-effect relationships among physical entities existing in that continuum is also unbounded—open, not closed.* This signifies that nature is not deterministic, and that events are "brought about" by both "cause" and "chance;" that they are in part predictable and in part unpredictable. A symbolic scheme used for prediction at one level of depth, does not in general apply directly at others. Natural laws are not universal, but limited, in the range and level of their applicability. The hope of scientists to be able to find the grand all-inclusive equation, by which the physical universe could be fully explained and its future

---

[6] I suggest that this be found to be true no matter at what level we may begin our exploration downward or upward, inward or outward.

[7] Bohm, opus cit., p. 139.

fully predicted, undoubtedly has had great motivating value, but it is doubtful that it is justified by any logic that takes into account the stubborn autonomies and limitless complexities in the depths of nature—as well as the implications of the next proposition.

P9. *There may now exist realms of physical reality with extension throughout space-time-depth of which we are not aware.* Certainly there are now realities to which man has no *direct* access through his senses, but which are known by indirect means. Magnetism is one of these. Electricity is another. Science was utterly unaware of the latter for a very long time, i.e. up to the seventeenth century; and yet how boundless and all-pervasive it is now known to be! To suppose that there may not be still others just as pervasive, yet still beyond our ken, would be foolhardy indeed. A break-through into one or more of them could happen at any time. The possibility, or even probability, that, however much we may know at any given time, there may be entire realms or kinds of reality the existence of which we are not even aware, together with the impossibility of ever knowing whether this is or is not actually the case, is an important aspect of the genuine mystery of *things as they are.*

P10. But there are also questions about *things as they are to be.* In all likelihood *nature is still in the making and new realms of reality will appear in time.* This has happened in the past; why not also in the future? Since there is no evidence that such becomings are at all predictable—except by vague and very general long-range extrapolation of past trends—here is another component of genuine mystery.

The last element of mystery we should consider here resides in the unavailability of ultimate explanation or understanding. As has been said many times, (P11) *science offers explanations in only a limited and immediate sense, namely in answer to questions of how things happen, not of why—in a final sense. The latter remain utter mystery which its endless succession of how-questions and answers points to, but does not resolve.* To answer the how-kinds of questions science identifies pertinent empirical functional relationships, so-called laws of nature, that do in fact exist among observed variables and constants, or events, and then points to these as the explanations. In seeking to understand the explanations or empirical laws, it then constructs symbolic systems called theories which enable it to see a number of laws as being related conceptually, and by which both they and the individual events can be derived (predicted) deductively. A scientist speaks then of "understanding" a body of many facts or phenomena when he can in this way show them to be derivable from one theory. While this is a most impressive and exceedingly fruitful kind of understanding, it still leaves unanswered the haunting question of *why* nature is so structured that science has been impelled toward *those* explanations and *that* understanding rather than others. Presumably the world could have been different. Why not? [8]

Let us now reflect briefly upon these findings in the hope of guarding against some unwarranted implications. We present three more propositions as points of departure for these reflections.

P12. *From the very nature of mystery, as we have conceived it, we must be forewarned that it is impossible either to demonstrate or deny its reality in nature by either formal logic or the usual verification processes of science.* This follows from its essential open-endedness, its unboundedness in space, time and depth. The discovery of lasting mystery as an objective quality of nature, is not an inevitable or certain consequence of scientific methodology.

---

[8] This question is considered most cogently from a somewhat different point of view by Thomas F. Green, "The Importance of Fairy Tales," in *The Educational Forum,* Nov. 1963.

On the other hand, (P13) *the evidence pointing to the reality of inexhaustible mystery can, and often does, become convincing, even if not compelling beyond any possibility of doubt, as it accumulates in time;* hence, the relevance of our earlier analysis.

It is now necessary to disavow an attitude toward the idea of ultimate mystery that was once widely prevalent, and is still not unknown in some quarters today. (P14) *The mystery of nature is not to be thought of as a realm that is sacrosanct, not to be invaded by human inquiry, "something we are not supposed to know." In the life and thought of man it has been a perpetually beckoning and challenging mystery to which the response has been a compound of wonder and the search for understanding by all available means, of confidence that the search will yield truth, and of a humble realization that, however many mysteries the search resolves and however much truth it does yield, the mystery still remains inexhaustible.* Science has been this kind of a response.

Many scientists shy away from, or even positively object to, applying the word mystery to nature. They insist that the "mystery of the heavens" has disappeared, or that the "mystery" of life, and of mind, is rapidly vanishing. I suspect, however, that such insistence represents for the most part a reaction against the taboo conception of, and attitude toward, mystery, rather than a denial of the basically mysterious quality of things. Certainly the mystery of life —as also of mind and many other components of nature—*is* vanishing in one sense. Yet in another it is increasing. The more we know about how things are in fact, the more is the wonder that in fact they are not otherwise.

It is of a piece with our conception of nature's mystery, i.e. in terms of the endless cascades of questions it calls forth, that the spirit of science is commonly held to be symbolized more adequately by its restless questing than by its successful finding. Science would cease if it ever lost its insistence that no answer is ever beyond further questioning. Surely this is attributable not simply to the scientist's psychological make-up by which he is sentenced forever to call things in question, but to the fact that the world he is trying to understand is inexhaustibly challenging—mysterious.

There are other aspects of nature about which we have been silent thus far. It not only builds up, but tears down. (P15) *Nature has apparently unbounded depths of destructiveness and inconsistency. This is one of the most perplexing components of nature's mystery.*

By its *destructiveness* we usually mean conflagration and flood, earthquake and tidal wave, hurricane and tornado, drought and famine, disease and epidemic. Though very real this is not all of it; witness, for instance, the prodigality of death in the so-called sabertooth-and-claw competition for survival.

The term *inconsistency* refers to nature's irrationality in working against itself much of the time. While it has developed marvelously ingenious mechanisms and processes for the qualitative improvement of the species and of life in general, it has at the same time produced others equally potent for deterioration. Thus it exhibits helpful symbiosis, i.e. a relationship of interdependence between, say, two species of animals in which each contributes to the other something that is indispensable and otherwise unavailable to it. Yet ironically there is also parasitism, in which one species lives on another, causing it much pain and suffering, and often even death. As an example of a less lethal, yet terribly agonizing kind of parasitism, Julian Huxley cites the case of fly maggots that live in the noses of various animals. A different kind of cruel inconsistency of nature is exemplified by the birth of monstrosities to normal parents.

331

In concluding this section I call attention, briefly without exposition, to three potent terms or concepts for which we are indebted to three theologians who have been doing much thinking about nature and science. Each of them denotes important shades of meaning beyond that of mere inconsistency, meanings that refer to aspects of nature that are objectively observable and very real. They do not enter the picture first through preconception or theory, but through direct experience. Bernard E. Meland speaks of nature as being characterized by both *manageability and unmanageability*. Paul Tillich's term is the *ambiguities of life,* and J. S. Habgood's the *untidiness of life*.[9]

V

The subject of this section is in a sense climactic for our study, for it shifts our attention to a much larger perspective, and connects history with nature. For the most part thus far our point of view has been terrestrial, even though we did mention astronomy briefly. We must now take a more explicitly transterrestrial look at nature, and adopt a cosmic stance. It seems trite to say that man cannot understand himself unless in an historic perspective. What seems to be forgotten too often, however, is that to be truly informing that perspective must take in more than human history, and must be seen in relation to the long sweeps of terrestrial pre-human history, and no less in the light of an all-inclusive cosmic history.

Many converging lines of evidence indicate that the earth's age is about two billion years. In order to give us some sense of proportion as to various developments within that time, G. M.

McKinley has worked out a remarkably enlightening time scale as follows.[10] Let the two billion years be represented by one calendar year, so that January 1 would be the beginning of terrestrial history, and December 31 the present. On this scale one day represents approximately 5,500,000 years, one hour somewhat more than 200,000 years, one minute about 4000 years, and one second roughly 65 years. According to contemporary understandings, on this scale the beginnings of life, in the form of self-replicating, long chain molecules, appeared in February. In April simple unicellular organisms emerged, and late in May the primitive invertebrates. Land plants came on the scene in the summer (midway in the two billion year span), and the large reptiles, brainy mammals and birds in the fall. "Then on the last day of the year, December 31, just some four hours before midnight, man appears walking gracefully erect and equipped with sensitive, marvelously sensitive hands. . . . An hour or so later he makes tentative efforts at social life, but it is not until the last minute of the year, that his first civilization is organized."

Clearly, human history is a very short interval in the totality of terrestrial history. This must not be lost sight of. And yet despite its brevity it is in many ways the most remarkable of intervals, considering how much has transpired within it. Apparently in no earlier interval of equal length was the rate of change ever so tremendous, and the frequency of emergence of novelty quite so high as in this one. Preparation for the appearance of mind took a very, very long time, but when it actually arrived on the scene activity took on an entirely new tempo and character, as when, after

[9] Bernard E. Meland, *The Realities of Faith,* Oxford University Press, 1962, p. 63; Paul Tillich, *Systematic Theology,* Vol. III, University of Chicago Press, Ch. I; J. S. Habgood, *Religion and Science,* Mills and Boon, London, 1964, Ch. I (soon to be published under another title by Holt, Rinehart and Winston, New York). Though now a clergyman, Habgood is a highly trained scientist, and his book is Number Eight in a series entitled *Science and Society.*

[10] G. M. McKinley, *Evolution: The Ages and Tomorrow,* Ronald, New York, 1956, p. 55 ff.

a full year's preparation of a small bud by a plant, there suddenly bursts forth in but a few moments a large, many-petaled, multihued flower. What this means is that human history must not be regarded as a relatively isolated, independent invasion of terrestrial history, but as an event inseparably a part of it, and causally an outcome of its processes.

It is equally true, however, that terrestrial history is itself but an integral part of, and a causal consequence of the processes of, transterrestrial, cosmic history; and without doubt it is but a short interval in it. Human history is then an even smaller fraction of cosmic history than it is of terrestrial history. A discovery of modern astronomy that for present purposes is especially significant is the high probability of the existence among the stars of myriads of planets suitable for habitation by beings with bodies and minds somewhat like ours. Harlow Shapley goes so far as to assert positively that *"millions of planetary systems must exist,* and billions is the better word," and that "we are not alone." If this is so, and there certainly seems to be no good reason for doubting it from a scientific point of view, terrestrial human history is not only an exceedingly small part of a much longer celestial history, but is only one of very many other human-like histories. Moreover, it seems likely that the origins of these did not coincide in time, and that therefore some—perhaps even many—human-like races of beings have existed elsewhere in space, and in their evolution have achieved high orders of physical, mental and social development, long before ours was born, perhaps even before our planet was born. One wonders whether some of them may not even have come *and gone,* in some sense, long ago. (P16) *There is good reason to suppose that human history covers but a minuscule span of time in the total history of nature, and that the terrestrial race of men is but one of many human-like races that have emerged in cosmic history, of whose individual histories some overlap in time, and others do not. Here is another component of nature's mystery: the mystery of other inhabitable worlds and their histories—in the past, present and future.*

VI

We now turn briefly to the question whether the scientific view of nature we have considered [11] can tell us anything about God. Might its imagery contribute significantly to the development of concepts and symbols of God that are truly meaningful in our time? Of course this is a far-reaching question that cannot be answered in a few pages, for, as I have suggested elsewhere, such conceptualization is formidable and demanding business, and requires the extensive exploration of three large areas of meaning with respect to the term "God;" meaning-by-empirical analysis, meaning-by-intuition, and meaning-by-postulation.[12] The first and third of these require the kind of formal and critical analysis we cannot go into here, and must reserve for another essay.

What we shall concern ourselves with now for the most part is the second meaning, that by-intuition. To focus our attention on this particular meaning is in a sense to ask our basic question in a somewhat different way: How may the insights of SV be helpful and illuminating as we think meditatively about God? The term *think* refers here not to the guarded, logically sequential reasoning that eventuates in carefully formulated conclusions, but to the more free-wheeling, yet no less potent, intuitive reflections and leaps of the imagination

---

[11] The scientific view of nature that is embodied in the propositions of preceding sections, and will hereafter be referred to by the symbol SV.

[12] Harold K. Schilling, *Science and Religion, An Interpretation of Two Communities,* Scribner's, 1962, Ch. IX.

that proceed without precise definitions and yield informal conclusions. It may at times even be an unconscious or subconscious awareness through "feelings in one's bones"—or what is sometimes called "thinking with the heart." It is the kind the psalmist must have been doing when he burst forth with "The heavens declare the glory of God; and the firmament showeth his handiwork. . . ."

In proceeding along these lines I shall quite frankly be thinking as a Christian, i.e. a member of a historic community in whose experience God has been, and continues to be, very real, and for whom therefore the concept of God is truly meaningful. I am not seeking more "evidence for the existence of God," but more insight and more meaningful symbols for reflecting upon and worshipping the God I am already aware of—and I am asking whether such additional insights, meanings, and symbols can come at least in part out of science. At no time have I said or supposed that nature "reveals" God, or can provide a "foundation" for faith in God; and I shall not now repudiate that view. I *have* said, however, that science points beyond its own definitive findings toward the reality of ultimate mystery—which is a different matter—and I shall now urge the view that nature, once it is regarded as the "ongoing creation of God" ("His handiwork"), does through the eye of faith yield important insights about God that are not discernible in any other way.

Remembering that we are now seeking meanings mostly with the eye of intuitive perception that sees things in wholes or in terms of over-all patterns without benefit of prior detailed analysis, what might a latter day psalmist mean if upon reflecting broadly on SV he were to sing out a contemporary equivalent of "The heavens declare. . . ."? What might his first reaction be upon "seeing" so much that his predecessors of long ago are not likely to have seen? I suspect that it would be a reaction of overwhelming wonder, with a sense of tremendous,

majestic, awe-full mystery; a mystery at once unbounded and unfathomable and yet perpetually beckoning and rewarding; a mystery that has yielded to the extraction of immense amounts of knowledge and truth and the resolving of countless mysteries, and yet remains essentially untouched and beyond understanding; a mystery of limitless spatial and temporal immensity, but also of innumerable dimensions and depths; a mystery displaying an infinity of qualitative variety, yet also of incredible cohesiveness and unity; consistency and ambiguity, order and disorder, causal predictability and pure chance.

What a grand vision and spectacle of mystery SV does present! Perhaps its most remarkable feature, however, is its being eternally pregnant with an inexhaustible potential for new actualities, together with a sensitive experimental adaptiveness to the needs of any particular situation, and an uninhibited openness toward the future. Moreover, looking back in retrospect upon its long developmental history, we can now see what no short range perspective could have shown; namely, that somehow the perpetual stirrings and pressures of new being within it, its moment by moment reactions and responses to situational dilemmas by tentatively trying now this, then that, and even its wasteful expenditure of substance and energy, have *in the long run* been goal-seeking, organizing and creatively constructive in character—and are therefore meaningful. While scientists still debate over the idea of any "purpose" or "goal" in nature, there is little disagreement that as a matter of fact successive major emergences have built upon, not cancelled or negated, preceding ones, and that therefore the long range developmental curve has been as consistently "upward," i.e. toward consciousness and sociality, as though these were actual goals.

Now I ask: Is it reasonable to suppose that from all this we can conclude nothing about God, as some theologians seem to insist when they say that we know nothing about God except what has been revealed through Jesus Christ? The ancient psalmists probably knew almost nothing about the remarkable aspects of nature portrayed in SV; even so for them nature did declare God's glory. Is it credible that if such knowledge and insight had come to them they would have written it off as of no significance for their conceptions of, or faith in, God?

There are of course more specific aspects of SV—aside from the more general ones of mystery, depth, openness and goal-seeking—that may signify something about God. Among them are the following ones: that the processes of genesis, emergence and developmental growth in nature have been operative for aeons upon aeons of time and in countless galaxies of planetary systems throughout endless space; and that in their depths all components of reality now seem to be dynamic rather than static, changing rather than fixed; and that their most basic constituent realities are now thought to be relationships, rather than substances in the old sense, and to be characterized by complexity more than simplicity.

To work out precisely these and many other implications of both the general and more specific aspects of SV for religious thought will, of course, require much more than the informal, intuitive "thinking with the heart" that we have engaged in here. For this task nothing less than the cold-blooded, critical, logically rigorous thinking, the empirical analysis and postulational theorizing of systematic theology, aided by the newer metaphysics and the resources of many other disciplines, will do. It is for just such a broad frontal cooperative attack upon the problem by many Christian scholars from many fields that I am pleading.

Finally I raise a question that reflects the "practical" mood of many people today, including many in the Church. What if the natural world does have many levels of depth, is unbounded and open, and truly mysterious—or not? Isn't this much ado about nothing? Does it really make any difference how we *think* theologically about God, and whether we do it in terms of mystery or not? What difference—in the way we work, play, love, hate, live and die? This question too demands much more rigorous thought than we can give it here. Perhaps it is the most difficult one of all. I offer then only a few brief remarks about it.

First there is a constant interaction between thought and act. Much more than is often realized, what we do is determined by how we think abstractly, *and* our abstract thought is determined by what we do. Much of this interplay is, of course, subconscious, and is known to be very potent in its effects—perhaps nowhere more so than in religion. This is of itself not sufficient, however, completely to shape the character of our attitudes and actions. To a large extent they are affected also by our conscious, deliberate thinking, including our "theoretical" thinking. Hence it does make a "practical" difference in our lives how we think consciously—theologically—about God. Some ways of conceptualizing God enrich our workaday lives and others impoverish them.

Second, it will make a very great difference whether we think of God as open, dynamic, creative mystery, or as a being whose nature can be known with considerable certainty and whose attributes can be specified by a closed and fixed doctrinal system. The one makes for intellectual and spiritual power, for adventurous faith, and expectant openness to the future, while the other tends to stultify, to substitute religious self complacency for faith, and to make difficult the acceptance of the new and the passage into the future. If SV with its new appreciation of mystery can to any extent impel us in the direction of the former of these conceptions its contribution to religious thought will be tremendous.

Its contribution would be even more significant, however, especially with respect to our situation today, if it helped us not only to see the theological implication of the reality of genuine mystery conceived intellectually, but to rehabilitate and sharpen our sensitivity to mystery intuitively perceived—and to the related mysterious qualities of unboundedness and depth. The older scientific views of nature, as shallow, closed and unmysterious, tended to denigrate and blunt that sensitivity, with rather serious consequences. The newer ones seem to me destined to change much of this—if men will respond to them. It is my fervent hope that Christian thought, including theology, will increasingly be found to be leading in this response.

Religion and Science: Bibliography

Baillie, John. *Natural Science and the Spiritual Life.* London: Oxford University Press, 1951.

Balthasar, Hans Urs von, *Science, Religion and Christianity.* Westminster, Md.: The Newman Press, 1958.

Barbour, Ian Graeme. *Christianity and the Scientist.* New York: Association Press, 1960.

Cohen, Morris W. *Reason and Nature.* Rev. ed. New York: The Free Press, 1953.

Lindsay, Alexander D. *Religion, Science and Society in the Modern World.* New Haven, Conn.: Yale University Press, 1943.

Mascall, E. L. *Christian Theology and Natural Science.* Hamden, Conn.: The Shoe String Press, 1956.

Needham, Joseph, ed. *Science, Religion and Reality.* New York: George Braziller, 1955.

Polanyi, Michael. *Science, Faith and Society.* Chicago: University of Chicago Press, 1964.

Richardson, Alan. *Science and Existence: Two Ways of Knowing.* London: SCM Press, 1957.

Russell, Bertrand. *Religion and Science.* London: Oxford University Press, 1935.

Raven, Charles. *Science and the Christian Man.* London: SCM Press, 1952.

Whitehead, Alfred N. *Science and the Modern World.* New York: The Macmillan Company, 1926.

VIII

Religion
and the Socioeconomic
and Political Orders

Introduction

Although no ultimate division exists, and no neat distinction can be drawn, between the theoretical and practical aspects of man's cultural activities, the previous sections have focused basically on man's concern to understand and appreciate reality while this final section centers largely[1] on his need to change reality as this need finds expression in the creation of socioeconomic and political orders. These orders generally have been of special concern to Christian thought about culture, and it is largely to them that Niebuhr refers in discussing the synthesist, dualist, and conversionist positions—positions which can be seen with particular clarity in this section. Consequently, the reader may find it helpful to review Niebuhr's account in section II. If, in the selections which follow, one were to move from Berger through Reinhold Niebuhr to Brunner and then to Kolb, H. R. Niebuhr, and Tillich, in which direction would one be moving along the spectrum between dualism and conversionism?

Perhaps we may add to Niebuhr's discussion in section II by making some comparisons with the natural law theory which is basic to the synthesist position of Murray. Murray follows Thomas Aquinas in holding that all relations are governed by the eternal law which is God's reason. That part of the eternal law which governs human relations is called natural law. Since man's reason is in some sense like or analogous to God's reason, man can recognize the natural law as it is *embodied in man and his institutions* and can see that it is normative.

Berger takes the position of Karl Barth that man can know God's reason only through revelation and not through any knowledge of man or of social institutions. According to Berger, God "did not create society," and human nature is simply "a social product, one that is socially relative depending upon the accidents of birth and biography."

Brunner thinks that Barth goes too far in holding that, in fallen man, God's image is completely shattered. Once he has received God's revelation in Christ, man can recognize God's further revelation in his creation, and God's creation includes his "created orders" in society —i.e., natural laws concerning the relations between male and female, for example, or between man and the state, or man and property. Even prior to the biblical revelation these orders may be perceived dimly, although not as God's creation.

The Niebuhrs believe that men can know something of God's natural law but, against the synthesists, they stress that the concepts in terms of which it is understood are always relative to a particular culture with its limitations and

---

[1] The first part of Kolb's article is a notable exception since it deals with the science of sociology. It is included here because of the contrast it provides with Berger's position.

biases. This means that the way in which the norms of natural law are understood in any particular culture must not be absolutized into norms valid for all cultures. The Niebuhrs differ, however, in their conception of God's relation to the natural law. For Richard Niebuhr God "is always in history; he is the structure in things," while, as he sees it, "for my brother, God is outside the historical processes." (In reading Richard Niebuhr one may recall the similar emphases on process in Roberts and Meland.)

Tillich expresses a view of natural law in terms of subjective reason and objective reason—the structure of the human mind and the corresponding structure of the reality known by it. He maintains, however, that "only the man who participates in the struggle of the 'elected group' against the class-society is able to understand the true character of being. . . . In all other spheres the general distortion of our historical existence makes it difficult, if not impossible, to find a *true insight into the human situation* and through it into being itself." [2]

Differences concerning natural law —differences concerning the extent to which there is an essential human nature (and a corresponding structure of justice) which can be known and followed as the true basis for our socio-economic and political activities—are not the focal point of most of the following selections, but these differences are important in understanding the issues which are raised. The most immediate comparisons may be found between Berger and Kolb,

and then between Reinhold Niebuhr, H. R. Niebuhr, and Murray.

In reading Brunner, one might compare his view of "the technical revolution" with the views of Cox and of White in section II. It may be instructive also to compare him with Tillich, on the one hand, and Berger, on the other, concerning what Tillich calls "the revolutionary consciousness." In this connection, how would you compare the implications of Brunner's statement that "every invention is an increase in power, and every increase in power within society is a danger to its balance and order" with Tillich's explanation of social change in terms of "elements belonging to a given structure which drive beyond this structure"? [3]

This question of revolutionary consciousness is closely related, in turn, to the role played in social change by self-deception. How does Tillich's belief that "the fate of self-deception . . . is inescapable, except in selected groups" compare with the views of Reinhold Niebuhr, Kolb, and Berger?

It may be noted, finally, that several writers in this section share the belief, with which we are now quite familiar, that important implications for theological thought are to be found in other areas of culture. One may compare, for example, Roberts' use of psychotherapy or Schilling's use of natural science with Berger's use of social science, Tillich's use of Marx or Kolb's belief that many aspects of theological thought about man can be tested within the discipline of sociology. Which positions have been least in agreement with this type of approach?

---

[2] Italics are the editor's.

[3] Note that Brunner also claims that "we should not look upon these inventions as the real causes of the technical revolution; they had to come because man wanted them."

EMIL BRUNNER

Modern Technology as an Expression of Rebellion*

. . . Amongst all the problems of civilisation with which we are dealing in these lectures, the problem of "technics" is the youngest. All the others have worried Western mankind and Christianity for centuries; not so technics. In earlier times people had hardly become conscious of it, much less did they think of it as a problem. To-day, however, it is in the front line, because—to a degree previously unheard of—technics—or shall I say technology?—determines the life of man, endangers the human character of civilisation, and even threatens the very existence of mankind. Whilst half a century ago the startling progress of technology was the basis of an optimistic philosophy of life and progress, since the two world wars, and particularly since the first atomic bomb was dropped on Hiroshima, the conception of technics has become more and more connected with gloomy, even desperate, perspectives for the future. . . . Whether civilisation and mankind will survive has become *the* problem of the hour, so that we cannot but start with it.

This fact—that technology has recently become the most urgent of all problems—contrasts strangely with the other fact that technics is as old as humanity. Human history begins with the invention of the first stone tool, that is, with technics. It is in the shape of *homo faber* that man first shows himself as a being transcending nature. From this beginning technics, that is, the creation and use of artificial tools serving the life of man, has increasingly distinguished man's life from that of the animal, and imprinted upon it a specifically human character. The his-

tory of technics from its beginning to, say, the time of James Watt, is characterised by an almost unbroken, more or less equable and, therefore, quite unobtrusive progress. Step by step man makes headway in solving the task which he recognises as his own, to subdue nature by his technical inventions.

We distinguish the first epochs of human history by their technical character, speaking of the stone age, the bronze age and the iron age, where an almost unnoticeable transition from one to the other makes the distinction difficult. The same is true of what we call historical man, as we find him first in the Delta of the Nile, in Mesopotamia, in the great valleys of China and of India, where the history of civilisation has its origin. Everywhere the development of technics is the hardly perceptible and therefore often forgotten basis of political, social and cultural change. Nowhere does this technical evolution assume a revolutionary aspect, never does it appear as a break with the past. All epochs and all nations in history are equally technical and therefore none is so in an outstanding sense. That is true also of Western history as it first appears as a characteristic unity in the Roman Empire; it is true of the Middle Ages and up to the beginning of the 18th century; but at that moment it is as if this underground current suddenly broke through the surface. The curve of development which hitherto had been a continuously and almost imperceptibly rising straight line, abruptly takes the form of a parabola becoming steeper and steeper. Technology begins to become a great revolutionary power and within the last few

* Reprinted with the permission of Charles Scribner's Sons and James Nisbet and Company from *Christianity and Civilisation*, Volume II, pages 1-15, by Emil Brunner. Copyright 1949, Charles Scribner's Sons.

decades it has taken the lead in the life of the Western nations, and even of the whole world. It has become the dominating factor of modern civilisation. The changes which technology has wrought in the last two centuries are beyond all comparison with those in previous ages. That is why our epoch is called the age of technics, and why the problem of technology, unknown to previous epochs, has suddenly become the most urgent problem of all.

Why is this so? We *might* answer this question first by pointing to the tempo of technical inventions and the changes created by them. The mad speed of technical progress makes mankind breathless; with one invention pressing fast on another, man cannot get any rest. The growth of technics is out of proportion to the progress made in other departments of life, and puts to shame all attempts of society to adapt itself to the technical change in order to make it useful and beneficent. It is like what happens when a youth suddenly begins to grow at a great pace. His spiritual development cannot keep pace with his bodily growth and therefore there are disturbances. There is a disproportion between bodily and spiritual growth, the one taking place at the cost of the other. This comparison, with its emphasis on the time-aspect of technical evolution, is certainly legitimate. It is true that technical evolution and change acquired such a speed that the balance of power within society was disturbed and that the social changes, which would have been necessary to adapt life to them, could not be made adequately. We might say that the mushroom growth of giant cities, with their apparent poverty of structure and their production of a mass-society and mass-psychology, was a kind of surprise-effect produced by lack of time for adaptation. In a similar way, one can attribute the preponderance of technical interest in our generation to this speedy development of technics.

But such an analysis remains wholly on the surface. More than that: it falsifies the picture of real history by making the cause the effect and the effect the cause. This idea of social adaptation lagging behind technical progress rather hides than reveals the truth. It is not technics which has created the modern man, but it is the modern man who has created technics. The technical man existed before technics. Take as an example the most famous novel hero of the age immediately preceding the technical revolution, Robinson Crusoe. Compare Robinson Crusoe with his colleague in suffering, Ulysses. How differently they face their identical lot of being cast by shipwreck on a solitary island! There is not much difference, technically, between Robinson Crusoe and Odysseus. Perhaps the most important difference is that Defoe's hero, in distinction from Homer's, has and uses gunpowder. But the main difference is this, and this is exactly what Defoe wants to show: how Crusoe masters technically his hopeless condition. This is the inspiring idea which has made the book a favourite of youth: the idea of the man who helps himself out of the difficulties, the man who—ingenious in quite another sense than Ulysses—is capable of subduing hostile nature step by step.

Behind the technical evolution of the last two hundred years there is a much deeper spiritual process, with which the first part of these lectures has dealt. This process begins with the Renaissance, leading on to the Enlightenment, and beyond it to the radically positivist secularised man of to-day. Modern technics is the product of the man who wants to redeem himself by rising above nature, who wants to gather life into his hand, who wants to owe his existence to nobody but himself, who wants to create a world after his own image, an artificial world which is entirely his creation. Behind the terrifying, crazy tempo of technical evolution, there is all the insatiability of secularised man who, not believing in God or eternal life, wants to snatch as much of this world within his lifetime as he can. Modern technics is, to put it crudely, the expression of the world-voracity of modern man, and the tempo of its development is the expression of his inward unrest, the disquiet of the man who is destined for God's eternity, but has himself rejected this destiny. The hypertrophy of technical interest, resulting in a hyperdynamism of technical evolution, is the necessary consequence of man's abandonment to the world of things, which follows his emancipation from God.

Let us return for a moment to those quiet periods which nobody would call technical, though even then technics had reached a high measure of development and was incessantly progressive. What do we mean by "technics"? In the first place, domination over nature, emancipation from its hazards by intensifying and multiplying the functions of bodily organs. The hammer and the crane are the fortified fist and the prolonged arm, the car is the improved foot, and so on. The whole of technics is a continuation of what nature has given to man as his particular character: upright walk. That is why technics is, as such, a task given to man by the Creator, that Creator who gave man the upright spine and thereby the freedom of the use of his hands and the eye directed to infinitude. God wants man to use his intelligence in order to rise above nature and *"subdue the earth"*. This phrase is found on the first page of the Bible. It immediately follows that other phrase in which the specific nature and destiny of man is expressed: *"and God created man in His own image"*. It is not by chance that the second precedes the first. The task of subduing the earth follows from the first. The task of subduing the earth follows from the nature and the destiny given to man by the Creator. It is most likely that the author of this first chapter of Genesis was thinking of the upright walk of man, but this physical presupposition of his

superiority is the expression of a deeper reason for superiority. Man is called to transcend nature, because he is called to be godlike. Technics is only one of the forms of nature-transcendence, but it is that which presupposes the others, higher civilisation and spiritual life.

So long as man does not use artificial means, he remains dependent on what nature gives, here and now. That is, he necessarily remains on a low, more or less animal, level of development. He is completely at the mercy of natural hazard and tied to the moment; he cannot look into the future, he cannot shape his life, he must live it as nature gives it. By the invention of artificial tools, man emancipates himself to a certain degree from the dictates of nature. The technics of housebuilding and agriculture make him independent of what nature gives at each particular time and place. With a roof over his head and four walls around him, he can defy the weather and live where he chooses. By agriculture he dictates to the earth what to produce for him and to produce it in such a measure that he can store up enough for the future. He makes water or wind drive his mill. He captures the wind in his sail and forces it to carry him over the seas. The spinning-wheel and the loom make him independent of the scarce animal-skins for clothing. One by one he cuts the thousand ties by which his body and its needs are linked to the fortuitous formation and production of the ground. The development of crafts of all sorts leads to differentiation of human society and to the specialised training and development of spiritual capacities; it leads to exchange, to the communal life of the city, to communication between town and town, between country and country. The crafts are at the same time a preparation for higher arts and, in the form of artistic trade, they play their part in aesthetic ennoblement.

Technical skill can be learned and, therefore, transmitted from generation

343

to generation. That is why in this sphere of life there is an unambiguous and more or less continuous progress. Each generation learns from the one before and adds new inventions. In this process of technical education the mind is trained for methodical work. The multiplicity of crafts makes for a rich differentiation of the spirit. It cannot be denied that cities, with their differentiated crafts, are pre-eminently the seats and nurseries of higher culture and education. All these organic types of technics —if I may so call them—are easily forgotten in our age of highly abstract mechanical and therefore inhuman technics. But they belong to the true picture and show the close relation between technics and truly human civilisation.

Even in this picture of pre-modern technics, however, there are traits of a more sinister quality. Closely related to the tool, and often expressed by the same word, is the weapon. The development of crafts almost everywhere gives rise to the development of war technics. There are exceptions to this rule, one of the most interesting being that of the older China, where an almost unique development of crafts did not lead to a parallel development of war technics, because war and fighting were stigmatised, culturally and morally. Not even the invention of gunpowder, which in Europe had such pernicious consequences, could become dangerous among this peaceful people. The moral discredit of war was so deep that gunpowder was never allowed to be used for war purposes, and its dangerous energy was puffed out in harmless fire-works. But apart from this most honourable exception, the development of technics generally resulted in increasingly dangerous weapons and wars. The Roman technics of roadbuilding was developed primarily for military purposes. The technics of shipbuilding created the navy, and so on. Still, all this remained within limits which prevented technics from being the dominating potential of war.

Another danger to society resulting from technical development is the formation of social classes. Technical, like military, superiority creates differences of property, social privilege and power. These differences, however, so far as they were conditioned by technics, did not become very dangerous in the pre-modern ages, because it was not so difficult to acquire technical skill and technical means. From all this, we can conclude that on the whole the positive, beneficial aspects of technical progress by far outweighed the negative or evil ones. In the "golden age of the crafts" nobody would have thought of technics as a serious danger or even a problem of civilisation.

All this is suddenly changed with the introduction of machine technics. It had a sort of prelude in the invention of gunpowder and its application to warfare. The consequences of this invention were far-reaching and could give a premonition of what further similar leaps in the development might mean. It is strange and somehow shameful that Christian Europe did not succeed in doing—perhaps did not even attempt to do—what had been achieved by the Chinese. At any rate, with gunpowder, technics begin to acquire a negative trait in European history. But incomparably more revolutionary was the invention of the steam engine and the locomotive, and later on the discovery and technical use of electricity and of petrol, the invention of light metals and the development of chemistry. Now begins the technical age. As we said before, we should not look upon these inventions as the real causes of the technical revolution; they had to come, because men wanted them. They had to develop at such an unparalleled rate, because men did not want to limit their development in any way. Still, once technics had become what it is now, its effects upon the social and spiritual life of mankind are tremendous.

It has often been said, and it is obviously true, that all the technical changes which took place in the life of men from the stone age to James Watt are not nearly as great as those since James Watt. The life of a farmer or craftsman before the invention of the steam engine was not so different from that of Jeremiah's time as from that under modern agriculture and industry. Machine industry in the broadest sense of the word, including transport and communication, has changed not only the life of Europe and America, but that of the whole surface of the world, in a tempo and in a measure completely unparalleled before.

This technical revolution has its positive as well as its negative side. By it man has indeed subdued the earth in a measure inconceivable before. By the radio he has eliminated distance completely, so far as mental communication is concerned; by the aeroplane he has eliminated it almost completely, so far as bodily communication is concerned. The techniques of production are capable of nourishing, clothing, housing every inhabitant of this earth in more than sufficient degree and with almost complete certainty. Hunger and want are no more inevitable. That they are still amongst us is entirely conditioned by political, social, international power-relations, preventing the reasonable use of technical possibilities. Medical and hygienic techniques would be sufficient to create everywhere conditions of life which would guarantee to a high degree a healthy life and development of the child and double the average age of man. The invention of cinema and radio, perfecting that of the printing-press, allows an almost unlimited spreading of cultural assets. In a measure then, present day technics places at the disposal of man the means which would safeguard a high standard of life and give access to cultural advantages to everyone capable of understanding and valuing them. Technical mankind has a superabundance of all things needed,

and a superabundance of means to transport them wherever they are needed. If there were no war, if there were only just and reasonable laws, if all men were well-intentioned, technics would provide, so it seems, almost a paradise. The technicians can claim that it is not their fault if, at this hour more than ever before, mankind presents features of the utmost misery and the most unworthy conditions. All this is meant by the phrase "technical progress", which up to recent years was used without hesitation. It seems as if technics—and particularly modern technics—was an indisputable gain for mankind.

Why is it, then, that nobody at this hour uses that word "progress" without hesitation, if at all? Let us be clear that there is no such thing as "technics in itself". The production of a cannon is a technical affair, but at the same time it is the expression of a certain political and military will. The production of dangerous narcotics is a matter of chemical industry, but it serves purposes which are medically and morally unsound and pernicious. Technics, therefore, is never purely technical. It always stands in the closest connection with the totality of social and cultural life and of man himself. "Technics" is an abstraction which does not exist. There are only men working technically for certain purposes. When modern man conceived the idea of redeeming himself and making himself master of his life by technics, he did not know or divine that such technics would have results of a very different order. What, then, are those effects of the technical revolution which an increasing majority of modern men abhor?

Modern technics does not mean merely a fantastic extension of man's power over nature; it also means millions of men working underground, uncounted millions of men massed together in soulless giant cities; a proletariat without connection with nature, without a native heath or neighbour-

345

hood; it means asphalt-culture, uniformity and standardisation. It means men whom the machine has relieved from thinking and willing, who in their turn have to "serve the machine" at a prescribed tempo and in a stereotyped manner. It means unbearable noise and rush, unemployment and insecurity of life, the concentration of productive power, wealth and prestige in a few hands or their monopolisation by state bureaucracy. It means the destruction of noble crafts with their standards of quality and their patriarchal working conditions; it means the transformation of the farmer into a specialised technician of agriculture, the rise of an office proletariat with infinitely monotonous work. It means also the speedy standardisation of all national cultures and the extinction of their historical originality. It means universal cliché-culture, the same films and musical hits from New York to Tokyo, from Cape Town to Stockholm, the same illustrated magazines all over the world, the same menus, the same dance-tunes. It means the increasing domination of quantity over quality, not only in production itself but also in the formation of social, political and international power.

Above all, there are two phenomena in very recent times which, like devilish monsters, rise from that progressively technified mankind: the modern totalitarian state and modern technical war industry. It cannot be said that the totalitarian state is the necessary product of technics, but its relation to technics is obvious. Without modern technics the totalitarian state is impossible. And the tendency towards totalitarianism lies within technical evolution: mechanisation, centralisation, mass-men. Modern war industry, however, is the direct product of modern technics. Let us remember it is not the technicians that are guilty, but man who has abandoned technics to itself, incapable of bridling its development, putting technics without hesitation, and, as if driven by necessity,

346

at the service of his political power-aims. This war machinery displayed its terrifying force in the first world war. The second world war manifested its increased destructive force; but since then there has come that last step or leap: the use of atomic energy, which means a sudden increase in the capacity of annihilation without analogy in the previous history of technics. Now the development of technical warfare has reached the point where nothing is impossible to it. Mankind for the first time faces possible universal suicide.

This is the other, the dark side of the picture. It shows how dangerous it is to speak of technics *in abstracto*. One could have known from the history of technics that every technical advance does not change merely man's relation to nature, but also man's relation to man. Every invention is an increase in power, and every increase in power within society is a danger to its balance and order. This fact could remain unnoticed so long as technical progress could be assimilated socially and ethically. It is the tragic fact of modern history that the technical revolution took place at a time when mankind was in a process of social dissolution and ethical confusion. It was the era of progressive secularisation and mass-atheism, when all ethical standards were relativised and men became metaphysically and ethically homeless. Cause and effect mutually interpenetrate each other. We have already seen that modern technics could not have developed without a certain spirit of rationalism and secularisation. It is, however, equally true that secularised humanity was not socially and ethically equal to the technical revolution. Only a society which was incapable of subordinating the profit motive to higher motives, a society which was ethically, and even aesthetically callous and enfeebled, could allow the growth of those soulless, ugly, giant cities, with their speculative building and their proletarian quarters. Only such a society could watch without protest the dissolution of all natural community, and accept as inevitable the development of modern war technics.

In this connection we have to point out grave fault on the part of the Christian Church. The Church ought to have been on the watch-tower. She ought to have seen what was going on behind those beautiful slogans of freedom and progress. The Church might have been expected to protect men from enslavement and from becoming automatons. The Church ought to have seen that in such conditions, which upset all the order of creation, the preaching of the Gospel became almost illusory. Is it not shameful for the Christian society that Confucian China was capable of suppressing the military use of gunpowder, while the Christian Church could not prevent, and did not even try to prevent, the development of a war machinery incomparably more dreadful?

European industrial history is not altogether devoid of indications of what might have happened if modern industry had developed within a truly Christian society. I am thinking of a certain phase in the industrial development of Great Britain and Switzerland. Within a few decades of the invention of the steam engine these countries experienced a physical and social devastation within the working population which was definitely alarming. But then moral and religious forces reacted and were called to the defence. By social legislation, by the trade-union and co-operative movements, and by something like an awakening of social consciousness through prophetic personalities, much of the damage was repaired in a comparatively short time. What had been called technical necessity proved quite unnecessary. The technique of fabrication, so often regarded as being beyond ethical control, was effectively put under such control. Many things remained bad enough, but yet the effect of this ethical-social reaction against the technical materialistic *laissez-faire* gives us a faint idea of what

could have been avoided if society had awakened in time to the ethical dangers of so-called progress.

Nobody can say how far the disease of uncontrolled, unassimilated technics has progressed already, whether the disease has reached the point where it becomes incurable or not. It is our duty, however, to open our eyes to the imminent threat to life and to do whatever we can to make technics serve human ends.

The nature of technics is to place at man's disposal the means for certain purposes. Of course, the production and use of technical means is in itself a purpose, but it is never a *Selbstzweck,* an ultimate purpose. It is essential to the health of a society that this order of ends and means should be known and recognised, so that technics as the sum of means is subordinated to man's life. Where the means become more important than the end, where technics becomes autonomous, a social disease develops, which is analogous to cancer: autonomous growths, not useful but injurious to the organism, which develop independently of the organic centre and finally destroy the organism. When, for instance, a country rejoices over the growth of a city of millions of inhabitants, this is as stupid as if someone were to rejoice over the growth of a cancer. Giant cities are merely symptoms, but they are obvious symptoms of autonomous technical growth which finally leads to destruction.

The positive meaning of a human civilisation depends on this subordination of means to ends. The reversal of this order, therefore, results in civilisation becoming inhuman and finally perverted. For this reversal of the order of ends and means, which produces a demonic autonomy of technics, secularisation is more to blame than technics. It is because the world and its goods become to men more important than God, eternal life and love, that men throw themselves into the production of material goods with that passion of which the human soul, destined for infinitude, is capable. Technics was merely the means by which this insatiable desire for material goods could be, or seemed to be, stilled, because technics is capable of unlimited development. Once brought into action, this process of unlimited increase and expansion could no longer be controlled. The machine invented by man began to control man's will; whether he liked it or not he had to obey the logic of technical development. It was exactly as in Goethe's symbolic ballad, *Der Zauberlehrling,* about the spying apprentice who had found out his wizard master's magic word which summoned obedient spirits to his service. For a while he revelled in the service of the water-carrying spirits; but before long he became afraid, because the spirits could no longer be controlled, so that by their very service the poor apprentice was in peril of being drowned —*Die ich rief, die Geister, werd ich nun nicht los*—a catastrophe from which the master's intervention saved him. This is very like our situation. Man has learned to control the immeasurable powers of nature. Modern man dominates nature to a degree unthinkable in previous ages. But whilst man controls nature by technics he no longer controls his own technics, but is more and more dominated by it and threatened with catastrophe.

Last century saw the climax of technical enthusiasm and of belief in progress by technics. It was then that people hoped technics would relieve man of all impediments and troubles connected with his body. "Our saviour is the machine", ran a sentence in a German newspaper. This enthusiasm for technics can still take hold of peoples whose technical development has lagged behind that of Western Europe. It can develop the more where the ground is prepared by secularist thinking which recognises only earthly and ma-

terial goods. In Western Europe, however, this enthusiasm has been followed by disillusionment, deep despondency and fear. The first part of the story of the *Zauberlehrling* is finished. The second part is in full process and, since the invention of the atomic bomb, is approaching its climax.

Such disillusionment and despair might bring about a real turn of the pendulum in the right direction, but only if man is capable of understanding something of the deeper causes of this fatal, automatic development of technics, if he comes to see the false order of means and ends—that is, secularisation, loss of faith in God and in eternal values—as the root of the whole matter. All other proposals to make technics subservient again to human ends, and all attempts to heal the damage to social and personal life produced by the technical revolution, are mere palliatives. I do not mean that they are worthless, they may even be necessary, as the treatment of symptoms—such as fighting the fever —is often necessary until more radical therapy can begin. But unless there is a basic conversion, technics will develop as before, and the tempo of its development will not decrease but increase, because nowadays men not only make inventions but have found the technique of making inventions. For this reason, all corrections coming from outside always come too late. The crazy tempo of technical revolution can only be reduced to a degree which is socially and personally supportable, if the whole scale of values of European nations can be changed. As long as material values indisputably take the first place, no change for the better is to be expected.

The perversion of the order of means and ends was caused by the decay of the consciousness of personality. And this in its turn was the consequence of the decay of Christian faith. In our time many have come to see, and are ready to admit, that moral values ought to be put in the first place. This insight is good, but not sufficient. Mere ethics has never displayed real dynamic. You cannot cure a demon-ridden technical world with moral postulates. In contrast to mere ethics and morality, Christian faith has the dynamic of passion, of surrender and sacrifice; it is capable of turning men to the eternal end, of unmasking demonic sin and thereby banning it, which no enlightened education is capable of doing.

Technics in itself is no problem for the Christian man. As long as technics is subordinate to human will, and human will is obedient to the divine will, technics is neutral, and as a means of goodwill is itself good. From the Christian point of view, there is no reason to condemn the machine and to return to the spinning-wheel. Even the use of atomic energy is not in itself harmful or bad. But we can hardly avoid the question whether technical evolution has not already passed the limits within which it is controllable by feeble, mortal men. This question cannot be theoretically decided. It is a question of the real dynamic. For us the only important question is whether mankind is ready, or may become ready, to perform that inward right-about-turn which alone will correct the fatal perversion of the order of means and ends.

PETER L. BERGER

Christian Faith and the Subversive Role of the Social Sciences*

There is a wealth of theological writing in the field of "social ethics," some of it dealing in a profound and challenging way with the moral problems faced by men in their social relationships. However, there is one thread that runs through many of these which is most likely to lead to a distorted view of social reality, and that is the understanding of social roles and institutions as given in very much the same way as natural phenomena are given. Thus ethicists will speak of "the family," "the state," or "the economy" as if these were hewn out of granite, while actually, as we have tried to indicate, they are manufactured out of the most precarious of fictions, assumptions, and "as if" agreements. This is most true, of course, when social institutions are conceived of as actually given in natural law, as in Catholic social doctrine, but also when they (or their ideal prototypes) are thought of as "orders of creation," as in Emil Brunner's ethics. There follows the almost irresistible tendency to speculate ethically not about men but about social roles. One then looks not at the moral problems of human beings engaged in government or warfare or agriculture,

* From *The Precarious Vision* by Peter L. Berger. Copyright © 1961 by Peter L. Berger. Reprinted by permission of Doubleday & Company, Inc.; pp. 191-208, 216-18.

but one theorizes about the ethics of "the statesman," "the soldier," or "the peasant." There is then only one step to the bad faith which provides moral alibis in the name of mythological entities such as "the state," "the law," "the system of free enterprise," and so forth. Of course the ethicist like the sociologist, or, for that matter, the man in the street will speak of institutions in these abstract terms, and furthermore such abstraction is a necessity of analytic thinking. The danger, as we have tried to show, begins when these abstractions are taken to exist as moral realities which supersede the moral imperatives of real human beings. We would suggest that the perspective on society developed in the first part of this essay may be helpful in avoiding this danger.

The confrontation with the living God of the Christian faith strips men of their alibis and disguises. The aprons of fig leaves spun with the lies of institutional ideologies cannot cover man's nakedness as God seeks him out in his hiding places. In this, indeed, all men are the children of Adam, who said, "I heard the sound of thee in the garden, and I was afraid, because I was naked; and I hid myself" (Gen. 3:10). Or, in the words of the Epistle to the Hebrews: "And before him no creature is hidden, but all are open and laid bare to the eyes of him with whom we have to do" (Heb. 4:13). The God "with whom we have to do" has not recognized the sovereignty of our card-house institutions or the extraterritoriality of the moral hiding places which men have concocted among themselves. He steps into the palace of the king and the judge's chambers, ignoring the royal mantle and the judicial robes, and addresses the naked man underneath the costume as He addressed Adam: "But the Lord God called to the man, and said to him, 'Where are you?'" (Gen. 3:9). And as kings and judges renounce their human brotherhood with their victims, pointing to the immunity of their office, God will

350

address them in words no different from those addressed to Cain: "What have you done? The voice of your brother's blood is crying to me from the ground" (Gen. 4:10).

Every literate man knows that certain positions in society entail responsibilities, privileges, and immunities. There are many books written about this, such as textbooks of ethics, codes of law, constitutions, and statutes. We would suggest that God, regrettably, has not read any of them. We would further suggest that this proposition of the illiteracy of God follows of necessity from the realization of God's truth as against the bad faith of social subterfuge.

To illustrate this proposition we might turn briefly once more to the case of capital punishment. We have looked before in some detail at the fabric of social fictions which provides moral alibis for all the individuals participating in this killing and which actually pretends that no individual did any killing at all. In a well-ordered modern state there are ample possibilities of documentation for this claim to personal immunity. The judge can point to the statute books, the governor to the constitution of the state, the warden to the prison regulations, and so forth. Any literate man can easily verify the authenticity of the claims. It is most unfortunate that God is illiterate. He has read neither statute books nor the constitution of the state, nor the prison regulations. Also, judges, governors, and wardens can point out to anyone that they have been duly appointed or elected to their respective offices; they have impressive documents to show that will verify this to any man who would question their jurisdiction or proper authority in the matter. It is again most regrettable that God is illiterate. The appointment of Judge Smith has been registered in all appropriate offices, published in the daily press, and entered in various official handbooks. God, alas, was not informed about the appointment. He continues to look upon Smith as a human being and judges him as human beings are judged in the divine presence. Since God is not only truth but also mercy, it is not beyond imagining that Smith's delusions about his own status may be a mitigating circumstance in the judgment. But God would not be God if He recognized these delusions as the truth.

This denuding character of the encounter between God and man is understandable in terms of the Christian doctrine of creation. God created the heavens and the earth. And then He created man. He did not create society. That latter achievement belongs entirely to man's own ingenuity. But God looks upon man and continues to address man as His creature. In other words, God addresses man as man and as nothing else. Even a human father will often find it hard to resist a smile when his son, whom he watched as a yelping infant on the day of his birth, steps up to him as a vice-president of the corporation or *aide-de-camp* to the commanding general. But human fathers, themselves part of the social drama, may eventually be taken in. God is above the social drama and is never taken in. Man enters into the world naked, without a name, without social roles, without involvement in the great institutions. For the remainder of his life he impresses upon others and upon himself the importance of his name, social roles and institutional positions. God remains unimpressed. In the words of Job: "Naked I came from my mother's womb, and naked shall I return" (Job 1:21). It would seem that no Christian understanding of society can dispense with this awareness of man's persisting nakedness beneath his social masquerades.

Perhaps the most terrifying aspect of the confrontation with God's address is not the judgment over man's sin but the profound challenge to his most cherished identifications. One dreams that one finds oneself on the street naked. One wakes up, shakes off the nightmare and the embarrassment, and repeats to oneself with pleasure one's repertoire of title roles: "I am Mr. James Sutherland Smith"—"I am the husband of Mrs. Alice Jennison Smith"—"I am vice-president of the Epitomy Manufacturing Corporation"—"I am a registered Republican," and so forth. Into this reassuring recital comes God's address —and returns one in an instant to nakedness. "And the foundations of the thresholds shook at the voice of him who called" (Is. 6:4). Not least the narrow thresholds which hold in our self-conceptions and our self-esteem!

But God's challenge is not only to the consciously contrived identifications of social one-upmanship. The challenge extends to the deepest, most taken-for-granted conceptions as to who and what one is. In the American racial situation it is easily said by Northern preachers of racial equality that God is "color-blind." This, of course, is quite true, in quite the sense intended by those who say it. But to grasp the weight of what is said one must realize the depths of self-identification involved in a Southerner saying to himself and to others, "I am white." Lillian Smith has given us a haunting description of this process of self-identification under the telling title "The White Man's Burden is his Own Childhood":

"So we learned the dance that cripples the human spirit, step by step by step, we who were white and we who were colored, day by day, hour by hour, year by year until the movements were reflexes and made for the rest of our life without thinking. Alas, for many white children, they were movements made for the rest of their lives without feeling. What white southerner of my generation ever stops to think consciously where to go or asks himself if it is right for him to go there! His muscles know where he can go and take him to the front of the streetcar, to the front of the bus, to the big school, to the hospital, to the library, to

351

hotel and restaurant and picture show, into the best that his town has to offer its citizens. These ceremonials in honor of white supremacy, performed from babyhood, slip from the conscious mind down deep into muscles and glands and on into that region where mature ideals rarely find entrance, and become as difficult to tear out as are a child's beliefs about God and his secret dreams about himself." [1]

The proclamation that God is "no respecter of persons," that He does not know the difference between "white" and "black," that the racial system of the South is a moral evil—this proclamation is not just a statement of inconvenient ethical injunctions but a shattering blow to the very roots of self-esteem. The Southerner whom Lillian Smith describes in the above passage may lose all he has, worldly goods and social position, perhaps even his sanity, but in the deepest recesses of his self there will be something that will say, "I am white." God's reply to this final self-affirmation is quite simple: "No—you are not white—you are a human being." In this confrontation the bad faith of the racial posture is sharply revealed. For "to be white," as any student of Southern society knows, is not a biologically objective fact of the pigmentation of the skin but rather a socially concocted myth. In a biological sense a man "is" this or that color. That, presumably, is a fact of nature. But in the socially relevant sense a man "is white" by the fiat of the myth. Enough has been written about the racial fantasies involved in this myth (as illustrated best by the case of very light-skinned "Negroes") to dispense with further elaboration. The crucial point is that "to be white" is not a biological fact but a social fiction. The system of oppression that appeals to this fiction is a system of bad faith. Both fiction and bad faith will not hold up in the confrontation with the God of truth. It goes without saying that the same argument applies to other racial, national, or ethnic identifications. Here too we have to deal with the illiterate God. Everyone knows very well that we have no choice in certain situations but to act "as white Southerners," "as Americans," "as Europeans," "as Jews," and so on. After all, this is what the social libretto says—here is our name and next to it it says in clear writing "a Jew," "a German," or whatever the play has cast us as. Again it is a great pity that this libretto has not come to God's attention. He thus remains inconsiderately uninterested in our description in the *dramatis personae*. Indeed, it is in the etymologically literal sense of the word (*persona*= dramatic mask) that God is "no respecter of persons."

It is in this society-shattering sense that we may understand Paul's declaration that in Christ "There is neither Jew nor Greek, there is neither slave nor free" (Gal. 3:28). And we are certainly justified if we regard this declaration as being of significance beyond the confines of the Christian community itself. The church, the community that confesses Christ, is to be in the world as a promise of the new human order that lies in the eschatological future. Christ is Lord over the world as well as over the church. The nonrecognition of ethnic and social identifications within the church foreshadows their nonrecognition in the world under the Lordship of the triumphant Christ. It gives one deep pause to read on in this same statement of Paul's and find it continues with the assertion that in Christ "there is neither male nor female." We would venture to suggest (at the risk of engaging in very daring exegesis) that there is much more involved in this final assertion than a call for equality between the sexes. We would suggest that, as God challenges all our social identifications, He also challenges our sexual identification. God refuses to recognize our protestations and

[1] Lillian Smith, *Killers of the Dream* (New York: W. W. Norton & Company, 1949), p. 91.

moral deductions to the effect that "we are Jews," "we are Greeks," "we are whites," "we are American citizens." He challenges no less our self-identifications as men and as women, our pretensions of virility and femininity. The divine answer to the statement "I am a man" is, once more, *"No—you are not a man —you are a human being."*

We would argue here somewhat analogously to the way in which we approached the relationship of fact and fiction in the racial situation. There are, of course, objective biological facts involved in human sexuality. Yet even a cursory glance at the wealth of anthropological literature on sexuality in different cultures will immediately show us that the complex of values, emotions, and moral ideals implied in the statement "I am a man" is not biologically given but socially learned. In other words, there are sexual roles just as there are other roles in society. Once more, the total identification of oneself with the sexual role is an act of bad faith. Any amount of delving into psychiatric literature about human sexuality will show us, even among the least "maladjusted," the tremendous precariousness of sexual identification. It would, for example, be of great interest to have Rorschach data available on the judges, jurors, and prosecuting attorneys who in Anglo-Saxon countries continue to this day to throw homosexuals in jail for years, and this frequently for acts engaged in discreetly and voluntarily by adults. The persecution of homosexuals is so vicious for very much the same reasons that racial persecution is. While the persecutor in the latter case uses his victim in bad faith to bolster his spurious self-identification as a member of a superior race, the persecutor in the former case forces upon and hence out of his victim the confirmation of his own usually shaky self-identification as a "normal" male. One beats the Negro to feel white. One

spits upon the homosexual to feel virile.

It is not our concern here to enlarge upon the question of a Christian ethic of sexuality, of the moral problems of homosexuality, or of the question as to the proper use of the police powers of the state in areas of private morals. We would only suggest that a truthful approach to these areas—that is, the only approach allowable in the confrontation of our existence with God—will make us wary of speaking very glibly about what is "natural," "normal," or "given" in the sexual roles of men and women. It is remarkable how Christian thought in these areas succeeds in going ahead happily as if the wealth of anthropological research on these matters in the last century, at least, had never happened. We might quote as an example not one of the worst cases but one of the best —the report on homosexuality of a committee set up a few years ago by the Church of England (a report, let it be added hastily, which is remarkable for its sensible and enlightened approach to this question):

"Right reason thus points to the ineluctable conclusion that the use of the sexual organs, being governed by the nature of sex itself and by the recognized purposes of coitus, is proper only in the context of a personal relation which is both heterosexual and specifically marital. Considered, then, in terms of objective morality, it is evident that homosexual acts are contrary to the will of God for human sexuality, and are therefore sinful *per se.*" [2]

We would suggest, as a helpful exercise, an examination in the light of the perspective on society developed in the first part of this essay of the phrases "recognized purposes," "specifically marital," and "objective morality"! The American reader, who has strong nerves and the will to carry problems to their "ineluctable conclusion" might amplify the exercise by reading, in succession, a

[2] D. S. Bailey (ed.), *Sexual Offenders and Social Punishment* (London: Church Information Board, 1956), p. 75.

good anthropological treatise on human sexuality,[3] the first Kinsey report, and some of the laws on sexual offenses now on the statute books of American states.[4]

A simple definition of a humanist ethic might be one which orients its conceptions and imperatives toward men rather than institutions. Thus, a humanist ethic, such as is generally accepted in Western democracies, would hold that political institutions exist for the welfare of men. Recent history has given us ample opportunity to observe the consequences of a contrary ethic that maintains that men exist for the welfare of the state. It is one of the ironies of history (and one of the consequences of the Babylonian captivity of the Christian faith in religious forms) that Christian ethical thought has frequently found itself in the antihumanist camp. We would suggest, from our understanding of society and of the Christian faith, that a Christian ethic will always be humanist in the sense just given. God is concerned with men. He addresses men. He addresses institutions only in the sense that men, in their real life in society, exist in institutional involvements. Thus different words must be addressed to the king and to the peasant. But both are addressed *as men*.

But Christian faith is relevant for social perception not only in such extreme cases as capital punishment or racial oppression (although the debunking, unmasking character of the Christian faith becomes very clear in the way it challenges the pretensions involved in such human situations). We would once more point to Bonhoeffer's assertion that Christ is Lord not only over the so-called "boundary situations" of human existence, but also Lord over the central areas of life (the "middle of the village," as Bonhoeffer called it). For, as we have seen, men come up against the problem of bad faith not only when they are jurors in sodomy cases or participants in other forms of legal lynching. Bad faith looms as a constant possibility over everyday life and its most ordinary pursuits. We might return here once more to the case of occupational or professional ideologies.

A good illustration of this might be the self-image of the advertising man in America, as it appears in his professional publications and gatherings, as well as in his speaking about himself personally. This self-image presents the adman as a rather gay, reckless figure, in some ways a professional fun-maker, descended in apostolic succession from the storytellers and town criers of olden times. He practices an art by which he gives color and amusement to people who might otherwise live very drab lives. Like all artists he has a measure of poetic license with the truth and mainly plays on the emotions rather than the intellect. In our own society this fun-maker also carries on a worthwhile, even crucial economic mission. His activities help move the goods, on which movement depends our prosperity. Advertising and abundance go together. The advertiser serves the public by showing it the way to a new, abundant life. Also, he serves as a bridge of communication between manufacturer and consumer. The adman represents the exuberance, the enterprise, and the confidence of our society.

It will be apparent to most non-admen that this self-image has a very shaky relationship with reality. The economic assumptions of the ideology are, at any rate, not beyond all reasonable doubt (that is, the notions about the economic beneficence of advertising). But its noneconomic aspects are shaky enough too. One may point out the discrepancy between the image of the fun-maker and

---

[3] Cf., for example, Bronislaw Malinowski, *The Sexual Life of Savages* (New York: Halcyon House, 1929) ; or, Margaret Mead, *Male and Female* (New York: Mentor Books, 1955).

[4] Cf. Morris Ploscowe, *Sex and the Law* (New York: Prentice-Hall, Inc., 1951).

the image of the communications expert. What is more, the apostolic succession of the first image is spurious. We are dealing here with the most synthetic of fun-making—based on careful market research, with a steady eye on the sales statistics and another eye peeking over the shoulder of the psychoanalyst for technical hints, the whole operation calculated for profit from beginning to end. Beyond that, the gay and reckless figure of the adman is not much in evidence when one has once looked a little more deeply into the world of Madison Avenue. This is a world of much anxiety and frustration, taking its grim toll of nerves, dreams, and ulcers. Finally, the license which the adman takes with the truth and with men's emotions is rarely poetic. It is the art of the sharp salesman, not that of the poet, which is in demand here.

Why is such an image adopted? This is not a very difficult question to answer. Men never like to face unpleasant aspects of their life. They invent ideologies to pretty up the picture. Groups of men reinforce each other in the conviction that the ideology is the truth. Advertising, as an occupation, presents a very high degree of conflict and tension. It demands a nervous, sharply competitive life. It involves the constant necessity of manipulating oneself and other people. If viewed under an ethical aspect it presents even greater doubts and anxieties. It is normal for men to shy away from anxiety and guilt. Occupational ideologies provide a convenient method for doing this.

Perhaps the problem of guilt is where the Christian faith relates most directly to this type of ideology. To ask men to see through their own ideological befogment is to push them into facing the moral ambiguity of their situation. The psychological tendency is, of course, to resist this attempt. Men tend psychologically either to suppress their guilt or to analyze it away. If the Christian faith involved only the proclamation of God's judgment, it would only reinforce this tendency (as, indeed, it has where it was mainly understood in this way—compare the Freudian paradise of the "Puritan mind"!). But the Christian faith primarily proclaims God's grace. The victory of Christ over sin and death involves the possibility that men may face their own guilt in a new way. Christian faith holds that man is justified by grace in the real world, as a real human being —that is, as a sinner. This belief makes it possible for man to face himself and to dispense with the narcotic of ideology. This can be a very liberating experience, not only emotionally but in the way in which it may now become possible to seek avenues of responsible action in one's situation. With this new freedom there is at least a chance of modifying some of the morally questionable features of the situation. As long as the situation is shrouded in ideology, there is not even a chance. Thus Christian faith is relevant not only to social consciousness but also to the (sometimes slim) possibility of social action. It is important to stress, however, that liberation begins in the realm of consciousness. Truly liberating action in society is dependent on this first liberation.

A few years ago a group of American military chaplains met in western Germany with a group of German churchmen to discuss problems of the military chaplaincy. This was the period when the new west-German army was just being organized and the problems were very timely. One of the American chaplains delivered a lecture describing and praising the chaplaincy in the American armed forces. He spent much time on the so-called "character guidance program," emphasized the close relationships among religion, morals, and patriotism, and finally stressed the direct contribution of the chaplain's work to military morale. The Germans were somewhat taken aback by this interpretation, which for them had rather disturbing similarities with views associated with a relatively recent past of German history. But there was little discussion immediately after the lecture. Some time later a group of the participants in this meeting were sitting together. Suddenly one of the German churchmen leaned over to the American who had given the lecture and asked him: "How does the function of the chaplain in the American army differ from that of the *politruk* in the Soviet army?" The import of the question did not immediately register with the American, because the question had to be translated and there had to be an explanation of the Russian term (*politruks* are Communist political officers attached to all units of the Soviet army, their task being the political guidance and morale of the troops). When the meaning of the question became clear to the American and his colleagues there was a long, painful silence. Then the Americans began to ask questions —not belligerently but in a mood of embarrassment and urgent curiosity. It was quite clear that the one question asked by the German churchman had suddenly opened up a completely new perspective on their situation to these chaplains. It would, of course, have been easy for them to defend themselves against the question within the categories of their professional ideology. That they did not do this, that they really listened to the question and tried to meet it, was not in small measure due to the Christian context in which both questioner and questioned faced each other. It is in this kind of encounter that the Christian faith can become liberating in the social perception and consciousness of men.

There is something radically "subversive" about this liberation. And, one might add, the Roman authorities showed great wisdom and political acumen in feeding the Christians to the lions (by the time the practice ended, of course, the Christians had become sufficiently domesticated to be innocuous to society). However, it would be erron-

eous to view the "subversion" of the Christian faith in the way in which, for instance, a Marxist would understand the development of revolutionary consciousness. Christian faith is radical because it challenges social assumptions at their very roots. Christian faith, as we have seen, can never exercise the conservative function normally assigned to religion. On the other hand, Christian faith takes a far too realistic view of man to be revolutionary in too many situations. Christian faith rejects the ideology of the conservative, because it sees through the fictitiousness by which the *status quo* rationalizes and maintains itself. Christian faith rejects the utopianism of the revolutionary, because it will not accept the fantastic hopes for the future with which revolutionary activity justifies its own existence. It is bad faith to oppress men in the name of conservative principles. It is also bad faith to engage in atrocities on the promise of a future justice, a promise for the fulfillment of which there is little rational hope. Thus the Christian view of social reality cannot easily be enlisted in the service of "liberalism" *or* "conservatism." In some concrete, real situations the political decisions of the Christian may be "conservative," in other situations "liberal." The Christian perspective will militate against delusions concerning the future as well as against those concerning the present. To pursue this further at this point would take us far beyond our immediate concerns, however, and it may be more profitable to return once more to the main thread of our argument.

It should be clear by this point that the challenge of the Christian faith to carefully cherished self-identifications is frequently a very shocking, disagreeable business. The natural inclinations of man lead him to take society for granted, to identify himself fully with the social roles assigned to him, and to develop ideologies which will organize and dispose of any doubts that might possibly arise. There is an instructive affinity between Christian faith and the analytic enterprise of the social sciences in that both serve to disturb this happy state of affairs. The Christian faith, in its prophetic mission, confronts man with a truth of such force that the precarious pretensions of his social existence disintegrate before it. The debunking effect of social-scientific analysis is far from contradictory to this prophetic mission. Indeed, it might be called its profane auxiliary. The smashing of idols, with whatever hammers, is the underside of prophecy.

But there is another aspect, perhaps one that might be called more positive, in the affinity between Christian and sociological "subversion." This aspect we have already touched upon in our discussion of role theory. It has to do with the extreme precariousness of human identity, not just of certain specific social identifications but of identity in any sense of the word. If we follow the insights of modern social psychology into the character of identity, we get a picture that makes it very difficult indeed to speak of "human nature" in any very meaningful sense. Human identity appears as a result of a socialization process in which it is others that "name" one—"name" in the fullest sense of the word. It is others, by their recognition, who bestow upon the child his sexual identity, his identities of race, nationality, and class, and the total complex of beliefs, categories, and values that goes with these several identities. "Human nature" (as soon as we get beyond strictly zoological facts) is a social product, one that is socially relative depending upon the accidents of birth and biography. But identity is not only produced socially. It is also sustained socially. Self-esteem, self-respect, and even the profounder levels of self-image depend upon the continuing recognition of their validity by other human beings. If this recognition is drastically withdrawn, it normally takes little time before the whole precarious edifice collapses into a whining misery of infantile terror. We are what we are by the recognition of others. Since all such recognition is, by its innate nature, highly precarious, so is whatever it is that we are. There is no more distressing realization of the contingency of our being than to understand that we are dependent for our very identity upon other human beings —creatures, that is, who may forget or change their minds, and creatures who will surely die.

This is not the place to speculate philosophically as to whether it would not be quite possible to get along without a metaphysical concept of the self. Nor is the writer qualified for such a philosophical task. It might be said, however, that a social-scientific slant on the question would certainly not induce one to tend toward the notion of the self as some kind of solid, stable entity persisting in time. If one looks at the bewildering repertoire of roles and "social selves" (William James) that any individual has, and then asks, "But who is he *really?*" there is no empirically satisfactory way of answering the question. The social psychologist (or, for that matter, the sociologist) will probably have to rule out the question and satisfy himself with the description of the repertoire as it develops in the individual's different social relationships. A psychologist might give an answer to the question in terms of something that could be called the individual's "nature," but unfortunately the likelihood is that, in doing so, the individual becomes either a zoological or a mythical entity which he himself has great difficulty recognizing once he is out of the social situation in which the psychologist makes the interpretation. An existentialist might possibly answer, "Ask him!" and add that an individual is that which he chooses himself to be. Which, if understood within a social frame of reference, is perhaps the best answer that could be given, unless one operates

357

with a concept of "soul" that has no relationship to the empirical self. But, as Sartre has pointed out, this means that there is no such thing as "human nature." Or rather, there is not—unless one posits God. It would seem that this Sartrian insight is significant for our argument here.

The reason why it is so difficult to answer the question "Who is he really?" is that there are no convincing criteria for deciding which recognition is definitive. After all, the individual in question is recognized by some as a virtuous man and by others as a crook, by some as sincere and by others as cynical, by some as endowed with a sense of humor and by others as a deadly bore. Even if there is a measure of consensus about him among his associates (as there usually is—or society could not go on), this is also an accident of the individual's situation. Remove him from the group that thought him virtuous and put him in some other context and very soon he may act the role of snarling villain. What is more, his own recognitions of himself are vague and contradictory. His picture of himself varies with the situations in which he finds himself. And if one psychologist calls him type A and another type B, there is no way of deciding which one is to be our authority.

Scholastic theology defined God as the only noncontingent being. And an Arabic proverb defines man as the one who forgets. God is the one who remembers. God calls man out of nothingness and gives him a name and remembers him for ever. Beyond the contingencies and precariousness of his identity, *man is he whom God addresses*. His being (his "nature," if one prefers) lies in that fact of God's address. His identity is that as which God addresses him. This is what Luther meant in his saying that man exists as long as God speaks to him, be it speaking in anger or in mercy. Or to put this in the terms used above, God's recognition is the definitive one.

Only in this perspective can we answer the question as to who we are. Let it be added here most emphatically that we are not presenting this at all as an argument for the existence of God. Such argumentation would once more be producing a *deus ex machina* in just the sense criticized by Bonhoeffer. What we are saying again, however, is that there is here too a certain affinity between the contingency of man's being, as understood by the Christian faith, and the precariousness of man's identity, as understood by the social-scientific enterprise.

There are important consequences to this perspective in terms of the social mission of the Christian church, that community in which the risen Lord is witnessed to in the world. Quite apart from what the church may or may not do in the way of social action, the church, if it is faithful to its mission, can play a vital role in society and its clash of ideologies. *The church is the place of truth.* When we say this, of course, we are fully aware that this is pretty much the opposite of what the empirical church normally is. But the church can be the place of truth when it stands on the ground of Jesus Christ and no other—that is, when it liberates itself from its social and psychological functionality. The church can then be not only the proclaiming church but the listening church, providing those rare opportunities in society where men can look truthfully at themselves and their roles. This too is an essential feature of the nonkerygmatic posture we discussed before. We would suggest that one of the most urgent tasks of the church in our present situation is the providing of such places of truth (be it in the local congregation or in other locales), places where men can think through in freedom the moral and human dilemmas of their social roles. The work of the European laymen's institutes since World War II has been a serious effort to realize this shape of the *Ecclesia audiens.* The demands of the American situation are not essentially different.

Even within the church there is often the idea that theological thought and understanding of society are strictly segregated activities of the Christian mind. Both theologians and sociologists spend much time erecting methodological fences which keep out the uninitiated (and, incidentally, imprison the initiates). We would suggest that the intellectual tasks of gaining an understanding of the Christian faith in depth and of gaining a broad perspective on society are related. . . .

To be ultimately serious about society means *ipso facto* to be caught within it. Thus even the revolutionary, who seeks to overthrow society and build a new one on the ruins of the old, is ultimately serious about his social involvements. Only a conception of man which transcends society can take social involvements with a grain of salt—or with tongue in cheek. Certainly the Christian faith is not the only such conception. But in the Christian understanding of man and of the nature of redemption lies an unusually fertile opportunity of gaining distance from the social problems pressing on one at the moment. Thus the refusal of taking society as ultimately serious (which means refusing to take it at the face value it usually puts on itself) not only is an experience of personal liberation but also has relevance to the effort to grasp society intellectually. . . . It is a commonplace observation, but still an important one, that a measure of distance allows one to see more clearly. The Christian faith, when it is true to itself and really is "in the world but not of it," provides distance from society and thus creates opportunities for perception. Thus the Christian faith relates to the enterprise of the social sciences not only because of its radical challenge to social delusions and alibis. In a more benign way, as it were, it relates to the "sociological imagination" (Mills) by way of the comic

perspective on the social carnival. The Christian sees man as having a destiny over and beyond society, man straddling two worlds, those two worlds that Simone Weil called those of gravity and grace. In thus transcending society, the Christian faith at the same time makes it possible to see society more clearly.

Dietrich Bonhoeffer made the important distinction between "ultimate" and "penultimate" concerns in his *Ethics.* The entire domain of social and political action, however serious its involvements may often be, will always be "penultimate" in the Christian economy. Thus the Christian will engage himself in action passionately, but he will not allow his commitment to blind him to the comic aspects of his situation. He will deal with men without forgetting that they were children not so long ago. He will protest against injustice, but he will not absolutize this protest or make it the basis of his existence. He will build for the future, but he will do so in full awareness of the precariousness of all human construction on the quicksands of history. Above all, he will remember that the central message of the Christian faith is not a call to struggle but a call to joy.

We quite miss the point if we only laugh at Don Quixote because he rides against windmills. The point is that, in the magic of the Quixotic universe, the windmills really cease to be windmills and are metamorphosed into a promise of glory. Of course, we know that "in this aeon," as the New Testament puts it, the ride of Don Quixote ends in a sad return to what we take for granted as reality. But the Christian faith means looking toward the aeon that is to come. The magic moment of comedy foreshadows this aeon, when redemption becomes the one overpowering reality of the universe. Christian faith, just because it strives for clear perception, cannot look at Don Quixote through the eyes of Sancho Panza. The windmills of the Quixotic attack are the battlements of the New Jerusalem, as yet dimly seen on the horizon. But it is toward this horizon that the human caravan is moving. Don Quixote rides toward the dawn of Easter morning.

WILLIAM L. KOLB

Sociology and the Christian Doctrine of Man*

PART I

The social sciences and sociology in particular are on the verge of betraying their great promise. Sociology came into being promising the liberation of man from certain of the social shackles under which he had lived for centuries. And now we seem to be much more interested in the possibility of *adjusting* man to the modern world and of leading him to abandon any hope of bringing about any change in it.

What is it in sociology which has led to this impasse or this loss of faith?

I think that there is a serious conflict between social sciences and religion, particularly if people who are committed to the Christian faith take their commitments seriously. Religion has frequently demeaned itself by buying the results of social science without questioning the assumptions lying behind that social science. Religion has become so grateful to the sociologist because he has finally found some functions for it; and there are a great many religious people who are interested in attempting to sell religion on the basis of the social functions which the sociologist has acknowledged it performs. All this has tended to conceal the potential conflict between sociology and religion.

I hope this conflict between sociology and religion will be a more edifying one than its ancestor, the conflict between the church and natural sciences in the 19th century. I hope those of us who are religious have learned something from the excesses of that earlier conflict which led our predecessors to take indefensible positions.

The conflict will have to be conducted in large measure by those people who are not only religious but who are also social scientists. Unfortunately, at the present time, we have a great many sociologists who are religiously committed but who believe they can separate their religious assumptions about the nature of man and society from their sociological assumptions about the nature of man and society into two separate, water-tight compartments and in this way avoid conflict. I find a great many of my colleagues in sociology among those who are in the ordinary sense of the word most religiously committed actually making use of the results of social sciences which violate some of their presuppositions and assumptions as Christians.

* Part I is from "The Verge of Betrayal" in *What Can This Charlatan Be Trying To Say?* Vol. I, No. I © 1964. Reprinted by permission of Charlatan Publications, Davenport, Iowa.

Part II is from *Faculty Forum*, No. 20 (March, 1962). Reprinted by permission of the Board of Christian Education of The Methodist Church and the Board of Christian Education of the Presbyterian Church, U.S.

On the other hand, we have to recognize that social science is empirical and that man, even in his religious behavior, can be studied empirically. There is no area of the empirical universe that is inaccessible to scientific investigation. We are even including in the empirical those things which used to be regarded as the primarily subjective. The fear I have regarding modern social science is not so much of the radical positivist who says there are no such things as values, no such things as decision making because these are all subjective phenomena which are not really real because they are not scientifically investigable. I am more concerned about the sociologist who does study values and decision-making in religion, but incorporates that study within a frame of reference which seems to me to deprive man of his basic dignity.

Nevertheless, we must recognize that, while empirical investigation is possible and that while we cannot always catch the nuances of the unique which obviously slip through the nets of generalization we establish, this does not mean we cannot study such things as consciences of men, their wishes, motivations, values, and so on. And we are constantly engaged in the process of studying them.

Moreover, we must insist on the possibility of systematic research carried on in the light of systematic theory, if we are going to carry on any sort of dialogue between theology and sociology. It means that we shall have to carry on systematic theology on the one hand and systematic sociology on the other.

My own work for the past several years has been fundamentally of this sort—an effort to conduct a criticism of sociology from within by placing into a state of tension with one another the Christian presuppositions about the nature and destiny of man on the one hand and certain sociological assumptions about the nature and destiny of man on the other hand. Sociology operates on the basis of several presuppositions and assumptions that must be taken into consideration. First, it extends the assumption of causality, of determinism, purely and completely into the human realm. Second, it thinks of society as being an organization of human relationships which can be explained within a causally deterministic framework. The sociologist has other models of man and of human society which he uses in his ordinary everyday life. And our society also has models of man and models of society which are the basis of our institutions. Our political institutions, our legal institutions, for example, are largely based upon the presupposition that man is not totally determined in his behavior. These assumptions are related in such a way that if you develop a sociology which explains human behavior in terms of cause and effect, and this comes to be applied in the courts, then tension arises between the old legal assumption of freedom of responsibility and the social scientific assumption that human behavior is determined by causal factors. I should like to give several illustrations all of which move in a common direction and to end with a basic argument that what we need in sociology is a new model of man and, as a consequence, also a new model of human society. I have attempted to derive that new model of man from Biblical tradition, and most of my own writing in recent years has been an attempt to show the theoretical relevance for sociology of the Judaic-Christian image of man, which incorporates certain different presuppositions and assumptions from the one which is now dominant in sociology at the present time. However, it is not a matter of dogmatic, authoritarian theological position saying to the sociologist, "We have the truth and you must abide by the truth, because we know what the truth is" (this is one of the mistakes of the dialogue that was carried on in the 19th century), but rather, "These are our ideas as committed Christians about the nature of man. We believe they have relevance for your understanding as a sociologist of man."

In the long run, the only way in which to test the relevance for sociology of the Judaic-Christian image of man will be whether or not it succeeds in ordering data better than the one presently being used. I believe that if one uses the Judaic-Christian image of man, one may order all of the data that other models of men are able to and in addition to order some data which these models cannot. I am talking now at the level of empirical observation, and am not trying to draw a distinction between what the social scientist can investigate on the one hand and what he cannot investigate on the other. Basically I am arguing, for example, that there must be an empirical corollary of the idea of sin and there must also be an empirical corollary of the idea of human freedom . . . that somehow or other these two dimensions must be introduced into the social sciences and not simply remain theological categories. The ultimate test will be whether or not this model of man does actually succeed in ordering what we observe about man better than the models we are presently using in the social sciences.

The reason why we ought to undertake this investigation is that in fact the social sciences are falling far short of their promise. The great problem of sociology and of all of the other social sciences is to help us understand our modern, urban, technical society, and perhaps to help us in rendering it more humane. This is the historical problem of sociology. I am not talking of building the abstract body of sociological principles, although this too is one of the tasks of social science. Rather, I am talking about the task of its great tradition: of what we have been attempting to understand. We offer courses in the underdeveloped areas of the world. We

know a good bit about older types of pre-literate societies; we know a great deal about feudal society; we know a great deal about 19th century American society; we know almost nothing really about 20th century American urban, technical society. The reason for this is that we are using a model of man which, in the limits it assigns to man, is not capable of appreciating the reality of this 20th century world. Thus for example, we tend to believe that man has always lived and therefore will always have to live in small isolated primary groups, that if he becomes geographically and socially mobile, he then becomes disturbed because he is deprived of primary group relations. To a considerable degree this is true.

The churches also have, to a considerable degree, bought this doctrine by essentially attempting to define Christian community as being synonymous with the sociological concept of the primary group. I think that one can make a very good argument that Christian love and Christian agape—the true brotherhood of Christ—is not always a matter of people nuzzling one another in close intimate physical relation. The Church has become convinced that it has to perform the function of the old rural village; thus the coffee klatch, good fellowship, and arriving at first-name basis in the first fifteen minutes after meeting, signs which, the Church thinks, are those of true Christian brotherhood and true Christian community. It got this idea basically from the kind of sociology which argues that man needs this sort of intimate personal relationship constantly.

One of the areas where this has been most clearly expressed has been in the area of family sociology. There is, for example, a book on modern marriage by Father Cervantes, a Roman priest, and C. C. Zimmerman of Harvard which is essentially a defense of the modern marriage system in the isolated one-class suburb. Basically the argument of the book is that people, in order to get along well together, in order to feel secure, in order to be adjusted, have to live in a culturally and socially homogeneous environment. This argument has been used in most of the courses in family sociology throughout the country and actually has received Christian sponsorship. There is a book by Sylvanus Duvall called *When You Marry* which was published under the sponsorship of the YMCA. This book has some Christian gems in it of the following sort: Marrying outside of your own social class is not necessarily bad but if you haven't fallen in love already, why don't you pick somebody in your own class and thus save yourselves trouble? This comes from the sociological image of man but it is sold as YMCA doctrine. But there is an even more beautiful sentence in Duval's book which goes something like this: There was a young man who, when he became interested in a girl, hired a private detective to investigate her background and her family's background, and while this may seem a little extreme, it does represent the fundamental attitude which a person should take in mate selection. The idea expressed in this sentence becomes known, I suppose, ultimately as marriage by questionnaire in which the primary thing of which you must be sure, because you are so weak and irresponsible and need primary relationships so much, is that your prospective mate must be someone who is as close to you, as much like you, as possible. Such writers haven't gotten up enough courage to recommend a violation of the incest taboo but this would seem to be the next suggestion if homogeneity is the requirement they think it is. Before I came to Carleton and was living in a big city in the South, I spoke at a meeting sponsored by the Council of Churches of that particular city. Two ministers in attendance proceeded to set forth the sociological orthodoxy as marriage advice to the young engaged couples who were present at the time without realizing that there was anything incompatible between this and the Judaic-Christian image of man.

There are other evidences of this decline. Back in the 1930's and 40's there was an Institute of Propaganda Analysis. Its influences still find their way into introductory sociology textbooks, which talk about card stacking, glittering generalities, manipulation, and other ways of propagandizing people in order to control them. The purpose of the Institute of Propaganda Analysis was to teach people about propaganda so that they could protect themselves against it whereas practically all of our efforts in this area today seem to go toward finding different and better ways of conducting propaganda campaigns. Again, I think this reflects a decline of faith in man's potentialities. The old idea was that man was partially rational; if you could educate him in the techniques of propaganda you could immunize him against it. But now we engage in propaganda making as a scientific specialty in sociology.

Another example of the same sort —this has been done mostly by the social psychologists who are our brothers—is the study of what might be called the eye-blink rate in the supermarket. We know, for example, on the basis of certain types of packaging studies that with certain types of color combinations you increase greatly the eye-blink rate of the ordinary American housewife when she goes to the supermarket. When the eye-blink rate increases, we know that she is falling into something of an hypnotic trance, at which point she is at the mercy of the packaging and can be persuaded to buy commodities which she perhaps does not really need. Here again is the basic use of social science as a manipulative device, not as a liberative device. The answer is not to destroy social science, adopting a know-nothing attitude toward social science is wrong—but the problem calls into question the kind of image of man and model of society

363

being used for analysis in social science.

Another area which is extremely important is the treatment of juvenile delinquency. In the 19th century when most good religious people were what I have liked to call moralistic Arminians and (an injustice to Arminius) held a doctrine of absolute human responsibility implying therefore that the punishment was supposed to fit the crime, our system of penal institutions was a pretty sorry affair, brutally conducted. When the idea first arose in social science that possibly the criminal or the juvenile delinquent was the product of his environment, it was liberative in its influence. Actually, this new idea was a reversion to an older Judaic-Christian image of man which held that men were never absolutely free but were creatures of necessity as well. But if you move toward the view that man is totally determined in his criminal behavior, you forget that under the old system of legal penology, even though the penalties were too severe, there was the idea that a man paid his debt to society and then in a sense was a free man. The punishment was for a limited period of time. But now we tend toward the indeterminate sentence, which means that since a man is determined in his behavior you can keep him in a penal institution as long as you have to, until he is well or because of the fact that he is ill. Another consequence of the deterministic image is that in the case of social work treatment of juvenile delinquents you are beginning to develop practices which concern lawyers a very great deal, e.g., the waiving of the use of hearsay evidence, i.e., the gradual eroding away of the old legal safeguards that were built upon the idea of the human being as a free and responsible person. What I am suggesting is that the doctrine of absolute determinism is perhaps as sadistic in its own way in the treatment of criminal behavior as the doctrine of absolute moral responsibility was in the 19th century. So far as the ordinary man

in the street is concerned, we still have a great residue of the absolute moralism of the 19th century. So far as the more sophisticated forms of social science treatment of prisoners are concerned, it seems to me that we are operating on the basis of a total determinism which of itself erodes human freedom and human liberty.

Some things that happen in the methods of sociological research are rather interesting and I think also reflect the image of man which we are using; it seems to me that people who have an image of man different from the one which is totally deterministic could not engage in such methods of research. One of the most famous recent instances of these methods was the matter of the "bugging" or placing hidden microphones in the jury room. Part of the institutions of our society, of course, is the norm that the deliberations of the jury are supposed to be absolutely secret and confidential. When this case became public, there was a great deal of concern about it. A sociologist made a study of the attitudes of lawyers and sociologists toward this particular method and found that about 50 per cent of a sample of lawyers condemned the "bugging" of the jury room and a large majority of a sample of sociologists defended it as being a legitimate exercise of the scientific method.

Similarly, we have people who pretend to join religious movements primarily for the purpose of studying them. Another case in the area of social psychology concerns the study of the ethical behavior of children. A study was made in which the investigators in order to discover whether or not the children were honest deliberately led them to believe that they were not being observed and that they could cheat in a particular game and get away with it. Nobody thought to raise the question of the honesty of the investigators toward the children.

There is also the matter of disguising

reality with language. In a recent review in the *New Republic* of "The Brig," a play concerning brutality in a military prison camp, the reviewer takes to task another critic for using the word "hoosegow." He objects to the word in the context of a review of the play because it deprives readers of really experiencing what the play was all about. In other words, the appropriate image is invoked more effectively by the term "concentration camp," which connotes brutality while "hoosegow" does not.

A great deal of sociological jargon is of the same sort. We cut ourselves off from experience by inventing a terminology and sometimes by pretending to an objectivity which removes the direct impact of the experience upon human beings. Here again we need to find some way of being objective in a way which might be called controlled passion rather than simple detachment. We need a language which will enable us to look at social reality as it actually is and yet permit us to respond to it in our full humanity.

Finally, let me say a word about the two primary models of society which exist in present day sociology. One of these is an old, old model. It has taken many forms and might be called the conflict model. This is the model of society generally held by social critics, and it emphasizes men's behavior as being determined by motives of self-aggrandizement and by the instruments of exploitation. There are many forms of this model. The Marxian model certainly falls into this particular category. A recent book by Peter Berger called *The Precarious Vision* employs essentially a power or conflict model of society. Basically the book's thesis is that society is a lie, an instrument of exploitation, and that human values are simply rationalizations of self-interest. This is what Peter Berger means when he says institutions are fictitious, including the church. In other words, the value systems of society are essentially rationalizations

of the self-interest of dominant and controlling groups. They may control either through economic power as in the case of Marx or they may control through the instruments of violence as in the case of Mosca, Michels and Pareto. In any event this has been one of the famous models of human society. It is not, incidentally, the dominant one in American sociology today. It is the one which C. Wright Mills used, for example, but it is certainly not the model of the modern functionalists, who are currently dominant in American sociological theory.

This latter model, called the consensus model, is based on human values and stresses that value consensus, moral consensus, is at the very center of society —that society is held together by moral agreement. I would argue that this particular model is naive with respect to its moral idealism. It regards power as being a facility of society by means of which society gets certain things done, but it does not investigate fully enough the exploitative aspects of power. More seriously, in recent years we have come to the idea that these moral value systems are not a result of the creativity of man but rather that society and its values have always been a going concern and that a person is born into the society, socialized into its values, and has no choice but to conform or to deviate. There is no theory of value creativity here at all but simply a doctrine of socialization, of indoctrination, of a person taking over the values of his particular society.

These are the two dominant models of human society in sociology today. Both of them have shortcomings. Fundamentally the Marxian model cannot be used to explain the Marxist revolutionary himself. It is very interesting that the people who use this model are inevitably moralists who are criticizing the social structure for its exploitative characteristics and therefore implying that *at least their values* are more than rationalizations of self-interest. In other words it seems to me that implicit in this very argument is the idea that men are capable of genuine moral commitments of a non-determined variety. In the case of the consensus theory of society, as I remarked earlier, what is lacking is an image of the brutalities of society, of the irrationalities of society, and of the way in which values can come into existence.

If we use a Judaic-Christian image of man we can order the same data which the power model orders. We are not surprised, it seems to me, as Christians, when we find out that even religion can be used to rationalize the self-interest of a particular social group, but at the same time we are aware that sometimes some people are at least partially capable of a genuine moral commitment. Sociologists of religion love H. Richard Niebuhr's book *The Social Sources of Denominationalism* and use it in many sociology of religion courses because it shows the influence of social class on theology and religion. They also love to point out how during the Civil War ministers on both sides prayed to the same God, absolutely convinced that God was on their side in that moral struggle. But what the sociologist of religion does not but could understand if he employed a broader image of man, is Niebuhr's book *The Kingdom of God in America* which shows the value system of religion as actually a dynamic independent force in the development of society. Similarly by employing a broader image of man he could also understand not only the ministers in the Civil War but also Abraham Lincoln's Second Inaugural Address, when Lincoln himself pointed out that the ways of God were not necessarily the ways of men and that probably guilt was involved on both sides of the struggle.

If the Judaic-Christian model of man is used in social scientific analysis then it would seem to me that we could no longer be so careless about our methods of research or about our uses of the results of social science. If, for example, we recognized the truth of the insight that human behavior is heavily conditioned and yet free, and I use the phrase "conditioned freedom" to refer to this particular assumption, we certainly then cannot take the position that the old 19th century moralistic Arminian took with respect to the penal system of the United States. At the same time we could not take the procedural safeguards protecting human freedom as lightly as did those who "bugged" the jury room. Lionel Trilling has said that men are neither absolutely free nor absolutely determined. We have to incorporate this reality into our social science. It may be difficult to bring about, but I am convinced that unless we find some way of bringing freedom as well as determinism into our scientific model in the human sciences—in the sciences of the human beings—the social sciences will continue to deteriorate. If we adopt this model of man it seems to me that we will certainly be more careful about our methods of research and will not do in an investigative situation something which violates the possibility of human freedom.

There are those who claim that you can't do this because science must use deterministic categories. Peter Berger is one of these who likes to use the two hats argument. He is both a theologian and a sociologist, and when he talks about man as a theologian he uses one language; when he talks about man as a sociologist he uses another language. I am claiming that ultimately you cannot use two languages: that ultimately these models have to be brought together at the levels of practice and of investigation. There are those who would say that the sociologist can only study man insofar as he is determined. I would argue that you cannot even understand the ways in which man is determined unless simultaneously you understand the ways in which he is free. Somehow or other we have got to bring these images together and through it I am convinced that we can be both better social scientists, i.e., we can order the data of our observations better, and at the same time we can make social science the instrument of our liberation that it was originally intended to be.

PART II

As a Christian who is also a sociologist, I am increasingly concerned about the overreaction of those Christians who totally condemn the involvement of the Christian church and the Christian religion with American culture. There can be little doubt that the church during the recent period of the revival of interest in religion has frequently served false gods. Efforts have been made by sociologists, laymen, and clergy to conceive and sell the Christian faith as an integrating factor in American life, both for society itself and for personality. But those who, in order to save the church and the faith from this idolatry, have argued that Christian faith may never serve the function of social integration and has no concern with the problem of mental health, are, I believe, in serious error. They are even in greater error when, because of a misunderstanding of both the sociology of religion and the nature of the Christian faith, they argue that since all religions must perform such functions as social and personal integration, the Christian faith should no longer be regarded as a religion.

In his recent work, *The Precarious Vision,* Peter Berger has held that the sociological imagination shows that all social institutions are fictitious, and that the Christian religion, like all religions, has been created by man in his self-centered search for ultimate meaning, for social and personal integration, for a cloak with which to conceal the fictitiousness of his institutions, and for a

device which will permit him to rationalize his bad faith. Against social institutions and all religion, he places the Christian faith which can never serve an integrative function for society or the person, which does not come from an inner religious experience but from the outside, and which can only shatter all institutions and religion. And further, the perspective of faith enables the person to see through the fictitiousness of social structure.

Now let us accept Berger's definition of religion as idolatrous and Christian faith as nonidolatrous, although I should prefer to speak of idolatrous and nonidolatrous faith. Christian faith, then, comes to us as a gift of Grace. Empirically, however, it is a human response and as such is inevitably involved in human finiteness and *only once* was it not involved in human self-centeredness. The involvement of faith in finiteness does not result in the creation of religion in Berger's sense. Furthermore the need for ultimate meaning, the need for integrated order in human personality, and the need for integrated order in society and hence for institutions are the result of human finiteness. The needs are exacerbated by human self-centeredness but they would be present even if man were without sin. Faith is a gift of grace but it is motivated like religion by the need for ultimate meaning and the need for personal integration. Moreover, faith performs these functions. It may have to shatter idolatrous ultimate meanings and the integration of life around false gods—indeed this is a never ending process—but with faith the self may be reborn. Despite the fact that Berger does not use the word function in the following passage, or speak of ultimate meaning and the ordering of personal life, are not all these implied: "In Jesus Christ we receive one brief glimpse of this divine mystery, but the mystery has such magnitude of splendor that this one glimpse is all we need to light our path for the remainder of our

367

days. We can now address God because we find that He has already addressed us. And we can dare to hope" (p. 273).

It is the same with institutions. Without sin, much of human activity would still have to be patterned and organized. There would still be social roles and complexes of norms, expressive and cognitive, if not moral. But these complexes of human behavior patterned and organized by roles and norms would be empty of fictitious elements due to self-centeredness; they would not be absolutized because the actors would recognize their own finiteness and hence proneness to error. These institutions would be organized around the love of God and man, and hence would constitute a pattern of social integration. In this context faith would serve a socially integrative function.

The possibility I have described is an impossible possibility, because men are self-centered. But what does this signify concerning the meaning-giving and integrating functions of faith in the actual world? It means that every response of faith is inextricably intermixed with religious responses; every man who is given faith worships *God* and *gods* simultaneously. The ultimate meaning which faith provides is clouded by the meanings religion provides. Finiteness is denied or exaggerated. Integration of the self by faith is marred by integration through religion, and now requires a moral code, which is itself ambiguous to the core. So also with social integration and its institutions. The Church if it affirms a set of common moral values, affirms values rooted in faith and values rooted in religion. The values are falsely absolutized, and social roles are given absolute value at the expense of human beings. Fictions, ideologies, and bad faith abound. Yet, if faith abides, it must affirm those meanings rooted in itself; it must affirm those moral values, personal and socially shared, to which it has given rise; and it must affirm those institutions or the elements in

them grounded in such values. To this degree it continues to perform socially and personally integrative functions. Simultaneously it must confront the religious meanings, the false values, the ideologies, and the institutional fictions.

I say confront rather than shatter for two reasons. The first reason I say it is because it is human beings who hold these meanings, values, ideologies, and fictions; and human beings require love as well as judgment from faith. The second reason is that it is not faith which confronts, but human beings with faith; and human beings with faith are human beings with religion even when they act as prophets. If the priest must affirm certain values and institutions only in fear and trembling because of his and their involvement in idolatrous religion, so also must the prophet deny in fear and trembling for he too is so involved.

Thus we must conclude that the situation is much more complex than [is recognized by] those who simply place Christ against culture, faith against social institutions and the integrated self. The faithful man and the faithful Church must affirm and participate in those modes of personal and institutional integration which themselves are rooted in faith; and must confront and deny those modes which are not. Yet such affirmation and confrontation cannot be absolutized for none are wholly faithful; man or church or secular institution. The ambiguity created by the mingling of faith and religion cuts deep. Institutions are ambiguous but not fictitious. The priest is required to affirm, but his affirmation is ambiguous because the values and institutions he affirms are ambiguous and because he is both a man of faith and a man of idolatry. The prophet is required to deny, but his actions too are ambiguous: the institutions and values he condemns have their elements of faith, and his prophecies have their element of religion. As prophet or priest we cannot

368

use the obvious of the symbols of faith to decide whether to affirm or to deny, for religion makes use of the same symbols as faith, and we have been told that not all who cry "Lord" will enter the Kingdom. Nor can we deny institutions or integrating values because the symbols of faith are absent, for we are told that God has not left himself without witness in any age or any place. Yet we must act; we must affirm and deny as responsibly as we can, remembering that whether priest or prophet we are not God, and that we too must be justified by faith and not by perfect knowledge or perfect deed.

JOHN COURTNEY MURRAY

Natural Law as the Christian Basis for Political Action*

THREE PSEUDO-PROBLEMS

My own terms of moral definition, argument, and judgment are, of course, those of the tradition of reason in moral affairs —the ancient tradition that has been sustained and developed in the Catholic Church. Consequently, listening to the public argument on morality and foreign policy, I have found it difficult to discover just what all the shooting is about. Three major issues have come to the fore. The trouble is that all three seem to me factitious. From where I sit, so to speak, in the moral universe, they are all pseudo-problems. Were I to enter the argument, this is the first point I should have to make.

The Protestant moralist is disturbed by the gulf between the morality of individual and collective man. He is forever trying somehow to close the gap. Forever he fails, not only in doing this but even in seeing how it could possibly be done. Thus he is driven back upon the simplist category of "ambiguity." Or he sadly admits an unresolvable dichotomy between moral man and immoral society.

I am obliged to say that the whole practical problem is falsely conceived in consequence of a defective theory. No such pseudo-problem arises within the tradition of reason—or, if you will, in the ethic of natural law. Society and the state are understood to be natural institutions with their relatively autonomous ends or purposes, which are predesigned in broad outline in the social and political nature of man, as understood in its concrete completeness through reflection and historical experience. These purposes are public, not private. They are therefore strictly limited. They do not transcend the temporal and terrestrial order, within which the political and social life of man is confined; and even within this order they are not coextensive with the ends

* From *We Hold These Truths: Catholic Reflections on the American Proposition* by John Courtney Murray, S. J. © Sheed and Ward, Inc., 1960; pp. 285-95, 297-98.

of the human person as such. The obligatory public purposes of society and the state impose on these institutions a special set of obligations which, again by nature, are not coextensive with the wider and higher range of obligations that rest upon the human person (not to speak of the Christian). In a word, the imperatives of political and social morality derive from the inherent order of political and social reality itself, as the architectonic moral reason conceives this necessary order in the light of the fivefold structure of obligatory political ends—justice, freedom, security, the general welfare, and civil unity or peace (so the Preamble to the American Constitution states these ends).

It follows, then, that the morality proper to the life and action of society and the state is not univocally the morality of personal life, or even of familial life. Therefore the effort to bring the organized action of politics and the practical art of statecraft directly under the control of the Christian values that govern personal and familial life is inherently fallacious. It makes wreckage not only of public policy but also of morality itself.

Again, the Protestant moralist is deeply troubled by the fact that nations and states have the incorrigible habit of acting in their own self-interest, and thus violating the fundamental canon of morality which sees in self-concern the basic sin. Here again is a pseudo-problem. I am, of course, much troubled by the question of the national interest, but chiefly lest it be falsely identified in the concrete, thus giving rise to politically stupid policies. But since I do not subscribe to a Kantian "morality of intention," I am not at all troubled by the centrality of self-interest as the motive of national action. From the point of view of political morality, as determined by the purposes inherent in the state, this motive is both legitimate and necessary.

There is, however, one reservation. I do not want self-interest interpreted in the sense of the classic theory of *raison d'état,* which was linked to the modern concept of the absolute sovereignty of the nation-state. This latter concept imparted to the notion of national self-interest an absoluteness that was always as illegitimate as it is presently outworn. The tradition of reason requires, with particular stringency today, that national interest, remaining always valid and omnipresent as a *motive,* be given only a relative and proximate status as an *end* of national action. Political action stands always under the imperative to realize, at least in some minimal human measure, the fivefold structure of obligatory political ends. Political action by the nation-state projected in the form of foreign policy today stands with historical clarity (as it always stood with theoretical clarity in the tradition of reason) under the imperative to realize the limits—narrow but real—of the possible. Today, in fact as in theory, the national interest must be related to this international realization, which stands higher and more ultimate in political value than itself.

No false theoretical dichotomy may be thrust in here. The national interest, rightly understood, is successfully achieved only at the interior, as it were, of the growing international order to which the pursuit of national interest can and must contribute. There is, of course, the practical problem of defining the concrete policies that will be successful at once in the national interest and in the higher interest of international order. The casuistry is endlessly difficult. In any case, one ought to spare oneself unnecessary theoretical agonies, whose roots are often in sentimentalism; as, for instance, the effort to justify foreign aid in terms of pure disinterested Christian charity. To erect some sort of inevitable opposition between the pursuit of national interest and the true imperatives of political morality is to create a pseudo-problem.

The third source of Protestant moral anxiety is the problem of power. The practical problem, as put to policy, is enormously complicated in the nuclear age, in the midst of a profound historical crisis of civilization, and over against an ideology of force that is also a spreading political imperialism. This, however, is surely no reason for distorting the problem by thrusting into it a set of theoretically false dilemmas—by saying, for instance, that to use power is prideful and therefore bad, and not to use it is irresponsible and therefore worse. The tradition of reason declines all such reckless simplism. It rejects the cynical dictum of Lenin that "the state is a club." On the other hand, it does not attempt to fashion the state in the image of an Eastern-seaboard "liberal" who at once abhors power and adores it (since by him, emergent from the matrix of American Protestant culture, power is unconsciously regarded as satanic). The traditional ethic starts with the assumption that, as there is no law without force to vindicate it, so there is no politics without power to promote it. All politics is power politics—up to a point.

The point is set by multiple criteria. To be drastically brief, the essential criterion is the distinction between force and violence. Force is the measure of power necessary and sufficient to uphold the valid purposes both of law and of politics. What exceeds this measure is violence, which destroys the order both of law and of politics. The distinction is teleological, in the customary style of the tradition of reason. As an instrument, force is morally neutral in itself. The standard of its use is aptitude or ineptitude for the achievement of the obligatory public purposes. Here again the casuistry is endlessly difficult, especially when the moralist's refusal to sanction too much force clashes with the soldier's classic reluctance to use too

little force. In any case, the theory is clear enough. The same criterion which governs the state in its use of coercive law for the public purposes also governs the state in its use of force, again for the public purposes. The function of law, said the Jurist (this is the title that Aquinas regularly gives to Ulpian), is to be useful to the community; this too is the function of force.

The community, as the Jurist knew, is neither a choir of angels nor a pack of wolves. It is simply the human community which, in proportion as it is civilized, strives to maintain itself in some small margin of safe distance from the chaos of barbarism. For this effort the only resources directly available to the community are those which first rescued it from barbarism, namely, the resources of reason, made operative chiefly through the processes of reasonable law, prudent public policies, and a discriminatingly apt use of force.

(Note here that Christianity, as I have already said, profoundly altered the structure of politics by introducing the revolutionary idea of the two communities, two orders of law and two authorities. But it did not change the nature of politics, law, and government, which still remain rational processes. To the quality of these processes Christian faith and grace contribute only indirectly, by their inner effect upon man himself, which is in part the correction and clarification of the processes of reason.)

The necessary defense against barbarism is, therefore, an apparatus of state that embodies both reason and force in a measure that is at least decently conformable with what man has learned, by rational reflection and historical experience, to be necessary and useful to sustain his striving towards the life of civility. The historical success of the civilized community in the continuing effort of the forces of reason to hold at bay the counterforces of barbarism is no more than marginal. The traditional ethic, which asserts the doctrine of the rule of reason in public affairs, does not expect that man's historical success in installing reason in its rightful rule will be much more than marginal. But the margin makes the difference.

AGAIN THE BASIC ISSUE

All this is the sort of thing that the theorist of natural law would have first to say were he to enter on the ground floor, so to speak, of the controversy about morality and public policy. He could not possibly argue concrete problems of policy in the moral terms of the ambiguist. Insofar as these terms are intelligible to him at all, they seem to him questionable in themselves and creative of pseudo-problems in the field of policy. In turn, the Protestant moralist, whatever his school, cannot possibly argue questions of policy in the moral terms of the tradition of reason. The tradition is alien to him at every point—in its intellectualism, its theological emphasis on the Reason of God, its insistence on the analogical character of the structures of life (personal, familial, political, social), its assignment of primacy to the objective end of the act over the subjective intention of the agent, and its casuistical niceties. At best, the whole theory is unintelligible; at worst it is an idolatry of reason and an evacuation of the Gospel.

It has also become customary to point out that, whatever the merits of the tradition, it is dead, in the sense of Nietzsche's dictum, "God is dead." So I was told recently. It happened that I wrote a little piece on the traditional moral doctrine on the limitations of warfare, as fashioned by the tradition of reason. . . . A friendly critic, Professor Julian Hartt of the Yale Divinity School, had this to say: "Father Murray has not, I believe, clearly enough come to terms with the question behind every serious consideration of limited war as a moral option, i.e., where are the ethical principles to fix the appropriate limits? *Where,*

not *what;* can we make out the lineaments of the community which is the living repository (as it were) of the ethical principles relevant and efficacious to the moral determinations of the limits of warfare?" This is a fair question.

After a look around the national lot, Professor Hartt comes to the conclusion that the American community does not qualify; it is not the living repository of what the tradition of reason has said on warfare. I am compelled regretfully to agree that he is right. Such is the fact. It may even be that the American community, especially in its "clerks," who are the custodians of the public philosophy, is not the repository of the tradition of reason on any moral issue you would like to name. This ancient tradition lives, if you will, within the Catholic community; but this community fails to bring it into vital relation with the problems of foreign policy. There seems, in fact, to be some reason for saying that the Catholic community is not much interested in foreign affairs, beyond its contribution in sustaining the domestic mood of anti-Communism.

But if it be the fact that the tradition of natural law, once vigorous in America, is now dead, a serious question arises. What then is the moral doctrine on which America is to base its national action, especially its foreign policy?

One could put the question in the first instance to the government. It is clear that the Department of Defense and its allied agencies find sufficient moral warrant for their policies in their loyalty to the good old Western-story maxim: "Don't shoot first." With the moral issue thus summarily disposed of, they set policy under the primatial control of that powerful dyarchy, technology and the budget, which conspire to accumulate weapons of mass annihilation that are morally unshootable, no matter who shoots first. Those who are disquieted by this situation—which is not ambiguous but simply wrong—are invited to find comfort in the emanations of crypto-pacifism from the White House, which seems to hold that we shall never shoot at all. The moral argument for this unambiguous position, whose simplism rivals that of the ambiguists, is never made clear. The inquiry into the moral bases of policy would probably produce other weird and wonderful answers, if elsewhere pursued— within the Department of State, for instance, with regard to disarmament, foreign aid, and diplomatic demarches among the uncommitted or emergent nations.

In any case, the question is perhaps more appropriately put to the American community at large. The theory of American government seems to be that public policies borrow, as it were, their morality from the conscience of the people. Right policies, as well as due powers, derive from the consent of the governed. Therefore, on what structured concept of the moral order does the American people undertake to fulfill its traditional public moral right and duty, which is to judge, direct, correct, and then consent to, the courses of foreign policy?

There is a sentimental subjectivist scriptural fundamentalism. But this theory by definition has nothing to say about foreign policy. It is at best a theory of interpersonal relationships and therefore irrelevant to international relations, which are not interpersonal. There is also moral ambiguism. But this, in the final analysis, is not properly a moral theory. It is perhaps a technique of historical analysis, highly doctrinaire in style; but it is not an ethical philosophy. It is an interesting paradoxical structure of rhetorical categories; but it is not a normative doctrine that could base discriminating moral judgments. All norms vanish amid the multiplying paradoxes; and all discrimination is swallowed up in the cavernous interior of the constantly recurrent verdict: "This action is morally ambiguous."

The school of ambiguist thought has done some useful negative service by its corrosive critique of older types of moral simplism and political utopianism. But it has no positive constructive power to fashion purposeful public policies in an age of crisis. It can throw rocks after the event, but it can lay no cornerstones. It points out all the moral hazards, and takes none. The self-contradiction inherent in sin is indeed a massive fact of the human condition; but not for this reason, or any other, does ambiguity become a virtue in moral judgment. Ambiguism can judge no policies save those that history has already judged. It can direct no policies because it can specify no ends toward which policy should be directed. And it can correct no policies since all policies deserve by definition the same qualification, "ambiguous," and what use is it to correct one ambiguous course by substituting another? We can discard ambiguism as the moral premise of public policy.

What is there left? There is, of course, the pseudo-morality of secular liberalism, especially of the academic variety. Its basic premise is a curious version of the Socratic paradox, that knowledge is virtue. It asserts that, if only we really could get to understand everybody, our foreign policy would inevitably be good. The trouble is that the past failures of the political intelligence of secular liberalism, and its demonstrated capacities for misunderstanding, have already pretty much discredited it.

Finally, there is the ubiquitous pragmatist, whose concern is only with what will work. But he too wins no confidence, since most of us have already learned from the pragmatist source of truth, which is history, that whatever is not true will fail to work. We want to know the political truth that will base workable policies.

It would seem, therefore, that the moral footing has been eroded from beneath the political principle of consent, which has now come to designate nothing more than the technique of majority opinion as the guide of public action—a technique as apt to produce fatuity in policy and tyranny of rule as to produce wisdom and justice. It was not always so. In the constitutional theory of the West the principle of consent found its moral basis in the belief, which was presumed sufficiently to be the fact, that the people are the living repository of a moral tradition, possessed at least as a heritage of wisdom, that enables them to know what is reasonable in the action of the state—in its laws, its public policies, its uses of force. The people consent because it is reasonable to consent to what, with some evidence, appears as reasonable. Today no such moral tradition lives among the American people. As Professor Hartt suggests, the tradition of reason, which is known as the ethic of natural law, is dead. Those who seek the ironies of history should find one here, in the fact that the ethic which launched Western constitutionalism and endured long enough as a popular heritage to give essential form to the American system of government has now ceased to sustain the structure and direct the action of this constitutional commonwealth.

The situation is not such as to gladden the heart. But at least one knows the right question in the present matter. It is not how foreign policy is to be guided by the norms of moral doctrine. It is, rather, what is the moral doctrine by whose norms foreign policy is to be guided?

THE ETERNAL RETURN OF NATURAL LAW

The news reported in the last chapter —that the tradition of natural law is dead—calls for some verification, before it is accepted as true. For one thing, it may be a case of mistaken identity; perhaps it was for some *contrefacon* of the doctrine that the funeral rites were held. This is possible. So many misunderstandings have conspired to obscure the true identity of the doctrine

that it is often mistaken for what it is not. Some of the misunderstandings are naive; others are of the learned sort. Some are the product of ignorance; others result from polemic bias. . . .

First, natural-law theory does not pretend to do more than it can, which is to give a philosophical account of the moral experience of humanity and to lay down a charter of essential humanism. It does not show the individual the way to sainthood, but only to manhood. It does not promise to transform society into the City of God on earth, but only to prescribe, for the purposes of law and social custom, that minimum of morality which must be observed by the custom, that minimum of morality which must be observed by the members of a society, if the social environment is to be human and habitable. At that, for a man to be reasonably human, and for a society to be essentially civil—these are no mean achievements. The ideal of the reasonable man, who does his duty to God, to others, and to himself, is not an ignoble one. In fact, it puts such a challenge to the inertness and perversity which are part of the human stuff, that Christian doctrine from the day of St. Augustine has taught the necessity of divine grace for this integral fulfillment of the natural law.

Second, beyond the fulfillment of the ideal of the reasonable man there lies the perennial question of youth, whatever its age. It is asked in the Gospel: "What do I still lack?" (Matthew 19:21). And there remains the Gospel's austere answer, put in the form of an invitation, but not cast in the categories of ethics, which are good and evil and the obligation to choose between them. The invitation opens the perspectives of a higher choice, to "be a follower of mine." For the making of this choice there is no other motive, no other inner impulse, than the free desire to respond to the prior choice of Him whom one chooses because one has been first chosen.

Third, the mistake would be to

imagine that the invitation, "Come, follow me," is a summons somehow to forsake the universe of human nature, somehow to vault above it, somehow to leave law and obligation behind, somehow to enter the half-world of an individualist subjectivist "freedom" which pretends to know no other norm save "love." In other words, the Gospel invitation, in so far as it is a summons to the moral life, is not a call to construct a "situation ethics" that knows no general principles of moral living but only particular instances of moral judgment, each one valid only for the instance; and that recognizes no order of moral law that is binding on freedom, but only a freedom that is free and moral singly in so far as it is sheer spontaneity.

Fourth, the law of nature, which prescribes humanity, still exists at the interior of the Gospel invitation, which summons to perfection. What the follower of Christ chooses to perfect is, and can only be, a humanity. And the lines of human perfection are already laid down in the structure of man's nature. Where else could they be found? The Christian call is to transcend nature, notably to transcend what is noblest in nature, the faculty of reason. But it is not a call to escape from nature, or to dismantle nature's own structure, and least of all to deny that man is intelligent, that nature is intelligible, and that nature's intelligibilities are laws for the mind that grasps them. In so far as they touch the moral life, the energies of grace, which are the action of the Holy Spirit, quicken to new and fuller life the dynamisms of nature, which are resident in reason. Were it otherwise, grace would not be supernatural but only miraculous.

H. RICHARD NIEBUHR

The Grace of Doing Nothing*

It may be that the greatest moral problems of the individual or of a society arise when there is nothing to be done. When we have begun a certain line of action or engaged in a conflict we cannot pause too long to decide which of various possible courses we ought to choose for the sake of the worthier result. Time rushes on and we must choose as best we can, entrusting the issue to the future. It is when we stand aside from the conflict, before we know what our relations to it really are, when we seem to be condemned to doing nothing, that our moral problems become greatest. How shall we do nothing?

The issue is brought home to us by the fighting in the East. We are chafing at the bit, we are eager to do something constructive; but there is nothing constructive, it seems, that we can do. We pass resolutions, aware that we are doing nothing; we summon up righteous indignation and still do nothing; we write

* Copyright 1932 Christian Century Foundation. Reprinted by permission from the March 23, 1932, issue of *The Christian Century;* pp. 378-80.

letters to congressmen and secretaries, asking others to act while we do nothing. Yet is it really true that we are doing nothing? There are, after all, various ways of being inactive, and some kinds of inactivity, if not all, may be highly productive. It is not really possible to stand aside, to sit by the fire in this world of moving times; even Peter was doing something in the courtyard of the high-priest's house—if it was only something he was doing to himself. When we do nothing we are also affecting the course of history. The problem we face is often that of choice between various kinds of inactivity rather than of choice between action and inaction.

Our inactivity may be that of the pessimist who watches a world go to pieces. It is a meaningful inactivity for himself and for the world. His world, at all events, will go to pieces the more rapidly because of that inactivity. Or it may be the inactivity of the conservative believer in things as they are. He does nothing in the international crisis because he believes that the way of Japan is the way of all nations, that self-interest is the first and only law of life, and that out of the clash of national, as out of that of individual, self-interests the greater good will result. His inactivity is one of watchful waiting for the opportunity when, in precisely similar manner, though with less loss of life and fortune if possible, he may rush to the protection of his own interests or promote them by taking advantage of the situation created by the strife of his competitors. This way of doing nothing is not unproductive. It encourages the self-asserters and it fills them with fear of the moment when the new competition will begin. It may be that they have been driven into their present conflict by the knowledge or suspicion that the watchful waiter is looking for his opportunity, perhaps unconsciously, and that they must be prepared for him.

The inactivity of frustration and

moral indignation is of another order. It is the way today of those who have renounced all violent methods of settling conflicts and have no other means at hand by which to deal with the situation. It is an angry inactivity like that of a man who is watching a neighborhood fight and is waiting for the police to arrive—for police who never come. He has renounced for himself the method of forcible interference which would only increase the flow of blood and the hatred, but he knows of nothing else that he can do. He is forced to remain content on the sidelines, but with mounting anger he regards the bully who is beating the neighbor and his wrath issues in words of exasperation and condemnation. Having tied his own hands he fights with his tongue and believes that he is not fighting because he inflicts only mental wounds. The bully is for him an outlaw, a person not to be trusted, unfair, selfish, one who cannot be redeemed save by restraint. The righteous indignation mounts and mounts and must issue at last—as the police fail to arrive—either in his own forcible entry into the conflict, despite his scruples, or in apoplexy.

The diatribes against Japan which are appearing in the secular and religious press today have a distressing similarity to the righteously indignant utterances which preceded our conflicts with Spain and with Germany. China is Cuba and Belgium over again, it is the Negro race beaten by Simon Legree; and the pacifists who have no other program than that of abstention from the unrighteousness of war are likely to be placed in the same quandary in which their fellows were placed in 1860, 1898 and 1915, and—unless human attitudes have been regenerated in the interim—they are likely to share the same fate, which was not usually incarceration. Here is a situation which they did not foresee when they made their vow; may it not be necessary to have one more war to end all war? Righteous indignation, not allowed to issue in action, is a dangerous thing—as dangerous as any great emotion nurtured and repressed at the same time. It is the source of sudden explosions or the ground of long, bitter and ugly hatreds.

If this way of doing nothing must be rejected the communists' way offers more hope. Theirs is the inactivity of those who see that there is indeed nothing constructive to be done in the present situation, but that, rightly understood, this situation is after all preliminary to a radical change which will eliminate the conditions of which the conflict is a product. It is the inactivity of a cynicism which expects no good from the present, evil world of capitalism, but also the inactivity of a boundless faith in the future. The communists know that war and revolution are closely akin, that war breeds discontent and misery and that out of misery and discontent new worlds may be born. This is an opportunity, then, not for direct entrance into the conflict, not for the watchful waiting of those who seek their self-interest, but for the slow laborious process of building up within the fighting groups those cells of communism which will be ready to inherit the new world and be able to build a classless international commonwealth on the ruins of capitalism and nationalism. Here is inactivity with a long vision, a steadfast hope and a realistic program of non-interfering action.

But there is yet another way of doing nothing. It appears to be highly impracticable because it rests on the wellnigh obsolete faith that there is a God—a real God. Those who follow this way share with communism the belief that the fact that men can do nothing constructive is no indication of the fact that nothing constructive is being done. Like the communists they are assured that the actual processes of history will inevitably and really bring a different kind of world with lasting peace. They do not rely on human aspirations after ideals to accomplish this end, but on forces which often seem very impersonal —as impersonal as those which eliminated slavery in spite of abolitionists. The forces may be as impersonal and as actual as machine production, rapid transportation, the physical mixture of races, etc., but as parts of the real world they are as much a part of the total divine process as are human thoughts and prayers.

From this point of view, naïvely affirming the meaningfulness of reality, the history of the world is the judgment of the world and also its redemption, and such a conflict like the present one is— again as in communism—only the prelude both to greater judgment and to a new era. The world being what it is, these results are brought forth when the seeds of national or individual self-interest are planted; the actual structure of things is such that our wishes for a different result do not in the least affect the outcome. As a man soweth so shall he reap. This God of things as they are is inevitable and quite merciless. His mercy lies beyond, not this side of, judgment. This inactive Christianity shares with communism also the belief in the inevitably good outcome of the mundane process and the realistic insight that that good cannot be achieved by the slow accretion of better habits alone but more in consequence of a revolutionary change which will involve considerable destruction. While it does nothing it knows that something is being done, something which is divine both in its threat and in its promise.

This inactivity is like that of the early Christians whose millenarian mythology it replaces with the contemporary mythology of social forces. (Mythology is after all not fiction but a deep philosophy.) Like early Christianity and like communism today radical Christianity knows that nothing constructive can be done by interference but that something very constructive can be done in preparation for the future. It also can build cells of those within each nation who, divorcing themselves from the program of nationalism and of capitalism, unite in a higher loyalty which transcends national and class lines of division and prepare for the future. There is no such Christian international today because radical Christianity has not arrived as yet at a program and a philosophy of history, but such little cells are forming. The First Christian international of Rome has had its day; the Second Christian international of Stockholm is likely to go the way of the Second Socialist international. There is need of and opportunity for a Third Christian international.

While the similarities of a radically Christian program with the communist program are striking, there are also great dissimilarities. There is a new element in the inactivity of radical Christianity which is lacking in communism. The Christian reflects upon the fact that his inability to do anything constructive in the crisis is the inability of one whose own faults are so apparent and so similar to those of the offender that any action on his part is not only likely to be misinterpreted but is also likely—in the nature of the case—to be really less than disinterested. He is like a father who, feeling a mounting righteous indignation against a misbehaving child, remembers that that misbehavior is his fault as much as the child's and that indignation is the least helpful, the most dangerous of attitudes to take; it will solve nothing though it may repress.

So the American Christian realizes that Japan is following the example of his own country and that it has little real ground for believing America to be a disinterested nation. He may see that his country, for which he bears his own responsibility as a citizen, is really not disinterested and that its righteous indignation is not wholly righteous. An inactivity then is demanded which will

378

be profoundly active in rigid self-analysis. Such analysis is likely to reveal that there is an approach to the situation, indirect but far more effective than direct interference, for it is able to create the conditions under which a real reconstruction of habits is possible. It is the opposite approach from that of the irate father who believes that every false reaction on the part of his child may be cured by a verbal, physical or economic spanking.

This way of doing nothing the old Christians called repentance, but the word has become so reminiscent of emotional debauches in the feeling of guilt that it may be better to abandon it for a while. What is suggested is that the only effective approach to the problem of China and Japan lies in the sphere of an American self-analysis which is likely to result in some surprising discoveries as to the amount of renunciation of self-interest necessary on the part of this country and of individual Christians before anything effective can be done in the east.

The inactivity of radical Christianity is not the inactivity of those who call evil good; it is the inaction of those who do not judge their neighbors because they cannot fool themselves into a sense of superior righteousness. It is not the inactivity of a resigned patience, but of a patience that is full of hope, and is based on faith. It is not the inactivity of the non-combatant, for it knows that there are no non-combatants, that everyone is involved, that China is being crucified (though the term is very inaccurate) by our sins and those of the whole world. It is not the inactivity of the merciless, for works of mercy must be performed though they are only palliatives to ease present pain while the process of healing depends on deeper, more actual and urgent forces.

But if there is no God, or if God is up in heaven and not in time itself, it is a very foolish inactivity.

REINHOLD NIEBUHR

Must We
Do Nothing?*

There is much in my brother's article, "The Grace of Doing Nothing" with which I agree. Except for the invitation of the editors of The Christian Century I would have preferred to defer voicing any disagreement with some of his final conclusions to some future occasion; for a casual article on a specific problem created by the contemporary international situation hardly does justice to his general position. I believe the problem upon which he is working—the problem of dissociating a rigorous gospel ethic of disinterestedness and love from the sentimental dilutions of that ethic which are current in liberal Christianity—is a tremendously important one. I owe so much to the penetrating thought which he has been giving this subject that I may be able to do some justice to his general position even though I do not share his conviction that a pure love ethic can ever be made the basis of a civilization.

He could not have done better than to choose the Sino-Japanese conflict, and the reactions of the world to it, in order to prove the difficulty, if not the futility, of dealing redemptively with a sinful nation or individual if we cannot exorcise the same sin from our own hearts. It is true that pacifists are in danger of stirring up hatred against Japan in their effort to stem the tide of Japanese imperialism. It is true that the very impotence of an individual, who deals with a social situation which goes beyond his own powers, tempts him to hide his sense of futility behind a display of violent emotion. It is true that we have helped to create the Japan which ex-

presses itself in terms of militaristic imperialism. The insult we offered her in our immigration laws was a sin of spiritual aggression. The white world has not only taught her the ways of imperialism but has preempted enough of the yellow man's side of the world to justify Japan's imperialism as a vent for pent up national energies.

It is also true that American concern over Japanese aggression is not wholly disinterested. It is national interest which prompts us to desire stronger action against Japan than France and England are willing to take. It is true, in other words, that every social sin is, at least partially, the fruit and consequence of the sins of those who judge and condemn it, and that the effort to eliminate it involves the critics and judges in new social sin, the assertion of self-interest and the expression of moral conceit and hypocrisy. If anyone would raise the objection to such an analysis that it finds every social action falling short only because it measures the action against an impossible ideal of disinterestedness, my brother could answer that while the ideal may seem to be impossible the actual social situation proves it to be necessary. It is literally true that every recalcitrant nation, like every anti-social individual, is created by the society which condemns it, and that redemptive efforts which betray strong ulterior motives are always bound to be less than fully redemptive.

My brother draws the conclusion from this logic that it is better not to act at all than to act from motives which are less than pure, and with the use of

* Copyright 1932 Christian Century Foundation. Reprinted by permission from the March 30, 1932, issue of The Christian Century; pp. 415-17.

methods which are less than ethical (coercion). He believes in taking literally the words of Jesus, "Let him who is without sin cast the first stone." He believes, of course, that this kind of inaction would not really be inaction; it would be, rather, the action of repentance. It would give every one involved in social sin the chance to recognize how much he is involved in it and how necessary it is to restrain his own greed, pride, hatred and lust for power before the social sin is eliminated.

This is an important emphasis particularly for modern Christianity with its lack of appreciation of the tragic character of life and with its easy assumption that the world will be saved by a little more adequate educational technique. Hypocrisy is an inevitable by-product of moral aspiration, and it is the business of true religion to destroy man's moral conceit, a task which modern religion has not been performing in any large degree. Its sentimentalities have tended to increase rather than to diminish moral conceit. A truly religious man ought to distinguish himself from the moral man by recognizing the fact that he is not moral, that he remains a sinner to the end. The sense of sin is more central to religion than is any other attitude.

All this does not prove, however, that we ought to apply the words of Jesus, "Let him who is without sin cast the first stone," literally. If we do we will never be able to act. There will never be a wholly disinterested nation. Pure disinterestedness is an ideal which even individuals cannot fully achieve, and human groups are bound always to express themselves in lower ethical terms than individuals. It follows that no nation can ever be good enough to save another nation purely by the power of love. The relation of nations and of economic groups can never be brought into terms of pure love. Justice is probably the highest ideal toward which human groups can aspire. And justice,

with its goal of adjustment of right to right, inevitably involves the assertion of right against right and interest against interest until some kind of harmony is achieved. If a measure of humility and of love does not enter this conflict of interest it will of course degenerate into violence. A rational society will be able to develop a measure of the kind of imagination which knows how to appreciate the virtues of an opponent's position and the weakness in one's own. But the ethical and spiritual note of love and repentance can do no more than qualify the social struggle in history. It will never abolish it.

The hope of attaining an ethical goal for society by purely ethical means, that is, without coercion, and without the assertion of the interests of the underprivileged against the interests of the privileged, is an illusion which was spread chiefly among the comfortable classes of the past century. My brother does not make the mistake of assuming that this is possible in social terms. He is acutely aware of the fact that it is not possible to get a sufficient degree of pure disinterestedness and love among privileged classes and powerful nations to resolve the conflicts of history in that way. He understands the stubborn inertia which the ethical ideal meets in history. At this point his realistic interpretation of the facts of history comes in full conflict with his insistence upon a pure gospel ethic, upon a religiously inspired moral perfectionism, and he resolves the conflict by leaving the field of social theory entirely and resorting to eschatology. The Christian will try to achieve humility and disinterestedness not because enough Christians will be able to do so to change the course of history, but because this kind of spiritual attitude is a prayer to God for the coming of his kingdom.

I will not quarrel with this apocalyptic note, as such, though I suspect many Christian Century readers will. I believe that a proper eschatology is necessary to a vigorous ethic, and that the simple idea of progress is inimical to the highest ethic. The compound of pessimism and optimism which a vigorous ethical attitude requires can be expressed only in terms of religious eschatology. What makes my brother's kind of eschatology impossible for me is that he identifies everything that is occurring in history (the drift toward disaster, another world war and possibly a world revolution) with the counsels of God, and then suddenly, by a leap of faith, comes to the conclusion that the same God, who uses brutalities and forces, against which man must maintain conscientious scruples, will finally establish an ideal society in which pure love will reign.

I have more than one difficulty with such a faith. I do not see how a revolution in which the disinherited express their anger and resentment, and assert their interests, can be an instrument of God, and yet at the same time an instrument which religious scruples forbid a man to use. I should think it would be better to come to ethical terms with the forces of nature in history, and try to use ethically directed coercion in order that violence may be avoided. The hope that a kingdom of pure love will emerge out of the catastrophes of history is even less plausible than the communist faith that an equalitarian society will inevitably emerge from them. There is some warrant in history for the latter assumption, but very little for the former.

I find it impossible to envisage a society of pure love as long as man remains man. His natural limitations of reason and imagination will prevent him, even should he achieve a purely disinterested motive, from fully envisaging the needs of his fellow-men or from determining his actions upon the basis of their interests. Inevitably these limitations of individuals will achieve cumulative effects in the life and actions of national, racial and economic groups. It is possible to envisage a more ethical society than we now have. It is possible

to believe that such a society will be achieved partly by evolutionary process and partly by catastrophe in which an old order, which offers a too stubborn resistance to new forces, is finally destroyed.

It is plausible also to interpret both the evolutionary and the catastrophic elements in history in religious terms and to see the counsels of God in them. But it is hardly plausible to expect divine intervention to introduce something into history which is irrelevant to anything we find in history now. We may envisage a society in which human co-operation is possible with a minimum amount of coercion, but we cannot imagine one in which there is no coercion at all—unless, of course, human beings become something quite different from what they now are. We may hope for a society in which self-interest is qualified by rigorous self-analysis and a stronger social impulse, but we cannot imagine a society totally without the assertion of self-interest and therefore without the conflict of opposing interests.

I realize quite well that my brother's position both in its ethical perfectionism and in its apocalyptic note is closer to the gospel than mine. In confessing that, I am forced to admit that I am unable to construct an adequate social ethic out of a pure love ethic. I cannot abandon the pure love ideal because anything which falls short of it is less than the ideal. But I cannot use it fully if I want to assume a responsible attitude toward the problems of society. Religious perfectionism drives either to asceticism or apocalypticism. In the one case the problem of society is given up entirely; in the other individual perfection is regarded as the force which will release the redemptive powers of God for society. I think the second alternative is better than the first, and that both have elements which must be retained for any adequate social ethic, lest it become lost in the relativities of expediency. But as long as the world of man remains a place where nature and God, the real and the ideal, meet, human progress will depend upon the judicious use of the forces of nature in the service of the ideal.

In practical, specific and contemporary terms this means that we must try to dissuade Japan from her military venture, but must use coercion to frustrate her designs if necessary, must reduce coercion to a minimum and prevent it from issuing in violence, must engage in constant self-analysis in order to reduce the moral conceit of Japan's critics and judges to a minimum, and must try in every social situation to maximise the ethical forces and yet not sacrifice the possibility of achieving an ethical goal because we are afraid to use any but purely ethical means.

To say all this is really to confess that the history of mankind is a perennial tragedy; for the highest ideals which the individual may project are ideals which he can never realize in social and collective terms. If there is a law in our members which wars against the law that is in our minds as individuals, this is even more true when we think of society. Individuals set the goal for society but society itself must achieve the goal and society is and will always remain sub-human. The goal which a sensitive individual sets for society must

therefore always be something which is a little outside and beyond history. Love may qualify the social struggle of history but it will never abolish it, and those who make the attempt to bring society under the dominion of perfect love will die on the cross. And those who behold the cross are quite right in seeing it as a revelation of the divine, of what man ought to be and cannot be, at least not so long as he is enmeshed in the processes of history.

Perhaps that is why it is inevitable that religious imagination should set goals beyond history. "Man's reach is beyond his grasp, or what's a heaven for." My brother does not like these goals above and beyond history. He wants religion and social idealism to deal with history. In that case he must not state his goal in absolute terms. There can be nothing absolute in history, no matter how frequently God may intervene in it. Man cannot live without a sense of the absolute, but neither can he achieve the absolute. He may resolve the tragic character of that fact by religious faith, by the experience of grace in which the unattainable is experienced in anticipatory terms, but he can never resolve in purely ethical terms the conflict between what is and what ought to be.

H. RICHARD NIEBUHR

The Only Way into
the Kingdom of God*

Editor *The Christian Century*

SIR: Since you have given me leave to fire one more shot in the fraternal war between my brother and me over the question of pacifism, I shall attempt to place it as well as I can, not for the purpose of demolishing my opponent's position—which our thirty years' war has shown me to be impossible—but for the sake of pointing as accurately as I can to the exact locus of the issue between us. It does not lie in the question of activity or inactivity, to which my too journalistic approach to the problem directed attention; we are speaking after all of two kinds of activity. The fundamental question seems to me to be whether "the history of mankind is a perennial tragedy" which can derive meaning only from a goal which lies beyond history, as my brother maintains, or whether the "eschatological" faith, to which I seek to adhere, is justifiable. In that faith tragedy is only the prelude to fulfilment, and a prelude which is necessary because of human nature; the kingdom of God comes inevitably, though whether we shall see it or not, depends on our recognition of its presence and our acceptance of the only kind of life which will enable us to enter it, the life of repentance and forgiveness.

For my brother God is outside the historical processes, so much so that he charges me with faith in a miracle-working deity which interferes occasionally, sometimes brutally, sometimes redemptively, in this history. But God, I believe, is always in history; he is the structure in things, the source of all meaning, the "I am that I am," that which is that it is. He is the rock against which we beat in vain, that which bruises and overwhelms us when we seek to impose our wishes, contrary to his, upon him. That structure of the universe, that creative will, can no more be said to interfere brutally in history than the violated laws of my organism can be said to interfere brutally with my life if they make me pay the cost of my violation. That structure of the universe, that will of God, does bring war and depression upon us when we bring it upon ourselves, for we live in the kind of world which visits our iniqui-

ties upon us and our children, no matter how much we pray and desire that it be otherwise.

Self-interest acts destructively in this world; it calls forth counter-assertion; nationalism breeds nationalism, class assertion summons up counter-assertion on the part of exploited classes. The result is war, economic, military, verbal; and it is judgment. But this same structure in things which is our enemy is our redeemer; "it means intensely and it means good"—not the good which we desire, but the good which we would desire if we were good and really wise. History is not a perennial tragedy but a road to fulfilment and that fulfilment requires the tragic outcome of every self-assertion, for it is a fulfilment which can only be designated as "love." It has created fellowship in atoms and organisms, at bitter cost to electrons and cells; and it is creating something better than human selfhood but at bitter cost to that selfhood. This is not a faith in progress, for evil grows as well as good and every self-assertion must be eliminated somewhere and somehow—by innocence suffering for guilt, it seems.

If, however, history is no more than tragedy, if there is no fulfilment in it, then my brother is right. Then we must rest content with the clash of self-interested individuals, personal or social. But in that case I see no reason why we should qualify the clash of competition with a homeopathic dose of Christian "love."

The only harmony which can possibly result from the clash of interests is the harmony imposed by the rule of the strong or a parallelogram of social forces, whether we think of the interclass structure or the international world. To import any pacifism into this struggle is only to weaken the weaker self-asserters (India, China or the proletariat) or to provide the strong with a facade of "service" behind which they can operate with a salved conscience. (Pacifism, on the other hand, as a method of self-assertion, is not pacifism at all but only a different kind of war.)

The method which my brother recommends, that of qualifying the social struggle by means of some Christian love, seems to me to be only the old method of making Christian love an ambulance driver in the wars of interested and clashing parties. If it is more than that it is weakening of the forces whose success we think necessary for a juster social order. For me the question is one of "either-or;" either the Christian method, which is not the method of love but of repentance and forgiveness, or the method of self-assertion; either nationalism or Christianity, either capitalism-communism or Christianity. The attempt to qualify the one method by the other is hopeless compromise.

I think that to apply the terms "Christian perfectionism" or "Christian ideal" to my approach is rather misleading. I rather think that Dewey is quite right in his war on ideals; they always seem irrelevant to our situation and betray us into a dualistic morality. The society of love is an impossible human ideal, as the fellowship of the organism is an impossible ideal for the cell. It is not an ideal toward which we can strive, but an "emergent," a potentiality in our situation which remains unrealized so long as we try to impose our pattern, our wishes upon the divine creative process.

Man's task is not that of building Utopias but that of eliminating weeds and tilling the soil so that the kingdom of God can grow. His method is not one of striving for perfection or of acting perfectly, but of clearing the road by repentance and forgiveness. That this approach is valid for societies as well as for individuals and that the opposite approach will always involve us in the same one ceaseless cycle of assertion and counter-assertion, is what I am concerned to emphasize.

PAUL TILLICH

Marxism and Religious Socialism*

Marxism has never been accepted indiscriminately and without a serious criticism by the religious-socialist movements. A large part of the theoretical foundation of religious socialism was dedicated to a thorough discussion of the doctrines of Marx and the Marxians.

The result of these discussions, in most cases, was partly a rejection, partly an acceptance and an essential transformation of the Marxist teachings by leading religious socialists. Has this situation changed? Has the gap between Christianity and Marxism deepened, either

* From *Christianity and Society*, Vol. VII, No. 2 (1941). Reprinted by permission of the Editor of *Christianity and Crisis*.

because Marxism has lost its significance and its power to interpret the present world, or because Christianity has developed in an entirely divergent direction? There are, indeed, elements in Marxism which have become obsolete, and there are developments in Christianity which tend to disrupt any connection between it and the ideas of Marx and his followers. But this does not mean that all elements in Marxism have lost their significance and that the entire Christian theology has turned against Marxism. On the contrary—it seems to me that important elements of the Marxist method of thinking are merged with theological thought to such a degree that they are not recognized any more as taken over from Marxism. This is especially true of the realistic and pessimistic interpretation of the human situation by neosupernaturalism and dialectical theology. In order to come to a decision about this question we must first remember why and in which respect Marxism was appreciated and criticized by religious socialism.

I. THE THEOLOGICAL APPRECIATION OF MARXISM

The main reason for the theological appreciation of Marxism is a striking structural analogy between the prophetic and the Marxian interpretation of history. This has often been carried through and needs only to be mentioned. Both prophetism and Marxism are historical interpretations of history, that is, interpretations in which history has a meaning of its own and is not only a continuation of the general natural process or a place of preparation for the supra-natural. History has an aim toward which it is moving and the fulfilment of which is the meaning of every historical event. And since history has an end, it also has a beginning and a center, a point where its meaning becomes visible and in the light of which an interpretation of history becomes

possible. Both prophetism and Marxism regard the fight between good and evil forces as the main content of history, describing the evil forces mainly as the forces of injustice and envisaging the ultimate victory of justice. This interpretation creates in both cases an eschatological mood, a tension of expectation, a directedness toward the future which is entirely lacking in all kinds of sacramental and mystical religion. Both prophetism and Marxism attack the existing order of society and personal piety as the expression of a universal evil in a special period. They passionately challenge concrete forms of injustice, threatening those responsible for it, especially the ruling groups, with the judgment of history and imminent destruction as the inescapable consequence of social injustice. Both prophetism and Marxism believe that the transition from the present stage of history into the stage of fulfilment will occur in a catastrophe or in a series of catastrophic events, the end of which will be the establishment of a kingdom of peace and justice and the symptoms of which are already recognizable to the divining or analytic spirit. The feeling that the catastrophic coming of the "new" is "at hand" is strong in both of them. Both prophetism and Marxism believe that certain minority groups within a selected nation or class are the real bearers of the historical destiny, that through their action the meaning of history is carried into reality. The free actions of these groups are considered as the instruments of the historical destiny. Freedom and historical destiny are not contradictory for prophetic and Marxist thinking. Mechanistic necessity, as well as accidental contingency of the process of history, is denied by both. Prophetic, as well as genuine Marxist, dialectics are above the level of this alternative.

The structural analogy between prophetism and Marxism is not confined to their interpretations of history. It also refers to main elements in their doctrines of man. This is true not only of the prophetic but also of the Christian doctrine of man generally. Man is not what he ought to be; his true being and his real existence contradict each other. Man is fallen, if not from an original actual goodness, at least from a stage of undeveloped innocence. He is estranged from himself and his true humanity, he has been dehumanized, he has become an object, a means of profit, a quantity of working power—according to Marx. He is estranged from his divine destiny, he has lost the true dignity of his being, the image of God, he is separated from his fellowman by pride, cupidity, and the will-to-power—according to Christianity. Christianity and Marxism agree that the nature of man cannot be determined from above history, that man's historical existence is decisive for every doctrine of man. And they agree that the nature of man cannot be determined by the characteristics of the individual man. Man is a social being, and his evil as well as his good is dependent on his social existence. Perdition and salvation are universal and historical. The individual as an individual cannot escape the former and cannot reach the latter. He is a part of a fallen world, whether the fall is expressed in religious or sociological terms; and he can become a part of a new world, whether this new world is conceived of in terms of a supra-historical or an infra-historical transformation. From this it follows that the idea of the truth in both Christianity and Marxism lies beyond the separation of theory and practice. The truth must be "done" in order to be recognized. Without a transformation of reality, no true knowledge of reality is possible. The situation of knowing is decisive for one's ability or inability to know. Only the "spiritual man" can judge everything, according to Paul, and only the man who participates in the struggle of the "elected group" against the class-society is able to understand the true character of being. Expressed in more

386

concrete terms, the church or the fighting proletariat is the place where truth has the greatest chance to be accepted. In all the other spheres the general distortion of our historical existence makes it difficult, if not impossible, to find a true insight into the human situation and through it into being itself. The fate of self-deception or—as Marx called it—of the production of ideologies is inescapable, except in selected groups which are predominantly composed of people in ultimate anxiety, despair, and meaninglessness. On the boundary of all human possibilities the new possibility arises and gains power. If all ideological veils are torn down and self-deception is no longer possible, truth can appear and can be acted upon. And it is revealed only in the measure in which it is acted upon. The protest of the reformers against the "self-made" gods or idols and the protest of Marx against the self-made ideas or ideologies challenge the same spiritual danger of man in his present existence: to make the truth a means of religious pride or political will-to-power. In all these points Christianity and Marxism are united in their opposition to a "Pelagian" or "harmonistic" optimism with respect to the nature of man.

II. THE THEOLOGICAL CRITICISM OF MARXISM

The basic difference between religious socialism and Marxism is rooted in their different attitudes toward the idea of transcendence. There is a kind of transcendence in Marxism, i.e., the limits of the present possibilities of human nature are transcended by the expectation of a coming stage of justice. A kind of miracle in the transition from the present to the future stage of mankind is presupposed, at least implicitly. And it is obvious that Marxism draws a great deal of its psychological power from this element of transcendence and faith. But this transcendence is not the absolute transcendence of Christianity. It remains in time and space, in history and politics. It is dependent on immanent processes. It transcends the present time, but not time as such. It does not know eternity breaking into time, shaking, turning, and transforming the temporal. Marxism never reaches this transcendence. It is suspicious of it. Religion, because of its supratemporal nature, is considered to be an ideology, i.e., a system of ideas and symbols which have no basis in reality but which are invented for the sake of making the misery of the disinherited classes more bearable to them and, consequently, for the sake of breaking their revolutionary impulse by a mystical opiate. This is the theory of religion in original, as well as in late, Marxism. Obviously, this theory had to be criticized sharply by religious socialism. Religions of this type are distortions of what religion essentially is. This distortion is always possible and has often become a historical power in the sense in which Marxism describes it. But such a description does not fit prophetic religion and its fight against the demonic powers of history and of the personal life. And even the "sacramental" element in religion is not simply ideology. It is also the basis of the prophetic element because only in the power of the Holy that is present can the Holy that is future be expected and realized. In any case, religious socialism follows the Christian and all great religious messages in affirming the transcendent, invisible, and eternal character of the ultimate fulfilment of history and human life. History is fulfilled above history, not within history.

From this follow some basic differences between religious socialism and Marxism. Although Marx had fought against what he called "utopian socialism," he himself and, even more, his followers did not escape dangerous elements of utopianism themselves. They did not expect, of course, that the class situation could be changed by persua-sion of the ruling classes, but they did expect that the economic process, in unity with the revolutionary impulse of the proletarian classes, would create the fulfilment of history—the classless society in which the main evils of the earlier mankind, of its "prehistory" as Marx called it, would be overcome. Religious socialism, on the contrary, has always maintained that the demonic forces of injustice, pride, and will-to-power never will be eradicated from the historical scene, although special manifestations of it, such as capitalism and nationalism, might be conquered. Therefore, religious socialism turned the anti-ideological criticism as much against itself and against all the other socialist and Marxist groups as against the enemies of socialism. The sharpest criticism of the socialist movement comes from religious socialism, while the lack of such a self-criticism, for instance, in the social-democratic parties, contributed much to their catastrophes. For the same reason, religious socialism, contrary to Marxism, upholds the importance of the personal life and its transformation for the revolutionary movement. The personal shortcomings of the leaders of the socialist groups and the lack of a profound education and discipline in the vanguards of the movement are due to the immanentist attitude of Marxism, to its overemphasis on the institutional, and to its lack of understanding of personal factors. For religious socialism the corrupted human situation has deeper roots than mere historical and sociological structures. It is rooted in the depth of the human heart. And in the same way the regeneration of mankind is not possible through institutional and political changes alone, but it also requires changes in the personal attitude of many people toward life. Therefore, for religious socialism the turning-point of history is not the rise of the proletariat but the appearance of a new meaning and power of life in the divine self-manifestation. These differences are of tremendous importance; but they do not prevent the inclusion of basic elements of the Marxist doctrines of history and man by prophetic Christianity.

III. RELIGIOUS SOCIALISM AND SCIENTIFIC MARXISM

Religious socialists have accepted many of the scientific results of the Marxian analysis of society, especially of economics, because they have found them to be true. And they have maintained and still maintain Marxist theories, as far as they can do so on scientific grounds. They were and are, at the same time, hospitable to any criticism of Marxist ideas as soon as such criticism seems to be demanded by the progress of scientific knowledge. Religious socialism rejects any dogmatism with respect to the Marxist principles. It subjects them to the criteria of every scientific procedure and, beyond this, to the methodical suspicion that they might have become ideologies themselves. But religious socialism rejects dogmatic anti-Marxism as well as dogmatic Marxism and subjects the scientific attack on the Marxian doctrines not only to scientific criteria but also to the suspicion of being an ideological escape. Especially in the present situation, in which Marx is pushed more and more into the background, has the question of ideological anti-Marxism increased in importance.

There are, above all, some philosophical principles in Marxism which can and must be maintained by religious socialism as discoveries of lasting significance, provided that their corrupted forms are recognized as such and rejected. The demand for the unity of theory and practice or, in more recent terms, for "existential thinking" is a lasting insight that Marx has discovered in his fight against theoretical idealism and materialism. But the distortion of this insight into a skeptical relativism, according to which all thinking is only

the expression of a special kind of being (psychological or sociological), must be considered not only as a corruption but also as the negation of existential thinking. In the same way it must be acknowledged by religious socialism that Marx is right in emphasizing material reproduction as the foundation of the whole historical process. But the distortion of this insight into a mechanistic economics or into a metaphysical materialism must be rejected. The economic sphere is itself a complex sphere, to which all other spheres essentially contribute, so that they cannot be derived from it, although they can never be separated from it. The dialectical method must be accepted as a method of describing the movements of life and history in their inner tensions, contrasts, and contradictions and in their trend toward more embracing unities. But the distortion of the dialectical method into a universal mechanism of calculable processes has nothing to do with reality and with the original meaning of this method. There are dialectical elements in all life and in every historical totality, namely, elements belonging to a given structure which drive beyond this structure. These structures can be described only in dialectical terms but not at all in terms of mechanical necessity. Existential thinking, historical materialism, and the dialectical method are achievements which should never be lost in religious socialism.

The same is true of several sociological and economic principles of scientific Marxism. Marx's method of analyzing economic phenomena is a sociological method; it takes into consideration, in every moment, the human and social factors and denies the escapist attitude of formal economics which hides the fact that economic action is human action. The recognition of this situation is the second highly important methodological contribution of Marxism. On the basis of this method Marxism has given that analysis of the contradictions of capitalistic society, which, more than anything else, has destroyed the harmonistic beliefs of bourgeois liberalism. Marx himself and most of his followers confined their analysis to the contrast of "capital" and "labor." In the last decades it has become obvious that there are many more contradictory elements in the later stage of capitalism and that the revolutionary vanguard is no longer identical with the proletariat or advanced groups within it. It has become evident that the lower middle classes and bureaucracy in state and business will play a much greater role than Marx anticipated. But all this does not invalidate the main point in his analysis, i.e., the insight into the contradictions in the structure of capitalism. On the contrary, this insight has been deepened and confirmed by the catastrophes of the present world. Any neoliberal attempt to re-establish a harmonistic interpretation of capitalistic society must be rejected by religious socialism. It is an obvious fact that, partly under the influence of Marxism, the economy of free competition has been restricted to a great extent by the increasing power of labor; by frequent and radical interferences of the state in all countries; by the general trend toward state capitalism and the rise of a centralizing bureaucracy. But this transformation, although invalidating some of the anticipations of Marx, is, at the same time, the confirmation of his basic vision. Nobody can understand the character of the present world revolution who has not been prepared for it by the Marxian analysis of bourgeois society, its contradictions and its decisive trends. Every day one may experience the fact that people who are lacking in Marxian education, directly or indirectly, are utterly confused by the rise of communism and fascism and by the present world catastrophe. They simply cannot understand the trends in the former structure of society which, with dialecti-

cal (not mechanical) necessity, have brought about the present situation. They explain it as the result of bad accidents created by bad men. Religious socialism, with the tool of the Marxian analysis of society brought up to date, is able to give a meaning to the present world transformation.

IV. MARXISM AS A LASTING PRINCIPLE AND RELIGIOUS SOCIALISM

It is understandable that ideas can become an element of the general consciousness to such a degree that their original significance is forgotten. Much of what they had to say and which was surprising in the beginning becomes natural. Other parts become antiquated; and so the whole system of ideas seems to belong to the past. A theory of social processes which has partly changed the actual processes may seem to have become wrong just because it was right at the time it appeared. But there are other spiritual creations, the effects of which are not exhausted by their historical successes. They have an infinite, inexhaustible meaning because they represent a lasting type of spiritual possibility. Such types are prophetism, Platonism, and Protestantism. Such types also are religious socialism and Marxism. They return again and again in different shapes, based on their original, classical appearance. Therefore, we must go back to their classical form, and we must reshape them in the light of actual experience. But we cannot dismiss them as merely forms of past history. They would return against our will. We cannot discuss Marxism as a movement of the past as long as we espouse the prophetic spirit as religious socialists. Religious socialism, if it is to keep any meaning and power, must not become another ideological justification of the present democracies, nor must it become a progressive idealism and a system of autonomous harmony. The breakdown of these ideas has created the present situation. Religious socialism, in the spirit of prophetism and with the methods of Marxism, is able to understand and to transcend the world of today.

Religion and the Socioeconomic and Political Orders: Bibliography

Barth, Karl. *Community, State and Church.* New York: Doubleday & Company, 1960.

Bennett, John C. *Christian Ethics and Social Policy.* New York: Charles Scribner's Sons, 1946.

Brunner, Emil. *Justice and the Social Order.* New York: Harper & Brothers, 1945.

Childs, Marquis W. and Cater, Douglass. *Ethics in a Business Society.* New York: Harper & Row, 1954.

Fromm, Erich. *The Sane Society.* New York: Holt, Rinehart & Winston, 1955.

Heimann, Eduard. *Freedom and Order.* New York: Charles Scribner's Sons, 1947.

Lindsay, A. D. *The Two Moralities.* London: Eyre & Spottiswoode, 1940.

Maritain, Jacques. *Scholasticism and Politics.* Image ed. New York: Doubleday & Company.

Muelder, Walter G. *Religion and Economic Responsibility.* New York: Charles Scribner's Sons, 1953.

Mumford, Lewis. *Technics and Civilization.* New York: Harcourt, Brace & World, [1934] 1963.

Niebuhr, Reinhold. *Christianity and Power Politics.* New York: Charles Scribner's Sons, 1940.

Samuelson, Kurt. *Religion and Economic Action.* Torchbook ed. New York: Harper & Row, 1964.

Tillich, Paul. *Love, Power and Justice.* Galaxy ed. New York: Oxford University Press, 1960.

West, C. C. *Communism and the Theologians.* New York: The Macmillan Company, [1958] 1963.

Index of Names

Index of Specific
Areas of Culture